Dear Reader,

The principles in SINGING ENERGY are the same principles that Robert Gansert has been teaching successfully for more than 15 years to students from all over the world. If you were in his presence, you would immediately see and hear the fantastic results of these revolutionary laws that he has discovered. His amazing results motivated him to record these principles in SINGING ENERGY in order to share these ideas which not only produce unbelievable volume and range in the human voice, but also enable the singer to develop a complete understanding of his instrument, and prevent him from "burning out" at an early age.

The principles in SINGING ENERGY are simple - like all great discoveries - but they require study and discipline, as, for example, the coordination of the body in such involuntary actions as yawning and vomiting. Since these are reflex acts, they require study to simulate in order to project sound from the bottom of the torso, thus involving the power of the body to generate and amplify the singing voice. The inability to see the vocal instrument, as opposed to the piano or any other concrete instrument, compounds the task of comprehension and, therefore, requires more focus of the reader in order to understand and apply the Gan-Tone Principles.

If you could hear Robert Gansert, or any of his students, produce the Gan-Tone sound, you would be thoroughly convinced that he is a pioneer in energizing the singing voice into a new dimension.

If you wish to sing or are a singer having problems and need help, Robert Gansert knows your problems and assures you that the answers to your problems are in his book, SINGING ENERGY. However, the skill involved in coordinating the body for producing the Gan-Tone sound obviously rests with the reader since, unfortunately, the author cannot accompany the book in order to demonstrate the amazing sound produced, that is, the instantaneous result in which all the Gan-Tone Principles are condensed and unified with lightning speed, producing great volume and an even range throughout the scale.

Understanding Jaw, Larynx, Body Fusion, which is comparable to the physical processes employed by the body in vomiting and yawning, is all you really need for increased range and volume. Page 77-79 Vocal Hook mini Table of Contents will enable the reader to understand how the vomiting and yawning processes are used in the Gan-Tone Method. To add dimension to your sound, study the Gan-Tone Pulsation section - Page 131- mini Table of Contents - for details.

GAN-TONE PRODUCTIONS

SINGING ENERGY
IN THE
GAN-TONE® METHOD of VOICE PRODUCTION

EXPLANATION OF LOGO THAT APPEARS ON COVER OF BOOK

The facial profile represents the mind that understands and applies the Gan-Tone Principles.

The uplifted position of the profile symbolizes a higher level of awareness regarding vibrations.

The triangle is symbolic of the points of concentration in the body for the maximum transmission, amplification and re-sounding of vocal cords and body vibrations, thereby producing maximum Singing Energy. Each angle of the triangle symbolizes the following:

The highest angle of the triangle points to the septum at the bridge of the nose, which is the most radiant area of resonance in the body, when the Jaw, Larynx, Body Fusion and the Gan-Tone Pulsations are applied with maximum intensity.

The lowest angle of the triangle points to the Sphincter ani externus muscle at the rectal-pelvic basin, which is the controlling center for the fusion of body parts and the compression, generation and magnification of vocal cords and body vibrations during the Compression Phase, or down-part of the Gan-Tone beat, and, also, the controlling center for the thrusting and focusing of vocal cords and body vibrations to the resonators for re-sounding on the Thrust Phase, or up-part of the Gan-Tone beat. The more intense the Compression Phase, or down-part of the Gan-Tone beat, on the fundamental vocal cords vibrations, the greater the utilization of breath, as a result of rapidly sinking the breath through Rectal-Pelvic Breath Control, which increases the speed of movement, amplification and thrust of vocal cords and body vibrations throughout the body and produces a more defined re-sounding of these vibrations in the apex of the triangle, which is the septum of the frontal sinus cavities. A projected sound of maximum dimensions is, therefore, produced with a minimum expenditure of breath.

The third, or mid, angle of the triangle points to the recesses of the oral, nasal and pharyngeal tracts which are fully expanded and utilized when the Jaw, Larynx, Body Fusion and the Gan-Tone Pulsations are maximally applied, allowing vocal cords and body vibrations to be maximally amplified and re-sounded in these cavities as well as in all the other body parts.

The circle represents a maximizing of the vibratory aura enveloping the body as a result of maximal amplification and resonance in the singing sound, when the Jaw, Larynx, Body Fusion and the Gan-Tone Pulsations are applied with maximum intensity.

SINGING ENERGY THROUGH BODY POWER

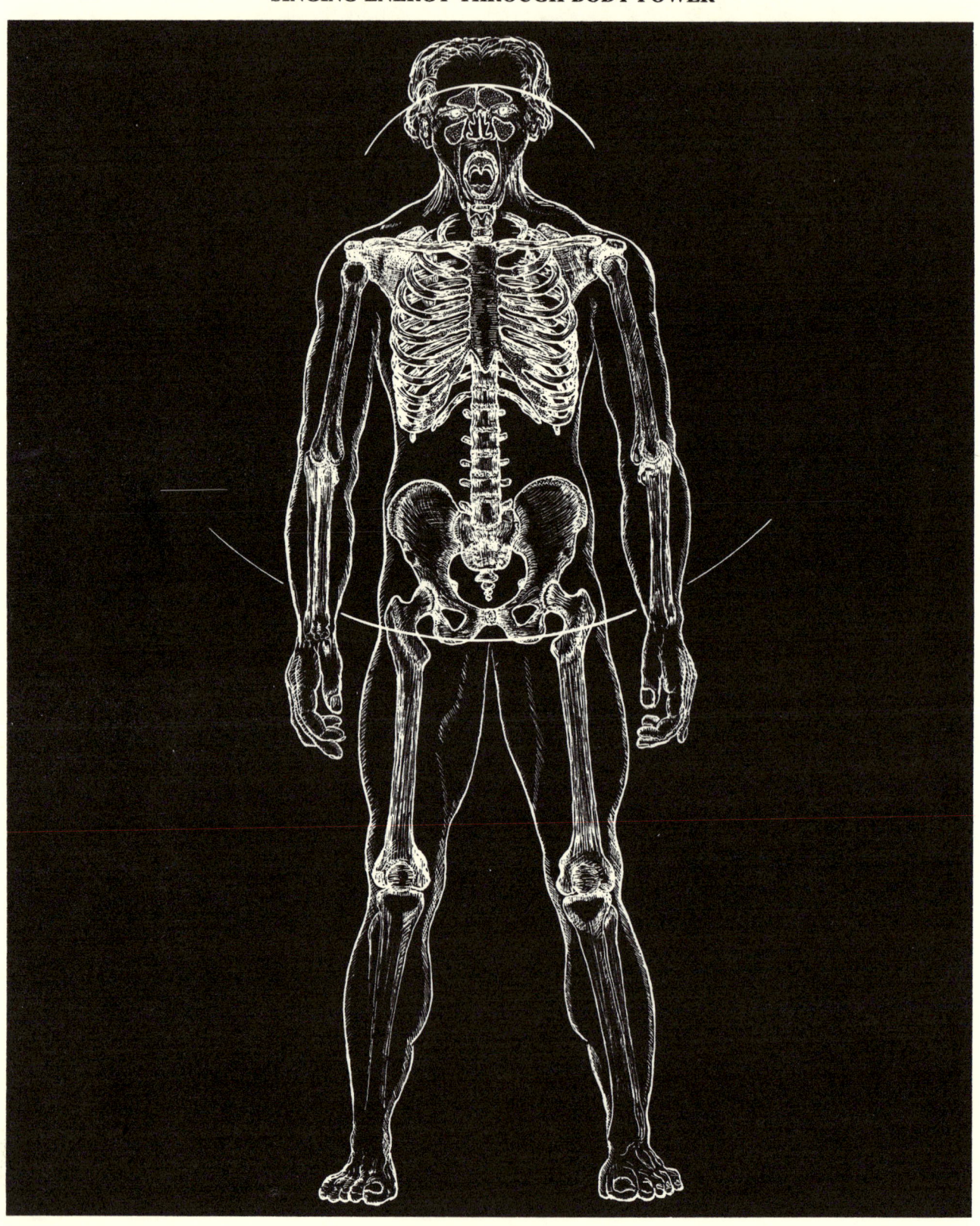

SINGING ENERGY

IN THE

GAN-TONE® METHOD of VOICE PRODUCTION

BY

ROBERT GANSERT

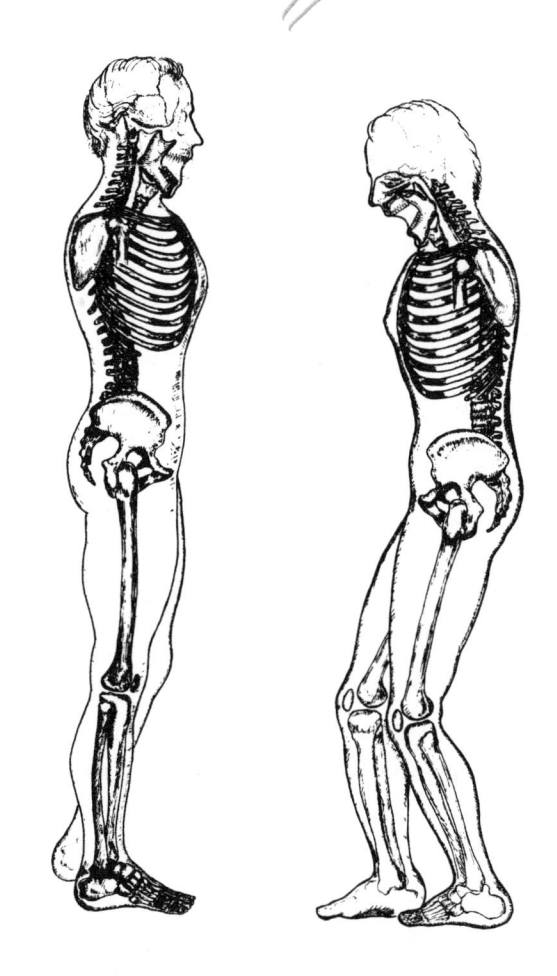

GAN-TONE PUBLISHING COMPANY

NEW YORK, NEW YORK

1981

The logo (Reg. # 994,211—registered 9/24/74) of the triangle and profile within the circle and the word Gan-Tone (Reg. # 1,035,940—registered 3/16/76) are trademarks of Robert Gansert, registered in the United States and other countries.

Copyright © Robert Gansert 1981

All rights reserved. No part of this book may be reproduced in any form or by any means, mechanical or electronic, including photocopying, recording or by any information storage and retrieval system, without permission in writing from the publisher or author.

Library of Congress Catalog Card Number: 81-80960
ISBN 0-939 458-00-4

Cover Design by Robert Gansert

Printed in the United States of America

*To my loving wife,
Carmela Capano Gansert,
for the long hours she has
devoted to the preparation
of the manuscript for
this book*

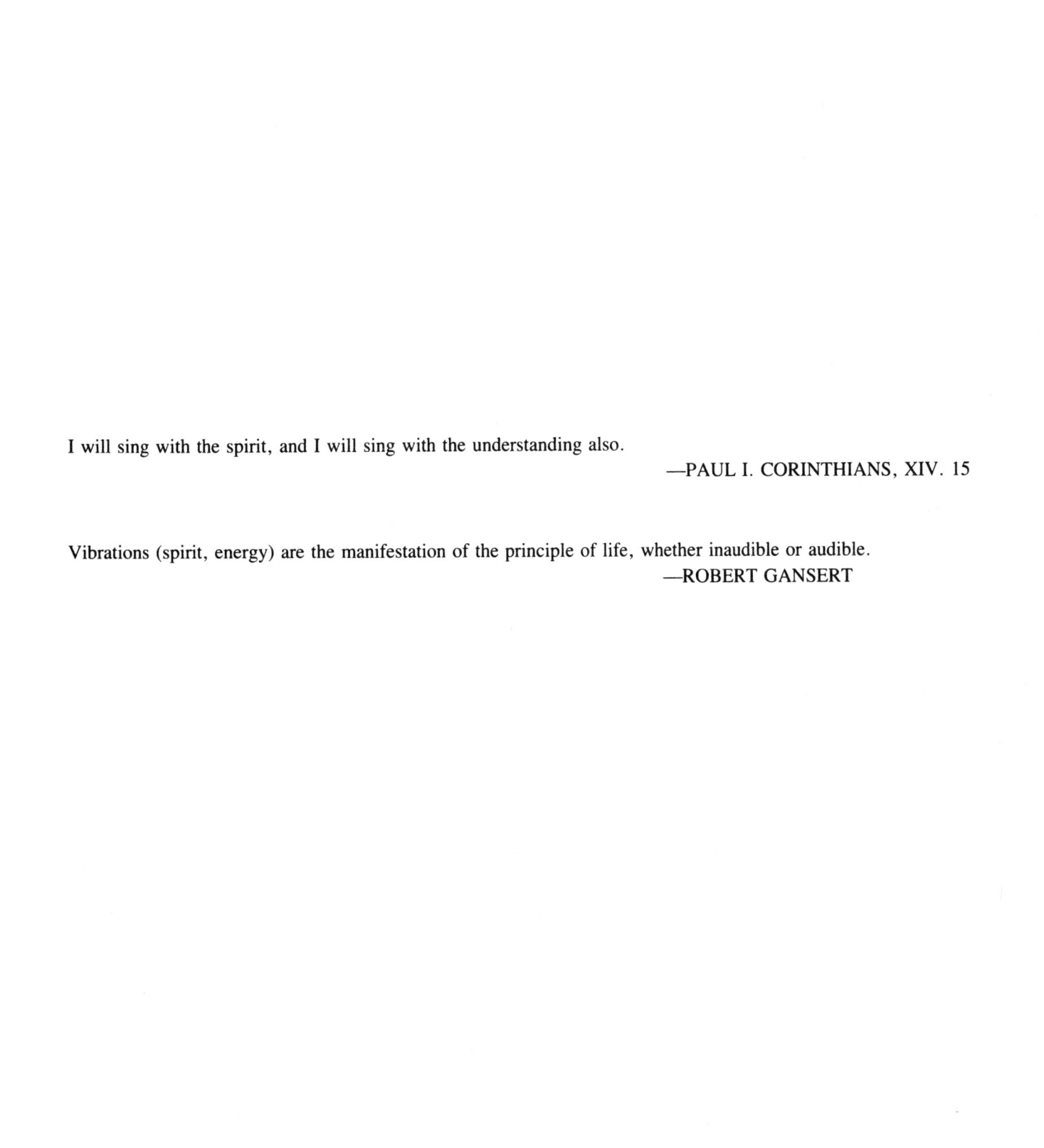

I will sing with the spirit, and I will sing with the understanding also.
—PAUL I. CORINTHIANS, XIV. 15

Vibrations (spirit, energy) are the manifestation of the principle of life, whether inaudible or audible.
—ROBERT GANSERT

CONTENTS

	Illustrations	xiii
	Preface	xvii
I.	Purpose of the Book	xxiii
II.	Some Current Beliefs Regarding Vocal Production Rejected by the Gan-Tone Method	1
	CONTENTS	5
III.	Why the Gan-Tone Method is a Scientific Method	17
	CONTENTS	19
IV.	Natural Singing in the Gan-Tone Method	43
	CONTENTS	45
V.	The Inner Laugh in the Gan-Tone Method	49
	CONTENTS	51
VI.	Popular and Classical Singing in the Gan-Tone Method	57
	CONTENTS	59
VII.	Rock and Roll in the Gan-Tone Method	69
	CONTENTS	71
VIII.	The Vocal Hook	75
	CONTENTS	77
IX.	The Jaw—Key to Scientific Singing	99
	CONTENTS	101

X.	The Gan-Tone—Revelation of Scintillating Singing	129
	CONTENTS	131
XI.	Vocal Focus—The Basis for Maximal Dimensional Singing	159
	CONTENTS	161
XII.	SUMMARY—Gan-Tone Principles in Sections IX, X, XI that Govern:	177
	Voice Projection	179
	Breath Control	179
	Range	180
	Register	180
	Resonance	181
	Volume	182
	Coloration	183
	Sound Configuration	183
	Brilliance	184
XIII.	Teaching the Gan-Tone Method	187
	CONTENTS	189
XIV.	Glossary	269
	CONTENTS	271

CONTENTS
ILLUSTRATIONS

	INTRODUCTION	207
I.	VOCAL HOOK	209
II.	LARYNX—FRONT VIEW	211
III.	VOCAL CORDS IN LARYNX—TWO VIEWS	213
IV.	CAVITIES OF MASK—FRONT VIEW	215
V.	CAVITIES OF MASK—LATERAL VIEW	217
VI.	TONGUE AND NECK MUSCLES INVOLVED IN THE SINGING PROCESS	219
VII.	FORWARD MANDIBULAR MOVEMENT IN JAW, LARYNX, BODY FUSION	221
VIII.	VERTICAL POSITION OF MANDIBLE IN JAW, LARYNX, BODY FUSION	223
IX.	HEAD MUSCLE THAT FUSES JAW AND BODY	225
X.	PTERYGOIDEUS LATERALIS MUSCLE—ORIGIN OF JAW, LARYNX, BODY FUSION—LATERAL VIEW	227
XI.	PTERYGOIDEUS LATERALIS MUSCLE—FRONT VIEW	229
XII.	FIVE ASPECTS OF MANDIBLE and Respective Positions of the Pterygoideus Lateralis Muscle	231
XIII.	LOCATION OF PELVIC-UROGENITAL DIAPHRAGM AND SPHINCTER ANI EXTERNUS MUSCLE	233
XIV.	REFERENCE POINTS FOR VOICE PROJECTION IN THE GAN-TONE METHOD OF VOICE PRODUCTION	235
XV.	BODY POSTURE IN ABSOLUTE JAW, LARYNX, BODY FUSION	237
XVI.	ROTATION OF HEAD, MANDIBLE AND PELVIS IN ABSOLUTE JAW, LARYNX, BODY FUSION	239
XVII.	MAXIMUM ROTATION OF HEAD AND PELVIS IN ABSOLUTE JAW, LARYNX, BODY FUSION	241
XVIII.	BODY CURVE IN ABSOLUTE JAW, LARYNX, BODY FUSION	243

XIX.	BODY POSTURE IN MODIFIED JAW, LARYNX, BODY FUSION	245
XX.	POSITION OF HEAD, MANDIBLE AND PELVIS IN MODIFIED JAW, LARYNX, BODY FUSION	247
XXI.	PRODUCTION AND AMPLITUDE OF GAN-TONE PULSATION	249
XXII.	EXTENSION OF AMPLITUDE OF NOTE BEING SUNG WITH APPLICATION OF GAN-TONE PULSATION	251
XXIII.	STRUCTURAL BOUNDARIES FOR PRODUCTION OF VOCAL SOUND WITH APPLICATION OF JAW, LARYNX, BODY FUSION AND GAN-TONE PULSATION	253
XXIV.	BODY AS A PISTON AND CYLINDER	255
XXV.	BODY AS EXTENSION OF VOCAL CORDS	257
XXVI.	KEY MUSCLES IN THE APPLICATION OF JAW, LARYNX, BODY FUSION AND GAN-TONE PULSATION	259
XXVII.	SYMBOL OF LARYNGEAL-PELVIC FUSION	261
XXVIII.	NATURAL FOCAL POINT OF VOCAL CORDS AND BODY VIBRATIONS	263
XXIX.	NASION CENTER—LATERAL ASPECT	265
XXX.	VIBRATORY AURA AS RESULT OF JAW, LARYNX, BODY FUSION AND GAN-TONE PULSATION	267

The logo and the illustrations in this volume
are reproduced from original drawings
by the author.

PREFACE

No form of energy is generated and transmitted in an unrelenting line, without relief, but is usually generated by vibrations, which provide a uniform release in the energy flow, thereby insuring a constant renewal of thrust which prevents rigidity, or the stifling of life, and promotes, instead, greater dimensions in the energy output. Rigidity consumes, confines and overwhelms energy, since it doesn't provide for the renewal of life, which can only be achieved in vibrational cycles.

Any augmentation of the dimensions of energy must, therefore, follow this natural principle and be structured in augmented vibrational frequency.

Awareness of this law, which is evident in the cosmos, whether it be microscopic or macroscopic, regarding the relationship of augmented vibrations to the augmentation of energy, or life, is the foundation of the Gan-Tone Method of Voice Production. The author is a pioneer in the augmentation of singing energy through augmented vibrational frequency, since awareness and mastery of the principles of the Gan-Tone Method enable the human to produce a singing voice of maximal dimensions through the utilization of an augmented compound frequency which results in multi-tones concomitantly with the dominant fundamental.

Tradition and convention in the art of singing are not aware of the effect of augmented vibrational frequency on the amplitude of the fundamental frequency, or the note being sung, since popular belief still adheres to the force of the air impinging on the vocal cords as being responsible for the changes in the dimensions of volume, depth and height in the singing voice and, therefore, refers to the strength or weakness of the vocal cords, lung power, chest size, arrangement of body parts and intestinal fortitude (guts) for affecting these dimensions.

The principles of the Gan-Tone Method, however, enable the singer to produce a compound frequency in the singing line by mentally superimposing 5 to 7 Gan-Tone beats per second on the beats of the fundamental pitch being sung. These imposed Gan-Tone beats extend the amplitude of the fundamental cycle from the vocal cords, downward through the body, to the Sphincter ani externus, the rectal muscle which is controlled by the human will, and is the distal border of the extended larynx. (The origin of the extended larynx, or voice box, is the plicae vocales, i.e., the true vocal cords.) The extension of the fundamental frequency to the rectal muscle occurs during the Compression Phase, or down-part of the Gan-Tone beat, causing the original vocal cords vibrations to be compressed to the rectal-pelvic basin without changing the pitch of the fundamental frequency.

However, the degree to which vocal cords vibrations are compressed to the bottom of the torso on the Compression Phase of the Gan-Tone beat is dependent on the skill possessed by the singer in applying the Jaw, Larynx, Body Fusion, which is the simulation of natural bodily functions that would utilize contractive muscular coordination of the thorax and abdomen to the pelvic basin at the rectal muscle.

Actually, contractive body action for the amplification of vibrations is dependent on the singer's control of the Pterygoideus lateralis muscle, near the temple of the head, which controls the necessary openings of the mandible (lower jaw) for coping with the pressure buildup in the throat area and thereby insuring maximal vibrational flow through this narrow opening which results in maximal re-sounding of these vibrations below and above the vocal cords. The Gan-Tone singer, therefore, becomes skilled in deftly positioning the lower jaw, or mandible, in anticipation of the increase of pressure and vibrations that accompany the increase in range, volume and dimension. The Pterygoideus lateralis muscle, through contraction, must maximally open the jaw to maximally open the mouth and throat for maximal re-sounding of vibrations. The lower jaw (mandible) must be maintained with a Feather-Touch Contact on the larynx during moments of great stress (loud, high notes) and must be opened prior to the re-sounding of vibrations in the cavities.

The higher the range and the greater the volume, the greater the skill required to contract the Pterygoideus lateralis muscle in order to insure the widest opening of the jaw, which will fuse the jaw to the body, thus creating the widest opening in the throat for the accommodation of vibrations and the dispersal of the accompanying pressure, away from the delicate throat area and onto the body, in the direction of the rectal-pelvic basin.

Great skill is required to condition, not only the Pterygoideus lateralis muscle, but the Sphincter ani externus, as well, since these two muscles must respond simultaneously to speed and contraction under stress. The Gan-Tone singer, therefore, becomes aware of the need to master the two diametrically opposed muscles of the body, the Pterygoideus lateralis in the head and the Sphincter ani externus at the bottom of the torso.

This muscle, the Sphincter ani externus, is the controlling center for producing the maximal dimensions of singing energy in the Gan-Tone Method, since maximal compression of vocal cords vibrations to this area on the Compression Phase, or down-part of the Gan-Tone beat, determines maximal thrust of these vibrations and, therefore, maximal re-sounding in the head vibrators and resonators on the Thrust Phase, or up-part of the Gan-Tone beat, resulting in maximum volume, depth and height in the singing voice.

However, the effectiveness of the compression of vocal cords and body vibrations to the rectal-pelvic basin on the Compression Phase of the Gan-Tone beat is dependent on the singer's skill in controlling the Pterygoideus lateralis muscle in the head for insuring the maximal flow and re-sounding of vibrations throughout the body. This path of control from the Pterygoideus lateralis muscle in the head to the Sphincter ani externus muscle at the rectal-pelvic basin represents the two extremities which make up the structure of the Compression Phase, or down-part of the Gan-Tone beat.

The degree of intensity in the compression of vocal cords and body vibrations to the bottom of the torso on the Compression Phase, or down-part of the Gan-Tone beat, results in an equal intensity of thrust of these vibrations to the sinus cavities on the Thrust Phase, or up-part of the Gan-Tone beat, thus augmenting the amplitude of the original vocal cords vibrations from the neck area to the body extremities, i.e., from the bottom of the torso to the head cavities, thereby augmenting the energy, or dimensions, of the singing line. The intensity of the Compression Phase determines the intensity of the Thrust Phase which, in turn, determines the dimensions of the emitted sound, exemplifying Newton's Law of Action and Reaction which states that for each action there is an equal and opposite reaction.

The Gan-Tone Method, therefore, negates the traditional beliefs that the strength of the vocal cords, lung power, chest size or intestinal fortitude determine vocal dimensions and declares, instead, that the whole body, ultimately, is the vibrator, amplifier, transmitter, re-sounder and projector of the vocal cords vibrations and functions like a bell.

Furthermore, the Gan-Tone Method declares that the point of reference for body fusion, compression, thrust, focus and direction of vibrations, cover of sound, center of tone, depth, height, volume, brilliance, breath control, projection, support, suppleness, resilience, sinking of the breath, coloration, and range is the Sphincter ani externus muscle at the rectal-pelvic basin, when coordinated with the Jaw, Larynx, Body Fusion and the Gan-Tone vibration.

The singer trained in the Gan-Tone Method becomes very alert to the coordination of body parts, by muscular contraction, in order to promote a maximal continuity of vibrational flow throughout the body and its resonators. Awareness of the role of the body in promoting vibrational flow makes the Gan-Tone singer conscious of the imperative need for speed and agility in positioning the jaw down and back (Jaw Sense) in order to attain maximal dimensions of depth and height in the singing line, since the Gan-Tone singer is aware that the jaw is the key to body involvement, or augmented vibrational frequency.

The Gan-Tone singer becomes aware of the great discipline that must be developed in the control of the Pterygoideus lateralis muscle in the head in order to keep the jaw open, down and back, with minimal muscular activity under great stress (loud, high notes).

The Gan-Tone singer realizes that it is not neck muscles that are the prime movers of the mandible (lower jaw) but, instead, the head muscle near the temple, the Pterygoideus lateralis, which must be controlled under stress in order to fuse the head to the body, thereby protecting the throat and neck muscles from strain under stress.

Tradition and convention focus on the many neck muscles as being responsible for the difficulties encountered by singers. However, the Gan-Tone Method declares that the Pterygoideus lateralis, a muscle which is in a superior position in relation to neck muscles, is really the muscle which controls and protects the network of neck muscles by lowering the mandible like a wing, during contraction, thereby sheltering these muscles during moments of stress (loud, high notes). The Pterygoideus lateralis muscle in the head, therefore, functions as a guardian of the jaw (the door for the emission of vocal cords and body vibrations) and as a protector of the numerous neck muscles by fusing them to the body during stress.

Current beliefs which stress the strength of the vocal cords, the focus of the jet of air on the vocal cords, lung power, or bone structure for achieving dimensions in the fundamental sound intensify pressure on the vocal cords and neck muscles ultimately distorting the projected sound and minimizing its integral parts. Distortion occurs when tightness and restriction in the throat area diminish the dimensions of the sound, producing rigidity which prevents the renewal of life, or energy, in the singing line.

The application of the Jaw, Larynx, Body Fusion and the Gan-Tone beat, however, release the rigidity by removing the focus from the vocal cords to the two new reference points, the Pterygoideus lateralis muscle in the head and the Sphincter ani externus muscle in the rectal-pelvic basin, shifting the pressure from the delicate throat area to the body.

Integral parts of the sound are magnified and their numbers increased during the Compression Phase, or down-part of the Gan-Tone beat, when all the body parts are fused as an extension of the vocal cords causing all body mediums, such as bones, cartilages, muscles and liquids, to vibrate, thereby reflecting their vibrant characteristics as undertones that are reflected as overtones, when they are re-sounded in the body (especially in the head cavities) during the Thrust Phase, or up-part of the Gan-Tone beat, producing an emitted sound that is characterized by multi-tones along with the dominant fundamental.

The intensity of focus in the vocal cords, which is the current belief, is now replaced in the Gan-Tone Method by an augmented frequency produced by Gan-Tone Pulsations which have a trip-hammer effect on the original vocal cords vibrations as they are transmitted, on 5 to 7 Gan-Tones per second, to the rectal-pelvic basin on the Compression Phase, or down-part of the Gan-Tone beat, and resounded throughout the body on the Thrust Phase, or up-part of the Gan-Tone beat, giving the emitted sound great dimensions of depth and height, from the softest to the loudest sounds. The singing voice projected through Gan-Tone Principles, therefore, has great suppleness, buoyancy, energy, brilliance and controlled abandon, since the augmented vibrational frequency provides a maximal renewal of life in the singing line through total body vibrations, creating an excitement for the listener, as a result of lifting him into a new vocal vibratory realm which makes the resultant sound transcend words in conveying a message.

Since the successive contractive muscular action from the Pterygoideus lateralis muscle in the head, downward through the body, to the Sphincter ani externus muscle at the rectal-pelvic basin involves the whole body in a simulated peristaltic action, while augmenting the original vocal cords vibrations on the Gan-Tone beat, vocal exercises in the Gan-Tone Method are broadened to include body exercises of a peristaltic nature. Involvement of the body extremities, through a peristaltic action that accompanies each Gan-Tone beat, requires that the singer develop a muscular flexibility through the body in order to transfer vocal cords vibrations, and the pressure that accompanies increased dimensions of sound, from the vocal cords to the body extremities, i.e., to the rectal-pelvic basin and the head resonators. The frequency of this peristaltic action, i.e., 5 to 7 Gan-Tones per second on the fundamental frequency, comprises the controlled vibrancy of the sustained sound in the Gan-Tone Method.

Flexibility in the peristaltic coordination, from the Pterygoideus lateralis muscle to the Sphincter ani externus muscle, takes time to develop, since there is a tendency for the singer to hold the rigidity of either end, causing the worm-like action to lack smoothness, and limiting the control and dimensions of the emitted sound.

Vocal exercises in the Gan-Tone Method are designed to promote flexibility in the internal contractive muscular action, downward through the body to the rectal-pelvic basin, while coordinating the Jaw, Larynx, Body Fusion throughout the range for maximal dimensions of sound, thus transferring stress and strain from the head and neck area to the body. A conspicuous absence of muscular strain in the neck is, therefore, evident in the Gan-Tone singer.

The peristaltic action of the body, while imposing Gan-Tone beats on the fundamental frequency, in order to augment the vibrational frequency of the fundamental, is not to be confused with the tremolo, which is a rapid fluttering of the tone; or with the vibrato, which is a slightly pulsating effect for adding warmth and beauty to the tone and for expressing changes in emotional intensity. The vibrato and the tremolo are created by muscles within the neck area, above and below the vocal cords. During moments of great vocal and emotional demands, the vibrato and the tremolo collapse, since neck and diaphragm muscles, of themselves, are not sufficient to withstand these demands; whereas, the augmented vibrational frequency produced by the Gan-Tone beat involves muscles of the body extremities, i.e., the Pterygoideus lateralis muscle in the head to the Sphincter ani externus muscle in the rectal-pelvic basin, thereby transferring great vocal and emotional demands from the congested area of the neck to the entire body, while protecting the neck muscles through fusion. These neck muscles become united to the body through fusion between the two reference points, i.e., the Pterygoideus lateralis muscle and the Sphincter ani externus muscle. The movement of vibrations throughout the body is controlled from these two reference points on the frequency of the Gan-Tone Pulsation which, in turn, controls the voluntary or involuntary vibrato, tremolo, wobble, or any other structural defect of the sound.

The Gan-Tone Method declares that the current beliefs which stress the dominance of throat muscles, i.e., supra-infrahyoid, etc., lock vocal cords vibrations in the neck area, producing limited dimensions in the emitted sound and localizing pressure in the neck area, while increasing the stridency of the tone and decreasing its musicality.

In the attempt to augment the dimensions of the voice, many singers gain excessive weight in order to add volume, depth and height to the emitted sound. This obesity strengthens the focus of stress in the neck area while adding some dimensions to the singing voice.

The Gan-Tone Method declares, however, that this obesity is unnecessary, since fusion insures maximal utilization of the entire body, from the sinus cavities to the soles of the feet. Excessive weight interferes with the necessary contractive muscular flexibility, from the Pterygoideus lateralis muscle in the head to the Sphincter ani externus muscle at the bottom of the torso, which the Gan-Tone singer must master in order to maximally augment the original vocal cords vibrations on the Gan-Tone beat. Body tonicity is essential in the Gan-Tone Method, and obesity interferes with tonicity. In fact, the Gan-Tone singer never fully experiences the complete sinking of the breath until the singer can discipline the focal point of compression and thrust, i.e., the Sphincter ani externus muscle, to the peristaltic action of the Gan-Tone beat *and can also maintain its involuntary tonic contraction under stress (loud, high, sustained notes). Contracting this muscle voluntarily under pressure produces rigidity in the pelvic area which stifles body resilience thereby diminishing the dimensions of the sound.*

The full beauty of the singing voice is realized only when the release is achieved in the singing line through the energizing quality of the Gan-Tone beat, magnifying multi-tones which cannot be heard until the Gan-Tone beat maximizes vibrational dimensions.

Although the author is a pioneer in the augmentation of singing energy through augmented vibrational frequency, whose amplitude extends to the body extremities, the Gan-Tone Principles should not be foreign to the reader, since these principles simply involve the simulation of natural bodily functions, such as, yawning, vomiting and any other action that forces the abdominal viscera to the bottom of the torso, i.e., to the Sphincter ani externus muscle.

The Gan-Tone Method is a break-through into a new dimension in the singing voice brought about by the unification of the body (Jaw, Larynx, Body Fusion) and an augmented compound frequency (imposition of the Gan-Tone beat on the pitch being sung) as opposed to the conventional belief of focusing on body parts (neck, diaphragm, intercostal muscles, lungs) and the fundamental pitch to produce vibrant energy in the singing line. Focus on the neck muscles, for ex., in attempting to attain depth, height and volume in the upper range ultimately results in a limited control of dimensions. These high notes become thin, strident and reedy, since they are utilizing the limited frequency of the fundamental as the vocal demand increases; whereas, the Gan-Tone Pulsation takes the fundamental pitch being sung and on rapid peristaltic action (5 to 7 Gan-Tones per second), from the Pterygoideus lateralis muscle to the Sphincter ani externus muscle, maximally utilizes the entire body for the compression, amplification and thrust of the fundamental vocal cords vibrations, defining the dimensions of depth and height in the projected sound thus producing vibrancy, buoyancy, resilience, brilliance and controlled abandon in the range, from low to high notes.

Therefore, the singer who seeks to achieve the ultimate in singing energy, whether it be in the popular (Rock and Roll, Folk, Pop) or classical (Opera, Operetta, Lieder) expression, will realize that the entire body is an extension of the vocal cords and that the singing line is the result of the resounding of the entire body whose bell-like ring is defined by the controlled frequency of the Gan-Tone Pulsation.

ROBERT GANSERT

PURPOSE OF THE BOOK

The purpose of this book is to reveal to the singer, teacher and student the coordinated interaction of mind, body and air and the relevant dynamics, resulting from this interaction, that are responsible for the phenomena, structure and variety of vocal sounds emanating from the human body.

The author avoids making appraisals of prominent popular and classical singers, past and present, since the Gan-Tone Method is a penetration and revelation of how vibrations, which are responsible for vocal sound, are affected by the dynamics resulting from the coordinated interaction of mind, body and air. Any student, aware of the Gan-Tone Principles involved in the production of vocal sound, is able to diagnose the vocal vibratory condition of any singer in order to determine the degree of effective, coordinated interaction of mind, body and air which, in turn, determines the singer's vocal quality. This awareness becomes the criteria for enabling the student to evaluate, not only the vocal skill of any singer without depending on the critic's appraisal, but, also, the degree of skill possessed by speakers as well.

The greater the degree of restriction of vocal cords vibrations in the vocal cords area, for ex., the more strident, reedy and hard the quality of the emitted sound.

The greater the freedom of the sound, the greater the skill possessed by the singer or speaker in extending the radii of vibrations from the vocal cords, omnidirectionally, throughout the body, rather than restricting vibrations at the vocal cords, resulting in a mellow, deep, resonant, buoyant, brilliant sound. As the vocal cords vibrations transmit omnidirectionally, the thrust of these vibrations penetrates the depths of the body giving the emitted sound not only a full-bodied quality but, also, great brilliance as a result of penetrating the head resonators.

This transmission of vibrations omnidirectionally is concomitant with the transference, moderation and elimination of vocal cords pressure and friction which is the essence of the Gan-Tone Method. Since the restricted area of the throat, which contains the vocal cords, is the most susceptible area for irritation and pressure in the process of singing or speaking, moderation of any form of friction in this area is absolutely essential for insuring vocal survival.

The vocal skill of any singer in the Gan-Tone Method is determined by his degree of awareness and utilization of the Jaw, Larynx, Body Fusion and the Gan-Tone Pulsation. The greater the fusion of the jaw, larynx and body, and the more efficient the application of the Gan-Tone Pulsation, the greater the propagation of vocal cords vibrations omnidirectionally and the greater the transference of pressure from the delicate vocal cords to the body enabling the singer to produce voluminous, full-bodied sound with a minimum of vocal cords pressure.

However, it is important to note that the degree to which the Gan-Tone Pulsations transmit vocal cords vibrations to the body extremities, i.e., from the rectal-pelvic basin to the sinus cavities, is dependent on the skill possessed by the singer in swiftly applying the Maximal (Absolute) Jaw, Larynx, Body Fusion. If, for ex., the singer has not mastered the maximum simulation of the yawn, i.e., the Feather-Touch Contact of the jaw on the larynx, during moments of great stress (loud, high, sustained sounds), then the penetration of vocal cords vibrations to the body extremities on the Gan-Tone Pulsations is diminished. This condition is comparable to the stifled state of the natural yawn when the jaw is not quite released down and back and resting, with a feather-touch, on the larynx.

Mastery of the Jaw, Larynx, Body Fusion, or the simulated yawn, makes the continuity of body fusion to the rectal-pelvic basin possible which enables the Compression Phase, or down-part of the Gan-Tone Pulsation, to transmit and amplify vocal cords and body vibrations to the Sphincter ani externus muscle, the lowest extremity of the torso (rectal-pelvic basin). This effective action makes possible an equally effective reaction, which is the thrusting of these vocal cords and body vibrations to the highest extremity of the body, the sinus cavities, thus maximizing overtones which are the direct result of undertones. The projected sound, therefore, is a product of the Gan-Tone two-phase cycle of Compression (undertones) and Thrust (overtones).

When the Jaw, Larynx, Body Fusion is ineffective, i.e., when the jaw is not resting on the larynx, with a Feather-Touch Contact, during moments of great stress (loud, high, sustained sounds), since the singer doesn't have control of the Pterygoideus lateralis muscle at the temple of the head, body fusion to the rectal-pelvic basin is diminished, stifling the movement of vocal cords and body vibrations, producing vibrational absorption and focusing the amplification and control of vocal cords vibrations in the throat area rather than the body. This condition localizes stress in the throat rather than diffusing it through the body.

By effectively fusing vocal cords vibrations downward to the rectal-pelvic basin on the Gan-Tone Pulsations, as a result of mastering the Jaw, Larynx, Body Fusion, body vibrancy increases, producing greater amplification of vibrations and greater resonating space in the body cavities resulting in greater volume of sound with less expenditure of breath, since the body becomes a bell. The degree of resilience of the body and its resistence to vibratory absorption is dependent on the degree to which the Jaw, Larynx, Body Fusion and the Gan-Tone Pulsations are applied involving the diaphragm and extending the utilization of the body to the Sphincter ani externus muscle, the lowest extremity (rectal-pelvic basin), as a controlling center for the transmission, amplification and thrust of vocal cords and body vibrations thus establishing the Gan-Tone Principle of Rectal-Pelvic Breath Control. The diaphragmatic muscle now becomes a part of the many abdominal muscles which are maximally utilized in muscular contraction for fusing body parts and vocal cords and body vibrations to the foundation of the pelvis on the Compression Phase, or down-part of the Gan-Tone beat.

In the Gan-Tone Method, mind swiftly coordinates body parts in the Jaw, Larynx, Body Fusion which yields the effective fusion of body parts and the compression of vocal cords and body vibrations to the lowest extremity of the body (Sphincter ani externus muscle at the rectal-pelvic basin) which, in turn, yields an equal reaction (Newton's Law of Action and Reaction) of thrust of these vibrations to the highest extremity of the body (sinus cavities), when the Gan-Tone Pulsation is applied which, in turn, yields a minimum expenditure of breath, or air, in producing sound, as a result of sinking the breath through Rectal-Pelvic Breath Control causing body resilience and thereby enabling the entire body to function as a bell. Without the application of the Jaw, Larynx, Body Fusion and the Gan-Tone Pulsation, Rectal-Pelvic Breath Control would be impossible.

This coordinated interaction of mind, body and air, in the Gan-Tone Method, causes vocal sounds of great depth, height, resilience and brilliance to emanate from the human body.

**SOME CURRENT BELIEFS REGARDING VOCAL PRODUCTION
REJECTED BY THE GAN-TONE METHOD**

GAN-TONE REJECTIONS

Incomplete knowledge of the natural mechanical laws utilized in vocal production has resulted in many current beliefs which the Gan-Tone Method of Voice Production will not only reject, but will replace with verifiable truths.

These current beliefs, essentially vague, incomplete or actually incorrect, will be summarized briefly in this section to motivate the reader to continue reading in order to learn how the principles of the Gan-Tone Method handle these beliefs.

CONTENTS

GAN-TONE REJECTIONS

I.	The method varies with the singer.	7
II.	Vocal instruction can be achieved through imitation.	7
III.	Voice placement can be attained without an understanding of the principles of body mechanics.	8
IV.	The diaphragm is the origin of support for effective vocal projection.	8
V.	The diaphragmatic muscle is the primary source for breath control.	9
VI.	Obesity is desirable for fine singing.	9
VII.	Loss of weight will result in loss of the voice.	9
VIII.	Throat sprays and liquor before performances will relax the artist and improve the quality of his vocal delivery.	9
IX.	Singing should be accompanied with smiling.	10
X.	Advancing years result in a decline of vocal prowess.	10
XI.	Advancing age results in the fallen voice characterized by a loss of high notes and a deepening, darkening quality in the voice.	10
XII.	Lifting the body while singing sustained phrases in the upper vocal register helps to attain security.	10
XIII.	Singing with the intellect rather than the emotions tends to make the singer uneasy.	10
XIV.	Many methods are needed to teach singing properly.	11
XV.	Vocalises are effective for positioning the voice accurately and developing perception.	12
XVI.	Adolescent voice students should not be exposed to arias and art songs, since the lack of physical development can cause damage to the vocal apparatus.	12
XVII.	There are three registers in the singing voice.	13
XVIII.	The tremolo, an excessively wide vibrato, becomes a common occurrence with the aging artist.	13

Singing Energy

XIX.	A classical singer can't do popular singing without the classical influence.	14
XX.	The falsetto voice is a false or artificial voice which lies above the male's natural voice.	15
XXI.	Proper singing involves tightening muscles in the area of the thoracic diaphragm.	15

I. Human expression through sound in the art of singing has long been considered a mysterious ability possessed by a chosen few. For generations, the stress has been placed on the natural gifts of the singer. This empirical approach can only result, obviously, in confusion and uncertainty for the voice student, thus perpetuating the mystery. This confusion has been augmented by the traditional lack of agreement regarding the method for producing the singing voice, since it is generally believed that the method varies with the singer.

A method, however, implies the application of principles, in an orderly procedure, resulting in similar reactions, if applied to similar subjects. Utilization of a methodology should result in similar reactions, if applied to similar subjects as, for ex., humans; otherwise, there are no rules and, ultimately, no method.

Utilization of valid principles in an orderly procedure (method) should result in beautiful singing in all those who are willing to exert the labor necessary to manifest excellence. Verifiable basic laws remove the mystery and promote the realization that a scientific understanding of vocal production, not only makes this skill available to all, but, also, enables singers to produce beautiful sound for many years. Understanding scientific principles results in vocal freedom, thus promoting harmony in vocal demonstration as opposed to confusion, uncertainty and inharmony.

Since all humans have similar physical structures, i.e., for ex., the nose, mouth and throat are similarly arranged, there are not many methods for producing the voice but, essentially, one method.

II. It is believed that the teaching customs of the 18th and early 19th century singing teachers were outstanding because they utilized no method but simply sang to their pupils and asked them to imitate the sound.

This practice actually has no truth in principles. Imitation alone can not be interpreted. Since there are no principles that can be utilized, the singer is always in a state of doubt regarding his ability to produce any sound. However, since all humans have similar physical structures, they can do similar things with their voices through the utilization of basic principles. Awareness of basic scientific laws, which will result in similar reactions in all humans, will not only enable each person to control his own vocal instrument securely and intelligently, but will also enable him to express his own unique vocal quality, which can only be attained when the vocal line is completely unimpeded.

Familiarity with scientific principles regarding the coordination of the graduated jaw and the yawn with body involvement (Jaw, Larynx, Body Fusion), for example, will insure that pressure will be removed from the vocal line resulting in a free sound, and application of the Gan-Tone Pulsation will result in a scintillating sound.

Any voice teacher who is aware of the scientific principles in the Gan-Tone Method will know exactly where each student is regarding his level of understanding. He will also realize that all students are different and must be approached differently. Some, for example, have naturally resonant parts of the voice. Some sing high, some low, and some have unlimited range. The Gan-Tone Method stresses the pursuit of these qualities along with the application of Gan-Tone Principles, without any superfluous anatomical preoccupation, in order to free each voice to express its own unique sound. Rapport between teacher and pupil is based on principle, and the teacher must, therefore, find common ground where he can operate through principles of voice production with his pupil.

Since the Gan-Tone Principles produce similar reactions in all humans, they are applicable to the very talented as well as to those who have vocal problems. Since the talented present no challenge, it is with those students having vocal problems that the Gan-Tone Principles prove themselves.

III. Voice placement is a vague and desperate term repeatedly verbalized by the voice teacher in order to obtain resonance, flexibility and control in the singing voice. He often attempts to achieve these results by suggesting to the student that he place the tone in a high position, sometimes referred to as putting the voice in the mask, or getting the tone up-and-over. The teacher's inability, however, to completely understand how to concretize the coordination of the principles of body mechanics, to achieve the many dimensions of sound possible in the human voice, leaves the student's demonstration to chance and further compounds the student's confusion regarding voice placement.

The application of Gan-Tone Principles, however, concretizes the mechanics that are absolutely essential for achieving the proper placement of the voice which will result in resonance, flexibility and control, the characteristics of the free sound.

Rather than suggesting to the student that he place the tone high in the mask or that he circulate or arch the tone or that he get the tone up-and-over, application of Gan-Tone Principles that coordinate the jaw, the mouth, the body, the vocal cords and the yawn, in its many positions, will automatically achieve this result. In ascending the scale, for example, the singer encounters increasing pressure after several notes that culminates in the so called "break" in the voice. Not understanding how to allay this pressure, he attempts to continue ascending the scale by pushing through this accumulating pressure causing much tightness or tension in the jaw, throat and body muscles, resulting in a change in vocal quality. He may reach high tones or negotiate the demands of a song, but the vocal result is not one of evenness, flexibility, control or free resonance.

The Gan-Tone Principles completely eliminate this "break" in registers by immediately enabling the student to begin ascending the scale in a high position rather than the low one just described thereby lifting above the friction. This freedom is obtained by the simultaneously coordinated involvement of the varied positions of the yawn, the jaw, pressure on the Adam's apple (larynx) and downward pressure through the body to the rectal-pelvic basin (Jaw, Larynx, Body Fusion) commensurately with the degree of pressure to be overcome in the vocal line, enabling the singer to diffuse the pressure rather than pushing through it. Realization of the importance of not letting the jaw ride up as one ascends the scale prevents the constriction of the throat, eliminating an undesirable condition. Introduction of the Gan-Tone, which is a superimposed pulsation on the natural vibrations of the voice, enables the singer to get the tone up-and-over with intelligence and security rather than chance.

Since all humans have similar physical characteristics, this simultaneous coordination of body mechanics will result in an unimpeded vocal line in all singers. This principle is scientific, since it is applicable to all humans. Essentially, the greatest difficulty of singers who have vocal problems can be traced to ignorance regarding this coordination of the yawn, the jaw, the body, (Jaw, Larynx, Body Fusion) and the Gan-Tone Pulsation. A thorough knowledge of these principles eliminates the mystery of voice placement and enables the singer to produce free sound with security.

IV. Voice projection, as it is currently understood and practiced, stresses the origin of support in the body at the diaphragmatic muscles. This belief is incomplete, since Webster's Dictionary defines the diaphragm as "a partition separating the cavity of the chest from that of the abdomen." This definition proves that the diaphragm divides the body in half, therefore, placing a limitation on the full understanding of body utilization in vocal projection.

In the Gan-Tone Method of Voice Production, the origin of support in vocal projection is not the diaphragm but the torso, down to the rectal-pelvic basin, which can be considered the cylinder of the body. This cylinder (torso) contains the piston, which is the act of grunting down through the torso, or cylinder. Exerting pressure downward through the torso to the rectal-pelvic basin causes the voice to be projected and makes the body a resilient agent for sustaining, propping, or supporting, the sound. The degree of grunting, or pressure exerted downward through the torso, concomitant with laryngeal pressure, the yawn and the graduated jaw, determine the varied dimensions of the sound. The piston-like action of the grunt through the cylinder (torso) is reflected in the superimposed beat, or the Gan-Tone Pulsation. Maximum utilization of these principles in any part of the singing scale will result in scintillating, vibrant and voluminous sounds.

V. Breath Control, that coveted secret of beautiful singing, involves the ability to sustain long phrases, execute intricate passages and simultaneously shade and color the sounds without running out of breath. The current belief that diaphragmatic breath control leads to this desired result is not incorrect, since the utilization of this diaphragmatic musculofibrous septum (thoracic-abdominal diaphragm) does contribute to breath control. This belief, however, is incorrect, if it is considered the primary source for developing the sustained sound.

In the Gan-Tone Method, creating a long breath line is dependent on the utilization of the whole body as a resilient support and magnifier of breath through the transmission of vocal cords and body vibrations to the bottom of the torso (rectal-pelvic basin) at the pelvic-perineum diaphragm on the Gan-Tone Pulsations made possible through the Jaw, Larynx, Body Fusion, thus including the diaphragm and establishing the Gan-Tone Principle of Rectal-Pelvic Breath Control.

The thoracic-abdominal diaphragm, in the Gan-Tone Method, is a part of the many body muscles which are maximally utilized in muscular contraction for fusing body parts and vocal cords and body vibrations to the bottom of the torso (rectal-pelvic basin).

The body resilience produced, as a result of sinking the breath through Rectal-Pelvic Breath Control, causes the body to function as a bell, thus requiring a minimum expenditure of breath in producing the singing sound.

VI. For generations the belief was held that obesity was desirable for fine singing.

Although size does play an important role in volume and quality of tone, as exemplified by the obvious disparity of sound between the baby grand and the concert grand pianos, size alone, however, is not essential for fine singing. The application of Gan-Tone Principles takes priority over size in producing volume and quality of sound.

The voice of an obese soprano, without an understanding of Gan-Tone Principles, for example, is inferior in volume and quality to the voice of a thinner soprano who applies these principles, since, for example, the thinner soprano is utilizing the complete body in vocal projection; whereas, the obese soprano is concentrating on partial body support at the diaphragm.

VII. It is also commonly believed that a loss of weight will result in loss of the voice as can be noted with several famous singers.

Although there is a temporary loss of vocal control, since weight loss will result in a change of balance and size of sound, application of scientific principles will result in vocal adjustment.

Volume, for example, can be increased through complete body utilization in vocal projection and a maximum application of vocal focus (Thrust Phase—up-part of Gan-Tone Pulsation).

However, it is fair to note that if an obese soprano applied the Gan-Tone Method of Voice Production and then had a weight loss, her readjusted voice would not be comparable in size and quality to the voice she possessed before the weight loss.

VIII. It is a popular belief that spraying the throat or imbibing liquors or wines before performing will relax the artist and thus improve the quality of his vocal delivery.

This practice is a poor substitute for the necessary scientific principles that promote secure vocal production. Although the artist may experience some anxiety prior to performing, knowledge of these principles insures the intelligent use of his vocal apparatus. Involvement with the operation of principles while singing causes the artist to draw attention away from himself and thus control anxiety.

IX. Many believe that singing should be accompanied with smiling.

A scientific application of principles in singing would make this belief incorrect, if it is used as a fundamental principle in tone production, since smiling tends to concentrate tone in the dental area resulting in a restriction of the open throat which, in turn, concentrates pressure on the vocal cords.

When vocal freedom is attained, the expression on the singer's face is free of anxiety and, therefore, presents a pleasant appearance. The singer can then assume various degrees of facial expressions including the smile, since outward expressions, such as grimaces and smiles, are imposed when the vertical-elliptical vocal structure is unnecessary, i.e., when the maximum dimensions of the soft as well as the loud sounds are not required.

X. It is commonly believed that advancing years result in a decline of vocal prowess.

This belief is incorrect, if the artist's health is intact. It would be more correct to state that the degree of vocal ability manifested by the artist is commensurate with his degree of understanding regarding the application of vocal principles.

Physical strength undoubtedly declines with advancing years and results in a devitalization of body functions. Since it is the decline of the physique rather than the vocal cords, maximizing scientific principles will result in minimizing body exertion thus extending the vocal skill of the aging artist. Complete involvement of the body as opposed to partial involvement (diaphragm) results in a more supported sound in the older artist that cannot be duplicated by the younger performer, since physical maturity plays a role in the settling of sound in the body.

XI. Many believe that advancing age (50 plus) results in the fallen voice characterized by a loss of high notes and a deepening and darkening quality in the voice.

This condition, however, implies that the aging artist has always utilized a tight and restricted position in producing sound, brought about by a rigidity of the jaw in an attempt to control the voice, as opposed to a flexible, graduated jaw opening that is commensurate with the vocal demand. Since strength wanes with age, the older artist is physically unable to continue manipulating the jaw in producing sound.

If the artist, however, had been aware of scientific principles, he would have known how to allay the pressures that result from a rigid jaw position. Furthermore, since sound settles in the body with advancing years, the older artist, if singing correctly, should possess a more mellow instrument of more than ample dimensions, thus by-passing the afflictions of the fallen voice.

XII. In the process of singing sustained phrases in the upper vocal register, artists lift their bodies, essentially their shoulders or heels, in order to attain security.

This practice is incorrect, since these parts of the body should be drawn downward, rather than upward, in order to attain maximum support.

Without any outward manifestation, pressure should be exerted downward, by contractive muscular action, with the inclusion of the diaphragm, to the bottom of the torso at the pelvic-perineum diaphragm. Packing the body by forcing pressure to the bottom of the torso is comparable to the vertical, downward propellent action of the rocket fuel on the launching pad. The intensity of downward pressure and the solidity of the launching pad determine the rocket's degree of thrust. The diffusion of thrust that occurs when lifting the body as opposed to packing the body downward to the bottom of the torso is analogous to the fate of the rocket if it were launched from a platform composed of sand. The downward thrust of the rocket engines would dig a hole in the sand and weaken the upward thrust of the rocket, thus making the lift-off unsuccessful.

The diffusion of thrust in producing sound, caused by lifting the body, curtails the support of the tone, resulting in a thin voice of limited size in the upper register.

XIII. Books focusing on the mechanics of voice production have a tendency to promote uneasiness in the singer causing him to rely on the intellect rather than upon feelings in expressing himself vocally.

This belief is vague and misleading to the voice student. Scientific principles should take precedence over emotion, since the gamut of emotional expression encompassed by the artist is dependent on the degree of facility he has with his instrument. More effective shading and coloring of sound to coincide with feeling or emotional expression, for example, require a freer vocal instrument. Facility with scientific vocal principles, ultimately, is the key to this freedom. Contrary to the belief that the singer sing with the heart to obtain a desired emotion, mental concentration on scientific principles should, instead, take priority. Scientifically maintaining a high order in the structure of the vocal line and imposing the particular emotion within the framework of this structure not only prevents any distortion of the sound, but also enables the artist to be in constant control of his vocal line.

Artistic production, therefore, requires the control of the instrument and the application of the emotion within the confines of this control. Furthermore, singers are role playing and are, therefore, seeking to simulate a high degree of authenticity rather than actually experiencing a particular emotion. Obviously, no performer would last physically if he experienced every emotion he expressed while role playing. This simulated emotion is controlled by the mental application of what one considers the characteristics of a particular feeling and, therefore, does not, ultimately, involve the heart.

Primitive singing was essentially an expression of emotions and was not concerned with the voice as an artistic instrument. Emphasis on singing as an art, however, requires that greater stress be placed on the vocal instrument rather than the emotion, that is, the balance must shift to understanding rather than instinct.

Appropriate involvement of the heart in singing should reflect the artist's utmost sincerity in seeking to achieve the greatest heights of vocal freedom in his demonstration, through a maximum understanding of principles, which would inspire and elevate his listeners.

XIV. Many incapable singing teachers destroy many excellent voices since they are aware of only a few methods of voice production and teach them in the same manner to all pupils. The exhaustive effacing of the incorrect method, when these students change teachers, often produces no improvement.

This belief not only further corroborates the confusion that exists regarding the application of methodology in voice production, but also provides an immediate excuse for a voice teacher's inability to correct problems. Application of a scientific method would not only eliminate the teacher's need to dwell on the condemnation of other teachers but would also eliminate his need to know where the student received the incorrect instruction. Overcoming the problem would be the teacher's only concern. Efficacious application of principles is not dependent on whether the student is a beginner or an advanced one having vocal difficulty, but, rather, on the level of the student's understanding of basic principles, since a method implies the application of definite principles that should be applicable to all; otherwise, there are no rules and, ultimately, no method.

The Gan-Tone Method rejects the belief that the exhaustive effacing of the incorrect method often results in no improvement. It was written that the tares should grow together with the wheat until the day of harvest, when you will reap the harvest and the tares will be eliminated. Rather than dwelling on the negative aspect, rise above the student's problem by concentrating on the principle that corrects the difficulty, and the problem will vanish. Vocal restriction, for example, is usually the primary problem that creates vocal difficulty; therefore, emphasis should be focused on scientific principles that free the instrument. Although no two voices are alike, the full beauty of each voice is achieved only when the vocal line is completely unimpeded.

The belief that there is often no improvement in attempting to correct vocal inharmony proves that the theory being applied is incorrect, since, if a principle is scientific, the result achieved should be harmonious. Although the approach to each student is different, in order to compensate for individual differences, the scientific principles applied, however, are the same for all.

XV. Vocalises have long been considered effective for practicing singing on vowel sounds. It is also believed that vocalises position and stabilize the voice accurately while promoting the singer's perception for singing extensive, superior and complicated melodies.

Vocalises, however, are an incorrect approach to placing and stabilizing the voice accurately, since they are not based on a scientific method for producing sound. Any positioning of the voice is merely left to chance, leaving the student unaware of the mechanics of voice production necessary for developing an even scale. Since there is no application of scientific principles for freeing the vocal line, the student may be learning and reinforcing a restricted production that will not only limit his vocal potential, but may also cause vocal impairment. Unless the student is observed carefully, in the process of vocalizing, by a knowledgeable voice teacher in order to make the student aware that every point of vocal pressure must be counteracted with scientific principles to overcome this stress, vocalises for placing and stabilizing the voice could be disastrous.

Vocalises to promote perception for singing extensive, superior and complicated melodies are impractical, since the application of a scientific method for producing sound enables the teacher to by-pass vocalises and promote perception in the student for singing these melodies as they appear in musical context, such as arias and songs. By applying Gan-Tone Principles to a singing line in an aria, rather than singing a vocalise, the student, under the watchful eye of the teacher, learns how to overcome the points of stress, thus insuring freedom in his vocal line and enabling him, therefore, to develop taste for singing many varied melodies.

Since vocalises are never sung in public and don't emphasize scientific principles for effective singing, they are of no intrinsic value to the voice student. However, the principles utilized in the Gan-Tone Method, such as the Jaw, Larynx, Body Fusion and the Gan-Tone Pulsation, can be applied to any vocalise to enlarge dimensions and promote vocal freedom.

In the Gan-Tone Method, dynamic exercises are applied in songs being sung. These exercises construct and produce the voice according to the desired vibratory effect at any given point in the melodic line.

XVI.   It is a popular belief that the adolescent voice student should not be exposed to arias and art songs since the lack of physical development at this age may cause damage to the vocal apparatus.

The application of scientific principles, however, makes this belief incorrect. Pressure, for example, focused on the vocal cords in negotiating intricate passages and broad melodic lines involving a wide vocal range is the outstanding factor contributing to damage of the vocal cords and muscular apparatus. Although adult voice students can take more abuse of the vocal cords and the muscular apparatus, since they have more physical development than the adolescent, constant friction on the cords, however, will also cause vocal impairment in the adult.

Rather than having the student push through vocal pressure, application of Gan-Tone Principles alleviates this stress by making the student aware of the scientific positioning of the physical apparatus essential for removing the friction. Awareness, for example, of the graduated jaw positions necessary for overcoming the various degrees of pressure prevents friction of the vocal cords.

The assimilation of scientific principles involved in body mechanics should precede the insertion of sound. Securing this "voiceless" position to prevent muscling and thereby avoid straining is comparable to constructing a building. The framework is built before adding the plaster, plumbing, etc. In the application of scientific principles, therefore, the student becomes aware of singing positions, rather than notes, in order to create the physical conditions necessary for freeing the vocal line, thus enabling the student to realize his own unique vocal potential.

In teaching the adolescent student, however, the voice teacher should be exceptionally attentive to making the student aware that every point of vocal pressure must be counteracted with scientific principles. Anxiety of facial expression and the aftercough, for example, are signs of vocal restriction. Gradual application of downward pressure through the body must be accompanied by a vertical-elliptical mouth opening and a wider opening of the jaw, since these jaw positions must correspond to the amount of intensity applied to the support, otherwise damaging stress on the student's vocal cords and surrounding area becomes evident, but more readily on the vocal apparatus of the immature adolescent. The principles applied to the adult voice student and the adolescent, however, are the same except that the teacher would introduce principles more slowly and carefully with the adolescent.

Any adolescent fortunate enough to practice these principles to adulthood will have an advantage over the student who begins instruction at a later age, since practice over a longer period of time will result in a higher degree of coordination of body mechanics which will produce a freer instrument. The degree of vocal freedom is commensurate with the degree of understanding and ease involved in the application of these principles. Practice at regular intervals over a longer period of time, obviously, insures greater facility with any skill.

XVII.   It is currently believed that there are at least three registers in the singing voice. These registers are categorized as low, middle and high, since the quality of the voice appears to change in the ascending and descending scale, and the positions of the larynx, palate and tongue are believed to change accordingly.

The Gan-Tone method, however, rejects this belief of the different registers and reveals, instead, that there is only one register in the singing voice applicable for the performance of acceptable music.

Since the difference in quality of tones produced, while singing the scale, delineates the different registers, eliminating this variation in tonal quality eliminates this differentiation. Any singer who experiences this tonal change in the singing scale is pushing up the voice rather than lifting it. He is applying a depressed position rather than an uplifted one. Pushing occurs when the jaw rides up against the pressure that naturally builds, while ascending or descending the scale, causing a constriction of the throat aperture and resulting in a variation in tonal quality.

Rather than registers, there are impasses in the singing scale which can be overcome by applying the principle of the graduated jaw and the yawning position. The high yawn and the graduated jaw positions (Jaw, Larynx, Body Fusion) necessary to overcome pressures prevent restriction in the throat, thus avoiding impasses and preventing any changes in tonal quality, which results in the even scale, or one register. This high position is comparable to an airplane that flies above the clouds in order to avoid the stresses of a raging storm.

Furthermore, rather than focusing on body parts, such as the vocal cords, surrounding throat muscles and diaphragm, it is the skill developed in coordinating the jaw in order to unite the body by fusion, from the rectal-pelvic basin to the head resonators, throughout the range that produces the even scale, or one register.

XVIII. It is believed that the tremolo, which is an excessively wide vibrato, becomes a common occurrence with the aging artist.

This belief is incorrect, since it is not advancing years, but the uncontrolled jaw and the depressed, or low, position of the vocal attack which results in the tremolo.

This excessive vibrato doesn't often occur in the younger artist, who may also be singing with a halted position of the jaw, since he has the strength to hold the jaw in place and the muscles to sustain the natural vibrato in the voice.

The aging artist, however, lacks this strength and, as a result, the jaw can't be held down, causing it to wobble. This undisciplined jaw interferes with the flow of sound causing a tremolo in the vocal line.

Although the aging artist may still be able to hold the jaw in place, a tremolo can still develop, as a result of the excessive muscular energy needed to combat pressure in the vocal line. (Muscles spasm under pressure.) Waning energy with advancing age causes a reduction of speed in the natural vibrato of the voice resulting in a tremolo. Obviously, then, will power alone is insufficient, since the artist no longer has the strength to hold muscles by sheer determination.

It is much easier, however, to correct the tremolo rather than dwell on its causes. As in mathematics, the problem will be solved only when the correct principle is applied.

In order to eradicate the tremolo in the aging artist, it is necessary to be aware of the Gan-Tone Principles, since the application of these principles will result in a voluntary, rather than an involuntary, control of the vibrato as, for ex., the utilization of the graduated jaw positions necessary to cope with the various pressures will eliminate the tight jaw, thus removing the need for excessive muscular strength in the neck, since the pressures of the singing line are transferred to the body.

Application of the Gan-Tone will enable the artist to mentally harness the vibrato. The Gan-Tone is a superimposed pulsation on the natural vibrations of the voice. It involves the mental imposition of a calculated beat, which is produced by the simultaneous action of the downward pressure through the body and the downward action of the jaw on the larynx (Adam's apple) along with the yawn (Jaw, Larynx, Body Fusion), while making a sound and then repeating it. The cycle of this beat, for example, is comparable to the cycle of the pulse beat. The speed of these beats, or Gan-Tones, is controlled by the singer in order to achieve a controlled vocal line and also add dimension, buoyancy, brilliance and scintillation to the voice. In addition, the yawn and the graduated positions of the jaw (to coincide with the pressure demands) relax the jaw, thus minimizing physical tension, since the artist can maintain a free passage in the throat area, rather than muscling through the points of stress. Utilizing a minimum of muscular strength and mentally applying the Gan-Tone Pulsation enable the singer to transpose the vocal line into a mentally controlled series of beats, or Gan-Tones.

Mastering this control early in the singer's career results in the avoidance of a tremolo with advancing years.

XIX. It is believed that if a student is trained to do classical singing (opera, art songs), he can't do popular singing without the classical influence.

The Gan-Tone Method of Voice Production, however, makes this belief incorrect, since adaptability of the voice to classical or popular singing is dependent on the degree of understanding of the Gan-Tone Principles. The application of principles would be the same except that moving from the popular to the classical would require a greater degree of understanding.

Popular singing requires less range, power, control and musicianship along with less knowledge regarding clean attacks of the vocal line thus making a thorough knowledge of the Gan-Tone Principles unessential.

In classical singing, the performance of long phrases involving a wide gamut of range and intricate passages with shading and coloration necessitates more knowledge and skill with these principles.

In both types of vocal expression, however, the singer is confronted with the problem of overcoming pressures of the vocal line and must, therefore, apply, in varying degrees, the principles of the graduated jaw coordinated with body support in order to counteract these stresses.

Since classical singing requires more range, the singer must become acquainted with the wider positions of the jaw in order to accommodate the greater pressures. Greater volume also necessitates more awareness of body support.

In singing popular songs, however, the classical singer fails to modify the principles of body mechanics to adjust to the more limited range and volume of popular singing. He applies the same degree of principles required for classical expression to the popular and the result becomes pompous, distorted and even comical. A modification in the utilization of the Gan-Tone laws of body mechanics would enable the classical artist to perform popular songs without sounding like a classical singer. To achieve a smooth transition from classical to popular singing, in training the student, the voice teacher should be skilled in enabling the classical student to experience the singing of different sounds produced with a variety of jaw and mouth positions coordinated with a variation in body support (Modified to Absolute Jaw, Larynx, Body Fusion) in order to prevent a rigidity in singing positions.

Application of the lifted position, which is the result of the Jaw, Larynx, Body Fusion and the Gan-Tone Pulsation, enables the singer, classical or popular, to produce an unimpeded vocal line resulting in the even scale, thus revealing the full beauty of the voice.

Often popular singers "burn out" early in their singing careers because they experience many problems with their vocal cords, as a result of their ignorance of the scientific principles that would counteract the pressures of the vocal line.

Awareness and application of Gan-Tone Principles eliminate vocal impedence, thus leaving the singer free to involve his own unique qualities in the interpretation of classical as well as popular music.

XX. Webster's Dictionary defines the falsetto voice as "a false or artificial voice, specifically, that voice of a man which lies above his natural voice."

The Gan-Tone Method of Voice Production proves this definition incorrect.

Falsetto is the diminutive in Italian for the word false. By definition, falsetto means slightly false, but not completely so. However, this so-called falsetto voice is not false at all, but extremely natural, and part of the vocal cords. It is false because man has imposed the belief that to apply pressure to the larynx while fusing the vocal cords gives a manly sound. This voice produced with fused vocal cords-laryngeal pressure can be sustained without collapsing up to a certain point in the range, usually a High C.

The voice produced in the "falsetto" manner can also be duplicated in the lower range and is not, therefore, "that voice of a man which lies above his natural voice." The lowest note in the natural range of the male, if sung with the jaw firmly placed downward on the larynx, or Adam's apple, will attain the same quality as the so-called falsetto voice, as long as the vocal cords are not fused to the larynx. Furthermore, in the yawn position, it is possible to ascend the scale into the falsetto range without any break in the scale. It is obvious, therefore, that this voice is not limited to the range that exists above the natural voice because the entire range of the male voice, without application of vocal cords-laryngeal pressure in the course of ascending the scale, naturally includes the so-called falsetto voice. Degree of body support is not a factor in creating the falsetto quality. A male can apply full body support and achieve the same quality as long as he is not applying vocal cords-laryngeal fusion.

When pressure is applied on the vocal cords and larynx, while ascending the scale, the quality characteristic of the manly voice is attained. However, in the process of ascending the scale, the pressure brought to bear on the larynx becomes increasingly intense and puts such strain on the muscular structure to the point where this structure collapses, thus removing the pressing-downward action on the larynx. When this pressure on the larynx is removed, volume collapses and the voice loses the bigness, i.e., the manly quality. By removing vocal cords-laryngeal fusion, strain is no longer focused on the cavity of the larynx, although the vocal cords are still being utilized.

Since the larynx functions as an amplifier, removing pressure from this area results in de-amplification, or in the so-called falsetto voice, even though body support is still being applied. The recipient of the sound from the vocal cords is no longer the larynx, since this focal point is now being by-passed. The sound, no longer focused on the larynx, moves to the head resonators as principle amplifiers. Although a big sound can be produced by applying body pressure, it is not a manly sound. Since this laryngeal fusion with the vocal cords no longer exists, the male can continue to sing to the highest end of his vocal cords.

The human, therefore, is not equipped to reach the highest end of his vocal cords, when the cords are fused to the larynx. Actually, God has given man more reach in his voice than he can grasp.

A Gan-Tone definition of the falsetto voice would, therefore, be as follows:

> The falsetto voice is not a false voice but the natural male or female voice through the entire gamut of the vocal cords produced by not fusing the vocal cords to the larynx. Application of pressure while fusing the vocal cords to the larynx results in the so-called manly sound but limits the range of the vocal cords that can be utilized, since increased range results in increased strain on the muscular, cartilaginous, ligamentous (vocal cords) structure of the larynx.

XXI. Proper singing involves tightening muscles in the area of the thoracic diaphragm.

This belief is incorrect, since tension in any part of the body, such as hands, toes, buttocks, leg muscles, stomach muscles, or any other muscles, as well as tense facial expressions, such as grimaces, produce rigidity. Tension in any part of the body, therefore, causes fatigue and stifles body resilience. Just as the human utilizes the leg muscles, for example, without tension (rigidity) in walking, so the muscles of the body must be coordinated, without tension, in the singing process.

The body should be considered a resilient agent. In supporting sound, the body acts as a spring. As pressure is imposed through the body by grunting downward, pressure naturally goes downward to the bottom of the spring, i.e., to the rectal area of the body. In its descending action, it involves the lungs, heart, diaphragm, liver, gallbladder, spleen, stomach, ascending, transverse, descending and sigmoid colons to the anus, also known as the rectal area. When greater volume or increased range are desired, the increased bodily stress which results can be minimized by concentration of support in the lower extremities at the pelvic-perineum diaphragm.

Maximizing body support and thrust by utilization of the torso to the rectal-pelvic basin not only facilitates greater vocal volume but also promotes buoyancy in the upper range.

Complete torso involvement also promotes diffusion of the increased laryngeal pressure which results when producing high tones.

This concentration of support in the lower extremities is also desirable for drawing pressure away from the vocal cords and the upper vital organs, such as the heart.

This maximum torso utilization is analogous to the position of a mechanical piston, which is a sliding cylinder within a cylindrical vessel. When the driving action of the piston reaches the bottom of the cylindrical vessel, maximum energy is produced. When maximum support and thrust are desired for emitting tones effectively in the ascending or descending scale, complete torso involvement is, therefore, imperative.

The variation in body pressure downward is controlled by the singer in the form of an imposed beat called the Gan-Tone. Each downward movement through the body to the rectal-pelvic basin is accompanied by a downward movement of pressure on the larynx, produced by the downward movement of the jaw, while yawning, creating Jaw, Larynx, Body Fusion. However, the depth and intensity of the downward packing of the body, comparable to the piston in the cylinder, determine the degree of body utilization involved in support and thrust. The body, therefore, becomes a resilient agent and pulsates like the heart beat. For every downward beat there is a release, thus preventing tension in any part of the body.

WHY THE GAN-TONE METHOD IS A SCIENTIFIC METHOD

CONTENTS

WHY THE GAN-TONE METHOD IS A SCIENTIFIC METHOD

I.	How the Gan-Tone Method fulfills the requirements of a Scientific Method	21
II.	The definition of Singing Energy in the Gan-Tone Method and how it relates to popular and classical singing	21
III.	The role of body mechanics, i.e., the Jaw, Larynx, Body Fusion and the Gan-Tone Pulsation, in extending the vocal cords throughout the body	22
IV.	The Three Phases of the Vibratory Structure of Vocal Sound in the Gan-Tone Method	22
V.	The Lack of feather-touch control between the Jaw, Larynx and Body and its effect on Vibrating air	23
VI.	The role of the Gan-Tone Pulsation in conjunction with the Jaw, Larynx, Body Fusion in producing Rectal-Pelvic Breath Control	24
VII.	Procedure for Maximizing Amplification of the Sound-Producing Cycle by the Gan-Tone Pulsation	25
VIII.	How Body Vibrations are Produced	25
IX.	The role of the Jaw, Larynx, Body Fusion and the Gan-Tone Pulsation in making the whole body, rather than the lungs, function as a bellows	25
X.	The role of the Gan-Tone Pulsation in conjunction with the Jaw, Larynx, Body Fusion in transforming the Limited Amplitude of the Fundamental Frequency to an Alternating Current whose Amplitude Extends to the Body Extremities	26
XI.	The Role of the Gan-Tone Pulsation in affecting the Vibrancy of Pitch	26
XII.	The role of the Jaw, Larynx, Body Fusion and the Gan-Tone Pulsation in maintaining the dimensions of the sound	27
XIII.	Voice Projection in the Gan-Tone Method	27
XIV.	Procedure for Rectal-Pelvic Breath Control and Vocal Thrust (Voice Projection) in Humans with the Gan-Tone Method	28
XV.	Body Resilience in the Gan-Tone Method	28
XVI.	Support (Appoggio) in the Gan-Tone Method	29

XVII.	Abdominal Breathing (Diaphragmatic Breath Control) in the Gan-Tone Method	30
XVIII.	The Falsetto Voice in the Gan-Tone Method	30
XIX.	Avoiding the Ill Effects of Vibrating Air Pressure in the Throat with the Gan-Tone Method	32
XX.	The Attack in the Gan-Tone Method	33
XXI.	Range in the Gan-Tone Method	34
XXII.	The Body Register in the Gan-Tone Method	34
XXIII.	Attaining the Center of Tone in the Gan-Tone Method	35
XXIV.	Mouth Opening in the Gan-Tone Method	37
XXV.	Areas of Resonance in the Gan-Tone Method	39
XXVI.	The Function of the Diaphragm in Breathing	40
XXVII.	The Function of the Diaphragm in Speaking	41
XXVIII.	The Function of the Diaphragm in Singing in the Gan-Tone Method	41

WHY THE GAN-TONE METHOD IS A SCIENTIFIC METHOD

I. Science, according to Webster, is concerned with observation and classification of facts, especially with the establishment of verifiable general laws, or principles, chiefly by induction, which is reasoning from a part to a whole, or from the individual to the universal; and by hypotheses, which involves making assumptions tentatively in order to explain certain facts and guide in the investigation of others.

The Gan-Tone Method of Voice Production can be considered scientific according to this definition, since verifiable laws, or principles, have been established in this method, as a result of observing the relationship between the singing sounds produced by the human and the coordination of the body parts that make up his vocal apparatus. Tentative assumptions were made that were applied to many humans and after getting similar reactions, whenever these assumptions were applied, verifiable general laws, or principles, were established.

A method requires an orderly process or a definite system of procedure of instruction to obtain a desired result. If a method is applied to similar subjects, that is, humans, similar reactions should result thereby proving the validity of the principles, or laws, that were applied in an orderly procedure. If the principles applied resulted in different reactions in similar subjects, that is, humans, there would be no basis for establishing an orderly process, or method, since the variety of reactions would make it impossible to validate the principles applied.

The Gan-Tone Principles, applied in an orderly process, do result in similar reactions in all humans thereby fulfilling the requirements of a method. Since the human body, which includes the vocal apparatus, is similar in all humans, there are not many methods for producing the human voice in singing and speaking but, essentially, one method. The physical path through which the mind guides the air through the body is similar in all humans, since, for example, the location of the jaw, vocal cords, and larynx is the same, and the area of the throat, through which the mind guides the air, is restricted and curved in all humans. Although there are countless variations in the shape of body parts, the location of these parts is the same in all humans, requiring one method, not many methods, to guide the interaction of mind, body and air involved in the singing process.

The singer's grasp of the mechanics, that is, physical principles, or science, involved in the production of sound, which leads to the innumerable interactions of mind, body and air, is the very basis, or structure, of the art of singing. The degree to which the mechanics involved in the production of the human voice are mastered, determines the degree and variation of vibrant energy in the vocal expression.

Creativity, based on mastery of scientific principles, leads to the learning pulsation, which consists of the application of principles and subsequent unfoldment, bringing into existence, by successive development, the ultimate in human thought.

Awareness of mechanics which is the realm of physical science produces harmonious functioning of body parts, evolving countless dynamics of mind, body and air, resulting in skillful vocal performance which is art, making science and art synonymous and essential for achieving the ultimate in singing energy.

II. In the Gan-Tone Method, singing energy is the audible manifestation of vocal vibrations, from the pure vocal cords sound to the full-bodied, open-throated, head-resonant sound, that is, from the least audible vibrations produced on the edge of the vocal folds to the extension of the vocal cords throughout the whole body, by means of the application of the Jaw, Larynx, Body Fusion and the Gan-Tone Pulsation, producing maximum amplification of the original vocal cords vibrations. The greater the penetration of vocal cords vibrations through the body, the more energetic the singing line, that is, the greater the radiance, buoyancy, resilience, flexibility, evenness, security, depth and height of the singing line.

In the Gan-Tone Method, singing is controlled, vibrant, vocal energy which progressively dominates the lyrics, or message, being communicated as the dimensions of vibratory energy expand. Classical singing provides the best vehicle for expanding the dimensions of vocal, vibratory energy, since maximum involvement of the body produces a vibrant, energetic line of sound of such dimensions and radiance that it becomes the dominant component of communication as opposed to words. In popular singing, which is essentially a conversation-like vocal expression, whose singing line contains minimal dimensions of vocal, vibratory energy, the words, or text, dominate communication. In the Gan-Tone Method, ordinary speaking is uttering words, or articulating sounds, through minimal vocal energy, making speech the dominant component of communication. Therefore, as vibrating energy increases in the singing line, the resultant sound transcends words in conveying a message.

Communication that is dominated by sound appeals to the higher spiritual and intellectual inclinations of the human, since the sound appears to be produced beyond the body, giving it an ethereal quality. The spiritual quality in the sound is the result of audible vibrations maximized to an extraordinary level made possible through minimal vocal cords involvement and maximal body involvement, which require intellectual awareness.

III. Great control in technical skill, or body mechanics, is required to initiate vibrations at the vocal cords, with a feather-touch, and transmit these vocal cords vibrations to the omnidirectional extremities of the body on the Gan-Tone Pulsation, generating and amplifying these vibrations through the body which re-sound, with great impact, in the body cavities and, in turn, are re-sounded in the atmosphere, causing the singer to appear surrounded by a vibratory aura. The quality of this aura is determined by the singer's ability to progressively minimize vocal cords vibrations and pressures, as the demand for amplification increases, causing vibrating energy to diverge outwardly to the extremities of the body, rather than being converged at the vocal cords, in the attempt to amplify sound. This divergence of vibrations produces great dimensions in the sound, giving it a spiritual quality. The convergence of vibrations at the vocal cords, however, shrinks the dimensional qualities of the sound, as a result of minimal vibratory energy, giving the sound a reedy, tight, hard, throaty quality devoid of resilience and buoyancy.

The skill involved in coordinating the jaw, larynx and body in order to transmit vocal cords vibrations through the body, with a feather-touch on the vocal cords, is analogous to a tight rope walker performing his feat at a great height from the ground. The farther the singer gets from the vocal cords, in the production and amplification of the singing voice, the greater the skill required in the coordination of the jaw, larynx and body, and the more ethereal and breathtaking the vocal result. The farther away from the ground the tight rope walker gets, without a net, the more skill is required in balance, and the more ethereal and breathtaking his feat.

IV. In the Gan-Tone Method, the impact of vocal sound in the atmosphere consists of three phases of vibratory structure occurring concomitantly. They are as follows:

Phase One - The first phase is the initial state of vibrations which occurs when a jet of air from the lungs activates the vocal cords to vibrate at a specific pitch as, for example, A above Middle C, which is 440 v.p.s., resulting in omnidirectional penetration of vibrations. The limited thrust, resulting from the jet of air, confines the vocal cords vibrations primarily to the throat area, where they are essentially absorbed in the muscles and bones of the throat. Those parts of the diverging, vibrating spheres not absorbed in the solid parts pass through the open throat and re-sound in the cavities of the larynx, trachea, head and chest simultaneously.

This first phase produces minimal amplification, thrust and re-sounding of vibrations, creating a vocal sound in the atmosphere of limited volume, depth and height.

Phase Two - The second phase of vibratory structure is produced by the coordination of the jaw, larynx and body, which results in body fusion, creating the strongest unification of the body for vibratory amplification and penetration, when the original vocal cords vibrations (1st phase) are imposed upon by the Gan-Tone Pulsation, a superimposed beat on the fundamental pitch being sung. The original vocal cords vibrations are fused through the body to the rectal-pelvic basin and are compressed and amplified during the Compression

Phase, or down-part of the Gan-Tone beat. At the peak of compression, maximum thrust is developed, resulting in the omnidirectional penetration of vibrations throughout the body, which includes the re-sounding of these vibrations in the body cavities.

The singer can impose the Gan-Tone beat six times per second, amplifying the dimensions and thrust of the original, fundamental vocal cords pitch. The combination of vibratory energy of phase 1, that is, the constant flow of vibrations of the fundamental pitch, which can be, for example, A above Middle C, or 440 v.p.s., plus the intervals of Gan-Tone Pulsations, of phase 2, which can be imposed six times per second on a sustained note, greatly multiply the dimensions of the fundamental pitch with each imposition of the Gan-Tone.

The fundamental pitch remains constant, but the volume of amplified vibrations is greatly increased with each Gan-Tone beat, as a result of fusion, compression and thrust of vocal cords vibrations omnidirectionally from the rectal-pelvic basin.

Phase Three - The aggregate of vibratory energy of phases 1 and 2, projected into the atmosphere, produces the third phase of vibratory structure, or total impact of vocal sound in the atmosphere.

At this point, the sound of the fundamental pitch is characterized by great volume, depth and height.

V. The degree of skill demonstrated by the singer in effectively fusing the body through the coordination of the jaw, larynx and torso determines the degree of effective application of the Gan-Tone Pulsation, which, in turn, determines the degree of effective Rectal-Pelvic Breath Control and vocal projection. The relationship between the Jaw, Larynx, Body Fusion and the Gan-Tone Pulsation is a basic, scientific principle in the Gan-Tone Method.

Maximum fusion of the body occurs when the jaw is down and back and resting on the larynx with a minimum of pressure, or feather-touch, that is, a minimum amount of muscle energy is exerted in order to keep the contact between the jaw, larynx, muscles and cartilages of the throat firmly and securely in place, especially under pressure (loud, high sounds).

Lack of feather-touch control between the jaw, larynx and body causes vibrating air to move erratically through the vocal hook, or irregular, curved path from the trachea to the facial apertures. Irregular mental coordination results in erratic movements of movable parts in the throat, such as the tongue, mouth, muscles and cartilages, interfering with the flow of vibrating air, causing a disturbance in the singing line, making it unstable and subject to distortion and collapse. This condition is comparable to the testing of stress and strain involving the aerodynamics on wings and other surfaces of airplanes. By adjusting air pressure and the relative positions of the wings and other surfaces, metal fatigue and collapse can be determined and avoided.

In the wind tunnel, when air is jetted parallel to the wing surface, a relatively smooth division of air exists simultaneously, with minimal turbulence, on either side of the wing. As the angle of the wing is increased, exposing the flat surface to the air blast, turbulence is increased, since the air passing rapidly over the wing sets up a pulsation which consists of compression and rarefaction, or vacuum, causing the wing to vibrate. The speed of the pulsation frequency is dependent on the speed of the air passing over the wing surface, which, in turn, determines the degree of stress, or fatigue, on the airplane. The more the air velocity and accompanying turbulence increase, the more the wing vibrates, increasing stress and resulting in eventual collapse of the metal.

As the pitch of the vocal cords vibrations and the strength of the jet of air increase, turbulence also increases. If the tongue, mouth, muscles and cartilages are not kept firmly and securely in place, they will vibrate, like the wing, disrupting the stability of the sound. Increased stress in the muscles, caused by increased pitch and air velocity, will eventually result in the collapse of the muscles and sound.

The angle, or pitch, of the wing is comparable to the frequency, or pitch, of the voice. Increased pitch in the wing or voice increases turbulence, even though the air pressure is constant. Accelerated air pressure compounds turbulence, and the wing, like the throat muscles, eventually collapses, as a result of fatigue.

Natural laws, or common denominators, appear to be evident in all sciences making parallels, for example, in aerodynamics and electricity, convenient and helpful in the explanation of the Gan-Tone Method as a scientific study of voice production.

VI. Feather-Touch Contact of the jaw, larynx and body produces maximum body fusion, insuring the most effective utilization of the human breath. Maximum body fusion produces the greatest amount of resonating space in the body while transmitting vibrations omnidirectionally through the body, but especially to the rectal-pelvic basin. Therefore, when the jaw is completely down and back and fused to the larynx, with a feather-touch, Rectal-Pelvic Breath Control is in operation. The pressure that is involved in the downward movement of the vocal cords vibrations through the body is anchored and controlled at the rectal-pelvic basin, as the singer imposes pressure to this area. This fusion of body parts and transmission of vibrations through the body, anchored and controlled at the rectal-pelvic basin, are the governing principles of Rectal-Pelvic Breath Control and also, are the principles that determine the degree of transmission and re-sounding of vibrations above the vocal cords.

Divergence of pressure from the vocal cords through the body to the rectal-pelvic basin, or body fusion, decreases the need for air to activate the vocal cords in order to amplify sound. Amplification of sound becomes the task of the body, diminishing the need for air pressure, since the amplifier of the vocal cords vibrations is no longer the vocal cords or the larynx, but the entire body. Less breath is, therefore, required to amplify sound, or vocal cords vibrations, since the natural law in operation is as follows:

> The more powerful the amplifier, the less the need for air pressure to amplify sound.

Two kinds of pressures are involved in the initial production of vocal cords sound. The degree of air pressure impinging on the vocal cords for the production and amplification of vibrations is one kind, and the other kind is the pressure required on the vocal cords to maintain the pitch. Both kinds of pressures are increased as turbulence increases. Focusing increased air pressure on the vocal cords to amplify sound is not only a limited method, but it also increases friction, pressure and turbulence which, in turn, require greater pressure on the vocal cords by the singer to maintain the pitch. Increased pressure on the vocal cords leads to restriction of vocal cords vibrations in the neck, muscle fatigue and eventual collapse of the sound structure.

These pressures, however, are controlled and minimized, in the Gan-Tone Method, by Rectal-Pelvic Breath Control which is produced with the application of the Gan-Tone Pulsation.

Rectal-Pelvic Breath Control is characterized by the following necessary actions:

> Vocal cords vibrations are compressed to the rectal-pelvic area through body fusion by means of the down-part of the Gan-Tone beat (Compression Phase), which is accomplished by grunting down to the rectal-pelvic basin, as in the processes of yawning and vomiting.

> It should be noted that effective compression of vocal cords vibrations to the rectal-pelvic basin occurs only when the Feather-Touch Contact of the jaw, larynx and body is mastered, especially under pressure (loud, high notes).

> The application of the down-part of the Gan-Tone beat sinks the breath, fusing vibrations and grounding them to the bottom of the torso (rectal-pelvic basin). This area of the body becomes the central point for the greatest control of omnidirectional vocal cords vibrations, transferring the vibratory aura from the head and throat to the entire body by maximizing compression and rarefaction, the phases of the vibrational cycle.

**Compression and Rarefaction on the Vocal Cords—
The Two Phases of the Sound-Producing Cycle**

Compression: A jet of air from the lungs impinges on the folds of the vocal cords. This pressure on the vocal cords impacts the air causing sound.

Rarefaction: The elasticity of the vocal cords aids in enabling them to spring back in the opposite direction causing rarefaction, or a vacuum.

Since the air pressure from the lungs is constant, the cycle is repeated. One cycle is equal to one vibration. The frequency of this cycle of compression and rarefaction, per second, determines the pitch.

Procedure for Maximizing Amplification of the Sound-Producing Cycle by the Gan-Tone Pulsation

VII. The cycle of sound, compression and rarefaction, repeated, for example, 440 times per second is the pitch of A above Middle C (440 v.p.s.). If this pitch is held for 10 seconds, i.e., 4,400 vibrations, and a Gan-Tone Pulsation is imposed 5× per second, this Gan-Tone beat is being imposed 50× during this 10 second period. It should be noted that the Gan-Tone Pulsation does not disturb the mental coordination necessary to maintain the desired pitch as, for ex., 440 v.p.s. (A above Middle C). Each down-part of the Gan-Tone beat (Compression Phase), for ex., in A above Middle C, is fusing 88 vocal cords vibrations through the body to the rectal-pelvic basin amplifying these vibrations commensurately with the degree of pressure that the singer imposes on each Gan-Tone beat.

A Gan-Tone Principle follows:

> The greater the intensity of the Compression Phase of the Gan-Tone beat (down-part of the beat), which fuses the fundamental pitch to the rectal-pelvic basin, the greater the amplification of vibrations.

Rarefaction, or vacuum, in the body cavities is maximized, as a result of the rapid contraction of muscles, causing the cavities to be extended, as a result of compression, which sinks the breath and body parts.

This amplification of vocal cords vibrations through the body, during the down-part of the Gan-Tone beat, relieves the vocal cords of vibratory and frequency pressures, by eliminating the turbulence that occurs when focusing excessive pressure on the vocal cords to amplify sound. The entire body, rather than the vocal cords, is now responsible for amplification.

VIII. Fusion of vocal cords vibrations through the membranes, muscles, cartilages and bones of the body produces additional vibrations in these parts which are also fused with the vocal cords vibrations to the rectal-pelvic basin. These body vibrations are subject to the same Gan-Tone Principle regarding compression, i.e., the greater the intensity of the Compression Phase of the Gan-Tone Pulsation, the greater the amplification of body vibrations. Therefore, the application of the Gan-Tone Pulsation, not only amplifies vocal cords vibrations, but it also picks up activated body vibrations. Both the vocal cords and body vibrations travel, essentially, the same compression path, simultaneously, to the rectal-pelvic basin. These activated vocal cords and body vibrations make the whole body vibrate, giving it the function of the bell.

When the vocal cords and body vibrations reach maximum compression at the rectal-pelvic basin, the reaction to this action occurs, which is the Thrust Phase, or up-part of the Gan-Tone beat. During this time, the vocal cords and body vibrations are thrust to the resonators with an impact commensurate with the intensity of the Compression Phase (down-part of the Gan-Tone beat), demonstrating Newton's Law of Action and Reaction which states that for every action, there is an equal and opposite reaction.

IX. As long as the vocal cords are being activated, vocal cords vibrations are constantly being re-sounded omnidirectionally in the body cavities, or resonators. However, the greatest thrust of vibrations to the resonators occurs when the entire body is utilized as a bellows. Ordinarily, the bellows are the lungs which supply the air stream that activates the vocal cords. However, the application of the Jaw, Larynx, Body Fusion and the compression and thrust phases of the Gan-Tone beat make the entire body function as the bellows. The air stream from the lungs is now strengthened, amplified and supported by the body, since compression of the lungs is now augmented by body compression, as a result of the Compression Phase of the Gan-Tone Pulsation (down-part of the beat).

The re-sounding of vibrations in the resonators produces a smooth line of sound as, for ex., A above Middle C, or 440 v.p.s., as a result of the tremendous speed at which these vibrations travel. However, sound is a series

26 **Singing Energy**

of vibrations and their speed, per second, determines the pitch. The Gan-Tone beat does not determine pitch. The frequency of application of the Gan-Tone beat is to amplify the dimensions of the sound. An average of 5 to 7 Gan-Tones, per second, can be applied for the maintenance of a smooth flow of sound.

X. During the Thrust Phase of the Gan-Tone Pulsation (up-part of the Gan-Tone beat), the dimensions of sound are maximized, since each Gan-Tone cycle is, essentially, an alternating current of vocal cords vibrations which moves through the body downwardly, by compression, for the purpose of amplifying vibrations, and upwardly, by thrust, in the opposite direction, mainly to the resonators, for the re-sounding of these vibrations.

The limited amplitude of the fundamental frequency, or original vocal cords vibrations, to the resonators is transformed to alternating current by the Gan-Tone beat, which in two phases fuses and amplifies the fundamental frequency, compressing it to the rectal-pelvic basin (down-part of the beat), and then thrusts and re-sounds it, producing brilliant peaks (up-part of the beat) which, in turn, gives the singer greater control of volume, resilience, buoyancy, depth, height and projection in the emitted sound. Sustaining a line of alternating cycles produces a sound that is much easier on the ear and, therefore, a desirable sound effect. A direct current is unrelenting and lacks release and resilience. However, the buoyant effect of the Gan-Tone Pulsation is most desirable for enjoyable listening, since it produces release and resilience in the singing line, two important characteristics for desirable voice production.

The maximum dimension of depth reached in the body, as a result of maximum compression of vocal cords and body vibrations, produces maximum re-sounding of vibrations which, in turn, produces maximum vibratory energy, giving the emitted sound maximum brilliance. When, for ex., 5 Gan-Tones are imposed, per second, on A above Middle C, or 440 v.p.s., 88 vocal cords vibrations of the fundamental frequency (440 v.p.s.) are being fused to the rectal-pelvic basin in each Gan-Tone cycle. The height of compression of these vibrations is reached halfway through the cycle, at 44 vibrations, which are thrust with great impact throughout the body, but especially to the body cavities, or resonators, for maximum re-sounding, creating a brilliant peak, or pulsation, of sound. The repetition of this Gan-Tone Pulsation creates a series of brilliant peaks which produces a smooth singing line of great vibrant energy characterized by great brilliance, depth, height, buoyancy and resilience.

A Gan-Tone Principle follows:

The greater the intensity of the compression action of vocal cords vibrations (down-part of the Gan-Tone beat), the greater the intensity of the thrust reaction of vocal cords vibrations to the resonators (up-part of the Gan-Tone beat), producing greater resonance.

The more brilliant the audible peaks of re-sounded vibrations, with an even repetition of Gan-Tone Pulsations, the more even and energetic the projected singing line.

Pitch and Vibrancy Variation

XI. The fundamental pitch can vary by decreasing (lower sound) or increasing (higher sound) vibrations per second.

The speed of the Gan-Tone Pulsation is determined by the singer and is imposed independently of the speed of the fundamental pitch.

The frequency, or speed, of the Gan-Tone beat can be increased or decreased. Maximum imposition, per second, is 7 Gan-Tones, which give maximum vibrancy to the emitted sound. Minimum, per second, is 5 Gan-Tones. The singing line becomes uneven, if less than 5 Gan-Tones, per second, are imposed.

The frequency of the Gan-Tone cycle, or beat, does not affect the pitch of the fundamental frequency.

The less Gan-Tones imposed, per second, the less numerous the peaks of vibrant sound, since brilliance is decreased, as a result of wider intervals between the brilliant peaks.

The more Gan-Tones are imposed, per second, the more numerous the peaks of vibrant sound, since brilliance is increased, as a result of shorter intervals between the brilliant peaks. Greater skill is required of the singer to increase the imposition of Gan-Tones on the singing line, since greater spontaneity and dexterity of application are required.

Variable of the Gan-Tone Frequency

The frequency of the Gan-Tone Pulsation can vary (5 to 7 per second) independently of the fundamental frequency.

The imposition of the Gan-Tone beats on the fundamental frequency can vary in intensity and speed, while the fundamental pitch is varied or constant. If, for ex., Middle C, or C^1 (256 v.p.s.), is sustained for 2 seconds, the singer can impose anywhere from 5 to 7 beats per second on this fundamental frequency. In order to produce a uniform singing line, the singer would select the number of beats per second and maintain a constant frequency.

The degree of intensity imposed on the Gan-Tone beat, and the number of beats imposed, per second, will determine the degree of vibrancy in the singing line. Maximum vibrancy and evenness in the singing line occur with the imposition of about 7 Gan-Tones per second.

Variable of the Fundamental Frequency

The frequency of the fundamental pitch of a sustained sound increases or decreases independently of the frequency of the Gan-Tone Pulsation.

XII. The more rapid the articulation of sounds and words in intricate melodies, the more difficult it is to maintain the dimensions of the singing line, as a result of the varied movements of the jaw, making it more difficult to impose the Gan-Tone beat. However, in the Gan-Tone Method, the Jaw, Larynx, Body Fusion is applied constantly in order to maintain a maximum of dimensions, even though much articulation is involved. This constant fusion to the rectal-pelvic area maintains constant solidity and depth in the sound, since vibrations are fused to the rectal-pelvic basin. Nevertheless, the varied movements of the jaw do diminish vibratory continuity, curtailing the dimensions of the sound.

The singer's skill in moving swiftly from consonants to vowels will determine the degree of jaw contact with the larynx which, in turn, will determine the degree of body fusion, or vibratory continuity (V.V.C.) which, in turn, will add more dimensions of sound to the intricate melodies.

However, the maximum dimensions of sound can be attained only in sustained notes of approximately one or more seconds in duration at which time 5 to 7 Gan-Tones can be imposed, since the jaw is completely fused with the larynx and body. Any divergence of the jaw from the Feather-Touch Contact with the larynx and body will diminish the dimensions of the sound.

Voice Projection in the Gan-Tone Method

XIII. The application of the Jaw, Larynx, Body Fusion and the Gan-Tone Pulsation, in the Gan-Tone Method, revolutionizes the traditional understanding regarding voice projection.

According to current belief, the bellows of the lungs determines the degree of force with which the singer directs the stream of air to the vocal cords in order to determine the volume of the emitted sound. It is believed that the ability of certain individuals to sing more loudly than others can be essentially attributed to greater lung power, more freedom in the laryngeal tract, and larger chest and resonating cavities.

The Gan-Tone Method, however, rejects these current beliefs regarding voice projection, since it is the Feather-Touch Contact of the Jaw, Larynx, Body Fusion and the Gan-Tone Pulsation that maximize voice projection. The whole body, rather than the lungs, becomes the bellows, since the fusion of body parts, as a result of the Feather-Touch Contact of the Jaw, Larynx and Body, and the Gan-Tone application, sinks the breath and vocal cords vibrations to the rectal-pelvic basin, increasing lung power by involving the body as a bellows. The whole body now becomes a bell, or total vibrator and resonator.

It is currently believed that the transmission and resounding of vibrations in the sinus cavities is negligible, as a result of their unfavorable positions and minute openings.

In the Gan-Tone Method, these cavities are highly utilized for attaining brilliant peaks in the sound, creating a singing line of great vibrant energy and dimension. The septum and the surrounding frontal sinus cavities become the highest points for vibrations and resonance in the mask.

However, the current belief of projecting sound from the lungs or diaphragm, or both, makes these areas impenetrable, since the thrust of vocal cords vibrations from the diaphragm lacks the impact for adequately penetrating the sinus cavities for resonance.

The intensity of the Gan-Tone application, however, fuses vocal cords vibrations to the solid floor of the rectal-pelvic basin, creating a powerful launching pad for the omnidirectional thrust of vocal cords vibrations throughout the body, but especially to the resonators, which include the sinus cavities. The intensity of this thrust insures the penetration of the sinus cavities. The frequency of the Gan-Tone Pulsation maximizes the impact of vibrations to these cavities where they are re-sounded with great brilliance and then projected and re-sounded in the atmosphere, producing a singing line of maximum carrying power.

A Gan-Tone Principle can, therefore, be summarized:
> Voice projection is the thrusting of vocal cords and body vibrations from the rectal-pelvic basin to all the body resonators through fusion of the Jaw, Larynx, and Body and the application of the Gan-Tone Pulsation.

The degree of compression of vocal cords vibrations to the rectal-pelvic launching pad (down-part of Gan-Tone beat) determines the degree of thrust (up-part of Gan-Tone beat) which, in turn, determines the degree of impact of these vibrations to the resonators which, in turn, determines the degree of resonance which, in turn, determines the degree of carrying power of the projected sound.

Procedure for Rectal-Pelvic Breath Control and Vocal Thrust (Voice Projection) in Humans with the Gan-Tone Method

XIV.

1 - SPARK — Jet of air to the vocal cords to produce vibrations, or sound. One vibration consists of compression and rarefaction, the two phases of the sound-producing cycle. Pitch of sound is determined by the number of vibrations per second.

2 - CONTACT — Feather-Touch Contact of the Jaw, Larynx and Body to produce the strongest path for the transmission of vocal cords vibrations through the body, or Vocal Vibratory Continuity (V.V.C.)

3 - FUSE — Gan-Tone application—Compression Phase—down-part of beat—to fuse vocal cords vibrations and body parts to the rectal-pelvic basin.

4 - COMPRESS — Vocal cords and body vibrations are compressed through the body to the rectal-pelvic basin maximizing amplification of these vibrations. Height of compression is reached halfway through the beat.

5 - THRUST — Vocal cords and body vibrations are thrust to body cavities, or resonators, amplifying sound—up-part of the Gan-Tone beat. Newton's Law of Action and Reaction, i.e., the intensity of the Compression Phase determines the intensity of the Thrust Phase.

6 - PROJECTED
    SOUND — Singing line of vibrant, vocal energy.

Body Resilience in the Gan-Tone Method

XV. The body's ability to resist deformation, which prevents the absorption of vibrations, determines its effectiveness as a conductor for the transmission and amplification of vocal cords and body vibrations.

The Feather-Touch Contact of the Jaw, Larynx and Body and the application of the Gan-Tone Pulsation make the body a highly resilient column, since they produce a fusion of body parts making these parts elastic and, therefore, capable of maintaining their shape. This elasticity, produced by fusion, allows vibrations to be transmitted through these body parts, rather than absorbed, thus maximizing the body as a transmitter and amplifier of vocal cords and body vibrations.

Fusion of body parts to the rectal-pelvic basin produces a spring-like action in the body making it function as a piston in a cylinder. The mind imposes pressure on the vocal cords to determine pitch, and the vibrations, which produce pitch, are fused through the body to the rectal-pelvic basin, concomitantly with the fusion of the jaw, larynx and body, on the Compression Phase, or down-part of the Gan-Tone beat. In the process of fusion, vocal cords and body vibrations are amplified and thrust from the solid floor of the rectal-pelvic basin on the Thrust Phase, or up-part of the Gan-Tone beat. These vibrations are thrust to the resonators, reverberating with an impact commensurate with the intensity of compression.

The body can be considered the cylinder. The piston is the pressure mentally imposed down through the body, on the Compression Phase, or down-part of the Gan-Tone beat, which compresses vocal cords and body vibrations to the rectal-pelvic basin, thrusting them to the resonators on the Thrust Phase, or up-part of the Gan-Tone beat. The uniform repetition of Gan-Tone Pulsations functions as a piston, or cylinder, moving up and down within the larger cylinder of the body.

Excess weight does not contribute to body resilience, since vibrations are absorbed. Obesity for singing is, therefore, unnecessary, if the singer has not developed the skill of the Feather-Touch Contact of the Jaw, Larynx and Body and the spontaneous application of the Gan-Tone Pulsation. Excessive weight is essentially uninvolved in the process of transmitting, amplifying, thrusting and re-sounding of vibrations, since there is minimal fusion of body parts.

However, if the obese singer developed skill in applying the Feather-Touch Contact of the Jaw, Larynx and Body and spontaneity in the Gan-Tone application, more body resilience would be created, which would make vibrations permeate the excess weight increasing the spring-like action of the body. The excess weight would, therefore, be connected with the pressure head at the rectal-pelvic basin, adding additional dimension to body power in amplification and thrust of vibrations. Increasing the size of the body cylinder naturally increases compression which, in turn, increases the output of vibrations to be re-sounded, thus increasing the dimension of body resilience.

Support (Appoggio) in the Gan-Tone Method

XVI. Support is the amount of Jaw, Larynx, Body Fusion and compression of vocal cords and body vibrations to the rectal-pelvic basin (Sphincter ani externus muscle) necessary to sustain a quantity of resonant sound. The degree of sound sustained is commensurate with the degree of body fusion and compression produced which is dependent on the intensity of the Gan-Tone application. The controlling center for the maximum support of sound is the rectal-pelvic basin. No other area of the body provides the long and extensive line, from the vocal cords to the rectal-pelvic area, for the compression, amplification, thrust and re-sounding of vocal cords and body vibrations, which results in maximally supported, resonant sound.

Maximum intensity in the application of the Gan-Tone beat maximizes support above and below the vocal cords, i.e., the head and body. The greater the amount of penetration of vocal cords and body vibrations to the rectal-pelvic basin, on the Compression Phase of the Gan-Tone beat, the greater the degree of thrust of these amplified vibrations in the opposite direction, to the resonators, on the up-part of the Gan-Tone beat, maximizing penetration of vibrations in the head, completing the cycle of fusion, compression, penetration and amplification down through the body, which is the action, and the thrust and penetration to the head, the reaction, which maximizes support of sound above and below the vocal cords, i.e., the head and body.

The current beliefs of supporting sound by tightening throat muscles, setting the jaw, "getting the tone high," increasing air pressure from the lungs, resting tone on the chest, sustaining at the diaphragm, focusing in the solar plexis area, tightening abdominal muscles, pushing the stomach in and out, engaging in general calisthenics, practicing abdominal panting or holding the breath for a long period of time, manipulating the chest cage by contracting intercostal muscles, focusing on chest or abdominal breathing, reflecting on the importance of nasal as opposed to oral breathing or focusing on yoga can not compete with the utilization of the whole body, above and below the vocal cords, for the support (appoggio) of sound.

Maximum support of sustained sound can only be achieved and maintained through the spontaneous action of the Feather-Touch Contact of the Jaw, Larynx and Body and the Gan-Tone Pulsation.

The current beliefs of concentrating on body parts for support of sound focus pressure on these parts as, for ex., making excessive demands on the chest for the support of sound can result in strain in this area, which can produce stress on the heart, an obviously undesirable condition; whereas, compression through the body, progressively to the rectal-pelvic basin, de-localizes pressure from vital organs, such as the vocal cords, heart and stomach. These pressures are gathered at the rectal-pelvic basin, where they are utilized in the magnification and thrust of vibrations while unifying the whole body as the supporting agent of sound. Withdrawing pressure from body parts, and unifying these parts with the whole body, enables them to perform their function with ease, giving the singer a sense of security in the support of sound.

Abdominal Breathing (Diaphragmatic Breath Control)

XVII. The current belief of abdominal breathing for the support and control of the singing sound doesn't fully utilize body potential for the propagation, amplification and thrust of vocal cords vibrations, since the focus of control for utilizing the breath is on the diaphragm or abdomen, thus relying on half the body for fusion, amplification, support and thrust of vibrations. Whatever air is focused on the vocal cords is not thoroughly involved in the amplification of vibrations. Since the whole body is not amplifying vocal cords vibrations, more air must be jetted from the lungs to the vocal cords to amplify sound. When the whole body is amplifying vocal cords vibrations, less air is required, since the body is producing the amplification, rather than the vocal cords. Reliance on the vocal cords for amplification creates more pressure in this area, more irritation and more restriction producing a reedy, tight, uncovered sound.

Focus of control of the breath at the rectal-pelvic basin fuses the vocal cords vibrations through the larynx to this basin, naturally involving the fusion of the diaphragm along with the lower parts of the body. Control of vibrations at the rectal-pelvic basin, not only enables the body to be involved in the amplification of vibrations but, also, makes possible the strongest foundation for thrusting vibrations, with maximum impact, to all the resonators, which include the sinus cavities of the head.

Control of vibrations at the diaphragm or abdomen for supporting, thrusting and re-sounding vibrations makes it impossible for the vibrations to penetrate the extremities of the body, i.e., the rectal-pelvic basin (compression penetration) and the head (thrust penetration). The compression and thrust of vibrations are not fully grounded, since the piston (compressed vocal cords and body vibrations and body parts) only goes halfway through the cylinder (body) dissipating the thrust, as a result of partially involved compression.

Falsetto in the Gan-Tone Method

XVIII. The falsetto voice is pure vocal cords sound produced without the fusion of the hyoid bone, muscles and surrounding cartilages. The pitch of the falsetto voice is determined by the degree of pressure applied to the vocal cords without laryngeal fusion. The pure vocal cords vibrations that produce the falsetto voice are the basic vibrations of all vocal sound before they are fused with body parts for vibrational amplification.

Whenever there is an abrupt change from the fused, or amplified, sound to the non-fused, or falsetto, sound in the singing line, the contrast is marked, since the structure that unites these two sounds spasms, or collapses, revealing the pure vocal cords sound which is intact, since it is not subject to the great pressures of fusion. Therefore, maintenance of the pure vocal cords sound, or falsetto, is easy. When this sound is fused with other body parts, it becomes more difficult to maintain, since the coordination and skill required to sustain this fused structure, as the pitch, or range, and volume increase, become more exacting. Great discipline is required to maintain the jaw down and back to insure the fusion of body parts, when singing higher pitch, as a result of the increasing pressures.

It is, therefore, natural to moderate these pressures by raising the jaw which, in turn, interrupts the continuity of body fusion, thus diminishing vibratory continuity, which results in diminished dimensions of the emitted sound. The extent of vibratory penetration becomes limited to the throat area making it easier to sing higher notes without laryngeal or body involvement. The sound, therefore, becomes more pure vocal cords sound, or falsetto, as the range increases with the raised jaw, since the larynx becomes less involved.

Many high voices, particularly tenors, stress an ungrounded application of the jaw as they increase range, i.e., the jaw is not completely down and resting on the larynx. However, increasing convergence of the jaws from the absolute jaw opening, when increasing range, interrupts body fusion which diminishes the manly sound and increasingly approximates the pure vocal cords sound, or falsetto voice.

The structure of the larynx is responsible for the pronounced difference between the male and female falsetto sound. In males, the larynx is larger than in females producing a greater difference between pure vocal cords sound, or falsetto, and fused, or amplified, sound. The components of the female vocal apparatus (larynx and cords) are closer together, making the contrast of pure vocal cords sound (falsetto) and fused (amplified) sound less vivid. Since there is a closer union between the vocal cords and the laryngeal cartilages, the larynx is more easily involved as range is increased. Usually, the male voice manifests a greater gamut of falsetto sound, since the components of his vocal apparatus (larynx and cords) are wider apart, making them easier to be operated individually, thus enabling the male to increase his range with little or no laryngeal involvement. His larger vocal cords also make possible a wider range of falsetto sound.

When the female pure vocal cords vibrations are somewhat fused to the larynx, the emitted sound approximates the male falsetto. However, when the pure vocal cords vibrations are fused to the body, the female voice develops a body sound, making it distinctly different from the male falsetto.

When the male pure vocal cords vibrations (falsetto) are fused to the body, there is a radical difference between the male and female sound.

The size of the larynx, vocal cords and body structure accounts for the lower pitch and resonance in the male voice. The male laryngeal cave is much larger than the female cave, and this difference in size produces a deeper sound in the male. This contrast is analogous to bells of different sizes. The larger the bell, the deeper the sound.

The smaller vocal cords in the female are responsible for higher-pitched vibrations making the female voice approximately an octave higher than the male voice, which means that vibrations, for every note sung by the female, are twice as much as those of the male. If, for ex., a tenor and a soprano are both singing a High A, the tenor is singing 440 v.p.s. while the soprano is singing 880 v.p.s., which is an octave higher.

Therefore, the smaller laryngeal cave and the naturally shorter, higher-pitched vocal cords, as opposed to the larger cave and longer, lower-pitched vocal cords, account for the differences in singing sounds between female and male voices.

In the pure vocal cords sound, or falsetto, the male can reach much more range than he can reach with the fused, or amplified, sound, since there is less pressure on the vocal cords enabling the cords and the larynx to stretch more when they are not fused with other body parts. This pure vocal cords sound has an effeminate quality, since it is not really fused with the components of the larynx and body. Vibrations don't penetrate the vocal folds too deeply. However, as range increases in the falsetto voice, the vibrations become more intense, particularly if the jaw is unhinged down and back but not fused to the larynx, making more of these vibrations penetrate the vocal cords, larynx, resonators and body adding more volume to the sound. The higher position of the larynx, created by its lack of fusion with the body, makes the emitted sound effeminate even though the volume is increased.

The pure vocal cords sound, or falsetto, is, therefore, voice produced without laryngeal fusion. The falsetto is more evident in the male as opposed to the female, as a result of the difference in size of the larynx, vocal cords and body structure.

Avoiding the Ill Effects of Vibrating Air Pressure in the Throat with the Gan-Tone Method

XIX. When vibrating air is passing through the throat without restriction, sound is moving freely out of the body. When the throat opening constricts, vibrating air is restricted in its movement. This restricted vibrating air, unable to move, builds up pressure omnidirectionally within the laryngeal cavity, distorting the membrane of the vocal cords by its turbulence which, in turn, disturbs the pitch making it necessary to apply more pressure on the vocal cords in order to maintain pitch. As the brain imposes more pressure on the vocal cords to maintain pitch, it also imposes air pressure from the lungs. This pressure causes friction and irritation which cannot be sustained by the delicate vocal cords.

Anxiety in the singer becomes a natural consequence, causing body tension to focus in the throat and vital organs, which is accompanied by fear. The more effort exerted by the singer to cope with this anxiety, and maintain the desired pitch in the singing line, the more he aggravates this undesirable condition. Repeated effort interferes with the flexibility of the vocal cords and the spontaneity of the vibrational flow causing muscle fatigue, which results in a diminishing of vibrational response and eventual collapse of the vocal structure.

The turbulence created by restricted vibrating air in the constricted throat can make the throat area susceptible to many ill effects, such as nodules on the vocal cords, as a result of pressure and friction, and laryngitis, which is an inflammation of the mucous membrane of the larynx, characterized by tickling sensations, dryness, heat, pain, dry cough, difficulty in swallowing, labored movements of throat muscles, and narrowed air passages, especially through the vocal cords, which halt the vocal vibratory response. Other more serious ailments of the larynx, throat and respiratory system can also occur, as a result of prolonged irritation which interferes with the metabolism of the respiratory system.

Restricted vibrating air decreases the payload of vibrations to the head, throat and chest resonators which decreases re-sounding, minimizing the body cavities as resonators and producing diminishing dimensions of depth and height, focusing, or converging, vibrations essentially in the constricted throat, thus making the emitted sound tight, reedy, inflexible and lacking in buoyancy and radiance. The degree of vibrational absorption in the throat is commensurate with the degree of vibrational restriction and is analogous to singing in a room with two partially closed doors. Beyond the partially closed doors (restricted throat), there are corridors (head and chest resonators). Although the singing sound (vibrations) can penetrate through the partially closed doors to the corridors (resonators), the degree of penetration and re-sounding of vibrations is commensurate with the degree to which the doors are opened, i.e., the door leading to the upper corridors (head resonators) and the door leading to the lower corridors (chest resonators).

In the Gan-Tone Method, the application of the Jaw, Larynx, Body Fusion and the Gan-Tone Pulsation releases the restricted, turbulent, vibrating air by opening the constricted throat area and stabilizes and strengthens the many movable parts in the throat that compound turbulence. The Gan-Tone beat maximizes body fusion, amplification of vocal cords vibrations and thrust of these vibrations to the resonators. This superimposed beat also opens the throat to its maximum for the free passage of these highly amplified and intensely thrust vibrations, minimizing vibrating air pressure restriction.

Releasing the turbulence of vibrating air and movable parts allows the pitch to be maintained with a minimum of mental pressure, since turbulence that would distort the pitch and require more physical pressure on the vocal cords is released. Pitch is, therefore, maintained with a minimum of tension on the vocal cords.

Mind also determines the amount of air pressure necessary to activate the vocal cords to vibrate the desired pitch. The amount of air pressure required of the lungs is decreased as turbulence is diminished, since the jet of air from the lungs is not opposed by the turbulence but, instead, moves freely through the opened throat for the smooth and natural flow of vibrations to the resonators.

The application of the Jaw, Larynx, Body Fusion and

the Gan-Tone beat stabilizes and strengthens movable body parts that would compound turbulence by compacting the epiglottis on the curve of the tongue which, in turn, is fused to the hyoid bone downward through the many movable parts of the larynx and trachea. Since these movable body parts are fused, they are no longer susceptible to spasms under pressure and, rather than functioning as weak links, they become one strong unit. The fusion of these parts also creates the widest opening in the throat for the maximum flow of vibrating air which, in turn, creates the ideal condition for the application of the Gan-Tone Pulsation. This superimposed beat on the fundamental vocal cords vibrations fuses, compresses, amplifies, thrusts and re-sounds these vibrations in the body cavities with an impact that is commensurate with the intensity of the Gan-Tone application.

Since the turbulence, resulting from the restricted vibrating air and fluttering movable parts, is stabilized, the singer is relieved of pressure, anxiety and fear. Since the vibrating air is moving freely and securely, friction and irritation in the throat, which cause such ill effects as nodules and laryngitis, are eliminated. The singer no longer has to fear the structural collapse of sound, since the many parts responsible for vocal vibratory continuity and amplification of these vibrations are fused creating a strong, stable column grounded at the rectal-pelvic basin. The singer is also free of anxiety stemming from the excessive pressure exerted on the vocal cords to maintain pitch and the excessive air pressure from the lungs to the vocal cords to maintain vibrations.

The principles of the Gan-Tone Method, therefore, enable the singer to attain security and harmony in the production of the singing voice, since the application of these principles removes pressure from the throat area and fuses it through the body, thus transferring the focus of pressure from the delicate vocal cords to the bottom of the torso, or rectal-pelvic basin, at the Sphincter ani externus muscle.

The Attack in the Gan-Tone Method

XX. The attack of any sound is made with as little pressure on the vocal cords as possible, i.e., just enough pressure to maintain the pitch and airflow to move the vibrations.

When the jaw is down and back, resting on the larynx, and the back of the tongue, hyoid bone and larynx are firmly fused with the body and grounded at the rectal-pelvic basin, the strongest structure for the attack of any sound is created, along with the condition necessary for the maximum application of the Gan-Tone Pulsation.

The spontaneity with which the singer applies the Gan-Tone Pulsation and articulates the consonants in order to get to the vowels as quickly as possible determines the effectiveness, or brilliance, of the attack. Great skill is required to attack a sound beginning with a consonant, when applying maximum thrust to vibrating air from the rectal-pelvic basin, since the great impact of vibrating air creates an explosion on the consonants, especially b, p, and k, causing this intense, vibrating air to reverberate on the vocal cords producing a spasm on the cords and possible soreness on the periphery of the cords at the rim of the glottis. In order to avoid this undesirable condition, the singer must develop great spontaneity in moving from the consonant to the vowel, when maximum thrust of vibrating air is involved, in order to release this intense pressure through the opened throat on the vowel, thus producing a vibrant, energetic, voluminous sound with a Feather-Touch Contact of the jaw, larynx and body, while minimizing vocal cords pressure.

The attack of any sound is controlled from the rectal-pelvic basin, which gives maximum vibratory response, maximum amplification of vibrations and maximum thrust to be utilized for the attack, thus taking the burden of providing strength, volume, thrust and impact from the vocal cords. A throat attack is, therefore, eliminated. This Gan-Tone approach utilizes the feather-touch, the Jaw, Larynx, Body Fusion and the Gan-Tone Pulsation, grounding vocal cords vibrations to the solid foundation of the rectal-pelvic basin, thus giving the greatest strength to the attack of the sound, while minimizing vocal cords pressure.

The degree to which the Gan-Tone approach is utilized determines the degree of effectiveness of the attack, giving great direction and definition to the areas of focus in the resonators and body regardless of the vowels being sung. The great magnification and thrust of vibrations from the rectal-pelvic controlling center makes this direction and definition possible.

The attack of sound, in the Gan-Tone Method, is produced with minimal pressure on the vocal cords and does not involve the manipulation of throat components, such as the false vocal cords, to produce guffaws, bawling, coarse sounds or non-pitched bellowing that mar the purity of the singing line. Scooping and swooping, in the attempt to maintain pitch security, also impair the singing line, since they focus vibrations and pressure in the throat, greatly minimizing the dimensions of the sound.

Since the Gan-Tone Pulsation supplies great control over vibrations above and below the vocal cords, dead center of the attack can be maintained, giving buoyancy to the emitted sound, as a result of the great depth of vibrational thrust from the rectal-pelvic basin which, in turn, produces a vibrant, energetic aura of great dimension that surrounds the singer during moments of great vocal demand, i.e., loud, high sounds.

The singing line produced by the Gan-Tone attack is characterized by great depth, height, vibrancy, volume, evenness, buoyancy and brilliance.

Range in the Gan-Tone Method

XXI. Range can be increased and made secure by developing the skill of coordinating the jaw, larynx and body. The impasse in the range, which prevents the free movement from low to high sounds, and vice versa, can be eliminated with understanding, since it is not the vocal cords which prevent the movement but, rather, the lack of awareness regarding the fusion of the jaw, larynx and body. The restricted position of the jaw restricts the movement of vibrating air causing an inability to ascend or descend the scale. Coordination of the jaw down and back frees vibrations by opening the throat, increasing the range and dimension of the sound.

The jaw is analogous to a door that opens to accommodate the passage of objects of different sizes. The bigger the objects, the more the door has to be opened. As more range and security are desired, the jaw, or door, must be opened wider to open the throat in order to permit more space for the passage of increased vibrations. At the same time, the Jaw, Larynx, Body Fusion, grounded at the rectal-pelvic basin, and the Gan-Tone beat give security to the sound, since pressure is removed from the throat area and dispersed through the body.

Lack of knowledge of the Jaw, Larynx, Body Fusion and the absolute opening of the jaw with the Feather-Touch Contact of the jaw on the larynx invariably focuses tone in the throat area, making it impossible to maximize the dimensions of sound uniformly throughout the range. In order to attain the maximum dimensions of sound throughout the range, the following is required:

> Maximum fusion of vocal cords vibrations through the body. Maximum compression and amplification of these vibrations grounded at the rectal-pelvic basin, where these vibrations are thrust through the open throat made possible by the Jaw, Larynx, Body Fusion, maximizing resonating space for the purpose of maximum re-sounding of vibrations. The intense thrust of these vibrations from the rectal-pelvic basin creates an impact in the resonators unattainable by any other bodily means. Maximum re-sounding in the resonators produces a uniform range, from low to high, of maximum dimensions.

The Body Register in the Gan-Tone Method

XXII. It is currently believed that the range of the human voice is divided into registers and that these registers are dependent on the adjustment of the vocal cords. In singing up the scale, the register changes at the point where the vocal cords readjust themselves to reach the higher tones. All tones below this point are considered the chest, or thick, register, and all tones above this point, the head, or thin, register.

The Gan-Tone Method rejects the belief that the vocal cords adjust themselves as range is increased and that there are chest and head registers. All vibrations activated in the vocal cords are transmitted omnidirectionally, whether the frequency, or pitch, is high or low. These vibrations are transmitted, amplified and thrust throughout the body on the Gan-Tone beat. The vibrations and intensity of pitches are simultaneously transmitted to the head and chest. It is easier to mistake lower-pitched vibrations as chest register, since the lower frequency of lower pitch is discernible in the chest vibrations. However, this lower frequency also re-sounds in the head cavities and permeates the skull. The skull bones, however, are more resilient and resist deformation, making their vibrating movement less obvious than the softer, less resilient components of the chest.

As the singer ascends the scale, the abrupt change encountered in the quality of sound is not the result of the vocal cords adjusting themselves and producing the transition from the chest to the head registers but, rather, a lack of coordination of the jaw that makes the body more or less involved. When the jaw, larynx and body are coordinated throughout the range, chest and head tones are one, irrespective of pitch. Lack of awareness regarding the coordination of the jaw in passing through, essentially, the middle range results in the interruption of the Jaw, Larynx, Body Fusion, causing the tone to change from a body sound to a disembodied one. These two different sounds are mistakenly considered chest and head registers.

As the so-called chest register terminates, and the pitch is increased, the speed of vibrations increases. Since the vibrations don't have a body involvement, they lose the depth of the chest and reverberate, with a minimal amount of resonance, in the head and chest, producing a disembodied sound. As the speed of the pitch increases, vibrations are less discernible to the sense of touch, since the intervals between the cycles are shortened and much more rapid.

With the application of the Gan-Tone Pulsation, the jaw is the door which admits greater or lesser quantities of vibrations, enabling them to pass freely back and forth. The increased vibrations produced by increased range require a wider throat opening. As the increased jaw opening accommodates the increased vibrations of increased range, an even line from low to high sounds is produced characterized by depth and height, without any change in quality, or breaks in the voice, proving that there are not several registers, but one body register. Vocal cords sounds, regardless of pitch, are extended throughout the body, producing an even range of sounds, as long as the throat is opened to accommodate the varying quantities of vibrations.

Attaining the Center of Tone in the Gan-Tone Method

XXIII. The center of tone is attained when the spheres of vibrations emanating omnidirectionally from the vocal cords maintain a common center. Maintenance of these concentric spheres gives uniformity and stability to the dimensions of depth and height, which projects the pure vocal cords sound with, or without, laryngeal and body involvement, giving the emitted sound resilience, buoyancy and abandon.

Distortion of the concentric circles of vibrational spheres produces eccentricities in the vibrating sound. This distortion is produced by unnecessary pressure on the vocal cords and reflects the singer's inability to maintain uniform minimal vocal cords pressure as the range and volume increase or decrease. Unnecessary pressure distorts the pattern of sound and introduces tightness, sharpness and flatness in the projected sound. The stress and anxiety of the vocal demand (loud, high sounds) causes the singer to tense the throat muscles in order to attain and maintain security, focusing body pressures in the throat area. This excessive pressure distorts the vibrational pattern, shifting the center of the tone, by giving eccentricity to the vibrational spheres which, in turn, distorts the pure vocal cords sound, thus limiting the potential dimensions of the fundamental sound and its accompanying harmonics and partials.

Tone, in the Gan-Tone Method, originates as inaudible vibrations imposed by the mind in the form of impulses to the vocal cords. These impulses are transmitted to the vocal cords through nerves that coordinate the arytenoid cartilages and other movable parts of the larynx in order to enable the vocal cords to function as vibrators of the nerve impulses. These impulses are registered as tension on the vocal cords. Tension is made up of inaudible vibrations. The degree of tension imposed on the cords (inaudible vibrations) is commensurate with the pitch, or the number of vibrations per second that produce the high or low notes. These impulses from the mind, transmitted to the vocal cords through nerves as inaudible vibrations, become audible when acted upon by a jet of air from the lungs.

In the Gan-Tone Method, sound is conceived as a

composite of coordinated inaudible and audible vibrations based on a chain reaction produced by action and reaction, which can be described as follows:

The inaudible vibrations are initiated by thought, which takes the form of a definite pitch (reaction) that the singer has heard and wishes to duplicate (action). If a singer, for ex., wishes to sing Middle C, the thought takes the form of 256 v.p.s. that are transmitted as impulses through the nerve tissue and are manifested as tension on the vocal cords, or inaudible vibrations, equal to the action and reaction of the cycles of thought and impulse vibrations. At this point, a singer can sing a melody in his mind without making any audible sounds.

The cycle of inspiration and expiration is a vibration. In normal breathing, seventeen respiratory cycles can occur in one minute. A cycle consists of one inhalation and one exhalation.

During inspiration, in the breathing cycle, the vocal cords are released from tension imposed by thought and impulse, or inaudible vibrations. This release is reflected in the mind as rest. The imposition of pressure on the vocal cords and the release of this pressure (expiration and inspiration) consists of an uneven vibration, since it depends on when the singer takes a breath.

During inspiration, the lungs are filling with air. When a normal amount of air is taken in by the singer, the expiration part of the cycle occurs, at which time, the mind imposes tension on the vocal cords in the form of inaudible vibrations that are commensurate with the v.p.s. of the desired pitch. The expired air activates these inaudible vibrations making them audible.

When spontaneity is applied to mind, impulse, vocal cords tension, adequate air pressure to activate the vocal cords to vibrate at a desired pitch, and extraneous pressures, essentially in the throat area, that are compounded by body involvement, are minimal, the vibrational spheres emanate, omnidirectionally from the vocal cords, evenly and concentrically. The center of tone is, therefore, attained, producing a uniformity of depth and height, giving the emitted sound resilience, buoyancy and spontaneity. Evenness in the sound is attained, as a result of the ability of the vibrations to move freely, above and below the vocal cords, since the vibrational spheres maintain concentricity, above and below the cords.

However, whenever excessive pressure is applied to the vocal cords, vibrating spheres become eccentric, disturbing the balance above and below the vocal cords, curtailing the movement of vibrations which, in turn, produces a tight, reedy sound that is not accurate in pitch. As long as the center of the tone is maintained, vibrational restriction is minimal, enabling a maximum amount of vibrations to be re-sounded in the resonators. Conversely, when the center of the tone is eccentric, a smooth movement of the vibrational spheres is interrupted, causing the restriction of vibrations in the throat area, reducing the amount of vibrations to be re-sounded in the resonators, thus diminishing the dimensions of the emitted sound. The restricted vibrations build pressure in the throat and affect the vocal cords by interfering with pitch, making the sound sharp or flat.

Counteracting this condition with increased pressure on the vocal cords, in order to maintain the pitch and the center of the tone, compounds this condition, making it increasingly difficult to maintain the proper pitch and center of the tone. At this point, the singer becomes tense and anxious.

Therefore, as a singer involves more range and volume and wishes to maintain accurate pitch, the coordination of body parts, such as the jaw, tongue, larynx and body, is essential in order to insure the Feather-Touch Contact on the vocal cords. It should be noted that the movement of vibrational spheres will be restricted, if the jaw is not opened sufficiently to allow free passage of these vibrations. The application of the Gan-Tone vibration insures the feather-touch by maximizing vocal cords vibrations through fusion of body parts, such as the tongue, hyoid bone, thyroid cartilage, cricoid cartilage and the torso, developing a compression head of these vocal cords vibrations at the rectal-pelvic basin with a minimum of pressure at the vocal cords. Since excessive pressure on the vocal cords necessitates greater mental energy to generate the pitch impulse, minimal pressure on the cords, made possible by the Gan-Tone beat, promotes a mental feather-touch in generating this impulse.

The application of the Gan-Tone vibration, which is a cycle of compression (down-part of the beat) and thrust (up-part of the beat) of vocal cords and body vibrations, maximizes the dimensions of these vibrations, while maintaining the center of the tone above and below the vocal cords.

The Jaw, Larynx, Body Fusion and the Gan-Tone vibration, therefore, maintain the center of the tone, maximum dimensions in the amplified vocal cords and body vibrations (Compression Phase—down-part of the Gan-Tone beat) and also re-sound these amplified vibrations (Thrust Phase—up-part of the Gan-Tone beat) with maximum impact in the resonators of the body.

The intense vibrational thrust generated from the rectal-pelvic basin gives the singer great control over the direction, impact, penetration and re-sounding of these vocal cords and body vibrations throughout the body, from the rectal-pelvic basin to the head resonators, regardless of the vowel being sung, while maintaining a Feather-Touch Contact on the vocal cords. This minimal pressure on the cords attains and maintains the concentric vibrational spheres which enable the singer to attain the center of tone. The emitted sound is, therefore, highly focused, since the concentric vibrational spheres are maintained while these vocal cords and body vibrations are being maximally amplified and thrust to the resonators on the Gan-Tone vibration.

Mouth Opening in the Gan-Tone Method

XXIV. Awareness of the size of the mouth opening in relation to the dimensions of the emitted sound enables the singer to produce a singing line of vibrant energy with control and assurance.

In the Gan-Tone method, the mouth is considered a highly variable opening between the nose and the chin that contains the lips, teeth, tongue and uvula, whose size and shape can be altered to accommodate varying amounts of vibrations for the purpose of re-sounding them in this chamber.

The periphery of the lips can move from a completely closed position to a wide-open position, while the jaw is down and back and completely unhinged, enabling the mouth opening to function independently of the jaw position.

The widest opening of the mouth occurs when the lips are maximally opened in a vertical-elliptical position, the corners of the mouth are relaxed and the jaw is down and back, in an unhinged position, and resting on the larynx. This maximum opening of the mouth and jaw produces the most effective structure for utilizing the body as a maximum amplifier of vibrations. Maximum amplification of vocal cords vibrations produces maximum volume, depth, height, resilience, buoyancy and brilliance in the emitted sound.

Maximum opening of the mouth and jaw enables body fusion to be maximized, since it causes the back of the tongue, the jawbone, hyoid bone, thyroid cartilage, cricoid cartilage and the subsequent structures of bones down through the body to be most efficiently fused. When the jaw is opened wide, it fuses with the larynx causing vocal cords vibrations to be fused through bones and cartilages, down through the body, to the rectal-pelvic basin. Weaker structures of the body, such as membranes and muscles, are shielded from potential pressures, in the singing process, since they are protected, through fusion, by the more solid parts, such as bones and cartilages, therefore, avoiding possible weak links in the vertical body column. As fusion progresses, from the unhinged jaw resting on the larynx to the rectal-pelvic basin, the strongest column for the transmission, amplification and thrust of vocal cords and body vibrations is produced. This maximum body fusion also creates the maximum opening of the head and chest resonators, since the jaw, mouth and throat are opened to their maximum, creating more resonating space. The mouth can be considered one of the bells of the body, since it vibrates and re-sounds vocal cords vibrations.

The mouth and jaw openings, the uplifted position of the uvula, the Feather-Touch Contact on the vocal cords, body fusion, compression and amplification of vocal cords vibrations, on the down-part of the Gan-Tone beat, and the thrust of these vibrations to the resonators, on the up-part of the Gan-Tone beat, determine the effective utilization of the resonators as re-sounding agents of the amplified vocal cords vibrations.

When the jaws and mouth are maximally opened, the

uvula in an uplifted position, and fusion, compression and thrust are maximum, vibrations are maximally amplified. Resounding areas are, therefore, largest and most efficiently utilized. This maximum position for maximum amplification of vibrations can be maintained throughout the range of the voice, from low, middle to high on all open vowels, such as a as in sat or a as in ma. Closed vowels, such as long e, can also be sung with an unhinged position of the jaw and a wide mouth opening in the middle and upper range. The unhinged position of the jaw for the long e vowel is not easily adaptable in the lower range. However, as range is increased, past Middle C of the male and female voices, the unhinged position of the jaw with the vertical-elliptical mouth opening, when singing long e, increases depth, height and brilliance in the voice.

Since the mouth can be opened and closed independently of the maximally diverged jawbones, it can be used as a lens while maintaining an unhinged position of the jaw down and back on the larynx. The fused position of the jaw to the larynx insures the greatest amplification of vocal cords and body vibrations to be re-sounded in the body cavities, i.e., the mouth, head and chest, in any part of the range, while the mouth positions can vary from wide-opened, as in the AH sound, to closed, as in the OO sound, where the lips approximate a whistle position.

In the AH position, i.e., wide-opened mouth, vibrations penetrate the entire skull, as well as the sinus and chest cavities, when body fusion and compression of vocal cords vibrations to the rectal-pelvic basin are maximized. With the aid of the simulated yawn, the nasal, oral and pharyngeal tracts are maximally opened; the nostrils are dilated; the uvula is lifted higher; and lung space is maximized. The curve of the tongue is pressed forward and downward, and body cavities are maximally opened for re-sounding of vibrations.

When the mouth is closed in the whistle position and maximum vibrations are amplified through the body, there is a diminishing of vibrational movement out of the body, since the mouth is closed, reducing the dimensions of the sound, even though the jaw is unhinged and maximally fused to the body. Vibrations are re-sounded in the mouth and emit through the nostrils. Vibrations are also re-sounded in other head and chest cavities. The lower notes, having a slower vibrational frequency, are felt in the mouth and the entire skull, as well as in the chest. As the singer ascends the scale, the vibrational frequency of notes is increased, making it more difficult to feel their frequencies in the head or chest. Although the mouth is closed, these vibrations penetrate the body and its cavities omnidirectionally from the vocal cords. Since the dimensions of these vibrations are stifled by the closed mouth position, resonance is emitted through the nasal cavities producing a sound that is characteristic of a high penetration of the skull, i.e., a deep penetration of the septum of the sinus cavities above the eyes, a deep penetration of the mask, a maximum re-sounding in the nasal chambers, such as the two fossae, and a diminishing of oral, pharyngeal and chest resonance, giving the emitted sound a very intense, brilliant, but muffled quality.

The OO position of the mouth, the unhinged jaw and maximum body fusion and compression of vocal cords vibrations (down-part of Gan-Tone beat) thrust these vibrations (up-part of Gan-Tone beat) high in the mask penetrating the base of the nose. As the range increases, vibrations penetrate deeper through the mask, sinus cavities and skull, emphasizing head and nasal resonance, giving the sound great brilliance and height, as a result of deep vibrational penetration in the skull and postnasal. Since the mouth opening is small, oral, pharyngeal and thoracic vibrations are restricted, diminishing resonance in these areas.

The mouth and jaw openings, in rapid conversation-like singing, can not be wide, since articulation is too rapid. However, conversation-like singing usually occurs in the low or middle part of the range, not making it necessary for the mouth and jaw to be opened widely, since vibrational intensity is reduced, as a result of the slower frequency of lower notes. Maximal dimensions of mouth and jaw openings, and maximal compression and re-sounding of vibrations can be attained in any part of the range except in rapid articulation. However, the application of Gan-Tone Principles, which includes the Gan-Tone Pulsation, yields great insight into the amplification, thrust and re-sounding of vocal cords vibrations throughout the body and leads to the skill of spontaneity in the application of these principles, giving the singer a deftness in maximizing the dimensions of sound, even in rapid, conversation-like singing as, for ex., swift consonant-to-vowel articulation.

The maximum opening of the mouth and jaw, in the Gan-Tone Method, is required only when there is a great vocal demand, such as loud, high, sustained sounds. However, a singer trained in the Gan-Tone Method realizes that whenever maximum dimensions of sounds are desired in any part of the range, whether they are loud or soft sounds, maximum mouth and jaw openings are required in order to attain maximum amplification of vibrations which, in turn, produces maximum resonance, i.e., great depth, height, resilience, buoyancy and brilliance in any loud or soft sound.

Maximum opening of the mouth and jaw, along with the application of the Gan-Tone beat, prevent constriction of the throat and resonators, thereby preventing restriction of vibrational movement, which insures maximum dimensions in the emitted sound.

Areas of Resonance in the Gan-Tone Method

XXV. Areas for the re-sounding of vocal cords vibrations (resonators) are created by the Feather-Touch Contact on the vocal cords, and the Jaw, Larynx, Body Fusion which includes the vertical-elliptical mouth opening and the uplifted position of the uvula. This fusion makes the body a resilient column for the transmission, amplification and thrust of vocal cords and body vibrations on the Gan-Tone beat, which maximizes total body vibrations and grounds them at the rectal-pelvic basin, thus providing the maximum quantity of amplified vibrations to be re-sounded in the resonating chambers of the body.

However, without fusion of body parts, vibrations move to certain areas of the resonators which are beyond the singer's control and are known as formants, i.e., natural resonating areas. A prominent body resonator is the mouth. The natural resonating areas, or formants, in the mouth resonate in response to certain frequencies, or pitches, and vowel sounds confining resonance dependent on these frequencies and vowel sounds to these formants, giving immobility and rigidity to vibrations, thus limiting vibrational movement to the throat area which, in turn, diminishes resonance and the resultant dimensions of the emitted sound.

Lack of body fusion, therefore, confines minimal vibrational resonance to the chest, throat and mouth, since the thrust of these vibrations is indefinite and minimal, creating minimal impact in the resonators and making it difficult for the singer to control and direct these vibrations to different areas of the resonators other than the so-called natural resonating areas, or formants. The natural movement of these vibrations to the particular formants is dependent on the vowel sounds and frequency, or pitch, being sung.

In the Gan-Tone Method, fusion and compression change the sound-producing structure and the size of this structure, i.e., the areas of amplification and re-sounding of vibrations are increased. The Feather-Touch Contact on the vocal cords, i.e., minimal tension on the cords to maintain pitch, minimal jet of air to activate the cords to audible vibrations, and minimal amount of pressure on the cords to maintain fusion of body parts, from the vocal cords to the rectal-pelvic basin, establish a new point of reference for the amplification, thrust and re-sounding of vocal cords vibrations.

Although the vocal cords are the initial vibrators of pitch, they are not the sole vibrators in the Gan-Tone Method. The lungs, of themselves, are not the power-supply for activating and thrusting vocal cords vibrations, and the larynx, pharynx, mouth and chest are not the sole resonators of the body.

Rather than the vocal cords, it is the body, through fusion and the Gan-Tone frequency, that vibrates the fundamental vocal cords frequency. Rather than the lungs functioning as the activators and thrusting agents, the Gan-Tone Method establishes the rectal-pelvic basin as the new point of reference, enabling vocal cords vibrations to be thrust from the rectal-pelvic controlling center, omnidirectionally, throughout the body, but especially to the body cavities, or resonators. The intense thrust attained by compression of vocal cords vibrations to the rectal-pelvic pad launches these vibrations, with great penetration, to all the resonators, emphasizing the deep penetration of the skull, which includes the highest sinus cavities. The sphere and magnitude of vibrational influence is extended from the lungs, vocal cords and mouth to the rectal-pelvic basin and the top of the skull. The vowel sounds and frequency, or pitch, being sung, therefore, are no longer the factors for determining the areas of natural resonances (formants).

If the dome, or roof, of the mouth is observed from a sideview, it resembles a natural indicator, and the degrees of vibrational intensity can be registered on its curve.

However, in the Gan-Tone Method, the roof of the mouth is no longer the point of reference for registering and controlling resonance. The indicator is now the rectal-pelvic basin. The degree of thrust from this pad determines the depth and height of the body that will be penetrated by vibrations, and the degree of registration in these bodily areas is determined by the intensity of the thrust. The lines of vibrational force move on radii that originate from the rectal-pelvic basin. The focus of these radii alternates, back and forth, from the septum of the sinus cavities to the posterior, nasal-pharyngeal tract, even though vibrations are being thrust omnidirectionally from the rectal-pelvic basin. This focus can be considered a triangular structure for the control of vibrational penetration. The lowest angle points to the rectal-pelvic basin, the highest angle points to the septum and the third angle points to the posterior nasal-pharyngeal tract.

The sweep and intensity of vibrational and resonant penetration produced by this triangle determines the efficiency with which the body cavities, above and below the vocal cords, re-sound vibrations which, in turn, determines the dimensions of the emitted sound.

The extreme points of reference, i.e., the rectal-pelvic basin and the top of the skull, maintain the strength of penetration of vibrations in the body extremities, which includes the control of these vibrations from the vocal cords to the roof of the mouth, eliminating the conventional, natural areas of resonance in the mouth, called formants, as the determining areas for re-sounding frequencies, or pitches. In the Gan-Tone Method, there are superior formants. The conventional, naturally resonating areas are the result of a lack of body coordination which constricts resonating areas of the throat, head and chest, diminishing vibratory continuity, amplification and thrust, restricting vibrations in the area of the vocal cords and throat, thus diminishing the dimensions of re-sounded vibrations in the body cavities, including the head, throat and chest.

Since the whole body vibrates, as a result of body fusion and compression of vocal cords vibrations to the rectal-pelvic basin on the Gan-Tone beat, the omnidirectional penetration of vocal cords vibrations to the body extremities is made possible, making the whole body, with its cavities maximally opened, resonate as a bell.

The bell is composed of the vibrator, which is the body, i.e., the wall which surrounds the cavities. The degree to which the body, or wall, vibrates is dependent on the degree of body fusion and compression of vocal cords vibrations.

When compression, amplification and thrust of vocal cords and body vibrations are maximum, all the resonators of the body resound. Rather than specific areas of the body, such as the formants in the mouth, the entire body resounds on all frequencies, or pitches, from low to high sounds, as a result of body coordination, body involvement and total vibratory impact in the resonators, causing the body to function as a bell.

The Function of the Diaphragm in the Gan-Tone Method of Voice Production

Although the diaphragm is considered by many to be the main source of control of the breath and voice, the Gan-Tone Method of Voice Production clarifies the proper function of the diaphragm in the entire gamut of inspiration and expiration of breath from the process of breathing and speaking to the maximum output of sound which is the singing voice.

Breathing

XXVI. In the breathing process, the musculofibrous diaphragm, which covers the abdomen, contracts downward during air inspiration, assuming a dome-shaped appearance and creating space in the lung area causing the lungs to expand and inspire air while the abdomen protrudes as a result of the downward pressure of the diaphragm. At the peak of air-intake, the abdominal muscles push the diaphragm upward toward the thoracic cavity, which is the area of the chest and lungs, deflating the lungs, and the breathing cycle is completed and repeated. When the abdominal muscles reach their peak in pushing against the diaphragm in the expiration of air, the diaphragm is in repose momentarily and has the shape of a wave-like letter M. It is essentially this expired air that produces the vocal sound.

The life of the human sound is produced by used and unused expired air, i.e., in the process of inspiring air, the tract leading from the mouth and nostrils into the sacs of the lungs is involved as follows:

> The air within the sacs of the lungs taken in during inspiration is utilized by the body and is exhaled during expiration as carbon dioxide. The tract leading from the lungs to the fork of the bronchials through the trachea to the vocal cords contains essentially unused air, i.e., air that has not been used by the body and is, therefore, emitted as oxygen rather than carbon dioxide. The amount of air that is used and converted into carbon dioxide is only that amount which is necessary to replenish oxygen to the blood stream, i.e., essentially that air which is drawn into the sacs of the lungs. This combination of unused air and carbon dioxide activates the vocal cords sound on the exhale through the windpipe.

In addition to the downward movement of the diaphragm expanding the area within the thoracic cavity, or chest, for drawing air into the lungs, chest muscles also aid in expanding the chest cavity.

Speaking

XXVII. In normal speaking, as pressure is maintained on the vocal cords, more air is being used than in the process of breathing. In sustaining the speaking sound, the essential points of pressure are the vocal cords and the larynx. This pressure is carried downward and imposed on the diaphragm giving support and stability to the vocal vibrations that resound in the head and body and are projected outwardly. The diaphragm moves downward in breathing and speaking and in its movement, it compresses the viscera of the abdomen squeezing out the sides of the abdomen and the movable muscles surrounding it, giving support and buoyancy to the emitted sound. For ordinary speaking, this diaphragmatic involvement is normal. However, when a greater amount of sound is required in the speaking process, a greater amount of diaphragmatic pressure is necessary.

Singing

XXVIII. The role of the diaphragm for the support, thrust and stability of the sound, in the Gan-Tone Method of Voice Production, is replaced ultimately by the involvement of the whole body. Present popular belief places the point of control of the sound at the diaphragm muscle.

In the Gan-Tone Method, the point of control shifts from the diaphragm to the solid foundation of the bottom of the torso, the muscles of the rectum as, for ex., the Sphincter ani externus, and the surrounding pelvic bones. As air pressure is imposed on the vocal cords, the action of the diaphragm causes a protuberance of the abdomen which ultimately diminishes the support, since the thrust of the sound is dissipated in the outward movement of the abdomen. This horizontal movement, or spread, of the abdomen is corrected by focusing and controlling the pressure at the bottom of the torso rather than at the diaphragm. Control at the bottom of the torso makes the path of support a straight line parallel to the body, perpendicular to the ground rather than diffusing horizontally, and plumb with the center of the earth thus using earth's gravitational pull to contribute more solidity to the compact column of the body, consequently, making the dynamic lines of pressure, sound and support fuse in a more direct line.

At the lower extremity, therefore, the foundation is solid for maximum control of thrust, which, in turn, causes the head resonators, at the upper extremity of the body, to function at their maximum as resonators of the vocal vibrations, enabling the body to function more efficiently as a bell.

Since the diaphragm is a partition dividing the body in half, emphasis on the diaphragm prevents the thorough involvement of the rest of the body to the bottom of the torso. However, involving the whole body by emphasis at the bottom of the torso, the diaphragm is kept under control, along with the viscera of the abdomen, forming the compact cylinder of the body. Just as the removal of partitions between rooms increases the resonance of sound, so the shift of emphasis from the partition of the diaphragm muscle to the bottom of the torso opens up greater dimensions for the support of sound, creating a firm foundation for greater fusion of the whole body, which produces greater vibrations, greater thrust, and greater resonance, thus insuring maximum volume and control of the sound since the body functions with maximum efficiency as a vibrator and resonator (bell factor).

A Gan-Tone Principle can, therefore, be summarized, as follows:

> As the vocal demand for louder, higher and more sustained sounds increases, the emphasis must shift from the thoracic diaphragm to the pelvic-perineum diaphragm at the bottom of the torso for the most efficient support of sound.

NATURAL SINGING IN THE GAN-TONE METHOD

CONTENTS

NATURAL SINGING IN THE GAN-TONE METHOD

I.	Conventional definition of Natural Singing	47
II.	Gan-Tone definition of Natural Singing	47
III.	The degree of mouth opening for attaining maximum volume of sound according to popular belief	47
IV.	The degree of mouth opening for attaining maximum volume of sound in the Gan-Tone Method	47
V.	The role of the unhinged jaw (maximally opened upper and lower jaw in the Jaw, Larynx, Body Fusion) in transferring vocal cords vibrations and pressure from the throat to the body, when producing a maximum volume of sound	47
VI.	The comparison of the unhinged jaw position, i.e., the Jaw, Larynx, Body Fusion, with the natural yawn	47
VII.	Common belief regarding great dimensions of depth and height in the singing voice	48
VIII.	Gan-Tone belief regarding great dimensions of depth and height in the singing voice	48

NATURAL SINGING IN THE GAN-TONE METHOD

I. It is commonly believed that singing naturally means singing without any knowledge of the vocal apparatus or the coordination of body parts, and that this "doing what comes naturally" approach is the most effective way to produce the most beautiful singing.

This belief is not acceptable in the Gan-Tone Method, since the singing line creates a focus of stress in the vocal cords and surrounding muscles, and this stress cannot be overcome without the conscious coordination of body parts which will release the pressure that is causing this stress and diffuse it throughout the body. A knowledge of this coordination of body parts in the process of singing, therefore, enables the singer to cope with the varying pressures that occur in the singing line by understanding how to coordinate parts of the body in order to minimize and eliminate these pressures, thus creating the impression that the singer is singing naturally, since no signs of strain or tension are evident.

II. Natural singing, in the Gan-Tone Method, means singing without any signs of stress, as a result of the conscious employment of natural movements of body parts to overcome pressures in the singing line. These same movements are unconsciously employed daily to overcome pressures that build up in the body.

III. It is commonly believed that a maximum volume of sound can be attained with the mouth partially opened. This belief is incorrect, since the maximum volume of sound produces great strain on muscles in the throat which can only be protected by shifting this pressure to solid parts (bones).

IV. This transference can only be achieved with a maximum opening of the mouth, i.e., an unhinged position of the jaw, since this position unifies the solid parts of the head, throat and body protecting the softer parts, such as muscles, from strain and allowing the original vocal cords vibrations to penetrate through the body.

V. Any divergence of the jaw from this unhinged position, while producing the greatest quantity of volume, decreases the penetration of vocal cords vibrations omnidirectionally throughout the body and particularly in the extremities of the body, such as the head resonators and the bottom of the torso, the two areas that add to the greatest dimensions of the vocal sound. Any divergence of the jaw from the vertical-elliptical mouth opening diminishes the function of the extremities as vibrators and resonators, since the vibrations, rather than moving to the extremities through solid parts, such as bones, are now absorbed in the softer parts, such as muscles. Since these extremities are not being fully utilized as vibrators and resonators, the sound lacks height and depth, reducing the dimensions of the sound to the throat area giving the sound a flat, reedy, tight, hard, throaty quality.

Furthermore, this focus of pressure in the throat area is detrimental to the vocal cords and surrounding muscles and cartilages of the throat and neck causing irritation in any or all of these parts.

VI. In the process of sustaining loud, high sounds, it is natural for the jaw to ride up towards a closing position, since it requires much jaw discipline to arrive at the supple positioning of the jaw in an unhinged attitude in order to maintain the necessary contact of the jaw with the larynx and body which, in turn, will transfer the pressure buildup from the throat to the body. The supple position of the jaw unhinged down and back is unconsciously and effortlessly achieved very naturally in the process of yawning which, in turn, diffuses and eliminates pressures in the body. A conscious application of this jaw position, however, requires much discipline to simulate in order to overcome pressure in the singing line.

When the discipline of the jaw is mastered and balanced with the diffusion of pressure throughout the body, during the process of singing, especially while encountering the greatest intensity of pressure during loud, high, sustained sounds, the singer appears to be singing naturally, without strain, since he has mastered a technique necessary not only for vocal survival, but also for vocal beauty.

VII. It is commonly believed that great dimensions of depth and height in the singing voice unfold naturally and are gifts bestowed on rare individuals.

VIII. This belief is unacceptable in the Gan-Tone Method, since a skillful application of the Gan-Tone Pulsation and the Jaw, Larynx, Body Fusion plays an important role in adding amplitude to the vocal line that enables any sincere seeker to achieve great dimensions of depth and height in the singing voice. When the Gan-Tone application is mastered, it appears as though the singer has great natural dimensions of depth and height in the voice, since the Gan-Tone Pulsation enables the whole body to be involved as vibrator and resonator of the original vocal cords vibrations, which are fused and compressed to the rectal-pelvic area on the down-part of the Gan-Tone beat, known as the Compression Phase, uniting the entire body as a vibratory agent. These vibrations have the greatest omnidirectional thrust from the rectal-pelvic basin, which is not only the center for the control of vocal pressure, but also, the center for the greatest propagation, thrust and transmission of vibrations through the body. These vibrations are most audible in the body resonators during the Thrust Phase, or up-part of the Gan-Tone beat.

When the discipline of the Jaw, Larynx, Body Fusion and the Gan-Tone Pulsation is mastered, enabling the whole body to be involved as a bell, the singer appears not only to be singing naturally, but also to produce great dimensions of depth, height and volume in the sound.

THE INNER LAUGH

CONTENTS

THE INNER LAUGH

I.	How the Natural Laugh is simulated in the Gan-Tone Method	53
II.	Similarities and Differences between the Natural Laugh and the Inner Laugh	53
III.	How Pitch is produced in the Natural Laugh	53
IV.	The Difference between the Giggle and the Deep Laugh	53
V.	How the simulated Inner Laugh affects the fundamental Vocal Cords Vibrations	54
VI.	How the position of the Jaw affects Newton's Law of Action and Reaction in producing Maximal-Dimensional Singing	54
VII.	The Negative Results produced by improper Fusion of the Jaw to the Body	54
VIII.	The Purpose of the Inner Laugh	55
IX.	How the Inner Laugh magnifies the Life of the Singing Voice	55

THE INNER LAUGH

I. The natural human laugh is a series of imposed vibrations on the natural frequency (vibrations) of the laugh's pitch, that is, a high-pitched or low-pitched laugh. The frequency and dimensions of the imposed vibrations are determined by the degree of emotional reaction to happiness, satisfaction, derision or thought sensation and are ultimately controlled and thrust from the rectal-pelvic area.

The natural laugh is simulated in the Gan-Tone Method of Voice Production with the imposition of the Gan-Tone Pulsations on the natural vibrations of the singing voice. The frequency and dimensions of this simulated laugh are determined by the alertness of the singer regarding the intervals between pulsations and the intensity of the application. The dimensions of the Gan-Tone Pulsations, or inner laugh, are ultimately controlled and thrust from the rectal-pelvic area.

II. The natural laugh is an emotional reaction to vibrational stimuli through the physical senses, such as sight, smell, hearing, touch, taste and thought sensation, and can also be the result of mixed emotions; whereas, the Gan-Tone Pulsations, or inner laugh, are the mental imposition of Gan-Tone Principles which control, at will, the vibrational amplitude of pitch, adding greater dimensions to the singing voice.

In the natural laugh, as well as in the inner laugh, there are essentially two frequencies of vibrations occurring concomitantly. The pitch of the voice is one frequency of vibrations, and the pitch of the natural laugh, that is, the number of times per second the laugh occurs, is another frequency of vibrations. The simulated inner laugh, or a series of imposed Gan-Tone Pulsations, is one frequency of vibrations, and the natural pitch on which the Gan-Tones are imposed is another frequency of vibrations.

The natural laugh is a series of vocal spasms and is, therefore, an interrupted line of sound; whereas, the inner laugh is a series of smooth pulsations imposed on the fundamental frequency and produces what appears to be an uninterrupted line of sound.

Unlike the natural laugh, which is the result of outer stimuli, the inner laugh is the result of principles operating from within, that is, controlled by the mind. The outer stimuli that produce the natural laugh evoke an emotional reaction from the mind which is unpredictable; whereas, the inner laugh, not affected by outer stimuli, is a purely mental reaction to principles and, consequently, is predictable and, therefore, capable of greater spontaneity, reliability and dimensions, when the principles are mastered.

III. The vibrations of the natural laugh, the result of outer stimuli, cause the mind to convulse vocal sound and body parts, such as the lungs, diaphragm and viscera of the abdomen. This convulsive action emits a frequency of vocal sound, the pitch of which is determined by the intensity of the laugh and the composition of the person's mind and body as, for example, a masculine laugh is pitched lower than a feminine one. The laugh is a series of interrupted pitches which can remain constant or go up-and-down in pitch according to emotional reactions. Each sound, or cycle of the laugh, is one convulsion, therefore, making the laugh an interrupted series of sounds, or cycles.

IV. The intensity of the laugh determines the amount of vibrational penetration through the body. If the laugh is confined to the vocal cords, it has small dimensions and, therefore, shallow. This shallow laugh can be considered the giggle. As the vibrations are amplified through fusion and compression of body parts, the laugh assumes greater dimensions, since more vibrations are being re-sounded in the body cavities causing the body to become more resilient. The more intense and penetrating the emotional reaction, the greater the penetration of vibrations through the body yielding a greater amplification of vibrations, as a result of greater fusion and compression of body parts producing, in turn, greater body resilience. The deeper the laugh, the more the body is involved in the penetration and amplification of vibrations, reaching the peak of body involvement at the rectal-pelvic area. The thrust of these vibrations from this area to the body resonators results in a roaring laugh.

However, if the vibrations of the natural laugh are confined to the vocal cords, the resultant sound, or giggle, is pure vocal cords sound, since the vibrations have not been fused, compressed and amplified through the bones and cartilages of the jaw, larynx and body. Regardless of the degree of body support, this natural laugh, that is, the giggle, sounds effeminate, shallow and usually denotes a silly mental state. The giggle can, therefore, be defined as follows:

> A laugh whose vibrations are confined to the vocal cords, producing pure vocal cords sound, incorrectly referred to as the falsetto. The giggle is characterized by a high-pitched, feminine quality with a complete absence of resonant depth in the laugh.

V. The simulated inner laugh, that is, the imposition of a series of Gan-Tone Pulsations, on the natural vibrations of the pitch maintained in the singing line transforms the dimensions of the singing voice by fusing, compressing and amplifying the original vocal cords vibrations through the body to the rectal-pelvic area on the downpart of the Gan-Tone beat, or Pulsation, known as the Compression Phase and then thrusting these vibrations, with equal intensity, from the rectal-pelvic area, the center of vibrational control and thrust, on the up-part of the Gan-Tone beat, or Pulsation, known as the Thrust Phase.

This fusion of the fundamental vocal cords vibrations to the rectal-pelvic area involves two different frequencies: the frequency of the pitch, or v.p.s., and the frequency of the Gan-Tone Pulsations. It should be noted that the frequency, or v.p.s., of the Gan-tone Pulsation is independent of the frequency of the pitch being maintained in the singing line, that is, the frequency of the Gan-Tone beat can vary (faster or slower), while the fundamental pitch is constant, or vice versa. As the fundamental pitch is being sustained, vibrations are propagating omnidirectionally and are re-sounding in the body cavities. Whenever a series of Gan-Tones, or Pulsations, are imposed (the simulated inner laugh), the fundamental vocal cords vibrations are amplified by fusion and compression through body components from the jaw, larynx and down through the body to the rectal-pelvic area, thus making the radii of amplified vibrations from the vocal cords penetrate omnidirectionally the greatest depth and height of the body below and above the vocal cords which, in turn, produce maximal resonance in the body cavities.

VI. The intensity developed by fusion and compression of vocal cords and body vibrations to the rectal-pelvic area is reflected in the thrust of these vibrations to the body resonators which demonstrates Newton's Law of Action and Reaction which states that for every action, there is an equal and opposite reaction. The intensity of the Thrust Phase is commensurate with the intensity of the Compression Phase. It should be noted that the effectiveness of the Compression Phase regarding amplification and transmission of vibrations is wholly dependent on the position of the jaw.

If the jaw rests firmly on the larynx with minimal involvement of throat muscles to maintain this position, vibratory continuity is most effective, and transmission and amplification of vocal cords vibrations during the Compression Phase are, therefore, maximized. The throat passage is also at its widest for the thrusting of these vibrations (up-part of the Gan-Tone beat), if the jaw is properly fused with the body, therefore, maximizing the re-sounding of these amplified vibrations to the resonators.

Maximal re-sounding of vocal cords vibrations transforms the dimensions of the singing line, giving the emitted sound great depth, height, resilience, buoyancy, spontaneity, radiance and brilliance, while diminishing anxiety, strain, fatigue and tension in the singer.

VII. Improper fusion of the jaw, that is, a divergence of the jaw, rather than resting firmly on the larynx with an absolute minimum of cervical muscle involvement in maintaining this position (collapse of the vertical-elliptical mouth opening), especially during moments of great stress (high, loud, sustained sounds), focuses pressure *immediately* on throat muscles. Absorption of vibrations in the soft parts (muscles) occurs as the hard parts (bones) separate causing the structure of vibratory continuity to weaken resulting in the following:

1. Focus of strain on the vocal cords and sur-

rounding muscles rather than diffused through the body.

2. Collapse of the vocal apparatus through muscle strain and spasm, as a result of the converging jaws.

3. Diminished amplification of vocal cords vibrations, as a result of diminished vibratory continuity.

4. Minimal effectiveness of compression, as a result of a limited amount of vibrations to be amplified.

5. Debilitated thrust, as a result of a limited payload of vibrations to be thrust to the resonators.

6. Restriction in the throat opening commensurate with the divergence of the jaw, restricting the movement of the decreased vibrations to the body resonators.

It should also be noted that any setting of the jaw, especially during loud, high, sustained sounds, causes undue muscle stress.

Although the simulated inner laugh is somewhat effective with a diverging jaw, it is obvious that the maximum resonant potential and dimension of the sound is greatly reduced, preventing the whole body from functioning as a bell.

The body functioning as a bell can be realized only when the body components, which includes the jaw, are properly fused during the application of the inner laugh, a series of imposed Gan-Tone Pulsations on the natural pitch of the singing line.

VIII. Since the purpose of the inner laugh, in the Gan-Tone Method of Voice Production, is to release tension, strain and anxiety in the singer, while producing resilience, buoyancy and brilliance in the singing voice, it is only natural that it would be a simulation of the natural laugh whose purpose also involves releasing tension and producing buoyancy in the human, while magnifying vibrations of life in the body.

Each pulsation in the natural laugh provides a fresh basis, or new life, for the continuation of activity. The deeper the natural laugh, the greater the release of body tension. As the laugh permeates the body, vibrations propagate omnidirectionally, fusing through the body on a wave of compression which magnifies the vibrations and simultaneously erases tensions. The body, under the influence of the laugh, is like a computer which, after the toil of computation, erases the figures and starts anew.

Each Gan-Tone Pulsation in the inner laugh erases body tensions, especially in the heart and stomach, since its downward wave to the rectal-pelvic area nullifies a belief that anxiety rides up through the body, gripping the vital organs. The inner laugh insures freedom from any localizing of anxiety that may occur, especially during moments of stress (loud, high, sustained sounds), and actually erases anxiety by "laughing" at it.

Without the application of the inner laugh on the singing line, vibratory continuity, that is, the process of amplifying and transmitting vocal cords vibrations throughout the body, is localized, usually in the throat area, preventing the utilization of the body as a vibrator and re-sounding agent (bell characteristics).

IX. The inner laugh magnifies the life of the singing voice by amplifying vibrations and resonance, creating a great pyramidal dimension, or structure, of sound whose reverberating base is the depth of the body (rectal-pelvic basin) and re-sounding height is the apex at the bridge of the nose which, in turn, activates the sinus cavities and surrounding areas to vibrate and resonate.

The efficient application of the inner laugh on the singing line causes the body to become highly vibrant, resilient and resonant, making the body transmit and re-sound many more vibrations omnidirectionally thus increasing the aura of vibrations that naturally envelops the body. Vibrations re-sound not only in the body cavities and emit through the facial apertures, but also transmit outwardly through the body, creating an aura of vibrations that envelops the entire body, since sound travels omnidirectionally.

The natural laugh and the simulated inner laugh are, therefore, similar processes which are conducive to stimulating life by magnifying vibrations in the human.

POPULAR AND CLASSICAL SINGING IN THE GAN-TONE METHOD

CONTENTS

POPULAR AND CLASSICAL SINGING IN THE GAN-TONE METHOD

I.	Why the application of Gan-Tone Principles is similar for popular and classical singing	61
II.	How the vocal needs of the singer affect the application of the Gan-Tone Principles of Jaw, Larynx, Body Fusion	61
III.	Why the maximum application of Jaw, Larynx, Body Fusion accommodates the greatest pressures involved in the singing line	61
IV.	Why popular singing doesn't present a great vocal demand for the singer	61
V.	Why knowledge of the absolute application of the Jaw, Larynx, Body Fusion is an advantage to the popular singer	61
VI.	Why the Gan-Tone Method rejects the current belief that a classical singer can't perform popular music without the classical influence	62
VII.	Why an opera singer trained in the Gan-Tone Method is able to move freely and fearlessly from the classical to the popular expression	62
VIII.	The role of the jaw in the Gan-Tone Method in promoting the flexibility of movement from the classical to the popular expression	62
IX.	How the Gan-Tone Principles of Jaw, Larynx, Body Coordination and Fusion prevent popular singers from "burning out"	63
X.	Why a singer should be able to move from the popular to the classical expression and vice versa	63
XI.	The role of the Jaw, Larynx, Body Coordination and Fusion in enabling a singer to move from the classical to the popular expression	63
XII.	The role of the Gan-Tone Pulsation in enabling the classical or popular singer to extend the dimensions of his sound after he develops a flexible coordination of the Jaw, Larynx, Body Fusion	64
XIII.	Procedure for transforming dimensions of the sound with the Gan-Tone Pulsation	64
XIV.	Why flexibility in the coordination of the jaw, larynx and body is essential	64

XV.	Procedure for producing and projecting sound with the feather-touch (essence of the Gan-Tone Method)	65
XVI.	Advantages of the skillful application of the Gan-Tone Pulsation to the popular or classical singer	65
XVII.	How a knowledge of Gan-Tone Principles gives the singer a wide gamut of vocal potential to choose from, whether popular or classical	65
XVIII.	Why the classical singer requires a greater involvement with Gan-Tone Principles than the popular singer	66
XIX.	Why it is practical for the singer to specialize in either popular or classical singing	67
XX.	Summary of advantages to the singer who gains facility with the Gan-Tone Principles	67

POPULAR AND CLASSICAL SINGING IN THE GAN-TONE METHOD

I. Since any form of singing, whether it be popular or classical, requires the coordination of the human vocal apparatus in order to cope with the pressures that are present in the singing line, the application of Gan-Tone Principles is similar for any form of singing except that the degree of involvement of the principles varies with the degree of intricacy, volume and range encountered by the singer whether his vocal expression is popular or classical.

The greater the degree of skill obtained with the Gan-Tone Method, the greater the flexibility the singer will demonstrate in moving from the popular to the classical, and vice versa, making his popular singing sound just as natural as his classical expression.

II. In order to obtain flexibility with the varied forms of vocal expression and avoid rigidity in the coordination of body parts (which would minimize flexibility), the Gan-Tone Principles of Jaw, Larynx, Body Fusion are applied to the extent necessary in order to cope with the vocal needs encountered by the singer. The greatest vocal demands are usually present in the classical expression, such as Opera and Lieder, since they usually contain the most intricate singing lines. However, great vocal demands in terms of range and volume can sometimes be present in Rock and Roll and, at times, this vocal demand (many high notes and difficult passages) can be equal to, or greater than, the classical expression, therefore, requiring a maximum application of the principles of Jaw, Larynx, Body Fusion to insure vocal survival.

III. An absolute, or maximum, application of Jaw, Larynx, Body Fusion Principles accommodates the greatest pressures involved in the singing line. Maximum fusion of the jaw and larynx with the body creates the widest opening in the throat in order to diverge the greatest amount of vibrations and pressure that occur in maximum range and volume. The widest opening of the jaw is necessary in order to achieve maximum fusion of the jaw with the body creating the strongest circuit for strengthening the transmission and amplification of vibrations omnidirectionally from the vocal cords throughout the body. The spontaneity with which the singer applies the Jaw, Larynx, Body Fusion determines how effectively he will counteract the vocal pressures. Since the jaw acts as a circuit maker, movement of the jaw downward towards the larynx creates a strong circuit between the vocal cords and body causing the divergence of vocal cords vibrations omnidirectionally throughout the body. Movement of the jaw away from the larynx breaks the circuit limiting the transmission of vibrations causing a convergence of these vibrations and pressure in the throat area. Therefore, when the vocal demand is great, complete fusion of the jaw, larynx and body is essential for minimizing pressure and insuring vocal survival.

IV. Popular singing, essentially, does not present a great vocal demand for the singer, since most of the singing line does not involve high range or great volume and is often a languid, dreamy, conversation-like form of expression found in Blues, Ballads, Spirituals, Rock and Roll, Country, Western and Folk singing, thus not requiring an absolute, or maximum, application of the Jaw, Larynx, Body Fusion Principles. The singing line in these forms of vocal expression creates, essentially, a minimal amount of vibrations and pressure, as a result of focus on the middle and low part of the range.

V. Although absolute fusion of the jaw, larynx and body is not essential, since the popular singer is not confronted with a great amount of vibrations and pressure in the throat area, knowledge of the absolute application of the Jaw, Larynx, Body Fusion Principles during loud, high, sustained sounds will insure the preservation of the vocal apparatus over the years and will also enable him to add greater depth, height and fullness to his vocal expression. Since complete body fusion amplifies the original vocal cords vibrations omnidirectionally throughout the body, maximum application of these Gan-Tone Principles in any part of the range will enable the popular singer to create new dimensions of vocal sound.

VI. It is currently believed that a singer who is trained in the classical form of vocal expression can not perform popular music without the classical influence. This belief is eliminated in the Gan-Tone Method of Voice Production with the realization that it is rigidity in the coordination of the jaw, larynx and body which is essentially responsible for the classical singer's inability to perform popular music effectively.

VII. The performance of Opera requires a greater understanding of voice production, which represents hundreds of years of vocal evolvement, and is, therefore, a highly developed manifestation of vocal awareness. Popular singing, in general, does not demand a great understanding of voice production and is, essentially, aimed at the masses who have little or no insight into the mechanics of voice production. The dictionary defines popular as "Suitable to the public in general; as: a) Easy to understand; plain." Since it requires much discipline to master the vocal demands of Opera, the classical singer develops a certain rigidity in the production of sound that makes it difficult for him to adapt to the popular forms of expression. Popular music does not demand this great discipline in the sound and, usually, a singer who develops this control wants to maintain it for the following reasons:

    1- He has spent many years mastering the discipline necessary to negotiate the classical vocal demand and is happy with the thought that he is functioning on a high level of vocal awareness.

    2- He believes he has mastered a high form of vocal expression and may resent expressing himself in vocal forms that require little or no discipline.

    3- He senses his inability to make this transition from the highly disciplined classical approach to the less disciplined popular forms, since he has developed rigid habits of vocal production.

    4- He may hesitate changing from a classical to a popular form of expression for fear of losing his voice.

However, an Opera singer trained in the Gan-Tone Method of Voice Production will develop a flexibility in the application of his vocal apparatus which will enable him to move freely and, therefore, fearlessly, from the classical to the popular expression, as a result of his thorough understanding of the interaction of mind, body and air, not only giving him greater insight into his vocal apparatus but, also, an invaluable ability to diagnose all forms of vocal expression, whether it be singing or speaking. His flexibility with the vocal apparatus will enable him to create new dimensions of sound in the vocal expression of his choice.

VIII. In the Gan-Tone Method, the jaw is the key to flexibility in enabling the singer to move from the classical to the popular expression without the classical influence.

The singer becomes extremely sensitive to the relationship of the varied openings of the jaw and their effect on vocal vibrations and pressures, rather than adhering to one rigid positon of the jaw. He also becomes sensitized to the supple coordination of the jaw, larynx and body along with the varying degrees of involvement of these parts in creating the desired sound.

The Opera singer who has a classical influence in his popular expression lacks the flexibility in the supple coordination of the jaw, larynx and body. He rigidly adheres to the exaggerated positions of the jaw, for example, in singing conversation-like passages, occurring in the medium and low range in Ballads or Folk Songs, that do not require these wide-open jaw positions giving a pompous, distorted quality to the sound. Fusion of the jaw, larynx and body, which occurs when the jaw is opened wide, produces greater dimensions of height and depth in the sound, as a result of greater body involvement, which is not required in popular singing. The degree of vocal cords vibrations and pressure produced in popular singing is generally not as extreme as it is in Opera, where the widest opening of the jaw is necessary in order to produce maximum volume and give great dimensions of height and depth to the sound in any part of the range. It should be noted that it is not the quality of the Opera singer's vocal cords that prevents him from singing a popular song effectively, or lead others to say that "he doesn't have the voice for it" but, rather, a rigid coordination of his vocal apparatus that makes it impossible for him to move from the classical to the popular expression successfully.

A classical singer trained in the Gan-Tone Method develops such a supple coordination of the jaw, larynx and body making it possible for him to move from the exaggerated jaw positions in sustained sound to the conversation-like involvement of the jaw thus taking the stigma of operatic influence out of his popular singing.

IX. Conversation-like singing in the popular expression, at times, rests in the high part of the range focusing pressure in the vocal cords and making it difficult to transfer the buildup of pressure from the delicate vocal cords to the body. Since the Gan-Tone Method makes the singer aware of pressure, and its harmful effects, he learns to coordinate the maximum opening of the jaw, in a supple, subtle manner, in order to transfer vocal cords vibrations and pressure to the body without distorting the singing line. When sustaining a high note in classical singing, rapid articulation of words is avoided; whereas, this rapid articulation of words on a high note or notes occurs frequently in popular singing, therefore, requiring a greater understanding of the supple, subtle positioning of the jaw, from the widest to the narrowest opening, in order to eliminate the classical influence and, at the same time, insure vocal survival. Obviously, popular singing, at times, requires a greater understanding of the jaw, larynx, body coordination than classical singing. Lack of understanding and application of this coordination by popular singers explains why these singers "burn out" and why there is a constant turnover of these singers.

X. Although classical vocal expression (Opera and Lieder) can be considered the highest form of vocal development, a rigid coordination of the vocal apparatus (jaw, larynx and body), in producing this sound, creates a barrier for the classical singer to the complete understanding and absolute exploration of the human voice.

Popular forms of vocal expression contain, for the most part, pure vocal cords sound without laryngeal and body involvement. The essence of the Gan-Tone Method is the involvement of pure vocal cords sound, which is activated with a minimum of pressure on the vocal cords, and the amplification of this pure vocal cords sound, or vocal cords vibrations, throughout the body with the fusion of the jaw, larynx and body causing the body to function as the amplifying, thrusting, re-sounding and projecting system for the original vocal cords vibrations, thus extending the dimensions of height, depth and volume of the original pure vocal cords sound.

Since pure vocal cords sound is the starting point of all vocal sound, it should be at the command of the singer, whether his expression is popular or classical. This pure vocal cords sound should be activated at the vocal cords with an absolute minimum of mind, body and air pressure and re-sounded, or amplified, throughout the range with the fusion of the jaw, larynx and body, diffusing vocal cords pressure to the body extremities and producing maximum dimensions of height, depth and volume in the original pure vocal cords sound through body involvement rather than pressure on the vocal cords. It, therefore, becomes the responsibility of the body, not the vocal cords, to extend the dimensions of the pure vocal cords sound through the skillful coordination of the jaw, larynx and body. The classical singer, who is unable to produce the pure vocal cords sound involved in popular singing, lacks the understanding necessary to move back and forth from the simple to the complex, that is, from the original pure vocal cords sound to the amplified dimensional sound.

XI. Rigidity in the coordination of the jaw, larynx and body in the process of producing sound is responsible for the classical singer's inability to move from the complex to the simple, that is, from the amplified dimensional sound to the original pure vocal cords sound, or from the classical to the popular form of expression. Flexibility in the coordination of the jaw, larynx and body involves understanding the innumerable vocal effects that can be produced by mentally varying pressure, in different degrees, on these parts as, for example, decreasing pressure of the jaw on the larynx, which is produced by closing the jaw to a conversation-like position, while easing throat and body fusion, produces a sound that approximates the pure vocal cords sound, since it has a minimum of laryngeal and body involvement. Moving the jaw away from the larynx breaks the circuit between the vocal cords and the body preventing the original vocal cords vibrations from being amplified through the body and causing these vibrations to be restricted in the throat area.

The innumerable positions of the jaw in relation to the larynx and body, the innumerable degrees of pressure imposed on the vocal cords and the innumerable degrees of pressure on the body reflect innumerable degrees of re-sounding of vocal cords vibrations in the body and its cavities creating a great gamut of coloration and volume in the human sound. Therefore, the singer who lacks the ability to coordinate the jaw, larynx and body flexibly lacks the complete understanding of his vocal instrument and the awareness of the absolute exploration of the human voice.

XII. When the classical or popular singer, trained in the Gan-Tone Method, has developed a somewhat flexible coordination of the jaw, larynx and body in producing the desired sound, whether it be a classical or popular expression, the singer has established the condition suitable for the effective application of the Gan-Tone, a superimposed pulsation on the natural vibrations of the notes being sung, which enables the singer to extend the dimensions of his sound by transforming the procedure in which original vocal cords vibrations are amplified.

XIII. This transformation occurs as follows:

The spark of sound is activated with a minimum of pressure on the vocal cords. The body is utilized as a cylinder, and the piston is the pressure the singer imposes, initially on the vocal cords and progressively downward through the body, anchoring this pressure and vocal cords vibrations in the Sphincter ani externus muscle at the rectal-pelvic basin through the imposition of the down-part of the Gan-Tone beat, which is known as the Compression Phase, since it fuses original vocal cords vibrations and pressure through the body to the rectal-pelvic basin.

Complete focus of pressure and vocal cords vibrations at the rectal-pelvic basin occurs at the height of the Compression Phase, at which time these vocal cords and body vibrations are amplified and thrust on the up-part of the Gan-Tone beat, known as the Thrust Phase, transmitting these vocal cords and body vibrations through the body and its cavities with maximum impact, causing these vibrations, through re-sounding, to produce maximum volume, resonance, brilliance, height and depth in the emitted sound. This procedure completes one cycle of the Gan-Tone Pulsation.

The repetition of this beat, whose speed is controlled by the singer, forms the structure of vocal sound, which includes the original vocal cords vibrations, fusion and compression of these vibrations through the body, amplification, thrust, resonance, or re-sounding, and projection of these vibrations as voluminous, brilliant sound.

XIV. Flexibility in the coordination of the jaw, larynx and body is required before the Gan-Tone Pulsation can be applied effectively, since flexibility in this coordination causes the most effective transference of vocal cords vibrations and pressure from the vocal cords to the body, that is, the singer has become sensitive to the jaw positions necessary to diffuse the vocal cords vibrations that occur in the singing line and the accompanying pressures that occur in the vocal cords and throat muscles.

Although a rigid setting of the jaw in a rather wide-open position does diffuse vibrations and pressure through the body, tension is evident in the face and neck, as a result of facial grimaces, rather than placidity, and the intense involvement of throat muscles, indicating that the structure of sound is being maintained in the throat; whereas, a flexible positioning of the jaw in relation to vibrations and pressure creates a placid countenance and requires a minimum of throat muscle involvement, indicating that the structure of sound is being maintained by the body.

When a skillful flexibility of the jaw is achieved, the jaw ultimately balances on the larynx with a minimum of muscular effort, whether the vocal demand is small or great. As the amount of air pressure that is focused on the vocal cords to maintain the pitch being sung is diminished, the more skillfully the jaw is balanced on the larynx, since vocal cords vibrations are not being restricted by tension in the throat area, enabling the singer to apply a feather-touch to the jaw and the vocal cords in producing sound. Ease in the constant transference of vocal cords vibrations and pressure to the body eliminates the singer's need to blatantly attack the vocal cords for volume and other dimensions of sound.

XV. The feather-touch for producing and projecting sound is the essence of the Gan-Tone Method and can be summarized as follows:

1- Flexible positioning of the jaw to achieve a balancing of the jaw on the larynx with a minimum of muscle activity regardless of the vocal demand.

2- Minimal pressure imposed on the vocal cords to determine pitch.

3- Minimal jet of air from the lungs for vibrating the pitch.

The effective transference of vocal cords vibrations and pressure to the body, as a result of the flexible jaw positions, coincides with the path of the Gan-Tone Pulsation. The more flexible the jaw positions in transferring vocal cords vibrations and pressure to the rectal-pelvic basin during the Compression Phase, or down-part of the Gan-Tone beat, the less the restriction of vibrations, causing a more instantaneous grounding of these vibrations at the bottom of the torso which, in turn, produces a more instantaneous thrust of these vibrations creating a great impact in the cavities, or resonators, of the body during the Thrust Phase, or up-part of the Gan-Tone beat. Instantaneous grounding of vocal cords and body vibrations at the rectal-pelvic basin (Sphincter ani externus muscle) followed by the intense impact of these vibrations in the body cavities produces highly resonant undulations of vibrations causing the body to function as a bell in producing and projecting multidimensional sound.

Skillful application of the Gan-Tone Pulsation by popular as well as classical singers enables them to produce a gamut of sound, from the lightest pure vocal cords sound to the full-bodied, open-throated, head-resonant sound, with a minimum of pressure, or feather-touch, on the vocal cords throughout the entire gamut of vocal sound.

XVI. Skillful application of the Gan-Tone Pulsation causes vocal cords vibrations and the accompanying pressures to be transmitted and diffused omnidirectionally throughout the body with maximum effectiveness, easing the focus of vocal cords pressure in the throat area and minimizing muscle fatigue, thus preventing the development of numerous undesirable throat conditions that can occur through irritation and which can lead to the eventual collapse of the vocal apparatus.

Skillful application of the Gan-Tone Pulsation enables the singer to project a maximum volume of sound with a minimum of physical effort by utilizing the body most effectively for amplifying and re-sounding vocal cords vibrations. The vocal cords become the microphone. The flexible jaw becomes the switch, or circuit breaker, for regulating the extent of body involvement. The body becomes the amplifier of the vocal cords vibrations, and the body cavities become the speakers, making the body the system responsible for increasing the volume of sound. The human has fabricated a system for amplifying sound based essentially on the three components found in his own natural amplifying system, such as, the microphone, which is comparable to the vocal cords, the amplifier, which is comparable to the body, and the speaker, which is comparable to the body cavity. The original activator of vibrations in the human is a current of air and in a basic man-made system, it can be a current of electricity.

XVII. A singer's awareness of the Gan-Tone Principles, therefore, gives him a wide gamut of vocal potential from which to choose, whether his vocal expression is popular or classical, since he develops a basic understanding of his vocal instrument. The degree to which he masters the flexible coordination of the jaw, larynx and body will determine the degree to which he utilizes the body as an amplifier of vibrations and a thrusting agent of these vibrations to the body cavities, making the body function as a cylinder and piston for amplifying, thrusting and re-sounding vocal cords and body vibrations which, in turn, will determine the degree of volume, height and depth that he will be capable of acquiring in his emitted sound.

The singer, trained in the Gan-Tone Method, will be in command of the pure vocal cords sound, essential for popular singing, with a reasonable degree of study. The degree of flexibility he demonstrates in moving to the classical expression effectively, however, requires a greater involvement with the principles, since a higher degree of vocal discipline is necessary to move from the pure vocal cords sound to the full-bodied, open-throated, head-resonant sound that contains a maximum of resounded vibrations, as a result of maximum involvement of the vocal cords, jaw, larynx and body. In order to extend the dimensions of the pure vocal cords sound, the classical singer has to develop the skill of fusing the vocal cords vibrations to the surrounding muscles, larynx and body. The degree of fusion of these parts is determined by the vocal effect desired by the singer. If he wants to produce a voluminous, multidimensional sound, he will require the strongest circuit, for the maximum transmission and amplification of vibrations, which is created by maximum fusion of these body parts, with the mental imposition of pressure on the back of the tongue, making the line of imposition coincide with the vertical body line, which, in turn, coincides with the line of gravity, a natural aid in fusion, since the gravitational pull naturally compresses physical objects. Another line of pressure, imposed by the singer, perpendicular to the vertical line of pressure, moves the tongue forward, creating a maximum opening of the throat, when the yawn is imposed with these lines of pressure.

The imposition of the Gan-Tone beat maximizes and stabilizes the voluminous, multidimensional sound by maximizing the amplification of vibrations and maintaining the structure of these vibrations on the calculated Gan-Tone beat whose frequency is controlled and stabilized by the singer.

Any divergence from the maximum fusion of the jaw, larynx and body produces a diminution of vibrations which results in diminished dimensions in the sound.

XVIII. Since the popular singer is not required to produce a full-bodied, open-throated, head-resonant sound, which is the height of vocal control, he is not required to develop the skillful coordination for maximal fusion of the jaw, larynx and body. However, the popular singer, trained in the Gan-Tone Method, who can produce the pure vocal cords sound, without body involvement, and also develops the skill for a minimal fusion of the jaw, larynx and body, for a sound of minimal dimension, as well as a maximal fusion of these body parts, for a multidimensional sound, can move from the popular to the classical, and vice versa, with ease, giving him complete control of his vocal instrument.

The classical singer, trained in the Gan-Tone Method, has to develop skill in articulating consonants clearly and quickly in order to maximize the length of the vowel sounds, since vowels create the widest jaw opening for moving the greatest amount of vibrations to the resonators which, in turn, produces the greatest dimensions in the sound. The speed with which consonants are articulated, and the speed with which the jaw is opened determines the dimensions of the emitted sound, that is, the faster the consonants are pronounced, concomitantly with the widest jaw opening, the greater the dimensions and duration of the emitted sound.

The popular singer does not have to develop the skill of articulating consonants quickly, while opening the jaw rapidly, since great dimensions of sound are not required in his conversation-like expression. He can slur his consonants into the vowel line, since the limited dimensions of the sound he produces depends on the degree of pressure he exerts in the throat area, which confines the development and movement of vibrations to the neck. However, a popular singer, trained in the Gan-Tone Method, can, by the supple and subtle application of principles, greatly enhance the dimensions of the singing sound by multiplying vibrations and eliminating pressures that would restrict the movement of vibrations and cause harm to the vocal cords. Developing skill in supple, subtle movements of the jaw, larynx and body prevents abrupt changes or exaggerated pompous sounds in the popular expression.

The classical singer has to develop skill in the spontaneous application of the coordinated jaw, larynx and body, along with the Gan-Tone beat, in order to transform pure vocal cords vibrations into multidimensional sound of great height and depth. Spontaneity in the application of the Gan-Tone beat maximizes the dimensions and duration of the sound by rapidly fusing and amplifying vocal cords and body vibrations. This instantaneous action results in the instantaneous reaction of thrusting and resounding these vibrations, with great impact, in the body cavities (resonators). Repetition of this Gan-Tone beat, whose frequency is controlled by the singer, produces a brilliant, scintillating, buoyant, vibrant, resonant line of sound which is greatly desired by the classical singer.

Since a singing line of such dimensions is not required in the popular expression, the popular singer doesn't have to develop the skill of spontaneous application of Gan-Tone Principles. Conversation-like vocal reactions dominate in the popular singing line with an almost total reliance on electronics for amplification.

The classical singer has to develop skill in attaining the absolute opening of the jaw, since this maximum opening leads to a jaw condition reached after the singer has achieved the ability to sustain the jaw down and back with a minimum of muscle activity, at which time the jaw balances on the larynx with a feather-touch, especially during moments of great vocal demand (loud, high, sustained notes), insuring complete involvement of the body as amplifier, thrusting agent and resonator. Application of the Gan-Tone beat, after this jaw position has been mastered, produces maximum resilience in the emitted sound, since the maximum unrestricted movement of vibrations made possible with the completely relaxed position of the jaw insures the spring-like action of the Gan-Tone beat through the body culminating in a decisively controlled vocal reaction.

The popular singer, trained in the Gan-Tone Method, is not required to develop the great skill of balancing the jaw on the larynx with a minimum of muscle activity for the most effective utilization of the Gan-Tone beat, which is required of the classical singer, since the singing line is essentially conversation-like and devoid of the extremely high, sustained, full-bodied sounds. However, the more freedom the popular singer develops in the flexible coordination of the jaw, the more vibrations he will free and amplify in the entire range of his voice, making available to him a greater gamut of vocal possibilities from which to create new dimensions of sound.

XIX. Although the Gan-Tone Method gives the singer insight into the principles required for vocal expression in the popular without sounding classical, and vice versa, it would be practical for the singer to specialize in either the popular or classical form of expression and focus on the Gan-Tone Principles to the degree necessary to cope with the particular singing demands. Attempting to master the gamut of vocal expression, from the popular to the classical, requires great capacity and, also, learning repertory in either category can be a monumental task. In the classical expression, this task is compounded by the foreign language requirement.

XX. However, facility with the Gan-Tone Principles will give the popular and classical singer a complete understanding of his vocal instrument, making him aware of vocal cords vibrations and pressure in the throat area and how to transfer them to the body, not only protecting his vocal instrument from irritation and possible collapse, but also, enabling him to determine the degree of dimensions he wishes to produce in his emitted sound. He will also become aware of the degree of Gan-Tone Principles that need to be mastered for effective vocal expression in the area of his choice and the skills necessary to move back and forth from the simple to the complex, that is, from the pure vocal cords sound to the full-bodied sound, or from the popular to the classical vocal expression, with flexibility and understanding.

ROCK AND ROLL IN THE GAN-TONE METHOD

CONTENTS

ROCK AND ROLL IN THE GAN-TONE METHOD

I.	Why the Gan-Tone Method thoroughly analyzes and handles any form of singing, whether it be Rock and Roll or Opera	73
II.	Why the Gan-Tone Method is the key to determining the level of vocal awareness of any singer, whether his vocal expression is Rock and Roll or Opera	73
III.	Why an awareness of Gan-Tone Principles extends the dimensional potential of the human voice and stabilizes the vocal structure necessary to maintain the singing line	73
IV.	Why Rock and Roll singers lose their voices	73
V.	The difference between the human vocal apparatus and the piano	73
VI.	How awareness of the Gan-Tone Principles enables the Rock and Roll singer to preserve his voice	73
VII.	The role of the jaw in the Gan-Tone Method for diffusing vocal cords pressure from the throat to the body	74
VIII.	How awareness of the Gan-Tone Pulsation enables the Rock and Roll singer to transform and augment the dimensions of his vocal sound	74
IX.	Why the Gan-Tone Method gives the Rock and Roll singer great flexibility in the degree of dimension he can attain in his sound	74
X.	Why it is advantageous for a child to be instructed in the Gan-Tone Principles at an early age	74

ROCK AND ROLL IN THE GAN-TONE METHOD

I. Human expression through the singing voice in any form is thoroughly analyzed and handled in the Gan-Tone Method of Voice Production, since any form of singing, whether it be Rock and Roll or Opera, requires the coordination of the human vocal apparatus in order to cope with the pressures that occur in the singing line and thus insure vocal freedom and security.

II. Knowledge of the Gan-Tone Method of Voice Production is the key to determining the level of vocal awareness of any singer regardless of his form of vocal expression, whether it be Rock and Roll or Opera. The singer's level of vocal awareness determines the extent of vocal cords involvement, the degree of body involvement, the degree of coordination of vocal cords and body, the degree of amplification of vocal cords and body vibrations, the degree of re-sounding of these vibrations and the degree of projection of vibrations and resonance from the body which, in turn, determines the quality, volume and freedom of the emitted sound.

III. Lack of understanding regarding the coordination of body parts when singing or speaking causes a convergence of pressure and vibrations in the vocal cords making the cords the amplifiers of vocal cords vibrations, not only limiting the dimensional potential of the human voice but, also, causing irritation in the vocal cords, fatigue in the surrounding muscles and eventual spasm and collapse of the vocal structure necessary to maintain the singing line.

Awareness of the Gan-Tone Principles of body coordination causes a divergence of pressure and vocal cords vibrations from the vocal cords omnidirectionally throughout the body making the entire body an extension, or amplifier, of the original vocal cords vibrations, not only extending the dimensional potential of the human voice but, also, minimizing irritation and muscular fatigue by diffusing pressure and vocal cords vibrations throughout the body, thus stabilizing the vocal structure necessary to maintain the singing line.

IV. Rock and Roll singing involves a blatant attack of the vocal cords in the singer's attempt to negotiate melodic lines and project voluminous, high sounds. He attacks the vocal cords with a degree of blatancy commensurate with the pressures involved in the singing scale. The higher the notes, the greater the vocal pressures and the more blatantly the singer attacks the vocal cords in order to cope with this condition. The louder the sound, the harder the attack on the cords creating a more blatant sound in order to cope with the need for more volume which results in a raucous sound known as Hard Rock. Since this sound is completely centered in the vocal cords, delicate membranous folds that are about half an inch long, this blatant attack of air and vibrations on these delicate membranes results in a buildup of pressure and irritation causing the Rock and Roll singer to experience much hoarseness and eventual collapse of his vocal structure which explains why there is such a constant turnover of Rock and Roll singers.

V. The human vocal apparatus is not a visible instrument, such as the piano, which contains systematic gradations of pitches from low to high, and where the structure of sound is mechanical and rigid. The piano can be considered a fabricated extension of the human mechanism and involves only a fractional part of the human dynamic potential. The human vocal apparatus is capable of an infinite variety of dynamics, as a result of the interaction of mind, body and air, and is less comprehensible than the piano to the senses, i.e., sight, touch and hearing. More insight and understanding is, therefore, necessary to reveal the many dimensions of the human vocal apparatus and to maintain its longevity.

VI. Awareness of the principles involved in the Gan-Tone Method of Voice Production enables the Rock and Roll singer to negotiate melodic lines with a feather-touch rather than a blatant attack on the vocal cords, since he realizes that a blatant attack on the cords does produce high or low sounds but does not give lasting structure and freedom to these sounds. The blatant attack on the cords makes the vocal cords responsible, not only for the fundamental pitch but, also, for the amplification, structure and security of the sound; whereas, the Gan-Tone Principles of Jaw, Larynx, Body Fusion treat the vocal cords as the initial spark for pitch applying a minimum of pressure on the cords to maintain the fundamental tone. The responsibility for the amplification, structure and security of sound is, therefore, transferred to the body, which is far more capable than the delicate vocal cords.

VII. The coordinated fusion of the jaw to the larynx with the vertical-elliptical mouth opening create a strong contact of vocal cords and larynx with the body which transmits and amplifies vocal cords vibrations from the vocal cords to the body on a strong vocal vibratory circuit by utilizing the jaw as a circuit maker. The more fused the jaw to the larynx and body, the more solid the vibratory circuit throughout the body diverging not only vocal cords vibrations from the vocal cords and surrounding muscles, but pressure as well. The less fused the jaw to the body, or any divergence of the jaw from the fused position, the less solid the vibratory circuit, or current of vibrations that would propagate omnidirectionally from the vocal cords throughout the body, causing vocal cords vibrations and pressure to converge on the vocal cords.

VIII. Awareness of the Gan-Tone beat, which is a superimposed pulsation on the natural vibrations of the voice, enables the Rock and Roll singer to transform and augment the dimensions of his vocal sound, making available to him more voice from which to create new sounds and new styles of singing with less effort and strain on the vocal cords.

Application of the Gan-Tone Pulsation fuses vocal cords vibrations on the Compression Phase, or down-part of the Gan-Tone beat, which reaches maximum compression and amplification of vibrations at the rectal-pelvic basin, followed by maximum thrust and transmission of vibrations onmidirectionally throughout the body, but especially to the head resonators, on the Thrust Phase, or up-part of the Gan-Tone beat, multiplying the original vocal cords vibrations by re-sounding them in the fibers and cavities of the body, thus creating more volume, range and dimensions of height and depth, as a result of the greater penetration of omnidirectionally transmitted vibrations.

IX. The natural quality of the Rock and Roll singer's voice is still present and is included within the wider dimensions of the Gan-Tone Pulsation enabling the singer to utilize the limited dimensions of his original natural sound at will. Since the Gan-Tone Pulsation is an extension and transformation of the natural sound, or original vocal cords vibrations, the end result of the skillful application of the Gan-Tone Pulsation yields a multidimensional sound which appears to be extremely natural to the listener. The Rock and Roll singer, however, is still free to resort to the limited dimensions of his original sound by not applying the Gan-Tone Method which, of course, includes the Gan-Tone Pulsation. Once having realized that the Gan-Tone Method gives greater freedom and dimension to the singing sound and that his vocal longevity depends on this method, he undoubtedly will be highly motivated to utilize the Gan-Tone Method of Voice Production.

X. If a child were exposed to the Gan-Tone Method at an early age, which is really the most malleable period, by the time he became a teen-ager, he would have a very supple application of the Gan-Tone Principles, and if he chose to sing Rock and Roll, or any other form of vocal expression, and became famous for his singing, he would be excellently equipped to handle the mental, emotional and vocal demands of a successful singer without fear of losing his voice in his twenties or thirties and without having to undergo re-orientation to a new method of singing that might be disastrous to his image, since the public might not recognize the change.

Starting a singing career with the Gan-Tone Method of Voice Production eliminates the need to change any famous singer's image, as a result of a malfunction in the singing instrument, since the singer will not develop vocal problems that will necessitate rehabilitation of his vocal instrument. Since he will be secure in his vocal expression, he will not experience the anxiety and tension that result from the inability to cope vocally, thus insuring vocal stability throughout his singing career.

THE VOCAL HOOK

CONTENTS

THE VOCAL HOOK

I.	Physical characteristics	81
II.	Why there can be only one method for mastering the aerodynamics in the Vocal Hook	81
III.	Why there is much confusion regarding the technique to be utilized in producing the singing voice	81
IV.	A great acoustical advantage of the Vocal Hook	81
V.	Concentration of vibrating air Above the Upper Teeth and on the Roof of the Mouth and its effect on tonal quality	81
VI.	Concentration of vibrating air on the Back of the Mouth and the role of the Uvular Tympany in affecting tonal quality	82
VII.	The effect of vibrating air on the Back of the Mouth, when the Uvular Tympany is not distended	82
VIII.	The effect of vibrating air on the Back of the Mouth, when the Uvular Tympany is distended	82
IX.	The Feedback of vibrating air	83
X.	Summary: Advantages of the Vocal Hook as a result of its curved shape	83
XI.	How the simulation and coordination of the natural principles of Yawning and Vomiting affect the Vocal Hook	83
XII.	Similar characteristics of Yawning and Vomiting	83
XIII.	Basic differences in Yawning and Vomiting	84
XIV.	Simulation of the First Similar Characteristic of Yawning and Vomiting: Fusion of the Jaw with the Body	85
XV.	The Vocal Cords Sound in the Gan-Tone Method	86
XVI.	Description of the Breathing Process	86
XVII.	How the Characteristics of Breathing are simulated in Diaphragmatic Breath Control	87

XVIII.	How shifting the emphasis from the Thoracic-Abdominal Diaphragm to the Pelvic-Perineum Diaphragm at the Rectal-Pelvic Basin gives the singer more Control of Breath and Support of Sound	87
XIX.	The role of the Abdomen in the Gan-Tone Method	87
XX.	The analogy of the Opened Parachute and the Structure of Body Support	88
XXI.	Why the emphasis of concentration should shift from the Thoracic-Abdominal Diaphragm to the Rectal-Pelvic Basin (Pelvic-Perineum Diaphragm)	88
XXII.	Gan-Tone Principle: The effect of Body Fusion on the Original Vocal Cords Sound	88
XXIII.	Simulation of the Second Similar Characteristic of Yawning and Vomiting: Dilated Nostrils	89
XXIV.	The effect of Dilated Nostrils on Resonance	89
XXV.	The Exterior Vocal Cords (lips) and the Interior Vocal Cords	89
XXVI.	The effect of Dilating and Contracting Nostrils on the quality of the sound	89
XXVII.	Simulation of the Third Similar Characteristic of Yawning and Vomiting: Distention of the Uvular Tympany	89
XXVIII.	The effect of the Uvular Tympany on the quality of the sound	90
XXIX.	The role of the Uvular Tympany in Direct and Indirect Resonance	90
XXX.	The analogy of a Person Sitting in a Room with Two Opened Doors	91
XXXI.	Simulation of the Fourth Similar Characteristic of Yawning and Vomiting: Pushing the Back of the Tongue and its root forward and downward	92
XXXII.	Gan-Tone Principle regarding the Back of the Tongue	92
XXXIII.	Simulation of the Fifth Similar Characteristic of Yawning and Vomiting: Grunting, or Pushing Down through the Body	93
XXXIV.	The role of Grunting, or Pushing Down through the Body (Fusion), in conjunction with the Gan-Tone Pulsation on the quality of the sound	93
XXXV.	The role of Fusion on the Movable Parts of the Vocal Hook and its effect on the quality of the sound	93
XXXVI.	The role of Fusion on Body Elasticity and its effect on the quality of the sound	93
XXXVII.	How the Larynx functions as a Vibrator	94
XXXVIII.	Why simulating the Natural Yawn is important in the Gan-Tone Method	94
XXXIX.	How the Gan-Tone Pulsation produces Resilient Sound, when the body is tension-free through the Yawning Process (Jaw, Larynx, Body Fusion)	95
XL.	Why the process of Ejection in Vomiting is simulated in the Gan-Tone Method	95

XLI.	Why Yawning is the Diametrically Opposed Process of Vomiting	96
XLII.	How the Expanding Process in Yawning contributes to the Bell Factor of the Body	96
XLIII.	How the Contracting Process in Vomiting aids in Ejection	96
XLIV.	How the Gan-Tone Method simulates and simultaneously coordinates the Diametrically Opposed Characteristics of Yawning and Vomiting	96
XLV.	Results of the Impingement Factor in the Gan-Tone Method	97
XLVI.	The Tongue English	98
XLVII.	Why the Principles of the Gan-Tone Method are natural, universal principles	98

THE VOCAL HOOK

I. Anatomically, the tract leading from the vocal cords, the larynx, the pharynx (back of the mouth), the pharyngeal curve, the vents of the mouth and nostrils (nares) to the tip of the jaw is shaped in a curve and can be referred to as the vocal hook. This curve-shaped area, comparable to the head of a poised cobra snake, is very irregular with its curves and channels causing vibrated air, or sound, passing through it to undergo much turbulence and agitation. It is this agitated, vibrated air, otherwise known as sound, passing through this tract, or vocal hook, enroute to emission, that must be mastered aerodynamically, if freedom is to be attained in the emitted sound, i.e., the singing voice.

If this tract, or vocal hook, were a straight path (i.e., from the larynx to the mouth and nostrils), the emitted sound would be different from the sound emitted from a curved path. The variety of surfaces to be found in the curved path provide many additional resonances for sound, augmenting the size and coloration of the sound. A straight path is less irregular and less impeded than a curved path and, therefore, incapable of producing the wide variety of sounds which is the truly remarkable feature of the curve.

II. Although this curved tract, or vocal hook, from the vocal cords to the mouth, nostrils and jaw, varies slightly with each individual, the basic structure is the same and characteristic of all humans implying that the method for mastering the aerodynamics in the vocal hook must be similar, if applied to similar subjects, i.e., humans.

The degree and variety of turbulence in the vibrated air, or sound, passing through the curve, or vocal hook, vary with the degree of irregularity to be found in this tract, which is slightly different in all humans, as, for example, the size of the jaw, nose, throat opening, mouth, larynx and its components. Although there are individual differences, the basic curve-shaped structure is evident in all humans.

The jaw complex of the vocal hook, which comprises the tongue, tonsils, epiglottis and opening to the larynx, along with the uvula, and other parts, is extremely flexible and mobile and, therefore, uniquely capable of harnessing the turbulent, vibrated air in order to produce many gradations of sound not possible in a straight path. Air passing through a smooth pipe, or straight path, will move with minimal turbulence or friction as a result of the unimpeded surface. Air passing through a curved pipe, i.e., vocal hook, whose surface is irregular and impeded as a result of the curve, will move with greater turbulence and the resulting eddies (i.e., "currents of air running contrary to the main current; one moving circularly; a whirlpool") are responsible for impeding the flowing sound.

III. Although the vocal hook is a perfect vehicle for the demonstration of many sounds, as a result of its curved structure, traditional and present ignorance regarding the aerodynamic principles involved in exploiting the advantages of this vocal hook has contributed not only to perpetuating the mystery regarding the singing voice, but has also caused much confusion regarding the technique to be utilized in producing the singing voice.

IV. A great acoustical advantage of the vocal hook is the cupola configuration, or concave shape, of the roof of the mouth which focuses sound within the cave of the mouth giving the emitted sound a bell-like quality not attainable if the roof of the mouth were not curved in shape.

V. Aerodynamically, as the vibrated air from the vocal cords strikes the concave-shaped roof of the mouth, the vibrated air, i.e., sound, bounces off and converges in the mouth. Since the roof of the mouth is shaped in a curve, each point on this area, from the uvula to the lips, produces its own particular reverberated sound. Apart from the general resonance of the roof of the mouth, particular resonance at a specific point can be stressed by mentally directing sound waves to a specific location as, for ex., above the upper teeth. Within the cupola of the mouth and above the upper teeth are two minor recesses, or cupolas, that give more intense focus to sound when air is concentrated intentionally in this area. This doubly concentrated air bounces off and converges causing intense focusing of sound which resounds in the mouth.

Since this area above the upper teeth is connected with the bones of the face, such as, the nose, cheeks and forehead, it can withstand great intensity of vibrating air, as a result of its bony structure and, more important, this bony surface creates a solidity which multiplies and intensifies resonance. Therefore, the more intensely air is guided to this area above the upper teeth, the more this vibrating air permeates and involves these bones causing them, in turn, to vibrate, resulting in maximum utilization of head resonance, giving more intensity and volume to the sound.

Another specific location for mentally directing sound waves is the hard palate, or roof the mouth.

Concentration of vibrating air in this area causes the rebounding air to be focused toward the center of the dome (roof of the mouth) resulting in a less intense sound. Since the concentrated air is somewhat removed from the area of the upper teeth which connects with the facial bones, this air can not be vibrated as intensely because of its distance away from the dense, bony structure of the mask (cheeks, nose, forehead). Furthermore, as the vibrating air is directed toward the hard palate (roof of the mouth) and away from the area of the upper teeth and base of the nose to the soft palate and folds of the mouth, the intensity of the sound diminishes as the density of the area decreases. The area near the upper teeth is composed of bone and cartilage. Bone is a strong vibrating agent and also an effective conductor of vibrations to connecting bones, which, in turn, carry these vibrations to other cavities of the head, such as the nasal and sinus cavities and the pharyngeal cavity. Multiple vibrations produced concomitantly in these areas result in maximum resonance. However, when the vibrating air is mentally directed away from the hard palate (roof of the mouth) toward the soft palate, the vibrating air further diminishes in intensity, since the composition of the roof of the mouth in this area is no longer bone but movable soft membrane. This composition does not vibrate air as intensely as bone, since it is a softer surface.

The mental concentration of air at the center of the hard palate (roof of the mouth), therefore, yields a combination of the extreme intensity of the area near the upper teeth and base of the nose along with the more mellow characteristic of the membranous area near the soft palate.

VI. Another specific location for directing sound is the back of the mouth.

The opening of the back of the mouth varies with the condition of the uvula and the surrounding membrane which can be referred to as the uvular tympany. Since the uvula is a flexible membrane capable of being distended, it functions as a tympany which the dictionary defines as an inflation or distention. This uvular distention, or tympany, can function as a wall, or dividing membrane, between the mouth and the pharynx, when the uvula is not distended but resting on the back of the tongue, making this membrane the back of the mouth. As the uvular tympany expands, the mouth cavity enlarges revealing the pharynx. When this uvular tympany distends to its maximum, it fuses with the pharynx which now becomes the back wall of the mouth making the pharynx an extension of the mouth thus adding length to the fundamental size of the mouth. Since the mouth chamber, or cave, has been increased in size, it now becomes capable of maximum resonance.

VII. When vibrating air is concentrated on the back of the mouth and the uvular tympany is not distended but closed, the sound, or vibrating air, is projected through the nasal passage and emitted through the nostrils, giving the tone certain qualities peculiar to the nasal tract.

If the tone is directed toward the nostrils, the sound will be more billiant, since it is concentrated in the bony area of the nose and eyes.

If the tone is directed toward the pharyngeal tract, the sound will be softer, deeper and less brilliant, since it is farther away from the bony area of the mask.

Guiding the air to positions between the nostrils and the pharyngeal tract will give a wide variety of coloration to the sound.

VIII. When the uvular tympany is distended, the fundamental cave of the mouth is elongated, since the pharyngeal cavity becomes an extension of the mouth.

By concentrating the vibrating air in this area, the sound is deeper, darker and less brilliant.

IX. Furthermore, concentrating the vibrating air in the pharyngeal cavity when the uvular tympany is distended, near the back of the tongue toward the larynx, as in the process of yawning, causes vibrating air, i.e., sound waves, to collide against the curved shape of the pharyngeal cavity and cupola of the mouth causing some of the sound waves to be fed back into the system (body) on the Gan-Tone cycle. The more intensely the Gan-Tone beat is applied, the greater the reverberation of sound waves against the pharyngeal-oral cavity causing a greater quantity of these sound waves to be fed back. This feedback of sound is added to the exhaled sound waves being emitted through the vocal cords resulting in increased volume of sound and decreased need to tax the vocal cords in attempting to multiply the sound, since this feedback contributes to this amplification.

Greater utilization of breath is also made possible through feedback, since resonance that would ordinarily be exhaled is fed back increasing the density and volume of sound. Compacting sound waves in the process of feedback affords greater thrust for greater projection of the voice.

Feedback of vibrating air, brought about by simulating the characteristics of the yawn, can be utilized wherever sound waves re-sound in the vocal hook, and the application of the Gan-Tone beat highly defines this process. As sound waves, or spheres, for example, are directed to the roof of the mouth while simultaneously simulating the natural yawn, feedback of sound waves occurs. Resonance in back of the upper or lower teeth, the base of the nose, the higher recesses of the nasal passage or combinations of these points can also be further re-sounded through feedback.

X. The vocal hook, therefore, has the ability, as a result of its curved shape and varied recesses, to vibrate, re-sound and feed back sound waves emanating from the vocal cords.

Since the anatomy of the vocal hook is similar in all humans, there are not many methods but, essentially, one method, or technique, to guide sound waves through this vocal hook for the most efficient production of the singing voice. The common anatomical structure of the vocal hook in all humans makes the aerodynamics encountered within this curved path similar for all humans producing similar acoustical effects as, for ex., focusing air on the center of the hard palate will yield a combination of the extreme intensity of the area near the upper teeth and base of the nose along with the more mellow characteristic of the membranous area near the soft palate.

XI. Although there are individual differences in the mental and physical characteristics of humans, such as inclination, sensitivity, size of the throat opening, vocal cords, etc., these differences are natural variables and contribute to the unique beauty of each voice when the basic, natural principles for producing the singing voice are uncovered and mastered. Mystery and confusion are eliminated with the realization that these natural principles are unconsciously operating in the human harmoniously in the two diametrically opposed processes of yawning and vomiting.

An involuntary action, the natural yawn occurs when the body draws in a deep inspiration of air. In vomiting, rather than drawing in, the body ejects undesirables from the stomach through the mouth. Yawning and vomiting are, therefore, diametrically opposed body processes, but they both result in a similar outcome—the maximum distention and opening of the vocal hook.

Simulation and coordination of the natural characteristics of the yawning and vomiting processes are the two most important aspects of the Gan-Tone Method of Voice Production.

Since all humans possess similar tracts, the methods of yawning and vomiting are similar for all. It follows, then, that since humans have vocal hooks that are generally alike, the method for guiding sound waves through this curved path to produce the singing voice has to be similar. Therefore, there are not many methods but, essentially, one method. Although cars have individual differences, the rules for driving them are the same.

XII. Since the acts of yawning and vomiting occur so naturally, it is important to examine the characteristics of these processes in order to become consciously aware of the body mechanics that must be simulated in order to consciously incorporate them in the singing process.

Although yawning and vomiting are opposite processes, they are similar in the following characteristics:

1. The jaw is opened wide—down and back—revealing recesses behind the hinges of the jawbone, causing the jaw to be so fused with the body that they both function as one, completely compacting the body.

As a result of this fusion in yawning, air and body pressure are directed to the deepest recesses of the lungs, stomach and downward to the bottom of the torso. The phenomenon of the complete yawn exists only when the jaw is fused with the body.

Similarly, in vomiting, fusion of the jaw with the body, as a result of the unhinged jaw along with a definite grunting, or pushing down through the body to the bottom of the torso, enables the body to gain and maintain the thrust for projecting and ejecting the contents of the stomach through the mouth. Again, this phenomenon would not be complete, if the jaw were not fused with the body.

2. The nostrils are dilated in yawning and vomiting.

Dilated nostrils in yawning enable the air to be directed to the nasal and sinus cavities, and other cavities of the head.

Dilated nostrils in vomiting permit maximum opening of the nostrils to facilitate passage of the ejected contents.

3. The uvular tympany is distended in yawning and vomiting.

This distention is nature's way of widely opening the vocal hook, or curved pathway, in order to provide for the maximum inspiration in yawning and the maximum ejection in vomiting. This complete distention of the vocal hook minimizes irregularities of the curve and compacts protuberances, such as the epiglottis and the back of the tongue.

4. The back of the tongue, and its root, is pushed forward and downward in yawning and vomiting.

This action opens the pharyngeal tract to its widest allowing maximum inspiration in yawning and maximum ejection in vomiting.

5. A grunting, or pushing downward, (contractive muscular action) through the body is common to both yawning and vomiting.

In yawning, the grunting, or pushing downward, takes place at the peak of the intake of air when the lower abdominal area expands followed by a downward pushing and compacting of the abdomen to the point of the closed rectal aperture (Sphincter ani externus muscle) in order to release pressure and tension in the body, which is one of the purposes of yawning.

In vomiting, the grunting down occurs when the abdominal muscles push down toward the rectum (Sphincter ani externus muscle) and the stomach contracts. This contraction against the compacted abdomen creates strong paroxysms, or spasms, which eject the contents of the stomach.

In both yawning and vomiting, the pushing downward of pressure to the rectum at the Sphincter ani externus muscle is the extreme point the two processes have in common for elimination. In yawning, tension is eliminated. In vomiting, undesirables ejected from the stomach through the mouth are thus eliminated. The culmination of the cycles of both yawning and vomiting is, therefore, projection, as a result of the pushing-down at the rectal area.

XIII. The basic differences in vomiting and yawning are as follows:

1. In yawning, there is a drawing-in.

In vomiting, there is an ejection from the stomach through the mouth.

2. In yawning, there is an expansion of the air tract from the nose to the lungs and a compacting of the abdominal viscera to permit maximum intake of air. This maximum air-intake, which expands the air tract, compacts the area surrounding this expansion making the air more dense and the surrounding lower viscera, such as the intestines and other organs, more solid.

In yawning, there is also an expansion of the lungs, as a result of contractive muscular action, in order to permit maximum intake of air.

In vomiting, there is the opposite of expansion taking place. Paroxysm, which is a violent involuntary contraction or series of contractions of the muscles, otherwise known as muscle spasm, contracts the stomach which, in turn, emits the undesirable contents through the mouth and nostrils.

XIV. Since an awareness has been developed of the body mechanics involved in yawning and vomiting with the description of the similar and dissimilar characteristics, the simulation of these characteristics in the Gan-Tone Method of Voice Production can now be described.

<u>Fusion of the jaw with the body, the first similar characteristic of yawning and vomiting described, is a fundamental principle in the Gan-Tone Method.</u>

Fusion of the jaw with the body is important, since it controls the variable pressures encountered in the singing process and also determines the degree of opening of the vocal hook and the amount of projected vocal sound.

When the jaw is completely unhinged—down and back—and, therefore, completely fused with the body, the greatest quantity of pressure can be allayed. In this position, the jawbone is fused with the collar bone; therefore, the pressure encountered in the projection of the maximum output of sound falls on the jawbone and collar bone. The closer the jawbone is to the collar bone and the body, the more solid the fusion of the vocal hook to the body. Any riding-up of the jaw from this position while sustaining maximum volume of sound will put pressure on neck and throat muscles rather than bone. The limp open hand, for example, is not capable of sustaining the power of the tightened fist. The jaw fused with the body is comparable to the tightened fist.

The unhinged jaw fused with the collar bone compresses the components in the vocal hook that are located between the jaw and the collar bone. The components, in their descending order, are the tongue and its root, the hyoid bone, the supra-infrahyoid muscles, the thyroid cartilage, the cricoid cartilage to the collar bone along with the epiglottis, which is compacted to the back of the tongue maximizing the opening of the larynx, allowing the unobstructed movement of the emitted sound. By keeping this curved path and these components compacted under stress, a balance is developed between the muscles and bones in which pressure is shifted from the muscles to the bones as needed. If, under great pressure, for example, the neck muscles are holding the jaw and setting it in a compromised position, the strain on the neck muscles will ultimately cause their collapse. To prevent collapse, the jaw should be completely unhinged—down and back—causing a compacting of neck muscles, thus preventing muscle strain by shifting this stress to cartilages and bones.

There are singers who hold the jaw in a set position, i.e., not completely unhinged during moments of stress, (high, sustained notes and maximum volume), thus placing great tension on neck muscles, restricting sound to the larynx, since the throat opening becomes constricted producing a tight sound and causing eventual vocal difficulties as the singers get older. This held position of the jaw arises from a natural tendency to control the sound by using muscles to tighten the jaw. The freedom and beauty of the sound is increasingly impeded as this muscle tension is increased, since the constriction of the throat opening, i.e., the laryngeal and pharyngeal tracts, restricts the sound. However, if the jaw is moved down and back as pressure and friction increase, this restriction of sound is minimized, since the throat opening is widened causing the sound to move more effortlessly. As the tone moves more freely through this tract, the stress of pressure can move more naturally to the bottom of the torso and the head resonators.

Therefore, it is the necessary openings of the jaw, in order to allay pressure in the vocal cords and larynx, and the downward pressure through the body to the bottom of the torso, to support the sound and fully utilize the head resonators, that give dimension, freedom and beauty to the emitted sound. As air is concentrated in the vocal cords and larynx and the sound is allowed to move freely by unhinging the jaw under pressure, emphasis of pressure is shifted from this area to the head resonators (sinus cavities, bridge of the nose, cheekbones, roof of the mouth, or hard palate, etc.) as a result of the involvement of the body. It is the balance of this emphasis—the co-ordinated jaw and body support, with sufficient pressure to activate the vocal cords, and the maximally opened vocal hook through the principles of vomiting and yawning—that determines the degree to which the body will function as a bell, i.e., as a resonating chamber for sound. If the body-supported sound is restricted in the laryngeal area, as a result of the tight jaw, causing less emphasis on pressure in the head resonators and body, the sound will be reedy, hard and tight.

Fusion of the jaw with the body also determines the amount of projected vocal sound. The unhinged jaw and the compacting of the components cause the maximum opening of the pharynx and larynx creating a greater area for resonance of vocal cords vibrations.

XV. Ultimately, the vocal cords sound is the result of the following:

The human body is made up of many freely moving parts, such as bones, cartilages, muscles, ligaments, liquids and membranes, and when these parts are fused, they determine the amount of solidity, vibration and resonance that contribute to the augmentation of the original vocal cords sound. The fusion of these parts varies in individuals, as a result of their differences in mental and physical makeup. However, these parts are similar in all humans. Therefore, the quality of the singer's vocal apparatus is evaluated properly only when there is a complete awareness of the degree of fusion of all these parts.

The audible singing sound in the human originates at the vocal cords and resounds in the surrounding cavities, i.e., the larynx, pharynx, head and chest. This vocal cords sound, devoid of any extraneous augmentation, is referred to as the falsetto voice and is the origin of all vocal sound before it is resonated in the cavities of the body through fusion. This pure vocal cords sound can be augmented by fusing the vocal cords to the laryngeal cartilages. In addition to the vocal cords vibrations and resonance, the involvement of the larynx produces a larger and more vibrant sound which multiplies resonances in the cavities of the body when this amplified sound is projected to these cavities.

By unhinging the jaw and resting it on the Adam's apple, which is the thyroid cartilage, the jaw fuses with the larynx. This fusion of the jaw and larynx, in turn, causes the fusion of the hyoid bone, which is between the jaw and the larynx, further augmenting the vibrations and resonance of the sound in the body cavities.

The fused vocal cords, larynx, jawbone and hyoid bone can now be fused to the body by further fusing these parts to the lower part of the larynx, the trachea, collar bone and chest bones.

This combined fusion causes further fusion through the body by pushing pressure downward to the Sphincter ani externus muscle at the rectal area causing a solidification of the body parts.

The fusion of the vocal cords and the larynx is comparable to the intensity gained by pressing the forefinger and the thumb together. As the different parts of the body are fused, the initial vibrations of the vocal cords sound are continually augmented throughout the body causing a continuous vibrating current.

The thoracic-abdominal diaphragm in the Gan-Tone Method of Voice Production plays an important role in further fusing the body parts to the rectal area in order to involve the whole body in breath control and support of sound as opposed to the current belief which stresses the diaphragm as the main source.

XVI. Diaphragmatic breath control, the present popular belief, is the simulation of the natural process of breathing while singing.

The process of breathing can be described as follows:

The diaphragm, a dome-shaped musculofibrous partition, separates the thoracic (chest) cavity from the abdominal cavity. The convex top of the diaphragm is the floor of the thoracic (chest) cavity. As the diaphragm moves downward onto the abdomen in the process of breathing, the abdominal parts (viscera) are compacted causing them to protrude. As the diaphragm descends on the abdomen, more space is created in the thoracic cavity causing air to rush into the lungs. Space created where there originally was no space causes air to rush in to fill the vacant space, which is the result of suction and atmospheric pressure and is characterized by breathing in, or inhaling.

When the lungs are completely filled with air and the diaphragm is in a downward position, the abdominal muscles ascend against the bottom of the diaphragm which, in turn, presses against the lungs emitting the air from the lungs, which is essentially carbon dioxide, and is characterized by breathing out, or exhaling. This inhalation and exhalation of air describes one cycle of breathing.

XVII. In diaphragmatic breath control, the characteristics of breathing are simulated as follows:

The vocal sound is produced on expired, or exhaled, air. This exhaled air passes through the vocal cords and by exerting tension on the vocal cords, through mental concentration, sound is produced in the same manner that mental intention causes the forefinger and the thumb to be pressed together, or causes any other coordinated movement of the human body. As the sound is emitted from the body, pressure is exerted downward to the diaphragm and onto the abdominal area causing the abdomen to protrude and giving support to the sound by solidifying the abdomen and its parts. This solidification of the body causes the sound to become more vibrant and resonant resulting in greater control of the breath, since the vibrated air, or sound, is being resonated in the body cavities rather than escaping rapidly through the mouth. Since only half of the body is involved in supporting sound in diaphragmatic breath control, singers usually gain weight in order to gain more control of the sound.

XVIII. Rather than gaining weight, a more efficient involvement of the body in supporting sound can be accomplished through the Gan-Tone Method of Voice Production which stresses the ultimate point of concentration at the rectal area (Sphincter ani externus muscle), rather than the diaphragm. In the process of speaking, the diaphragm is adequate as support for sound and for breath control. However, singing requires a greater utilization of the body for support. Therefore, the diaphragm is more efficiently used when considered a part of the body, rather than the ultimate source of support and breath control. When the diaphragm is used as the main source of support and breath control, the abdominal area beneath it is pushed out as the diaphragm descends causing the support to spread horizontally, making it impossible to use the whole body as a vertical column of support, or to efficiently utilize the body as a piston and cylinder.

In order to utilize the whole body (from head to toes), when the need for maximum support arises (higher notes and louder sounds), the point of concentration should be at the rectum, which has the following effect:

Rather than the walls of the abdomen falling out horizontally, depleting the support, maintenance of concentration at the Sphincter ani externus muscle, which is the base of the rectum, keeps the lines of muscles and pressure vertically directed to the rectum, holding the walls of the abdomen compacted in an inward and downward direction, thus involving the body below the diaphragm, causing the whole body to be utilized for support and breath control.

Shifting the emphasis from the thoracic-abdominal diaphragm to the pelvic-perineum diaphragm for control of breath and support of sound causes the whole body to be fused, amplifying the vocal sound by giving it greater support, since the body now becomes involved as a vibrator and resonator whose vibrations and resonances are reflected in the body, which includes the cavities of the head and chest.

As the body becomes more vibrant and resonant, the amount of air that is utilized in making the sound at the vocal cords decreases, since the initial vibrations from the cords are further vibrated in the fused parts, and these accumulated vibrations are further augmented as resonance in the cavities of the body. As the air is vibrated, resonated and concentrated, it is not being emitted rapidly from the mouth, resulting in maximum breath control.

XIX. Much confusion exists among voice teachers regarding the role of the abdomen. Some teachers feel that the abdomen should be pushed out when singing; others feel it should be pushed in. Some teachers suggest that both procedures should be used. Other teachers feel that panting exercises and calisthenics are important for strengthening this area; while still other teachers feel that pushing against weights on the abdomen while lying on the back will strengthen the abdominal support.

However, as the need for strengthening the support for the singing sound increases, concentration at the rectal-pelvic basin as the ultimate point of support makes the line of body support compacted vertically, which automatically includes the abdomen, removing the confusion regarding the role of the abdomen. Since this organ is compacted in an inward and downward direction toward the rectal area, it no longer has to be pushed out or drawn in toward the backbone, even when concentration at the rectal area is not needed, i.e., when the vocal demand does not require such support. However, as more support is needed, concentration at the rectal area removes the need to manipulate the abdomen.

XX. The structure of the support is analogous to the shape of an opened parachute. The umbrella part of the opened chute is comparable to the diaphragm pressing down on the abdomen. The cords are the muscles of the abdomen which converge at the rectum. At this converged point in the parachute, the passenger is in complete control of the chute by manipulating the cords. Similarly, the rectal area becomes the focal point of controlled support by drawing the lines of pressure through the body to this point, thus utilizing the whole body as a compacted column for the most solid and efficient support of sound.

It is obvious, therefore, that the alternating action of the abdomen, inwardly toward the spine and outwardly, is not only tiring, but completely unnecessary in the Gan-Tone Method of Voice Production. Concentration of support at the thoracic-abdominal diaphragm utilizes only half of the body as opposed to concentration at the Sphincter ani externus muscle, (pelvic-perineum diaphragm) in the rectal area which completely aligns the body as a compacted column of support.

XXI. The vacillating action of concentration at the thoracic-abdominal diaphragm and the rectal-pelvic basin determines the degree of body support. It should be noted that much of singing does not require such complete body support to the rectal area and, therefore, involvement of the thoracic-abdominal diaphragm is sufficient. However, as the need for greater support increases (higher, louder, sustained sounds), the pressure moves from the thoracic-abdominal diaphragm through the abdomen to the pelvic-perineum diaphragm. The most complete body support involves concentration at the rectal area, rather than the thoracic-abdominal diaphragm, where the concentration of pressure fuses the abdominal viscera most effectively to the bones of the spine and pelvic area, fusing, in turn, the bones and joints of the hips and legs, which, in turn, fuse to the floor. It is important to note that this movement of pressure from the thoracic-abdominal diaphragm through the abdomen to the rectal-pelvic basin not only fuses the whole body and creates a foundation which is strongest at the rectal area, but it also, by its downward course, eliminates pressures from the upper extremities and organs (heart, lungs, abdomen, etc.) of the body.

The earth's gravitational pull is a natural aid in the fusion of the components of the body, when the body is in a direct line with the pull of gravity.

XXII. The following Gan-Tone Principle can, therefore, be stated:

> Each body component creates vibrations and resonances, when fused to the original vocal cords sound. Each component produces its own vibrations and resonances whose characteristics can be detected in the sound.
>
> The degree of definition applied to the fusion of all the components in the solidification of the body as a whole determines the degree to which the body functions as a bell.
>
> The degree to which the body functions as a bell determines the degree of accumulated vibrations and resonances, which determines the dimensions of the vocal sound. The more involved the components, the greater the vibrations and resonances of the amplified pure vocal cords sound (falsetto voice). A universal truth is, therefore, quite evident. The more united the members, the stronger the voice of the body. In the Gan-Tone Method of Voice Production, the degree of involvement of these components comprises the vocal apparatus.

XXIII. <u>Dilated nostrils, the second similar characteristic of yawning and vomiting already described is another important involvement in the Gan-Tone Method.</u>

XXIV. Dilated nostrils, to a great extent, regulate the amount of resonance in the nasal chamber, since opening and closing the nostrils determine the size of the vestibules of the nostrils. As the nostrils are dilated, the vestibules are enlarged, expanding the area and making it more taut, resulting in increased resonance, thus adding to the cumulative resonances of the vocal hook.

More sound is carried to the cavities of the head not only by the increased resonance in the vestibules, but also by the fusion of the nostrils with the cartilages and bones of the face. The degree to which the nostrils are dilated determines the degree of solidity of the nostrils to the bones in this area. Bones produce vibrations which resonate in the cavities of the body. The degree to which cartilages and muscles are vibrant is determined by their degree of tautness. Dilation of the nostrils produces tautness in the nostrils which, in turn, fuses them to the bones, cartilages and muscles of the mask causing a fusion of their vibrations which, in turn, is resonated in the cavities of the head, resulting in increased amplification of sound.

XXV. The tautness of the muscles in the process of fusion, for producing vibrations and resonances, is analogous to the tightening of the lips in whistling brought about by the contraction of the Orbicularis oris, which is a sphincter muscle. The lips can be considered two anterior (external) vocal cords similar to the two interior vocal cords, which are muscle-controlled ligaments.

The sounds produced by the lips, to a great extent, are dependent on their degree of tautness. Air striking the lips, i.e., the periphery of the mouth, when the lips are compressed, produces a shrill sound, which is the fundamental principle of the whistle. The degree to which the lips are brought together, or taut, determines the degree of vibrations. The more taut the lips, the faster the vibrations, resulting in a higher-pitched whistle. The less taut the lips, the lower the pitch of the whistle, as a result of the slower vibrations. The volume of the whistle depends on the degree of air pressure impinging on the lips. The greater the air pressure, with the pitch remaining constant, the more solid the fusion of the lips to the hard, bony areas of the face, making the whole area more vibrant and resonant.

Similarly, air striking the interior vocal cords vibrates the cords producing the human voice. The more taut the cords, the higher the pitch. The less taut the cords the lower the pitch. The greater the air pressure, the bigger the sound.

XXVI. Dilating and contracting the nostrils affect the quality of the sound. When the nostrils are dilated, the sound moves out more freely. When the nostrils are contracted to the point of closing, the sound produced in the nasal passage can not be emitted through the nose and is emitted, instead, with the sounds of the oral cavity that exit through the mouth. As the openings of the nostrils move from dilated to constricted, the emitted sound becomes more reedy, since the sound is restricted to the nasal area.

The constriction of the walls of the nostrils produces this reedy sound, similarly as the concentration of sound in the vocal cords, the result of a tight jaw, produces a reedy quality in the voice.

Although the sound has the characteristic peculiar to the area of restriction, the reedy quality is also present. Constriction, for example, in the nose, as a result of constricted nostrils, gives the reedy sound a nasal quality as opposed to a free-flowing sound, when the nostrils are opened. Restriction in the vocal cords produces tightness in that area giving the reedy sound a strident quality as opposed to the resonating sound produced in the body cavities, when the sound is not restricted to the vocal cords, but is magnified in these cavities. The tight jaw adds a tightness to the impeded reedy sound.

The role of the reed in the wind instruments operates on the same constriction principle. As the air passes through the narrow opening of the mouthpiece and reed, the air is restricted to this area causing the reed to vibrate, resulting in a tight, shrill sound.

XXVII. <u>The distention of the uvular tympany, the third similar characteristic of vomiting and yawning described is important in the Gan-Tone Method.</u>

The uvula and the surrounding membrane can be referred to as the uvular tympany. Since the uvula is a flexible membrane capable of being distended, it functions as a tympany which the dictionary defines as an inflation or distention. The two muscles that comprise the uvular tympany are the Palatoglossus and the Palatopharyngeus muscles.

In the process of singing, the uvular tympany becomes a relay for controlling sound out of the body through the pharyngeal-nasal tract, the mouth, or both.

The maximum distention of the uvular tympany, combined with the opened pharyngeal-nasal tract, affords the widest passage for the emission of sound, when this tract is kept opened, since the vocal hook is now completely involved.

In singing, the sound can be regulated, either through the pharyngeal-nasal tract or through the mouth, by controlling the degree of distention of the uvular tympany. When the uvular tympany is distended to its maximum, the nasal passage can be closed off, since the uvular tympany can be joined to the back wall of the pharynx. The membranes of the tympany blend with this back wall, creating the maximum opening of the cave of the mouth, which connects with the part of the pharyngeal tract that leads to the larynx. Concentration of the sound in the cave of the mouth and pharynx gives the sound depth. Complete distention of the uvular tympany, without closing off the nasal passage, gives the sound a free path which adds height to the depth of the sound.

XXVIII. The uvular tympany, therefore, determines the quality of sound in the following ways:

1- If the uvular tympany blends with the tongue, closing off the mouth cavity, the tone is colored by the characteristics of the pharyngeal-nasal tract giving it a more deep and nasal sound.

2- As the tympany distends, it permits tone to exit through the mouth. However, the degree of concentration in the mouth is now dependent upon the balance of the opening of the pharyngeal-nasal tract and the mouth, which the uvular tympany controls. The greater the pharyngeal-nasal opening, the greater the head resonance, which is characteristic of this tract, and the greater the consumption of air required to maintain resonance in this area. The wider the tympany distends, extending the mouth area, the greater the area available for re-sounding vibrations. By balancing the pharyngeal-nasal tract with the oral tract, a variety of tonal colors can be achieved. Thus the degree of resonance in either chamber is determined by the activity of the uvular tympany.

3- By distending the uvular tympany to its maximum, this tympanic membrane blends with the back wall of the mouth, or the pharynx, cutting off the passage of tone from the pharyngeal-nasal tract. Although the sound proceeding from the cords now goes directly to the oral cavity, or mouth, it can not go directly to the pharyngeal-nasal passage, where it could resonate. However, the degree of air pressure resonating sound on the roof of the mouth determines the amount of vibrations and their degree of penetration of the bone and cartilage on the roof of the mouth through the floor of the pharyngeal-nasal tract, which results in indirect resonance in that tract.

Therefore, even though the pharyngeal-nasal tract is cut off, as a result of the fusion of the uvular tympany to the back wall of the mouth, or pharynx, vibrating sounds concentrated on the hard palate, or roof of the mouth, vibrate the maxilla, palatine bones and the cartilage of the septum whose vibrations resound in the two major fossae, or caves, of the nasal tract, which, in themselves, are a marvel of acoustical accommodation in that their many minor caves and passages vibrate perfectly an infinite variety of sounds.

The nasal-pharyngeal tract and the oral tract eventually merge as one tract to the larynx. The physical characteristics of these tracts are acoustically designed as perfect resonators for any conceivable vocal sound.

XXIX. The degree of activity, therefore, of the uvular tympany determines the degree of direct and indirect resonance. Direct resonance is the result of direct vibration of sound passing through the channels of the vocal hook, i.e., the vocal cords sound re-sounded in the larynx, pharynx, mouth and pharyngeal-nasal tract along with the cavities of the chest. Indirect resonance is the result of vibration of sound penetrating the walls of the vocal hook into chambers, or cavities.

In the process of breathing simultaneously through the nasal and oral passages, the uvular tympany has sufficient opening for permitting the passage of vibrations to be re-sounded in the cavities of the vocal hook.

The employment of the uvular tympany as a dividing point determines the degree of direct-resonance involvement, since this tympany can close off the back of the mouth, by blending with the tongue, preventing the re-sounding of direct vibrations in the mouth. Since the back of the mouth is closed, even though the lips are opened, the recipient of direct vibrations and resonance is the nasal tract. However, indirect resonances, via the nasal tract, penetrate the roof of the mouth downward producing indirect resonance in the mouth. By distending the uvular tympany to the wall of the pharynx, these membranes join, closing the passage to the nasal tract and the recipient of direct resonance is the mouth. However, the vibrating air on the roof of the mouth penetrates the roof, bones and cartilages of the sinus and nasal cavities, producing indirect resonance in the nasal cavities, as sound in one room penetrates the walls and re-sounds in another room.

It is obvious, therefore, that the uvular tympany apportions, or allocates, direct and indirect vibrations and resonances to the nasal and mouth cavities. The degree of uvular tympany distention also controls the vibrations and resonances in the pharyngeal tract which are ultimately reflected in the whole body.

XXX. These occurrences are analogous to a person sitting in a room which has two opened doors. The room is the mouth. The front door is the opening of the mouth through the lips. The rear door is the opening at the uvula tympany. Beyond the opened rear door is a hall, which is the pharyngeal tract. There is a staircase leading to the room above. The staircase is the pharyngeal tract, and the room above is the nasal tract.

The room above is partitioned into two rooms having two front doors that are opened. These front doors are the nostrils, or nares, leading to the outside.

Someone is singing in the corridor downstairs, which is the voice proceeding from the larynx. These vibrations, travelling at more than 1,120 feet per second, resound almost simultaneously in the rooms because the doors are opened. (Sound travels faster in the vocal hook than in the atmosphere, since these vibrations are being thrust by the body.) However, the difference in travelling time that it takes the vibrations to reach the two upper rooms, since the upper rooms are farther away, partially accounts for the variation in overtones and harmonics that occur.

Essentially, the efficiency of these rooms (mouth and nasal cavities) as resonators is dependent upon the projection of sound, which is determined by the degree of intensity of the Jaw, Larynx, Body Fusion and the Gan-Tone Pulsation, since the greater the intensity, the greater the thrust that projects the sound through the vocal hook. The body is the force, or the battery, that drives the current of sound to the resonators of the vocal hook, and the Gan-Tone Pulsation insures the maximum utilization of these resonators (rooms).

When the door leading to the lower room, or the mouth cavity, is closed, the tone passes freely to the upper room, or the nasal cavity. This condition occurs when the uvular tympany blends with the back of the tongue closing the opening to the back of the mouth. The quality of the sound takes on the nasal characteristics of the nasal cavity.

The uvular tympany, therefore, controls the amount of vocal sound resounding in the oral and nasal rooms by closing either level or opening both of them.

The amount of air utilization in these processes is as follows:

> The concentration of sound in the mouth requires the least amount of air utilization.
>
> The concentration of air in the nasal tract requires more air and more thrust, since, anatomically, it is farther removed from the vocal cords.
>
> The simultaneous utilization of both cavities (oral and nasal) is dependent on the role of the uvular tympany in maintaining the maximum opening of these two passages as tributaries of the pharyngeal tract (which is an extension of the laryngeal tract), requiring greater thrust and, ultimately, a greater consumption of air.

The fundamental sounds that are made in the various chambers are existent in principle, even if not audible to the human ear, and the amplitude of these sounds and their accompanying overtones, or harmonics, become audible by increasing amplification and maintaining freedom in the flow of sound through the vocal hook.

XXXI. Pushing the back of the tongue and its root forward and downward, the fourth similar characteristic of vomiting and yawning described, is another important aspect that is simulated in the Gan-Tone Method.

In order to achieve a maximum opening of the vocal hook, it is essential that the back of the tongue and its root be pushed forward and downward. At the same time, the lower jaw is unhinged down and back and resting against the throat. In this position, the throat can accommodate the passage of the loudest sounds, since it is the widest opening. In this same position, there is also a fusion of the solid parts, such as, the jawbone, hyoid bone and larynx. This fusion magnifies the resonance of the tones emitted, since the sound that emanates from the vocal cords through the muscles, cartilages and bones that have been fused is now further amplified, as a result of going through these fused parts.

This increased resonance is comparable to the increased volume achieved in the grand piano as opposed to the console. Since the grand piano has a larger case, it has more area that can be amplified as opposed to the smaller area of the console which limits the area of amplification.

Furthermore, the fusion of the component parts that occurs (when the back of the tongue and its root is pushed forward and downward, and pressure is exerted on these parts in the process of grunting down through the body to the bottom of the torso) welds the body into a more resonant agent, just as the pieces of the piano are fused together and, in certain areas, laminated, under thousands of pounds of pressure, in order to get the ultimate amount of resonance and thrust. However, there is a variable factor present in the human that can't be duplicated by the rigidity of certain fundamental components of the piano. Since the piano is man's creation, it only represents, in part, an extension of the human. The sound produced by the human undulates in waves to, more or less, fuse the body as a resonator; whereas, the piano case as a resonator is inflexible, since the boards of the case cannot change at will. The resilient composition of the body, however, can change at will, since the mind determines the degree of pressure to be imposed on the body. The degree of pressure that the body fuses determines the degree to which the body functions as a bell.

XXXII. The following Gan-Tone Principle can, therefore, be summarized:

Pushing the root of the tongue downward and forward and, from this point, imposing pressure through the body (Jaw, Larynx, Body Fusion), while producing vocal sounds, compacts the body which causes the body to become a resonant extension of the vocal cords by an orderly process of fusion.

The body as a bell is dependent upon the intensity of the fusion of the parts. The greater the fusion, the greater the resonance. The action of the tongue forward and downward, with the jaw down and back, determines the degree of intensity with which the parts will be fused. The degree of fusion will determine the degree to which the body functions as a resonator of the sound that is produced in the vocal cords.

The degree of fusion also determines the degree of thrust, thus applying Newton's Law of Action and Reaction which states that every action has an equal and opposite reaction. The degree of intensity of the downward action determines the degree of thrust the body exerts in carrying sound in the opposite direction to the head resonators, such as, the nasal, oral and sinus cavities. The greater the thrust, the greater the reverberation of sound in these cavities, resulting in increased volume of sound.

Maintaining downward pressure through the body to the bottom of the torso (from the fusion of the larynx and the surrounding parts, as a result of pushing the root of the tongue downward and forward), i.e., Jaw, Larynx, Body Fusion, is the keystone to the body as a resonator, the body as a thrusting agent and the body as a projector of sound.

The degree of vocal resonance, thrust and projection of sound determines the degree to which the body functions as a bell.

XXXIII. Grunting, or pushing down through the body, the fifth similar characteristic of vomiting and yawning, certainly plays an important role in the Gan-Tone Method, since it is a basic characteristic of Jaw, Larynx, Body Fusion.

XXXIV. As pressure is exerted downward to the bottom of the torso, simultaneous coordination of pressure in the larynx is necessary in order to fuse the component parts of the vocal hook (vocal cords, cartilages of the larynx, accompanying and surrounding muscles, ligaments and bones) in order to give stability to the sound under pressure by preventing cracking, or collapsing, of the vocal sound. An indefinite fusion of the parts produces an indefinite sound; whereas, solidification of these component parts of the vocal hook, by mental imposition of pressure, results in control of the tract leading out through the larynx, thus contributing to definite, brilliant, resonant sound. Fusion of the bones, cartilages, ligaments and muscles of the vocal hook is comparable to the fusion of the component parts of the hand which results in a solid fist. The lack of fusion is comparable to the limp hand.

It should be noted that imposition of pressure on these parts, producing the fusion of these parts and causing them to be more resonant, does not result in the production of a tight sound, since it is the imposition of the Gan-Tone Pulsation (a mentally imposed beat on the natural vibrations of the singing line) through these fused components that not only produces more resonance, as a result of body solidity, but a more resilient sound as well. The body becomes a resilient medium through which the mind imposes pressure in the form of a beat. This beat (Gan-Tone), imposed and released, projects a resilient current of sound. The alternating cycle of the beat is a natural phenomenon. The downward-pressure part of the cycle furnishes thrust. The upper part of the cycle, or release of the pressure, results in projection of the sound, thus completing one cycle. The speed and volume of this alternating cycle is mentally controlled by the singer. The speed of the cycle depends on the number of beats the singer wishes to utilize per segment of sound, per second.

XXXV. If the imposed pressure through the body is maximum and the imposed pressure on the larynx is eased, the resultant vibrations through the head resonators are less brilliant, since the vibrator (larynx) is not operating to maximum capacity.

If the vibrator is being imposed upon by pressure and fused to its maximum, in the singing process, and the imposed line of pressure descending through the body is eased, then the laryngeal sound lacks the thrust afforded by the maximum descending pressure and results in less brilliant head resonance and projection.

A Gan-Tone Principle can, therefore, be stated as follows:

The basis for determining the most efficient utilization of the body as support and thrust for sound, and the efficiency of the head resonators as reverberators of the vocal sound rests with the condition of the laryngeal tract.

The greater the volume of sound produced, the greater the need for fusion of the movable component parts of the vocal hook.

XXXVI. The body is an elastic medium upon which the brain imposes variable pressures in the process of involving the body as a solid support and resonant extension of the vocal sound. As the mind causes the tips of two fingers of one hand to impinge upon one another in the pinch and, similarly, with the two fingers of the other hand, the mind also coordinates other pressures not apparent to the eye, such as, laryngeal pressure and body pressure, in a simultaneous action in which the pressure on either is equal, or variable, or independent of one another.

The elasticity of the body, in coordination with the movement of the jaw in fusing with the body, determines the payload of sound which is thrust to the head resonators.

The body as a bell includes two essential areas of resonance: one which extends from the vocal cords upward through the larynx to the resonators of the head, and the other from the vocal cords downward through the larynx to the bottom of the torso and the pelvic area. It is the degree to which the body as an elastic medium, from the vocal cords to the bottom of the torso, is solidified by pressure that determines the kick, or thrust, of the vocal payload, which is comprised of body resonance and head resonance, that successively determines the quality, i.e., the depth, height, volume and brilliance, of the projected sound.

XXXVII. The larynx as vibrator functions as follows:

> Attached within the larynx are two ligaments known as the vocal cords. When pure vocal cords sound is produced, without the fused involvement of the larynx, a light sound is evident.

When the vocal cords sound is fused with the cartilaginous, shell-like structure of the larynx, through the contraction of laryngeal muscles, the larynx vibrates with the vocal cords, amplifying the vocal cords sound.

The more the area above the vocal cords is fused solidly, the greater the vibratory quality of the tract leading from the cords to the head resonators. These accumulated vibrations reverberate in the cavernous chambers of the pharyngeal, oral and nasal tracts. This is the area of fusion above the vocal cords.

The fusion below the vocal cords occurs when the pure vocal cords sound, which is essentially a light sound, is fused through muscles and the cartilaginous, shell-like structure of the larynx. This fusion causes the larynx to vibrate and amplify the pure vocal cords sound. Fusion of this laryngeal sound through the cricoid cartilage, downward through bones, cartilages and muscles of the entire body comprises the second area of vocal fusion.

The degree of fusion of the larynx and the body, therefore, determines the degree to which the entire body functions as a sound-producing agent, i.e., as an extension of the vocal cords.

XXXVIII. The basic differences in vomiting and yawning already described play an important role in the Gan-Tone Method of Voice Production. The essence of vocal projection is achieved, in the Gan-Tone Method, when the maximum body-supported sound passing out of the larynx through the vocal hook on the principle of the vomit is simultaneously opposed by the action of the incoming yawn.

In yawning, there is a drawing-in of air down through the body, as a result of the contraction of muscles, which provides additional space in the openings of the body for air to be inspired. This additional space creates vacuums which are filled with air by the force of atmospheric pressure. At the peak of air intake, the muscles are maximally contracted downward after which the expiration part of the yawn results in muscle contraction upward, thus completing the yawning cycle and causing the body to relax.

The essential difference between yawning and the ordinary process of breathing is as follows:

> Yawning releases body pressures, tensions and anxieties and, at the same time, relaxes the brain; whereas, the process of ordinary breathing does not release pressures, tensions and anxieties, and, therefore, they accompany breathing.

In yawning, as the muscles contract, air is drawn down through the body creating an expansion of the body cavities and flesh, which not only releases constriction in the body by eliminating tension and improving circulation, but, also, provides a freer path for the transmission and amplification of vocal cords vibrations. This yawning process is a sympathetic phenomenon reaching its height at the peak of inspiration, which tends to relax the body and mind and is, therefore, a highly desirable condition to utilize by simulation during the singing process, since this complete relaxation eliminates obstructions, enabling the singer to be more completely absorbed with the principles involved.

The stretching of muscles by the contractive action of antagonistic muscles, in the process of yawning, releases tensions as follows:

> As the body fibers expand, tension that develops in the fibers of the muscles (knotting up) disappears, in the same way that news of a joyous event creates a buoyant release throughout the fibers of the body.
>
> The mind imposes anxieties in the muscle fibers

of the body in the form of tension which constricts the muscles, thus restricting their normal function, which is to coordinate the body in daily activities. Stretching the muscles through yawning, however, restores the normal function of the muscles by making them tension-free and, therefore, better adapted to coordinate the daily activities of the body.

Body expansion, which occurs with the deep inspiration of air into the blood stream, combined with the greater thrust of the heart beat carry a greater amount of oxygen and blood to the channels of the brain, where the process of expansion and contraction, reflected in these channels, results in relaxation of the brain. During the yawning cycle, the expansion characteristics of the body are reflected in the action of the heart beat. If the heart beats six times during the course of the yawn, for example, these expanded beats are reflected six times within the walls of the arteries of the brain, and this expansion of the arteries causes tension to vanish. This release of tension and binding gives greater resilience and capacity to the brain's activities.

XXXIX. Since the body is now tension-free, it is susceptible to the greatest degree of resilience and is, therefore, in the most desirable state for utilizing the Gan-Tone Pulsation which, in turn, produces the highest degree of resilient sound.

The Gan-Tone produces pulsations of pressure down through the body similarly as the heart pumps blood throughout the body in a series of pulsations. When the superimposition is made on the vocal cords vibrations in the form of a Gan-Tone, or beat, these vibrations are carried in the direction of the bottom of the torso, on the down-part of the Gan-Tone beat, according to the amount of body support required, which is dependent on the amount of volume or intensity desired in the sound. The greater the volume, the greater the imposition of the Gan-Tone beat through the body which, in turn, produces a greater payload of sound to the resonators of the head and chest and, ultimately, causes the whole body to function as a resonator (up-part of Gan-Tone beat).

Every Gan-Tone beat through the body carries with it a reaction in the form of one beat of resonance throughout all the resonators. A series of these beats, or Gan-Tones, constitutes the sustaining quality in the melodic line. The Gan-Tones are constantly imposed on the vocal cords vibrations by the singer on light and fast moving passages, where pressure is mainly confined within the larynx, and on loud, sustained sounds, where the imposition of pressure starting at the vocal cords penetrates deeply to the bottom of the torso.

The effective utilization of the Gan-Tones eliminates the tight, or rigid, restricted sound. As air passes through the bellows of the lungs (ultimately the body is the bellows), the air impinges upon the periphery, or edge, of the vocal cords creating natural vibrations for a given pitch which are carried to the resonators. At the same time, the Gan-Tones, imposed by the singer on the vibrations of the fundamental, carry these natural vibrations to the depths of the torso during the downward parts of the Gan-Tone beats, and then to the resonators on the upward parts of these Gan-Tones.

One complete cycle of the Gan-Tone occurs when the beat, or Gan-Tone, imposed by the singer on the vibrations of the pitch, transmits these vibrations, first to the depths of the torso, on the downward part of the Gan-Tone and then projects them to the resonators on the upward part of this beat.

The imposition of the Gan-Tones on the natural vibrations of the singing line provides a free-flowing path for extending the amplitude of these vibrations from the depths of the body to the head resonators, minimizing the restriction of sound in the area of the vocal cords. Imposing about six Gan-Tones per second on the fundamental pitch concomitantly with the Absolute Jaw, Larynx, Body Fusion maximizes the vibrational impact of this pitch throughout the body, but especially to the head resonators, producing maximum depth, height, volume and buoyancy in the singing line.

XL. Vomiting, the diametrically opposed process of yawning, does not involve drawing into the body but, instead, ejecting. The role of vomiting involves cleansing the alimentary tract of undesirables. The thrust of the vomit has its depth at the pelvic-perineum diaphragm in the rectal-pelvic basin. The natural phenomenon of the thrust for ejection in the vomit is utilized in the Gan-Tone Method for the projection of sound.

The thrust from the bottom of the torso is the aspect of the vomit that is simulated. The spasmodic waves resulting from the convulsive contracting and expanding of the stomach, however, are omitted. In the Gan-Tone Method, the alimentary tract is used together with the rest of the body, as pressure is imposed down through the body, making the alimentary tract another part of the structure for the support and thrust of sound.

Since the process of vomiting is purgative in nature, a most thorough elimination is achieved through the laryngeal opening, pharyngeal tract (which includes the moving forward and downward of the tongue in order to further open the pharyngeal tract), the oral and nasal tracts and the dilated nostrils.

The process of ejection in vomiting opens the vocal hook to its maximum, thus identifying the simulated principle of vomiting to be mastered in the Gan-Tone Method.

XLI. Yawning, the diametrically opposed process of vomiting, does not involve ejection but, instead, the expansion of the body cavities, viz., the sinuses, nasal, oral, pharyngeal, laryngeal, tracheal, bronchial and lung cavities, in order to permit maximum intake of air. This air, which expands the cavities, compacts the areas surrounding this expansion making the air more dense and the surrounding lower viscera, such as the intestines and other organs, more solid.

XLII. The expansion, to the maximum, of the facial vents, i.e., the nostrils and the vertical-elliptical mouth opening, is characteristic of the first phase of the yawn cycle. This expanding process is carried on a wave of pressure imposed downward through the body, but especially to the cavities, which includes the lungs, thus mixing air and space more solidly. As this process expands the cavities of the body, compacting the body downward, in the process of singing with the Gan-Tone Method, vibrations and resonance are consequently multiplied, as a result of increased density and resilience. As the cavities reverberate the vibrations of the vocal cords, the application of the Jaw, Larynx, Body Fusion transmits these vocal cords vibrations through the body making it an extension of the cords and larynx, causing the whole body to become the total vibrator.

This reverberation of vocal cords vibrations throughout the body produces the bell factor, which is the ratio of vibrations to resonance. As the body becomes more or less vibrant, the cavities become more or less resonant. It is this ratio that determines the degree to which the body functions as a bell. Thus the fusion of the vocal cords sound, through the root of the tongue (pressed downward and forward), the hyoid bone, the cartilages and muscles of the larynx to the muscles at the base of the torso, essentially determines the dimensions of vocal vibrations. The greater the fusion of the body, the greater the solidity and amplitude of the vocal cords vibrations and, consequently, the greater the reverberation in the cavities.

XLIII. In vomiting, there is the opposite of expansion taking place, which is contraction. The sensory nerves on the back of the tongue trigger an alarm system that detects an undesirable chemicalization fermenting in the stomach which leads to contractive spasms of the abdominal muscles and the diaphragm. These spasms contract the stomach resulting in emesis, or the ejection of the contents of the stomach through the esophagus and mouth, which can include the nostrils. The support and thrust of this ejection is controlled by the Sphincter ani externus muscle in the pelvic-perineum diaphragm.

Contractive spasms of the stomach are not utilized in the Gan-Tone Method of Voice Production, since the focus of pressure is at the Sphincter ani externus muscle through the Jaw, Larynx, Body Fusion which uniformly aligns pressure from the Pterygoideus lateralis muscle in the head to the Sphincter ani externus, which includes the stomach, thus removing any localized tension in this area.

XLIV. The simulation of the yawning and vomiting functions, two diametrically opposed body processes, are coordinated simultaneously in the Gan-Tone Method in order to further multiply the dimensions of sound through the impingement factor.

Grunting down through the body, the common characteristic of both yawning and vomiting, coordinated simultaneously with the opposing characteristics of yawning and vomiting, i.e., inspiring air during the yawning process and ejecting, or emitting, sound during the vomiting process, maximize the opening of the vocal hook, which comprises the laryngeal and pharyngeal tracts, the tongue forward and downward, the lower jaw down and back, the uvular tympany distended, the oral and nasal tracts, dilated nostrils and vertical-elliptical mouth opening.

Yawning in the process of ejecting is essential in the Gan-Tone Method, since yawning while vomiting, i.e., projecting the vocal sound, produces the impingement factor which maximizes the impact of reverberating vibrations through compression, or condensation, and rarefaction. The degree of body compression and rarefaction through the Jaw, Larynx, Body Fusion and the Gan-Tone Pulsation determines the degree of atmospheric condensation and rarefaction, i.e., the degree of depth, height and volume in the projected sound.

As the tone is being projected outwardly and the nostrils and uvular tympany are distending creating vacuums, air is being drawn inwardly. The collision, or impingement, of these two actions increases the dimensions of sound. Yawning, or inspiring air into the body, against vomiting, or projecting sound out of the body, increases space and density in the body cavities resulting in greater dimensions of vibrations and resonance.

This impingement factor is analogous to two cars approaching each other on a highway, in opposing directions, traveling at sixty miles per hour. The collision factor here is doubled, as a result of the two cars hitting each other head-on rather than one car hitting a wall at this speed. Consequently, the sound produced on impact is doubled in the case of the two colliding cars.

Only when the Jaw, Larynx, Body Fusion and the Gan-Tone Pulsation are mastered can the opposing characteristics of yawning and vomiting be fully understood and efficiently simulated in the singing process.

XLV. Utilization of the impingement factor in the Gan-Tone Method produces the following results:

1. The resonators of the body are opened to their maximum insuring maximum vibrations and reverberation of sound (bell factor).

2. The resonators are solidified to their maximum enabling the entire body to function as a bell.

3. The principle of feedback is more evident, as the principle of impingement is more definite.

A Gan-Tone Principle can, therefore, be stated:

The degree of thrust of vocal cords vibrations determines the degree of resonance which, in turn, determines the degree of feedback to the vibratory source which, in turn, regenerates and embellishes the vocal result, i.e., the greater the thrust of the vocal cords vibrations to the resonating chambers, the greater the resonance. The greater the resonance, the greater the re-echoing of this sound to the output, or vocal cords, the source of the sound, adding more vibrations to the output (vocal cords), thus regenerating the fundamental sound, overtones, harmonics and partials.

The essence, therefore, of vocal projection is achieved when the maximum body-supported sound (from the rectal-pelvic basin) passing out of the larynx through the vocal hook on the principle of the vomit characteristic (ejection) is simultaneously opposed by the action of the incoming yawn.

By varying the intensity of the Jaw, Larynx, Body Fusion and the Gan-Tone Pulsation and also by varying the balance of the opposing processes (vomiting and yawning characteristics), volume, brilliance and color are at the command of the singer enabling him to project his sound with the greatest degree of control.

As definition and skill are attained in the simulation of the vomit and yawn characteristics, they can be controlled so that either vomit or yawn characteristics can dominate. When these charactcristics oppose each other to the greatest degree, maximum projection is achieved which results in maximum volume.

The condition of the voice is at its healthiest when these two opposing characteristics are operating simultaneously, since impinging on each other results in more sound, more space within the cavities, more compacting of the walls of the cavities, as a result of their more efficient expansion, and more body support, producing more vibrancy in the cavities and the body as a whole. Increased vibrancy in the cavities and the body produces greater resonance and greater thrust for vocal projection.

The Tongue English

XLVI. As in playing billiards or other sports, the application of English, which is "the spinning or rotary motion around the vertical axis given to a ball by striking it to the right or left of its center,"[1] can also be applied to singing.

The tongue would be comparable to the ball, and the movement of the tongue, from the root to the tip, in certain positions to attain a certain sound would be comparable to English in singing.

The cue is to the ball in billiards what the vibrating air, or sound, is to the tongue in singing, i.e., the angle at which the cue hits the ball determines the nature of the shot. The angle at which the vibrating air hits the tongue determines, to a great extent, the degree of freedom in the sound.

In moving the cue, the ball functions as an impedence. The angle at which the cue hits the impedence (ball), other than dead center, which is English, determines the nature of the shot.

The attitude of the tongue—the whole tongue, not just the surface—in relation to the propelled sound, determines, to a great extent, the brilliance, volume, freedom and flexibility of that sound.

Furthermore, intensifying fusion of the tip of the tongue (through the action of the Genioglossi muscles) with the back of the lower teeth and gum stabilizes the tongue, thereby dilating and stabilizing the vocal hook, and also aids in the fusion of the mandible to the larynx under stress (loud, high, sustained notes).

XLVII. The coordination that is required in the Gan-Tone Method has been experienced involuntarily by all humans in the yawning and vomiting processes.

Simulated yawning in the Gan-Tone Method is known as the Jaw, Larynx, Body Fusion and simulated vomiting is the Gan-Tone Pulsation.

Fusing vocal cords and body vibrations to the rectal-pelvic basin on the Compression Phase, or down-part of the Gan-Tone beat, is the action that produces the equal reaction of thrust, or ejection, of these vocal cords and body vibrations to the body resonators on the Thrust Phase, or up-part of the Gan-Tone beat. The degree of intensity in the application of the expanding process, which is the Jaw, Larynx, Body Fusion and the Compression Phase, or down-part of the Gan-Tone beat, determines the degree of intensity in the contracting process, which is the Thrust Phase, or up-part of the Gan-Tone beat.

Since yawning and vomiting are involuntary processes, it requires much discipline to consciously simulate these processes for effectively ejecting the singing sound.

In the Gan-Tone Method, voice projection is dependent on the injection of vocal cords and body vibrations to the rectal-pelvic basin (yawning—Jaw, Larynx, Body Fusion), which yields the opposite process of ejection (vomiting—Gan-Tone beat) of these vibrations to the body resonators, which yields the projected sound. The more intense the injection, the more intense the ejection and, therefore, the greater the depth, height, volume, resilience and brilliance of the projected sound.

In the Gan-Tone Method, the pitch of the vocal cords vibrations is not affected, when the dimensions of the projected sound are increased by extending the amplitude of the vocal cords vibrations to the body extremities, i.e., from the Sphincter ani externus muscle at the pelvic-perineum diaphragm, with the Jaw, Larynx, Body Fusion and the Compression Phase, or down-part of the Gan-Tone beat, to the head resonators on the Thrust Phase, or up-part of the Gan-Tone beat, thereby creating an unobstructed path for these vibrations through the Vocal Hook and involving body power for energizing the singing sound.

---

[1] Dictionary definition.

THE JAW—KEY TO SCIENTIFIC SINGING

CONTENTS

THE JAW—KEY TO SCIENTIFIC SINGING

I.	The Importance of the Jaw in the Gan-Tone Method	103
II.	The Role of the Jaw in Voice Projection	104
III.	The Role of the Jaw in Breath Control	106
IV.	The Role of the Jaw in Range	112
V.	The Role of the Jaw in Register	114
VI.	The Role of the Jaw in Resonance	118
VII.	The Role of the Jaw in Volume	119
VIII.	The Role of the Jaw in Coloration	122
IX.	The Role of the Jaw in Sound Configuration	123
X.	The Role of the Jaw in Brilliance	127

The Importance of the Jaw in The Gan-Tone Method

I. The jaw, in the Gan-Tone Method, is the key to the scientific production of the singing voice, since the jaw determines the degree to which the body will be fused, and this body fusion affects all the characteristics of the singing voice. The jaw governs the body as a medium for propagating and transmitting vocal cords vibrations. When the jaw is unhinged, down and back, and resting on the larynx, the strongest contact is created for the transmission of vocal cords vibrations through the body. Any divergence of the jaw from this position diminishes the transmission of these vibrations which, in turn, affects voice projection, breath control, range, register, resonance, volume, coloration, sound configuration and brilliance, the characteristics of the singing voice.

Voice Projection - The jaw plays an important part in voice projection, since it is the key to the fusion of the head, throat and torso. When the jaw is completely down and back and resting on the larynx, complete fusion of these body parts occurs, resulting in complete body involvement in projecting vibrating air to the head and chest resonators with maximum force, producing the maximum re-sounding of vibrations. The emitted sound, therefore, has maximum depth, height and carrying power which are the most effective characteristics of voice projection.

Breath Control - The jaw plays an important part in breath control, since the maximum opening of the jaw, down and back, fuses the jaw to the larynx and body causing the thrust vibrating air to be focused in the resonating areas of the head and chest with great speed, requiring less air expenditure, thus providing more air reserve for the singer.

Range - The jaw plays an important part in range, since the degree to which the jaw is moved down and back, while ascending or descending the scale, determines the degree of dilation that will take place in the throat to counteract restriction which eliminates any impasse, thus enabling the singer to discover more range.

Register - The jaw plays an important part in eliminating abrupt changes in tonal quality resulting in one register, or scale, from high to low sounds. The movement of the jaw downward opens the throat, and this movement widens the throat passage which, in turn, eliminates the restriction responsible for changes in tonal quality and register breaks.

Resonance - The jaw plays an important part in resonance, since it determines the amount of vocal cords and body vibrations that will be re-sounded in the resonators. When the jaw is down and back and fused with the larynx and body, the original vocal cords vibrations penetrate deeper into the body, above and below the vocal cords, producing a maximum amount of vibrations to be re-sounded in the resonators. The maximum opening of the jaw also creates the widest path in the throat area for the greatest amount of vibrations to be re-sounded in the resonators, resulting in maximum resonance.

Volume - The jaw plays an important part in volume, since it produces body fusion which multiplies the original vocal cords vibrations, resulting in greater resonance, thus increasing the volume of the singing voice. When the jaw is unhinged, or down and back, it is fused to the larynx and body causing the body to be completely involved in the magnification of the original vocal cords vibrations.

Coloration - The jaw plays an important part in coloration, since the unhinged position of the jaw, down and back, fuses the whole body, extending the original vocal cords vibrations throughout the body, causing the body to be completely involved as vibrator and resonator, thus enabling the singer to select from a great variety of shades and hues in depicting a tonal picture.

Sound Configuration - The jaw plays an important part in sound configuration, since an understanding of the jaw positions, from the graduated movements in limited volume and vowel sustenance to fusion of the jaw with the body in maximum volume and vowel sustenance, determines the effective control of the endless variety of sym-

104   Singing Energy

metrical, varicolored sound patterns produced in the process of singing vowels and consonants.

Brilliance - The jaw plays an important part in brilliance, or the radiant brightness of sound, since the unhinged position of the jaw, down and back, fuses the jaw to the larynx and body causing the fusion of vocal cords vibrations through the body, making the body an extension of the vocal cords. The degree to which these vocal cords vibrations are compressed through the body determines the thrust, or impact, of these vibrations to the resonators which, in turn, determines the brilliance of the emitted sound.

Since the fusion of the lower jaw (mandible) to the larynx and torso is essential for the scientific production of the singing voice, the singer must master the vertical-elliptical mouth opening and the unhinged jaw position under stress (loud, high, sustained notes) in order to maintain body involvement.

Mastery of the lower jaw does not involve focus on neck muscles, but, rather, on a head muscle, four centimeters deep from the lateral surface of the skull near the hollow of the temple behind the zygomatic arch, known as the Pterygoideus lateralis muscle, the PRIME MOVER of the mandible (lower jaw). The skill developed in the contractive action of this head muscle under stress maintains the vertical-elliptical mouth opening and allows the lower jaw to be fused to the larynx and torso, causing minimal tension in throat muscles which prevents a rigid setting of the lower jaw, especially while singing loud, high, sustained sounds.

The Role of the Jaw in Voice Projection

II.   Voice projection, in the Gan-Tone Method of Voice Production, is the thrusting of sound from the body through the coordination of the following:
1. Body Support
2. Head and Chest Resonators
3. Jaw, Larynx, Body Fusion

Maximum intensity in this coordination gives the greatest carrying power to the emitted sound.

1. Body Support

The body provides the thrust which flings and sustains the sound from the activated vocal cords to the head and chest resonators. The degree of body involvement determines the amount of rap of air to the resonators, which function like bells. The body supplies the power to the sound, which is comparable to the hammer that rings the bell. The power of the stroke exercised by the hammer on the bell determines the degree of ring.

In electricity, the body would be equivalent to the battery which determines the force that drives the current through a conductor which, in turn, lights the bulb. The body is the battery which supplies the force that determines and sustains the current of air to the varied resonating terminals, which are the head and chest resonators.

2. Head and Chest Resonators

The head and chest resonators are bells that ring, thus augmenting the activated vocal cords, resulting in amplification of sound, when these resonators are fused with the whole body, thereby determining the amount of vocal projection.

The head resonators, which are the cavities above the vocal cords, consist primarily of:
    a.) superior, middle and inferior conchae (nasal apertures)
    b.) sinus cavities
    c.) hard palate (roof of the mouth)
    d.) rear of upper and lower teeth
    e.) posterior wall of the pharynx (back of the mouth)
    f.) base of the nose
    g.) portion of the larynx above the vocal cords

The chest resonators, which are cavities below the vocal cords, consist primarily of:
    a.) lungs
    b.) bronchial tubes
    c.) trachea (wind pipe)

d.) portion of the larynx below the vocal cords

The thorough involvement of these head and chest resonators, from their sole importance to their varied combinations, will determine the dimensions of vocal support.

In electricity, the terminals are the bulbs to be lighted by the electrical current driven by the battery. The force of the electrical current will determine, not only the number of bulbs that will be lighted, but also, the wattage, i.e., the brilliance of each bulb.

In singing, the terminals are the head and chest resonators that ring, as a result of the current of air whose force is determined by the body. The amount of body support, or force produced, determines the number of resonators that are utilized, and the degree of brilliance that is rendered by each resonator. Therefore, efficiency in body involvement plays an important role in vocal projection, since it supplies the power which thrusts sound to the head resonators.

Popular belief limits body involvement in the projection of sound to the diaphragm, thus preventing maximum utilization of body support. Since, by dictionary definition, the diaphragm is a partition separating the cavity of the chest from that of the abdomen and is, therefore, midpoint in relation to the bottom of the torso, concentration at this point results in partial body involvement, concentrating pressure at the diaphragm, rather than at the bottom of the torso, thus preventing the whole body from functioning as a resilient agent for the support and solidity of sound. Preoccupation with the diaphragm limits the amount of total body support available, thus limiting the degree of ring in the resonators which, ultimately, limits the amount of vocal projection potential. Partial body support is also detrimental, since it focuses the burden of stress on a smaller radius, thus placing undesirable pressure on vital areas, such as the heart, the vocal cords, and the stomach muscles. Complete body involvement to the bottom of the torso, however, prevents this convergence of pressure, thus drawing stress away from vital areas, such as the heart.

3. **Jaw, Larynx, Body Fusion**

The jaw is the key to maximum utilization of the head as resonator and the body as support in the projection of sound, since it acts as a faucet in determining the quantity of air that will be passed to the resonators with the least amount of impedence. Since the neck, by nature, is a restricted part of the body, the nozzle, or jaw, is the door which determines the amount of passable air. Placement of the jaw down and back in order to insure the unhinging of the lower jawbone, producing the largest recess in front of each earlobe, i.e., the maximum opening of the jaw and mouth, concomitantly with a maximum simulated yawn, results in the maximum fusion of the jaw, larynx and body causing the whole body to function as one unit, thus insuring complete body involvement.

Popular belief stresses undue importance of the larynx as a vibrator, and the vocal cords as the principle sound makers. The larynx, however, is the vibrator in the initial stage, but as it consolidates with the body, the larynx is infinitely augmented, since it fuses with the body, promoting the diffusion of laryngeal pressure, thus reducing friction, or stress, in this vital area.

The vocal cords are the source of the human voice, but not the ultimate in the production of the emitted sound. In the Gan-Tone Method, the vocal cords act as the spark, rather than the sole source of sound, demonstrating the Gan-Tone Principle of minimizing concentration on the vocal cords and maximizing other areas of the body as vibrators, above and below the vocal cords. After sound is made at the cords, it is supported and amplified throughout the body, taking the burden of stress off the vocal cords.

Complete body involvement, the result of maximum jaw opening, is utilized only when the greatest vocal pressure must be allayed. High-pitched notes, such as High C for sopranos and tenors, and extremely loud sounds usually create the greatest vocal pressure and must, therefore, be performed with a maximum opening of the jaw causing the larynx to fuse with the body.

Although the greatest vocal pressure is present at the highest range of the scale and the loudest volume, varying degrees of pressure are evident in the gamut of the singing scale. Through trial and error, the student, having realized the security obtained in emitting sound through the Jaw, Larynx, Body Fusion, will become sensitive to the role of the jaw in overcoming pressure points in the gamut of singing sounds, i.e., in the process of testing the reality of the position of the jaw to the pressure encountered in the singing scale, he will become sensitive to the gradations of the jaw necessary for overcoming the degrees of pressure (Jaw Sense). This coordination of the graduated jaw and body-supported sound, in allaying vocal pressure, can only be accomplished through continuous practice, that is, a singer must live with this principle in order to gain the facility of automatic response.

The degree to which the projected vocal line manifests carrying power, freedom, dimension and endurance is commensurate with the ability of the singer to coordinate the body with the graduated positions of the jaw, along with the full utilization of the head and chest resonators.

The Role of the Jaw in Breath Control

III. Breath control, in the Gan-Tone Method of Voice Production, involves the agile conversion of a quantity of air into resonating sounds in the singing process in order to utilize a minimum of air in activating the vocal cords and transmitting this sound to resonating areas of the body and head with speed and efficiency, thus enabling the singer to sustain long phrases, execute intricate passages and simultaneously shade and color the sounds without running out of breath.

Maximum efficiency and agility in this conversion of air is dependent upon the following:

    1. Jaw, Larynx, Body Fusion
    2. EXINVAC—Exhale, Inhale and Vacuum
    3. Jaw, Mouth, Nose Coordination

Jaw, Larynx, Body Fusion

The coordination and fusion of the jaw, larynx and torso, the components of body support, are essential for determining the solidity necessary for thrusting sound to the head resonators with the greatest degree of speed and efficiency. The jaw plays an important role in maximum body support, when it is completely fused with the larynx and body. If the jaw is not fused with these parts, when there is great vocal demand, pressure will be focused on the vocal cords, larynx and surrounding areas, rather than diffused through the body, creating a weak link in the over-all hook-up of body support.

Complete utilization of the body in the support of sound is dependent upon the necessary fusion of the jaw, larynx and torso. The degree of downward pressure exerted on the jaw which, in turn, is applied to the larynx and then to the body results in the fusion of the jaw, larynx and torso causing these parts to act as one unit, thus promoting maximum solidity, from the jaw to the bottom of the torso. Consolidation, or fusion, of these parts (jaw, larynx, torso) promotes more instantaneous thrust for sound as the degree of downward pressure is increased.

The Gan-Tone Principle in operation is as follows:

> The degree to which the downward pressure through the body is applied determines the definition of the thrust sound to the head resonators. Conversely, the diminishing of pressure downward through the body, i.e., a relaxation of pressure from the jaw to the larynx to the torso, diminishes the thrust of the supported sound to the head resonators causing a weaker vocal signal, since the solidity of body support is debilitated, resulting in a devitalized sound.

Maximum body support is analogous to bouncing a rubber ball on a cement floor. The solidity of the cement floor causes the ball to move quickly and definitely. Debilitated body involvement, however, is analogous to bouncing a rubber ball on sand. The sand's lack of solidity causes the ball to move slowly and indecisively.

In the singing process, the more definite the support,

the less air is utilized, thus enabling the singer to corral a reserve of air, resulting in a longer breath line.

Observation of the rubber ball on the cement floor, as opposed to the sand floor, will concretize this Gan-Tone Principle. The instantaneous reaction of the ball on the cement floor is analogous to the instantaneous reaction of the sound that is thrust from a solid body support. The ball and the sound cover the distance with more agility and power, thereby utilizing less air. Conversely, the indefinite reaction of the ball on the sand floor is analogous to the unsupported sound. The devitalized reaction of the ball on the sand floor is analogous to the slow reaction of the sound that is thrust from a weakened body support. The ball and the sound move sluggishly, requiring more air and more effort in order to attain any power. Furthermore, in attempting to produce a big sound without complete body involvement, the radius of support from the larynx to the bottom of the torso diminishes, focusing stress on the vocal cords, larynx and surrounding area, causing friction and irritation, a highly undesirable condition in this sensitive area.

The governing Gan-Tone Principle is as follows:

> Maximum efficiency in the singing process involves a minimizing of pressure, or stress, in the vocal cords and surrounding areas, and a maximizing of the jaw, larynx, body involvement, along with the head and chest resonators for ultimate support and amplification of the sound that originates in the vocal cords.

Efficiency of air conversion into resonance is commensurate with rapidity of sufficient air concentration necessary to resonate specific areas, such as, the roof of the mouth, the back of the mouth, the back of the upper and lower teeth, the base of the nose, the nasal and postnasal areas, and the sinus cavities, individually, in combination, or collectively. The intensity of focus involved in the concentration of air to these resonating areas is dependent upon the packing of the body, or the solidity of body support, and this support can be thoroughly realized only when there is a complete fusion of the jaw, larynx and body. Therefore, the Gan-Tone Principle in operation is as follows:

> The greater the intensity of focus to the resonating areas, the more brilliant the sound and the less air expenditure thus providing more air reserve for the singer.

EXINVAC—Exhale, Inhale and Vacuum

Exinvac—the Gan-Tone Principle that precedes the awareness and mastery of the Jaw, Larynx, Body Fusion and the Gan-Tone Pulsation—enables the singer to attain the body register and to get the most out of his breath by utilizing the air that would ordinarily be emitted from the mouth and nose, i.e., unresonated air, and converting it into resonating sound, thus gaining greater control of the breath.

Unless the singer is consciously focusing air in the resonating areas during the singing process, the breath is not only expended quickly, but it is also emitted unresonated, causing the singer to run out of breath prematurely and resulting in a dull, breathy voice, since more air is being emitted than is being converted into resonating sound.

Exinvac is the conscious application of a simulated yawn (inhalation) each time the singer exhales in the singing process. <u>Ex</u>hale is the emitted air and sound. <u>In</u>hale and <u>Vac</u>uum are characteristics of the natural yawn.

The beginner in the Gan-Tone Method is taught the Exinvac Principle, which is the first stage of the Jaw, Larynx, Body Fusion. By simulating the natural yawn, the beginner becomes aware of the characteristics that are involuntarily utilized by the body in the natural yawn, which can be described, as follows:

> a) There is a deep inspiration of air, while the jaw opens progressively down and back to its widest unhinged position, causing a depression in front of the tragus, just above the ear lobe.

> b) At the same time, the nostrils distend, permitting a maximum quantity of air through the nasal apertures.

> c) The mouth opens to its widest position, filling this cavity with air.

> d) The circumference of the mouth (lips) opens wider exposing the teeth in a natural effort to inspire the greatest amount of air.

> e) As air moves toward the back of the mouth

(pharynx), the uvula and soft palate (Uvular Tympany) are lifted.

f) At the same time, contractive muscular action within the body (condensation) makes space, creating vacuums in the body cavities, such as, the mouth, nose, pharynx, larynx, trachea and lungs.

g) As these cavities expand, space is created producing vacuums (rarefactions) for the duration of the inhaled air, causing this air to fill these vacuums.

h) When the abdominal muscles are contracted and pulled toward the backbone, the inspired air is concentrated high in the chest area. When the abdominal wall expands, the inhaled air is pulled deeper into the torso. However, the degree to which the inhaled air is drawn to the various depths and heights of the body is dependent on the degree to which body fibers are stretched in all directions, but especially downward through the body, i.e., fused to the bottom of the torso.

i) The vacuums originate at the points of expansion, i.e., the head, vocal hook and chest, when the thoracic diaphragm descends in contraction, causing air to be drawn in, or inhaled, to these points in order to fill these vacuums.

j) The release of contracted viscera and muscles, such as, the diaphragm, at the peak of inhalation, results in the final stage of the natural yawn cycle.

Since the air is drawn away from the mouth and nasal apertures to the back of the mouth during the natural yawn, simulating this condition in the singing process prevents much air from escaping unused. This air is directed toward resonating areas, such as the postnasal, the roof of the mouth, and the pharynx (back of the mouth), and pulled deeply into the chest cavity to be fused with the body in the support of sound. As the muscles contract, during the projection of sound, air is exhaled through the body cavities toward the oral and nasal apertures, but it is opposed by the distended Uvular Tympany (Inhale). This distension creates space (vacuums) in the head, vocal hook and chest, causing the unresonated air, that would ordinarily be emitted from the mouth and nose, to be converted to resonance.

Vocal sound produced through the Exinvac Principle, therefore, increases breath control through increased utilization of breath, while minimizing body constriction and vibrational restriction.

Although the natural yawn promotes maximum relaxation in anticipation of sleep, the simulated yawn in singing also promotes relaxation but, unlike the natural yawn, prevents drowsiness, since the simulated yawn is a voluntary action produced by mental intention.

The exhalation of sound through muscle contraction with body support while inhaling (yawning) through the Exinvac Principle promotes increased concentration of air in the vocal tract causing the air to become a greater conductor for sound, since air density increases air pressure which accelerates sound movement to resonating areas, resulting in greater impact and amplification.

The maximum utilization of breath, or the height of breath control, however, is achieved only when the singer masters the Jaw, Larynx, Body Fusion (which involves Exinvac), since body fusion to the Sphincter ani externus muscle is the basis for the application of the Gan-Tone Pulsation. The Compression Phase, or down-part of the Gan-Tone beat, is imposed on the vocal cords vibrations, transmitting these vibrations while sinking the breath to the pelvic-perineum diaphragm on the Jaw, Larynx, Body Fusion. These vibrations are ejected (vomiting characteristic) to the body resonators on the Thrust Phase, or up-part of the Gan-Tone beat, thereby maximally utilizing the body as vibrator and resonator, while maximally controlling the breath.

Jaw, Mouth, Nose Coordination

The jaw, mouth and nose can be considered regulators for controlling the quantity and quality of the sound, when coordinated with the larynx and body, along with an efficient application of the Exinvac Principle, since they will enable the singer to get the most out of his breath.

Jaw

During the maximum yawn position (Exinvac Principle), the jaw is down and back, or completely unhinged, the back of the tongue is placed as forward as possible, and the tip of the tongue is placed against the back of the lower teeth and lip in order to increase the throat opening. The uvula is lifted, and its continuing membrane is expanded allowing a maximum flow of air, since the throat is now completely opened. This maximum yawn position, or completely opened throat, is imperative in the accommodation of the greatest vocal stress, i.e., the loudest sounds, through the gamut of the scale, but especially in the upper range of all voices. Since there is a natural tendency to deviate from this position, when producing and sustaining these sounds, it is essential to discipline this position during these moments of great stress in order to prevent a restriction of the sound and harm to the vocal organs (larynx, vocal cords and throat).

As the jaw rides up, leaving the position of maximum opening, the Jaw, Larynx, Body Fusion deteriorates, resulting in a lack of solidity in the body structure necessary for sustaining the greatest vocal demand. The fusion of the jaw with the body is, therefore, absolutely essential during the production and sustenance of the loudest sounds, especially in the upper range. It is obvious then, that maximum quantity of sound is dependent upon maximum opening of the jaw. When this jaw position strays, while producing a maximum quantity of sound, body structure deteriorates; pressure is focused on the throat muscles, rather than diffused through the body; and the ability to sustain loud, high sounds withers. It is, therefore, important to keep the following Gan-Tone Principle in mind:

> Any closing movement of the jaw from its maximum opening, in the process of singing loud or high sounds, should be preceded by the easing of body pressure, not only to prevent the natural build-up of stress in the throat area, but also to enable the sound to flow effortlessly, thus expending less air and enabling the singer to sustain a longer breath line.

Quality of sound is affected by the degree to which the jaw impedes or releases the flow of sound. If the jaw does not allay the pressure encountered in the process of singing, the emitted sound will be strident and tight, since the air is being forced through a constricted area. However, maximum opening of the jaw, when singing soft as well as loud sounds, will insure maximum fullness of these sounds, since this maximum jaw opening insures the widest utilization of the mouth cavity, thus creating more resonance, which results in maximum dimensions of sound.

It is, therefore, obvious that the jaw functions as a regulator, since it determines the quantity and quality of sound and air that will be emitted in the singing process.

Mouth

The mouth also operates as a regulator, since the gamut of positions, from closed or from minimum to maximum openings, in coordination with the varied positions of the jaw determine the quality of the emitted sound. When the jaw and the mouth are wide open during the production of a sustained sound, for example, the mouth can function as a regulator independent of the jaw, since it can be dilated and contracted, i.e., opened and closed without disturbing the unhinged position of the jaw. The lips, or periphery of the mouth, act as regulators for controlling the quantity and quality of the sound. Awareness of the following Gan-Tone Principle is, therefore, desirable:

> The degree of intensity on the periphery of the mouth, for a given opening, determines the degree of focus and resonance at that point and the amount of air utilized in the production of sound.

Tightening or releasing the lip muscles affects the degree of brilliance of the emitted sound. Resonance is produced when the lips are tightened, since muscle tautness causes the lips to function as a resonator. This tightened position causes the lips to fuse as one with the teeth, promoting maximum solidity and resonance in this area. Conversely, releasing the lip muscles, while singing, diminishes solidity in this area which, in turn, reduces resonance. Attempting to produce this resonance without tightening the lips not only results in failure to attain resonance, but also causes a rapid expenditure of air, and the singer, therefore, runs out of breath prematurely. Furthermore, activating the lips as an area of resonance results in less stress on the vocal cords, a highly desirable condition in the process of singing.

The coordination of the jaw and mouth, where the mouth can function independently without affecting the unhinged position of the jaw, can be attained in the following manner:

a) Open the jaw down and back to its unhinged position with the mouth also open.

b) Select an easily sung note and produce an AH vowel sound with a minimum of voice.

c) Proceed from the AH sound to the OOM sound holding the M position in order to close the mouth completely, thus covering the gamut of the varied mouth positions from completely opened to completely closed.

d) Maintain the jaw in a completely unhinged position throughout this exercise.

e) Place a finger in the hollow, in front of the tragus just above either earlobe, in order to maintain the unhinged position of the jaw during the AH to OOM exercise. Any closing movement of the jaw can be detected, since the hollow will disappear as the jaw closes.

It is important to note that an optical illusion is created, when proceeding from the AH to the OOM position. Facial muscles are pulled back in the direction of the ears during the AH sound, and these muscles are pulled forward during the OOM position, creating the appearance that the jaw is closing. However, in reality, the jaw is not moving and is completely unhinged.

Acquiring this coordination of the jaw and mouth at an early age promotes greater and more permanent facility with this skill, enabling the very young singer to accomplish vocal feats ordinarily considered harmful because of the lack of physical development in the vocal apparatus, and enabling the older singer to avoid the detrimental effects of the wobbling jaw and the fallen voice.

This coordination of the jaw and mouth, where the mouth functions independently of the unhinged jaw, requires training, since it is a difficult skill to master. Therefore, it is advisable to practice without the application of the voice, until the mechanical coordination is attained.

Awareness, mastery and application of this coordination in the singing process results in the following advantages:

a) Maximum fullness of loud sounds throughout the gamut of the AH to OOM positions.

Conversely, even if body support is constant, any degree of jaw closure, while singing loud sounds, causes restriction of sound and air in the throat, since this jaw movement deteriorates the Jaw, Larynx, Body Fusion, preventing the diffusion of pressure throughout the body. The recipient of this pressure is now the throat area. The sound loses its fullness, since it is severed from body involvement. Although body support is applied, the closing of the jaw under pressure separates this support, resulting in a devitalized, thin sound.

b) Maximum fullness of soft sounds throughout the gamut of the AH to OOM positions.

The unhinged jaw position, while singing soft or loud sounds, creates the maximum area for mouth resonance; whereas, the closing of the jaw diminishes the size of the mouth cavity as a resonator.

c) Prevention of pressure buildup in the throat, protecting the vocal cords, larynx and surrounding muscles from harmful irritation.

Since the unhinged jaw position causes a fusion of the jaw, larynx and body, pressure is diffused throughout the body, rather than focused on the larynx, vocal cords and neck muscles.

Although the vocal apparatus of the adolescent student is not fully developed, stress, which ordinarily accompanies the execution of intricate or sustained phrases, can be eliminated by making the student aware of the coordination of the mouth and the unhinged jaw. This skill can be taught effectively by having the student sing a song softly in a comfortable part of the range, and whenever a sustained note occurs, the student is instructed to replace the word with the AH vowel sound, while the jaw is unhinged, thus assuming the simulated yawn position (Exinvac Principle). This condition results in the Jaw, Larynx, Body Fusion, eliminating pressure from the delicate, immature throat and elevating the position of the emitted sound. Emphasis placed on the maximum opening of the jaw, by stressing the AH sound, (vertical-elliptical mouth opening), makes the student aware of the most effective position for eliminating pressure in the throat area. It is very important to stress with the adolescent that any movement of the jaw from the complete yawn position in the sustaining of a note, especially a high one, should be preceded by a release of body pressure in order to prevent strain in the throat area. While maintaining an unhinged position of the jaw, the student should be taught to sing the vowels (a,e,i,o,u). It will be noted that the degree of ease and clarity attained varies, since the position of the tongue and mouth changes with each vowel. The ē position is the most difficult to master, since ē is a closed vowel and ordinarily involves jaw closure. It is imperative that the adolescent become sensitive to the role of the jaw in overcoming pressure points. Maximum pressure must be allayed by maximum jaw opening or reduction of body pressure. However, in singing sustained, high notes, the jaw must be completely unhinged in order to prevent throat damage. Mastery in assuming positions, rather than singing sustained notes, until the adolescent learns how to overcome pressure points is absolutely essential.

Ultimately, facility in combining the Gan-Tone Principles with the voice will insure not only the protection of the vocal apparatus of the adolescent, but will also enable him to produce sounds of varied dimensions.

d) Maintenance of stability in the emitted sound, since the jaw is not wobbling.

When the jaw in unhinged, or down and back, it does not obstruct the movement of sound and air emitted from the larynx. However, any interference of the jaw puts pressure on the neck and jaw muscles causing the jaw to wobble, if the singer can't hold it firmly in varying positions. This wobbling jaw is more evident in older singers, since they lack the physical strength to maintain these positions.

The unsolidified jaw is comparable to sustaining a weight in one hand, at shoulder height, that is, at arm's length away from the body. The muscles supporting the arm and weight yield to fatigue and collapse. However, when the hand holding the weight is held close to the chest, the muscles supporting the arm and weight will not yield to fatigue as readily, since the body is involved in assuming the burden of the weight.

e) Release of pressure from the head and neck enabling the singer to exert less physical energy.

f) Facility in attaining tone coloration, i.e., diminishing a sustained sound from loud to soft, or vice versa.

The unhinged position of the jaw independent of mouth movements, along with the yawn, adds depth and height to the sound, at any part of the range, enabling the singer to have great control of volume, since there is maximum utilization of mouth resonance in the soft as well as the loud sounds.

g) Maximum utilization of head and body resonators.

The unhinged jaw, independent of mouth movements, assures the fusion of the jaw with the larynx and torso, causing vocal cords vibrations to be thrust from the depths of the body to the resonators with great impact.

Nose

The nose, in coordination with the jaw and the mouth, operates as a regulator, since it regulates the amount of sound that will be further amplified in the nose and provides maximum utilization of any unused air, thus enabling the singer to get the most out of his breath.

The position of the jaw, in coordination with body support, determines the strength of the resonance that will be produced in the nose. When the jaw is completely down and back, or unhinged, it is fused with the larynx and the torso, assuring the maximum thrust of sound to the head resonators, such as, the oral, nasal and sinus cavities. Since the larynx is a vibrator, the fusion of this voice box with the jaw and the body further augments its vibratory function. When this augmented sound is focused in the bony channels of the nose, increased amplification occurs as the sound resounds further in this area.

The sound emitted from the larynx, in the singing process, can move toward the nose in two paths simultaneously, or alternately, depending on the coloration desired by the singer.

The sound moves out of the voice box through the pharyngeal cavity to the fork (uvular tympany) which divides the mouth from the posterior entrance of the pharyngeal-nasal channel. At this point, the sound can be directed through the mouth via the rear of the tongue and focused on the palate area above the upper teeth to the base of the nose resonating the nasal and sinus cavities through fusion, or the sound can be directed through the posterior entrance of the pharyngeal-nasal channel directly into the nasal fossae and onto the sinus cavities. However, the path to the sinus cavities is not as direct or solid, when approached through the posterior nasal channel.

When the singer mentally focuses sound to the nose via the mouth, the following mechanical coordination should be noted:

> The degree of Jaw, Larynx, Body Fusion involvement, and the degree of intensity on the periphery of the mouth, or tightening of the lips, (particularly the upper lip, since it fuses with the upper teeth below the nose) determine the solidity and focus of vibrant energy at the base of the nose. Tautness of the upper lip can be attained by pinching at the base of the nose. This focus of vibrant energy at the base of the nose can be oscillated back and forth between the nasal base and the sinus bones and re-sounded in the sinus cavities, maintaining intensity at the base of the nose by tightening, or pinching, the upper lip and tightening the nostrils, thereby producing the highest and most concentrated focus, since the sinus cavities are the highest resonating cavities in the head. Therefore, augmented laryngeal sound that is further amplified in this area via the mouth is characterized by height and brilliance and is essentially frontal tone.

When the singer mentally focuses sound to the nose via the posterior entrance of the nasal channel, with the J.L.B. involvement and the tightened lips, particularly the upper lip, the sound is influenced by nasal resonance, since it is focused in the nasal cavities, as it moves toward the nose. This sound is, therefore, also characterized by height and brilliance, but depth is added, since the concentration is on the postnasal as opposed to the frontal nasal area.

Therefore, the following Gan-Tone Principle should be evident:

> The depth, or coloration, of a given tone is determined by the position of the oscillation from the frontal concentration of resonance in the sinus cavities to the postnasal concentration in the posterior nasal channel.

> The darker, or deeper, the sound, the greater the involvement of the posterior nasal channel. Conversely, the less dark, or deep, the sound, the greater the involvement of the frontal nasal area, or sinus cavities.

In seeking the desired coloration, it is important for the singer to be aware of the following Gan-Tone Principle with reference to air expenditure in sustaining tone in the highest and deepest nasal chambers:

> The deeper, or darker, the sound in the gamut of the singing scale, the more breath is needed to sustain these tones, since more resonating cavities are being utilized, necessitating more air.

> The higher the pitch, the deeper the sound, and the more intense the body involvement, the more rapid the consumption of air.

This Gan-Tone Principle is analogous to the projection of the rocket out of the earth's gravitational pull. The greater the pull to be overcome by the rocket, the greater the amount of fuel and thrust it will need to leave the earth and be projected into space.

Similarly, the voice tends to be bound in the area of the vocal cords limiting the use of the highest and deepest nasal chambers. However, greater projection of sound to these areas can be attained by increasing thrust through Jaw, Larynx, Body Fusion, thereby adding more dimensions to the sound by delivering a greater payload of sound to the resonators.

More breath is also available to the singer, since the Jaw, Larynx, Body Fusion sinks the breath to the depths of the body and thrusts it to the body resonators for re-sounding, rather than being emitted through the facial apertures unused.

The Role of the Jaw in Range

IV. Range, in the Gan-Tone Method of Voice Production, is that gamut of voice produced through the vocal cords without laryngeal pressure and through a limited portion of the vocal cords with laryngeal pressure.

The voice that emanates from the vocal cords without laryngeal pressure is that sound that tradition considers the falsetto voice. However, it is not false at all, but pure vocal cords sound, since it is produced by the vocal cords without any support from the vibrator (larynx).

The vocal cords are two pairs of ligaments which project into the cavity of the larynx. The upper pair (superior, or false, vocal cords) are thick and are not directly concerned in the production of the voice. The passage of breath between the edges of the lower pair (inferior, or true, vocal cords; also called vocal folds), when drawn tensely and approximated together, produce the voice. The larynx functions as an organ of the voice by vibrating and resonating the sound that initially is produced by the inferior, or lower, pair of vocal cords. The vocal cords that produce the sound are encased within the larynx, and when pressure is applied to the internal and external laryngeal muscles, the larynx functions as a voice box, since it now becomes an amplifier by vibrating the pure vocal cords sound, causing the voice to be magnified.

The larynx is comparable to an electronic amplifying system. When sound is projected into a microphone, it is enlarged. When sound is projected from the vocal cords into the larynx, it is also enlarged.

Magnification of sound is produced in the electronic amplifying system through three steps:

    a) the sound through the microphone

    b) the amplification, as a result of the power of the electrical components (amplifiers)

    c) the utilization of speakers of various sizes

Magnification of the human voice is produced through three steps:

    a) the sound originating in the vocal cords

    b) the vibration of the larynx fused with body power for resonating and amplifying the vocal cords sound

    c) the utilization of speakers, or resonators, of the head, such as, the nasal and oral cavities

The larynx, composed of nine cartilages, amplifies pure vocal cords sound, when these cords are fused to the larynx by the contraction of intrinsic laryngeal muscles. When looking down on the larynx from above, it is a wedge, or v-shaped container. The point of the wedge (apex) is located in the front of the throat (Adam's apple), and the wide points are in the back of the throat. This v-shaped contour (larynx) forms a hard casing around the vocal cords, and when pressure is applied to this larynx and its parts, such as, the two arytenoid cartilages and the vocal cords, they fuse to vibrate and magnify the sound. Exerting pressure on the larynx is comparable to focusing pressure on the thumb against a hard surface, or table, to compact, or solidify, the area between the bone of the thumb and the table.

When pressure is not applied to the larynx, it is not fused to the attached vocal cords. This condition is comparable to a megaphone that is held at arm's length from the mouth, while producing a sound, as opposed to fusing the megaphone to the mouth by applying pressure to the megaphone against the mouth, while producing a sound. Fusion of the mouth and megaphone produces amplification of sound causing greater volume. Lack of fusion of the mouth and megaphone, while producing sound, whether speaking or singing, nullifies amplification.

The degree of range, or vocal cords involvement, is dependent on the degree of laryngeal pressure that is employed. As the singer ascends the scale, or attempts to utilize the upper range of the vocal cords, with a maximum degree of laryngeal pressure (which is applied when the greatest volume, or amplification, is desired) along with the unhinged jaw and maximum body support, the structure of the fused vocal cords and larynx becomes increasingly difficult to maintain because of the buildup of pressure on the muscles that fuse the larynx as an amplifier causing these muscles to collapse, removing the amplifying function of the larynx.

The apparent change in the quality of the voice, as one ascends the scale, is referred to as a "break" in the voice. It is important to note that as long as air is activating a sound in the healthy vocal cords, in the singing process, there is no "break" in the voice. The break in the vocal line occurs in the involvement of the larynx. If, by nature, a person involves little or no laryngeal pressure, in singing a scale, the emitted sound will be limited in volume, and the possibility of a "break" is minimal. If, by nature, a person manifests much laryngeal pressure in ascending the scale, the likelihood of a "break" in the voice is great, unless laryngeal pressure is eased, and the jaw is fused to the body in order to diffuse this inevitable buildup of pressure which causes an abrupt change in the quality of the voice.

The abrupt change occurs when pressure on the larynx can no longer be maintained, and the structure of the fused vocal cords and larynx collapses. Removal of laryngeal pressure causes a change in the quality of the voice revealing the pure vocal cords sound, known as the falsetto voice, since the larynx is no longer vibrating the vocal cords sound.

Since the structure of the larynx varies in humans, the sounds produced and the abrupt changes, or "breaks," also vary.

However, wherever the break, the remedy is similar for all humans with the following Gan-Tone Principle:

> As the break in the voice approaches, i.e., the inability to maintain the fusion of the larynx and vocal cords, decrease laryngeal pressure and increase body involvement through the opening of the jaw (Exinvac Principle) to alleviate throat pressure by transferring this pressure through the body. By coordinating the decrease of laryngeal pressure with the jaw opening, no break will occur, since the jaw is now fused with the larynx and body, making the body the vibrator and resonator of the vocal cords sound, rather than the larynx.

The jaw plays an important part in determining the amount of range that can be reached with laryngeal pressure. The increased opening of the jaw, with increased range and volume, dilates the vocal hook and utilizes the body as vibrator and resonator of the vocal cords sound, thereby removing the focus of pressure from the larynx that is responsible for the natural impasse which limits range in voices. Lack of understanding regarding the role of the jaw at the point of impasse causes singers to push through this obstruction, producing strain in the throat and causing them to believe that the point of impasse is the limit of their range. In reality, it is only a small part of their range potential.

The problem can be summarized as follows:

> In ascending the scale, the constricted throat area restricts the movement of the vocal sound causing an impasse and preventing the pursuit of further range. In order to open the constricted area for the passage of the vocal line, without any obstruction, increase the jaw opening while ascending the scale.

The following Gan-Tone Principle eliminates the natural impasse, making it possible to reach more range:

> The degree to which the jaw is moved down and back, while ascending the scale, determines the degree of dilation that will occur in the throat to counteract restriction which prevents the impasse.

The higher the range, the greater the need for the jaw to rest firmly down and back, as close as possible to the larynx and collar bone, in order to counteract the increasing restriction of vibrations that occurs with increasing range.

The Role of the Jaw in Register

V. Register, in the Gan-Tone Method of Voice Production, is the range of the vocal cords, from low to high sounds, produced in a smooth and unbroken line without any change in quality revealing that there is only one register applicable for the performance of acceptable music and rejecting the current belief that there are at least three registers in the singing voice. Since the difference in quality of tones produced, while singing the scale, delineates the different registers, eliminating this variation in tonal quality would eliminate this differentiation. In reality, there are not many registers of the sound produced by the vocal cords any more than there are gradations marked on the vocal cords that determine vocal registers.

In singing very low to very high notes, the cords produce an even flow of sound. Rather than the cords, it is the curved, irregular path of the vocal hook that causes turbulence in the vibrating air resulting in registers and breaks in the voice. The flow of sound through the vocal hook is analogous to the flow of water in a stream. The water flows over pebbles and stones creating irregular patterns in the energetic lines of moving water. As the water passes on, the stream widens and encounters more irregularities until it comes to a waterfall (the curve of the tongue). The eddies and whirlpools created, as the water tumbles over the fall, greatly change the pattern of momentum, pitch, intensity and force of the water's movement, just as the eddies created by the irregular curved path of the vocal hook greatly change and distort the original vibrations, the resultant resonances, and the structure, movement, freedom and dimension of the sound.

When the singer ascends the scale, there are various

points in the scale where the tonal quality changes abruptly resulting in the so-called registers of the voice, since the emphasis of resonance appears to shift from the chest to the head as the main resonator of sound above the abrupt changes. Breaks in the voice occur when the structure of the tone cannot be maintained by the singer causing a crack, or break, in the sound resulting in a disembodied, or light, sound.

The difference between register breaks and pressure breaks is as follows:

> Abrupt changes in tonal quality as the singer ascends the scale is referred to as register breaks and is responsible for the age-old belief that there are different registers in the voice. Register breaks can occur several times in the process of ascending the scale.

> The inability of the singer to maintain a uniformity of quality in sustained, loud, high sounds, or other sounds, in any part of the scale, without collapsing the structure that maintains the uniformity of sound throughout the singing line, is referred to as pressure breaks in the voice.

The Cause for the Popular Belief of Registers in the Ascending Scale

It is essentially the inability of the singer to coordinate movements of the jaw and mouth, movable parts, pressure points on the surface of the tongue and surrounding throat muscles, which would guide the sound smoothly through areas of turbulence and pressure, that results in register breaks. The turbulence of vibrating air in the neck caused by the uneven curve of the vocal hook distorts the sound being emitted from the vocal cords leading others to conclude that there are register breaks in the voice. Although this distortion of vibrating sound is reflected back to the vibrating vocal cords, the initial vocal cords sound is not the originator of the turbulence and ultimate breaks in the vibrating vocal sound.

The Cure for Register Breaks

In the Gan-Tone Method of Voice Production, the jaw plays an important role in eliminating abrupt changes in the tonal quality resulting in one register, or scale, from high to low sounds. The movement of the jaw downward opens the throat, and this movement minimizes constriction in the throat which, in turn, reduces restriction in the same manner as opening the door wider to pass an object that otherwise would be restricted for lack of space. This jaw movement is accompanied by pressure applied to the points of greatest restriction on the surface of the curve of the tongue. By coordinating the movements of the jaw while imposing pressure forward and downward on the curve of the tongue to the thyroid cartilage, or Adam's apple, the vocal line will pass more freely, i.e., as the singer ascends the scale and a change in tonal quality is imminent, as a result of increased pressure brought on by the turbulence created in the irregularities of the vocal hook, especially at the curve of the tongue, the singer, anticipating this change, increases the space in the vocal hook at the curve of the tongue by moving the jaw downward and applying pressure on the curve of the tongue causing the curve to be pressed downward and outward contributing to the enlargement of this space, thus enabling the sound to be emitted without restriction. The absence of this restriction prevents a change in tonal quality eliminating the so-called register breaks.

However, further aids in enabling the sound to be emitted freely are as follows:

> 1- The simulation of the yawn (Exinvac Principle) increases space in the vocal hook by lifting and guiding the sound through the curved path.

> 2- The utilization of the apertures of the face, i.e., the mouth and nostrils, but especially the mouth, employed as lenses, not only determines the quantity of sound, as a result of their expansion, but also the quality, as a result of more vibrational movement made possible by this expansion.

A Gan-Tone Principle can, therefore, be summarized:

> The coordination of jaw movements, pressure points on the tongue, the simulation of the yawn (Exinvac Principle), and the utilization of the facial apertures as lenses are the basic ingredients for sufficiently eliminating restriction in the vocal hook which will prevent changes in tonal quality, thus eliminating the so-called registers in the ascending scale.

Although the physical structures of humans vary, as for example, the vocal hook (the size and shape of the

116   Singing Energy

component parts, such as the larynx, hyoid bone, tongue, etc., and the arrangement of these parts), application of this principle varies according to the structure that is peculiar to the individual and his ability to absorb the principle. However, the principle, or method, for eliminating changes in tonal quality, when ascending the scale, is the same for all humans, although the degree of application is dependent on individual differences.

The Cause of Pressure Breaks in the Singing Line

The inability of the singer to maintain a uniformity of quality in sustained, loud, high sounds, or any other sounds, without collapsing the structure that maintains the uniformity of sound throughout the singing line is referred to as pressure breaks in the voice. This condition is caused by the singer's lack of concentration on the following:

1- Positions of the jaw that will fuse the movable parts in the vocal hook.

[2]2- Tension on the vocal cords for determining the pitch of the sound.

[2]3- Air pressure on the cords for determining the size of the vocal signal.

4- Pressure on the curve of the tongue for achieving the proper throat opening.

5- The principle of the yawn for expanding the size of the vocal hook.

6- The facial apertures, i.e., the mouth and nostrils, and their role as lenses.

The Cure for Pressure Breaks

The curved line, from the vocal cords to the tip of the tongue, which rests against the lower teeth and lip, is the surface that must be mastered in order to permit the free-flow of sound without breaks, or cracks, in the voice. It is on this surface that the singer will learn to impose pressure along with the coordinated downward movement of the jaw. When the jaws are closed and the teeth are together, this surface has the widest curve. When the jaw (mandible) is lowered, this curved surface becomes smaller. The size of the curve determines the dimension of the sound. The wider the curve, the less the dimension of free-flowing sound, and the more the jaw approaches a closed position. The tighter the curve, the greater the dimension of free-flowing sound, and the more the jaw approaches a wide-open position. The widest opening of the jaw produces the tightest curve and the largest opening for the free passage of sound. This position is seen most clearly when the button of the jawbone, or chin, is as close as possible to the button of the thyroid cartilage, or Adam's apple. Maximum strength, dimension, and freedom of sound are attained, since this position creates the maximum opening of the throat producing the maximum passage of vibrating sound to be apportioned and focused in the head resonators.

As a result of this maximum opening, the throat muscles and cartilages of the larynx are fused in a solid mass by putting the pressure of the vocal demand on solid structure, i.e., the button of the jawbone, or chin, moving downward as close as possible to the button of the Adam's apple (thyroid cartilage) fuses all the parts in-between, such as, flesh, muscles, membranes, cartilages and bones, giving the inside of the curve its greatest strength.

If there is a riding-up of the jaw under pressure causing these two buttons (chin and Adam's apple) to diverge, the pressure of the vocal demand shifts to muscles rather than bones. These muscles cannot sustain the vocal demand and thus cause the structure to fatigue and collapse, resulting in a pressure break, or crack, in the vocal line.

The riding-up of the jaw under pressure of the vocal demand is analogous to extending the arm parallel to the ground while holding a weight in the extended hand. The muscles soon fatigue causing the arm to collapse. The same weight, however, carried on the shoulder can be sustained for a long period of time.

The outside of the curve, i.e., that part of the tongue which constitutes part of the tube of the throat, requires just as much control as the inside of the curve.

Although the complete surface of the vocal hook, from the vocal cords through the epiglottis to the tip of the tongue, requires awareness of pressure points, the curve of the tongue toward the back of the mouth is the most critical location for the imposition of pressure along with

---

[2]Tension on the lips of the vocal cords coordinated with air pressure impinging on the tensed cords determine the pitch and size of the vocal signal.

utilization of the jaw positions, since this sharp curve produces an abrupt change in the path of the sound and, therefore, requires skillful maneuvering in order to permit sound to pass through it unimpeded. Greater sensitivity to the balancing of these pressure points is, therefore, required of the singer in order to avoid breaks in the singing line. Through trial and error, the proper points for imposed pressure on this critical surface will be mastered.

Consequently, elimination of register and pressure breaks is not the task of the vocal cords in adjusting but, rather, the task of the singer in keeping the sound moving as smoothly as possible through the curved area of the vocal hook, which is analogous to a car on a race track travelling at a high speed and attempting to negotiate a curve. The ability to negotiate this curve, at various speeds, depends upon the driver's understanding of the coordination of certain elements, such as, the speed, size and weight of the car plus the size and surface of the track, in order to constantly adjust these elements, by applying more or less focus on them as needed, to insure their balance, thus enabling the driver to negotiate the curves smoothly and continue the race. However, if, through lack of awareness and skill, this balance is not maintained, he will cause a break in the continuity of movement and smash into the wall where, hopefully, bales of hay will prevent a possible tragedy.

The car is comparable to the sound emanating from the vocal cords. If the car is functioning normally and is unable to negotiate the curve, it isn't the car's fault for breaking the smooth movement and registering a mishap. Maneuvering the car is the driver's responsibility. The driver with more awareness and skill will have less breaks registered.

Similarly, the coordination the singer learns, in the Gan-Tone Method, is to guide the voice successfully through the vocal hook by becoming aware of the following:

> 1- The variations in the jaw movements which will insure the free movement of the vibrating air.
>
> 2- The coordination of varying pressure on the movable and immovable parts along with the focusing of vibrating air on these parts which will give structure and freedom to the tone.
>
> 3- The control of the back of the tongue, and its curve, along with the pharyngeal opening, the uvula, (to be lifted as high as possible, while keeping the tract open from the pharynx through the nasal tract), and other movable parts, in order to allow maximum space in the constricted vocal hook which will aid in determining freedom as well as volume of sound.
>
> 4- The control of the facial openings to be used as focusing agents or lenses. The mouth is to the emitted sound what the lens of the eye is to the incoming light.

Control of these parts is analogous to the control required in the game of billiards. By hitting the ball in many spots, the ball can be made to curve or to move in strange patterns. This skill of maneuvering the ball is called English. By developing the skill of applying pressure on the curve of the tongue and controlling the size of the area leading out of the mouth and nose from the vocal cords, English guides the sound through the irregular terrain of the vocal hook.

Through practice, a skill is developed which results in the alignment of the dynamic lines of vibrating air, in a continuous flow, through the vents of the vocal hook. The skill required in taking the racing car smoothly around the curve is quite visible, since the curve is readily seen by the driver. The skill required in moving sound smoothly through the vocal hook is not visible to the singer, since the curve in the vocal hook and the vibrating air cannot be seen, but they are just as real as the curve in the track and the racing car. Certainly the car will not move around the track without the driver's ability to coordinate the pressure points, such as, pressure on the steering mechanism, to guide the car smoothly around the curve, and pressure on the gas and brake pedals, to produce the most efficient speed for negotiating the curve.

Similarly, the voice will not move through the vocal hook successfully without the singer's awareness of the following:

> The imposition of pressure on the vocal cords by the singer varies in all individuals. However, through practice, the coordination that determines the strength of the vocal signal can be developed.

118   Singing Energy

The degree to which the vocal signal is fused with the larynx, surrounding muscles, cartilages and bones varies with the individual; similarly, the anatomical structure and arrangement of component parts of the entire body, and, specifically, those of the vocal hook, vary according to the individual.

The ability to manifest smoothness in the flow of sound, in the process of singing, varies with the individual. The coordination necessary for this smooth flow can be developed and controlled.

The ability to sense the need for guiding sound smoothly through the vocal hook varies with the individual, since everyone's level of sensitivity is different. However, the faculty of sensitivity can be developed.

The following Gan-Tone Principles can, therefore, be summarized:

It is not the vocal cords that determine air turbulence, breaks, or registers. It is essentially the curve of the vocal hook, with its accompanying irregularities, that breaks the straight flow of the sound. It is the coordination and fusion of the jaw with the tongue, the hyoid bone, the cartilages and muscles of the larynx along with the simulated yawn (Exinvac Principle) and utilization of the facial apertures as lenses that "straighten out" the curve and eliminate breaks of the so-called chest and head registers, which ultimately results in a smooth transition from low to high sounds otherwise known as the even scale, thus denoting one register in the singing voice.

The more efficient the coordination and fusion of the parts of the vocal hook, the more even and undistorted the vocal sound, as a result of less restriction in the less constricted vocal hook, maximizing the flow of sound and minimizing pressure on the cords, while maintaining a steady flow of sound.

It should be noted that Webster's Dictionary defines Register as follows:

"a. The compass, or range, of a voice or instrument.

b. The series of tones produced by a particular adjustment of the vocal cords. In singing up the scale, the register changes at the point where the vocal cords readjust themselves to reach the higher tones; all tones below this point being considered to be the chest, or thick, register, all above, the head, or thin, register."

This dictionary definition is incorrect according to the Gan-Tone Method of Voice Production. Register is the compass, or range, of a voice, but it is not a "series of tones produced by a particular adjustment of the vocal cords," since it is not the vocal cords that adjust but, rather, the singer who must guide the sound smoothly through an irregular, curved surface in order to prevent a change in quality, thereby producing an even scale by revealing a smooth, unbroken transition from low to high notes.

A Gan-Tone definition would, therefore, be as follows:

Register is the compass, or range, of a voice produced in a smooth and unbroken line, without any change in quality, by minimizing throat constriction and vibrational restriction through increasing the jaw opening concomitantly with increasing fusion below and above the vocal cords, while ascending or descending the scale.

The Role of the Jaw in Resonance

VI. Resonance, in the Gan-Tone Method of Voice Production, is the amount of vocal cords vibrations resounded in the cavities of the head, chest and body commensurate with the degree of fusion of the jaw, larynx and torso and the imposition of pressure through the body which result in the fusion of vocal cords vibrations with the body, increasing the body's role as a vibrator and resonator, thus demonstrating the principle of the bell.

The body, like the bell, becomes the vibrator and resonator of its own sound, since it has vibrators and chambers for resounding its vibrations.

The vibrator, in the body, is the fused body through Jaw, Larynx, Body Fusion. The sound vibrations of the vocal cords are fused with the surrounding larynx whose cartilaginous structure subsequently vibrates the surrounding muscles, bones and cartilages. These vibrations are solidified throughout the body by lowering the jaw downward in the direction of the Adam's apple and collar bone making, as in electricity, a strong circuit, thus solidifying a greater area below and above the vocal cords. As the singer imposes pressure down through the body, the degree of fusion that occurs determines the amount of vibrations throughout the body, or the degree to which the body vibrates as a bell. The greater the fusion, the greater the vibratory penetration, and the greater the degree to which the body becomes a medium for vibrations. The more the body vibrates, the more the vibrations are resounded in the resonating chambers and body, which results in greater resonance.

The vibrator in the bell is the cupola-like structure of its own configuration. The solid structure of this cupola is impinged upon by a hammer causing it to vibrate. The solidity of the cupola's structure, comparable to the solidity of the fused body, produces vibrations that resound off its walls.

The man-made bell reflects the utilization of basic fundamental principles of the human bell (body) without the intricacies of flexibility in dimension that are made possible throughout the body, as a result of brain involvement. Subconsciously, the human invented the bell patterned after his own natural characteristics, thus logically utilizing, in part, the qualities of his own master bell. The body, viewed as a master bell, is capable of being tuned into an infinite variety of pitches and dimensions of coloration and volume, as a result of the variation of pressure throughout its many parts.

The jaw plays an important role in maximizing the function of the body as a bell, since it is the fusion of the jaw with the larynx and the components of the throat that determines the effective utilization of the vocal cords sound, of the body as vibrator, and of the body cavities as resonators. However, to attain this fusion, the mouth is opened in a vertical-elliptical position, and the jaw is lowered in order that the button of the jaw, or chin, approximates the button of the thyroid cartilage, or Adam's apple. When these two buttons meet, the path that provides the greatest solidity for vocal vibrations is attained. This path (fused chin and Adam's apple) is the connecting link of the original vocal cords vibrations from the bottom of the torso to the top of the head, thereby extending the amplitude of these vibrations to the body extremities. As this fusion is maintained while pressure is imposed down through the body, the original vocal cords vibrations penetrate deeper into the body, below and above the cords.

A Gan-Tone Principle can, therefore, be summarized:

> It is the degree of orderly fusion of the jaw, tongue, hyoid bone, larynx, cartilages of the trachea, elements of the chest, diaphragm muscle and abdomen to the rectal and pelvic areas that determines the degree to which the body will function as a vibrator, below and above the vocal cords, which is the basis for determining the efficiency of the body cavities as resonators of these vibrations that emanate from the vocal cords.

Application of the Gan-Tone, which is the action of imposing a pulsation on the vocal line down through the body, in the process of singing, produces the reaction of thrusting the vocal cords sound to the resonating chambers of the body with an intensity that is commensurate with the intensity of the Gan-Tone.

The Role of the Jaw in Volume

VII. Volume, in the Gan-Tone Method of Voice Production, is the fullness or quantity of tone determined by the amount of vibrations and resonances created through fusion in the body of the original vocal cords vibrations. Intensity of fusion increases throughout the body as the singer applies increased pressure on the fused parts, below and above the vocal cords, commensurate with the degree of volume desired, since it is the degree of accumulated vibrations that produces resonance which results in volume.

A Gan-Tone Principle can, therefore, be stated:

> The greater the application of fusion throughout the body, the greater the amount of vibrations which, in turn, produces greater resonance, thus increasing the volume of the singing voice.

The conventional belief, however, is as follows:

> The degree of volume produced in the singing voice is dependent on the degree of force with which the singer directs the jet of air to the vocal cords thereby influencing the vibrational amplitude.

This statement, although not false, is incomplete and misleading. Incomplete since it involves only a small part of the vibrating and resonating area of the body involved in producing volume. This area is the vocal cords, which is the initial source of sound and, although important, is not the complete vibrating and resonating system of the body. Misleading in that it confines the amplitude of vocal vibrations to the degree of force with which the singer directs the stream of air to the vocal cords.

The human voice originates in the brain and is manifested in the vocal cords. The mind tenses the cords to a desired pitch, just as the mind causes the impingement of pressure on the thumb and index finger. The mind directs the stream of air to the vocal cords that are tensed to a certain pitch, just as it also directs air to the oral cords, or lips, in the whistle, producing sound. However, it is not the force of this stream of air to the vocal cords that ultimately determines the loudness of the sound or even the dimensions of the soft sound. It *is* true that the sound originates in the cords, and that a greater force of air impinging on the tense cords *can* produce a somewhat louder sound. However, it is ultimately through the fusion of body parts, which the original vocal cords vibrations penetrate, that the greatest amount of sound can be realized.

Body fusion multiplies the vocal cords vibrations by extending these vibrations throughout the fused area of the body. The accumulation of these vibrations and the depths through which they penetrate the body determine the amount of resonance that will be reflected in the cavities of the body which, in turn, determines volume. It is obvious, therefore, that the vocal cords (a little more than 1/2" in the adult male) as a volume-producing agent must yield to the whole body as the ultimate vibrator and resonator of sound. Since the whole body (bell) is greater than any of its parts, the body can, logically, bear the burden of stress which cannot be sustained by the delicate vocal cords, nor can the cords create vibrations and resonance comparable to the ability of the body, the master vibrator and resonator.

A conventional belief can be stated as follows:

> The degree of volume evident in the singing voice is dependent on the degree of lung power the singer possesses.

This statement is incomplete, since lung involvement, though an integral part, is not the sole agent that supplies the force which directs the stream of air to the vocal cords, nor, by itself, does it constitute the complete bellows system in producing the greatest dimensions of sound. It is unfair to see the lungs as the providers of the greatest force to the stream of air, anymore than it is fair to look upon the bellows as being sufficient to fire the furnace, since it is the force, or compression, of the whole body through Jaw, Larynx, Body Fusion that supplies force to the stream of air impinging upon the cords, augmenting the bellows of the lungs. It is not the power of the man-made bellows that determines the efficiency with which the furnace is fired but, rather, the power of the bellows rests with the manipulator who involves his hands, arms, or whole body, if necessary, in order to thrust the air with maximum efficiency. In both cases, the involvement of the whole body is essential for the greatest amount of thrust.

The two processes, in the Gan-Tone Method, that constitute the bellows system of the body, i.e., supplier of air to the vocal cords, are natural compression and body fusion.

Compression, by which the lungs supply air to activate the vocal cords, is extended throughout the body by fusion, making the whole body a bellows for the control, strength, resilience, thrust, balance and stability of the air.

Compression of the lungs occurs in the process of breathing. In the exhaled part of breathing, the air in the lungs is compressed by the collapsing of the lungs with the aid of the chest, abdomen and diaphragm. The fibers of the chest that are distended in the process of inhalation are contracted during exhalation. The action of the diaphragm moving downward over the abdomen, which opens the thoracic cavity (chest) during inhalation, returns upward to a position of repose before the beginning of the next breathing cycle, thus aiding in compression of the lungs causing air to be directed to the vocal cords. The action of the diaphragm pushing down, dome-like over the abdomen during inhalation, compresses the abdomen. During exhalation, the compressed abdomen expands upward, aiding in the movement of the diaphragm upward toward the chest cavity, compressing the lungs and causing air to be directed to the vocal cords.

Body fusion, the other process involved in the bellows system of the body, has never really been considered or treated properly by voice experts but, in the Gan-Tone Method, body fusion is absolutely essential for maximizing vibrations which, in turn, creates increased resonance, thus producing the greatest quantity or volume of sound.

Body fusion for maximum volume cannot be fully attained without the thorough understanding and involvement of the following processes:

    1- The union of the jaw, larynx, bones, cartilages and muscles of the lower part of the neck with the upper part of the torso, while maintaining the vertical-elliptical mouth opening.

    2- The fusion of sound through this united area down through the body to the rectal-pelvic area produced by the singer through imposition of pressure (Jaw, Larynx, Body Fusion).

The union of the neck area is brought about, primarily, through the control of the jaw and, secondarily, by pressure on the vocal cords and surrounding muscles and cartilages of the throat, many of which are united through the downward movement of the jaw. When the jaw is unhinged down and back and resting on the larynx (Adam's apple), as close as possible to the structure at the top of the torso, such as, the collar bone, fusion of bony structure occurs making the throat area very solid and, therefore, able to withstand the demand of maximum volume, since the stress of pressure is now on bones and cartilages and, therefore, the sound-producing structure is more solid, vibrant, stable and controlled. However, if the jaw strays from this solid unification, i.e., the jaws converge, during moments of great pressure, such as, maximum volume, the emphasis of stress shifts to neck muscles, and the sound diminishes in strength, stability, structure, size and volume, since the muscles are soft and, therefore, cannot produce the vibrancy characteristic of solid bones. More important, since muscles cannot sustain the pressure of bones, they become a weak link under stress and collapse, breaking the unity of body fusion. The union of the jaw, larynx, bones, cartilages and muscles of the neck to the upper part of the torso is, therefore, essential for insuring the fusion of the head, throat and body, with the jaw as the connecting link for maximizing the body's role as vibrator and resonator which, in turn, results in maximum volume.

When the neck is properly fused, as a result of the downward movement of the jaw, with the vertical-elliptical mouth opening, the vibrations produced through this fusion penetrate somewhat the area below and above the vocal cords. As the singer increases pressure downward through the chest muscles, diaphragm and abdomen to the Sphincter ani externus muscle at the pelvic-perineum diaphragm, the vibrations in the fused area of the throat further fuse through the solid body, and the strength of these vibrations is felt and supported at the rectal muscles.

Maximal dimension and volume in the sound are dependent on the singer's ability to coordinate and balance the two areas of pressure—the larynx, within which the vocal cords vibrations are fused, and the Sphincter ani externus muscle, where body fusion and vocal cords vibrations are focused. This balance becomes more critical as pitch and volume are increased, since there is a commensurate increase in pressure which must be displaced between these two points, rather than localized at one point. Localizing pressure, either at the larynx or the Sphincter ani externus muscle, rather than balancing it between these two points, restricts body resilience.

When the throat is fused with the downward position of the jaw, while singing the loudest sounds without the involvement of fusion through the body, the resultant resonance in the body chambers is limited to the vibrations created in the throat area, and the dimension of the loud sound is shallow, throaty, less brilliant, less stable, less resilient and less resonant thereby curtailing its volume.

When pressure is imposed downward through the body, and the fusion of the jaw is fully employed, vibrations penetrate deeper into the body, since the downward pressure imposed by the singer fuses the body components more solidly. When solidification of the body increases to the rectal area, body components vibrate according to the molecular structure peculiar to each part. As pressure is imposed down through the body, sound vibrations mix with the vibrant body components causing a more intense and resilient thrust of vibrations to the resonators of the chest, pharynx, mouth, nasal-pharyngeal tract and head. The combination of these maximum vibrations and resultant resonances are responsible for maximum volume.

In considering the body a bell, the hammer that strikes the bell, when it is rung, is analogous to the air that strikes the cords. The amount of vibrations produced, when the hammer hits the bell is dependent on the solid vibrancy of the bell and its acoustical structure. These factors determine the resounding degree of the vibrations within the cave of the bell and its outer walls. As the air strikes the cords and is vibrated throughout a solid body by fusion, the total body vibrations are reflected as resonance within the cavities of the body which, in turn, results in the loudness of sound, or volume.

Since body fusion determines the amount of vibrations and resonances, which equals volume, and since this fusion depends on the role of the jaw, a Gan-Tone Principle can, therefore, be summarized as follows:

> Volume, the result of vibrations and resonances produced through body fusion by the imposition of pressure through the body, hinges on the efficient movement of the jaw down and back which, in turn, fuses the larynx and throat to the head and body.

The Role of the Jaw in Coloration

VIII. Coloration of sound, in the Gan-Tone Method of Voice Production, is the variety in tonal quality of human voices dependent on the degree of vibrations and resonance which is produced by mental focus of vocal vibrations on vibrant and resonant areas throughout the body.

Since coloration of the emitted sound is affected by the vibrations and resonances focused in different areas of the body, the mind plays an important role in the tone-color selection of the emitted sound.

The gamut of tone coloration cannot be fully demonstrated without the complete understanding of body fusion, since it is only through complete body utilization as vibrator and resonator that the infinite variety of tone colors can be manifested. Body fusion produces the ultimate in vibrations and resonances which enables the singer to select from a great variety of shades and hues in depicting a tonal picture.

Body fusion, therefore, is essential for providing the greatest gamut of tone coloration, but this body fusion is not possible without the important role of the jaw which unifies the whole body and extends the vocal cords vibrations throughout the body.

The position of the jaw down and back resting on the collarbone with the jawbone straddling the larynx, the vertical-elliptical mouth opening, and the surface of the curve of the tongue focusing toward the Adam's apple, or button of the larynx, fuse the muscles, cartilages and bones (especially the jawbone and hyoid bone) downward through the body, solidifying the area below and above the vocal cords. This body solidification produces the ideal condition for generating the greatest quantity of vibrations and resonance, since the vocal cords vibrations can now be extended through the fused components to the rectal-pelvic area. However, should the jaw diverge from its fused position with the collarbone, the components (larynx, hyoid bone, throat muscles, cartilages and spinal column) become separated and isolated causing vibrations to be absorbed in the throat muscles, resulting in a diminution of vibrations and a lessening of their penetration throughout the body. This diminution is commensurate with the diverging movement of the jaw. As the jaw rides up, it exposes the angle of vulnerability which can be described as follows:

> The degree to which the jaw diverges from its fusion with the Adam's apple and the collarbone determines the degree to which pressure focuses on the vocal cords and throat muscles, restricting the production of vibrations to the vocal cords. The diverging jaw acts as a circuit breaker, breaking the fusion of vibrations throughout the body, making it impossible to ground and support a maximum of vocal vibrations at the rectal-pelvic area.

When the jaw is not fused to the body, vocal cords vibrations become restricted to the throat area, greatly limiting the coloration potential of the emitted sound. Since body fusion has collapsed, the vocal cords now have the responsibility of coloration that can only be accomplished through body involvement. Since tone coloration is produced from a constricted position of the throat opening, the movement of sound vibrations are restricted causing a tight, reedy sound. Tight, as a result of the constricted throat opening, and reedy, as a result of undue focus on the vocal cords. The restricted sound produced by the diverging jaw limits the body's role in supporting, thrusting and vibrating the sound, placing maximum stress on the neck, making this delicate area vulnerable to fatigue and collapse.

When the jaw is fused to the body, vocal cords vibrations are fused downward to the rectal-pelvic area, the point of greatest support and thrust, resulting in maximum coloration potential of the emitted sound. The vocal hook is now thoroughly opened, since the area from the vocal cords to the mouth has its widest vent for the passage of vocal vibrations. The fusion of these vibrations to the rectal-pelvic area and the penetration of these vibrations through the body determine the coloration of these vibrations to be reflected in the cavities of the body.

A Gan-Tone Principle can, therefore, be stated:

> The greater the degree of penetration of vocal cords vibrations throughout the body, the greater the degree of coloration of vibrations to be resounded in the body resonators producing a variety of tonal colors in the emitted sound.

Coloration, or pigmentation, of the vocal sound is affected by the various components of the body. Solids, liquids and gases make up body components. Bones, cartilages, tendons, muscles and membranes are the solids of the body. Blood and water can be considered the body liquids. Air constitutes the basic gas of the body. It is the mixture of these components, by fusion and compression, that determines the influence these components have on the coloration, or pigmentation, of the emitted sound.

Focusing vibrations through bones, as, for example, in the facial mask, gives more brilliance to the sound, since bone produces more vibrations which, in turn, magnify resonance.

Focusing vibrations to the cartilaginous roof of the mouth, or floor of the nasal chambers, produces mouth-roof resonance which is colored by less intensity of vibrations, since cartilage is softer than bone, mellowing the vibrations in the oral cavity.

Focusing vibrations in the pharynx (back of the mouth), which can be considered a membranous, muscular cave, yields less vibrant tone coloration, since membranes and muscles are softer than cartilage. A deeper tonal quality is also evident, as a result of its cavernous structure.

Therefore, by fusing vibrations through the body and then mentally focusing these vibrations in different areas of the body, such as, the maxillary bone at the base of the nose, the facial mask, the bridge of the nose, the roof of the mouth, the two cupolas behind the upper teeth, the uvula, the area behind the lower teeth, the surface of the tongue curvature, the fossae of the nasal tract, the sinuses, the pharynx, the larynx, the trachea, the chest, the diaphragm, the abdomen, the rectal-pelvic area, or combinations of these parts, an infinite variety of coloration, or pigmentation, can be given to the vocal vibrations and resultant resonance which is reflected in the emitted sound.

A Gan-Tone Principle can be summarized as follows:

> The degree of intensity of the Jaw, Larynx, Body Fusion, coordinated with the degree of intensity of focus of vibrations to the various parts of the body, along with the degree to which the mouth focuses these vibrations, determine the variations in coloration, or pigmentation, of the emitted sound.

The Role of the Jaw in Sound Configuration

IX.   Sound configuration, in the Gan-Tone Method of Voice Production, is the control of the endless variety of symmetrical, varicolored sound patterns, produced in the process of singing vowels and consonants, made possible through the understanding of the jaw positions, from the graduated movements in limited volume and vowel sustenance, to fusion with the body in maximum volume and vowel sustenance.

Regardless of the vowels and consonants being sung, the fusion of the jaw with the body provides the greatest amount of vibrations, emanating spherically from the vocal cords and permeating the body omnidirectionally. The dynamic movement of vibrations omnidirectionally from the vocal cords is balanced and controlled by body fusion and thrust to produce an infinite variety of vibrations to be shaped into vowels and consonants by the coordination of the nostrils, mouth, jaw, lips, teeth, tongue, uvula and throat muscles. Therefore, the fused body provides the maximum vibrations. The resonators provide the subsequent maximum resonance, and the resultant sound is emitted in the form of consonants and vowels shaped by the coordination of the nostrils, mouth, lips, jaw, teeth, tongue, uvula and throat muscles, which can be considered the instruments for shaping words in the singing line.

Fusion of the jaw with the body is required only when the greatest amount of sound is required on the vowels of the singing line. As volume is increased, body fusion is necessary in order to provide more vibrations. If volume is increased without fusion, the body, which is the amplifier of vibrations, is divorced, restricting the amplification of these vibrations to the throat muscles, which cannot sustain the strain, causing eventual collapse of these muscles. However, when maximum volume is not required, maximum structure is not required, i.e., the jaw need not be fused with the body, since the body as an amplifier for producing maximum vibrations and freedom of the sound is not necessary.

Jaw involvement, while shaping vowels and consonants in the singing sound, can vary from the natural position of the jaw in normal conversation involving minimal movement of the lips and jaw, to the progressive movement of the jaw downward as the need arises for more volume, security and vowel sustenance. Fusion of the jaw with the body occurs when the chin is moved downward by muscle contraction and resting on the larynx (Adam's apple) close to the collar bone, causing the strong parts (jaw, larynx and body) to be the recipients of pressure, rather than the throat muscles which are now protected by this fusion.

Fusion of the jaw with the body can be maintained while shaping any vowel in the singing line, thus producing maximum volume on any vowel. This fusion is attained, without rigidity of the jaw and throat components, by placing the jaw downward, through the contractive action of the Pterygoideus lateralis muscle which, when mastered, makes possible the fusion of the jaw with the larynx and torso with minimal throat-muscle involvement, making the fused body the recipient of pressure, rather than the throat muscles. Maximum involvement of the jaw, larynx and body on any vowel requires that the mouth attain a vertical-elliptical shape to insure that the transmitting vibrations from the rectal-pelvic area penetrate the highest resonating point, i.e., the septum above the bridge of the nose that separates the two frontal sinus cavities. As the jaw is moved downward, the mouth opens wide in a vertical-elliptical position with the surface of the teeth covered by the lips. This position allows the widest opening of the mouth, keeping the dynamic lines of vibrations (thrust from the rectal-pelvic area, the deepest point in the body) moving directly to the highest point, the septum, for the maximum amount of resonance to be reflected in the singing vowels which are shaped by the coordination of the nostrils, mouth, lips, teeth, tongue, uvula, jaw and throat muscles, the instruments for shaping words in the singing line.

Maximum volume on any sustained vowel and maximum duration of any vowel sound is dependent on the speed with which the singer moves from the consonant of a word to the vowel and vice versa, while coordinating body fusion with the vertical-elliptical position of the mouth. Slow coordination, on the other hand, diminishes maximum volume that can be attained on any sustained vowel, since sluggish movement of the jaw, for example, makes the jaw work as a tap, restricting the movement of vibrations, thus limiting the fullness of the vibrations and resultant resonance for the duration of the sustained sound. Spontaneity in the coordination of the jaw, larynx and body with the vertical-elliptical position of the mouth produces instantaneous maximizing of vibrations as resonance for the duration of the sustained vowel. The unhinged position of the jaw (Jaw, Larynx, Body Fusion) makes possible open-throated, body-supported resonance. Any drifting away from this position during maximum volume and sustaining of vowels diminishes the vibratory and resonant characteristics of any vowel.

Singing vowel sounds, while maintaining an unhinged position of the jaw, i.e., the vertical-elliptical mouth opening, during loud, high, sustained sounds requires discipline along with the skill of utilizing the nostrils and lips as lenses and the control of the different positions of the tongue and uvula for shaping the different vowels.

In the shaping of every vowel (a,e,i,o,u), care must be taken to insure that the jaw is completely unhinged. Dilation of the nostrils increases the vibration and resonance of vowel sounds.

In singing the AH sound, the tongue lays on the floor of the mouth with the tip of the tongue touching the lower teeth and back of the lower lip. The AH sound is the easiest sound to produce with the unhinged jaw since the positions of the tongue and mouth are easy to assume and maintain under pressure.

The long ā sound is made with the forward movement of the tongue and consists of two sounds (ĕ as in them and ē as in we) as in the word say. Skill is required in maintaining the unhinged position of the jaw while going from the first to the second sound. Skill is also required in the coordination of the lips and tongue.

The long ē sound is an extremely difficult sound to sing with the unhinged jaw position, since there is a tendency to close the mouth, show the teeth, spread the lips horizontally in a smiling position and protrude the jaw. Although this position can be utilized during notes that produce minimal stress (notes of lower pitch and intensity), it is detrimental during notes of maximum stress (notes of higher pitch and intensity) for the following reasons:

1. The departure of the jaw from body fusion removes body support from the fundamental vocal cords vibrations placing stress in the throat area, diminishing the strength of the structure of vibrations and resonance, and constricting the throat opening.

2. The closed mouth puts the pressure of maintaining the structure of sound on the teeth, the vocal cords and throat muscles.

3. The uncovered teeth and horizontally expanded lips (smile) spread the tone, limiting the dimensions of the sound.

Therefore, the sound becomes tight, as a result of constriction; less vibrant, as a result of less amplification of vibrations; reedy, as a result of restriction to the throat area; thin, as a result of lack of dimensions that are possible only through body fusion; brittle, as a result of the clenched position of the jaw and the lack of body thrust, making the sound more susceptible to fatigue and collapse, as a result of reliance on throat muscles.

In order to maintain the unhinged position of the jaw during the ē sound, and thus involve the body, from the rectal-pelvic area to the septum of the frontal sinuses, the long ē must be articulated within the framework of the unhinged jaw, and this articulation can only be demonstrated when the singer learns to lift the back of the tongue in coordination with the unhinged jaw in order to articulate the ē sound and, at the same time, create a direct line for the fused vibrations to the rectal-pelvic area to be thrust to the highest point (septum) with the greatest impact. The vertical-elliptical position of the mouth and lips furnishes the strongest facial configuration for maximum strength in sustaining the ē vowel, since this position is parallel to the line of support and thrust from the rectal-pelvic area to the frontal sinuses, the two extremities of the body. The spreading of the mouth in the horizontal-elliptical position produces a spreading of the tone, jeopardizing the vertical line from the rectal-pelvic area that produces the greatest dimension in vibrations, support, thrust and height in resonance.

The long i vowel is made up of two pure vowels (ah as in pa and e as in me). Skill is required in maintaining the unhinged position of the jaw, while going from the first to the second sound. The tongue must assume the position that corresponds to the desired sound. With practice, the tongue can be disciplined to articulate the purity of the desired sound within the structure of the unhinged jaw.

The long ō sound is made up of two sounds (o as in no and oo as in who). Skill is required in maintaining the unhinged position of the jaw, while dilating and contracting the lips in moving from the first to the second sound.

The long ū vowel is made up of two sounds (y as in you and oo as in who). Skill is required in saying the first sound, which is the consonant y, since it involves a rapid movement of the jaw on this letter along with emphasis on the oo sound, while coordinating the contraction of the lips with the unhinged jaw.

It should be noted that whatever vowels are sung, whether they are long, short, open or closed, it is essential that the singer develop a sensitivity to changing pressures that occur in going from one sound to another. Under great stress, the jaw is unhinged and the mouth is in a vertical-elliptical position, while the tongue and lips articulate any particular vowel sound desired or required. By unhinging the jaw, the singer insures the involvement of body fusion for producing maximum vibrations, support, thrust, open throat, resonance and cover for the emitted sound. Through maximum fusion, the dimensions of the sound are deepest and highest, creating an aura, or cover, around the sound not possible without maximal fusion of vocal cords vibrations with the body.

In singing a word, under pressure, that begins with a vowel, the spontaneity and agility with which the singer moves the jaw down and back determines the degree of body fusion that will be involved which, in turn, determines the dimension of the vowel being sung. The degree to which the jaw is kept from riding into the sound determines the purity of the line.

If the word ends with a vowel, the uniformity of fusion (jaw, larynx, body coordination) should be maintained to the end of the word in order to insure the purity of the vowel. The uniformity of the vowel ending can be achieved by maintaining the structure of the vowel sound to its completion without the addition of any other extraneous vowel sound.

In sustaining vowels that have two different sounds, with the jaw unhinged, such as a, i and o, the tongue movement from the first to the second sound must be instantaneous, if maximum volume is to be evenly maintained. If the movement is indecisive, the transition from one sound to the other will interfere with the evenness of the singing line. Furthermore, when sustaining a high note or maximum volume, emphasis should be placed on the first sound of the sustained vowel, and the second sound should be pronounced rapidly at the end of the sustained vowel in order to achieve an even, unbroken singing line. When this second sound is articulated, pressure of the sustained vowel is terminated. If the pressure is not terminated and the jaw closes in articulating the second sound, support shifts immediately from the body to the muscles of the neck and vocal cords, placing pressure and strain in the neck area, interrrupting the evenness of the singing line and changing the quality of the sound. When the jaw closes, the quality of the second sound changes, since it is no longer an open-throated, body-supported sound. The uniform quality of the two different sounds no longer exists.

The closing jaw interferes with the movement and amplitude of vibrations, since the jaw becomes divorced from the body. The amplification of vibrations through body fusion no longer exists. The throat opening becomes more constricted confining the movement of vibrations to this area causing the second sound to become tight and reedy, since it is devoid of the amplified dimensions of body vibrations and head resonance.

However, if the second sound of the vowel is made rapidly, preventing the jaw from closing under pressure, the two sounds will maintain a uniform quality, since both sounds have the support of body fusion, which produces a maximum of amplified vibrations, an open throat for the uninterrupted passage of these vibrations, and maximum thrust from the rectal-pelvic area for maximum resonance in the body resonators.

A Gan-Tone Principle can, therefore, be summarized:

> The degree to which the jaw rides up, when singing loud, high, sustained sounds, or when shifting from one vowel sound to the other will determine the degree to which the quality of the singing line will be altered.
>
> The more the jaw rides up while sustaining a vowel, and the more sluggish the movement, when shifting from one vowel sound to another, in any part of the scale, the more the spherical penetration of vibrations through the body diminishes causing the center and control of vibrations to be shifted from the rectal-pelvic area to the vocal cords and surrounding muscles, diminishing the dimensions of the emitted sound.
>
> The more spontaneous the movement from one vowel sound to the other, the greater the fusion of the jaw to the body maintaining the continuity of maximum vibrations, maximum support and thrust, and maximum throat opening for the free passage of vibrations and resonance in the body cavities, below and above the vocal cords, resulting in a uniform quality in the sustained sounds.

This Gan-Tone Principle is a basic truth in the Gan-Tone Method of Voice Production and when applied to the singing of any language (American, Italian, French, German, etc.), whether the vowels are pure or otherwise, this principle will yield the maximal degree of vibrations, resonance and coloration which produces the greatest freedom, dimension and purity in any singing sound.

Since consonants play a very important role in the configuration of sound for communicating words in any language, whether singing or speaking, it is important that the singer be aware of the rapid articulation of consonants in order to maintain the dimension of the sound and the purity of the singing line.

During the pronunciation of consonants in any language, the singing line as well as the speaking line is interrupted, since consonants, unlike vowels, close the mouth and throat opening with the aid of the lips, teeth, tongue and uvula. Since the singing line is interrupted, it is essential that the singer learn to condense and articulate consonants as rapidly and distinctly as possible, whether it be one consonant (b) or consonant blends (schl). A high order of sound cannot be maintained, if there is a sluggish movement in the pronunciation of consonants.

A Gan-Tone Principle can, therefore, be stated:

> The degree of spontaneity with which the consonants in words are condensed and articulated in coordination with the Jaw, Larynx, Body Fusion determine the degree to which the consonants will affect the singing line.

> The slower the pronunciation of consonants, the shorter the duration of the singing line, as a result of the excessive interference created by the prolonged consonants which, in turn, interferes with the application of the Jaw, Larynx, Body Fusion, narrowing the dimensions of the emitted sound.

> Conversely, the more condensed and instantaneous the pronunciation of consonants (single or multiple), the more spontaneous the application of the Jaw, Larynx, Body Fusion, producing a longer singing line of greater dimensions.

The Role of the Jaw in Brilliance

X. Brilliance, in the Gan-Tone Method of Voice Production, is the radiant brightness of sound produced by the fusion of the vocal cords vibrations through the body made possible by the fusion of the jaw to the larynx and body while maintaining the vertical-elliptical mouth opening.

Maximum amplification of vocal cords vibrations is achieved by fusing these vibrations through compression to the rectal-pelvic area, where they are grounded and then thrust to the resonators with great impact insuring the maximum utilization of these resonators for the focusing and shaping of these vibrations which, in turn, insures the maximum brilliance, or radiant brightness, of any emitted sound. Efficient involvement of the resonators insures the most effective re-sounding of vibrations resulting in the greatest degree of brilliance, or radiant brightness, in the vocal sound. The degree of intensity in the action of fusion and compression determines the degree of reaction in the thrusting and resultant magnification of vibrations. The greater the impact of the thrust, the more efficiently the resonators are being utilized to re-sound vibrations.

The highest degree of brilliance in the singing line can only be attained through the fusion of the jaw to the larynx and body, since the fusion of the jaw results in the complete involvement of the body as a bell in extending the vocal cords vibrations, making the body an extension of the vocal cords. The maximum vibrations produced through body involvement along with the maximum thrust of these vibrations from the bottom of the torso involve the body as a battery of great force for transmitting these vibrations to the resonating areas. The gounding of vibrations at the Sphincter ani externus muscle in the pelvic-perineum diaphragm provides a momentum for thrusting to the resonators <u>not</u> possible, if the vibrations were grounded at the thoracic diaphragm.

The compression of vocal cords vibrations through the body to the bottom of the torso is comparable to the piston in the cylinder. The piston is the compression, and the cylinder is the body. As the compression proceeds from the vocal cords through the cylinder of the body, it reaches its highest degree of compression at the rectal-pelvic area, which results in the highest degree of thrust, producing, in turn, the highest degree of amplification of vibrations in the resonators. These amplified vibrations result in the highest degree of brilliance in the vocal sound, when these vibrations are focused in the most vibrant areas of the resonators, such as the bony parts at the bridge of the nose that connect with the head resonators, the bony parts of the mask and the resonators beyond the mask, such as the skull cap and its sinuses.

Effective penetration of these vibrations, by focusing in the vibrant areas, and the re-sounding of these vibrations is dependent upon the Jaw, Larynx, Body Fusion. When the jaw is down and back and resting on the larynx (Adam's apple) approximating the collar bone, the whole body becomes involved in the amplification of vocal cords vibrations. Any divergence of the jaw from the larynx results in a disengagement of the body, a diminishing of vibrations, and a restriction of these vibrations to the throat area, reducing the efficiency of the body as an amplifier of vibrations and as a thrusting agent of these vibrations to the resonators. Inefficient involvement of the resonators causes ineffective re-sounding of vibrations which results in diminished brilliance in the emitted sound.

The position of the jaw down and back fuses the jaw to the larynx and body causing a maximum opening of the vocal hook which, in turn, insures a relatively unobstructed path for the movement of amplified vibrations to the resonators of the head and body. When the jaw is in a halting position, the vocal hook is constricted, restricting the free movement of vibrations which have already been diminished as a result of the absence of body fusion. These diminished vibrations, further weakened by restriction in the vocal hook, do not have the momentum of thrust to effectively penetrate the resonators resulting in minimum brilliance in the emitted sound.

A Gan-Tone Principle can, therefore, be summarized:

The degree to which the jaw is fused to the larynx and body determines the degree to which the vocal cords vibrations are fused and compressed through the body and grounded at the rectal-pelvic area.

The degree of compression determines the degree of thrust of these vibrations to the resonators of the head and body where they are focused and re-sounded for brilliance in the vocal sound.

The greater the fusion of the jaw to the larynx and body, the greater the fusion and compression of the vocal cords vibrations resulting in a greater degree of amplification of vibrations, producing a greater degree of thrust and impact to the resonators which, in turn, causes a higher degree of re-sounding of these vibrations in the resonators, resulting in greater brilliance in the emitted sound.

THE GAN-TONE—REVELATION OF SCINTILLATING SINGING

CONTENTS

THE GAN-TONE—REVELATION OF SCINTILLATING SINGING

I.	Meaning of the Gan-Tone	133
II.	Procedure for the Application of the Gan-Tone Pulsation	135
III.	The Role of the Jaw in the Imposition of the Gan-Tone Pulsation on the Fundamental Vibrating Pitch of the Voice	136
IV.	Why the Gan-Tone is Neither a Vibrato Nor a Tremolo	138
V.	The Role of the Gan-Tone in Voice Projection	140
VI.	The Role of the Gan-Tone in Breath Control	142
VII.	The Role of the Gan-Tone in Range	144
VIII.	The Role of the Gan-Tone in Register	145
IX.	The Role of the Gan-Tone in Resonance	147
X.	The Role of the Gan-Tone in Volume	149
XI.	The Role of the Gan-Tone in Coloration	151
XII.	The Role of the Gan-Tone in Sound Configuration	153
XIII.	The Role of the Gan-Tone in Brilliance	157

Meaning of the Gan-Tone

I. The Gan-Tone is a superimposed pulsation on the natural vibrations of the voice which is voluntary and controlled by the singer. A series of these Gan-Tones, imposed by the singer on the singing line, increases the magnitude of vibrations of the original vocal cords sound which results in greater singing energy. When the singer sings a note, for example, at 440 vibrations per second, and this note is sustained for five seconds, he can impose the Gan-Tone thirty times during a five second period, without altering the 440 v.p.s.

These pulsations, or Gan-Tones, stabilize the fusion of the vocal cords and their vibrations to the surrounding membranes, muscles and larynx and carry these vibrations downward through the body. The Gan-Tones mix with vibrations created in the body, when pressure is imposed through the body in the process of superimposing these Gan-Tones on the natural vibrations of the voice. The body is made up of membranes, tendons, ligaments, cartilages and bones which vibrate at different frequencies. By the imposition of Gan-Tones, the vibrating vocal cords sound is fused through the larynx down through the body and blends with the vibratory quality of the body, i.e., the Gan-Tones, fused with the vocal cords, cause this area to vibrate along with the components below and above the vocal cords, such as, membranes, ligaments, muscles, cartilages and bones of the head, mask or chest. The vibratory characteristics of these components mix with the fundamental pitch of the vocal cords sound. Therefore, by imposing Gan-Tones on the natural vibrations of the voice, the fundamental pitch of the vocal cords sound is strengthened, enabling it to permeate the body below and above the cords. This original vocal cords sound, or fundamental pitch, mixes with the vibrations that are peculiar to the components below and above the vocal cords. The frequencies of these components are affected not only by their elasticity and density, i.e., whether they are muscles or bones, but also by the degree of pressure imposed on them by the singer in the process of fusing the body. Elasticity and density of bones, cartilages, ligaments, tendons and membranes vary according to the degree of pressure imposed on them by the mind which, in turn, affects their vibratory characteristics.

The imposition of the Gan-Tone fuses the original vocal cords sound throughout the body consciously enabling the singer to control the support for the sound at the deepest part of the body, i.e., at the rectal-pelvic area.

The imposition of the Gan-Tone transforms the singing voice by giving it greater dimensions not possible without it. The Gan-Tone enables the body to become a mass of vibrations and resonance which, in turn, results in maximum volume. No matter what the dimensions are in a voice before the imposition of the Gan-Tone, once having incorporated the Gan-Tone, the voice assumes unimaginable dimensions in terms of flexibility, coloration, brilliance, spontaneity, buoyancy, agility and, above all, volume, placing singing energy at the command of the singer.

The Compression Phase of the Gan-Tone cycle is the downward pressure exerted through the body from the vocal cords to the bottom of the torso in a piston-like movement.

In the movement of pressure downward, the simultaneous fusion of vocal cords sound and body compression is maintained. As pressure is imposed on the pitch, the frequency of the Gan-Tone on this fundamental sound, i.e., original vocal cords vibrations, is variable. The speed of the Gan-Tone can be slow or fast for the duration of a sustained sound regardless of its pitch as, for example, if a pitch of 500 vibrations per second is being sung for 5 seconds, the Gan-Tone may be imposed 25 to 35 times, or at an amount that the singer wishes to control without changing the pitch or smoothness of the fundamental sound.

When first attempting to impose the Gan-Tone, the singer may manipulate the structure of the vocal cords and throat muscles to accent the sound for embellishment, which is really a vibrato. It is not the Gan-Tone, since only the vocal cords are vibrators through the contraction of laryngeal muscles. The Gan-Tone involves the coordinated action of the fundamental sound with the jaw, larynx and torso, making the whole body the vibrator of the original vocal cords vibrations, rather than just one part.

The more intense the Compression Phase of the Gan-Tone cycle, the more intense the vibrations produced throughout the body. These vibrations are thrust to the resonators with increased force, resulting in a greater re-sounding of these vibrations in the resonators, or cavities, of the body, producing greater volume and bringing to light the clarity of harmonics and partials, which are integral, multiple sounds of the fundamental vibrations.

As the sound is freed and magnified through the Gan-Tone, other characteristics of the fundamental sound, such as, harmonics and partials, are more clearly heard.

The coordination of the jaw, larynx and body is the key to the fusion of pressure throughout the body, shifting the emphasis of pressure from the delicate vocal cords (a little less than 1/2" in the female) to the body and creating the most desirable condition for the application of the Gan-Tone. The imposition of the Gan-Tone Pulsations on the fundamental pitch fuses these vibrations through the body and grounds them at the rectal muscles, causing the pelvic bones to vibrate, and these vibrations are felt as pulsations at the Sphincter ani externus muscle by the singer.

The imposition of Gan-Tone Pulsations on the original vocal cords vibrations, therefore, extends the amplitude, or boundaries, of these vibrations from the area of the vocal cords to the body extremities, i.e., from the bottom of the torso to the head resonators, without changing the pitch being sung, and this amplitude becomes the structure of the sound.

The purpose of the Gan-Tone is to utilize the entire body, rather than its parts (vocal cords, larynx, lungs, thoracic diaphragm), as a vibrator and resonator of the original vocal cords sound, thereby augmenting singing energy.

A Gan-Tone Principle can, therefore, be summarized:
> The manifestation of the vibrating body depends upon the imposition of pressure through the body, by the singer, as Gan-Tones (pulsations), fusing and amplifying the original vocal cords sound throughout the body by uniting the vibrating parts and making the body a mass of vibrations and resonance resulting in maximum volume and causing the body to function as a bell.

The imposition of Gan-Tones on the natural vibrations of the voice increases singing energy by playing an important role in the following:

1- <u>Voice Projection</u> - As a result of downward pressure through the body, thrust is increased and felt in all directions but essentially in the opposite direction, i.e., from the bottom of the body to the head resonators, giving the sound greater projection.

2- <u>Breath Control</u> - As a result of downward pressure through the body, more efficient utilization of breath is made possible through increased magnitude of vibrations, producing more sound with less breath.

3- <u>Range</u> - As a result of the coordination of the jaw, larynx and body, which is essential for the imposition of the Gan-Tone, the natural impasses in the voice are eliminated enabling the singer to discover more range.

4- <u>Register</u> - As a result of the imposition of the Gan-Tone on the fundamental note, the singer ultimately realizes that register breaks, abrupt changes or cracks in the voice are due to lack of understanding, rather than initial changes in the vocal cords.

5- <u>Resonance</u> - As a result of the fusion of the vocal cords sound throughout the body, the magnitude of vibrations of the fundamental pitch is increased and reflected as resonance in the body cavities whose walls are also permeated by these vibrations which are transmitted through the walls and beyond.

6- <u>Volume</u> - As a result of the downward pressure through the body, the original vocal cords sound is fused through the body, and the magnitude of this fundamental pitch is increased resulting in increased resonance, which yields greater volume.

7- <u>Coloration</u> - As a result of varying the coordination of the Gan-Tone with the jaw, larynx and body, sound can be colored in innumerable ways as, for example, when the Gan-Tone is imposed to the bottom of the torso and the jaw is opened wide, the color of the sound will be characterized by depth.

8- <u>Sound Configuration</u> - As a result of the superimposed pulsation on the natural vibrations of the voice, uniformity of vibrations for any vowel is controlled for greater dimension.

9- <u>Brilliance</u> - As a result of the Gan-Tone,

more intense vibrations of a given frequency are evident in the singing line. Focus of these vibrations along with increased thrust to the resonators give greater scintillation and brilliance to the sound.

Procedure for the Application of the Gan-Tone Pulsation

II. The Gan-Tone, a superimposed pulsation on the natural vibrations of the singing voice, is applied as follows:

1- Activate the vocal cords to vibrate at a desired pitch by mentally directing a stream of air to the vocal cords. This pitch re-sounds in the walls of the larynx and in the body cavities, such as, the chest and head.

2- Fuse these fundamental vibrations of the vocal cords by exerting pressure from the vocal cords down through the body on the down-part of the Gan-Tone beat similarly as pressure is forced down through the body when vomiting or yawning.

3- At the same time, place the jaw in an unhinged position, down and back, achieving the same position of the jaw that is evident in the process of vomiting or yawning. This unhinged position of the jaw fuses the movable parts in the throat to the body, giving all the parts strength by uniting them with the whole body, and makes the maximum compression of vocal cords vibrations to the rectal-pelvic area possible.

4- Compress the body downward from the curve of the tongue to the hyoid bone, larynx, trachea, collar bone, chest, abdomen and on to the rectal-pelvic area. This process is evident in vomiting. Body compression carries the fundamental vocal cords vibrations down through the body anchoring them at the rectal-pelvic area. This fusion and compression of body parts and vocal cords vibrations occurs during the down-part of the Gan-Tone beat known as the Compression Phase. The fundamental vocal cords vibrations of a given note are amplified to their maximum on this down-part of the Gan-Tone beat. The degree of intensity of body fusion and the degree of body compression determine the amount of amplification of vocal cords vibrations and the degree of thrust to the resonators that these vibrations will achieve during the up-part of the Gan-Tone beat.

5- Thrust the amplified, fundamental vocal cords vibrations to the various resonators of the body through the open throat by means of the unhinged position of the jaw, which must be maintained for maximum freedom in the passage of these vibrations through the throat area.

It should be noted that the fusion and compression of body parts and vocal cords vibrations to the rectal-pelvic area, during the down-part of the Gan-Tone beat, appears to be occurring simultaneously with the thrusting of these vibrations to the resonators. However, fusion and compression precede thrust, since the degree of thrust is dependent on the degree of fusion and compression demonstrating Newton's Law of Action and Reaction which states that for every action there is an equal and opposite reaction.

6- Apply the Gan-Tone beat (down-part and up-part) on the fundamental vocal cords vibrations in slow motion, in the beginning, until the following is evident:

Skill is achieved in activating the vocal cords vibrations with minimal pressure, while amplifying these fundamental vocal cords vibrations to their maximum by fusion of body parts and compression of these vibrations to the rectal-pelvic area (down-part of the beat).

Skill is achieved in thrusting these amplified vocal cords vibrations from the rectal-pelvic basin to the resonators through an unhinged jaw position in order to insure maximum freedom in the passage of these vibrations through the throat area (up-part of the beat).

It should be noted that the penetration of the down-part of the Gan-Tone beat, which carries with it the fundamental vocal cords vibrations to the rectal-pelvic area requires much practice before maximum compression and penetration of these vibrations to this area are possible. The beginner will encounter difficulty in keeping the jaw unhinged and in penetrating to the bottom of the torso during the down-part of the Gan-Tone beat. He will also encounter difficulty in maintaining the unhinged position of the jaw during the thrusting of these vibrations to the resonators (up-part of the Gan-Tone beat), since the natural tendency is for the jaw to close.

Much practice is required to coordinate the unhinged jaw with the Compression and Thrust Phases of the Gan-Tone beat. This coordination is essential for the following reasons:

    a. The unhinged position of the jaw down and back, revealing recesses near the earlobes, along with the head tilted downward results in the fusion of body parts, such as, the curve of the tongue, hyoid bone, thyroid and cricoid cartilages. This fusion enables the vocal cords vibrations to be extended beyond the area of the larynx down to the bottom of the torso during the down-part, or Compression Phase, of the Gan-Tone beat, making the whole body the vibrator of the vocal cords vibrations.

    b. The unhinged position of the jaw is essential for maximum amplification of vocal cords vibrations, since any divergence from this unhinged position breaks the continuity of resilience, thus diminishing the amplification of vocal cords vibrations regardless of the amount of body compression achieved.

    c. The unhinged position of the jaw is essential for efficiency in the thrusting of these amplified vocal cords vibrations, since any divergence from this unhinged position diminishes the impact of the vibrations in the resonators, regardless of the strength of the thrust, as a result of the diminished payload of amplified vocal cords vibrations brought about by the lack of vibratory continuity in the body. If the jaw is not fused with the body, or unhinged down and back, the throat area becomes less resilient for the propagation and amplification of vocal cords vibrations, and these vibrations are absorbed in the throat area rather than amplified on the Compression Phase of the Gan-Tone beat. Since there are less vibrations involved in the Compression Phase, there are less vibrations to be thrust to the resonators on the Thrust Phase.

    d. The unhinged position of the jaw is essential for the release of pressure in the throat area in order to insure the unobstructed passage of the greatest quantity of magnified vocal cords vibrations.

The Role of the Jaw in the Imposition of the Gan-Tone on the Fundamental Vibrating Pitch of the Voice

III. The Gan-Tone, a superimposed beat which adds fusion and extends the structure of the fundamental pitch, is applied in coordination with the downward movement of the jaw and the vertical-elliptical mouth opening. As the need for a greater manifestation of Gan-Tones arises, and the intensity of the Gan-Tones increases, it is imperative that the jaw be down and back and resting on the Adam's apple in order to fuse the chin with the throat and body. This maximal jaw opening under pressure is dependent on mastery of the Pterygoideus lateralis muscle in the head, since this muscle is the prime mover of the mandible (lower jawbone).

As the pressure of the Gan-Tone is imposed down through the body and ultimately grounded in the rectal muscles and pelvic bones, the jaw must be down and back against the thyroid cartilage and as close to the collar bone of the body as possible in order to make the structure for the support of tone near the neck area very solid. In the process of increasing the imposed pressure of the Gan-Tone through the body, particularly in grounding the pressure to the bottom at the rectal-pelvic area, the singer must be sure that the jaw is resting securely in order that the sharp part of the jaw, i.e., the chin, is as close as possible to the solid parts of the larynx and collar bone. In this position, the burden of stress is assumed by the hard components, such as the bone of the chin and the hard cartilages of the larynx and collar bone.

As the chin moves toward the collar bone, the structure of the jawbone straddles and covers the larynx. Although the larynx is made up of ligaments, cartilages and muscles and can withstand much pressure, the jawbone does protect the larynx. When the jawbone approximates the collar bone, the structure produced relieves the throat and neck muscles of the strain imposed by the maintenance of loud sounds and deep body support.

If the jaw rides up during moments of great stress (loud, high, sustained sounds), pressure immediately shifts from the more solid structure of the bones to the less solid cartilages and muscles of the throat. As the more solid parts of the jaw, larynx, throat and collar bone spread apart, the structure that supports the sound becomes less solid, since the structure is now being supported by muscles, rather than bones, causing the sound to be less solid and vibrant. Continued pressure on the muscles, rather than bones, causes fatigue in the muscles and eventually results in the collapse of the structure.

When the Gan-Tone is properly applied, i.e., the imposition of a pulsation on the fundamental vocal cords vibrations (5 to 7 per second) down through the body to the rectal-pelvic area, the amount of pressure needed to maintain the jaw down and back to the thyroid cartilage is minimal, since the pressure is not localized by the intense holding of the jaw. Rigidity of the jaw, in the attempt to hold the sound solidly in the neck area, is no longer required and is replaced by the coordinated jaw movements down and back, as pressure increases in the throat. The pressure ordinarily focused on the vocal cords, larynx and throat muscles is now sustained by the body through fusion, enabling the muscles to join together the hard parts (jaw, larynx, collar bone) relieving the muscles of strain. Under these conditions, pressure is diffused down through the body, rather than being restricted in the neck area, leaving the muscles free to move the jaw down and back, with little effort, consequently enabling the pressure that would ordinarily harm the vocal cords, larynx and neck muscles to be focused on the rectal-pelvic area of the body during moments of great stress.

The essence of the Gan-Tone Pulsation is to minimize pressure in the vocal cords, larynx and throat, produced by loud, high, sustained sounds, and diffuse this pressure throughout the body to the rectal-pelvic basin, thereby involving the lower extremities through compression of vocal cords vibrations and fusion of body parts, while minimizing tension in the throat area.

The Gan-Tone, or superimposed pulsation, is neither a tremolo nor a vibrato, since the Gan-Tone ultimately employs the use of the whole body for dimensions of the Gan-Tone sound. The coordination of the jaw with the body is the key, or controlling factor, regarding the degree of vibrations the body as a whole can utilize as resonance. Under the stress of singing loud sounds the jaw must be down and back in order for the sound to reach its greatest dimension in volume. The jaw is like a door. If the dimensions of the object to be admitted through the door are small then the door opening can be small. If the dimensions are great then the door must be opened or the object collides with the door. If the singer wishes to emit a loud sound, the door, or jaw, must be widely opened to permit the free passage of the greatest quantity of vibrating sound and to disperse the buildup of pressure in the vocal cords, larynx and throat that would restrict the movement of sound vibrations.

When the jaw is not down, but is somewhere between opened and closed, under moments of great stress, the jaw, which is like a tap for the control of the flow of sound out of the throat during projection, cuts off the flow of sound and prevents the efficient utilization of the Gan-Tone. The laryngeal area (neck) is, physically, extremely narrow and, with improper use of the jaw, becomes even more constricted, causing a great deal of the sound to be restricted to this area, preventing its free movement, creating friction and causing the sound to become tight, resulting in a throaty, reedy, hard quality. This restricted sound, caused by the restricted movement of the jaw, i.e., not sufficiently downward during loud, high sounds, causes the vibrations that are re-echoed in the resonating cavities to manifest the characteristics of the restricted sound, i.e., tight, hard, reedy and lacking in volume.

A Gan-Tone Principle can, therefore, be summarized:
> The degree to which the Gan-Tone Pulsation is imposed through the body is commensurate with the degree to which the jaw is imposed downward on the larynx and body.

Maximum dispersement of pressure throughout the body is dependent on maximum application of the Gan-Tone with maximum opening of the jaw.

The more pressure is dispersed throughout the body, the greater the diffusion of sound to be colored, embellished and magnified.

Why the Gan-Tone is Neither a Vibrato nor a Tremolo

IV. The Gan-Tone, the vibrato and the tremolo are similar in that they are all pulsations. However, the Gan-Tone is neither a vibrato nor a tremolo since, unlike the vibrato and the tremolo, the Gan-Tone involves an orderly fusion of the fundamental vibrations of the vocal cords throughout the body. This fusion unites, in an orderly fashion, all the parts of the body in order that the body can become totally vibrant and resonant, making the stress that accompanies the production of vibrations and resonance dependent on the unification of the body and not on any particular throat muscles, nor on manipulation of the jaw, larynx and vocal cords for the size and shape of the sound.

The vibrato and the tremolo, on the other hand, both deal essentially with the manipulation of muscles, rather than fusion of the entire body as does the Gan-Tone. The function of the muscles in the vibrato and the tremolo is essentially for the manipulation of the beat on the vocal cords. As the vocal demand increases (loud, high, sustained sounds), the muscles can't sustain the burden of the increased pressure and are doomed to fatigue causing the eventual collapse of the vocal line. The function of the muscles in the Gan-Tone is to unify the parts of the body in fusion. By fusing the body, stress is shifted from the vocal cords and surrounding muscles to the bones, cartilages, ligaments and membranes of the entire body.

The vibrato is a slightly tremulous or pulsating effect on the vocal cords, controlled by the singer, for adding warmth and beauty to the tone or for expressing changes in emotional intensity. The extent of body involvement of the vibrato is confined to the vocal cords, two flat folds of ligaments, limiting the role of the vibrato to a superficial involvement of the body, thus curtailing its ability to add warmth and beauty to the tone and to express changes in emotional intensity.

The vibrato is usually considered an enhancement on the vocal line, but the tremolo is viewed as undesirable, although the degree of stability of both the vibrato and the tremolo determines to what extent they are alike, i.e., the degree to which muscles are manipulated in maintaining a steady vocal line determines when the vibrato becomes a tremolo. As the muscles fatigue with pressure or age, affecting their elasticity and responsiveness, the intervals in the frequency of the pulsations become exaggerated. As this exaggeration increases, the vocal line loses its steadiness and the vibrato now becomes a tremolo. Some people, for example, manifest, by nature, an evenly spaced, pleasant sounding vibrato, or pulsation, in the singing line. Others consciously impose a pulsation on the vocal line in order to enhance the sound. This action is essentially brought about by the vocal cords and adjoining muscles. Where the pulsation is evenly spaced, the result is a pleasant one, even though the sound may be limited in dimensions. However, when the production of a loud sound is required and the resultant stress is on throat muscles, the evenness of the sound can be maintained only as long as the coordinated response of the muscles is constant as, for example, an athlete, at a certain age, begins to lose his muscle responses making him unable to react effectively. The singer is subject to the same problem. When these muscle responses deteriorate, the ability to hold the sound intact, especially loud, high, sustained tones, diminishes, since the vocal line now manifests exaggerated intervals in the frequency of the pulsations, resulting in the tremolo.

Another way in which the vibrato can occur on the singing line is through the manipulation of the jaw on the vocal cords and surrounding muscles by moving the jaw up-and-down, voluntarily or involuntarily (jaw oscillation), producing a pulsation on the natural vibrations of the voice. The pulsation of the resultant vibrato manifests the same frequency which is evident in the up-and-down movement of the jaw, whether it is slight or excessive. While singing a certain frequency of sound, if the jaw moves twenty times in a five-second period, the singing line will manifest twenty vibratos at the same time. The degree to which this jaw-action is imposed can vary the volume of the sound.

The frequency of jaw movements up-and-down (action) is equal to the reaction of the vibrato on the singing line. Each movement of the jaw up-and-down is reflected in one beat of the vibrato. If this action results in a pleasant and even sound, it is acceptable. The ability to maintain the evenness of sound is commensurate with the ability of the throat muscles to hold a firm and stable vocal line. However, these muscles are eventually affected by strain or the aging process (as in the athlete) which deteriorate the quiver of the vibrato that was initially pleasant. A quiver implies a slight shake, making the interval in the frequency of the pulsation slight, therefore, not impairing the vocal line. This quivering in the vocal line, whether it is voluntary or involuntary, is referred to as the vibrato. When the interval in the frequency of the quiver increases, whether it is done voluntarily or involuntarily, the vocal line loses the evenness causing an exaggerated interval in the pulsations which is known as the tremolo.

The singing line that is imposed upon by the tremolo results in the evidence of two different pitches. The fundamental pitch that is required in the sustaining of a note is accompanied by an alternate, lower pitch in the process of each cycle of the tremolo, i.e., in the course of sustaining the vocal line on a particular pitch imposed upon by the tremolo, each tremolo is composed of the requisite pitch and an alternate pitch. Double pitches on the vocal line are a result of the following action:

>   When the mind imposes pressure on the vocal cords, at a particular pitch, the singer imposes the tremolo, while sustaining the fundamental pitch. When the singer imposes the thrust of the tremolo to maintain the intensity in the pitch of the beat, this thrust tone has the desired pitch. During the release phase of the tremolo, there is a release of tension in the throat muscles, larynx and especially in the vocal cords. Release of tension in the vocal cords produces a lower pitch. This lower pitch is the alternate pitch that accompanies the fundamental pitch and is the low phase of the tremolo cycle. The introduction of this alternate pitch impairs the vocal line.
>
>   Even though the interval of the frequency of the tremolo is exaggerated and accompanied by the alternate pitch, the vocal line could maintain a pleasant quality, which would be the result of a single pitch, if the low phase of each pulsation were not sung. Elimination of this low phase would produce one pitch.

The application of the Gan-Tone, which is a calculated pulsation on the natural vibrations of the voice, can eliminate the low phase of the tremolo thus removing this undesirable condition from the vocal line. Fusion results in the unification of the movable parts, such as the jaw, larynx and surrounding muscles, anchoring these parts to the bottom of the torso during maximum stress, thus taking the strain away from the vocal cords and surrounding muscles which would ordinarily weaken, when limited to the vibrato, and eventually cause the tremolo. The security produced by the fusion of the Gan-Tone to the bottom of the torso provides a strong structure for the thrust of the total vocal cords and body vibrations to be re-sounded in the head and body cavities, or resonators, thereby not allowing a slackening of the vocal cords on the down-part of the beat that produces the alternate pitch in the low phase, thus eliminating the tremolo, and highlighting the up-part, or Thrust Phase, of the beat, which eradicates the deviation from the fundamental pitch, thus eliminating the double frequency.

The Gan-Tone (pulsation) is imposed through the body to the rectal-pelvic area, thus involving the whole body as a vibrator and resonator of the vocal cords vibrations, extending the dimensions of these vibrations in a coordinated order from the vocal cords throughout the body. The effective application of the Gan-Tone beat is dependent on the fusion of the jaw, larynx and body with the jaw being the key to the effective fusion of the body during the imposition of the downward part of the pulsation known as the Compression Phase of the Gan-Tone cycle. The most intensive application of the Gan-Tone involves the fusion of the initial vocal cords vibrations through the body to the rectal-pelvic area, and the thrust of these vocal cords and body vibrations from this solid base to the head and body resonators with an intensity of resonance that is equal to the thrust, causing the Gan-Tone to involve the body as a bell.

However, it is fair to emphasize that in order to achieve

the suppleness in the body, for enabling it to function as a vibrator and resonator of vocal cords vibrations through the Gan-Tone imposition, much discipline is required.

Preoccupation with tension in the face, throat, shoulders, limbs, diaphragm and abdomen prevents the free movement of fusion to the rectal-pelvic area. The disciplining of the jaw down and back to fuse the larynx with the torso requires much attention in order to apply the direct movements which result in a minimum of muscular activity. The fusion of the jaw, larynx and body, ultimately, the result of the feather-touch, produces the greatest compression at the bottom of the torso, and the greatest thrust of the combined vocal cords and body vibrations to the resonators, giving sound unimaginable dimensions not possible with the vibrato, which is confined to adding a slightly tremulous or pulsating effect on the vocal cords.

It is obvious, therefore, that the scope of the Gan-Tone Pulsation is such that it can eliminate the tremolo and incorporate the desirable characteristics of the vibrato into the method that produces the greatest magnification of pulsations of the human voice, by giving the greatest clarification to the dominant fundamental and its integral parts.

The Role of the Gan-Tone in Voice Projection

V. Projection of sound, in the Gan-Tone Method of Voice Production, is dependent on the intensity and spontaneity with which the Gan-Tone (pulsation) is imposed on the natural vibrations of the voice and fused through the body to the rectal-pelvic area, intensifying vibrations which are thrust to the head and body resonators, such as, the chest, pharynx, mouth, postnasal and sinus cavities, resulting in greater resonance which is projected to the audience as voluminous sound.

The Gan-Tone transforms the concept of voice projection by focusing support at the pelvic-perineum diaphragm in the rectal-pelvic area which involves the complete torso and legs, as opposed to the popular belief which focuses support at the thoracic diaphragm, involving only half of the torso. The solidity of grounding support in the rectal-pelvic area adds greater stability and thrust to the total vocal cords and body vibrations, unattainable if the thoracic diaphragm were the focus of support. These magnified vibrations of the fundamental vocal cords sound, augmented by body vibrations, are re-sounded in the cavities of the body, resulting in augmented resonance.

Efficacious vocal projection involves the application of the Gan-Tone with the coordination of the jaw, larynx and body. The Gan-Tone is imposed on the fundamental pitch at a frequency determined by the singer. Every imposition of the Gan-Tone is fused to the vocal cords, surrounding area below and above the vocal cords and down to the pelvic area in one phase. During the down-part of the beat, pressure is exerted downward to the rectal-pelvic area, fusing the body to the bottom of the torso, while compressing vocal cords vibrations to this area. Simultaneously, vibrations that are not being fused are being transmitted through the vocal cords, larynx and surrounding muscles, and bones and cartilages of the throat and head. Collectively, these vibrations comprise the total vocal cords and body vibrations. The action of the downward part of the beat is the Compression Phase of the Gan-Tone cycle which essentially involves producing body vibrations that mix with the fundamental pitch of the vocal cords sound and fusing these vibrations to the Sphincter ani externus muscle. The intensity of this fusion determines the distance of the projected sound.

The pressure exerted down through the body on the Gan-Tone determines the amount of augmentation of vocal cords and body vibrations and the degree of thrust of these vibrations to the resonators. The stronger the pressure and vibrations through the body, the greater the thrust of vibrations to the resonators, and the greater the projection of sound. The action of imposing the Gan-Tone with intensity (fusion) produces the reaction of maximum thrust (projected sound).

The creation of fusion and thrust is analogous to pressing downward on a spring. The further the spring is contracted by pushing down on it, the more potential for thrust is created. At the peak of contraction, the depth of compression is reached, resulting in the greatest thrust of the spring, demonstrating Newton's Law of Action and Reaction which states:

Every action results in an equal and opposite reaction.

The fusion of vocal cords sound with body vibrations to the pelvic area results in an equal and opposite reaction to the head and body resonators.

One Gan-Tone cycle can, therefore, be summarized as follows:

1- The admission of air by inhalation.

2- The conversion and fusion of air as sound vibrations compressed to the rectal-pelvic area and throughout the body during the down-part of the beat, which comprises the action. (Compression Phase)

3- The stroke, or thrust, of the total vibrations to the resonators during the up-part of the beat, which is the equal and opposite reaction. (Thrust Phase)

It should be noted that the process of fusion to the rectal-pelvic area and consequent reaction to the resonators appear to be simultaneous actions, but they are not, since the principle of action and reaction is actually operating, i.e., the action precedes the reaction.

Maximum thrust of these vibrations to the cavities, or resonators, of the head and body results in a projected sound that manifests maximum brilliance, depth, vibrancy, buoyancy, security, stability, agility, flexibility, solidity, coloration, endurance, maximum volume, uniformity of the vocal line and carrying power.

This projected sound, produced with a maximum intensity of the Gan-Tone, is characterized by maximum brilliance, since the total vocal cords and body vibrations are thrust with the greatest intensity from the greatest depth of the body to the greatest height in the resonating cavities of the head.

This projected sound has maximum depth, since the deepest part of the torso, i.e., that part that connects the rectal-pelvic area and the legs, unifies the total body and provides the greatest source for grounded, supported, amplified sound.

This projected sound has maximum vibrancy, since the maximum application of the Gan-Tone achieves total body vibrations, i.e., vocal cords and body vibrations, through fusion.

This projected sound has maximum buoyancy, since the calculated pulsation of the Gan-Tone, with the coordination of the jaw, larynx and body, plus body fusion kick the sound, per beat, to the highest resonating points in the body with a calculated frequency of about 6 cycles per second, thereby maintaining the highest order of buoyancy.

This projected sound has maximum security, since the Gan-Tone fuses the vocal cords sound with the components of the larynx and throat, and these components, in turn, are fused downward through the chest, the diaphragm muscle, the abdomen and its viscera, fusing the vocal cords vibrations with the body vibrations to be grounded and supported at the rectal-pelvic area. The sound produced initially in the vocal cords, therefore, has the greatest security through the support of the entire body by fusion, which is the constant upon which the Gan-Tone beat is imposed.

This projected sound has maximum stability, as a result of the control of the frequency of the Gan-Tone and the coordination of the jaw in relation to pressure, fusion and volume of sound. The structure of the sound is increased by fusion which transfers the pressure that develops in the vocal cords and surrounding area to the entire body, making the initial area of vibrations (vocal cords and larynx) dependent on the body for steadiness and firmness which, in turn, makes the sound more continual and constant, since it is not dependent on the delicate vocal cords and surrounding muscles, thus preventing undesirable and unexpected changes in the sound.

This projected sound has maximum agility, since the Gan-Tone Method stimulates mental quickness in the application of principles, such as, the Jaw, Larynx, Body Fusion and the Gan-Tone Pulsation, which quickly unites all the parts of the body, giving a more instantaneous and resilient reaction to the projected sound. Singing energy is increased by the elimination of localized strain through the diffusion of pressure, creating a resilient body.

This projected sound has maximum flexibility, since the sound is not limited to the area of the vocal cords, thus decreasing the amount of tension, tightness, stiffness, reediness and hardness. By the diffusion of pressure through the body, the tone becomes more elastic. Control of this elastic quality through the body, from the Pterygoideus lateralis muscle in the head to the Sphincter ani externus muscle, permits a wide dimension of flexibility in the sound.

This projected sound has maximum solidity, since vocal cords vibrations are compressed to the pelvic-perineum diaphragm through the fusion of the jaw, larynx and body on the Compression Phase of the Gan-Tone beat. Grounding these vibrations at the rectal-pelvic area connects the torso to the floor by means of the legs insuring the maximum solidity in the support of the projected sound.

This projected sound manifests a greater dimension of coloration, as a result of the orderly fusion involved in the Gan-Tone. The sound of the original vibrating pitch of the vocal cords is fused to the surrounding muscles, cartilages of the larynx, throat muscles and bones, head, jawbone, collar bone, skull, chest bones and muscles, diaphragm, abdomen, spinal column, pelvic area and legs, etc. Wherever fusion occurs, from the vocal cords throughout the body, the quality of the sound is affected by the degree to which fusion penetrates the body as, for example, if the tone is limited to the area of the vocal cords and larynx, the sound will be hard and reedy. If the sound is fused to the area of the chest and diaphragm, the sound will be more mellow, buoyant and flexible. If the whole body is involved, the quality of the sound achieves maximum vibrancy, depth, support, resilience, resonance, etc.

This projected sound has maximum endurance, since the application of the Gan-Tone beat, by the fusion of the fundamental sound throughout the body, shifts emphasis from the vocal cords and surrounding area to other parts of the body in order that a minimum of pressure is exerted on the delicate vocal cords and surrounding muscles in the process of building volume. The application of the Gan-Tone makes the body, as a whole, sustain the burden of vocal stress, allowing the vocal cords to vibrate with a minimum of distortion, while maintaining sufficient pressure on the vocal cords and larynx to fuse with the body. Since stress, pressure, strength and support of the sound are removed from the vocal cords and determined, instead, by body involvement, the lasting quality of the vocal cords sound is prolonged and characterized by freshness and brightness, thus illustrating the essence of the Gan-Tone Method, which is to exert a minimal amount of pressure on the vocal cords sufficient to maintain fusion with the body, and to maximize the understanding that the body diffuses pressure and augments vocal cords vibrations, giving greater dimension and endurance to the vocal cords sound.

This projected sound is capable of maximum volume, since the whole body is hooked up by fusion during the Compression Phase of one Gan-Tone Pulsation, and the ultimate focusing point of the total pressure of this fusion is the rectal-pelvic area, maximizing vocal cords and body vibrations. Maximum fusion, applied as action down through the body, produces the maximum reaction of thrust to the head and body resonators, resulting in maximum re-sounding of vibrations, which becomes maximum volume. It is the repetition and strength of the Gan-Tone that determines the sustained sound, and the intensity with which the Gan-Tone is applied to the rectal-pelvic area that determines the volume of sound projected.

This projected sound is characterized by maximum uniformity of the vocal line. Since the Gan-Tone is a superimposed pulsation on the natural frequency of the voice, the control of these pulsations by the singer determines the evenness of vibrations of the singing line. In the Gan-Tone Method, the vocal line is made up of a series of Gan-Tones whose frequency is consciously regulated by the singer, thus enabling the singer to include the vibrato as part of the dimensions of the Gan-Tone Pulsations and to eliminate the tremolo or any other problem that would distort the uniformity of the vocal line.

This projected sound has maximum carrying power, since the Gan-Tone makes possible a maximum of vocal cords and body vibrations and maximum fusion of these vibrations to the rectal-pelvic area, creating maximum thrust, which results in maximum resonance through the maximum opening of the vocal hook, making possible the greatest carrying power of the projected sound.

The Role of the Gan-Tone in Breath Control

VI. Breath control, in the Gan-Tone Method of Voice Production, cannot be fully utilized unless the process of applying the Gan-Tone is fully understood and mastered. The spontaneity with which the Gan-Tone Pulsation and the vocal cords sound are fused through the body, with the simultaneous action of the jaw, larynx and body, determines the most efficient utilization of breath with the least amount of air pressure and strain on the vocal cords.

The fusion of the vocal cords sound through the body must be concomitant with the fusion of the jaw, larynx and body. The degree of speed with which the tone is fused, and the degree of pressure applied to this fusion to the rectal-pelvic area determine the degree of vocal cords and body vibrations produced, since the body now becomes a total vibrator functioning like a bell.

A Gan-Tone Principle can, therefore, be summarized:
> The degree of speed applied in the coordination of the Gan-Tone with the Jaw, Larynx, Body Fusion, and the degree of pressure applied to the fusion at the rectal-pelvic area determine the degree to which the body functions as a total vibrator, or bell, making the body an agent for the total conversion of breath into sound.

The orderly fusion of sound through the body, produced by the application of the Gan-Tone (down-part of the beat in the Compression Phase), and the pressure anchored at the rectal-pelvic area determine the amount of air that will be converted into vocal cords and body vibrations.

Elasticity and density in the contents of the bell are responsible for the vibrations and resonance produced.

The quality of elasticity, or resilience, implies the ability to spring back, or to recover size and shape after deformation. Density of a material implies its degree of compactness and impenetrability. The greater the density, or compactness, of a material, the greater its elasticity. Since elasticity implies compression and extension, the more compact, or dense, the material, the more it resists deformation, i.e., the more it is compressed, the more it springs back, and the more it is extended, or taut, the more it springs back, causing a greater amplification of vibrations. Fusion makes these vibrations more audible.

When a loosely compacted material is struck, vibrations are inaudible, since the material is deformed, absorbing the vibrations, rather than causing them to spring back. When striking a piece of cloth, as opposed to iron, vibrations are inaudible, since the cloth does not resist deformity and, therefore, absorbs the vibrations.

Similarly, the degree of elasticity and density that is created in the body determines the degree to which the body functions as a bell. Body fusion, in the Gan-Tone Method, creates elasticity and density in the body which produce the bell characteristics. Fusion, however, is a variable dependent upon the degree to which the singer applies it which, in turn, determines to what degree the body will function as a bell.

The two qualities of elasticity, i.e., compression and extension, are fully realized in the Gan-Tone Method. As fusion is applied through the body, to the greatest depth, i.e., to the rectal-pelvic area, the Compression Phase in the Gan-Tone Method is completed, causing a maximum of density, or compactness, in the body which, in turn, produces maximum elasticity, since the greater the compression to the rectal-pelvic area, the greater the extension, or springing back, of the body components which consitutes the up-part of the Gan-Tone beat, otherwise known as the Thrust Phase. At the height of the Compression Phase (down-part of the Gan-Tone beat), the singing line is elongated to its maximum as a string of sound stretching from the vocal cords to the rectal-pelvic area. The extension of this fused sound to this area followed by the Thrust Phase (up-part of the Gan-Tone beat) produces maximum air conversion into sound vibrations.

Very little air escapes unused, since the Gan-Tone harnesses the air immediately by fusion, enabling the singer to direct the air, or vibrations, to resonating areas of the head and body with a minimum of breath, making the whole body the source of breath control. However, the success of fusion (Compression Phase of the Gan-Tone cycle) depends upon the mastery of the jaw position down and back to insure fusion with the larynx, creating a strong structure in the irregular area of the vocal hook in order to protect the muscles and ligaments that are prone to stress.

It should be noted that the pelvic-perineum diaphragm in the rectal-pelvic area (not the thoracic diaphragm) is the <u>only source</u> from which sound can be directed throughout the body. The rectal-pelvic area connects downward to the legs and upward, in a direct line, through the abdomen, diaphragm, chest, trachea, larynx, throat and head. Only from the rectal-pelvic area can the fundamental sound be completely magnified in the resonating cavities of the body, thus making audible other integral parts, such as, harmonics, overtones, and other partials, of the fundamental pitch.

Only as breath is controlled in the form of vocal sound, fused through the imposition of the Gan-Tone and amplified throughout the body, can man thoroughly understand and utilize his body acoustics.

Therefore, the ability to sustain long phrases and loud sounds, to execute intricate passages and simultaneously shade, focus and color sounds, without running out of breath, does not depend on lung power, chest size, vocal cords strength or size of resonators, but, rather, on the unified body.

In the Gan-Tone Method, lung power is reinforced and amplified through body fusion, making the body the bellows for determining the vocal power of the singer. Through fusion of the Gan-Tone, the importance of the chest is controlled by the body at the rectal-pelvic area, which is the deepest source of support and the deepest involvement of breath control. The orderly fusion of sound augments the vocal cords by making the whole body the vibrator of vocal sound, shifting the importance of vocal cords strength in the constricted neck area to body power, thus removing the responsibility of volume from the delicate vocal cords to the body, thereby relieving the vocal cords, and surrounding area, of unnecessary strain.

The efficiency of resonators is most thoroughly realized not by their size, but by the most efficient conversion of breath through the instantaneous application of the Gan-Tone, which produces maximum vibrations, maximum thrust and maximum focus of the sound to such resonating areas as the base of the nose, back of the upper teeth, hard palate, pharynx, and nasal passage with a minimum of breath, resulting in a maximum utilization of breath as vibrating sound.

The Role of the Gan-Tone in Range

VII. Range, in the Gan-Tone Method of Voice Production, is most fully realized when the singing line (vocal cords vibrations) is imposed upon uniformly by a series of Gan-Tones (pulsations) that fuse and control the throat muscles in coordination with the fusion of the jaw, larynx and body to the bottom of the torso, making a solid structure for the entire range and eliminating natural impasses, enabling the singer to discover more range.

Through the most intense application of Gan-Tones, range manifests maximum volume as well as maximum support, i.e., the entire range reflects the depths of penetration of fusion to the rectal-pelvic area. Grounding of the vocal cords vibrations at the rectal-pelvic area results in the greatest control of thrust of these vibrations to the resonating areas of the head and body throughout the range, which can be summarized in the following Gan-Tone Principle:

> The amount of agility and spontaneity with which the Gan-Tone fuses vocal cords vibrations to the rectal-pelvic area, and the degree of pressure exerted to this area (Jaw, Larynx, Body Fusion) determine the strength of the thrust of these vibrations to the resonating cavities of the body which, in turn, determines the volume produced throughout the range.

To insure the deepest penetration of Gan-Tones to the bottom of the torso (Compression Phase, or down-part of the beat), the jaw must be completely fused with the larynx and body, i.e., the jaw must be unhinged down and back and resting against the thyroid cartilage close to the collar bone placing pressure on the solid structure of bones rather than muscles. This solidity of the fused area gives greater strength to sound and relieves the vocal cords and surrounding muscles of strain. If this fusion is not maintained, natural impasses, register changes, or breaks will occur in the ascending and descending scale, accompanied by fatigue in the throat area.

When the position of the jaw is idling, somewhere between opened and closed, the singer experiences difficulty in ascending the scale and, before reaching much range, experiences the natural impasse in the voice, preventing the singer from going any higher. The protruding jaw causes a constriction in the throat, like a faucet that turns off the flow of water, limiting the movement of sound in the ascending scale. This non-directed position of the jaw is analogous to placing the car in neutral gear. In this position, the car can go neither forward nor backward. However, by shifting to the driving gear, the car will move forward.

When impasses are evident in the ascending scale, they are eliminated by moving the jaw down and back, opening the throat and permitting an unobstructed passage of tone, thus revealing much greater range potential. Ignorance regarding the position of the jaw down and back while ascending the scale prevents many singers from realizing how much range they really possess. In most cases, the range potential is much greater than can possibly be imagined, since the natural impasse is evident in most voices and can be eliminated only by the understanding of the coordinated movements of the jaw, while imposing the Gan-Tone. Although most singers manifest an impasse, in varying degrees, this obstruction will continue until the coordination of the Jaw, Larynx, Body Fusion is mastered.

It should be noted that even though a singer can cover the gamut of the scale, from high to low, without any apparent impasse, a lack of understanding regarding the fusion of vibrations through the body greatly limits the dimensions of sound throughout the range, since the lack of fusion severs the laryngeal sound from the body, producing a devitalized voice.

The larynx is the original vibrator and resonator of the vocal cords vibrations and is not sufficient, of itself, to bear the pressure that accumulates in ascending the scale. Muscles, sustaining the increasing intensity in ascending the scale, collapse, preventing the singer from ascending further. Imposition of the Gan-Tone prevents pressure in the throat muscles, while ascending the scale, by shifting this pressure from these muscles to the body. As the beat (Gan-Tone) is imposed (Compression Phase) on the vocal cords vibrations, while ascending the scale, the fullness and depth of the tone is maintained, since these vibrations and the beat are grounded in the rectal-pelvic area, rather than in the neck.

The maximum thrust of vocal cords and body vibrations emanates from the greatest depths and passes through the larynx and pharynx freely because the jaw is down and back, opening the vocal hook to its utmost, not only delivering the greatest amount of vibrations to the resonators (Thrust Phase), but also enabling the singer to reach more range with security, since the natural impasse is eliminated. Furthermore, notes in any part of the range are sustained by the repetition of the frequency of the Gan-Tone which gives these notes depth, height, brilliance and buoyancy.

The Role of the Gan-Tone in Register

VIII. Register, in the Gan-Tone Method of Voice Production, is synonymous with the range of the vocal cords, from low to high sounds, produced without any change in quality, as a result of the application of the Gan-Tone Pulsation in coordination with the fusion of the jaw, larynx and body.

Breaks in the voice are completely eliminated with the application of the Gan-Tone, revealing that there are not several registers in the ascending scale, but only one register, which is the range of the voice.

As the singer ascends the scale, there is a change in tonal quality resulting in the popular belief that there are several registers in the voice. In order to eliminate these changes in tonal quality, mastery of the fusion of the jaw, larynx and body is essential. When this coordination is achieved, the imposition of the Gan-Tone beat on the vocal cords vibrations of the resultant even scale will further secure it from the possibility of tonal changes, i.e., register breaks.

The inability to coordinate sound out of the vocal hook, throughout the entire range from low to high, is responsible for the changes in tonal quality, while ascending the scale. As a singer pursues more range, the tonal quality abruptly changes, as a result of restriction of the vibrational movement in the constricted area of the throat. In order to relieve this constriction, which otherwise produces more restriction when ascending the scale, the jaw must be lowered down and back, since this downward movement of the jaw opens the throat. The opening of the throat dilates the constriction, creating more space. This increased space frees the restricted vocal line allowing the same quality of sound to be perpetuated throughout the ascending scale.

This unrestricted sound is now fused through the body concomitantly with the fusion of the jaw to the larynx and downward to the rectal-pelvic area of the body with the imposition of one Gan-Tone in the Compression Phase (down-part of the beat). In order to impose the Gan-Tone, the jaw must be down and back in order to fuse the vocal cords sound through the body to the rectal-pelvic area. At the same time, this unhinged position of the jaw assures an open throat which prevents restriction in the sound, insuring the elimination of tonal changes in the ascending scale by producing an even vocal line.

The imposition of the Gan-Tone and the fusion of the jaw, larynx and body, at the point in the scale where the tonal change would ordinarily occur, prevent this change by opening the throat and relieving the restriction.

The Compression Phase of the Gan-Tone cycle fuses this sound to the rectal-pelvic area making the resultant vocal cords and body vibrations very solid by shifting the emphasis of vocal support from the vocal cords to the bottom of the torso. This combination of vocal cords and body vibrations thrust from the rectal-pelvic area with maximum intensity to the resonators produces a maximum of resonance, which not only insures an even scale, but also, a maximum volume of open-throated, body-supported, resonant sound.

Associated with the different "registers" are the sensations of vibrations in different parts of the body, such as the chest and head. Awareness of vibrations in the chest area accompanies the chest register popularly believed to be the lower range of the voice, and awareness of vibrations in the head are believed to be the result of the higher range.

In the Gan-Tone Method, these chest and head vibrations do not occur at different parts of the range but are present in all parts of the range. Although the lower notes vibrate more prominently in the chest, as a result of the lower frequency, they also vibrate simultaneously in the head. In ascending the scale, there is an orderly transference of focus of these vibrations from the chest to the head as a result of increased frequency, intensity and thrust, making the sensation of vibrations prominent in the head, even though the vibrations are also present in the chest area. Furthermore, the imposition of the Gan-Tones causes the whole body to vibrate the frequency of the Gan-Tone Pulsations, regardless of the pitch of the notes.

Actually, the following Gan-Tone Principle can be stated:

Vibrations propagate and dominate in various parts of the body and throughout the whole body in proportion to the pitch of the sound and the intensity of the application of the Gan-Tone.

Another reason for the belief in "registers" is the singer's inability to sustain loud, high sounds without a change in quality referred to as pressure breaks. When the singer cracks, the laryngeal contact is broken, revealing the pure vocal cords sound, which causes an abrupt change in quality resulting in a devitalized sound, since it is devoid of the vibrations and resonance provided by the larynx. Although the pitch is the same, the amplitude of vibrations diminishes, even though the body support for the tone is constant, since the support is only involved in the pure vocal cords sound which is not amplified by the vibrating larynx.

In the Gan-Tone Method, pressure breaks and cracks in the voice are overcome through the fusion of the vocal cords sound through the fused larynx and jaw and downward through the body. This fusion relieves the vocal cords, larynx and surrounding neck muscles of unnecessary pressure by shifting this pressure to the body. During the production of any sounds, but especially loud, high ones, if pressure is isolated in throat muscles, due to a lack of body fusion, the muscles that connect the vocal cords sound solidly to the larynx, and the muscles that control the movements of the larynx fatigue and spasm, causing the larynx to be divorced from the vocal cords, thus collapsing the structure of the vocal line. Since the vocal cords and larynx can move up and down, lack of proper anchoring of these parts to the body makes them vulnerable to strain, spasm and collapse which results in the abrupt change in tonal quality. In the Gan-Tone Method, this instability of parts is corrected by grounding the vocal cords and larynx to the body, thereby placing the stress of sounds, especially loud, high ones, on the solid body, rather than on muscles. This grounding has its foundation at the rectal-pelvic area by fusing the vocal cords sound through the larynx and body. With the downward position of the jaw, the muscles that control the movements of the vocal cords and larynx are stabilized by being fused to the body, giving the vocal cords vibrations vibrant continuity to the bottom of the torso.

The spontaneous application of the Gan-Tone Pulsation immediately establishes the security of the vocal line and perpetuates it by the repetition of the Gan-Tone cycle. Whenever the Gan-Tone Pulsation is applied, the fundamental pitch of the vocal cords sound is fused to the larynx and surrounding muscles protecting the vocal cords and these muscles from strain. Fusion of the vocal cords ligaments with the laryngeal cavity and adjoining laryngeal muscles and cartilages, along with the downward movement of the jaw create compression in this area, causing all these parts to be united in a natural and orderly procedure. Membranes and muscles, which under stress become strained, are now protected by the union of the jaw with the body. The Gan-Tone cycle consists of one beat in two phases. The Compression Phase is the down-part of the beat through the body which generates and propagates vibrations. The Thrust Phase is the up-part of the beat which projects the vibrations to the head and body resonators. The repetition of this Gan-Tone cycle (5 to 7 per second) diffuses pressure and vibrations throughout the body and re-sounds these vibrations in the resonators.

It is the pull and strain in the throat muscles that bring fatigue, instability and collapse to the vocal line. The application of every beat of the Gan-Tone through the body transfers the responsibility of support from throat muscles to the body insuring a constant security of the vocal line, thus preventing pressure breaks and cracks in the voice.

The Role of the Gan-Tone in Resonance

IX. Resonance, in the Gan-Tone Method of Voice Production, is demonstrated, to the highest degree, with the application of the Gan-Tone Pulsation which produces the greatest degree of conductivity in the body for vocal cords vibrations and the greatest degree of support and thrust of these vibrations to the resonators, resulting in maximum resonance.

The body's role as a conductor of vibrations that emanate from the vocal cords is fully utilized with the unification of the head, larynx and body. The effectiveness of this union is dependent upon the position of the jaw which functions as a circuit maker for conductivity. As the jaw is moved downward to the larynx (Adam's apple) and collar bone, the circuit of the head, larynx and body attains its strongest connection. Any divergence of the jaw from this downward position, especially during moments of great pressure, weakens this circuit. The imposition of the Gan-Tone beat on the natural vibrations, or pitch, of the vocal cords sound fused through this circuit, with maximum pressure, results in the anchoring of this pressure and vocal cords vibrations to the rectal-pelvic area, producing the ideal condition for enabling the body to function as a maximum conductor of maximum vibrations throughout the body, below and above the vocal cords.

During the Gan-Tone cycle of one beat, the body provides conductivity, amplification, support, thrust and resonance. The imposition of the Gan-Tone is the Compression Phase of the cycle, or down-part of the beat. As the Gan-Tone is imposed on the vocal line and fused through the body to the rectal-pelvic area, compression results which provides the greatest anchoring and support for the vocal cords vibrations. This compression (down-part of the beat) also provides the greatest amount of amplification and thrust of vocal cords vibrations, from the bony area of the pelvis throughout the body. This thrust takes the vibrations below and above the pelvic area, i.e., to the legs, and especially to the resonating chambers of the head and body (up-part of the beat).

A Gan-Tone Principle can, therefore, be stated:

> The degree of spontaneity and intensity of the Gan-Tone application determines the intensity of compression of the vocal cords vibrations to the bottom of the torso.
>
> The degree of intensity of this compression determines the degree of amplification, support and thrust of these vibrations to the resonators of the body which, in turn, determines the degree of resonance.

The effectiveness of the resonators is dependent upon

the degree of intensity, thrust and focus of the fused vibrations, since the power with which these vibrations are delivered to the resonators determines the degree to which they will result in resonance. The greater the intensity of the thrust of the vibrations, the greater the utilization of the body as a hammer for ringing the bells (resonators). Thrust is dependent on the intensity with which the Jaw, Larynx, Body Fusion is applied simultaneously with the fusion of the vocal cords vibrations to the rectal-pelvic area. However, the effectiveness of the Jaw, Larynx, Body Fusion is dependent upon the spontaneity with which these body parts are coordinated. The quicker the fusion of the jaw, larynx and body with the imposition of the Gan-Tone on the vocal cords vibrations to the rectal-pelvic area, the more definitely the body, as a hammer, wraps the bells (resonators). The body is the battery that supplies the force to the current (vibrations) which permeates omnidirectionally, or spherically, from the vocal cords but is audibly evident in the resonators (bells) to the degree that the body (battery) supplies the force.

Sound vibrations propagate omnidirectionally, or spherically. Although vocal cords vibrations propagate spherically, the transmission of these vibrations is affected by various mediums, such as, air, membranes, muscles, cartilages, bones, and combinations of these mediums. As vibrations extend outwardly, they pass through the medium of air and re-sound in the chest cavity, bronchial tubes, trachea, larynx, pharynx and head cavities. The portions of the expanding spheres of sound vibrations that are not carried by the air are absorbed by the mediums they strike. The degree of absorption is dependent upon the degree of density and elasticity of these mediums, as, for example, muscles are less dense and elastic than bone and, therefore, absorb the vibrations. These vibrations would ordinarily be lost in the production of resonance. With the application of the Gan-Tone, however, these vibrations are fully utilized, thus contributing to greater resonance.

Through the Compression Phase of the Gan-Tone beat, mediums that would absorb vibrations now play the opposite role and propagate them instead. As a result of the Compression Phase, such mediums as muscles, membranes, cartilages and bones become more dense and, therefore, more elastic enabling these mediums to magnify vibrations rather than absorbing them. As the Compression Phase descends, in a piston-like action, from the vocal cords, larynx and surrounding muscles, density, elasticity and vibrations increase. When maximum compression is reached, maximum density and elasticity are also attained, which result in maximum body vibrations. This maximum compression also gives maximum support and ultimate thrust from the bones of the rectal-pelvic area.

These vibrations, that would ordinarily be lost without the application of the Gan-Tone, are now further amplified in the resonators of the head and body, producing increased resonance which results in maximum sound. The amplified focus to various areas of the resonators, such as, behind the upper teeth on the hard palate, the roof of the mouth, the soft membranous posterior part of the hard palate, the pharynx, the base of the nose, the nasal-pharyngeal tract opening, the bridge of the nose, the sinus cavities and the chest cavity, magnifies the tonal qualities characteristic of these areas that would ordinarily not be discernible to the ear, along with harmonics and other integral parts of the fundamental vibrations. This amplified focus also enables the sinus cavities to be utilized to their utmost as resonators of vibrations, with the septum that separates the frontal sinus cavities providing the peak in the pyramidal structure of resonance.

In the Gan-Tone Method, the pyramidal structure of resonance consists of the Compression Phase of the Gan-Tone cycle (down-part of the beat) which compresses the vocal cords vibrations to the rectal-pelvic area, the foundation for the structure of vocal cords vibrations and resonance and, also, the base of the pyramid. This rectal-pelvic area provides the greatest support for the compression and thrust of vocal vibrations to be reflected throughout the resonators (up-part of the beat). The resultant resonance culminates at the apex of the pyramid which is the septum that divides the frontal sinus cavities. This septum is the highest and most intense recipient of vocal cords vibrations and resonance. The thrust of the Gan-Tone applies the force and direction from the rectal-pelvic area that progressively fuses vocal cords and body vibrations and resonances upward through the chest, larynx, pharynx, mouth, and nasal cavities and culminates in the frontal sinuses, with the septum between the two sinuses being the highest recipient of vibrations and resonance. Of course, this apex of the pyramid (septum) is fully utilized only with the most intense application of the Gan-Tone Pulsation which provides the maximum thrust necessary to completely vibrate and resonate the highest point of the pyramid. This septum, or partition, between the frontal sinuses is the highest sound-producing area in the human.

Since the resonators are located in different parts of the body, as, for example, the chest cavity is situated below the sinus cavities, sound vibrations are delivered more effectively with less intensity of thrust to this cavity (chest) as opposed to the sinus cavities, since the chest cavity is closer to the rectal-pelvic area, the ultimate support-and-thrust-control source of the vibrations.

A Gan-Tone Principle can, therefore, be stated:

> The location of the resonators in relation to the source of support and thrust, i.e., the rectal-pelvic area, determines the degree of thrust needed for effectively resonating the cavities (resonators).
>
> The closer the resonators to the rectal-pelvic area, the less need for intensity of the Gan-Tone application.
>
> Conversely, the farther the resonators from the rectal-pelvic area, the greater the need for intensity of the Gan-Tone application.
>
> Maximum intensity of the Gan-Tone application results in maximum vibrations that are thrust with maximum efficiency to all the resonators of the body resulting in maximum resonance, enabling the body to function as a bell.

The Role of the Gan-Tone in Volume

X. Volume, in the Gan-Tone Method of Voice Production, is the maximum fullness, or quantity, of tone resulting from maximum vibrations and resonance produced through maximum body fusion by the most swift and intense application of Gan-Tone Pulsations, making the body function as an extension of the vocal cords, causing the entire body to vibrate and resound like the bell. Vibrations and resonance are at a maximum when the body functions as a bell, thus producing maximum volume.

Application of the Gan-Tone Pulsation develops the body as a bell, and continuous application of this Pulsation perpetuates the body's role as a bell in generating maximum vibrations and resonance. Although there are individual differences in body components, such as, the size of the cavities, chest, nose, head, etc., these differences are not fully exploited without the involvement of the Gan-Tone. A singer, for example, may have large resonating cavities but, if the Gan-Tone Pulsation is not utilized, maximum vibrations cannot be produced. Since the resonators do not have maximum vibrations to resonate, they are not being fully exploited. On the other hand, a singer with smaller resonators who is utilizing the Gan-Tone, and, therefore, producing maximum vibrations, is fully harnessing the smaller cavities to greater advantage.

The speed and intensity with which fusion maximizes the rectal-pelvic area of the body as a thrusting agent for harnessing the body as a vibrating hammer, and the frequency of the imposition of the Gan-Tone Pulsation determine the impact of this hammer, per pulsation, on the resonators, which results in continual re-sounding of maximum vibrations, producing maximum volume and making the singing line a uniform repetition of Gan-Tone Pulsations. The frequency with which these Gan-Tones are applied is determined by the singer. Spontaneous application of the Gan-Tone produces instant compression, support and intensity, and they are grounded at the rectal-pelvic area. Swift application of the Compression Phase of the Gan-Tone (down-part of the beat) determines the degree of speed and force of the Thrust Phase (up-part of the beat) which, in turn, determines the impact of the vibrations to the head and body resonators.

Essentially, the Gan-Tones, i.e., superimposed pulsations on the fundamental vibrations that emanate from the vocal cords, fuse these vocal cords vibrations through the body to its lowest extremity (rectal-pelvic area and below) and fling them to its highest extremity (septum with its adjoining frontal sinus cavities), thus fully utilizing all the body components as vibrators and resonators, making the body a complete bell. Without the application of the Gan-Tone, body components, i.e., vibrators (vocal cords, larynx, muscles, bones, etc.) and resonators (nasal cavities, pharynx, mouth, etc.), function in isolation, since they are not fused, making the singer unable to realize their role in enabling the body to function as a bell.

Volume potential cannot possibly be fully realized with the current belief that the thoracic diaphragm is the main source of breath control. Diaphragmatic breath control, with, or without, the assistance of chest-cavity expansion as a bellows in providing the intensity of air to the vocal cords for producing amplitude of vibrations, greatly limits volume potential according to the Gan-Tone Method. The downward movement of the diaphragm onto the abdomen tends to expand the abdominal walls. This diffusion ultimately creates an unstable, indefinite, debilitated support for voice projection, thus limiting the volume potential. In the process of speaking, the diaphragm aids more appropriately in projecting the voice. Where a limited amount of singing sound is required, diaphragmatic support may also be sufficient, since a great degree of volume, or power, is not necessary.

However, when the need arises to fully exploit volume potential through body involvement, the thoracic diaphragm becomes a part of the sound-producing mechanism, and not the ultimate source, yielding its importance to the pelvic-perineum diaphragm in the rectal-pelvic area. Concentration at the thoracic diaphragm for vocal projection creates an awareness of only half the body, isolating and dividing the lower half, thereby diminishing the projecting power of the body which prevents the body cavities from being fully utilized as resonators.

In the Gan-Tone Method, fusion of the whole body in an orderly process (which includes the thoracic diaphragm) to the rectal-pelvic area on the Gan-Tone Pulsation carries vibrations omnidirectionally, below and above the glottis and vocal cords, making these fused areas more vibrant. As this fusion is carried to its ultimate at the rectal-pelvic area, body vibrations are magnified to their utmost vibrating and resonating the extremities of the body, from the floor to the head, naturally including the sinus cavities, thus rejecting the following statement:

> It is conventionally believed that sinus tone production is insignificant since the air sinuses of the head are ineffective as a result of their limited and variable sizes, unfavorable locations and extremely small openings.

The degree to which the resonators, or cavities, of the body resonate is dependent on the degree of force with which vibrations are projected to the resonators. In projecting from the thoracic diaphragm, resonators that are farthest removed from this area, such as, the sinus cavities, are ineffective in producing resonance, since this diaphragm is unable to generate sufficient vibrations and projection of these vibrations. However, the compression produced by the Gan-Tone at the pelvic-perineum diaphragm (whose focal point is the Sphincter ani externus muscle) in the rectal-pelvic area magnifies body vibrations and produces the intensity of thrust from this diaphragm necessary to vibrate the farthest resonators, such as, the sinuses, making the septum that partitions the frontal sinus cavities the highest point for vibrations, causing maximum resonance in these frontal sinus cavities, regardless of their size.

In the Gan-Tone Method, there are two points of focus in the production of sound. The first point of focus is the Sphincter ani externus muscle which receives a nucleus of vibrational energy as a consequence of compression (down-part of the Gan-Tone beat). The second point of focus is the nucleus of resonance at the septum and cavities of the frontal air sinuses, as a result of the thrust of this vibrational energy to the resonators (up-part of the Gan-Tone beat).

These two points constitute the boundaries of depth and height (amplitude) of the dominant fundamental.

The control of these two points through the Gan-Tone Pulsation, made possible with the Jaw, Larynx, Body Fusion, causes the body to function as a cylinder, or barrel, for directing and cannonading a nucleus of vibrant energy to the head resonators.

The Role of the Gan-Tone in Coloration

XI. Coloration of sound, in the Gan-Tone Method of Voice Production, is the scope of tonal pigmentation in human voices dependent on the emphatic mixture of vibrations and resonance, which can only be achieved by the imposition of the Gan-Tone Pulsation. Mentally focusing these vibrations to vibrant and resonant areas throughout the body gives a wide variety of coloration potential to the emitted sound.

Spontaneity and intensity in the application of the Gan-Tone to a particular area of the body defines the clarity of the vibrations in that area and affects and colors the re-sounding of the fundamental pitch in the body cavities.

Various substances in the body, such as, bones, cartilages, tendons, muscles, membranes, fluids and air, provide mediums for vibrations to become more vibrant. The body can be considered a bell which is composed of many laminations of various substances which, in themselves, are mediums for the propagation of vocal cords vibrations. These mediums, when fused, produce the total vibrations which are reflected in the tonal quality of the bell (body). The body as a bell has a greater advantage than the man-made bell, since mental focus, and the intensity of this focus, create innumerable combinations of mediums through fusion of the fundamental vocal cords vibrations by the application of the Gan-Tone, coloring the vibrations in countless ways which, in turn, are reflected in the coloration potential of the emitted sound. The man-made bell, however, is inanimate and fixed and, therefore, limited to the basic mediums of its contents which, by their rigidity, cannot be varied, greatly limiting the coloration of its vibrations and resultant resonance which, in turn, greatly limits the coloration of its emitted sound. The human, on the other hand, can modify tonal color at will by the spontaneous focus of the Gan-Tone which vibrates, by fusion, a particular medium for a particular color.

The agility with which the Gan-Tone Pulsation is imposed through the body determines the effectiveness of the fused laminations of the various mediums. As the fundamental vocal cords vibrations are fused downward, through the downward movement of the jaw resting on the larynx, more areas are fused with the vocal cords vibrations. As this fusion continues downward to the rectal-pelvic area, these vibrations pass through many mediums, such as, muscles, cartilages and bones. The area of focus of this fusion of vocal cords vibrations is mandated by the mind and occurs during the Compression Phase of the Gan-Tone (down-part of the beat). Where the concentration of focus occurs determines the color of the vibrations as, for example, if the focus is on the chest area, during fusion, the vibrations are affected by such mediums as bones, ligaments and muscles. Bones give more brilliance to vibrations. Muscles and ligaments give less brilliance, since they are softer than bone. The vibrations from these varied mediums, therefore, reflect a combination of brilliance from the resilient medium of bone and a more mellow quality from the softer mediums of muscles and ligaments.

The degree of intensity with which the Gan-Tone is imposed through the various mediums of the body determines the degree of clarity regarding the coloration characteristics of each medium which are distinctly defined, as long as the Gan-Tone beat is efficiently imposed, i.e., when the Gan-Tone is applied with spontaneity and intensity, the vibratory characteristics of each medium are magnified accordingly. Similarly, the vibratory characteristics of the body are amplified to the highest degree through maximum fusion, reflecting the total coloration characteristics peculiar to the various mediums of the body. When vocal cords vibrations are imposed upon by the Compression Phase of the Gan-Tone, they are fused through the various mediums and are brought to the bottom of the torso. In their movement through the mediums, these vocal cords vibrations collect the coloration characteristics of each medium, all of which are grounded at the rectal-pelvic area and are transmitted to the resonators of the body during the Thrust Phase (up-part of the beat). The degree of their thrust is dependent on the intensity of the Compression Phase.

During the Thrust Phase, all these amplified vocal cords vibrations are re-sounded in the body cavities with great impact, since they have been launched from the solid basin of the body. This intense impact of amplified vocal cords vibrations on the resonators results in maximum resonance which produces a maximum scope of coloration. The singer, therefore, as a result of the Gan-Tone imposition, has access to the greatest amount of vibrations through compression, the greatest amount of thrust from the rectal-pelvic area, and the greatest amount of resonance. The singer also has maximal access to the resonators for mixing vibrations and resonance to determine the tonal colors of the projected sound. The resonant characteristics of each resonator are distinctly different as, for example, the resonant characteristics of the oral cavity differ from those of the pharyngeal cavity and the sinus cavities, etc. By directing vocal cords and body vibrations to various areas of the resonators, features of each resonator are more clearly defined by amplification.

Without the application of the Gan-Tone, magnification of vibrations is not possible, since the entire body is not vibrating. Therefore, the resultant resonance is limited which, in turn, limits the scope of tonal-color potential. The delineation of the distinct characteristics of each resonator is never realized, since amplification of vibrations does not occur, thus preventing the magnification of resonant characteristics.

A Gan-Tone Principle can, therefore, be stated:

> The degree of amplification of vibrations is dependent on the degree of Gan-Tone application which, in turn, determines the degree of magnification of the resonant characteristics of each resonator.

Through the maximum application of the Gan-Tone Pulsation, the greatest amount of vibrations and thrust can be utilized which, in turn, yields the most efficient involvement of the resonators in resonating these vibrations thus enriching the tonal mixtures, which result in a wide range of tonal colors in the emitted sound. It should be noted that as maximum vibrations and resonance are attained, through the imposition of the Gan-Tone, all the tones of the fundamental sound, i.e., the fundamental tone, harmonics and other partials, are also magnified and, therefore, more easily delineated and heard.

Coloration of sound, such as, messa di voce, which is the swelling of sound from soft to loud and back to soft, can be demonstrated to its greatest dimension with the Gan-Tone, through the Jaw, Larynx, Body Fusion which fuses the vocal cords vibrations, from the most limited involvement of the vocal cords (softest dimension) to the deepest involvement at the rectal-pelvic area (loudest dimension) and back to the least involvement of the body which is at the vocal cords (softest dimension). Messa di voce is considered a vocal feat, but with the Gan-Tone application, it becomes a relatively simple exercise. Muscle control in the neck is utilized, at present, to perform this vocal feat, and it usually takes many years to develop these muscles. This muscle control, confined to the neck area, limits the coloration dimension of the sound. In the Gan-Tone Method, however, control of the messa di voce is transferred to the body, rather than isolated at the neck muscles, giving greater dimension to the coloration potential through the Jaw, Larynx, Body Fusion and compression of vocal cords vibrations to the rectal-pelvic area.

In the Gan-Tone Method, coloration of sound, such as, the messa di voce, is produced in the following manner:

> As tone is expanded or contracted, i.e., as volume is increased or decreased, the movement of the jaw downward, by placing it, without rigidity, as close as possible to the Adam's apple and collar bone, fuses the throat components (tongue, jaw, larynx and trachea) with the body to provide the strongest structure for the widest dimension of tonal coloration. As volume is increased, this position creates the widest throat opening for the greatest emission of vibrations. Fusion of the jaw, larynx and body makes possible the maximum utilization of body vibrations in the augmentation of the fundamental vocal cords vibrations, the maximum compression of these vibrations to the rectal-pelvic area, and the greatest amount of thrust of these vibrations through the unrestricted throat opening to be freely focused and guided in the different areas of the resonators for the maximum expansion of resonance in the coloration of the messa di voce.

Since many parts in the throat are movable, omnidirectionally, such as, the larynx, throat muscles, cartilages, hyoid bone and jaw, it is imperative that the singer fuse these components to each other and to the body without rigidity for the following reasons:

1. To minimize pressure on any particular component

2. To prevent any part from drifting away from its fused position with the body which would break the continuity of body vibrations

3. To prevent constriction of the throat opening which would restrict the movement of vibrations

causing a tight, reedy sound, limiting the colorable dimensions of this sound

Although many singers perform the messa di voce with a floating position of the jaw and larynx, the ultimate stability and coloration is minimal, since the control of this skill is focused in the neck area. As the pressure builds in the process of coloring the sound (increasing volume), these parts (jaw and larynx) must be fused with the body in order to prevent the focusing of pressure in the neck which isolates this area from the body, creating a weak link. This riding-up of pressure not only separates the larynx from body fusion, focusing undue strain on the larynx and surrounding muscles, but also creates constriction in the throat opening, restricting the movement of vibrations. The farther away the larynx moves from the fused body, the thinner the tonal coloration, since the source of amplified vocal cords vibrations, which is the body, is progressively becoming uninvolved.

Furthermore, fusion of the components protects weaker parts, such as, muscles and membranes, since the harder parts (bones) provide the structure for body involvement. The muscles, having performed their function in uniting the stronger parts (bones), can rest securely within the structure. As body fusion diminishes, the muscles no longer have the protection of the body and become the target for stress and strain, greatly limiting the dynamic movement of vibrations which, in turn, restricts the colorable dimensions of the messa di voce.

Therefore, the dimensions of the swelling and diminishing sound in the messa di voce are equal to the descending pressure created by the Jaw, Larynx, Body Fusion and the Gan-Tone Pulsation. The greater the fusion through the body, the greater the compression of vocal cords and body vibrations to the pelvic-perineum diaphragm, generating and directing more vibrational energy to the resonators for greater dimensions in the messa di voce.

The Role of the Gan-Tone in Sound Configuration

XII. Sound configuration, in the Gan-Tone Method of Voice Production, is the control of the greatest dimensions of the varicolored sound patterns produced in the process of singing vowels and consonants made possible through the imposition of the Gan-Tone on the fundamental vocal cords vibrations.

Regardless of the vowels and consonants being sung, the more instantaneous the pronunciation of the consonant, followed by the instant application of the Gan-Tone Pulsation on the vowel, the greater the dimension and duration of the sound, as a result of the maximum amplification of vibrations produced through instant body fusion, due to the speed of the Gan-Tone application and the lack of consonantal interference in the singing line.

The imposition of the Gan-Tone Pulsation gives the greatest dimensions to the vibrations, i.e., depth and height, as well as omnidirectional dimensions from the vocal cords. Jaw, Larynx, Body Fusion and the imposition of the Gan-Tone on the fundamental vocal cords vibrations to the rectal-pelvic area determine the omnidirectional dimensions of these vibrations.

Total body vibrations are controlled from the rectal-pelvic area through the involvement of the Jaw, Larynx, Body Fusion and the Gan-Tone imposition to this area, extending the vocal cords vibrations to the bottom of the torso.

The Gan-Tone application gives the greatest amount of support to these fused vibrations, since the basin of the rectal-pelvic area provides the greatest foundation for the support and launching of vibrations throughout the body, including the spinal cord and legs.

The fundamental vocal cords vibrations are fused by tension on the vocal cords to the surrounding muscles and larynx and further fused to the torso by placing the jaw (chin) close to the Adam's apple (laryngeal button) which, in turn, approximates the collar bone in order to stabilize the movable parts of the throat to the body. This fusion is grounded at the basin of the rectal-pelvic area during the Compression Phase (down-part of the beat) of the Gan-Tone Pulsation. It is from this basin that the greatest reaction to this compressive action occurs, i.e., the maximum thrusting of vocal cords and body vibrations, which is the Thrust Phase of the Gan-Tone Pulsation (up-part of the beat), producing the greatest impact in all the body resonators.

Maximum vibrations produced by the Gan-Tone application enable the singer to form a great variety of sound patterns. The focus and impact of these maximum vibrations to the different areas of the various resonators are made possible through the thrusting of these vibrations from the rectal-pelvic area (Thrust Phase, or up-part of the Gan-Tone beat). The body, through the imposition of the Gan-Tone, becomes the battery that furnishes the power for transmitting these vibrations to the resonators to be re-sounded and shaped into vowels and consonants with the aid of the nostrils, mouth, jaw, lips, teeth, tongue, uvula and throat muscles. Any divergence of body fusion upward from the rectal-pelvic area (abdomen, diaphragm, chest, neck) diminishes the dimensions, support and thrust of vocal cords vibrations, and weakens the focus and amplification of these vibrations in the body resonators, leaving the vocal cords vibrations to be focused, essentially, by the stream of air impinging on the vocal cords thus causing these vibrations to resound in the body cavities with a minimum of resonance, definition and coloration. The body involved as a battery, however, provides great thrust which can focus the vibrations in any area of the resonators.

The dominance of vowels, the mixture of consonants and vowels, and the dominance of consonants in the production of voice are explored to the utmost in the Gan-Tone Method by the Jaw, Larynx, Body Fusion and the imposition of the Gan-Tone on the fundamental pitch of the vocal sound.

The greatest dimensions of vocal sound, i.e., highest, loudest and most brilliant, are produced by the spontaneous articulation of consonants and the most intense and instantaneous imposition of the Gan-Tone on vowels along with the Jaw, Larynx, Body Fusion.

Uniformity in coloration of the emitted sound, i.e., sustained vowels, is stabilized and emphatically accented through the application and frequency of the Gan-Tone Pulsations. The application of these pulsations gives the greatest impact to any area of resonance, and the frequency of the Gan-Tone on the sustained vowels produces a singing line of uniform pulsations. The frequency of this pulsation is controlled by the singer.

The impact of vibrations to the resonators is commensurate with the intensity with which the Gan-Tone is imposed to the rectal-pelvic area during the Compression Phase (down-part of the beat) while maintaining the vertical-elliptical mouth position, which assists in aligning the thrust and focus of vibrations for the greatest utilization of the frontal sinuses, thereby producing the greatest dimensions of resonance (depth and height) in the sustained vowel sounds.

The stability of the Jaw, Larynx, Body Fusion must also be maintained during the Gan-Tone cycle (Compression and Thrust Phases) in order to realize the maximum amount of vocal cords and body vibrations to be delivered to the resonators. Any riding-up of the jaw, for example, will decrease body fusion and vocal cords and body vibrations, giving less payload of vibrations to be thrust to the resonators.

The frequency of the Gan-Tone Pulsation gives the sustained vowels maximum dimensions. The cycle of each Gan-Tone consists of two phases. The Compression Phase produces maximum vocal cords and body vibrations which are grounded at the rectal-pelvic area. The Thrust Phase from the basin of the rectal-pelvic area provides maximum thrust and impact of the aggregate vibrations to all the body resonators. It is the framework of the vertical-elliptical mouth position, the Jaw, Larynx, Body Fusion and the Gan-Tone imposition on the fundamental vocal cords vibrations grounded at the rectal-pelvic area which provides the power to the body for supplying the amplitude and intensity of vibrations to any part of the resonators to be re-sounded, shaped and colored into any vowel. Only with such body power can the realization of maximum support and thrust be achieved for directing vibrations to the highest points of resonant areas in the body. The frequency with which the Gan-Tone is imposed, i.e., the number of times per second the Gan-Tone cycle is applied, determines the order, smoothness and continuity of the singing line. The more frequently and intensely the Gan-Tone can be imposed, the less interruptions in the flow of the Gan-Tone sound, since the intervals between the Gan-Tone upbeats (Thrust Phases, when the vibrations are delivered to the resonators with the greatest impact) become shorter.

The alertness and spontaneity of the singer in imposing these Gan-Tones on the singing line will determine the evenness, sparkle and brilliance of the emitted vowel sounds, eliminating the possibility of the undesirable tremolo.

An example of the frequency of the imposition of the Gan-Tone on the fundamental vocal cords vibrations of a sustained vowel is as follows:

> The pitch of the note, A above middle C, is achieved by approximately 440 vibrations per second. If this A pitch is sustained for one second, while five Gan-Tones are maximally imposed on this fundamental A pitch of 440 vibrations, then five times during this second, these 440 vibrations (A pitch) are imposed upon, fused and amplified by compression through the components (vocal cords, surrounding muscles, laryngeal cartilages, jawbone, chest bones and components, diaphragm, abdomen and viscera, etc.), grounded at the rectal-pelvic area and thrust with the greatest impact to the highest resonators, giving the greatest impact of vibrations to all the resonators, including the frontal air sinus resonators, the lower air sinus resonators, the nasal-pharyngeal cavity, the mouth, the pharynx, the larynx below and above the vocal cords, the trachea and chest cavity.
>
> The down-part of the beat, or Compression Phase of the Gan-Tone cycle, provides amplification of vocal cords and body vibrations, and the up-part of the beat, or Thrust Phase, provides the impact of these vibrations to the resonators and is considered the sound amplifier of the fundamental vocal cords vibrations which, in this case, is the A pitch, or 440 vibrations per second. These 440 pulsations per second, produced by air blowing on the tensed vocal cords, somewhat permeate the surrounding muscles, the area below and above the vocal cords, the larynx, and other resonators to some degree. These vibrations are constant during the imposition of Gan-Tones, therefore, not affecting the speed (v.p.s.), or pitch, of the sound. The imposition of Gan-Tones alters the dimensions of the sound, while the pitch remains constant.

The evenness of the singing line is comparable to the evenness of light waves coming from the sun or emanating from an incandescent bulb. The frequency of pulsations of light waves from the sun are determined by a supreme intelligence. The frequency of pulsations from the light bulb are arranged and determined by human intelligence and are of lower frequency than the pulsations of light waves. In both cases, however, the speed of the frequency is sufficient to insure an orderly, even, smooth emanation of light with no apparent interruptions.

Any laxity in the frequency of the pulsations would cause light waves to flicker and is comparable to the tremolo.

The flicker in the light waves produces two different degrees of light. The brighter light occurs where the frequency of vibration is more rapid. The tremolo produces two different sounds in a wobbly pattern. The high part of the wobble contains the desired frequency. The low part of the wobble, or release, produces another sound, or a second pitch, which is undesirable.

The sun is to light vibrations what the body is to vocal sound vibrations. The sun supplies light vibrations, and the depth of these vibrations is focused in and thrust from its center. These vibrations are transmitted spherically and permeate all surrounding space. These vibratory spheres are affected by various mediums in space which, in turn, affect the fundamental pulsations of light waves emanating from the sun. The thrust of these vibrations is determined by the sun's mass and the heat it currently generates. The degree of this thrust determines the degree of penetration and resultant brilliance of light waves, or spherical pulsations.

The body, like the sun, supplies the maximum vibrations, and the depth of these vibrations is focused in its center, i.e., the rectal-pelvic area. These body vibrations are transmitted spherically permeating the body. These body vibrations are affected by the various mediums of the body (muscles, bones, cartilages, ligaments, etc.). The body's mass as a vibrator of the vocal cords sound is determined by the Compression Phase of the Gan-Tone, and the thrust is dependent on the intensity of the Compression Phase which, in turn, determines the penetration in the resonators giving the resultant sound brilliance and volume.

A Gan-Tone Principle can, therefore, be summarized:

> The frequency, intensity and thrust with which the Gan-Tone Pulsation is imposed on the sustained vowel sounds determine the evenness, smooth-

ness, clarity, brilliance, coloration, cover, or aura, and volume of the emitted sound.

The slower the frequency, intensity and thrust of the Gan-Tone Pulsation on the sustained vowel sounds, the greater the interval between the resonant sounds, causing an interruption in the singing line and a diminishing of the resonant aura.

Conversely, the greater the frequency, intensity and thrust of the Gan-Tone Pulsation on the sustained vowels, the more even and smooth the singing line and the greater the dimensions and aura of the emitted sound.

The imposition of the Gan-Tone Pulsation can produce unusual dimensions in the singing line even though consonants and vowels are being mixed.

In the mixture of consonants and vowels, there is a slow and constant movement of the jaw in the articulation of consonants, and a slow transition into the vowel sounds coordinated with the movements of the lips and tongue, causing the vowels to be chewed in order to articulate the word that is being sung. This chewing, or wavelike movement, of the jaw, lips and tongue is normal in speaking and is permissable in singing, when there is no demand for maximum volume and intensity, i.e., loudest and highest sounds. As long as this chewing of the vowel exists, there is no definite Jaw, Larynx, Body Fusion, therefore, limiting the potential for producing maximum vibrations, resonance, and maximum dimensions in the sound.

However, the application of the Gan-Tone to the indefinite involvement of the Jaw, Larynx, Body Fusion can produce greater dimensions in the sound not possible without the Gan-Tone application. The chewing action in the slow movement of the jaw makes complete fusion of the jaw to the larynx and body impossible, since fusion is constantly being interrupted by the slow articulation of consonants and vowels. Nevertheless, during the Compression Phase (down-part of the beat) in the Gan-Tone cycle, there are enough vocal cords and laryngeal vibrations that are fused through body components, downward to the rectal-pelvic area to be amplified and grounded in this area and transmitted to the resonators during the Thrust Phase (up-part of the beat). The unfused jaw, however, closes the throat opening causing the limited vibrations to be further restricted in this area, further reducing the payload of vibrations to the resonators. Vocal cords and laryngeal vibrations would be more magnified, if the jaw were fused with the larynx and body. When this fusion is indefinite, vibrations are transmitted and magnified through neck muscles, rather than through fused hard parts (bones), causing these vibrations to be absorbed, rather than transmitted and magnified.

However, a limited amount of fusion can still produce enough vibrations to be magnified and thrust from the rectal-pelvic area, with the Gan-Tone application, to utilize the resonators for ample resonance, resulting in dimensions in the sound not possible without the Gan-Tone application.

A Gan-Tone Principle can, therefore, be summarized:

The mixture of consonants with vowels, in articulating words in the singing line, debilitates the Jaw, Larynx, Body Fusion which is permissable, if maximum dimensions in the sound are not necessary. However, the Gan-Tone Pulsation applied to the indefinite Jaw, Larynx, Body Fusion will produce greater dimensions in the singing line not possible without the Gan-Tone application.

Attention to the articulation of consonants is essential in the Gan-Tone Method in order to insure the most effective and efficient application of the Gan-Tone which, in turn, will produce maximum dimensions in the emitted sound. The skill of pronouncing consonants with agility, conciseness and spontaneity is essential in order to eliminate superfluous sounds when articulating initial consonant blends, as, for example, when singing the initial blend br in the word brown, care must be taken to move quickly from one consonant to another and on to the vowel, rather than prolonging the consonants with a heavy, sluggish stress on either consonant (buhrrown). In the articulation of consonant blends of two, three or four letters as, for example, st and thr in American and schl in German, the time element involved in pronouncing these letters should be equivalent to the time necessary to pronounce one consonant, as a result of the instant condensation of these consonants.

Moving swiftly from the initial consonants to the vowels of words insures the most efficient utilization of the

Gan-Tone which can only be fully realized on vowel sounds, since the Jaw, Larynx, Body Fusion is not possible, if the singer dwells on consonants. Sluggish articulation of consonants results in the absence of the unification of the jaw, larynx and body, since the jaw rides up, when pronouncing consonants, making fusion with the larynx impossible. Rapid articulation of consonants, on the other hand, enables the jaw to be fused to the larynx and body immediately, causing instantaneous, maximum vibrations, as a result of the instant contact of the vocal cords vibrations to the rectal-pelvic area with the imposition of the Gan-Tone Pulsation. The open-throated position created by the instant fusion of the jaw, larynx and body along with the thrust produced, as a result of the compression of vocal cords vibrations (Compression Phase—down-part of the Gan-Tone beat), enable these vocal cords and body vibrations to be transmitted to the resonators with maximum power, focus and impact, since the path from the rectal-pelvic area to the resonators is now opened for the passage of unrestricted vibrations. Therefore, compression and fusion of vocal cords vibrations and support and thrust of these vibrations are maximized, resulting in maximum resonance to be shaped and focused for maximum dimensions in the projected vocal sound.

It should be noted that the fusion of the jaw, larynx and body is a supple condition that is achieved with practice, which results in an absolute minimum of pressure and tension in the vocal cords and throat area. Undesirable pressure and tension are transferred and diffused through the Compression Phase of the Gan-Tone beat which grounds these forces in the pelvic basin, causing the excessive pressure in the throat area, that accompanies the production of the human voice, to be removed. This transference of pressure, from the delicate vocal cords and surrounding muscles, to the rectal-pelvic area is the essence of the Gan-Tone Method. Sensitivity to the presence of pressure in the singing process followed by immediate coordination of fusion and compression with the Gan-Tone involvement prevent the concentration of pressure in the neck. It is this awareness that the singer must develop, if he is to insure maximum vibrations for utilization in shaping maximum sound with a minimum of throat tension. Rapid articulation of consonants insures a diffusion of this pressure from the throat area.

A Gan-Tone Principle can, therefore, be summarized:

The more rapid the articulation of consonants, the more rapid the fusion of the jaw, larynx and body, resulting in a more efficient application of the Gan-Tone cycle.

Rapid articulation of consonants yields rapid Jaw, Larynx, Body Fusion which, in turn, yields rapid fusion and compression (down-part of the Gan-Tone beat) causing the solid grounding of vocal cords vibrations to the rectal-pelvic area which, in turn, results in maximum thrust of unobstructed vocal cords and body vibrations through the open throat (up-part of the Gan-Tone beat) to the resonators, below and above the vocal cords, with the greatest impact, causing maximum re-sounding of these vibrations in all the openings of the body, making the body function as a bell in producing maximum resonance for focusing and shaping the emitted sound.

The Role of the Gan-Tone in Brilliance

XIII. Brilliance, in the Gan-Tone Method of Voice Production, is the intense scintillation and brightness achieved in the vocal sound by the spontaneous and forceful application of the Gan-Tone Pulsation on the fundamental pitch of the vocal cords vibrations which causes these vibrations to be intensely amplified and then thrust and focused from the rectal-pelvic area to the most vibrant parts of the resonators and the bony junctures of the mask adjoining the resonators.

The action of immediate compression of vocal cords vibrations to the rectal-pelvic area (Compression Phase—down-part of the Gan-Tone beat) causes the reaction of thrust of these vocal cords vibrations to the resonators with maximum impact (Thrust Phase—up-part of the Gan-Tone beat), resulting in maximum re-sounding of these vibrations. The speed, or frequency of repetition per second, of this Gan-Tone cycle constitutes the structure for producing buoyancy, smoothness and scintillation in the emitted sound, since each repetition of this cycle causes a compression of vocal cords vibrations to the bottom of the torso, giving a greater thrust of these vibrations to the body cavities, thus insuring the most efficient utilization of these resonators.

The more frequently the Gan-Tone is applied, the more constant the buoyancy of the focused vocal cords and body vibrations, insuring more intense re-sounding of these vibrations in the resonators which, in turn, produces greater scintillation, evenness and brilliance in the emitted sound. The frequency of the Gan-Tone application (6 per second), therefore, insures a continuity in the brilliance of the emitted sound, since the greater the frequency, the shorter the intervals between the upbeats, or Thrust Phases, thus insuring constant transmission, impact and penetration of vocal cords and body vibrations to the resonators.

Continuity of brilliance of the emitted sound in relation to the frequency of the Gan-Tone application is comparable to the continuity of brightness in a light bulb in relation to the alternating current of electricity. The cycle of alternating current produces a pulsation causing the filament in the light bulb to alternate between burning and dimming. The more frequent the application of the cycles of alternating current, the shorter the interval between burning and dimming in the filament, causing a more constant brightness in the light bulb. Maximum frequency in the alternating current results in maximum brilliance in the light bulb.

Each cycle of the Gan-Tone maximally applied provides the greatest amount of amplification of vocal cords and body vibrations through compression to the rectal-pelvic area which, in turn, produces the greatest amount of thrust of these vibrations to the resonators resulting in maximum impact and penetration. The intense impact of these vibrations re-sounding in the cavities causes their penetration throughout the body, making the whole body vibrate. These amplified, focused vibrations represent an extension of the original vocal cords vibrations which produce maximum brilliance in the emitted sound. The imposition of the Gan-Tone cycles, therefore, magnifies the original vocal cords vibrations through compression and supplies the greatest force of thrust of these vibrations to the resonators, giving the greatest degree of amplification to the resonance of the emitted sound. The repetition of this compression and thrust in each Gan-Tone cycle causes these vocal cords and body vibrations to be constantly buoyed.

The elasticity and effectiveness of this buoyancy is dependent upon the degree of intensity, speed, or frequency, with which the Gan-Tone is applied which, in turn, determines the degree of intensity of the Compression Phase, the degree of thrust, or force, exerted on the up-beat of the Gan-Tone, and the degree of resonance attained.

Speed in the Gan-Tone application results in a spontaneous reaction in the resonators, since the vocal cords vibrations are fused quickly and intensely throughout the body. The spontaneity of intense fusion of vocal cords vibrations to the deepest part of the body, followed by the intense thrust of these vibrations from this point, insures maximum resonance in the resonators and constitutes one Gan-Tone cycle which, when repeated, sustains the elasticity and brilliance of the emitted sound. Resilience in the sound, therefore, is made possible through the imposition of the Gan-Tone. The more frequent the application of the Gan-Tone cycle, the more elastic and resilient the sound.

A Gan-Tone Principle can, therefore, be summarized:
> The more frequent and intense the application of the Gan-Tone Pulsation on the fundamental vocal cords vibrations, the more elastic, resilient and brilliant the emitted sound.

VOCAL FOCUS—THE BASIS FOR MAXIMAL DIMENSIONAL SINGING

CONTENTS

VOCAL FOCUS—THE BASIS FOR MAXIMAL DIMENSIONAL SINGING

I.	The Meaning of Vocal Focus	163
II.	The Role of Vocal Focus in Voice Projection	164
III.	The Role of Vocal Focus in Breath Control	165
IV.	The Role of Vocal Focus in Range	165
V.	The Role of Vocal Focus in Register	167
VI.	The Role of Vocal Focus in Resonance	168
VII.	The Role of Vocal Focus in Volume	169
VIII.	The Role of Vocal Focus in Coloration	170
IX.	The Role of Vocal Focus in Sound Configuration	172
X.	The Role of Vocal Focus in Brilliance	174

The Meaning of Vocal Focus

I. Vocal focus, in the Gan-Tone Method of Voice Production, is the thrusting and centering of vocal cords and body vibrations in the most vibrant and resonant areas of the body, through the concomitant application of the JLB Fusion and the Gan-Tone beat, in order to amplify and resonate these vibrations, making the body function as a complete bell and giving maximum dimensions to the vocal sound.

Maximum focus of vocal cords and body vibrations in the most vibrant and resonant areas of the body is dependent on the amount of amplification and the intensity of thrust of these vibrations to these areas. The degree to which the vocal cords vibrations are fused through the body and centered at the rectal-pelvic area depends on the intensity of compression of these vibrations. This compression of vocal cords vibrations occurs during the application of the JLB Fusion with the Gan-Tone Pulsation. The down-part of the Gan-Tone beat provides the Compression Phase in which the fundamental vocal cords vibrations are fused, amplified and compressed to the rectal-pelvic area. At the height of the compressive action, the consequential reaction of thrust of these vibrations to the most vibrant and resonant areas of the body occurs as, for example, in the body cavities and the junctures adjacent to these resonators.

The intensity of thrust of these vibrations to the resonators of the body determines the degree of focus these vibrations will attain. The greater the focus of these vibrations in the cavities, the more intense the amplification of these re-sounding vibrations, which results in more effective projection of the vocal sound, more efficient utilization of breath, greater dimension in range, more evenness throughout the entire register, greater resonance, greater volume, more varied coloration, greater possibilities in sound configuration, and greater brilliance in the emitted vocal sound.

The degree of focus of vocal cords and body vibrations in the most vibrant and resonant areas of the body is dependent on the degree of thrust that occurs during the up-part of the Gan-Tone beat, and is the reaction to the action that transmits the fundamental vocal cords vibrations, by fusion and compression, to the rectal-pelvic area, which occurs during the down-part of the Gan-Tone beat, demonstrating Newton's Law of Action and Reaction which states that for every action, there is an equal and opposite reaction. Transmission and propagation of vocal cords vibrations is dependent upon the efficiency of the Compression Phase to the bottom of the torso. Transmission and propagation of amplified vocal cords and body vibrations to the resonators is dependent upon the efficiency of the Thrust Phase.

The Gan-Tone cycle, or beat, is analogous to the piston and the cylinder. The piston, in its initial movement of compression through the cylinder, is comparable to the Compression Phase, or down-part of the Gan-Tone beat, in which the vocal cords vibrations are compressed and transmitted through the body, as the Compression Phase moves toward the bottom of the torso, or cylinder. Upon reaching the point of maximum compression at the rectal-pelvic area, the Thrust Phase, or up-part of the Gan-Tone beat, reaches its maximum force, focusing the vocal cords and body vibrations in the body cavities, or resonators, with an intensity that is commensurate with the strength of the Gan-Tone application.

Compression and thrust of vibrations begin at the vocal cords but are realized, to the utmost, by the JLB Fusion which is constantly maintained as the Gan-Tone is applied, making the center of compression and thrust the rectal-pelvic area. When air impinges on the vocal cords, without the application of body fusion and the Gan-Tone beat, a degree of compression and thrust of vibrations occurs in the larynx and surrounding muscles, localizing and focusing these vibrations in the neck area. These vibrations are transmitted to the resonators, but they lack amplification and intensity of thrust. Consequently, there is a minimum of focus in the resonators, limiting the dimensions of the emitted vocal sound. However, the application of the JLB Fusion as a constant with the imposition of the Gan-Tone beat on the vocal cords vibrations creates a duo-action that is transferred downward through the chest, diaphragm, abdomen and grounded at the rectal-pelvic area. The degree of focus of vocal cords and body vibrations in the cavities, or resonators, of the body is dependent on the degree of compression of vocal cords vibrations. The greater the involvement of the body in the compression and thrust of these vibrations, the more intense the focus of these amplified vibrations to the vibrant and resonant areas of the body.

It should be noted that the thrust of vibrations to the vibrant and resonant areas of the body is present as soon as compression occurs in the slightest way. However, the degree of intensity of thrust is commensurate with the degree of intensity of compression which, in turn, determines the degree of focus of these vocal cords and body vibrations in the body cavities. Maximum compression of vocal cords and body vibrations to the rectal-pelvic area results in maximum thrust of these vibrations to the most vibrant and resonant areas of the body, resulting in maximum focus, intensity and amplification of vibrations, producing maximum resonance, thus giving the emitted vocal sound maximum brilliance.

A Gan-Tone Principle can, therefore, be summarized:

> The degree of focus of vocal cords and body vibrations in the most vibrant and resonant areas of the body is dependent upon the speed and degree of intensity of the application of the JLB Fusion as a constant and the imposition of the Gan-Tone Pulsation.
>
> The greater the intensity and speed of the concomitant action of the JLB Fusion and the Gan-Tone application, the more intense the focus of vocal cords and body vibrations in the most vibrant and resonant areas of the body, resulting in a greater amplification of vibrations, thus producing greater resonance which, in turn, insures greater brilliance, resilience, volume and color in the emitted sound.

The Role of Vocal Focus in Voice Projection

II. Vocal focus, which is the thrusting and centering of vocal cords and body vibrations in the most vibrant and resonant areas of the body through the application of the JLB Fusion as a constant and the Gan-Tone beat, transforms the concept of voice projection by focusing on the body resonators for the maximum amplification of vibrations, producing maximum resonance, which is projected to the listener as multidimensional sound.

The volume and projection of the voice is currently believed to be determined by the size and strength of the lungs, as a bellows, to provide a stream of air that activates the vocal cords to vibrate, producing sound which is re-sounded in the body resonators and, in turn, projected to the audience.

In the Gan-Tone Method, the body is the bellows, which includes the lungs. The body is the vibrator, which includes the vocal cords. The body is the resonator, i.e., the solid parts, bones, muscles, etc., along with the cavities, constitute the structure for resonance. The fundamental vocal cords vibrations propagated and disseminated throughout the body, and the re-sounding of these amplified vibrations in the body cavities cause the body to function as a bell, since the body, like the bell, has the characteristics for producing vibrations and resonance.

Vocal cords vibrations are multiplied and transmitted throughout the body. The amplification, thrust and focus of these vibrations in the body resonators are reflected as amplified resonance, which is projected as amplified vocal sound.

Projection of the voice is dependent on the intensity of thrust of vocal cords vibrations to the resonators. Since the greatest agent of thrust of vocal cords vibrations is the body, localizing thrust to the lung area prevents the full utilization of the body as a thrusting agent whose centering and grounding for thrust is the rectal-pelvic area. Transference of focus from the lungs to the body greatly magnifies the power of the lungs by making the whole body an extension of the lungs, while simultaneously magnifying the vocal cords vibrations through compression (down-part of the Gan-Tone beat). As the vibrations are compressed through the body, they are amplified and reach the height of amplification at the rectal-pelvic area, at which time the thrust of these vibrations (up-part of the Gan-Tone beat) from this depth is capable of delivering these vibrations with great impact to the resonators, thus fully utilizing these cavities. The amount of vocal projection is equal to the impact of thrust of these vibrations to the resonators. The greater the thrust of these vibrations to the resonators, the greater the penetration of these vibrations in the bones of the mask and head resonators giving greater brilliance to the projected sound.

Localizing the focus of thrust to the lungs, thoracic

diaphragm, or any other part of the body, rather than using the whole body, diminishes amplification of vibrations, thrust and resonance which, in turn, diminishes vocal projection.

A Gan-Tone Principle can, therefore, be summarized:

The degree of focus of vocal cords and body vibrations in the resonators determines the degree of vocal projection.

The greater the fusion and compression of vocal cords and body vibrations to the rectal-pelvic area, the greater the thrust and impact of these amplified vibrations to the resonators which, in turn, produces amplified resonance that is reflected in amplified vocal projection.

The Role of Vocal Focus in Breath Control

III. Vocal focus, which is the thrusting and centering of vocal cords and body vibrations in the most vibrant and resonant areas of the body through the application of the JLB Fusion as a constant and the Gan-Tone, increases breath control by requiring less air to amplify and direct these vibrations to the resonators which, in turn, re-sound these vibrations, converting them to maximum resonance, which is reflected in voluminous sound.

Through fusion and compression of vocal cords and body vibrations to the bottom of the torso, with the Gan-Tone application, the whole body becomes a vibrator and amplifier of these vibrations, requiring less intensity of air to activate the vocal cords, thus enabling the singer to sustain longer phrases without running out of breath.

When air is impinged on the vocal cords, they vibrate, producing a constant pitch of uniform vibrations per second that is re-sounded in the resonators through the throat opening. However, the imposition of the Gan-Tone takes the fundamental vocal cords vibrations and fuses them to the bottom of the torso, amplifying these vibrations, causing the whole body to become the vibrator of the vocal cords vibrations. Re-sounding these vibrations in the resonators results in maximum amplitude of resonance, since it reflects the fusion of total vocal cords and body vibrations causing the body to function as a bell with a minimum expenditure of breath.

However, without fusion and compression, vocal focus in the resonators would not be maximized. Reliance on the larynx as sole vibrator and resonator would limit the dimensions of the resultant sound and would require more breath to attain more volume, since the larynx is only one part of the body and is, therefore, limited in its ability to produce vibrations in great dimensions. The larynx is also limited in its ability to produce fusion, compression and thrust of vibrations, requiring more air to increase volume. The role of the larynx as a bell cannot be compared to the role of the body as a bell, since the whole is greater than any of its parts.

The significance of the jet of air to the vocal cords as an amplifier diminishes, as vocal focus is more efficiently utilized. Since the air impinges on the vocal cords with a feather-touch, friction in the vocal cords and surrounding muscles diminishes, as a result of amplifying vibrations through fusion and compression, with the JLB Fusion and the Gan-Tone application, rather than increasing volume by intensifying the jet of air through the tensed vocal cords.

A Gan-Tone Principle can, therefore, be summarized:

The degree of speed and intensity with which the vocal cords and body vibrations are thrust to the resonators with the JLB Fusion and the Gan-Tone beat determines the efficiency of breath control.

The greater the thrust and focus of vocal cords and body vibrations to the resonators, the less breath is required to project and re-sound vibrations in the resonators, producing maximum volume with a minimum of breath.

The Role of Vocal Focus in Range

IV. Vocal focus, which is the thrusting and centering of vocal cords and body vibrations in the most vibrant and resonant areas of the body through the application of the JLB Fusion as a constant and the Gan-Tone Pulsation, not only makes possible the maximum exploration of the dimensions of sound, i.e., depth, height, volume, coloration, buoyancy, resilience, fullness and brilliance throughout the range, but also increases the degree of range in all voices.

The application of the Gan-Tone is necessary for the

focusing of vocal cords and body vibrations in the most vibrant and resonant areas of the body. In applying the Gan-Tone, the coordination of body parts, their relationship to each other as fusing agents, and the role of body power in generating vibrant energy are essential. This awareness enables the singer to discover more range.

In attempting to ascend the scale, for example, most voices experience a pressure buildup which results in the appearance of an impasse, preventing singers from exploiting their full range potential. However, the application of the Gan-Tone requires the movement of the jaw down and back while ascending the scale, since it fuses the jaw to the body which, in turn, automatically eliminates the impasse, transferring the pressure buildup from the localized area of the throat to the body by fusion and compression (down-part of the Gan-Tone beat). Diffusion of pressure through the body eliminates the impasse enabling singers to continue ascending the scale thus discovering not only more range than was imagined, but also, an evenness in the entire range, rejecting the current belief of distinct registers in the singing scale.

The evenness in the entire range occurs as a result of body fusion and the maintenance of the open throat throughout the scale. As pressure mounts with the ascending scale, the throat becomes constricted, thereby restricting the movement of vibrations. This occurrence is analogous to a person throwing a pail of water through an open door. If the door is not opened wide enough, there is an abrupt change in the quantity of water that gets through the door, since the partially opened door prohibits much of the water from going through, limiting the original quantity of the water. The limited vocal vibrations produce limited dimensions in the vocal sound, resulting in a change in quality and more reliance on the pure vocal cords sound (falsetto voice) as the singer ascends the scale.

The focus of vocal cords and body vibrations in the more resonant areas of the body, such as, the bones and cavities of the head and chest, made possible through the Gan-Tone application (up-part of the Gan-Tone beat), results in a maximum of omnidirectional vibrations which, in turn, produces the greatest dimensions of sound throughout the range, i.e., depth, height, volume, coloration, resilience, buoyancy, fullness and brilliance.

A maximum of omnidirectional vibrations is produced by the amplification of the original vocal cords vibrations through fusion and compression (down-part of the Gan-Tone beat); these vibrations are supported and projected to the most vibrant areas of the body (up-part of the Gan-Tone beat).

The degree of dimensions achieved in the sound throughout the range is dependent on the unrestricted movement of vocal cords and body vibrations to the most vibrant and resonant areas of the body. Maintaining the focus of vocal cords and body vibrations in these areas of the body, in the upper range of the voice, requires great skill in coordinating the jaw downward with a minimum of pressure while maintaining the vertical-elliptical mouth opening in order to sustain the open throat for the smooth passage of vibrations, since it is a natural tendency to close the jaws as pressure mounts with increasing range. If the throat is closed, vocal cords and body vibrations cannot be projected and focused in the most vibrant and resonant areas of the body. Lack of vibrations in these areas limits re-sounding which, in turn, limits depth, height, volume, coloration, resilience, buoyancy, fullness and brilliance, the characteristics of vocal dimensions.

Although the maintenance of intensity in the thrusting and focusing of vocal cords and body vibrations in the most vibrant and resonant areas of the body becomes increasingly difficult with increased range, it will be mastered with constant practice in the coordination of body parts (fusion of the jaw, larynx, tongue and body) and strict adherence to Gan-Tone Principles as, for example, in singing a high note, the singer concentrates on the Gan-Tone Principles that will position the body, rather than trying to reach for the note. As anxiety rides up through the body in anticipation of the high note, the singer concentrates on the elimination of anxiety by fusing and unifying the body downward to the rectal-pelvic area (jaw, larynx, body coordination).

A Gan-Tone Principle can, therefore, be summarized:
> The degree of intensity that is achieved in the thrusting and focusing of vocal cords and body vibrations in the resonators with the JLB Fusion and the Gan-Tone, while ascending or descending

the scale, determines the degree of dimensions that will be evident in the range.

The greater the intensity in the thrusting and focusing of vocal cords and body vibrations in the resonators while ascending or descending the scale, the greater the depth, height, volume, coloration, resilience, buoyancy, fullness and brilliance in the range.

The Role of Vocal Focus in Register

V. Vocal focus, which is the thrusting and centering of vocal cords and body vibrations in the most vibrant and resonant areas of the body through the application of the JLB Fusion as a constant and the Gan-Tone, makes possible the Gan-Tone belief that there is only one register in the singing voice, and this register is similar to the range of the vocal cords, rather than the current belief of several registers. Range and register, in the Gan-Tone Method, are, therefore, one and the same.

Changes in tonal quality and pressure breaks which occur in the process of ascending and descending the scale, especially in the middle range, are responsible for the belief of many registers in the singing voice, and they are viewed as very natural phenomena. However, the disparity in the quality of the sound between the lower and higher notes, which is the basis for the origin of registers, is the result of ignorance regarding pressure buildup and how to allay this pressure. In the Gan-Tone Method, changes in tonal quality and pressure breaks known as registers in the voice can be completely overcome and are, therefore, non-existent with the utilization of vocal focus.

In order to apply the Gan-Tone and thus thrust, direct and center vocal cords and body vibrations in the most vibrant and resonant areas of the body, it is essential that the jaw be coordinated with the increase of vibrations and accompanying pressures that occur in ascending the scale, i.e., as the vibrations increase, the jaw must be moved down and back, closer to the body, with the vertical-elliptical mouth opening to create a wider opening for the passage of these increased vibrations, thus eliminating the pressure buildup. This jaw movement produces strength in the throat area by relieving strain, particularly in the muscles attached to, and surrounding, the vocal cords and in the muscles that move the jaw and larynx upward and downward. If pressure is not allayed by the fusion of the jaw to the body, with the increased vibrations, muscles that hold the sound stable become strained, spasm and collapse, causing changes in tonal quality, pressure breaks and a disembodied sound. Moving the jaw down and back in ascending and descending the scale strengthens all the muscles of the larynx and throat by unifying them with the body, shifting the pressure from the weaker components (throat muscles) to the body, thus relieving the throat area of pressure, making it possible for the vocal cords to function at their maximum by making the body an extension of the vocal cords.

The singer who is trained in the Gan-Tone Method is not disturbed by the traditional belief that there are several registers in the voice, since he learns how to overcome pressure, which is the culprit responsible for changes in tonal quality and breaks, when ascending or descending the scale.

Registers are also determined by the frequency of vibration and the physical area that is producing the maximum vibrations as, for example, the chest or head. Low notes are usually characterized by chest vibrations and high notes by head vibrations, causing the belief in chest and head registers. Undue importance is focused on registers in the singing voice, since it is believed that these registers are involuntary reactions and beyond the control of the singer. Although it may be evident that the slow frequency of vibration in low notes causes chest vibrations to be more obvious and that the rapid frequency of vibration of high notes stresses head vibrations, the ultimate control of vibrations and resonance in the various parts of the body, in the Gan-Tone Method, is dependent on the singer's understanding and application of the JLB Fusion as a constant and the Gan-Tone Pulsation which will thrust and focus vibrations uniformly throughout the range, from low to high, eliminating the marked distinctions, within the entire range of the voice, that have resulted in the belief of chest and head registers.

Fusion and compression of vocal cords vibrations to

the bottom of the torso, during the down-part of the Gan-Tone beat, magnify vocal cords vibrations throughout the body. The thrusting of these vibrations through the pressure-controlled open throat (vocal focus), during the up-part of the beat, no longer emphasizes vibrations in the chest or head, but involves, instead, the whole body, since these vibrations are being thrust to the most vibrant and resonant areas of the body throughout the range. Mastery of the maximum coordination of the Gan-Tone, i.e., down-part and up-part of the beat, causes the body to become an elastic medium and thrusting agent, resulting in maximum focus of vibrations in the highest resonators of the body throughout the range, i.e., in the frontal air sinuses of the mask and adjoining cavities, as well as in the pharynx and larynx.

A Gan-Tone Principle can, therefore, be summarized:

The degree of intensity and freedom that is achieved in the thrusting and focusing of vocal cords and body vibrations in the resonators, while ascending or descending the scale, is dependent on the degree of efficiency of the Jaw, Larynx, Body Fusion as a constant and the Gan-Tone Pulsation which, in turn, determines the following:

1 - The degree of pressure that will be allayed which, in turn, will determine the relative absence of pressure breaks in the range.

2 - The degree of evenness that will be maintained in the vibrational amplitude from low to high tones, eliminating the marked distinctions within the entire range, thus removing the belief in chest and head registers, since the free passage of vocal cords vibrations involves the chest and head simultaneously with the rest of the body.

The Role of Vocal Focus in Resonance

VI. Vocal focus, which is the thrusting and centering of vocal cords and body vibrations in the most vibrant and resonant areas of the body through the application of the JLB Fusion as a constant and the Gan-Tone Pulsation, maximizes resonance, since the greatest amount of vocal cords and body vibrations are being re-sounded in the chambers of the body, adding maximum dimensions, i.e., depth, height, coloration, flexibility, resilience and volume, to the emitted sound.

It is currently believed that resonance is the result of vibrations emanating from the vocal cords which are produced by a jet of air impinging on the vocal cords, via the bellows of the lungs, and re-sounded in the body cavities. However, in the Gan-Tone Method, this belief is limited and cannot, of itself, produce the maximum dimensions of resonance, i.e., depth, height, coloration, flexibility, resilience and volume, since the lungs cannot, of themselves, produce the intensity or control of the jet of air made possible through vocal focus, nor can the re-sounding of vocal cords vibrations in the body chambers have the magnitude and volume made possible through vocal focus. The obvious parts, such as the lungs, vocal folds and mouth, cannot produce the dimensions of resonance made possible through body power with vocal focus in the Gan-Tone Method.

Through the application of the JLB Fusion and the Gan-Tone Pulsation, the dimension of the vocal cords extends to the rectal-pelvic area, and this extension is reflected in the amplification of the fundamental vocal cords vibrations. Therefore, the degree of amplified vibrations produced is dependent on the singer's understanding and effective application of the Gan-Tone which, in turn, insures the complete involvement of the body as the agent of vibrations, rather than isolated parts, such as, the vocal cords and lungs.

Current belief limits the contraction of the walls of the lungs and surrounding muscles as the means for producing intensity in the jet of air impinging on the vocal cords which, in turn, determines the amplitude and thrust of vocal cords vibrations that re-sound (resonance) in the body cavities. In the Gan-Tone Method, fusion and compression of body parts greatly increase lung capacity in thrusting and controlling the jet of air impinging on the vocal cords, since the resilience of the lung walls and surrounding muscles extends to the rectal-pelvic basin with the application of the Gan-Tone (Compression Phase, or down-part of the Gan-Tone beat), giving greater dimension to the bellows of the lungs which are now extended to the bottom of the torso. The structure that produces the strength in the jet of air impinging on the vocal cords has its ultimate grounding in the pelvic-perineum diaphragm (Thrust Phase, or up-part of the Gan-Tone beat). Therefore, it is not lung size, lung power, vocal cords or resonator characteristics that determine the ultimate resonance of the projected sound but, rather, vocal focus, in the Gan-Tone Method, which utilizes fusion and compression to harness the whole body for producing maximum vibrations and resonance.

Current belief states that the thrusting of vocal cords vibrations to the resonators is dependent on the contraction of the muscles adjacent to the lungs. With the application of the Gan-Tone, the contraction of the lungs is greatly supported and strengthened through fusion and compression, and this contraction develops its greatest thrust from the rectal-pelvic basin, as a result of the fusion of muscles and bones. This basin becomes the solid foundation for the thrust and transmission of vibrations throughout the body during the Thrust Phase, or up-part of the Gan-Tone beat, which is also known as vocal focus.

A Gan-Tone Principle can, therefore, be summarized:

The degree to which the body is utilized as an extension of the vocal cords and lungs in the amplifying, thrusting and centering of vocal cords and body vibrations in the resonators determines the degree of resonance, i.e., depth, height, coloration, flexibility, resilience and volume, in the emitted sound.

Maximum utilization of the body as an extension of the vocal cords and lungs in the amplifying, thrusting and centering of vocal cords and body vibrations in the resonators yields maximum resonance in the emitted sound.

The Role of Vocal Focus in Volume

VII. Vocal focus, which is the thrusting and centering of vocal cords and body vibrations in the most vibrant and resonant areas of the body through the application of the Gan-Tone Pulsation on the JLB Fusion, produces maximum volume in the emitted sound, since the greatest quantity of vocal cords and body vibrations are being resounded in the chambers of the body. Maximum resounding of maximum vibrations results in maximum volume.

The amplification of vocal cords vibrations is made possible through the Compression Phase, or down-part of the Gan-Tone beat, which fuses the fundamental vocal cords vibrations through the body to the rectal-pelvic basin. The more definite and intense the fusion and compression of body parts and vocal cords vibrations to the rectal-pelvic basin, the greater the amplification of these fundamental vocal cords vibrations which are now extended and compressed to the rectal-pelvic basin. This process occurs during the application of the down-part of the Gan-Tone beat which is known as the Compression Phase. The degree of compression of vocal cords vibrations and body pressure determines the degree of thrust of these vibrations to the resonators (vocal focus).

Efficient compression of vocal cords and body vibrations, however, is dependent on the effectiveness of the Jaw, Larynx, Body Fusion. When the jaw is fused to the body, i.e., unhinged down and back, the strongest vibratory continuity exists between the vocal cords and the body, as a result of fusion of body parts into one solid structure, making compression of vocal cords and body vibrations to the rectal-pelvic basin most effective and, at the same time, creating the widest path in the throat area (vocal hook) for the passage of the greatest amount of amplified vocal cords vibrations.

The unhinged position of the jaw creates the greatest vibratory continuity for the amplification of vocal cords and body vibrations during the Compression Phase, or down-part of the Gan-Tone beat, and simultaneously creates the greatest space in the throat area (vocal hook) for the transmission of these amplified vocal cords and body vibrations throughout the body.

The degree of speed and intensity of fusion of body parts and compression of vocal cords and body vibrations determines the impact at the rectal-pelvic basin, specifically, at the Sphincter ani externus muscle, the focal point. The degree of impact of these vibrations to the rectal-pelvic basin (action) determines the degree of thrust (reaction) of these vibrations to the resonators. The more intense the thrust to the resonators (vocal focus), the more vibrations are being amplified resulting in a greater resounding of these vibrations which, in turn, produces greater volume in the emitted sound. The degree of compressive impact to the rectal-pelvic basin, therefore, is the key to the amount of vibrations that will be produced and amplified, which is the basis of vocal projection in the human. The controlling center of vocal projection is the rectal-pelvic basin, since there is no other place in the entire body where vibrations can be amplified to their utmost and launched, or thrust, to the varied resonators of the body. This launching pad (rectal-pelvic basin) is the controlling center for enabling the singer to direct vibrations, at will, to the desired resonators, resulting not only in increased volume of the emitted sound, but also enabling the singer to focus, with great control, on the varied mediums of the body, which have their own peculiar vibratory characteristics, in order to produce a great gamut of coloration in the emitted sound.

A Gan-Tone Principle can, therefore, be summarized:

The degree of speed and intensity in the fusion of body parts and the compression of vocal cords and body vibrations with the JLB Fusion and the Gan-Tone beat determine the impact of these vibrations to the rectal-pelvic basin (action). The impact of these vibrations to the rectal-pelvic basin determines the thrust and transmission of these vibrations throughout the body (vocal focus, reaction), which, in turn, determine the volume of the emitted sound.

The greater the fusion and compression of vibrations to the rectal-pelvic basin, the greater the thrust of these vibrations to the resonators which, in turn, yields increased amplified vibrations, resulting in increased volume of the emitted sound.

The greater the compressive impact of vocal cords and body vibrations to the rectal-pelvic basin, the greater the vocal focus which, in turn, yields greater volume and, therefore, more effective vocal projection.

The Role of Vocal Focus in Coloration

VIII. Vocal focus, which is the thrusting and centering of vocal cords and body vibrations in the most vibrant and resonant areas of the body through the concomitant application of the JLB Fusion and the Gan-Tone Pulsation, regulates the quality of the emitted sound by utilizing the peculiar vibratory characteristics of the varied mediums of the body (bones, cartilages, muscles, membranes, fluids, etc.), as desired by the singer, for producing a wide gamut of coloration in the singing sound. The controlling center for the transmission of these vibrations to the desired mediums is the pelvic-perineum diaphragm in the rectal-pelvic basin.

The thrusting and centering of vibrations in the resonators (vocal focus) for coloration requires the singer's direction of these vibrations to the various mediums for achieving certain desired characteristics (color) in the emitted sound.

By directing vibrations to the roof of the mouth after launching them from the rectal-pelvic basin, which provides the greatest control for the thrust of these vibrations, the vibratory characteristics of the hard palate, or roof of the mouth, are emphasized in the emitted sound. The degree of emphasis, however, is dependent on the degree of thrust from the rectal-pelvic basin and the position of the jaw. The color of the emitted sound, as a result of focus in the area of the hard palate, is characterized by brilliance, since the bony part of the hard palate is involved; and mellowness, as a result of the involvement of the soft palate and membranes of the mouth. The greatest degree, or intensity, of thrust of vibrations to the hard palate will emphasize the vibratory characteristics of this area to the utmost provided the jaw is unhinged, i.e., fused with the body. Any divergence of the jaw diminishes the amplification of the fundamental vocal cords vibrations and negates fusion of these vibrations, even though compression at the rectal-pelvic area is intense, causing a throaty quality in the voice, as a result of restriction in the throat.

Varying positions of the jaw, other than unhinged and fused with the body, while producing loud, high sounds, will affect the color of the sound regardless of the degree, or intensity, of thrust. Any attempt to hold the magnitude of the sound by a set position of the jaw will color the sound with a throaty, reedy, tight, strident quality, since vibrations and pressure are limited to the vocal cords. Although a high degree of intensity exists in the thrusting of vocal cords and body vibrations to the sinus cavities, for example, the vibratory characteristics of these cavities, i.e., brilliance and height, are not audible as a result of the diminished vibrations caused by the diverging jaw which breaks JLB Fusion. The open circuit produced when the jaw is diverged from the larynx and torso diminishes vibratory continuity and the ability to amplify vocal cords vibrations through compression. The thrust of these vibrations from the rectal-pelvic basin, although intense, transmits a small amount of vocal cords and body vibrations through a more restricted throat area, as a result of the diverging jaw. Therefore, the transmission and penetration of these vibrations to the sinus cavities are insignificant in coloring the sound with the characteristics of these cavities (brilliance and height).

The human vocal apparatus is different from any other instrument in coloring sound, since the human has a brain which enables him to focus, at will, vibrations in wave-like patterns from the rectal-pelvic basin, which is the controlling center for these vibrations, to any medium of the body.

Thrusting vocal cords and body vibrations from the rectal-pelvic basin and focusing them on the chest area colors the sound with a deep quality that is characterized more by depth, rather than brilliance.

Focusing vibrations to the pharynx (back of the mouth) colors the sound with a cave-like, mellow quality, as a result of emphasis on the back of the mouth and throat which are far removed from the bony structure of the mask.

Focusing vibrations deep in the postnasal (upper section of the back of the mouth) colors the sound by height rather than depth.

Focusing vibrations at the bridge of the nose causes these vibrations to move downward into the mask and upward into the sinus cavities, coloring the sound with brilliance and height.

Focusing vibrations at the base of the nose vibrates the maxillary bone penetrating the bony area of the mask, giving the sound much brilliance.

Focusing vibrations behind the lower teeth produces a moderate brilliance in the emitted sound, since this area is removed from the main structure of the mask.

Thrusting vibrations from the rectal-pelvic area enables the singer to reach the highest resonating area of the body, the septum and bones of the frontal air sinus cavities. By penetrating the sinus resonators, vibrations are re-sounded in all the cavities, or resonators, of the head giving the emitted sound the maximum dimensions in depth and height. Furthermore, penetrating the sinus cavities with the greatest degree of thrust causes the peculiar vibratory characteristics of the body mediums to be maximally magnified in the undulating waves of vibrations (fundamental imposed upon by the Gan-Tone beat) passing down and up through the body (rectal-pelvic basin to the sinus cavities), thus giving the greatest dimensions of coloration to the emitted sound.

Like the prism that brings out the spectrum of colors in light, the Compression Phase of the Gan-Tone application activates the vibratory characteristics of all the mediums through which the fundamental vocal cords vibrations penetrate. The degree of intensity with which the vocal cords and body vibrations are compressed to the rectal-pelvic basin determines the intensity with which these vibrations will permeate and vibrate the mediums, which, in turn, determines the range of color that is audible in the projected sound. The Gan-Tone application enables the body to function as a prism for making audible the gamut of colors in the projected sound that would otherwise be inaudible to the human ear for lack of magnification.

Vocal focus, in the Gan-Tone Method, clarifies and transforms the dimensions of coloration in the singing sound. It establishes, beyond a doubt, that the controlling center for the coloration of the projected sound is the rectal-pelvic basin from which vocal cords and body vibrations receive the greatest magnification and thrust. It also clearly defines and differentiates the peculiar vibratory characteristics of the various mediums of the body (bones, cartilages, tendons, muscles, etc.) that are brought to greater audibility, as a result of the increased compression of vibrations to the rectal-pelvic basin which, in turn, are thrust with equal intensity to the varied resonators of the body. Thus, the resultant sound is a combination of the vibratory characteristics of the mediums of the body, through which vibrations are transmitted, and the characteristics of the body resonators, within which vibrations are re-sounded.

Control of the vibrations at the rectal-pelvic basin insures the maximum involvement of the body, which completely transforms the dimensions of coloration in the singing sound, since the utilization of the body, which includes the vibratory characteristics of the varied mediums, adds maximum dimensions in depth, height, brilliance and volume to the emitted sound. Without the compression of vibrations to the rectal-pelvic basin and the resultant thrust of these vibrations from this controlling center, the maximum dimensions in coloration cannot be realized, since this lack of complete body utilization restricts the involvement of vibrations, and their amplification and thrust, to the lungs and throat which, in turn, greatly minimizes the involvement of the varied mediums of the body, limiting the potential dimensions of coloration in the emitted sound.

A Gan-Tone Principle can, therefore, be summarized:

The degree to which vocal cords and body vibrations are compressed to the rectal-pelvic basin on the JLB Fusion and the Gan-Tone beat determines the extent to which the peculiar vibratory characteristics of the varied mediums of the body will be audible in tonal coloration, since it is only from this controlling center (rectal-pelvic basin) that vibrations can be amplified and thrust to the varied mediums of the body to utilize most efficiently their vibratory and re-sounding characteristics.

The greater the compressive impact of vocal cords and body vibrations to the rectal-pelvic basin, the greater the thrust of these vibrations (vocal focus), resulting in the greater involvement of the mediums and resonators of the body which, in turn, yields greater coloration in the emitted sound.

The Role of Vocal Focus in Sound Configuration

IX. Vocal focus, which is the thrusting and centering of vocal cords and body vibrations in the most vibrant and resonant areas of the body through the application of the JLB Fusion and the Gan-Tone Pulsation, makes possible the greatest quantity of vibrations to be re-sounded and shaped into vowels and consonants for articulating the singing sound. Those areas of the body where vibrations don't ordinarily penetrate effectively as, for example, the irregular surface of the vocal hook, are activated by vocal focus to propagate, amplify and re-sound vibrations that are shaped into the singing word. Vocal focus also enhances these patterns, since these vibrations reflect the greatest dimensions of depth, height and brilliance.

Although vocal cords vibrations are always being thrust and transmitted omnidirectionally (otherwise, there would be no sound), the Compression Phase of the Gan-Tone (down-part of the beat) makes possible the greatest quantity of vibrations by extending the vibratory tract to the rectal-pelvic basin, while simultaneously fusing vocal cords vibrations to this basin. Maximum compression in this area results in maximum amplification of vocal cords and body vibrations, since this compression increases the vibratory capacity of the body (density and resilience), causing these vibrations to be magnified. At the height of compression, which is the action, the maximum thrust of these vibrations to the mediums and resonators of the body occurs (up-part of the beat, Thrust Phase, or vocal focus), giving the singer a maximum output of magnified fundamental vocal cords vibrations to re-sound and utilize in the shaping of vowels and consonants.

Through vocal focus, those areas, where vibrations don't ordinarily penetrate effectively, become involved in the propagation, amplification and re-sounding of vibrations. Without fusion and compression of body parts, such as, the jaw, larynx, chest bones and down to the rectal-pelvic area, the body, below and above the vocal cords, lacks vibratory continuity. Fusion and compression of body parts, however, unites the body as a vibrator, making all the bones and the rest of the body vibrate for the propagation and amplification of vibrations. The Thrust Phase of the Gan-Tone (up-part of the beat, or vocal focus), whose effectiveness is dependent on the intensity of the Compression Phase, delivers the total amplified vocal cords and body vibrations, below and above the vocal cords, concomitantly, reaching areas where re-sounding of vibrations are weakest, as a result of a lack of payload and thrust of vibrations. The degree of intensity of the thrust determines the degree to which the body, and all its parts, is activated. The more intense the thrust of these vibrations from the rectal-pelvic basin, the greater the body involvement (bell factor).

Vocal focus, therefore, permits the singer to utilize the body as a bell in producing a maximum of vocal cords and body vibrations, since the body becomes an extension of the vocal cords, enabling the singer to reach the extremities of the body in re-sounding these vibrations, as a result of thrusting them from the rectal-pelvic basin, the center which supplies the intensity for reaching areas where vibrations would not ordinarily have the carrying power to be audible to the human ear. This maximum resonance gives the singer boundless freedom to shape vowels and consonants with ease.

Depth, height and brilliance are reflected in the singing sound of any language, when vocal focus is applied. The Compression Phase of the Gan-Tone (down-part of the beat) not only reaches the extremities of the body by fusing vocal cords and body vibrations to the rectal-pelvic basin, but, also, in the process of fusion and compression, vibrations that penetrate the mediums, such as, bones, cartilages, tendons, etc., reflect the peculiar characteristics of these mediums, giving greater dimensions of coloration to the singing sound in any language. For example, the deeper these vibrations penetrate bone, the more brilliant the emitted sound. The Thrust Phase of the Gan-Tone beat, or vocal focus, enables these vibrations to deeply penetrate the resonators of the body, giving profound resonance to the articulated sound, i.e., depth, height and brilliance.

The greatest dimensions in the singing word can be achieved only through vocal focus, which insures the greatest quantity of amplified and re-sounded vocal cords and body vibrations. Vocal focus, however, is dependent on JLB Fusion which provides the circuit for the application of the Gan-Tone, since it creates the open throat necessary for the passage of these vibrations to be re-sounded. In shaping vowels, such as AH and long O, it is relatively simple to maintain the lower jaw fused with the body. However, in shaping closed vowels, such as, long E and A, there is a natural tendency for the lower jaw to diverge from the body, breaking the vibratory continuity, or circuit, between the jaw and the body, thus diminishing the amplification of vibrations to be re-sounded, since the vibratory continuity to the bottom of the torso is broken. The singing word, therefore, is characterized by diminished volume, depth, height and brilliance. The singer, however, can retain the dimensions of the singing words that contain these closed vowels by maintaining the vertical-elliptical mouth opening and the fused position of the jaw to the body (open throat), while singing these closed vowels, thus insuring vibratory continuity in the body for efficiently applying the Compression Phase of the Gan-Tone (down-part of the beat) which, in turn, results in effective vocal focus.

Although it is awkward, in the beginning, to maintain an unhinged position of the jaw while singing the closed vowel, long E, which is the most difficult vowel to sing in this position, practice and mastery of this vowel becomes the criteria for measuring the depth, height and brilliance of all the other vowels, since it maximally expands the pharyngeal cavity. The skill acquired in singing a high, voluminous sound on this vowel with the unhinged position of the jaw will aid greatly in developing sensitivity to pressure and how to allay it in attaining the maximum resonance on this, or any other vowel. This skill in the Gan-Tone Method is known as Jaw Sense.

Maintaining vocal focus while shaping vowels and consonants in any language augments the components of sound. Each sound is composed of two or more simple tones. The lower tone determines the pitch and is called the fundamental. The other tones are called upper partials, or overtones. In addition to the fundamental and its partials, the Gan-Tone, an imposed vibration which has its own integral parts, can be imposed about six times per second on the fundamental as, for example, 440 vibrations per second (first A above middle C). The fundamental cycle of the Gan-Tone pitch (6 v.p.s.) is produced during the Compression Phase, or down-part of the beat, which is the undertone, and the overtone is produced during the Thrust Phase, or up-part of the Gan-Tone beat. The singing sound, therefore, which contains not only the components of the fundamental vocal cords vibrations, but those of the Gan-Tones as well, transforms the dimensions of the singing line by creating new points of reference (rectal-pelvic basin to the septum of the sinus

174 Singing Energy

cavities) regarding the propagation, amplification, penetration and thrust of vibrations to be re-sounded and shaped into vowels and consonants.

A Gan-Tone Principle can, therefore, be summarized:

The degree to which vocal cords and body vibrations are compressed to the rectal-pelvic basin on the JLB Fusion and the Gan-Tone frequency determines the quantity of amplified vibrations (undertones) that will be thrust to the resonators (vocal focus) to be re-sounded and shaped into vowels and consonants.

The greater the compressive impact of vocal cords and body vibrations to the rectal-pelvic basin, the greater the quantity of amplified vibrations (undertones) that will be thrust to the resonators to be re-sounded for shaping the singing word.

The degree of dimensions in the configurated sounds, i.e., singing words, is dependent on the degree of fusion, compression, amplification, thrust, re-sounding and projection of vocal cords and body vibrations; these vibrations reach the highest degree of intensity and compression at the rectal-pelvic basin, the controlling center for vocal focus.

The overtone of the Gan-Tone Pulsation is the dominant vibratory characteristic of all the components, or integral parts, of the fundamental pitch and is dependent on the degree of intensity of the Thrust Phase of the Gan-Tone application (up-part of the beat).

The greater the degree of thrust of vibrations to the resonators, the more dominant the overtone of the Gan-Tone Pulsation in the vowels and consonants of the emitted sound.

The Gan-Tone sound is a duo-pitch which consists of the fundamental pitch as, for ex., A above Middle C, whose frequency is 440 hertz and the Gan-Tone fundamental whose frequency is 6 per second imposed on the 440 hertz.

The frequencies of these fundamentals can increase or decrease independently of each other as, for ex., the pitch can change to A^2 above Middle C whose frequency is 880 hertz, and the Gan-Tone frequency can remain at 6 hertz or change to 5 or 7 Gan-Tones per second without affecting the fundamental 880 hertz.

The Role of Vocal Focus in Brilliance

X. Vocal focus, which is the thrusting and centering of vocal cords and body vibrations in the most vibrant and resonant areas of the body through the application of JLB Fusion and the Gan-Tone Pulsation, makes possible maximum brilliance in the singing sound by producing maximum impact and penetration of vocal cords and body vibrations throughout the body and its resonators.

Vocal focus maximizes the involvement of body components by making the whole body a highly resilient medium for the amplification, thrust and re-sounding of vocal cords and body vibrations, giving the greatest dimensions of brilliance to the emitted sound. Since the compression and fusion of body parts (Compression Phase, or down-part of the Gan-Tone beat) causes density and resiliency in the body, absorption of vibrations is minimized, making possible the greatest amplification of vocal cords and body vibrations.

In the Gan-Tone Method of Voice Production, brilliance is dependent upon the intensity of the Gan-Tone application, since this intensity determines the degree to which the body components, and their characteristics, will be involved in the quality of the emitted sound. When the Compression Phase of the Gan-Tone (down-part of the beat) is applied with maximum intensity, an orderly involvement of all the body components results, with maximum pressure and vocal cords and body vibrations focused at the rectal-pelvic basin. Equal intensity of thrust (up-part of the beat) of these vibrations occurs, making it possible for the highest head resonators, such as, the sinus cavities, to be involved in the re-sounding of these vibrations, resulting in maximum brilliance in the emitted sound.

Without an intense application of the Gan-Tone Pulsation, however, these extremities, which are capable of producing the highest degree of brilliance in the emitted sound, are vaguely involved. This triangular structure between and above the eyes (septum and sinus cavities) is, therefore, not unified with the pyramidal structure of the body that is utilized as a vehicle for producing brilliant sound. The basin of the rectal-pelvic area is the base of the pyramid whose sides converge through the body, reaching the apex, or highest point, of the pyramid at the septum of the sinus cavities above the bridge of the nose. Therefore, by extending vocal cords and body vibrations through the body to the rectal-pelvic basin, the vibrant depth of the body, and then thrusting these vibrations to the septum which vibrates the sinus cavities, the vibrant height of the body, the greatest radiance of brilliance is achieved in the emitted sound, since the septum, or apex, vibrates the most resonant areas of the body (sinus cavities) which are now fully utilized thereby adding the sharpest point to the vibrations of singing energy. Complete involvement of the body, from its depth to its height, as a vehicle for generating and transmitting vocal cords and body vibrations causes these vibrations to reflect the colors of the varied mediums through which they pass, as, for example, mellowness, when passing through muscles, and depth, when passing through the lower extremities of the body. When these vibrations are re-sounded in the varied body cavities, therefore, the emitted sound reflects a composite of the varied characteristics of the body mediums through which these vibrations penetrate.

Regardless of body weight, size, shape or strength, effective utilization of the body as amplifier and thrusting agent (vocal focus) of vocal cords and body vibrations can not be realized without the coordination of fusion and compression of body parts.

When the jaw is placed close to the larynx and maintained with a minimum of effort, during the Gan-Tone application, while singing sustained notes, the vibratory continuity of the vocal cords and body vibrations is maximized, since the hard parts, such as, bones and cartilages of the jaw and larynx, fuse with the body causing the strongest circuit for vibratory continuity, as opposed to vibratory absorption in softer mediums, such as, muscles. The body, therefore, utilizes its weight, size, shape and strength most effectively in amplifying and thrusting vocal cords and body vibrations to the resonators which, in turn, yields the greatest impact of these vibrations to the resonators, resulting in maximum brilliance in the emitted sound.

If the jaw, however, is not fused with the body in order to maintain vibratory continuity, from the vocal cords to the rectal-pelvic basin, while maintaining the vertical-elliptical mouth opening, vocal focus is diminished resulting in diminished brilliance in the emitted sound. Pressure immediately focuses on weaker substances, such as, muscles, causing undesirable strain, weakening the structure and support of vibrations, since fusion of bony parts no longer exists. Vibrations that would be amplified through fusion of hard parts, such as, bone, are now absorbed in the softer, less vibrant muscles, as the hard parts diverge, minimizing the advantages of body weight, size, shape and strength, as a result of the weakened vibratory continuity and amplification. Divergence of the jaw also restricts the throat opening, diminishing thrust and re-sounding of vibrations in the body resonators, particularly in the sinus cavities above the bridge of the nose, which provide the greatest magnitude of brilliance as long as the JLB Fusion and the Gan-Tone are applied with maximum intensity.

A Gan-Tone Principle can, therefore, be summarized:

The degree of intensity of the Gan-Tone application with the JLB Fusion determines the degree of penetration of vocal cords and body vibrations, omnidirectionally, to the body extremities which, in turn, determines the degree of brilliance in the emitted sound.

The greater the intensity of the Gan-Tone application, the deeper the penetration of vocal cords and body vibrations, omnidirectionally, to the body extremities which, in turn, produces maximum brilliance in the emitted sound.

The degree to which the coordination of fusion and compression of body parts is applied determines the degree of effectiveness of vibratory continuity, as opposed to vibratory absorption, which, in turn, determines the degree of effective utilization of body weight, size, shape and strength.

The more efficiently the body parts are fused and compressed, the greater the transmission of vocal cords and body vibrations through the body, minimizing any absorption of vibrations in the softer body mediums which, in turn, insures the most efficient involvement of body weight, size, shape and strength for generating, transmitting and re-sounding vibrations to produce the greatest degree of brilliance in the emitted sound.

If vibrations are absorbed, rather than transmitted, as a result of inefficient coordination of fusion and compression of body parts, body strength, size, shape and weight are ineffective, since the body has only a limited amount of vibrations to be reflected in the vocal sound.

Jaw, Larynx, Body Fusion and the Gan-Tone Pulsation, therefore, maximize the role of vocal focus through the maximal utilization of the body resonators which produces maximal brilliance in the emitted sound, since the body resounds as a bell.

SUMMARY OF THE GAN-TONE PRINCIPLES THAT GOVERN VOICE PROJECTION, BREATH CONTROL, RANGE, REGISTER, RESONANCE, VOLUME, COLORATION, SOUND CONFIGURATION AND BRILLIANCE, THE CHARACTERISTICS OF THE SINGING VOICE

VOICE PROJECTION

1 - The degree to which the projected sound manifests carrying power, freedom, dimension and endurance is commensurate with the ability of the singer to coordinate the body with the graduated positions of the jaw along with the full utilization of the head and chest resonators.

2 - Maximum efficiency in the singing process should involve a minimizing of pressure, or stress, in the vocal cords and surrounding areas, and a maximizing of the jaw, larynx, body involvement for ultimate support of the sound, along with the head and chest resonators for ultimate amplification of the sound that originates in the vocal cords.

3 - The degree to which the jaw diverges from the solid structure of the converged jaw (fused jawbone and Adam's apple approximating the collar bone) impairing the vertical-elliptical mouth opening determines the degree to which pressure focuses on the vocal cords and throat muscles, restricting the production of vibrations to the vocal cords. The diverging jaw acts as a circuit breaker, breaking the fusion of vibrations throughout the body, making it impossible to ground and support a maximum of vocal cords vibrations at the rectal-pelvic area.

4 - The degree to which the downward pressure through the body is applied determines the definition of the thrust sound to the head resonators. Conversely, the diminishing of pressure downward through the body, i.e., a relaxation of pressure from the jaw to the larynx and torso, diminishes the thrust of the supported sound to the head resonators causing a weaker vocal signal, since the solidity of body support is debilitated, resulting in a devitalized sound.

5 - One Gan-Tone Cycle:
    a - The admission of air by inhalation.
    b - The conversion and fusion of air as sound vibrations compressed to the rectal-pelvic area and throughout the body during the down-part of the beat, which comprises the action (Compression Phase).
    c - The stroke, or thrust, of the total vibrations to the resonators during the up-part of the beat, which is the equal and opposite reaction (Thrust Phase).

6 - The degree of focus of vocal cords and body vibrations in the resonators (vocal focus) determines the degree of vocal projection.

The greater the fusion and compression of vocal cords and body vibrations to the rectal-pelvic area, the greater the thrust and impact of these amplified vibrations to the resonators which, in turn, produces amplified resonance that is reflected in amplified vocal projection.

BREATH CONTROL

7 - Any closing movement of the jaw from its maximum opening, in the process of singing loud, high, sustained sounds, should be preceded by the easing of body pressure, not only to prevent the natural buildup of stress in the throat area, but also, to enable the sound to flow effortlessly, thus expending less air and enabling the singer to sustain a longer breath line.

8 - The efficiency of resonators is more thoroughly realized, not by their size, but by the most efficient conversion of breath through the instantaneous application of the Gan-Tone beat which ultimately produces maximum vibrations, maximum thrust, and maximum focusing of the sound to such resonating areas as the base of the nose, back of the upper teeth, hard palate, pharynx, nasal passage, or other parts of the body with a minimum of breath, resulting in a maximum of breath as vibrating sound.

9 - The degree of speed applied in the coordination of the Gan-Tone beat with fusion through the body, and the degree of pressure applied to the fusion at the rectal-pelvic area determine the degree to which the body functions as a total vibrator, or bell, making the body an agent for the maximal conversion of breath into sound.

10 - The deeper, or darker, the sound in the gamut of

the singing scale, the more breath is needed to sustain these tones, since more resonating cavities are being utilized, necessitating more air.

The higher the pitch, the deeper the sound, and the more intense the body involvement, the more rapid the consumption of air.

11 - The degree of intensity on the periphery of the mouth for a given opening determines the degree of focus and resonance at that point and the amount of air utilized in the production of sound.

12 - The greater the intensity of focus to the resonating areas, the more brilliant the sound and the less air expenditure, thus providing more air reserve for the singer.

13 - The degree of speed and intensity with which the vocal cords and body vibrations are thrust to the resonators determines the efficiency of breath control.

The greater the thrust and focus of vocal cords and body vibrations in the resonators, the less breath is required to project and re-sound vibrations in the resonators, producing maximum volume with a minimum of breath, when the JLB Fusion and the Gan-Tone Pulsation are swiftly applied.

RANGE

14 - The degree to which the jaw is moved down and back while ascending the scale determines the degree of dilation that will take place in the throat to counteract restriction which prevents the impasse.

The higher the range, the greater the need for the jaw to rest firmly down and back, close to the larynx and collar bone, in order to counteract the increasing restriction that occurs with increasing range.

15 - As the break in the voice approaches as, for ex., in the middle range, decrease laryngeal pressure and increase the opening of the jaw. By coordinating the decrease of laryngeal pressure with the jaw opening, no break will occur, since the jaw is now fused with the larynx causing solidity in the laryngeal parts which produces solidity in the sound.

16 - The amount of agility, spontaneity and intensity with which the Gan-Tone beat fuses the vocal cords sound to the rectal-pelvic area on the constant under-drone of the JLB Fusion determines the strength of the thrust of vibrations to the resonating cavities of the body which, in turn, determines the volume produced throughout the vocal range.

17 - The degree of intensity that is achieved in the thrusting and focusing of vocal cords and body vibrations in the resonators (vocal focus), while ascending or descending the scale, determines the degree of dimension that will be evident in the range.

The greater the intensity in the thrusting and focusing of vocal cords and body vibrations in the resonators (Thrust Phase—up-part of the Gan-Tone beat), while ascending or descending the scale, the greater the volume, depth, height, coloration, resilience, buoyancy, fullness and brilliance throughout the range.

REGISTER

18 - It is not the vibrating vocal cords that determine air turbulence, breaks or registers. It is essentially the curve of the vocal hook, with its accompanying irregularities, that breaks the straight flow of the sound. The fusion of the jaw with the tongue, the hyoid bone, the cartilages and muscles of the larynx along with the simulated yawn and utilization of the facial apertures as lenses "straighten out" the curve and eliminate breaks of the so-called vocal registers, which ultimately results in a smooth transition from low to high sounds, otherwise known as the even scale, thus denoting one register in the singing voice.

The more efficient the fusion of the parts of the vocal hook, the more pure and undistorted the vocal sound, as a result of less restriction in the less constricted vocal hook, maximizing the flow of sound and minimizing pressure on the cords, while maintaining a steady flow of sound.

19 - The coordination of jaw movements, pressure points on the tongue, the simulation of the yawn, and the utilization of the facial apertures as lenses are the basic

ingredients for sufficiently eliminating restriction in the vocal hook, which will prevent changes in tonal quality, thus eliminating the so-called registers in the ascending scale.

20 - It is the pull and strain in the throat muscles that bring fatigue, instability and collapse to the vocal line. The application of every beat of the Gan-Tone through the body transfers the responsibility of support from throat muscles to the body, insuring a constant security of the vocal line, thus preventing pressure breaks and cracks in the voice.

21 - Vibrations propagate and dominate in various parts of the body, and throughout the whole body, in proportion to the pitch of the sound and the intensity of the Gan-Tone application.

22 - The imposition of pressure on the vocal cords by the singer varies in all individuals. However, through practice, the coordination that determines the strength of the vocal signal can be developed.

The degree to which the vocal signal is used with the larynx and surrounding muscles and cartilages varies with the individual; and, similarly, the anatomical structure and arrangement of component parts of the entire body, and, specifically, those of the vocal hook, vary according to the individual.

The ability to manifest smoothness in the flow of sound in the singing process varies with the individual. The coordination necessary for this smooth flow can be developed and controlled.

23 - The degree of intensity and freedom that is achieved in the thrusting and focusing of vocal cords and body vibrations in the resonators (vocal focus), while ascending or descending the scale, is dependent on the degree of efficiency of the Jaw, Larynx, Body Fusion as a constant and the Gan-Tone beat which, in turn, determines the following:

    a. the degree of evenness in the scale (one register)

    b. the degree of pressure that will be allayed which, in turn, will determine the relative absence of pressure breaks in the range

    c. the degree of evenness that will be maintained in the vibrational amplitude, from low to high tones, eliminating the marked distinctions within the entire range, thus removing the belief in chest and head registers, since the free passage of vocal cords vibrations involves the chest and head simultaneously with the rest of the body

RESONANCE

24 - The unhinged jaw position, while singing soft or loud sounds, creates the maximum area for mouth resonance; whereas, the closing of the jaw diminishes the size of the mouth cavity as a resonator.

25 - It is the degree of orderly fusion of the jaw, tongue, hyoid bone, larynx, cartilages of the trachea, elements of the chest, diaphragm muscle, and abdomen to the rectal-pelvic basin that determines the degree to which the body will function as a vibrator, below and above the vocal cords, which is the basis for determining the utilization of the body cavities for re-sounding these vibrations that emanate from the vocal cords.

26 - The degree of spontaneity and intensity of the Gan-Tone application determines the intensity of compression of vocal cords vibrations to the bottom of the torso.

The degree of intensity of this compression (Compression Phase—down-part of the Gan-Tone beat) determines the degree of support and thrust of these vibrations to the resonators of the body (Thrust Phase—up-part of the Gan-Tone beat) which, in turn, determines the degree of resonance.

27 - The location of the resonators in relation to the source of support and thrust, i.e., the rectal-pelvic area, determines the degree of thrust needed for effectively resonating the cavities (resonators).

The closer the resonators to the rectal-pelvic area, the less need for intensity of the Gan-Tone application.

Conversely, the farther the resonators from the rectal-pelvic area, the greater the need for intensity of the Gan-Tone application.

Maximum intensity of the Gan-Tone application results in maximum vibrations that are thrust with maximum efficiency to all the resonators of the body, resulting in maximum resonance, enabling the body to function as a bell.

28 - The degree to which the body is utilized as an extension of the vocal cords and lungs in the amplifying, thrusting and centering of vocal cords and body vibrations in the resonators determines the degree of resonance, i.e., depth, height, coloration, flexibility, resilience and volume, of the emitted sound.

Maximum utilization of the body as an extension of the vocal cords and lungs in the amplifying, thrusting and centering of vocal cords and body vibrations in the resonators yields maximum resonance in the emitted sound.

29 - The degree of focus of vocal cords and body vibrations in the most vibrant and resonant areas of the body (vocal focus) is dependent upon the degree of speed and intensity of the application of the Gan-Tone Pulsation.

The greater the intensity and speed of the Gan-Tone application, the more intense the focus of vocal cords and body vibrations in the most vibrant and resonant areas of the body, resulting in a greater amplification of vibrations, thus producing greater resonance which, in turn, insures greater brilliance, resilience, volume and color in the emitted sound.

VOLUME

30 - Volume, the result of vibrations and resonances produced through body fusion by the imposition of pressure through the body, hinges on the efficient movement of the jaw down and back which, in turn, fuses the larynx and throat to the head and body.

31 - The unhinged position of the jaw, independent of mouth movements, along with the yawn assure depth and height in the sound at any part of the range enabling the singer to have great control of volume, since there is a maximum utilization of mouth resonance in the soft as well as the loud sounds.

32 - The degree to which the Gan-Tone beat is imposed through the body is commensurate with the degree to which the jaw is imposed downward on the larynx and body.

Maximum dispersement of pressure throughout the body is dependent on maximum application of the Gan-Tone with maximum opening of the jaw.

The more pressure is dispersed throughout the body, the greater the diffusion of vibrations to be colored, embellished and magnified.

33 - The greater the application of vocal cords fusion through the body, the greater the amount of vibrations which, in turn, produces greater resonance, thus increasing the volume of the singing voice.

34 - The manifestation of the vibrating body depends upon the imposition of pressure through the body by the singer as Gan-Tones (pulsations), amplifying the original vocal cords sound throughout the body by uniting the vibrating parts and making the body a mass of vibrations and resonance, resulting in maximum volume and causing the body to function as a bell.

35 - The speed and intensity of the fusion of body parts and the compression of vocal cords and body vibrations determine the impact of these vibrations to the rectal-pelvic basin (Compression Phase—down-part of the Gan-Tone beat—action). The impact of these vibrations to the rectal-pelvic basin determines the thrust and transmission of these vibrations throughout the body (vocal focus—Thrust Phase—up-part of the Gan-Tone beat—reaction) which, in turn, determine the volume in the emitted sound.

The greater the fusion and compression of vibrations to the rectal-pelvic basin, the greater the thrust of these vibrations to the resonators which, in turn, yields increased, amplified vibrations, resulting in increased volume of the emitted sound.

The greater the compressive impact of vocal cords and body vibrations at the rectal-pelvic basin, the greater the vocal focus which yields greater volume and, therefore, more effective vocal projection.

COLORATION

36 - The degree of intensity of the Jaw, Larynx, Body Fusion coordinated with the degree of intensity of vibrational focus to the various parts of the body, and the degree to which the mouth focuses these vibrations determine the variations in coloration, or pigmentation, of the emitted sound.

37 - The degree of amplification of vibrations is dependent on the degree of Gan-Tone application which, in turn, determines the degree of magnification of the resonant characteristics of each resonator.

38 - Messa di Voce

As the tone is expanded or contracted, the movement of the jaw downward, by placing it, without rigidity, as close as possible to the Adam's apple and collar bone, fuses the throat components (tongue, jaw, larynx, trachea) with the body to provide the strongest structure for the widest dimension of tonal coloration. As volume is increased, this position creates the widest throat opening for the greatest emission of vibrations. Fusion of the jaw, larynx and body makes possible the maximum utilization of body vibrations in the augmentation of the fundamental vocal cords vibrations, the maximum compression of these vibrations to the rectal-pelvic area, and the greatest amount of thrust of these vibrations through the unrestricted throat opening to be freely focused and guided in the different areas of the resonators for the maximum expansion of resonance in the coloration of the messa di voce.

39 - The greater the degree of penetration of vocal cords vibrations throughout the body, the greater the degree of coloration of vibrations to be re-sounded in the body resonators, producing a variety of tonal colors in the emitted sound.

40 - The depth, or coloration, of a given tone is determined by the focus of oscillation from the frontal concentration of resonance in the sinus cavities to the postnasal concentration in the posterior nasal-pharyngeal channel.

The darker, or deeper, the sound, the greater the involvement of the posterior nasal-pharyngeal channel. Conversely, the less dark, or deep, the sound, the greater the involvement of the frontal nasal area and/or sinus cavities.

41 - The degree to which vocal cords and body vibrations are compressed to the rectal-pelvic basin determines the extent to which the peculiar vibratory characteristics of the varied mediums of the body will be audible in tonal coloration, since it is only from this controlling center (rectal-pelvic basin) that vibrations can be amplified and thrust to the varied mediums of the body to utilize, most efficiently, their vibratory and re-sounding characteristics.

The greater the compressive impact of vocal cords and body vibrations to the rectal-pelvic basin, the greater the thrust of these vibrations (vocal focus), resulting in the greater involvement of the mediums and resonators of the body which, in turn, yields greater coloration in the emitted sound.

SOUND CONFIGURATION

42 - The degree to which the jaw rides up when singing loud, high, sustained sounds, or when shifting from one vowel sound to the other will determine the degree to which the quality of the singing line will be altered.

The more the jaw rides up while sustaining a vowel, and the more sluggish the movement when shifting from one vowel sound to another, in any part of the scale, the more the spherical penetration of vibrations throughout the body diminishes causing the center and control of vibrations to be shifted from the rectal-pelvic area to the vocal cords and surrounding muscles, diminishing the dimensions of the emitted sound.

The more spontaneous the movement from one vowel sound to the other, the greater the fusion of the jaw to the body, maintaining the continuity of maximum vibrations, maximum support and thrust, and maximum throat opening for the free passage of vibrations and resonance in the body cavities, below and above the vocal cords, resulting in a uniform quality in the sustained sounds.

43 - The degree of spontaneity with which the consonants in words are condensed and articulated in coordination with the Jaw, Larynx, Body Fusion determines the degree to which the consonants will interfere with the singing line.

The slower the pronunciation of consonants, the shorter the duration of the singing line, as a result of the excessive interference created by the prolonged consonants which, in turn, interferes with the application of the Jaw, Larynx, Body Fusion, narrowing the dimensions of the emitted sound.

Conversely, the more instantaneous the condensation and pronunciation of consonants (single or multiple), the more spontaneous the application of the Jaw, Larynx, Body Fusion, producing a longer singing line of greater dimensions.

44 - The more rapid the articulation of consonants, the more rapid the fusion of the jaw, larynx and body, resulting in a more efficient application of the Gan-Tone cycle.

Rapid articulation of consonants yields rapid Jaw, Larynx, Body Fusion which, in turn, yields rapid fusion and compression (down-part of the Gan-Tone beat) causing the solid grounding of vocal cords vibrations to the rectal-pelvic basin which, in turn, results in maximum thrust of unobstructed vocal cords and body vibrations through the open throat (up-part of the Gan-Tone beat) to the resonators, below and above the vocal cords, with the greatest impact, causing maximum resonance of these vibrations in all the openings of the body, making the body function as a bell in producing maximum resonance for focusing and shaping the emitted sound.

45 - The frequency, intensity and thrust with which the Gan-Tone Pulsation is imposed on the sustained vowels determines the evenness, smoothness, clarity, brilliance, coloration, cover, or aura, and volume of the emitted sound.

The slower the frequency, intensity and thrust of the Gan-Tone Pulsation on the sustained vowels, the greater the intervals between the resonant sounds causing an interruption in the singing line.

Conversely, the greater the frequency, intensity and thrust of the Gan-Tone Pulsation on the sustained vowels, the more even and smooth the singing line, and the greater the dimensions of the emitted sound.

46 - The mixture of consonants with vowels, in the rapid articulation of words in the singing line, debilitates the Jaw, Larynx, Body Fusion, which is permissable, if maximum dimensions in the sound are not necessary. However, the Gan-Tone Pulsation applied to the indefinite Jaw, Larynx, Body Fusion will produce greater dimensions in the singing line and less pressure in the vocal cords not possible without the Gan-Tone application.

47 - The degree to which vocal cords and body vibrations are compressed to the rectal-pelvic basin determines the quantity of amplified vibrations that will be thrust to the resonators (vocal focus) to be re-sounded and shaped into vowels and consonants.

The greater the compressive impact of vocal cords and body vibrations to the rectal-pelvic basin, the greater the quantity of amplified vibrations that will be thrust to the resonators to be re-sounded for shaping the singing word.

The degree of dimensions in the configurated sound (lyrics) is dependent on the degree of fusion, compression, amplification, thrust, re-sounding and projection of vocal cords and body vibrations which reach the highest degree of involvement and control at the rectal-pelvic basin, the controlling center for vocal focus.

The overtone of the Gan-Tone Pulsation is the dominant vibratory characteristic of all the components, or integral parts (fundamental and overtones), and is dependent on the degree of intensity of the Thrust Phase of the Gan-Tone application (up-part of the beat).

The greater the degree of thrust of vibrations to the resonators, the more dominant the overtone of the Gan-Tone Pulsation in the vowels of the emitted sound.

BRILLIANCE

48 - The degree to which the jaw is fused to the larynx and body determines the degree to which the vocal cords

vibrations are fused and compressed through the body and grounded at the rectal-pelvic area.

The degree of compression determines the degree of thrust of these vibrations to the resonators of the head and body where they are focused and re-sounded for brilliance in the vocal sound.

The greater the fusion of the jaw to the larynx and body, the greater the fusion and compression of vocal cords vibrations, resulting in a greater degree of amplification of vibrations that produces a greater degree of thrust and impact of these vibrations to the resonators which, in turn, causes a higher degree of re-sounding of these vibrations in the resonators, yielding maximum brilliance in the emitted sound.

49 - The more frequent and intense the application of the Gan-Tone Pulsation on the fundamental vocal cords vibrations, the more elastic, resilient and brilliant the emitted sound.

50 - The degree of intensity of the Gan-Tone application determines the degree of penetration of vocal cords and body vibrations, omnidirectionally, to the extremities of the body which, in turn, determines the degree of brilliance in the emitted sound.

The greater the intensity of the Gan-Tone application, the deeper the penetration of vocal cords and body vibrations, omnidirectionally, to the extremities of the body which, in turn, produces maximum brilliance in the emitted sound.

The degree to which the coordination of fusion and compression of body parts is applied determines the degree of effectiveness of vibratory continuity, as opposed to vibratory absorption, which determines the degree of effective utilization of body weight, size, shape and strength.

If vibrations are absorbed, rather than transmitted, as a result of inefficient coordination of fusion and compression of body parts, body strength, size, shape and weight are ineffective, since the body has only a limited amount of vibrations to be reflected in the vocal sound.

The more efficiently the body parts are fused and compressed, the greater the transmission of vocal cords and body vibrations through the body, minimizing any absorption of vibrations in the softer body mediums which, in turn, insures the most efficient involvement of body weight, size, shape and strength for generating, transmitting and re-sounding vibrations to produce the greatest degree of brilliance in the emitted sound.

TEACHING THE GAN-TONE METHOD

CONTENTS

TEACHING THE GAN-TONE METHOD

I.	STUDENT OBSERVATION AND ANALYSIS	191
II.	PROCEDURE OF INSTRUCTION	194
III.	GAN-TONE REALIZATIONS	197
	Maximal (Absolute) Jaw, Larynx, Body Fusion	201
	Rectal-Pelvic Breath Control (Sinking the Breath)	202
	Modified Jaw, Larynx, Body Fusion	202
	Application of the Gan-Tone Pulsation	202
	Vocal Exercises for Applying the Jaw, Larynx, Body Fusion and the Gan-Tone Pulsation	203

Vocal Student Observation and Analysis

I. In approaching the student, the voice teacher trained in the Gan-Tone Method of Voice Production would utilize the following procedure:

1. <u>Obtain a sampling of the voice by having the student sing a few scales that would encompass the student's present vocal range.</u>

2. <u>Analyze this vocal sampling in order to determine the natural characteristics, such as:</u>

   a. strength of vocal signal produced
   b. existence of breaks in the voice
   c. smoothness and evenness of the vocal line
   d. degree of impedence in the vocal projection, i.e., any obstruction that results in a tight, restricted sound
   e. degree of involvement, if any, of the jaw, larynx and body
   f. intonation to pitch

   Although there are individual differences among students, it is certain that if the student is experiencing difficulty in range and volume, showing abrupt changes in quality, cracks in the voice, otherwise known as breaks, lack of breath control, fatigue, hoarseness, or blanking out of the sound in the process of singing, that the student is unaware of the basic Gan-Tone Principle involving the Jaw, Larynx, Body Coordination.

3. <u>Observe the symptoms present in the student who lacks the understanding of the Jaw, Larynx, Body Coordination Principle, such as:</u>

   a. lack of air to carry the vocal line effectively
   b. physical strain while attempting to sing loudly
   c. limitation in range, coloration, flexibility
   d. facial expression of anxiety and tension
   e. tight, raised shoulders while singing
   f. tension in various parts of the body, such as, arms, hands, legs and stomach
   g. rasping sound as a result of irritation
   h. absence of jaw coordination necessary to overcome the natural pressures that cause tension in the neck and throat muscles

4. <u>Focus on the student's inability to coordinate the jaw with the vocal demand, since it is this lack of understanding that essentially causes the symptoms observed.</u>

The jaw acts as a door for the emission and projection of the vocal sound.

The jaw must be down and back, resting on the larynx, when <u>the greatest degree of loudness, i.e., volume, is desired in any part of the range, but especially where the pressure is greatest, i.e., in the ascending scale, or when the greatest freedom in the flow of sound is desired for it is only in this position that the fully open-throated sound is demonstrated.</u>

This maximum opening of the jaw is not required in speaking, since long lines of sustained sound on vowels are not necessary in ordinary conversation. The unhinged position of the jaw down and back, resting on the larynx, causing recesses in front of the earlobes, thereby denoting maximum opening of the jaw, must be maintained during moments of great vocal demand (loud, high, sustained notes). Any compromising position, where the jaw moves away from the larynx, will jeopardize the security of the sound by immediately transferring the support from the solid union of the jaw and larynx to the neck muscles which can't sustain the intense vocal demand causing these muscles to become tense and tired, collapsing the security of the sound and causing the symptoms observed in the student.

It is important that the student and teacher be aware of any drifting of the jaw from this maximum position, while demonstrating the greatest volume in any part of the range, the highest part of the scale, or the greatest freedom in the flow of the sound.

This jaw movement will create a wobbling jaw which is the result of placing the stress mainly on muscles rather than on the solid contact of the jawbone and the larynx. This wobbling jaw constantly interrupts and impedes the flow of vibrations causing tightness in the student's sound which, in turn, causes body tension and fatigue and can only lead to eventual vocal collapse.

The following Gan-Tone Principle should, therefore, be noted:

> The degree of movement away from the vertical-elliptical mouth opening and the unhinged, down and back position of the jaw during moments of great stress, i.e., maximum volume and high notes, determines the degree of constriction (tightness and squeezing) that will occur in the open throat position causing a commensurate amount of vocal restriction (confinement) in the laryngeal area.

It naturally follows that the intense air pressure produced during the emission of maximum volume or high notes formerly released as sound through the open throat is now confined to the laryngeal area, as a result of closing the jaw during these moments of great stress.

The following condition occurs:

> The intense air pressure, or vibrating air, now confined to a restricted area, produces heat. As the jaw continues to ride into this pressure, the heat intensifies causing irritation in the larynx, the vocal cords and surrounding membranes. The delicate membranes of the vocal folds now become swollen from the burning intensity and do not respond normally any longer. In order to continue, the singer drives harder compounding the irritation, and the condition worsens.

The health of the vocal cords, therefore, is dependent on the position of the jaw in relation to the vocal demand. The maximum jaw opening is for the emission of the greatest pressure present during the projection of the maximum volume and the highest notes in full voice.

Subsequently, as pressure diminishes in the vocal demand (i.e., less volume and lower notes require less pressure), the jaw can stray from its maximum open position placing this diminished pressure on muscles without any harmful effects to the vocal cords and surrounding areas.

The jaw, in its maximum open position, i.e., unhinged, during the greatest vocal stress is comparable to supporting a five pound weight against the chest. The jaw riding up during moments of great stress is comparable to supporting this five pound weight at arm's length parallel to the ground.

The unhinged jaw, opened wide to sustain the greater weight of stress, is analogous to the five pound weight against the chest. In both cases, the weights are solidly sustained by the body.

The straying jaw is analogous to the book held at arm's length. In both cases, strain is focused on muscles rather than on solid structures (larynx and chest). Muscles, however, can't sustain pressure as well as solid body structures.

It is important to note that the graduated jaw positions to the maximum opening, i.e., the jaw sitting squarely on the larynx, determine the degree of fusion, or oneness, of the jaw, larynx and body. The maximum fusion of these parts causes the greatest support of the tone, since this fusion results in the transfer of stress away from the vocal cords and onto the body, i.e., from the larynx to the bottom of the torso. This deep body support causes the sound to be more easily projected to the head resonators, i.e., nasal, mouth and sinus cavities. Consequently, not only is pressure being drawn away from the delicate vocal cords, but this projection of sound through the body results in a maximum amplification of sound.

5. <u>Observe the student's facility in encompassing range, i.e., ascending and descending the scale. Note if there are evidences of the following:</u>
   a. breaks in the voice
   b. discomfort
   c. scraping
   d. fear
   e. strain
   f. lack of inclination to ascend the scale

Limitation in range often is the result of timidity and lack of awareness regarding the vocal potential. It will be noted that vocal students have much more range than they realize, and their limitation is the result of <u>a lack of understanding of the relationship of the jaw to range.</u>

Since each individual's nature is different, each one reacts differently vocally. Although vocal cords may be similar, the degree of range varies greatly with individuals.

Some students, for example, may encompass a wide range without any conscious involvement of the jaw. Their mental inclination appears to overcome the natural barriers that most individuals encounter when ascending or descending the scale. Individuals in this category are rare. However, it is important to note that their dimensions in volume and vocal freedom are, of necessity, limited. Ignorance regarding the role of the jaw in encompassing range will, ultimately, lead to collapse of the vocal structure, since the buildup of pressure that results from too much tension on neck muscles while ascending the scale, rather than diffusing this tension through the body, inevitably results in muscular collapse, preventing the singer from realizing more range and volume. Neck muscles are attempting to maintain an open throat position for the emission of unimpeded sound. However, the neck muscles can't sustain the burden of continuous singing, especially when sustaining loud, high notes.

This condition is analogous to the example of a person holding a five pound weight at arm's length parallel to the ground that was already cited. Since the muscles alone are sustaining this weight, fatigue is inevitable, to the point of collapse, in a matter of minutes. By bringing this weight to the chest, it can be sustained indefinitely, since the emphasis is now shifted from the muscles to the body in supporting the weight.

In order to eliminate the strain on neck muscles and diffuse this stress to the body, thus making it possible for the student to realize and demonstrate more range and volume, it is essential that the singer be aware of the importance of the coordination of the jaw opening to the degree of pressure involved. As the singer ascends the scale, the jaw must be opened wider to accommodate the increasing pressure. The further down and back the jaw is placed, the greater the fusion of the jaw to the body, causing the stress to be diffused to the body and away from the neck muscles.

Most voices have breaks, or impasses, while ascending or descending the scale. A break in the voice occurs when the opening of the throat, from the laryngeal tract to the pharynx (back of the mouth), is constricted, thus impeding the flow of sound. By instructing the student to move the jaw down and back and to push the back of the tongue forward along with the root of the tongue, which are some of the physical characteristics involved in vomiting, the maximum opening of the throat will be achieved. This extreme position will accommodate the highest and lowest notes plus the greatest volume, thus enabling the student to reach the gamut of his vocal cords potential, since this position eliminates pressure from neck muscles and transfers it to the body.

6. Observe whether or not the quality of the voice changes as the student ascends or descends the scale.

It will be noted that students often think they have "two, three or more voices" because of the pronounced change in quality, while ascending or descending the scale.

The vocal cords, however, do not cause any change in the quality of the voice. It is, instead, the flow of air through the varying positions of the laryngeal tract, of the back of the tongue, and of the postnasal tract, as the mouth positions vary, that determine the quality of the sound. As the shape of that area changes, the sound becomes more or less impeded. In order to enable the air to flow with no impedence, i.e., a free-flow of uninterrupted sound, it is important to coordinate the jaw with the muscles of the vocal hook. The jaw moved down and back along with the simulated yawn (Exinvac Principle), and the back of the tongue pushed forward and downward (vomiting characteristics), to create a maximum throat opening, will result in an unimpeded flow of vibrant air which, in turn, will eliminate the changes in vocal quality resulting in an even, smooth, unbroken line, while ascending or descending the scale.

Essentially, the curvature at the back of the mouth, in the vocal hook, causes the various turbulences of vibrant air according to the degree that the throat is opened or closed. In order to remove the turbulences, it is necessary to attempt to make that curve as straight and wide as possible in emitting sound. By coordinating the jaw with the pressing forward of the back of the tongue (vomiting characteristics) plus the simulated yawn (Exinvac Principle), the air flows in a freer manner because the passageway is now more widely opened.

7. Observe the strength of the student's vocal sound, i.e., whether he is producing the pure vocal cords sound with no laryngeal fusion, which is usually a light sound, or the augmented sound produced with laryngeal fusion, which is a more vibrant, powerful sound.

It will be noted that most beginners, and often many who have studied, have small voices which is usually the result of unawareness regarding the role of the larynx in augmenting the vocal cords sound.

Although vocal cords may be similar, the degree of vocal cords contact and laryngeal involvement varies greatly with individuals. Since the sound is preceded by the thought, the condition of that thought is an important factor in determining the quality of that sound. A timid person, for example, may activate a very weak signal in his vocal cords without any amplification of the larynx as vibrator; or a person's thought may not coordinate air properly through the vocal cords, and the result would be a feeble signal devoid of laryngeal involvement. Another person's nature may focus excessively in the vocal cords with strong laryngeal involvement without the ability to de-activate the larynx as vibrator to reveal only the vocal cords sound. These few examples represent a very limited number of variations regarding individual differences to be found in students. Actually, it is impractical to enumerate the countless differences that exist, since each student is a unique individual.

Considering the individual differences in thinking and the conditions that stimulate these differences, there is a relationship between the pure vocal cords sound and the degree of involvement of the larynx as a vibrator of this pure vocal cords sound among humans. No laryngeal fusion in the pure vocal cords sound results in the so-called falsetto voice; whereas, variations in laryngeal involvement determine the degree of amplification of this pure vocal cords sound. Maximum laryngeal involvement results in the antithesis of the falsetto voice, which is the maximally amplified voice.

By making the student aware of the role of the larynx as secondary vibrator and primary resonator, the student's sound can be amplified, i.e., a small voice can be changed to a big voice. (The vocal cords are the primary audible vibrators.)

Teaching the student to utilize some characteristics of the natural vomit will enable him to compact and solidify the cartilages, muscles and ligaments of the larynx thus augmenting the vibrating ability of the larynx which, in turn, multiplies the original vocal cords sound. By pressing forward and downward on the back of the tongue and its root, while simultaneously lowering the jaw, the area beneath the jaw, i.e., the neck area, solidifies with the larynx causing the larynx to fuse with the body. This fusion causes the body to be involved as a vibrator and resonator along with the larynx, resulting in more resonance, since the vibrating quality of the larynx has now been joined solidly to other parts, i.e., the jaw and the body.

This extension is comparable to the addition of more wood, lyre and resonant area to the grand piano, as opposed to the upright piano, in order to increase the output of sound. Another example involves amplifiers and speakers. The bigger the speaker, the greater the output of sound. The speaker in a pocket-sized radio, which is a few inches long, can't produce the resonance of a large speaker whose dimensions are measured in feet.

8. <u>Observe the student for any signs of tension in any parts of the body, such as the face, hands, arms, legs and stomach, since this tension denotes anxiety and the lack of dependence on principle.</u>

Procedure of Instruction

II. Select a simple scale, as for ex., B natural below middle C, E flat and F sharp returning to E flat and B natural to complete the scale, and ascend a half tone at a time. Each complete scale is to be sung within 3 beats at a metronomic speed of 76. The student takes a breath between each scale on the fourth metronomic beat.

As the student shows signs of cracking or thinning of the voice while ascending the scale, advise the student to bring the jaw further down and back thus insuring security in ascending the scale. The maximum opening of the jaw is required for the highest notes and the greatest volume, since the jaw is now fused with the larynx.

Instruct the student to press the back of the tongue forward and downward in order to create an open throat and stronger laryngeal contact.

Do not proceed past the point of strain, i.e., the higher notes in the ascending scale, until the strain is properly allayed through the proper coordination of the jaw, i.e., as the strain increases, the jaw must be more definitely down and back.

It will be noted that the student will react favorably to the instruction requiring the jaw to be sustained in the open position commensurate with the vocal pressure, since the student will become aware of the diminishing pressure away from the cords and the transfer of this pressure to the body, as he coordinates the jaw with the vocal demand.

This transfer of pressure from the vocal cords to the body is the essence of the Gan-Tone Method.

Stress with the student the importance of guiding the sound to re-sounding areas (body and head resonators, such as, the chest, mouth and sinus cavities), not only to increase volume, resonance, coloration, flexibility, support, resilience and freedom of the voice, but also to combat the buildup of pressure that accompanies the singing process.

Have the student observe that the quality of the sound is deeper and fuller, when the jaw is down and back while singing loud or soft sounds.

It is currently believed that singing a high note in maximum volume (fortissimo) and then diminishing it to a very soft sound (pianissimo) is a very difficult vocal feat. However, by disciplining the jaw to a maximum opening, while singing a high note from a fortissimo to a pianissimo, it will be noted that even a beginning student will be able to negotiate this vocal skill with little difficulty.

Make the student aware that the process of moving the jaw down and back, in order to gain freedom and security for the emitted sound, is coordinated with the action of pushing the root of the tongue forward and downward enabling the tip of the tongue to rest against the back of the lower teeth and gum. This coordinated action will not only ultimately control the tongue, preventing it from moving uncontrollably, but will also make a more solid connection to the jawbone. This extreme control is essential for maximal dimensions of soft and loud sounds and for extreme conditions, i.e., moments of great pressure (loud, high, sustained notes and great intensity), for it is at this time that anxiety, muscle tension and air pressure culminate to produce detrimental symptoms, such as, jaw spasm, involuntary tongue action, throat restriction, tightness and cracks in the sound.

Make the student aware that the distance between the lower teeth and the vocal cords is shortened when the jaw is down and back thus compacting the jaw and the tongue to the body, making the structure for the sound more solid. The surface of the tongue, from the larynx to the tip, is also compacted downward and forward, not only opening the throat more widely, but also fusing the parts of the jaw, the tongue, its root, the larynx, and the body, resulting in a highly desirable condition for preventing the destruction of the vocal structure during moments of great pressure, thus preventing confusion and anxiety by enabling the singer to produce sound that is secure and free.

The teacher will notice that the student will have a tendency to close the jaw while singing. This condition is natural. From the moment that one learns how to speak, the jaw is constantly moving up-and-down rapidly to accommodate the articulation involved in speaking.

Singing involves the sustained, graduated positions of the jaw that are not ordinarily applied to speaking. The range, intensity, focus, coloration and sustaining required in singing are unnecessary in speaking. However, the application of Gan-Tone Principles in speaking will bring inestimable freedom, security, beauty, nuance and volume to the speaking voice not realized through ordinary methods of speech. Utilizing the Gan-Tone Principles, and, specifically, those that involve Jaw Sense, is naturally less demanding in speaking than in singing, since the following is involved in speaking as opposed to singing:

1) No sustaining of the graduated positions of the jaw, as a result of rapid articulation.

2) Little need for maximum jaw opening, since there is little range and no sustaining on vowels, requiring minimal JLB Fusion and Gan-Tone Pulsation.

3) Less body involvement, less Vocal Vibratory Continuity and less projection, since the voice is utilized strictly for verbal communication; whereas, in singing (classical), communication requires a highly evolved control of vibrational energy and vocal artistry.

4) Less intensity, focus and nuance to be main-

tained, since speaking doesn't require the vibrant energy necessary in singing.

In order to enable the student to discipline the jaw in singing, instruct him in the analysis and mastery of the simulated yawn (Exinvac Principle). In the beginning, stress only one characteristic of the yawn, i.e., the jaw completely down and back with the upper and lower jaws maximally diverged and a vertical-elliptical mouth opening.

Have the student place his forefingers in front of the earlobes, holding this position for a few seconds at a time as the jaw opens completely, without making any sound. With the widest opening of the jaw, the student will feel a deep recess in front of each tragus above each earlobe. In this position, the student will note that the throat opens wide for the inspiration of large quantities of air as in the natural yawn.

Have the student maintain this position, and this time select a medium note that is comfortable for the student to sing. Have the student sing this note for five seconds at a time on the vowel AH.

Make sure the student's jaw, when opened to its maximum, is vertically lined with the body and not off to one side. If any inclination to pull the jaw to one side is noted, have the student consciously align the jaw by studying himself in the mirror, as he sustains the note on the vowel AH with the jaw completely down and back. Have the student continue studying his jaw position in the mirror, with and without sound, until he aligns the jaw vertically with the body.

This maximum opening of the jaw automatically results in a deeper feeling of support and a release of tension in the neck, since the jaw has now become fused with the body, drawing the pressure away from the neck muscles and onto the body. Much singing can be sustained, without fatigue, by dependency on neck muscles which means that the jaw doesn't have to be completely down and back at all times. However, as the pressure grows in the throat, the emphasis must shift from the overworked muscles to a more solid base, i.e., the body. The progressive movement of the jaw down and back commensurate with the increased pressure will relieve the tired feeling that is present in the neck area, since the body now assumes the stress originally focused on neck muscles.

The muscle that the student must master in order to keep the jaw down and back under pressure is not a neck muscle, but a head muscle near the temple and behind the zygomatic arch known as the Pterygoideus lateralis. The contractive action of this muscle keeps the jaw opened and fused to the larynx and also aligns the numerous neck muscles in the descending body fusion. When this muscle is swiftly contracted under pressure, the neck muscles are protected by being amalgamated to the hard parts, such as, bones, thereby preventing muscle strain.

As the student attains the deeper support through the maximum opening of the jaw, he will note that his voice has more volume, depth, height and freedom, when singing the AH sound. This condition can be reversed by raising the jaw, since this movement constricts the throat which restricts vibrating air resulting in less depth, height, resilience, volume, flexibility and freedom.

When the student has some control of the jaw in its maximum opening on the AH sound, have him sing a simple exercise. Start with middle C and ascend to E and G then descend to E and C on the Ah vowel. Progress in half steps until the gamut of the student's range is reached making sure that the student is maintaining his jaw at its maximum opening in a uniform position throughout the scale. The student's face should assume the expression evident during the natural yawn, i.e., the lips relaxed, the teeth covered, the mouth in a vertical-elliptical position and no signs of tension in the face or body.

It is common for the beginner to be inclined to close his jaw on high notes, where the pressure is greatest, since anxiety caused by the pressure tends to make him set the jaw with neck muscles rather than release it, i.e., move it down and back as the pressure builds, through mastery of the Pterygoideus lateralis muscle.

By constantly correcting the jaw for drift during moments of great pressure, the student will eventually, with teacher guidance, discipline the jaw to the point where he becomes less aware of singing notes and more aware of singing position, i.e., rather than becoming anxious at the thought of singing a loud, high, sustained note, he concentrates on the Gan-Tone Principle that will insure the successful demonstration of the high note, shifting his feeling from anxiety to confidence in the principle, as follows:

> As pressure builds in the neck area while ascending or descending the scale, movement of the jaw down and back will shift the emphasis of stress from the neck area to the body enabling the singer to overcome the accumulating pressure of the vocal line and thus uncover more range.

Rather than reinforcing this Gan-Tone Principle only through exercises or vocalises, maintain the student's interest by rehearsing this principle in contexture, i.e., through actual songs that are currently popular and which appeal to the student.

Traditionally, it was believed that singing vocalises was the best technique for developing the voice. However, teaching only through vocalises causes the student to establish certain coordinations of the jaw, larynx and body which result in very limited concepts of the variable jaw that are not necessarily applicable in the actual singing of songs. It is for this reason that care must be taken to use passages of songs as exercises in order to make the student realize the importance of learning many positions, i.e., gradations of the jaw that are necessary in order to create and maintain freedom, volume and coloration of the sound. Innumerable jaw positions occur in the spinning out of a melody, as a result of the variations in vowels and range; therefore, the sooner the student becomes acquainted and sensitive to this coordination of the jaw to pressure at a given point in the melodic line, the more ease he will develop in singing.

As the student keeps rehearsing the Gan-Tone Principle of the jaw down and back at points of pressure, he will notice a marked degree of freedom in his ability to handle passages of songs that were originally difficult for him.

The Gan-Tone teacher can introduce the imposition of the Gan-Tone Pulsation on the fundamental frequency, when the following has been accomplished:

> 1 - The student has developed Jaw Sense, i.e., sensitivity and speed regarding the relationship of the jaw positions to the pressures encountered in the singing line which occur with increased range and volume.

> 2 - The student can control neck pressure by placing the jaw down and back, with the upper and lower jaws maximally diverged and the mouth in a vertical-elliptical opening. This condition is produced by contracting the Pterygoideus lateralis muscle near the temple of the head under stress (loud, high, sustained sounds), causing the transfer of stress from the neck area to the Sphincter ani externus muscle at the bottom of the torso.

> 3 - The student has developed an awareness of the two Gan-Tone reference points, i.e., the Pterygoideus lateralis muscle in the head for lowering the mandible on the larynx which initiates the Jaw, Larynx, Body Fusion, and the Sphincter ani externus muscle, at the rectal-pelvic basin, which is the point of compression head, as a result of the Jaw, Larynx, Body Fusion.

> 4 - The student is able to apply the Jaw Check with speed and accuracy, that is, he is able to locate the recesses, the mandibular fossae, while sustaining loud, high tones in order to make sure that the jaw is securely down and back, resting on the larynx and fused to the body in order to create the strongest vibratory circuit and insure that pressure produced by loud, high, sustained tones is diffused through the body.

The Jaw Check is essential for grasping the significance of Vocal Vibratory Continuity, since the fused jaw under stress insures the involvement of the body extremities in maximally extending the amplitude of vocal cords and body vibrations.

Gan-Tone Realizations

III. Vocal exercises in the Gan-Tone Method unify vocal cords vibrations with the body causing the whole body to function as a bell in the production of the singing sound. This unification makes the body a highly resilient agent for countering vibrational absorption by creating a spring-like effect of the body, as a result of fusing the body from the Pterygoideus lateralis muscle near the temple of the head downward to the Sphincter ani externus muscle at the rectal-pelvic basin made possible with the application of the Jaw, Larynx, Body Fusion and the imposition of the Gan-Tone Pulsation.

The primary agent that counters vibrational absorption in the body is the Gan-Tone Pulsation, since its structural reference points are the Pterygoideus lateralis muscle in the head and the Sphincter ani externus muscle at the bottom of the torso creating the greatest dimension for the fusion, amplification, thrust and re-sounding of vocal cords and body vibrations, thus augmenting the amplitude of the fundamental frequency (original vocal cords vibrations) by extending it to the body extremities, i.e., from the rectal-pelvic basin to the head resonators.

However, the effectiveness of the Gan-Tone Pulsation in augmenting the fundamental frequency to the body extremities is dependent on the singer's skill in applying the Jaw, Larynx, Body Fusion and, specifically, the speed with which the Pterygoideus lateralis muscle is contracted for fusing the mandible (lower jaw) onto the body, which is the initial stage of the Jaw, Larynx, Body Fusion.

The structure of the Jaw, Larynx, Body Fusion and the Gan-Tone Pulsation consists of a series of contractive muscular actions from the Pterygoideus lateralis muscle in the head downward to the tongue and throat muscles, thoracic and abdominal muscles to the Sphincter ani externus, the muscle at the bottom of the torso.

The contraction of the Pterygoideus lateralis muscle starts the Jaw, Larynx, Body Fusion as it lowers the mandible (lower jaw) onto the complex of supra-infrahyoid muscles, causing these throat muscles to be fused to the body, thereby relieving them of the burden of stress that results from excessive vocal demands (loud, high, sustained notes).

A Gan-Tone Principle can, therefore, be stated as follows:

> The speed with which the singer applies the contractive action of the Pterygoideus lateralis muscle for positioning the mandible onto the supra-infrahyoid complex of throat muscles in the singing process, but especially under excessive vocal demand (loud, high, sustained notes), determines the degree to which this complex of muscles will be protected from stress.

The greater the speed in positioning the mandible by contractive muscular action of the Pterygoideus lateralis muscle in anticipation of vocal pressure and dimension, the greater the freedom from stress in the throat muscles, cartilages and ligaments (vocal cords), and the greater the dimension of sound, as a result of fusing the body to the extremities, i.e., from the Pterygoideus lateralis muscle in the head to the Sphincter ani externus muscle at the bottom of the torso.

Complex of throat muscles

16 muscles, or 8 pairs, are involved in this complex—one of each pair on each side of the throat:

Suprahyoid muscles (above the hyoid bone)
a) 2 Digastricus   c) 2 Mylohyoideus
b) 2 Stylohyoideus   d) 2 Geniohyoideus

Infrahyoid muscles (below the hyoid bone)
a) 2 Sternohyoideus   c) 2 Sternothyroideus
b) 2 Thyrohyoideus   d) 2 Omohyoideus

The speed with which the singer contracts the Pterygoideus lateralis muscle for fusing the mandible to the body, with a feather-touch contact, determines the degree of involvement of the vocal cords as an extension of the body, causing the vocal cords to be unified to the body, rather than functioning in isolation, thus minimizing friction and pressure in the vocal cords by dispersing this pressure to the pelvis.

The contractive muscular action, or peristalsis, from the Pterygoideus lateralis muscle in the head to the Sphincter ani externus muscle at the bottom of the torso, in rapid succession (5 to 7 Gan-Tones per second), constitutes the sustained singing line.

Conditioning the Pterygoideus lateralis muscle to maintain contraction in order to suspend and stabilize the mandible, or lower jaw, with a maximal opening of the jawbones, creating a jaw condition of suspended animation in the sustained singing line, especially under pressure (loud, high, sustained notes), requires much practice, since there is a natural tendency for the mandible to ride up under pressure, transferring this stress to neck muscles in direct proportion to the degree that the jaws converge.

In the Gan-Tone vocal exercises, the focus, therefore, is not on throat muscles, which is the conventional belief, but, rather, on the Pterygoideus lateralis, the muscle near the temple of the head.

The student concentrates on opening the mandible via the Pterygoideus lateralis muscle with a minimal use of neck muscles, i.e., just enough to anchor the chin dorsally to the spinal column. In this position, the mandibular fossae (recess on either side of the head just above and in front of either earlobe) are maximal in size, as a result of the Pterygoideus lateralis muscle pulling the condyle, or highest protuberance of the jaw, forward, causing these pits to be evident. In this position, there is no evidence of tension or protuberance of head, face and neck muscles, since these muscles are aligned with the two reference points, i.e., the Pterygoideous lateralis muscle in the head and the Sphincter ani externus muscle at the bottom of the torso.

This position is characterized by the vertical-elliptical mouth opening. The Gan-Tone teacher observes the student very carefully in the process of singing notes throughout the range with special care to maintaining this vertical-elliptical mouth opening in the upper range, since the student has a tendency to collapse this vertical-elliptical position to a horizontal spread in the upper range causing immediate evidence of facial and cervical stress, as a result of muscle tension in these areas.

This stress becomes the security system not only of students but of singers in general who are not aware of the Jaw, Larynx, Body Fusion.

Whatever exercises are utilized, whether they be standard vocalises or just notes that encompass the range, the teacher must be constantly alert to this vertical-elliptical mouth opening for launching the Jaw, Larynx, Body Fusion which will immediately involve the body as an amplifier, transmitter, thrusting agent and re-sounder of vocal cords vibrations, giving the student more range and volume in a relatively short time.

In the Gan-Tone Method, body fusion, created by the Jaw, Larynx, Body Fusion initiated by the contraction of the Pterygoideus lateralis muscle, establishes and stabilizes range and volume, since it eradicates muscular spasms that result in registers, cracks and breaks in the voice thus enabling the singer to encompass more range, with an even scale throughout the range. The vertical-elliptical mouth opening creates a vertical line of fusion through the body between the two reference points (the Pterygoideus lateralis muscle in the head and the Sphincter ani externus muscle at the rectal-pelvic basin), eradicating constriction in the throat and restriction of vibrational energy in this narrow opening, through fusion, enabling the singer to utilize more dimensions of the vocal cords.

Since the ability to sing songs with an even scale is dependent on the student's grasp of the vertical-elliptical mouth opening, it is more practical to practice this mouth position (which is really the skillful contraction of the Pterygoideus lateralis muscle) in the phrases of popular songs, rather than standard vocalises, since the singer becomes immediately involved with the dynamics that are peculiar to each song and how to maximize singing energy and freedom at each point of the song. Focusing on the dynamics of each song through Gan-Tone Principles, whose ultimate reference points are the Pterygoideus lateralis muscle in the head and the Sphincter ani externus muscle at the bottom of the torso, provides a resolution to all vocal problems, giving the student great understanding, buoyant confidence and ability to perform these songs in public, with or without electronic amplification.

Mastering the ability to harness the vertical-elliptical mouth opening and to adhere strictly to the two reference points (Pterygoideus lateralis and Sphincter ani externus muscles) enables the student to move into more complicated dynamics of more complicated singing, such as opera, and, also, to move from the popular to the classical, and vice versa, demonstrating the appropriate characteristics of each vocal expression.

Maintenance of the vertical-elliptical mouth opening throughout the singing process is essential in the Gan-Tone Method, since this position maintains the line of fusion from the Pterygoideus lateralis muscle in the head to the Sphincter ani externus muscle at the bottom of the torso, causing the head and body to be unified.

In maximal, or absolute, Jaw, Larynx, Body Fusion, the head is tilted forward in order to create maximal fusion, or maximal approximation of body parts, for the maximal compression of vocal cords and body vibrations on the Compression Phase, or down-part of the Gan-Tone beat, which will yield the maximal thrust of these vibrations to the head resonators on the Thrust Phase, or up-part of the Gan-Tone beat, thereby producing maximal singing energy, which includes maximal volume and dimension in the projected sound.

In order to maintain the vertical-elliptical mouth opening throughout the singing process and thereby maintain fusion to the bottom of the torso, it is important that the Gan-Tone teacher develop the student's skill in moving swiftly from the consonant to the vowel while maximally positioning the mandible (Jaw, Larynx, Body Fusion) for maximal dimension of sound, from fortissimo to pianissimo. In singing words, for ex., that contain multiple consonants, such as SCHL in German, the singer must move the mandible and the tongue with the same speed that it takes to move onto the vowel when words have a single initial consonant demonstrating the following Gan-Tone Principle:

> The greater the speed in moving the mandible down and back to create the vertical-elliptical mouth opening in the process of singing consonants, the greater the dimensions of the emitted sound, since this mouth opening, the position for singing vowels, produces the Jaw, Larynx, Body Fusion which creates the most resilient path for the movement of vocal cords vibrations throughout the body concomitantly with the dispersal of laryngeal pressure to the body extremities.

Initial consonants should be performed with great swiftness and definition, since sluggishness in the pronunciation of consonants, especially under pressure (loud, high, sustained sounds), causes trauma to the vocal cords by excessive air stroking the rim of the glottis, which is, essentially, the configuration of the vocal cords.

When consonants are sluggishly pronounced, the movement of air is interrupted causing undue compression of air in the throat area (vocal hook), producing excessive air pressure in the glottis (hole between the vocal cords) and, consequently, irritating, or shocking, the mucous membrane covering the ligamentous vocal cords which is, essentially, the rim surrounding the glottis. Excessive air pressure buildup, through sluggish pronunciation of consonants, especially in moments of extreme adduction of the vocal cords, i.e., when the vocal cords approximate during high notes, causes this air pressure to be further restricted, compounding the irritation of the vocal cords.

Maintaining speed and agility in pronouncing consonants enables the singer to stress the vowels, regardless of the language being sung, thereby maintaining the vertical-elliptical mouth opening which, in turn, insures the maximal Jaw, Larynx, Body Fusion and the dispersal of pressure to the pelvis, while simultaneously minimizing vibrational absorption and insuring maximal Vocal Vibratory Continuity, i.e., maximal singing energy.

The Gan-Tone teacher develops the student's skill in moving quickly from the consonant to the vowel initially in phrases of popular songs, carefully watching the student to make sure that he learns how to move the mandible swiftly down and back in order to maximize Jaw, Larynx, Body Fusion on sustained notes, i.e., vowels whose duration can vary, for ex., from a fraction of a second to about fifteen seconds. When the student has mastered the ability to maximize Jaw, Larynx, Body Fusion on the least sustained sound, maximal dimensions are maintained in rapid passages where the suspension of the jaw is impossible, since he maintains contact with the two reference points, i.e., the Pterygoideus lateralis muscle in the head and the Sphincter ani externus muscle at the bottom of the torso.

The student may question how he can articulate words with an open jaw, and the Gan-Tone teacher must clarify this confusion by making the student realize that he must learn to move the jaw swiftly in order to maintain Jaw, Larynx, Body Fusion, i.e., contact with the two reference points, for maximal body involvement and maximal diffusion of laryngeal pressure.

The student will observe with practice that maintenance of the vertical-elliptical mouth opening, or skill developed in contracting the Pterygoideus lateralis muscle swiftly, will enable him to reach more range and attain more volume and evenness in the singing line. He will also become aware of freedom from pressure in the throat area and greater breath control, since Jaw, Larynx, Body Fusion insures body involvement.

The student will realize that in order to maximally involve the body, he must become sensitive to areas of pressure buildup in the body that are detrimental to the production of sound, such as, facial tension which includes the tightening of eyes, head, cheek and mouth muscles; neck tension which includes the tightening of a complex of throat muscles; tension in the shoulders, limbs, thorax and abdomen; tension caused by the isolation of body parts, as opposed to fused body parts, and the riding up of body parts, such as, lifting the shoulders, the head, or rising on the toes, during moments of great vocal demand (loud, high, sustained notes).

The Gan-Tone teacher realizes that when the student masters the Jaw, Larynx, Body Fusion under pressure, i.e., loud, high, sustained sounds, the student will be aware of focusing all pressure downward to the Sphincter ani externus muscle in the rectal-pelvic basin, thereby maintaining fusion downward through the body, making the Gan-Tone singer appear tension-free in the face, neck, chest and abdomen. Rather than lifting the shoulders, the head, or rising on the toes, the Gan-Tone singer will fuse all these parts downward in line with the natural gravitational pull in order to maximize density, resilience and elasticity of the body, from the soles of the feet to the top of the head.

Maximal (Absolute) Jaw, Larynx, Body Fusion

Jaw, Larynx, Body Fusion, in the Gan-Tone Method, can be applied in a modified or a maximal position.

Maximal Jaw, Larynx, Body Fusion, rather than the modified, is introduced to the beginning student by the Gan-Tone teacher in order to achieve maximal dimensions, i.e., volume, depth and height in the singing sound on any vowel in any part of the range, since it is only from this maximal position that the jaw, larynx, mouth, and body can be coordinated for an infinite variety of vocal sounds. Furthermore, once having mastered the Absolute Jaw, Larynx, Body Fusion, it is easy for the student to apply a modified position, which is the one that is most frequently utilized, since most singing doesn't require the maximal dimensions of volume, depth and height. However, if maximal dimensions are desired by the singer, the Absolute Jaw, Larynx, Body Fusion is required.

In the maximal position, the head is tilted forward and downward. The pelvic area is tilted upward producing a cranial, pelvic, spinal curve. The knees are bent, one knee slightly in front of the other, with the feet solidly planted on the ground. The mandible is diverged maximally from the upper jaw and resting, with a Feather-Touch Contact, down and back, on the larynx. The student is taught to coordinate the Body Drop which involves dropping slightly and swiftly on the bent knees, when sustaining a loud, high note and maintaining the Absolute Jaw, Larynx, Body Fusion. This coordination involves an important principle of projection, which is that of recoil. When the bent knees are dropped concomitantly with the Absolute Jaw, Larynx, Body Fusion, the power created in the drop of the body produces the opposite reaction of power in the projected sound, which demonstrates Newton's Law of Action and Reaction. The attack of the note and the Body Drop must be spontaneous and simultaneous in order to completely involve the added body weight in the sound that occurs for the moment that the body is dropped.

Coordination of the Absolute Jaw, Larynx, Body Fusion with the Body Drop does the following:

1 - increases body weight
2 - increases vibrant areas in the body
3 - extends and increases body resilience and density
4 - minimizes vibrational absorption
5 - amplifies vocal cords and body vibrations
6 - increases thrust, re-sounding and projection of vocal cords and body vibrations

The greater the spontaneity and immediacy applied by the Gan-Tone student in coordinating the Maximal Jaw, Larynx, Body Fusion and the Body Drop on the loud, high, sustained sound, the greater the volume, resilience, vibrancy, buoyancy and controlled abandon of the emitted sound, since the body is functioning as a bell.

The Gan-Tone teacher teaches this spontaneous coordination of the Absolute Jaw, Larynx, Body Fusion and the Body Drop in the passages of popular and art songs or arias that contain loud, high, sustained notes. This coordination can be used in any part of the range, when maximum dimensions in the attack of the sound are desired.

The Body Drop is not introduced until the student has mastered the Feather-Touch Contact of the jaw on the larynx and can maintain this position under pressure. This mastery also includes the ability to simultaneously coordinate the contractive action of the two Gan-Tone reference points, i.e., the Pterygoideus lateralis muscle in the head and the Sphincter ani externus muscle in the rectal-pelvic basin.

Rectal-Pelvic Breath Control (Sinking the Breath)

The beginning student will experience difficulty in attempting to involve the Sphincter ani externus muscle in the singing process, since, in order to involve this muscle, body resilience between the two Gan-Tone reference points (Pterygoideus lateralis muscle in the head and the Sphincter ani externus muscle at the bottom of the torso) must first be achieved. In order to attain body resilience, tension in the body must be controlled from the two Gan-Tone reference points in order to eliminate localized restriction, which is the result of facial, cervical, thoracic, abdominal, and/or pelvic tension.

Involvement of the Sphincter ani externus muscle is tantamount to sinking the breath, which can be described in the Gan-Tone Method as the expiratory excursion, from the activated vocal cords down to the rectal-pelvic basin and up to the air sinuses of the head, completing one cycle of the Gan-Tone Pulsation. Therefore, to involve the Sphincter ani externus muscle, and deeply sink the breath to the rectal-pelvic basin, the student must master the application of the Gan-Tone beat, since the degree of intensity of the Gan-Tone Pulsation determines the degree of expiratory excursion from the activated vocal cords to the Sphincter ani externus muscle at the pelvic-perineum diaphragm and up to the air sinuses, which is known as Rectal-Pelvic Breath Control in the Gan-Tone Method.

The application of the Gan-Tone Pulsation is not introduced until the Gan-Tone student has mastered the Absolute Jaw, Larynx, Body Fusion.

Modified Jaw, Larynx, Body Fusion

In the Modified Jaw, Larynx, Body Fusion, the head is not tilted, but the jaw maintains contact with the larynx in order to insure fusion of the jaw, larynx and body. The pelvic area is not tilted upward from its vertical position. One knee is forward and slightly bent. One foot is solidly planted on the ground. The mandible is diverged maximally from the upper jaw and resting, with a Feather-Touch Contact, down and back, on the larynx.

In this modified position of the Jaw, Larynx, Body Fusion, contact is maintained between the two Gan-Tone reference points (Pterygoideus lateralis muscle in the head and the Sphincter ani externus muscle at the bottom of the torso), but the intensity of their involvement is modified, as opposed to their maximum involvement in the Absolute Jaw, Larynx, Body Fusion.

Although the Gan-Tone beat is applied in the modified J.L.B. Fusion, a maximal manifestation of vocal cords and body vibrations cannot be attained, i.e., maximal volume, depth, height and resilience, in the emitted sound. Nevertheless, these modified dimensions are ample for most types of singing, giving the sound unusual volume, depth, height and resilience in rapid as well as in slow, sustained, vocal passages.

Application of the Gan-Tone Pulsation

When the student masters the Absolute Jaw, Larynx, Body Fusion, he is ready for the application of the Gan-Tone Pulsation on the fundamental frequency.

The Gan-Tone Pulsation is a superimposed beat on the fundamental frequency, i.e., on the vibrations per second which produce the pitch being sung. Imposition of the Gan-Tone Pulsation on the fundamental frequency, or vibrations of the pitch being sung, extends the amplitude of this frequency from the vocal cords area downward to the pelvic basin on the down-part of the Gan-Tone beat known as the Compression Phase and upward to the head resonators on the up-part of the Gan-Tone beat known as the Thrust Phase, causing these vocal cords vibrations to be extended to the body extremities.

The teacher selects a note in a comfortable part of the range and has the student sustain this note while applying the Absolute Jaw, Larynx, Body Fusion and imposing 3 Gan-Tones per second[3] on the fundamental frequency, i.e., on the vibrations per second of the pitch

---

[3]The Gan-Tones per second can be increased (5 to 7), when the rapid contractive muscular action from the Abdominals to the Sphincter ani externus is achieved.

being sung, carrying this frequency down through the body to the rectal-pelvic basin. These fundamental vocal cords vibrations move from the vocal cords, through the chest, diaphragm, abdomen, and spinal cord to the rectal-pelvic basin on the Compression Phase, or down-part of the Gan-Tone beat, i.e., these vibrations are transmitted from the vocal cords through the body to the Sphincter ani externus muscle at the bottom of the perineum (the pelvic-perineum diaphragm).

This transmission of vocal cords vibrations to the bottom of the torso occurs only when the student has mastered the control of the Pterygoideus lateralis muscle, i.e., the contractive action of this muscle, which enables the mandible to diverge maximally from the upper jaw and fuse downward onto the larynx with a Feather-Touch Contact, creating a strong circuit through the body, from the head to the bottom of the torso (J.L.B. Fusion).

If the contractive action of the Pterygoideus lateralis muscle is sluggish and inaccurate, while the student is sustaining a high note and attempting to apply 5 to 7 Gan-Tones per second on the fundamental frequency in a wave-like contractive muscular action through the body, as in coughing, vomiting or laughing, signs of muscular tension appear immediately in the lateral and anterior cervical muscles and in the facial muscles, such as, the muscles of the brow, eyes, cheeks, mouth and shoulders. This tension is indicative of constriction in the vocal hook, i.e., in the throat area, and restriction of vocal cords vibrations in this area.

The complete contraction of the Pterygoideus lateralis muscle allows the mandible to be fused to the larynx, which shifts pressure from the neck muscles to the body in the direction of the pelvic basin.

The incomplete contraction of the Pterygoideus lateralis muscle breaks this circuit of body fusion by causing the mandible to be disengaged from the body, thereby interrupting the flow of vocal cords vibrations to the bottom of the torso and causing, instead, vocal vibrational absorption in the neck area where this open circuit occurs.

While maintaining the pitch of the sustained note and the Absolute Jaw, Larynx, Body Fusion, the student is directed by the teacher to repeat the progressive descent of contractive muscular action, which is produced when 5 to 7 Gan-Tones are imposed upon the fundamental vocal cords vibrations, causing the amplitude of these vibrations to be extended downward to the pelvic basin on the Compression Phase, or down-part of the Gan-Tone beat, and upward to the head resonators on the Thrust Phase, or up-part of the Gan-Tone beat. This coordination involves conditioning body muscles to respond voluntarily to a grunting-down process which occurs involuntarily during vomiting and yawning.

To insure complete fusion of the jaw to the larynx and body, the student places his fingers in the mandibular fossae, i.e., the hole which occurs just above each earlobe in front of the tiny protuberance called the tragus. The chinbone is moored dorsally in the direction of the spine and the neck muscles are relaxed, i.e., in a state of non-contraction, except for their minimal involvement in mooring the mandible dorsalward.

The Gan-Tone student becomes aware that the vocal cords vibrations that are compressed to the pelvic basin on the Compression Phase, or down-part of the Gan-Tone beat, are thrust naturally, on the Thrust Phase, or up-part of the Gan-Tone beat, to the nasion, the bridge of the nose, which is the merging point of a complex of cavities and partitions of the face and head, making the body a perfect agent, by its cylindrical shape, for applying Newton's Law of Action and Reaction for utilizing these resonators. The body controls the amplification of vocal cords and body vibrations on the down-part of the Gan-Tone beat which fuses these vibrations to the bottom of the torso and thrusts them naturally from this pelvic basin, on the up-part of the Gan-Tone beat, essentially upward to the head resonators as resonance and to other parts of the body as vibrations, making the whole body resound as a bell.

Vocal Exercises for Applying the Jaw, Larynx, Body Fusion and the Gan-Tone Pulsation

Vocal exercises for applying the Jaw, Larynx, Body Fusion and the Gan-Tone beat start in the middle of the voice, at about the C note, for it is usually at this point in the range that the impasse becomes evident. The impasse is that point in the range where the student experiences a change in vocal quality, since the throat muscles can no longer produce an even scale beyond this note. This point of impasse varies with each student. Some students do not experience an impasse in the range and can ascend and descend the scale without any tonal change. However, without the awareness of the Gan-Tone reference points (Pterygoideus lateralis muscle in the head and the Sphincter ani externus muscle in the rectal-pelvic basin), they are utilizing neck muscles, rather than the body, limiting their vocal potential.

In the Gan-Tone Method, in order to continue ascending the scale without a change in tonal quality or the use of neck muscles, the student must become acquainted with the skill involved in contracting the Pterygoideus lateralis muscle in the head, which involves the lowering of the mandible on the larynx with a minimal involvement of neck muscles. In this position, the student assumes the vertical-elliptical mouth opening as he ascends or descends the scale in a soft voice, producing an even range and eliminating tension in the head, face and throat.

At the point of impasse, which could be the C note, in the middle of the range, the Gan-Tone teacher guides the student to assume the vertical-elliptical mouth opening while descending the scale in a legato line from C to A, F and back to A and C in a soft voice on the AH sound, continuing downward in the scale in half tones to about G, E, C and back to E and G. While singing these Gan-Tone exercises, the student must avoid the natural temptation to have the mandible ride up, since this action produces tension in the neck area and changes in vocal quality (impasses).

After singing these Gan-Tone exercises down to about G, E, C and back to E and G in a legato line, breathing between each exercise and maintaining the vertical-elliptical mouth opening, at a metronomic speed of about 60 for each exercise, the Gan-Tone teacher guides the student to ascend the scale in a legato line using the same exercises. The student continues singing these exercises, in a soft voice, beyond the original impasse (C) to about 3 or 4 notes above this point, accenting the highest note of each exercise by increasing compression to the bottom of the torso. Body fusion must be intensified with increased range in order to maintain the dimensions of depth and height in the range.

Some students can maintain the vertical-elliptical mouth opening without difficulty as they ascend the scale and can, therefore, reach higher notes.

Those students who have difficulty maintaining the discipline of the jaw or who hang on tenaciously to neck muscles as they ascend will experience tonal changes and limitation of range until they learn to let go of neck muscles by maintaining the vertical-elliptical mouth opening.

The student who hangs on to neck muscles may appear to make more sound and to be more secure. However, this neck sound cannot ultimately compete with the sound produced by the resilient body whose reference points are the Pterygoideus lateralis muscle in the head and the Sphincter ani externus muscle in the rectal-pelvic basin which align all the body muscles, including neck muscles, for maximal structural resilience.

The determining factor for volume and dimension of sound, in the Gan-Tone Method, is body resilience and not the neck and its muscles. Body resilience involves the contractive muscular action, or fusion, from the Pterygoideus lateralis muscle in the head, through the neck muscles, to the chest and abdominal muscles, downward to the Sphincter ani externus muscle at the bottom of the torso.

The student or singer who clings to neck muscles for the structure of the vocal sound never experiences the full dimensions of the sound in regard to body involvement, and with advancing years is unable to control these neck muscles which results in vocal problems.

The Gan-Tone student will experience an increase in volume as he develops skill in fusing the jaw, larynx, and body along with the Feather-Touch Contact on the vocal cords, while singing the Gan-Tone exercises, since the body becomes an amplifier as vocal cords vibrations penetrate through the body to the bottom of the torso.

Accenting the highest note of each Gan-Tone exercise by increasing compression to the rectal-pelvic basin and, specifically, to the Sphincter ani externus muscle with the Jaw, Larynx, Body Fusion, as the student ascends the scale, is really the implementation of the Gan-Tone cycle, i.e., the Compression Phase, or down-part of the Gan-Tone beat, and the Thrust Phase, or up-part of the Gan-Tone beat. It can be considered a current of vocal vibratory energy carried on a contractive muscular pulse from the Pterygoideus lateralis muscle in the head to the Sphincter ani externus muscle at the pelvic-perineum diaphragm.

As the student keeps practicing the Gan-Tone exercises and accenting the highest note of each exercise by increasing compression at the rectal-pelvic basin, he will progressively experience control of five centers. They are as follows:

1 - Pterygoideus lateralis muscle in the head
2 - vocal cords—Feather-Touch Contact
3 - thorax (diaphragm)
4 - abdomen—network of powerful abdominal muscles
5 - pelvic-perineum (pelvic-urogenital) diaphragm and, specifically, the Sphincter ani externus muscle that pierces the pelvic-perineum floor

When the student masters the control of these five centers, while singing the Gan-Tone exercises rapidly, with an increase of compression to the Sphincter ani externus muscle on the highest note of each exercise, the compression to the bottom of the torso can be attained by singing only the highest note of the exercise 5 to 7 times per second and eliminating the two previous lower notes, enabling the student to maximize the singing sound on a smooth, or legato, line. Singing the highest note of the Gan-Tone exercise 5 to 7 times per second is the imposition of the Gan-Tone frequency on the fundamental pitch. Each cycle, i.e., the Compression Phase, or down-part of the Gan-Tone beat, and the Thrust Phase, or up-part of the Gan-Tone beat, is comparable to sinking the breath to the pelvic-perineum diaphragm.

Fusion from the Pterygoideus lateralis muscle to the Sphincter ani externus muscle naturally produces a fused amalgamation of vocal cords vibrations, body vibrations, bones, cartilages, membranes, air and liquids to the bottom of the torso. The sinking of the breath, in the Gan-Tone Method, is the compacting of the breath along with vocal cords and body vibrations to the rectal-pelvic basin on the Compression Phase of the Gan-Tone Pulsation, extending the boundaries of the bellows from the lungs to the bottom of the torso and is known as Rectal-Pelvic Breath Control.

The degree of sinking of the breath and amplifying of vocal cords and body vibrations is commensurate with the intensity of the Gan-Tone Pulsation.

INTRODUCTION TO ILLUSTRATIONS

Since the Gan-Tone Method establishes new reference points regarding the role of the body in the production of the singing voice, the author has created Gan-Tone illustrations which emphasize the anatomy involved in the application of Gan-Tone Principles in order to provide pictorial awareness and clarification.

Each illustration contains an explanation of the body parts involved and the role they play in the application of Gan-Tone Principles.

A luminous reflection of each illustration is provided in order to enhance and vivify the Gan-Tone Principles.

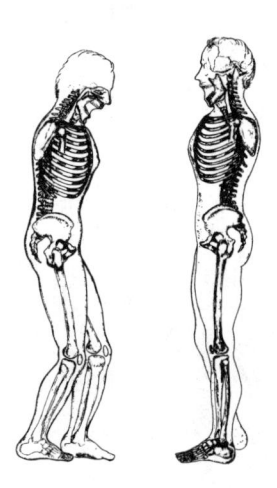

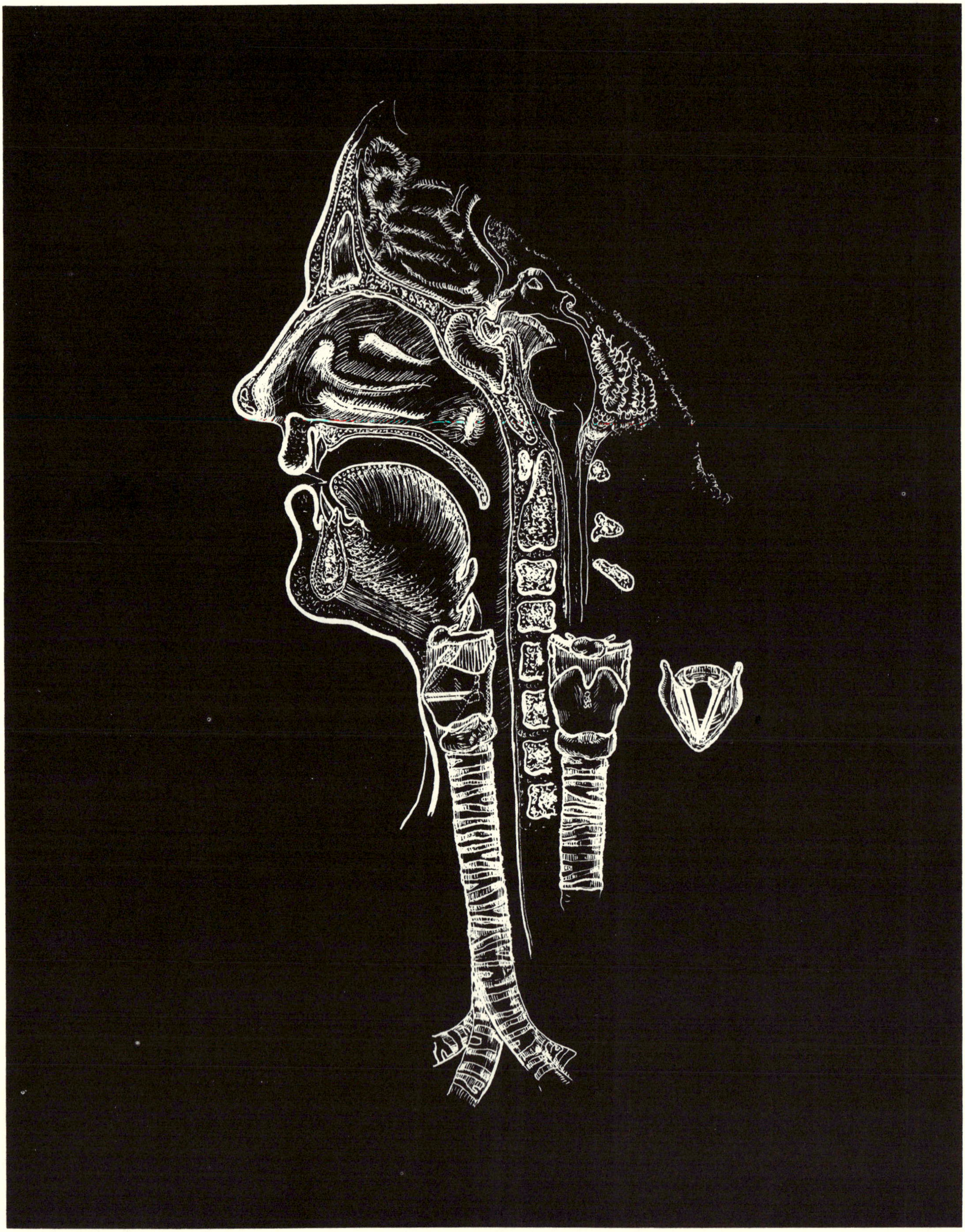

I. VOCAL HOOK

MASTERY OF JAW, LARYNX, BODY FUSION AND GAN-TONE PULSATION MAXIMALLY OPENS VOCAL HOOK FOR AMPLIFICATION, TRANSMISSION AND RE-SOUNDING OF VOCAL CORDS AND BODY VIBRATIONS.

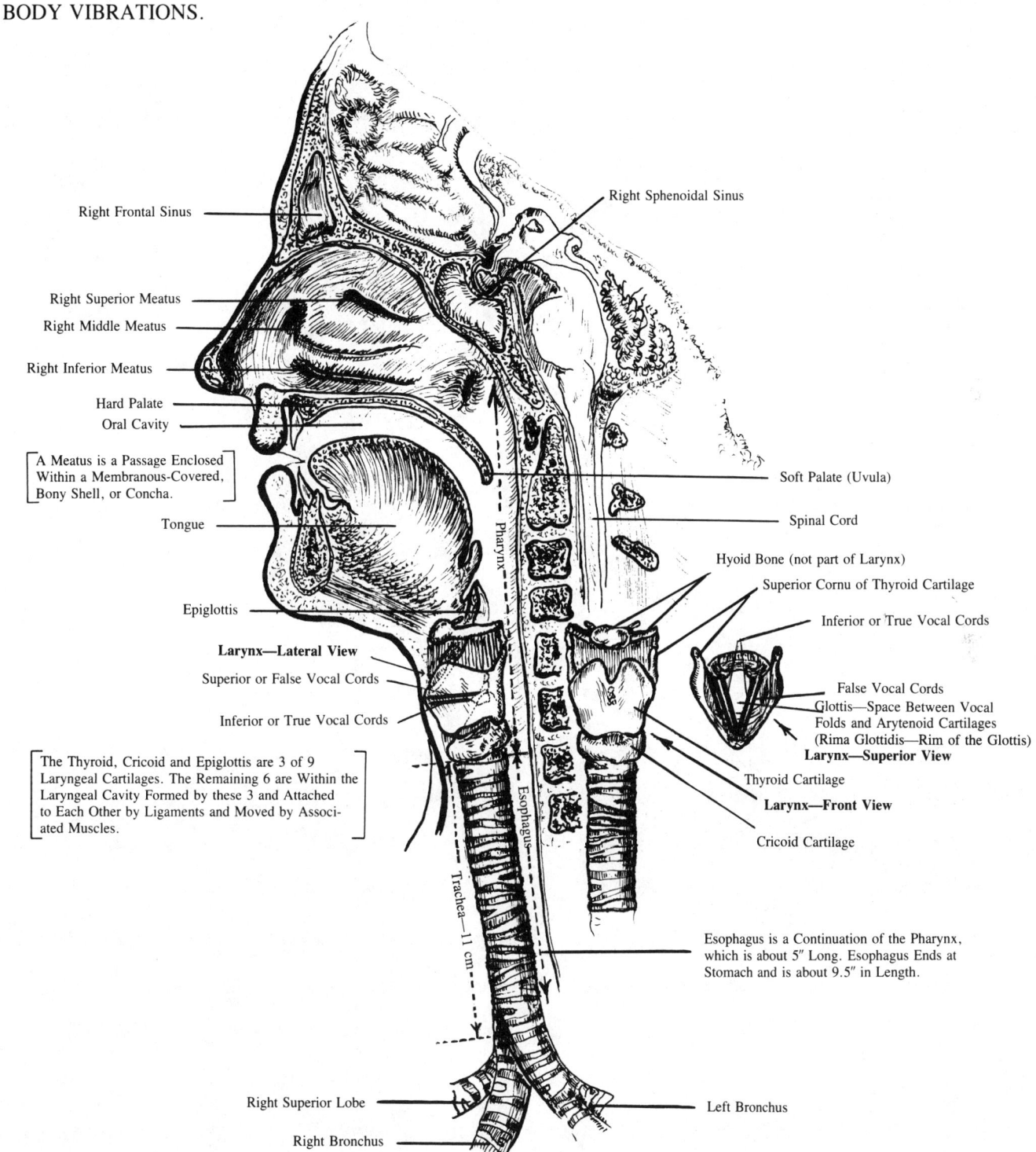

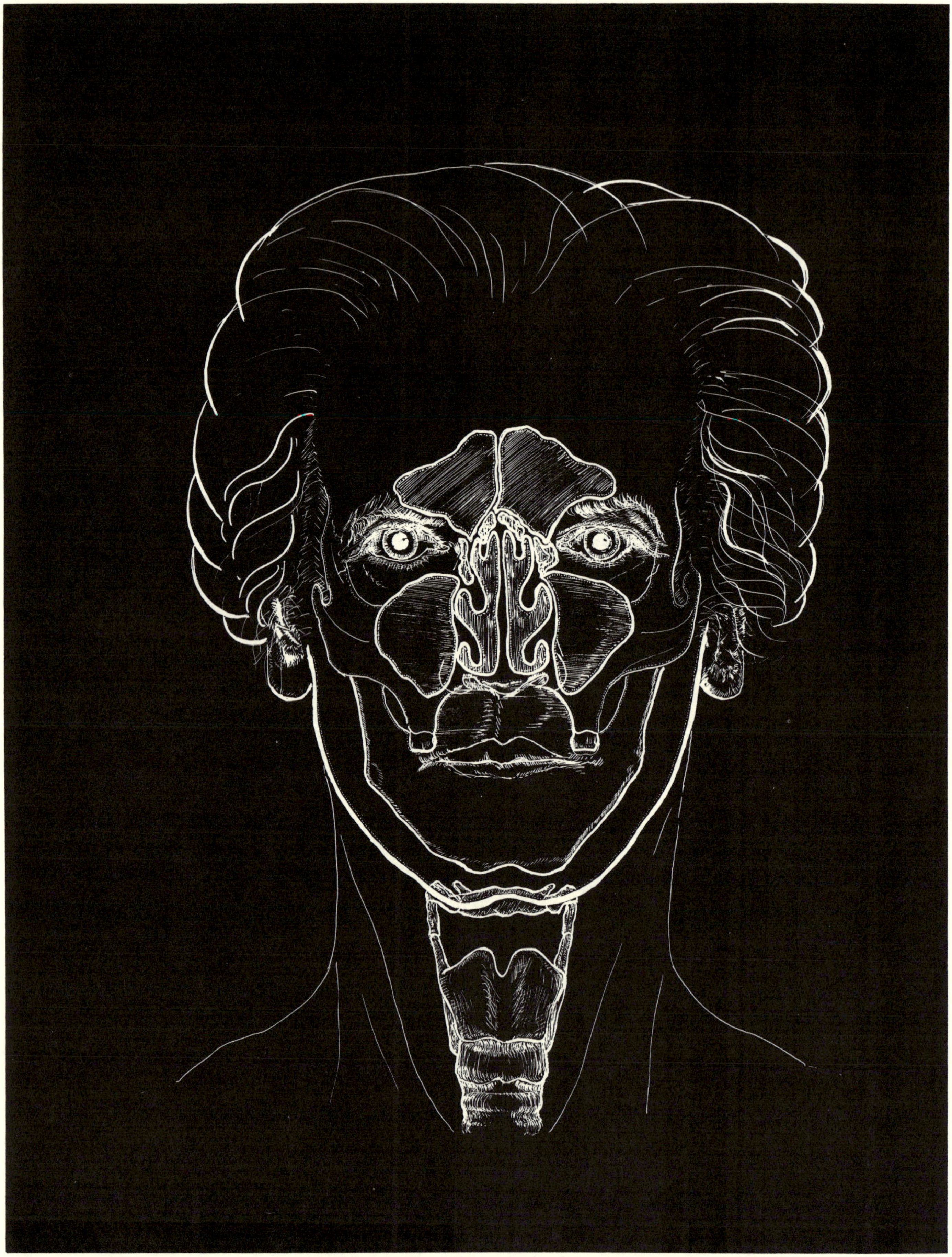

II. LARYNX—FRONT VIEW

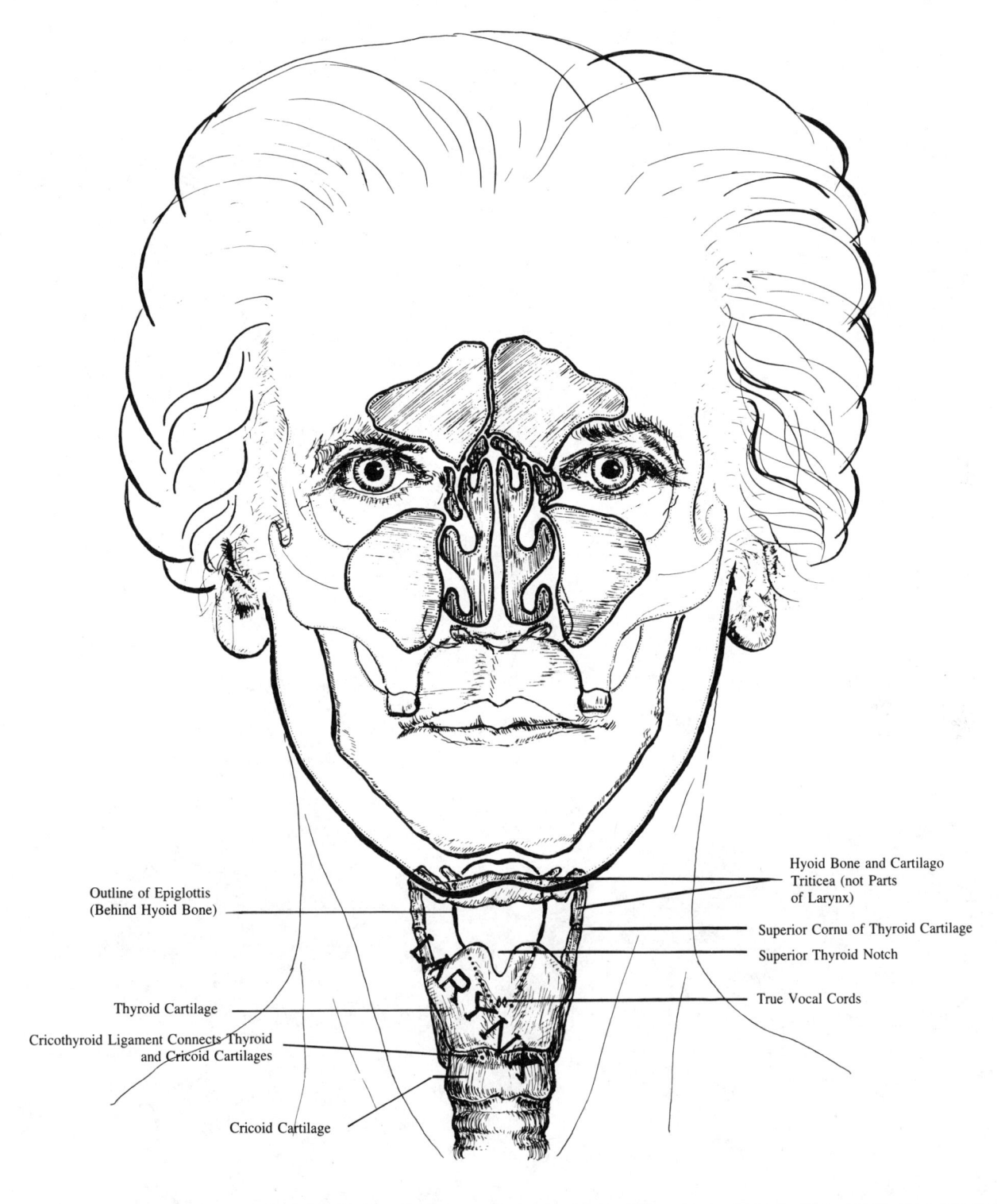

- Outline of Epiglottis (Behind Hyoid Bone)
- Thyroid Cartilage
- Cricothyroid Ligament Connects Thyroid and Cricoid Cartilages
- Cricoid Cartilage
- Hyoid Bone and Cartilago Triticea (not Parts of Larynx)
- Superior Cornu of Thyroid Cartilage
- Superior Thyroid Notch
- True Vocal Cords

THE LESS FUSED THE VOCAL CORDS TO THE LARYNX, THE MORE EVIDENT THE FALSETTO VOICE.

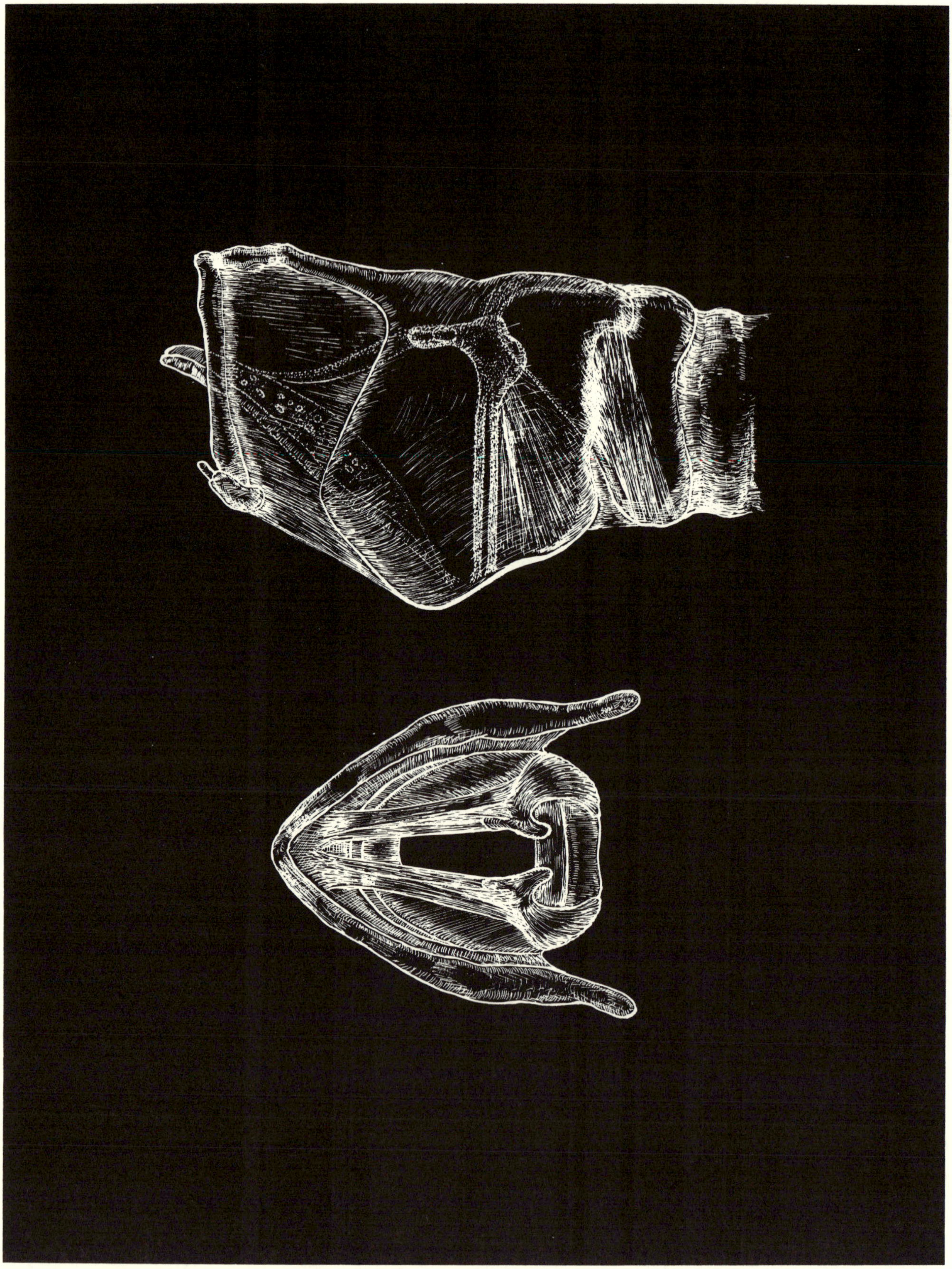

III. VOCAL CORDS IN LARYNX—2 VIEWS

THE VOCAL CORDS ARE THE PRIMAL VIBRATORS OF THE VOCAL SOUND AND THE LARYNX THE PRIMAL RESONATOR. THROUGH FUSION, THE BODY BECOMES THE PRINCIPAL VIBRATOR AND RESONATOR OF THIS ORIGINAL SOUND.

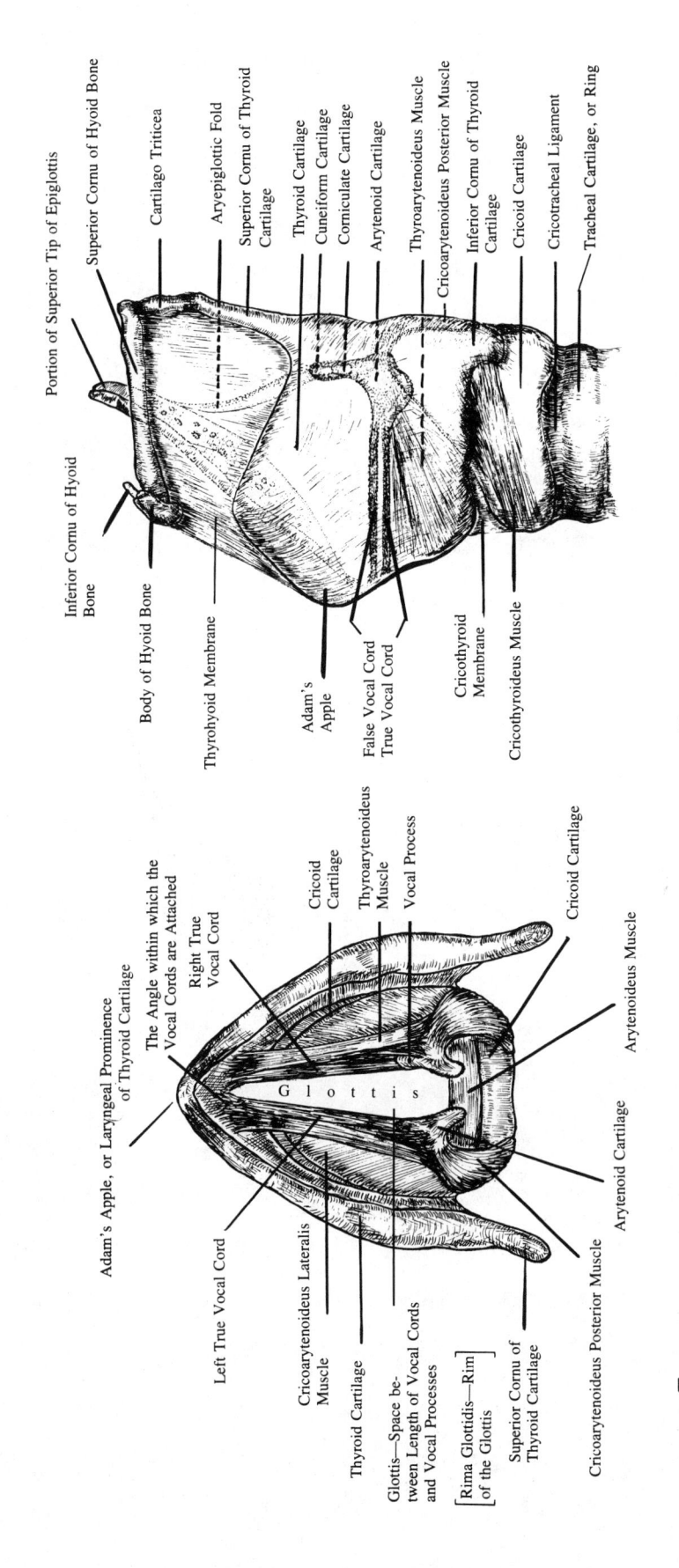

Larynx Viewed from Left Side

- Portion of Superior Tip of Epiglottis
- Superior Cornu of Hyoid Bone
- Cartilago Triticea
- Aryepiglottic Fold
- Superior Cornu of Thyroid Cartilage
- Thyroid Cartilage
- Cuneiform Cartilage
- Corniculate Cartilage
- Arytenoid Cartilage
- Thyroarytenoideus Muscle
- Cricoarytenoideus Posterior Muscle
- Inferior Cornu of Thyroid Cartilage
- Cricoid Cartilage
- Cricotracheal Ligament
- Tracheal Cartilage, or Ring
- Inferior Cornu of Hyoid Bone
- Body of Hyoid Bone
- Thyrohyoid Membrane
- Adam's Apple
- False Vocal Cord
- True Vocal Cord
- Cricothyroid Membrane
- Cricothyroideus Muscle

Larynx Viewed from Above

- Adam's Apple, or Laryngeal Prominence of Thyroid Cartilage
- The Angle within which the Vocal Cords are Attached
- Right True Vocal Cord
- Cricoid Cartilage
- Thyroarytenoideus Muscle
- Vocal Process
- Cricoid Cartilage
- Left True Vocal Cord
- Cricoarytenoideus Lateralis Muscle
- Thyroid Cartilage
- Glottis—Space between Length of Vocal Cords and Vocal Processes
- [Rima Glottidis—Rim of the Glottis]
- Superior Cornu of Thyroid Cartilage
- Cricoarytenoideus Posterior Muscle
- Arytenoid Cartilage
- Arytenoideus Muscle

[True Vocal Cords are part of the Rima Glottidis.
Rima Glottidis is a Little Less than 1" in the Male; a Little Less than 3/4" in the Female.
True Vocal Cords are a Little More than 1/2" in the Male; a Little Less than 1/2" in the Female.]

213

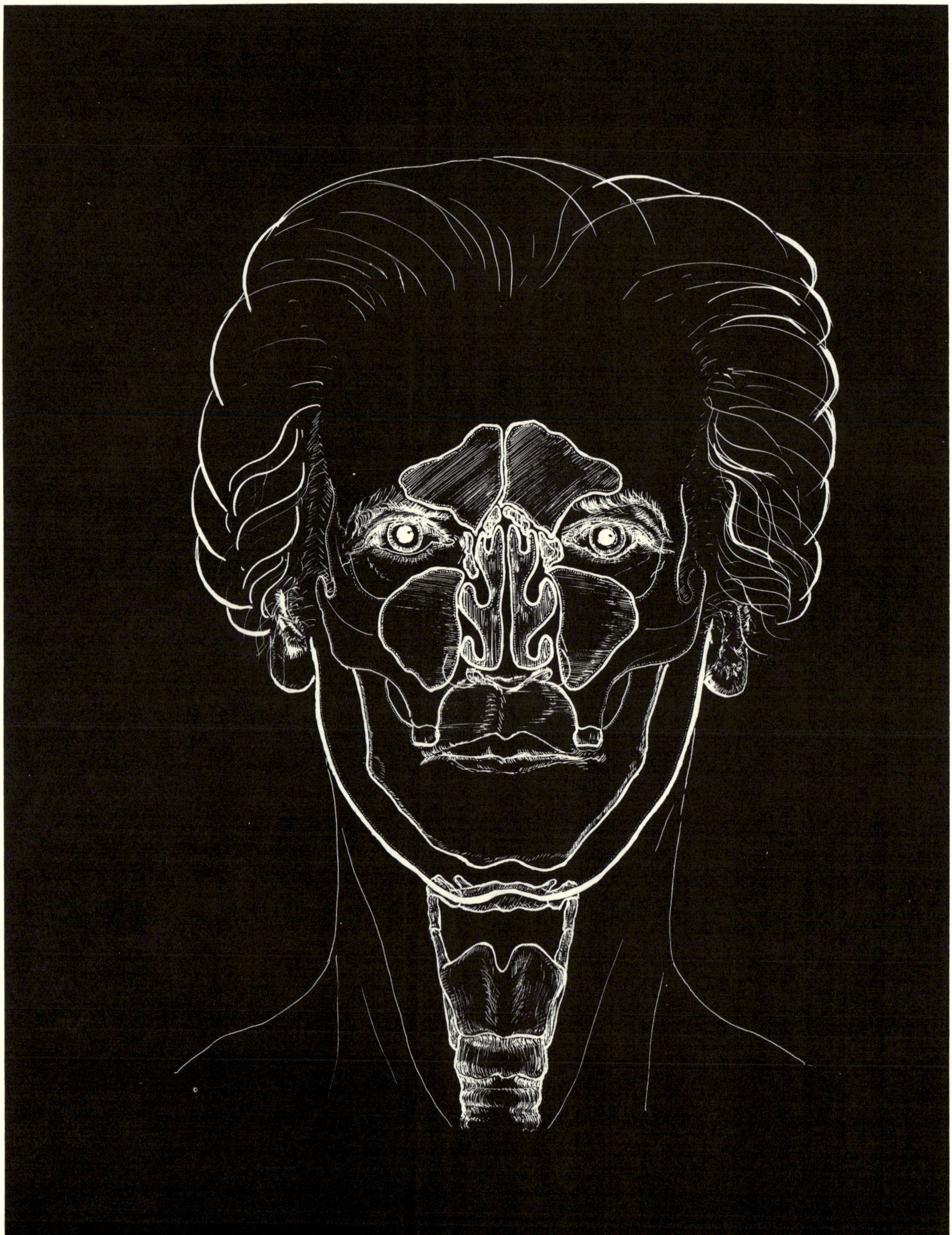

IV. CAVITIES OF MASK—FRONT VIEW

THE DEGREE OF INTENSITY APPLIED TO THE JAW, LARYNX, BODY FUSION AND THE GAN-TONE PULSATION DETERMINES THE DEGREE TO WHICH THE FACIAL RECEPTORS, OR CAVITIES, WILL RING.

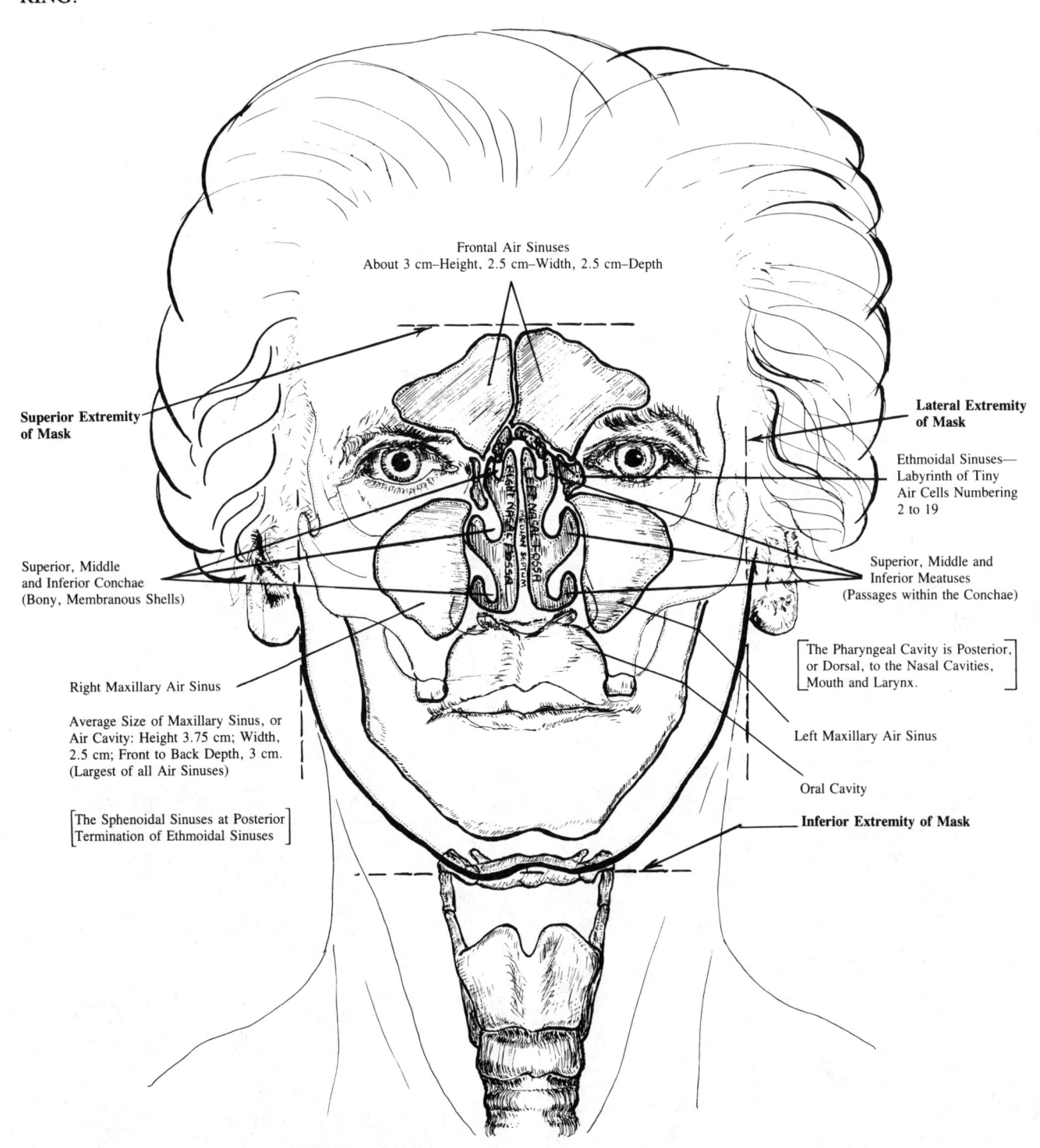

Frontal Air Sinuses
About 3 cm–Height, 2.5 cm–Width, 2.5 cm–Depth

Superior Extremity of Mask

Lateral Extremity of Mask

Ethmoidal Sinuses—Labyrinth of Tiny Air Cells Numbering 2 to 19

Superior, Middle and Inferior Conchae (Bony, Membranous Shells)

Superior, Middle and Inferior Meatuses (Passages within the Conchae)

[The Pharyngeal Cavity is Posterior, or Dorsal, to the Nasal Cavities, Mouth and Larynx.]

Right Maxillary Air Sinus

Average Size of Maxillary Sinus, or Air Cavity: Height 3.75 cm; Width, 2.5 cm; Front to Back Depth, 3 cm. (Largest of all Air Sinuses)

Left Maxillary Air Sinus

Oral Cavity

Inferior Extremity of Mask

[The Sphenoidal Sinuses at Posterior Termination of Ethmoidal Sinuses]

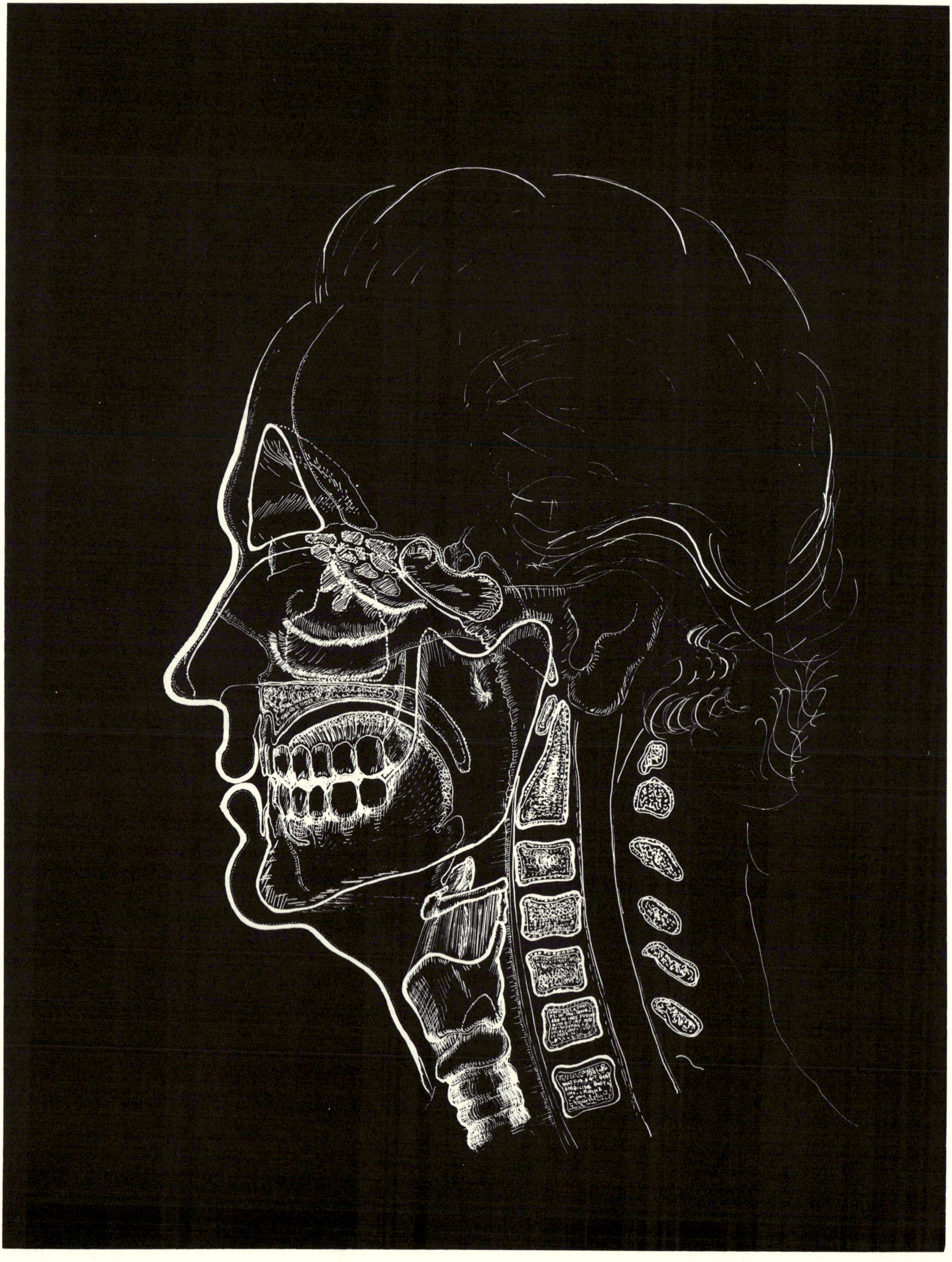

V. CAVITIES OF MASK—LATERAL VIEW

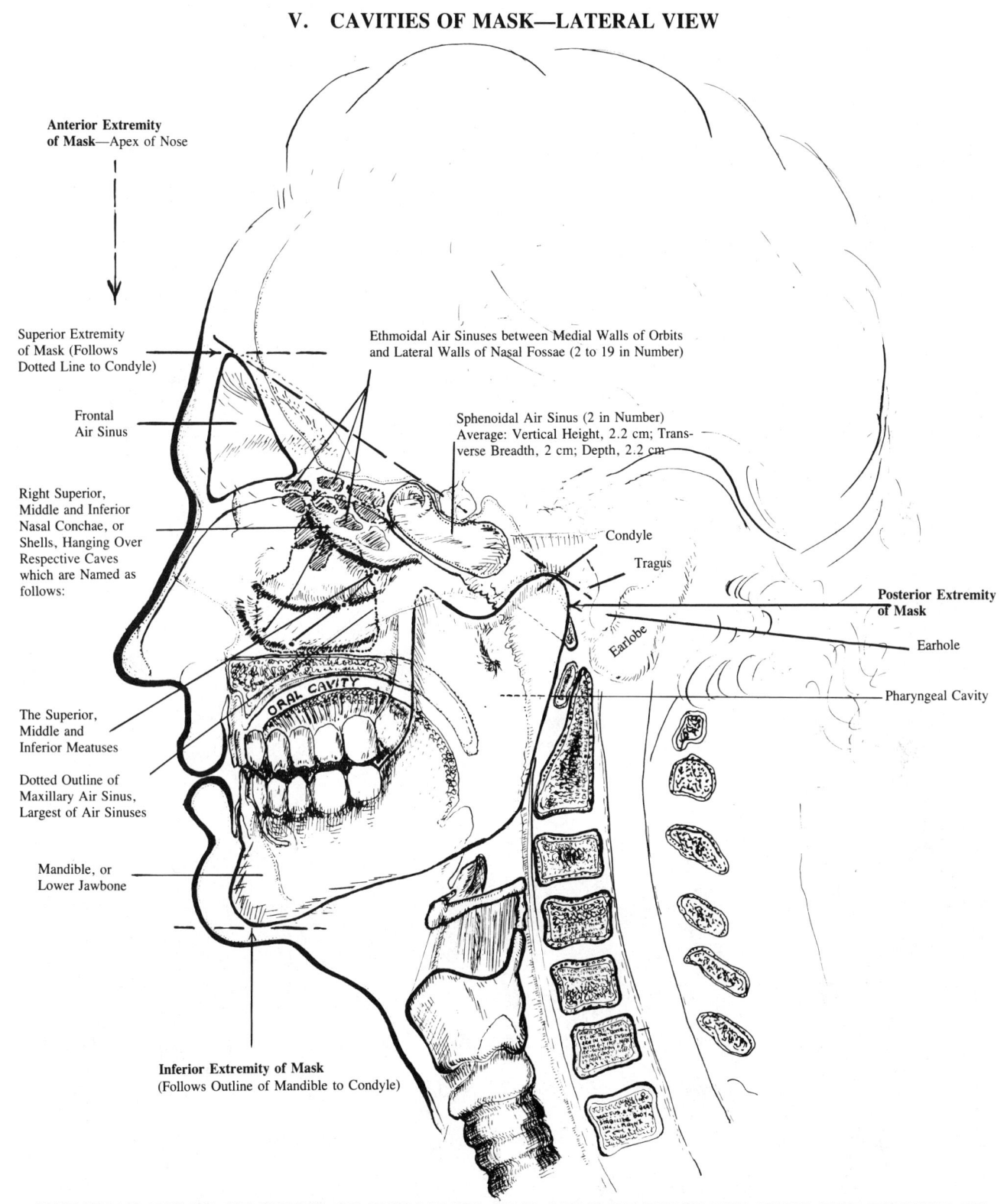

Anterior Extremity of Mask—Apex of Nose

Superior Extremity of Mask (Follows Dotted Line to Condyle)

Ethmoidal Air Sinuses between Medial Walls of Orbits and Lateral Walls of Nasal Fossae (2 to 19 in Number)

Frontal Air Sinus

Sphenoidal Air Sinus (2 in Number) Average: Vertical Height, 2.2 cm; Transverse Breadth, 2 cm; Depth, 2.2 cm

Right Superior, Middle and Inferior Nasal Conchae, or Shells, Hanging Over Respective Caves which are Named as follows:

Condyle

Tragus

Posterior Extremity of Mask

Earlobe

Earhole

Pharyngeal Cavity

The Superior, Middle and Inferior Meatuses

Dotted Outline of Maxillary Air Sinus, Largest of Air Sinuses

Mandible, or Lower Jawbone

Inferior Extremity of Mask (Follows Outline of Mandible to Condyle)

THE HEAD BELLS (CAVITIES OF THE MASK) CAN ONLY BE RUNG THROUGH THE THRUST OF VOCAL CORDS AND BODY VIBRATIONS FROM THE BOTTOM OF THE TORSO ON THE GAN-TONE PULSATIONS.

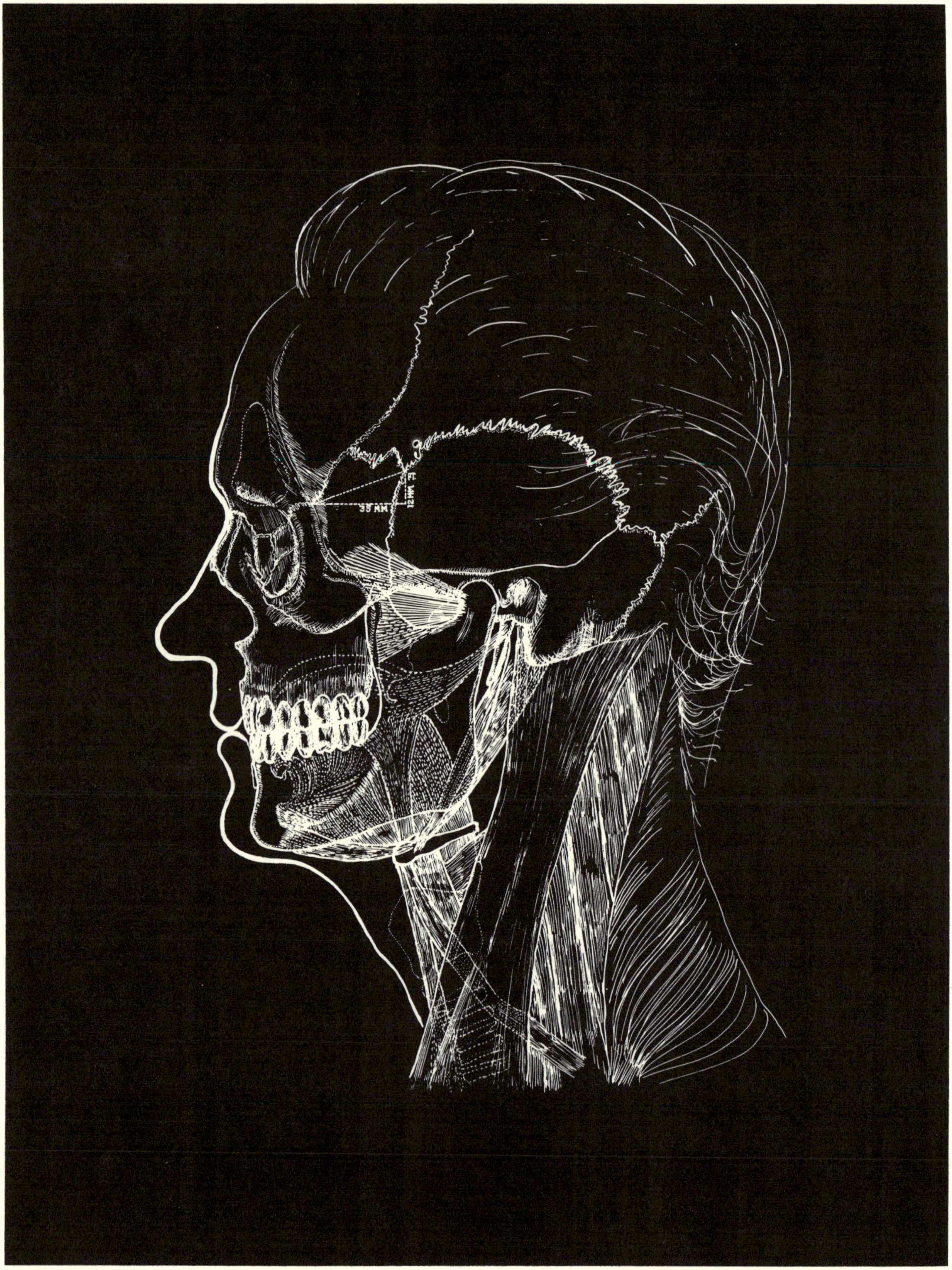

VI. TONGUE AND NECK MUSCLES INVOLVED IN THE SINGING PROCESS

THE PTERYGOIDEUS LATERALIS, A HEAD MUSCLE, IS THE KEY TO THE CONTROL OF TONGUE AND NECK MUSCLES DURING THE SINGING PROCESS.

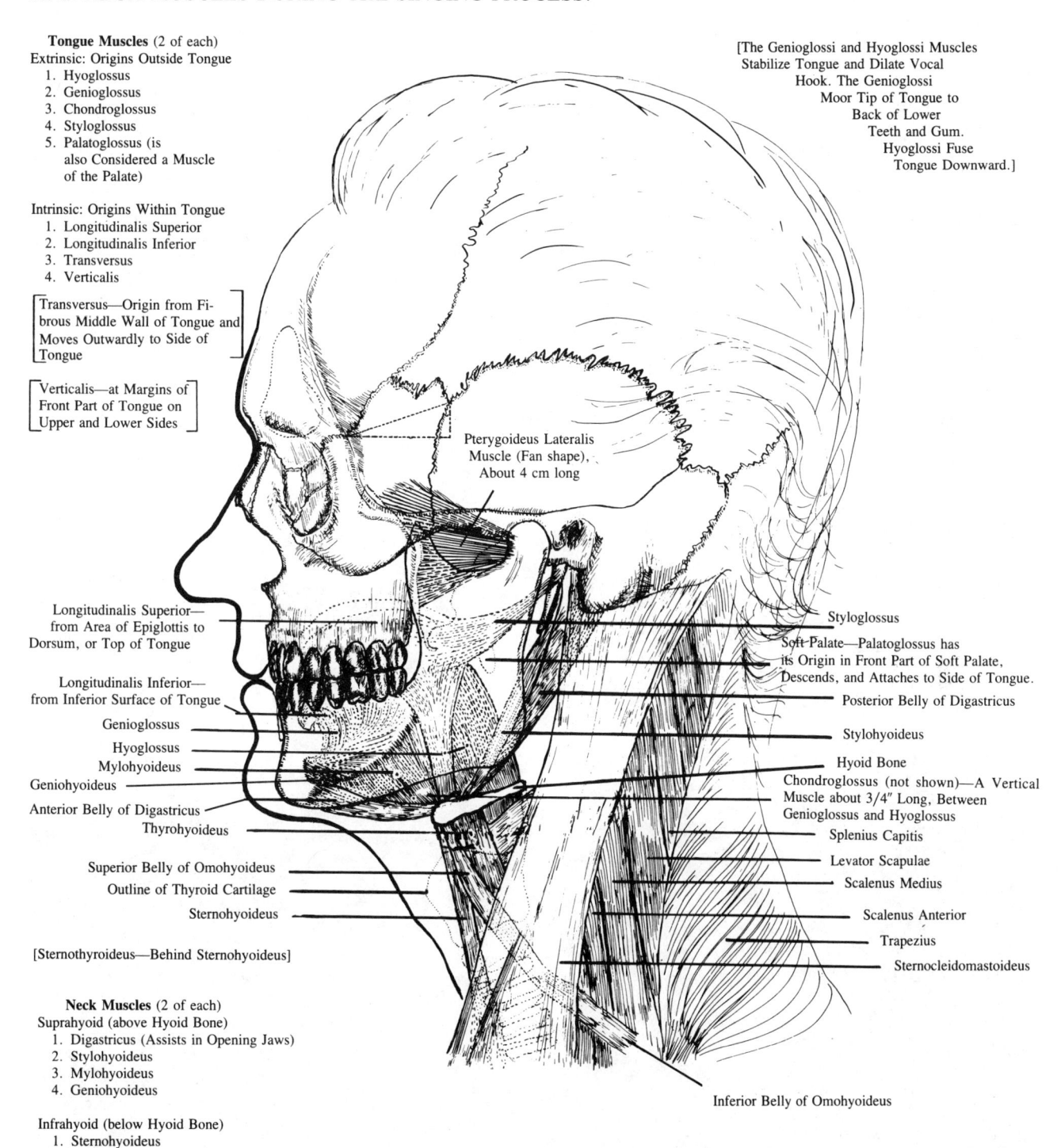

Tongue Muscles (2 of each)
Extrinsic: Origins Outside Tongue
1. Hyoglossus
2. Genioglossus
3. Chondroglossus
4. Styloglossus
5. Palatoglossus (is also Considered a Muscle of the Palate)

Intrinsic: Origins Within Tongue
1. Longitudinalis Superior
2. Longitudinalis Inferior
3. Transversus
4. Verticalis

[Transversus—Origin from Fibrous Middle Wall of Tongue and Moves Outwardly to Side of Tongue]

[Verticalis—at Margins of Front Part of Tongue on Upper and Lower Sides]

[The Genioglossi and Hyoglossi Muscles Stabilize Tongue and Dilate Vocal Hook. The Genioglossi Moor Tip of Tongue to Back of Lower Teeth and Gum. Hyoglossi Fuse Tongue Downward.]

Pterygoideus Lateralis Muscle (Fan shape), About 4 cm long

Longitudinalis Superior—from Area of Epiglottis to Dorsum, or Top of Tongue
Longitudinalis Inferior—from Inferior Surface of Tongue
Genioglossus
Hyoglossus
Mylohyoideus
Geniohyoideus
Anterior Belly of Digastricus
Thyrohyoideus
Superior Belly of Omohyoideus
Outline of Thyroid Cartilage
Sternohyoideus

[Sternothyroideus—Behind Sternohyoideus]

Styloglossus
Soft Palate—Palatoglossus has its Origin in Front Part of Soft Palate, Descends, and Attaches to Side of Tongue.
Posterior Belly of Digastricus
Stylohyoideus
Hyoid Bone
Chondroglossus (not shown)—A Vertical Muscle about 3/4" Long, Between Genioglossus and Hyoglossus
Splenius Capitis
Levator Scapulae
Scalenus Medius
Scalenus Anterior
Trapezius
Sternocleidomastoideus

Inferior Belly of Omohyoideus

Neck Muscles (2 of each)
Suprahyoid (above Hyoid Bone)
1. Digastricus (Assists in Opening Jaws)
2. Stylohyoideus
3. Mylohyoideus
4. Geniohyoideus

Infrahyoid (below Hyoid Bone)
1. Sternohyoideus
2. Sternothyroideus
3. Thyrohyoideus
4. Omohyoideus

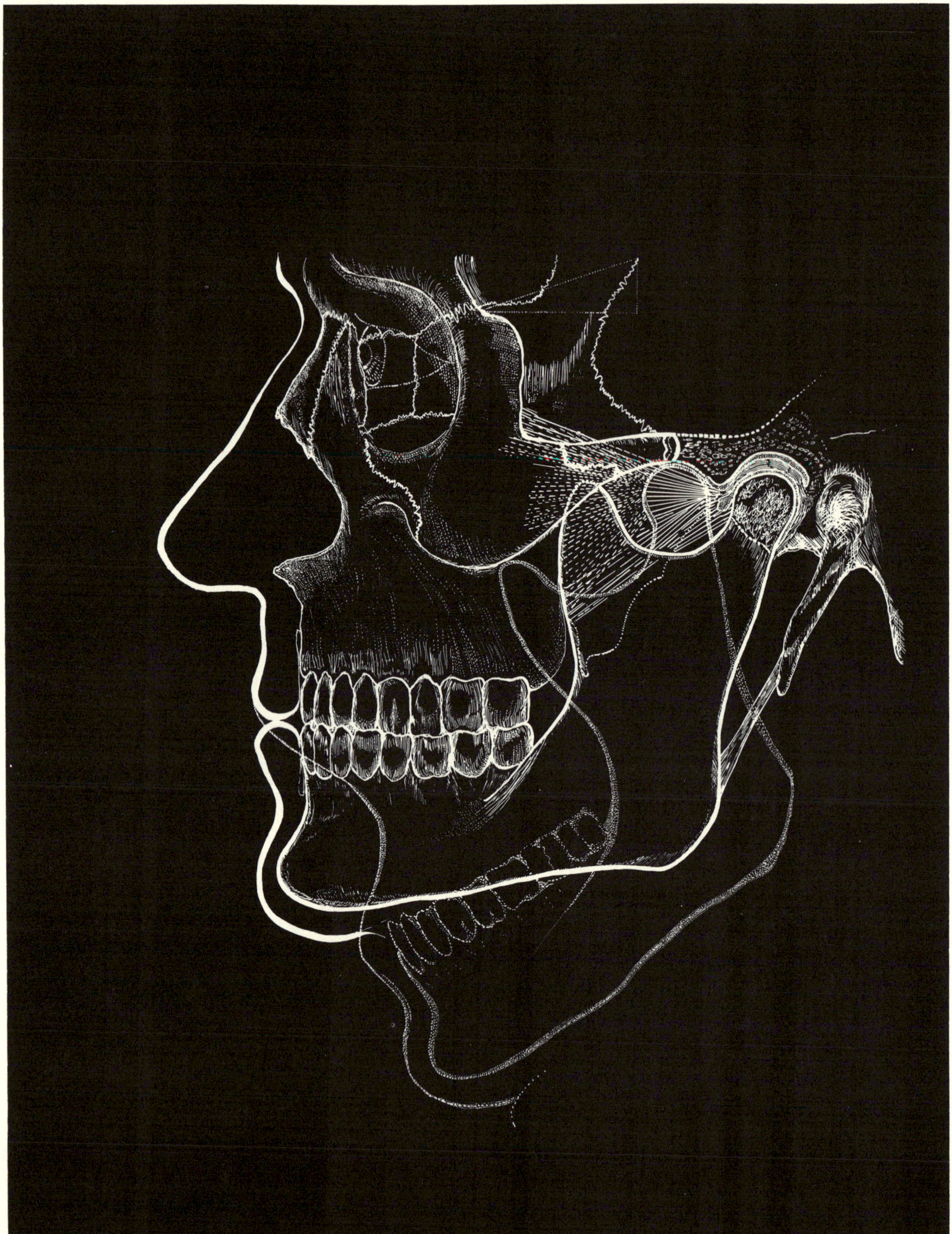

VII. FORWARD MANDIBULAR MOVEMENT IN JAW, LARYNX, BODY FUSION

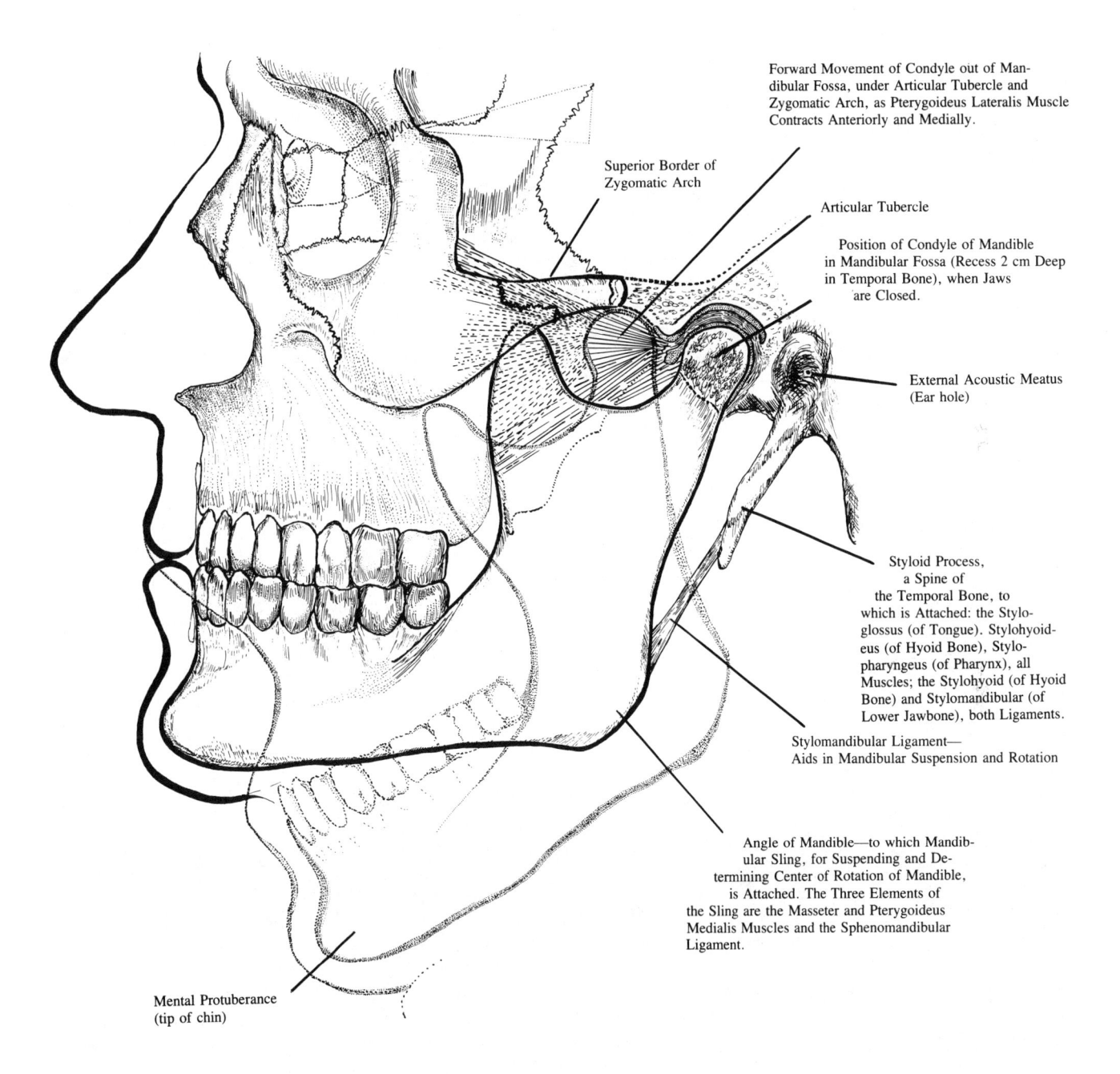

Forward Movement of Condyle out of Mandibular Fossa, under Articular Tubercle and Zygomatic Arch, as Pterygoideus Lateralis Muscle Contracts Anteriorly and Medially.

Superior Border of Zygomatic Arch

Articular Tubercle

Position of Condyle of Mandible in Mandibular Fossa (Recess 2 cm Deep in Temporal Bone), when Jaws are Closed.

External Acoustic Meatus (Ear hole)

Styloid Process, a Spine of the Temporal Bone, to which is Attached: the Styloglossus (of Tongue). Stylohyoideus (of Hyoid Bone), Stylopharyngeus (of Pharynx), all Muscles; the Stylohyoid (of Hyoid Bone) and Stylomandibular (of Lower Jawbone), both Ligaments.

Stylomandibular Ligament— Aids in Mandibular Suspension and Rotation

Angle of Mandible—to which Mandibular Sling, for Suspending and Determining Center of Rotation of Mandible, is Attached. The Three Elements of the Sling are the Masseter and Pterygoideus Medialis Muscles and the Sphenomandibular Ligament.

Mental Protuberance (tip of chin)

MANDIBLE FUSED TO LARYNX WHEN JAWS ARE OPENED WIDE BECOMES SWITCH THAT CONNECTS HEAD TO TORSO. WHEN MANDIBLE IS FUSED TO LARYNX, HEAD IS TILTED FORWARD, AND CONDYLE AND MENTAL PROTUBERANCE FORM A PERPENDICULAR LINE TO THE GROUND.

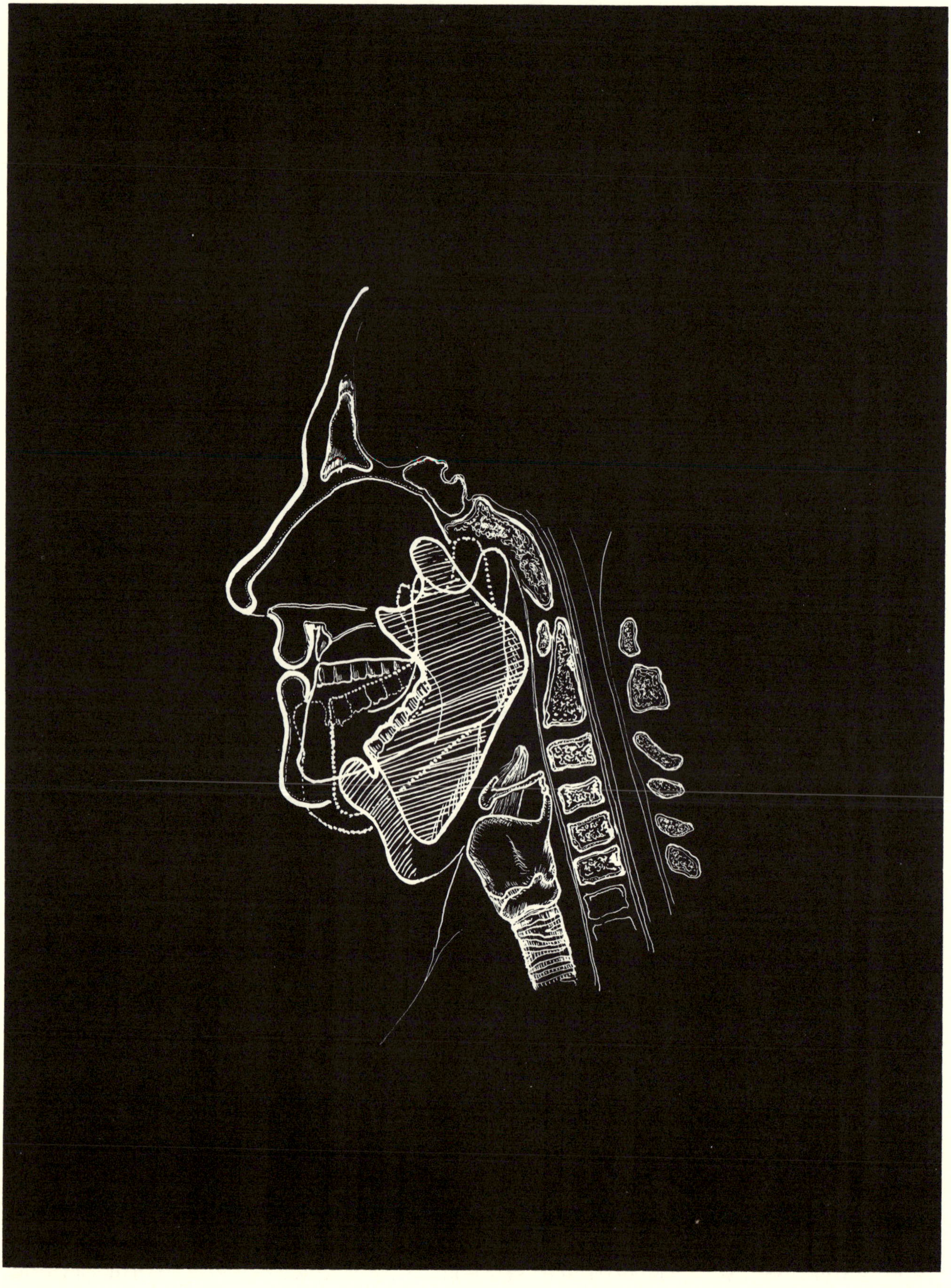

VIII. VERTICAL POSITION OF MANDIBLE IN JAW, LARYNX, BODY FUSION

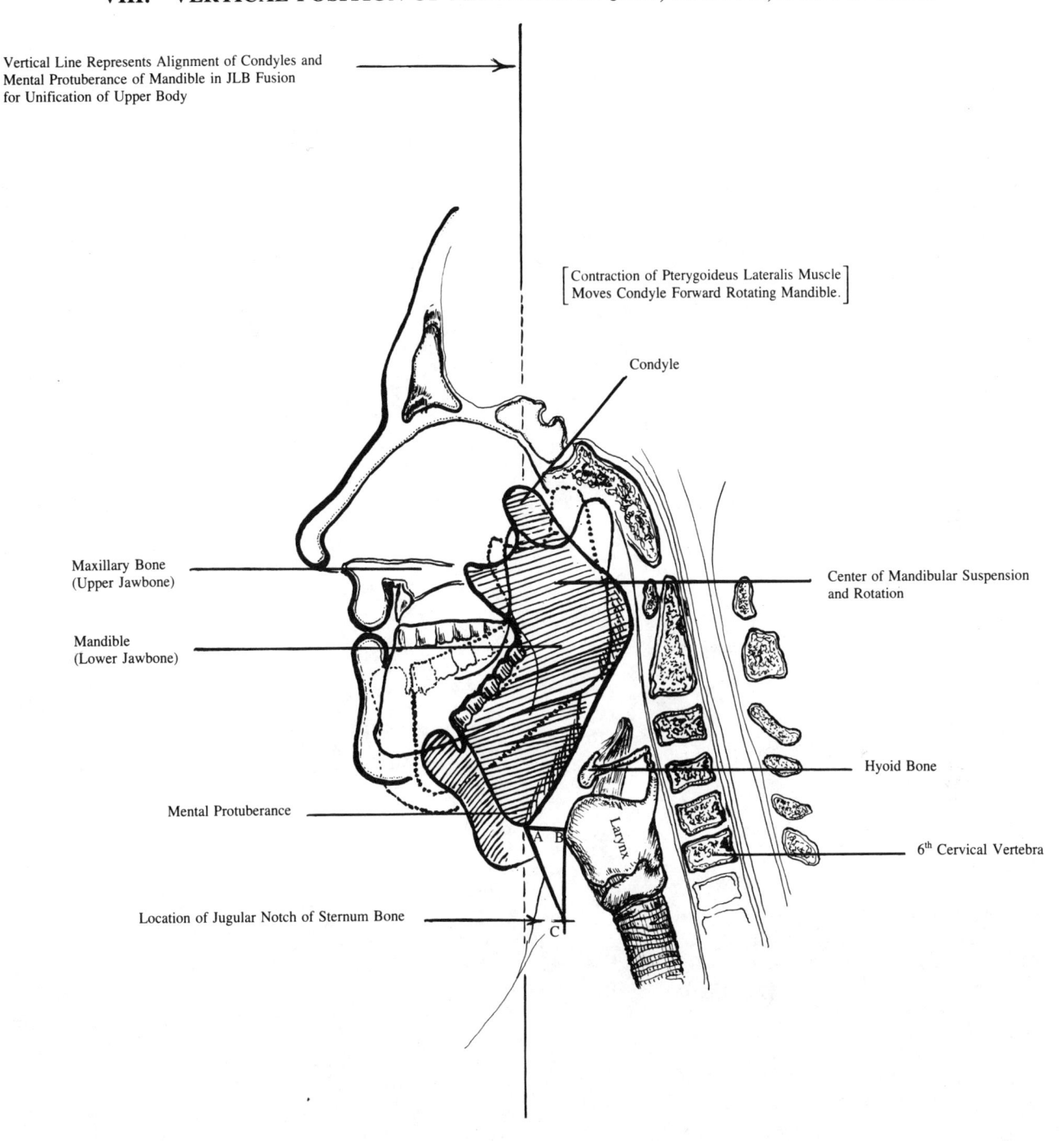

Vertical Line Represents Alignment of Condyles and Mental Protuberance of Mandible in JLB Fusion for Unification of Upper Body

[Contraction of Pterygoideus Lateralis Muscle Moves Condyle Forward Rotating Mandible.]

Condyle

Maxillary Bone (Upper Jawbone)

Center of Mandibular Suspension and Rotation

Mandible (Lower Jawbone)

Hyoid Bone

Mental Protuberance

6th Cervical Vertebra

Location of Jugular Notch of Sternum Bone

THE NEARNESS TO EACH OTHER OF THE THREE NOTCHES, I.E., TRIANGLE ABC (A—MENTAL, B—LARYNGEAL, C—JUGULAR), REGULATED BY THE DEGREE OF JAW OPENING AND HEAD TILT, DETERMINES THE DEGREE OF BODY UNIFICATION AND VOCAL VIBRATORY CONTINUITY. THE WIDER THE JAW IS OPENED AND THE MORE THE HEAD IS TILTED FORWARD, THE MORE THE TRIANGLE IS REDUCED, PRODUCING A GREATER AMPLIFICATION, FLOW AND RESOUNDING OF THE SINGING VOICE.

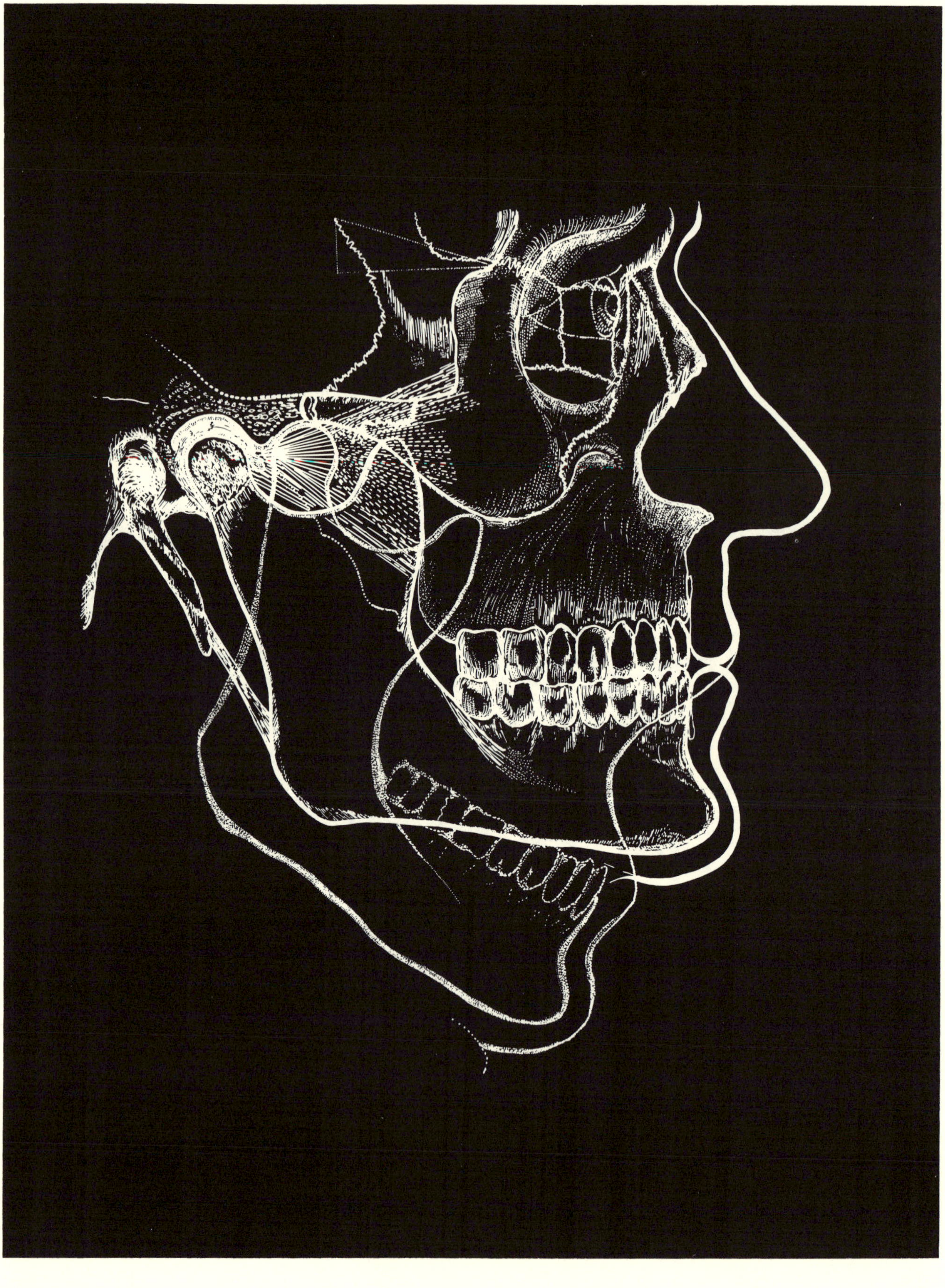

225

IX. HEAD MUSCLE THAT FUSES JAW AND BODY

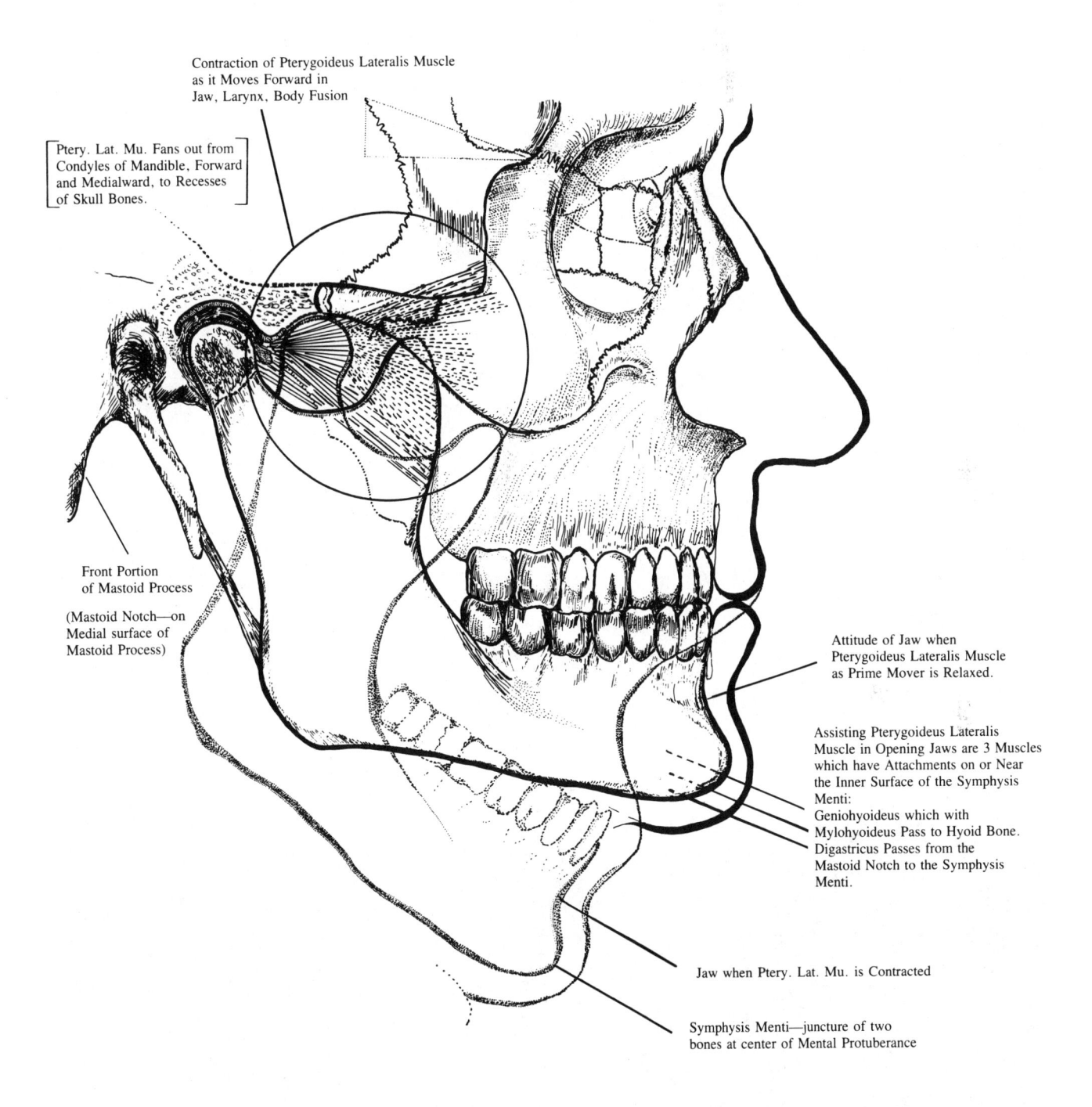

Contraction of Pterygoideus Lateralis Muscle as it Moves Forward in Jaw, Larynx, Body Fusion

[Ptery. Lat. Mu. Fans out from Condyles of Mandible, Forward and Medialward, to Recesses of Skull Bones.]

Front Portion of Mastoid Process

(Mastoid Notch—on Medial surface of Mastoid Process)

Attitude of Jaw when Pterygoideus Lateralis Muscle as Prime Mover is Relaxed.

Assisting Pterygoideus Lateralis Muscle in Opening Jaws are 3 Muscles which have Attachments on or Near the Inner Surface of the Symphysis Menti:
Geniohyoideus which with Mylohyoideus Pass to Hyoid Bone. Digastricus Passes from the Mastoid Notch to the Symphysis Menti.

Jaw when Ptery. Lat. Mu. is Contracted

Symphysis Menti—juncture of two bones at center of Mental Protuberance

COMPLETE CONTRACTION OF THE PTERYGOIDEUS LATERALIS MUSCLE FUSES MANDIBLE AND NECK MUSCLES TO THE BODY CAUSING NECK MUSCLES TO BECOME PART OF THE BODY IN DIFFUSING VOCAL STRESS TO THE BODY EXTREMITIES RATHER THAN ISOLATING THIS STRESS IN THE NECK.

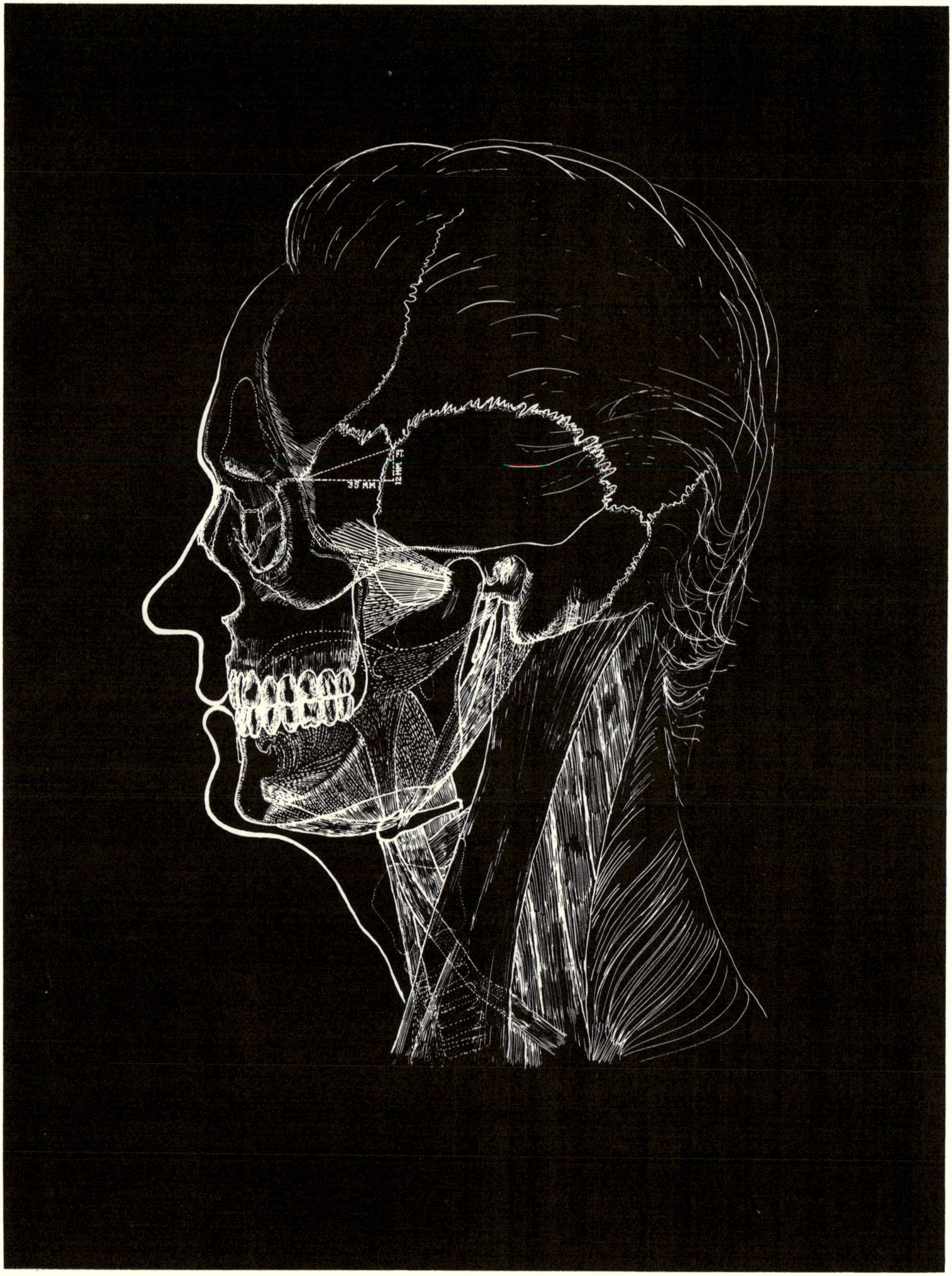

X. PTERYGOIDEUS LATERALIS MUSCLE—ORIGIN OF JAW, LARYNX, BODY FUSION—LATERAL VIEW

THE COMPLETE CONTRACTION OF THE PTERYGOIDEUS LATERALIS MUSCLE UNDER STRESS (LOUD, HIGH, SUSTAINED NOTES) PRODUCES THE MOST BRILLIANT RE-SOUNDING OF VOCAL CORDS AND BODY VIBRATIONS IN THE NASION CENTER (HIGHEST HEAD RESONATORS), WHEN JLB FUSION AND GAN-TONE PULSATION ARE MAXIMALLY APPLIED.

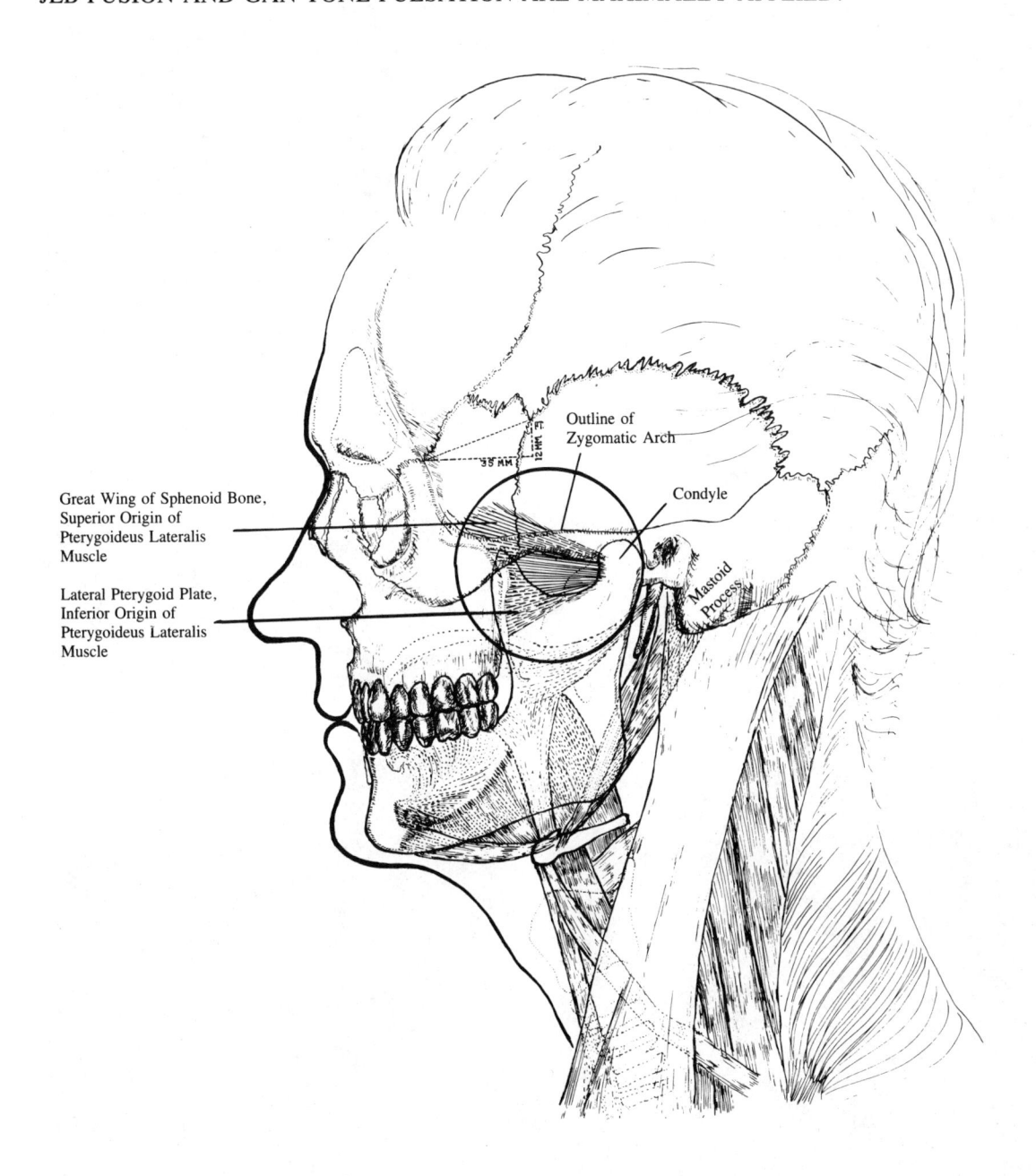

Origin of Pterygoideus Lateralis Muscle: The Deep Recesses of the Skull Bones Behind the Zygomatic Arch about 4 cm Deep from Each Side of Head—Converges Backward and Lateralward and Attaches to Condyle (One Muscle on Each Side of Head).

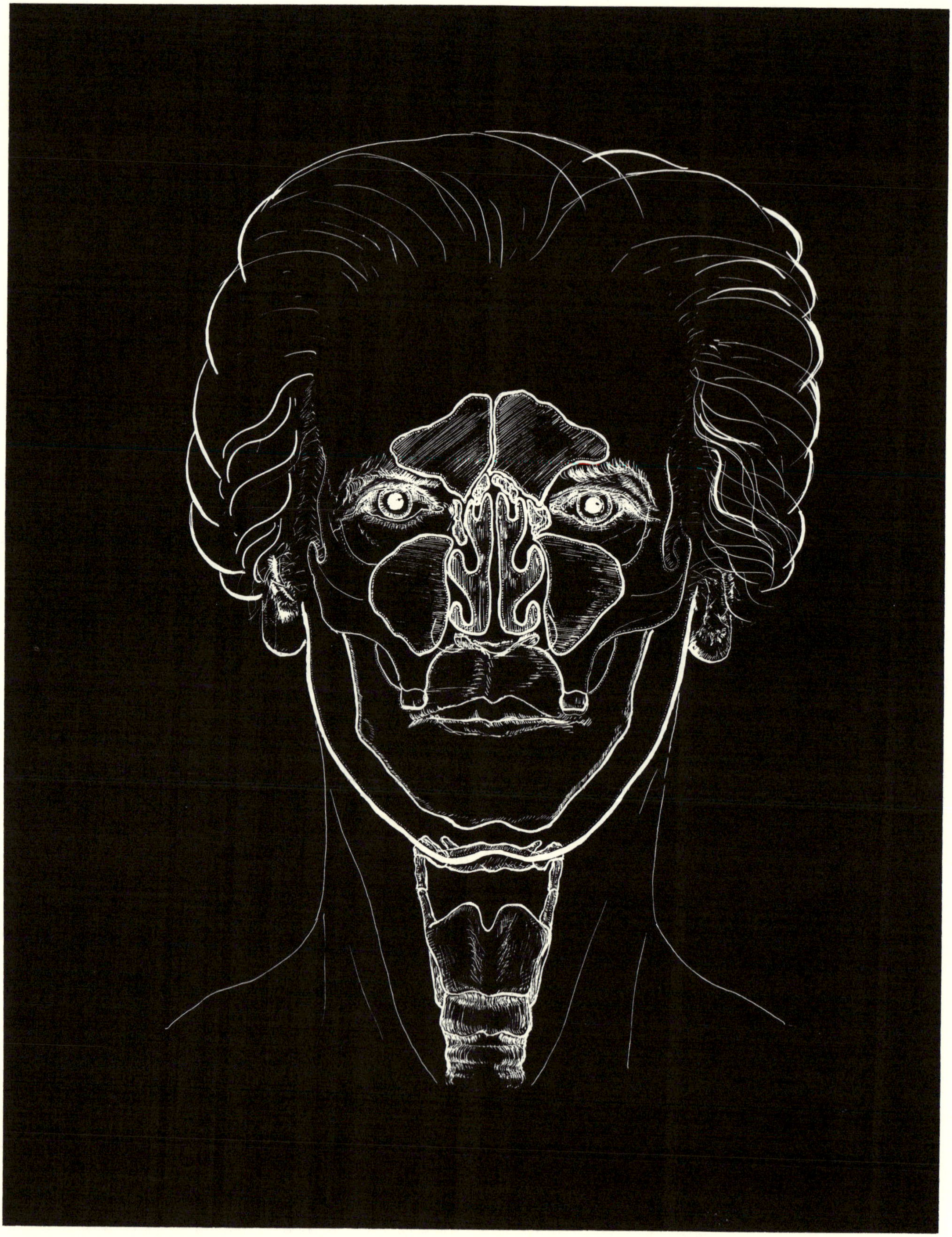

XI. PTERYGOIDEUS LATERALIS MUSCLE—FRONT VIEW

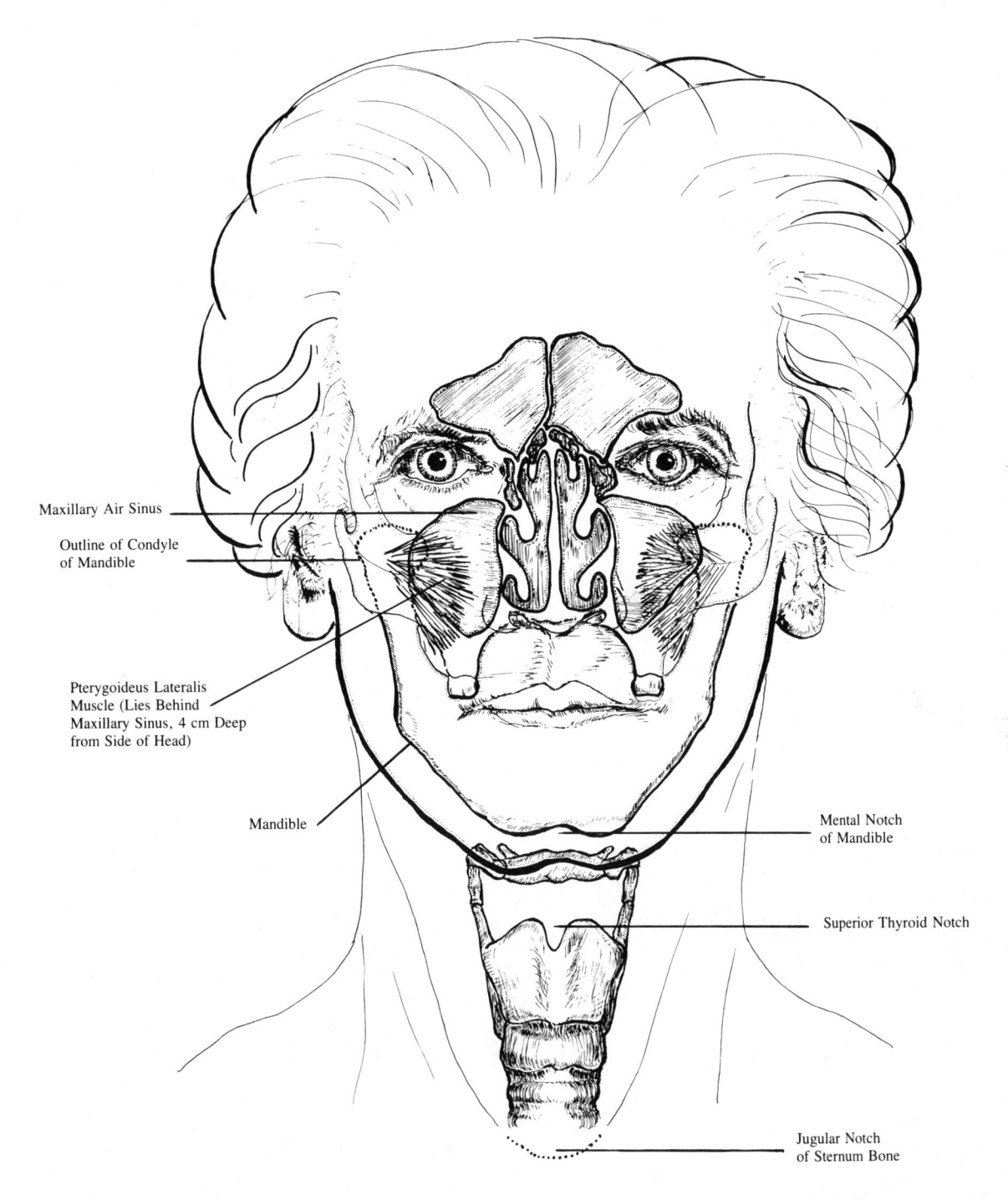

Maxillary Air Sinus

Outline of Condyle of Mandible

Pterygoideus Lateralis Muscle (Lies Behind Maxillary Sinus, 4 cm Deep from Side of Head)

Mandible

Mental Notch of Mandible

Superior Thyroid Notch

Jugular Notch of Sternum Bone

THE DEGREE OF SKILL THE SINGER ACHIEVES IN MAINTAINING THE COMPLETE CONTRACTION OF THE PTERYGOIDEUS LATERALIS MUSCLE UNDER THE PRESSURE OF VOLUME AND RANGE WILL DETERMINE THE DEGREE OF VOCAL VIBRATORY CONTINUITY THROUGHOUT THE BODY.

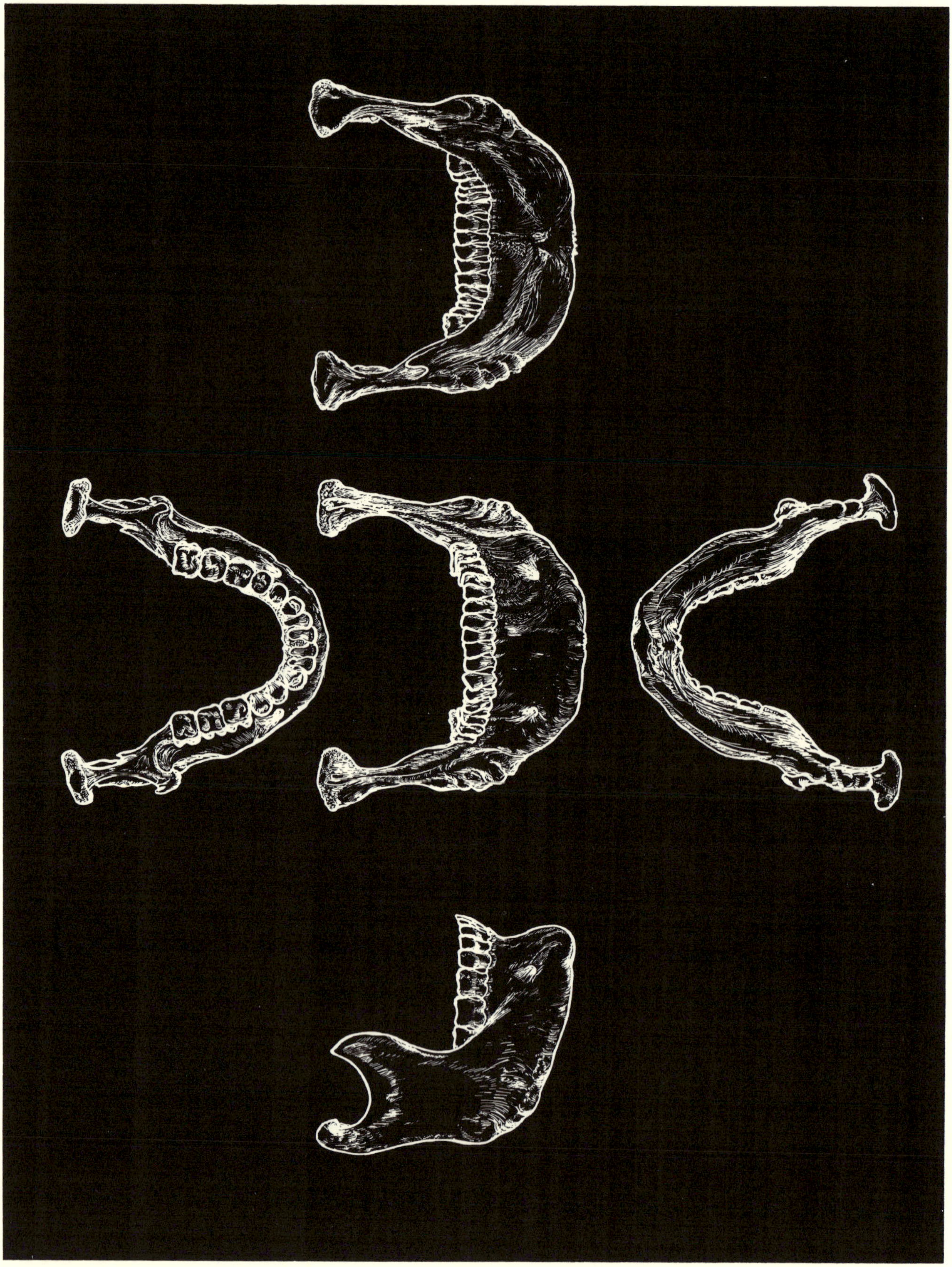

XII. FIVE ASPECTS OF MANDIBLE AND PTERYGOIDEUS LATERALIS MUSCLE ATTACHMENT

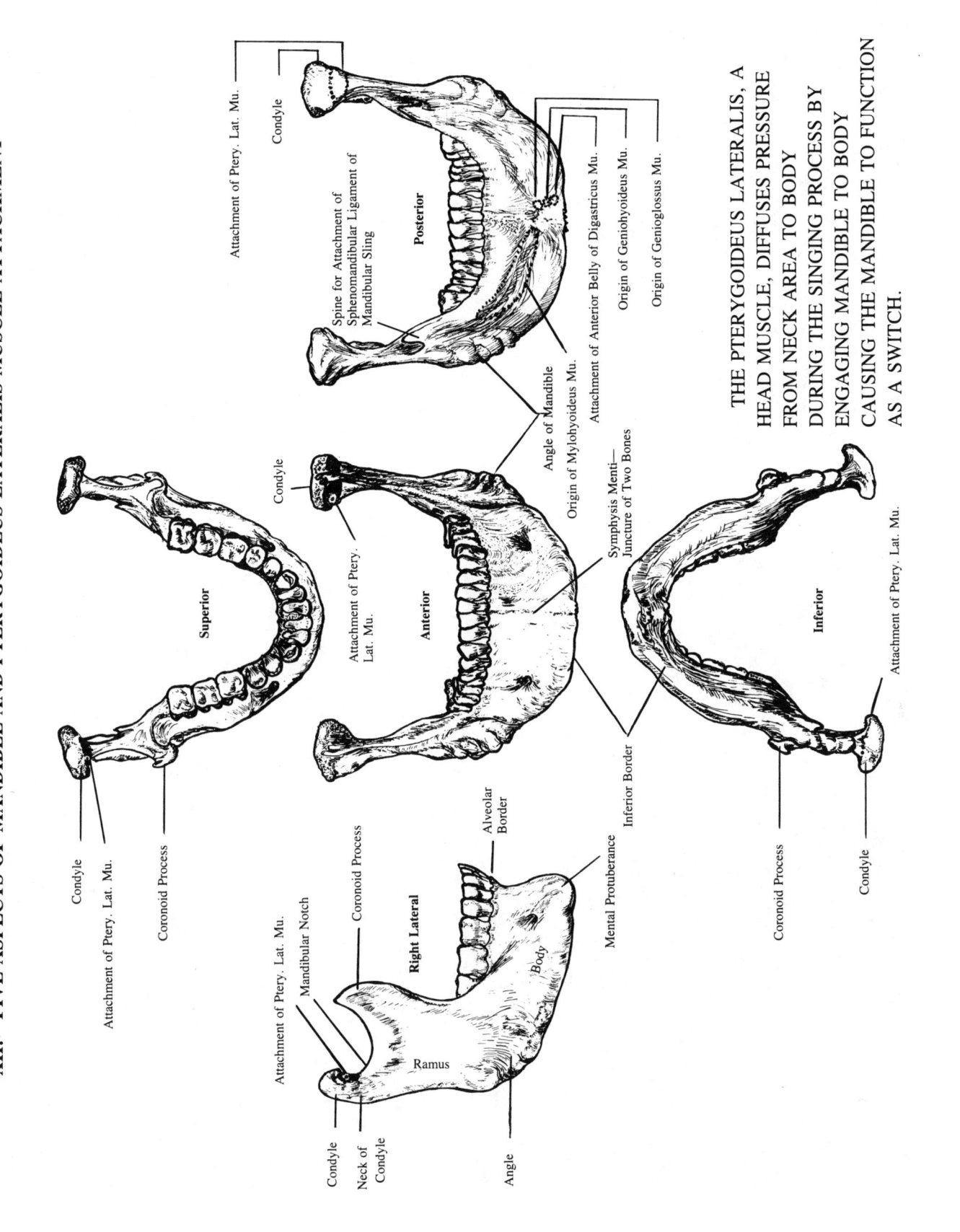

THE PTERYGOIDEUS LATERALIS, A HEAD MUSCLE, DIFFUSES PRESSURE FROM NECK AREA TO BODY DURING THE SINGING PROCESS BY ENGAGING MANDIBLE TO BODY CAUSING THE MANDIBLE TO FUNCTION AS A SWITCH.

231

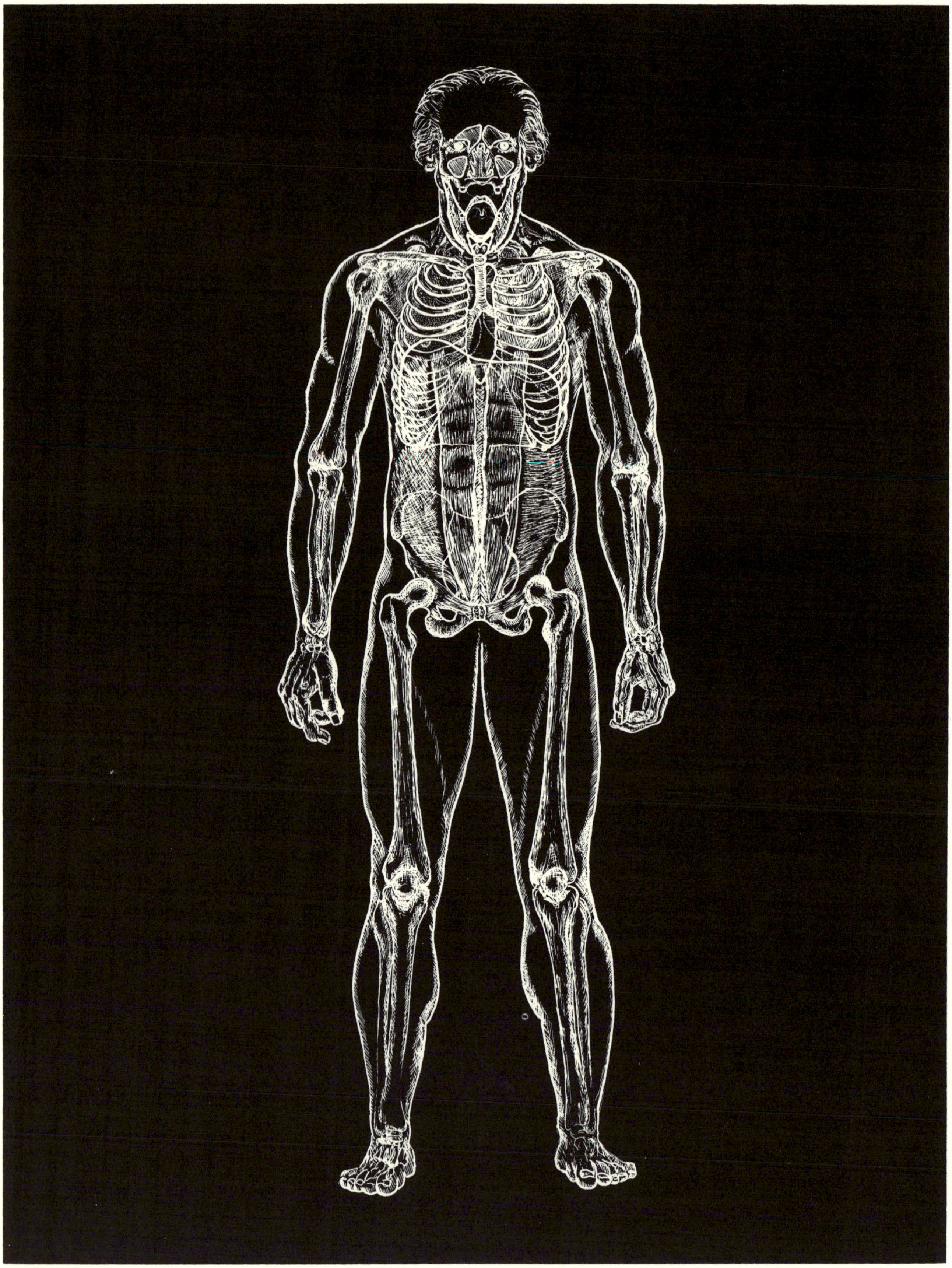

XIII. LOCATION OF PELVIC-UROGENITAL DIAPHRAGM AND SPHINCTER ANI EXTERNUS MUSCLE

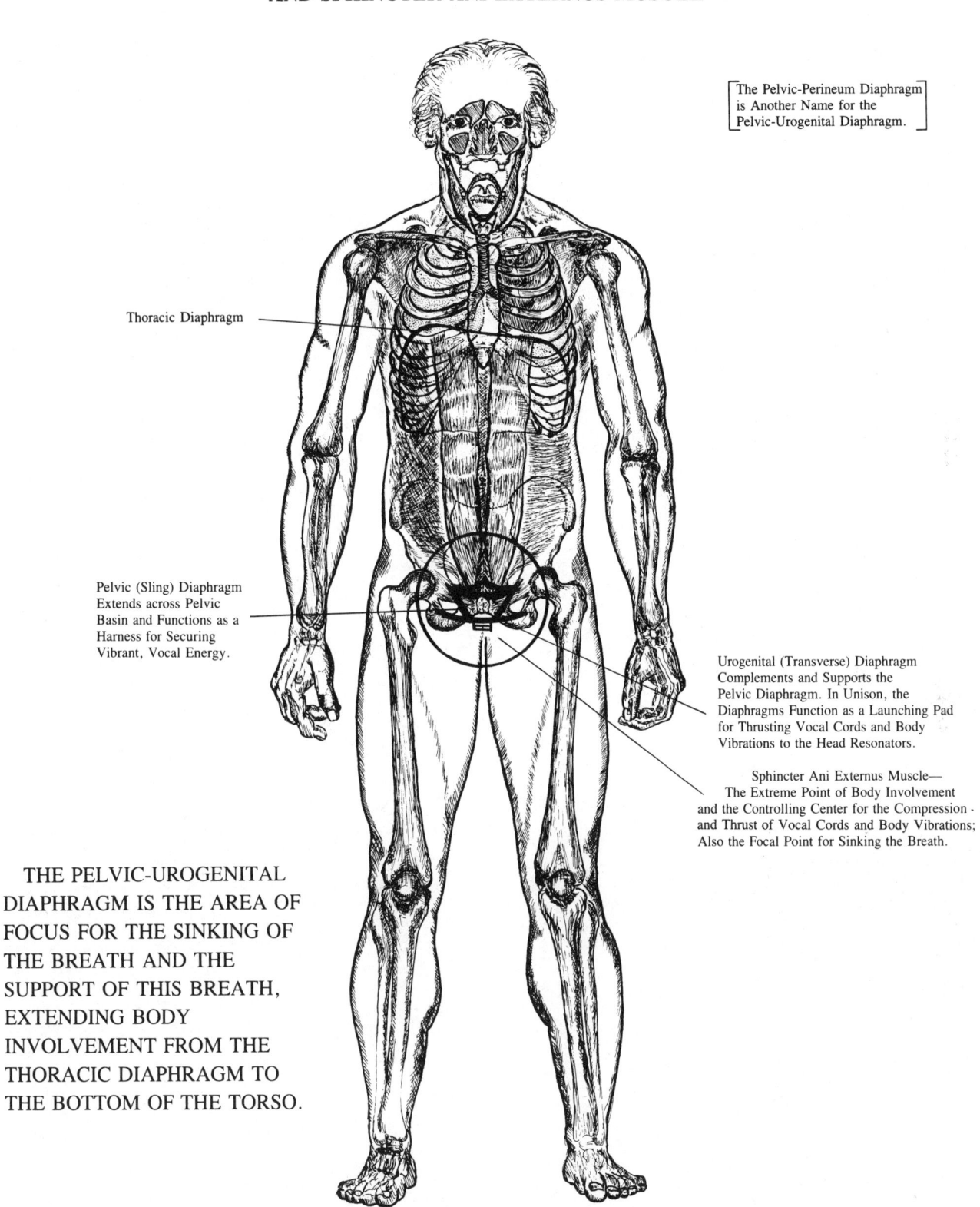

The Pelvic-Perineum Diaphragm is Another Name for the Pelvic-Urogenital Diaphragm.

Thoracic Diaphragm

Pelvic (Sling) Diaphragm Extends across Pelvic Basin and Functions as a Harness for Securing Vibrant, Vocal Energy.

Urogenital (Transverse) Diaphragm Complements and Supports the Pelvic Diaphragm. In Unison, the Diaphragms Function as a Launching Pad for Thrusting Vocal Cords and Body Vibrations to the Head Resonators.

Sphincter Ani Externus Muscle— The Extreme Point of Body Involvement and the Controlling Center for the Compression and Thrust of Vocal Cords and Body Vibrations; Also the Focal Point for Sinking the Breath.

THE PELVIC-UROGENITAL DIAPHRAGM IS THE AREA OF FOCUS FOR THE SINKING OF THE BREATH AND THE SUPPORT OF THIS BREATH, EXTENDING BODY INVOLVEMENT FROM THE THORACIC DIAPHRAGM TO THE BOTTOM OF THE TORSO.

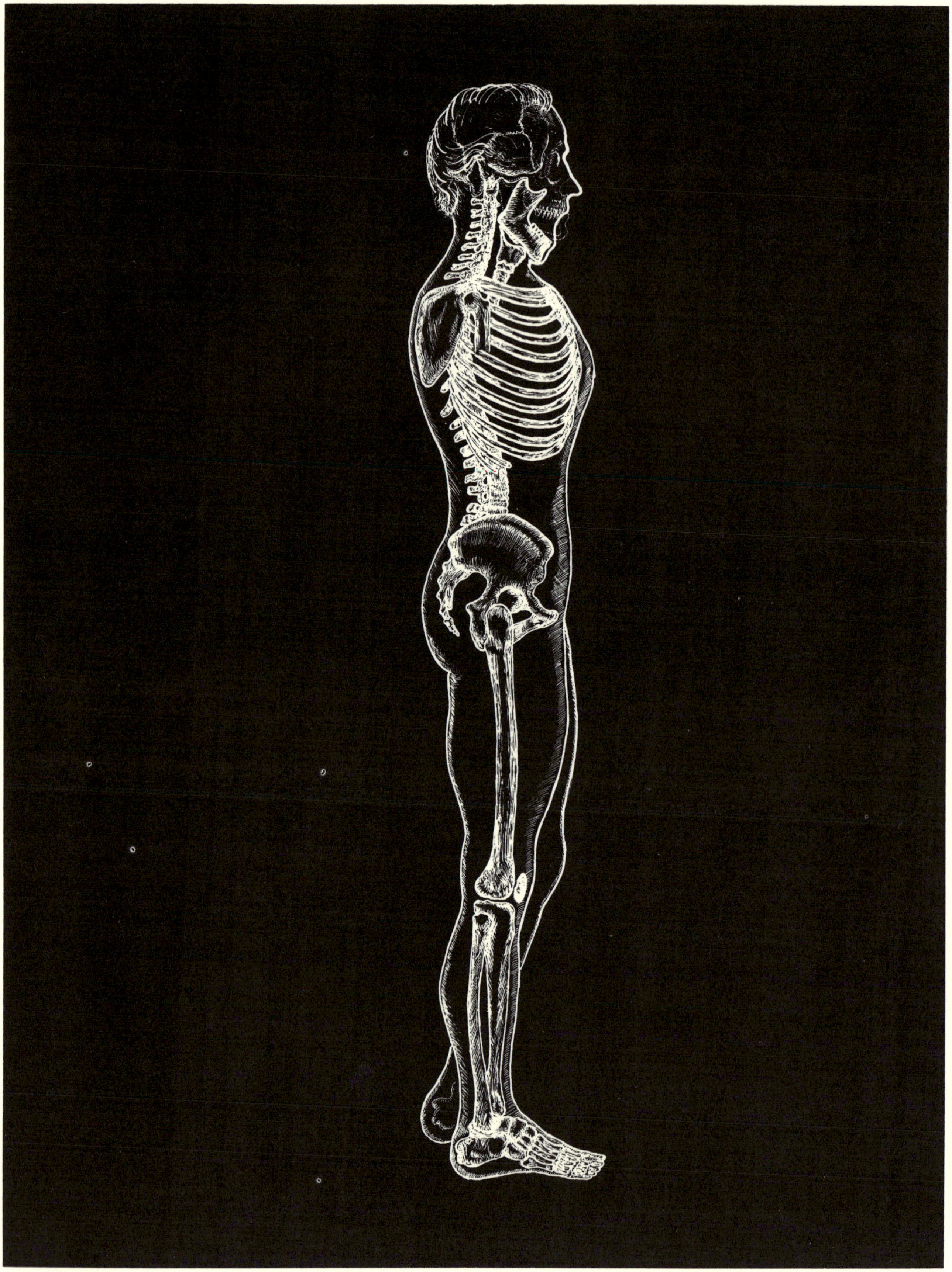

XIV. REFERENCE POINTS FOR VOICE PROJECTION IN THE GAN-TONE METHOD OF VOICE PRODUCTION

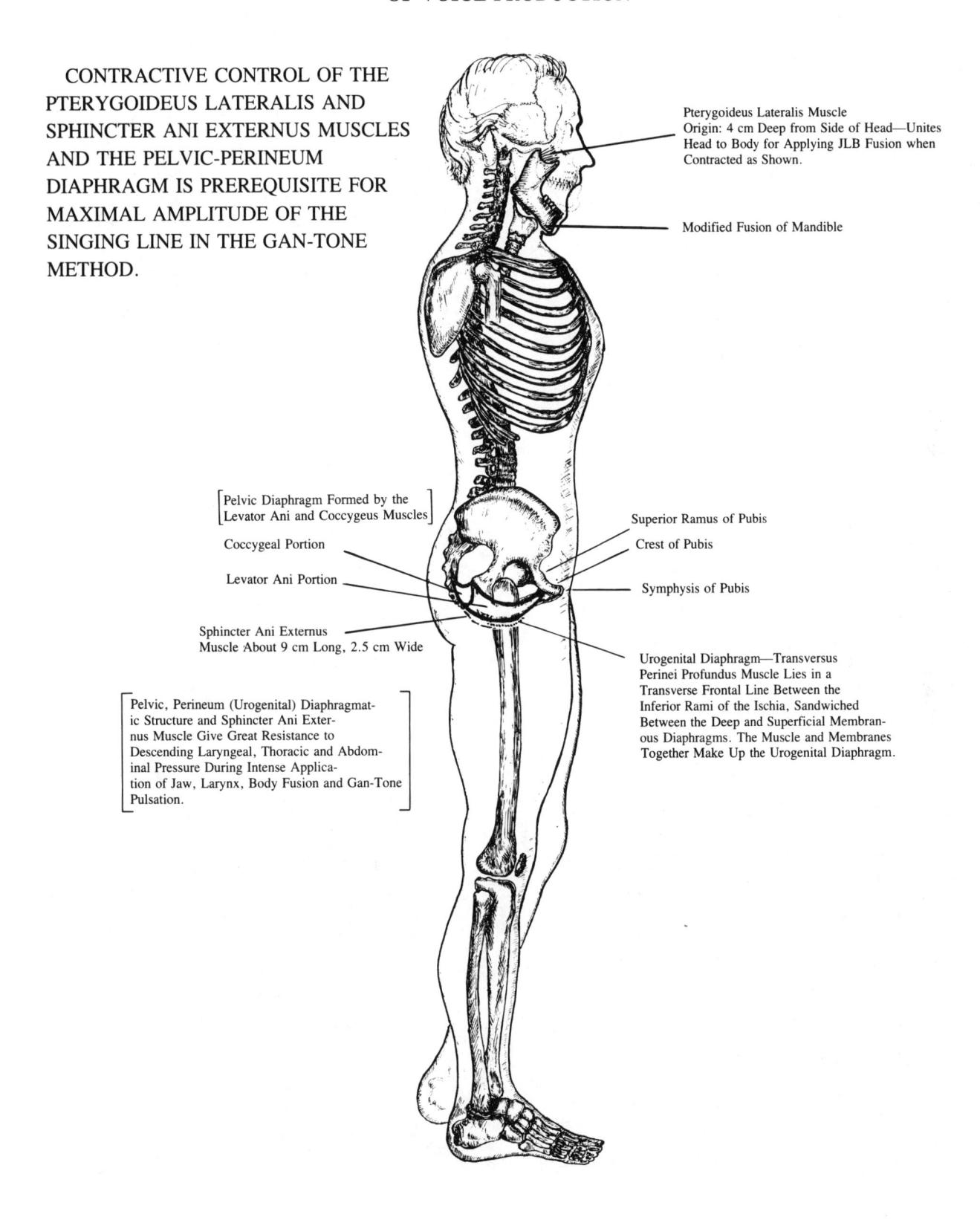

CONTRACTIVE CONTROL OF THE PTERYGOIDEUS LATERALIS AND SPHINCTER ANI EXTERNUS MUSCLES AND THE PELVIC-PERINEUM DIAPHRAGM IS PREREQUISITE FOR MAXIMAL AMPLITUDE OF THE SINGING LINE IN THE GAN-TONE METHOD.

Pterygoideus Lateralis Muscle Origin: 4 cm Deep from Side of Head—Unites Head to Body for Applying JLB Fusion when Contracted as Shown.

Modified Fusion of Mandible

[Pelvic Diaphragm Formed by the Levator Ani and Coccygeus Muscles]

Coccygeal Portion

Levator Ani Portion

Sphincter Ani Externus Muscle About 9 cm Long, 2.5 cm Wide

Superior Ramus of Pubis

Crest of Pubis

Symphysis of Pubis

Urogenital Diaphragm—Transversus Perinei Profundus Muscle Lies in a Transverse Frontal Line Between the Inferior Rami of the Ischia, Sandwiched Between the Deep and Superficial Membranous Diaphragms. The Muscle and Membranes Together Make Up the Urogenital Diaphragm.

[Pelvic, Perineum (Urogenital) Diaphragmatic Structure and Sphincter Ani Externus Muscle Give Great Resistance to Descending Laryngeal, Thoracic and Abdominal Pressure During Intense Application of Jaw, Larynx, Body Fusion and Gan-Tone Pulsation.]

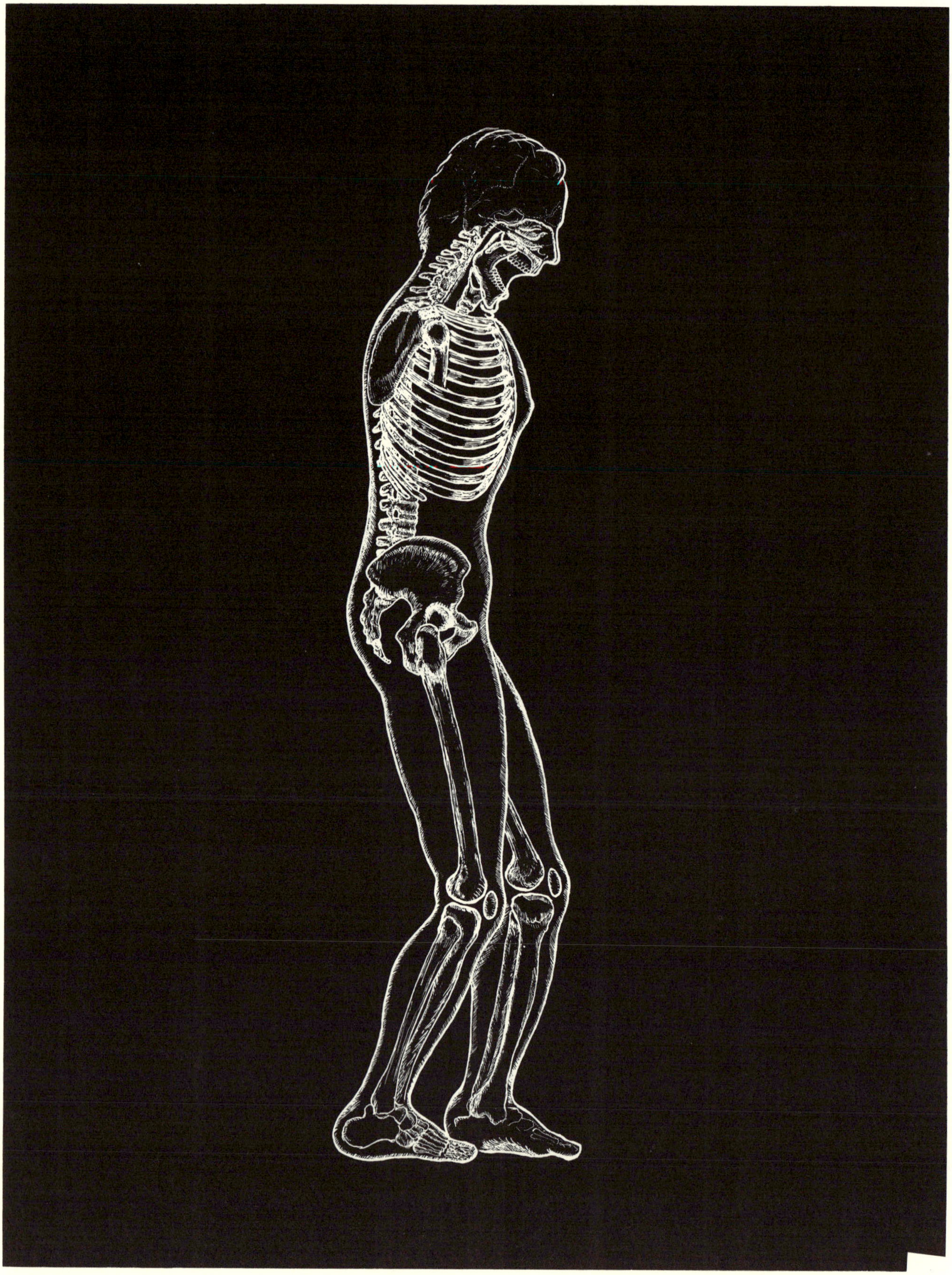

XV. BODY POSTURE IN ABSOLUTE JAW, LARYNX, BODY FUSION

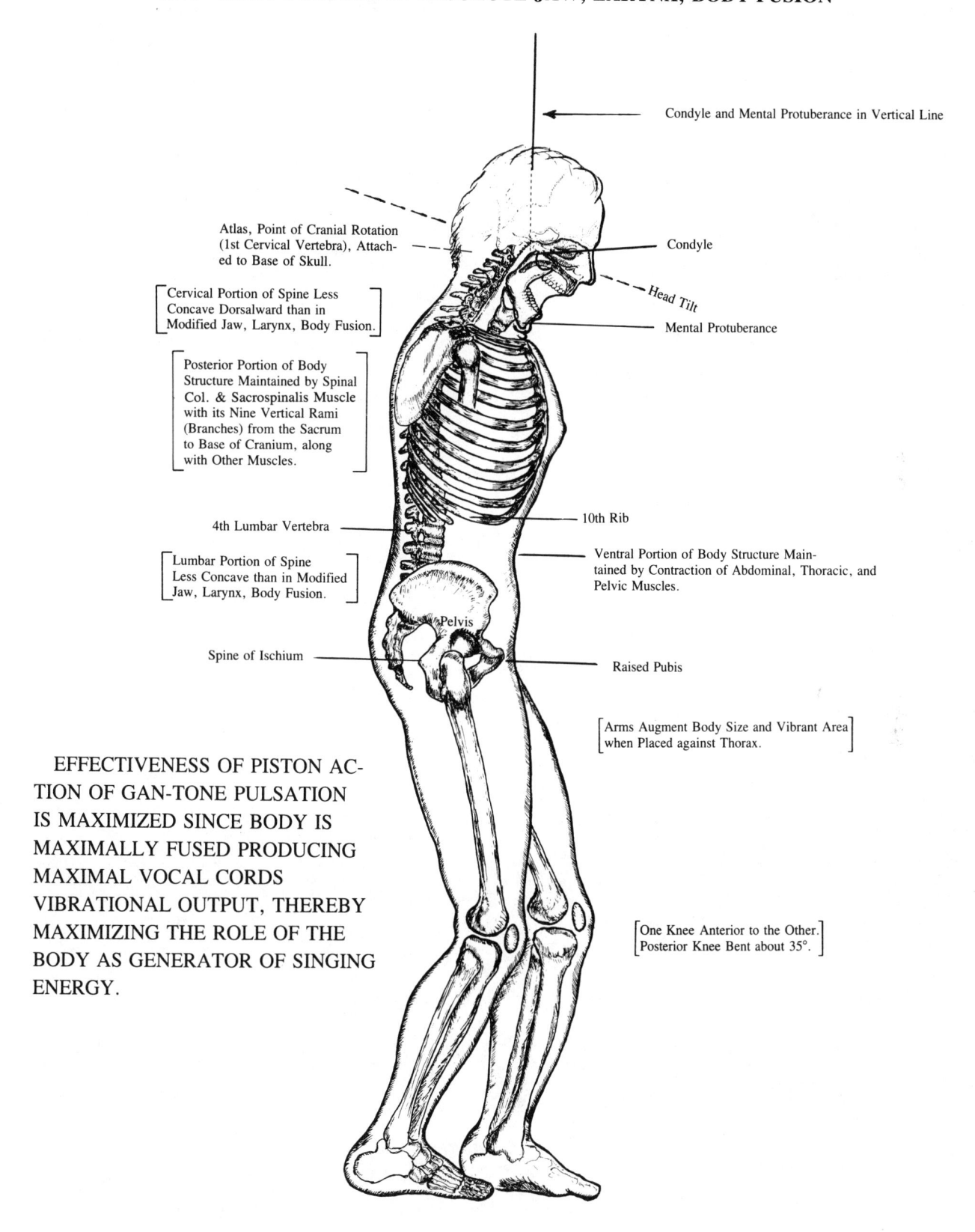

Condyle and Mental Protuberance in Vertical Line

Atlas, Point of Cranial Rotation (1st Cervical Vertebra), Attached to Base of Skull.

Condyle

Head Tilt

[Cervical Portion of Spine Less Concave Dorsalward than in Modified Jaw, Larynx, Body Fusion.]

Mental Protuberance

[Posterior Portion of Body Structure Maintained by Spinal Col. & Sacrospinalis Muscle with its Nine Vertical Rami (Branches) from the Sacrum to Base of Cranium, along with Other Muscles.]

4th Lumbar Vertebra

10th Rib

Ventral Portion of Body Structure Maintained by Contraction of Abdominal, Thoracic, and Pelvic Muscles.

[Lumbar Portion of Spine Less Concave than in Modified Jaw, Larynx, Body Fusion.]

Pelvis

Spine of Ischium

Raised Pubis

[Arms Augment Body Size and Vibrant Area when Placed against Thorax.]

EFFECTIVENESS OF PISTON ACTION OF GAN-TONE PULSATION IS MAXIMIZED SINCE BODY IS MAXIMALLY FUSED PRODUCING MAXIMAL VOCAL CORDS VIBRATIONAL OUTPUT, THEREBY MAXIMIZING THE ROLE OF THE BODY AS GENERATOR OF SINGING ENERGY.

[One Knee Anterior to the Other. Posterior Knee Bent about 35°.]

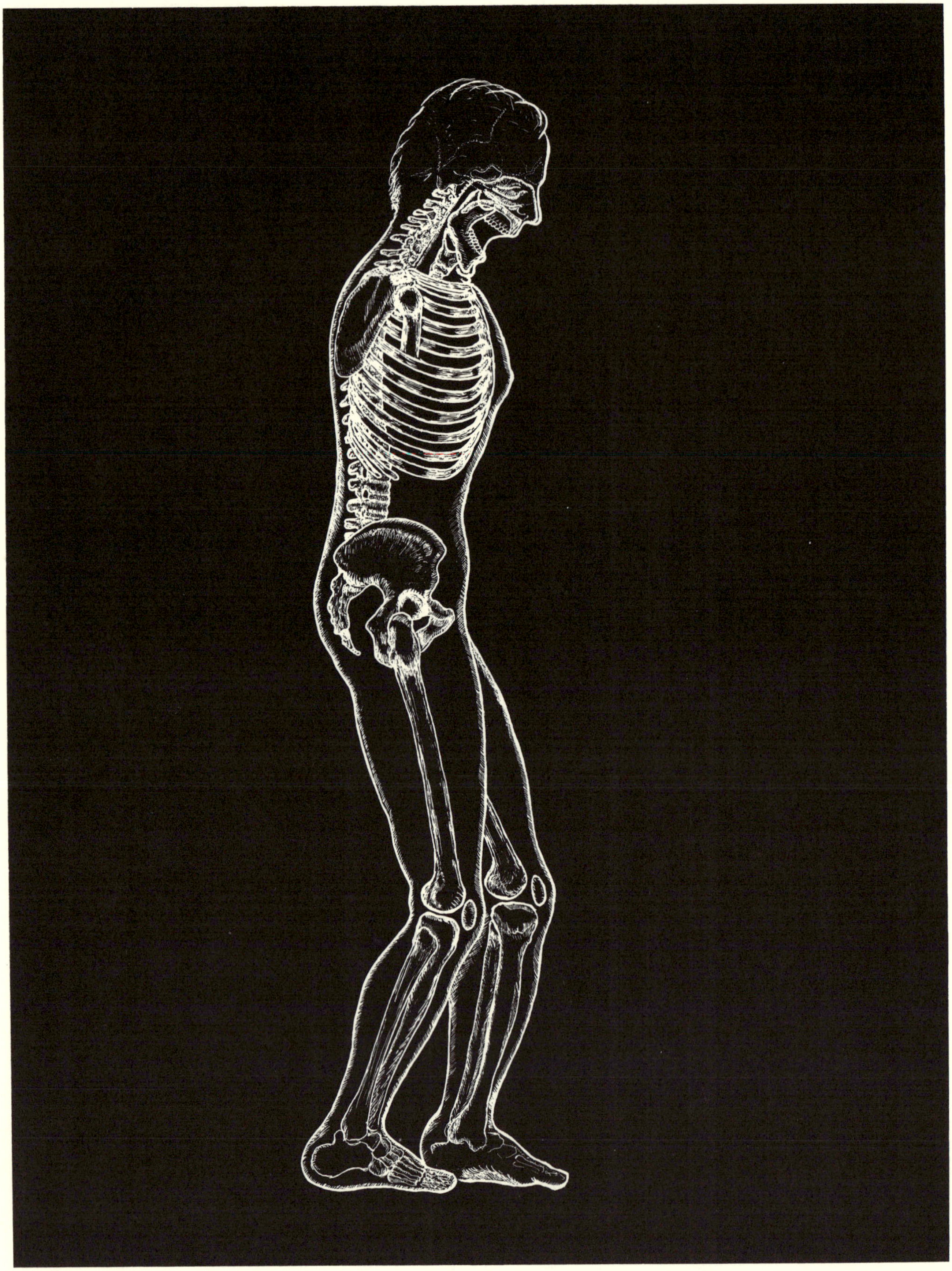

XVI. ROTATION OF HEAD, MANDIBLE AND PELVIS IN ABSOLUTE JAW, LARYNX, BODY FUSION

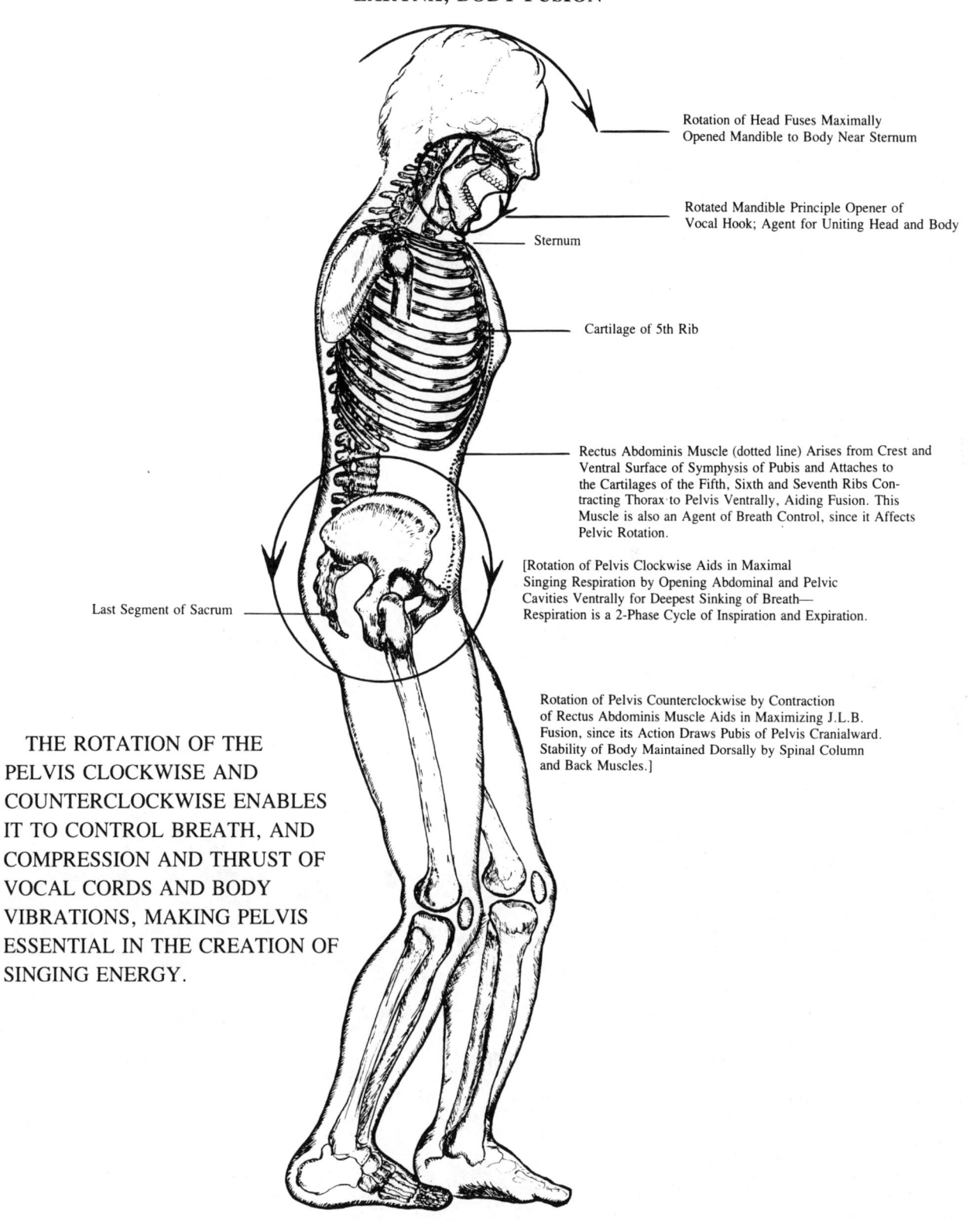

Rotation of Head Fuses Maximally Opened Mandible to Body Near Sternum

Rotated Mandible Principle Opener of Vocal Hook; Agent for Uniting Head and Body

Sternum

Cartilage of 5th Rib

Rectus Abdominis Muscle (dotted line) Arises from Crest and Ventral Surface of Symphysis of Pubis and Attaches to the Cartilages of the Fifth, Sixth and Seventh Ribs Contracting Thorax to Pelvis Ventrally, Aiding Fusion. This Muscle is also an Agent of Breath Control, since it Affects Pelvic Rotation.

[Rotation of Pelvis Clockwise Aids in Maximal Singing Respiration by Opening Abdominal and Pelvic Cavities Ventrally for Deepest Sinking of Breath—Respiration is a 2-Phase Cycle of Inspiration and Expiration.

Last Segment of Sacrum

Rotation of Pelvis Counterclockwise by Contraction of Rectus Abdominis Muscle Aids in Maximizing J.L.B. Fusion, since its Action Draws Pubis of Pelvis Cranialward. Stability of Body Maintained Dorsally by Spinal Column and Back Muscles.]

THE ROTATION OF THE PELVIS CLOCKWISE AND COUNTERCLOCKWISE ENABLES IT TO CONTROL BREATH, AND COMPRESSION AND THRUST OF VOCAL CORDS AND BODY VIBRATIONS, MAKING PELVIS ESSENTIAL IN THE CREATION OF SINGING ENERGY.

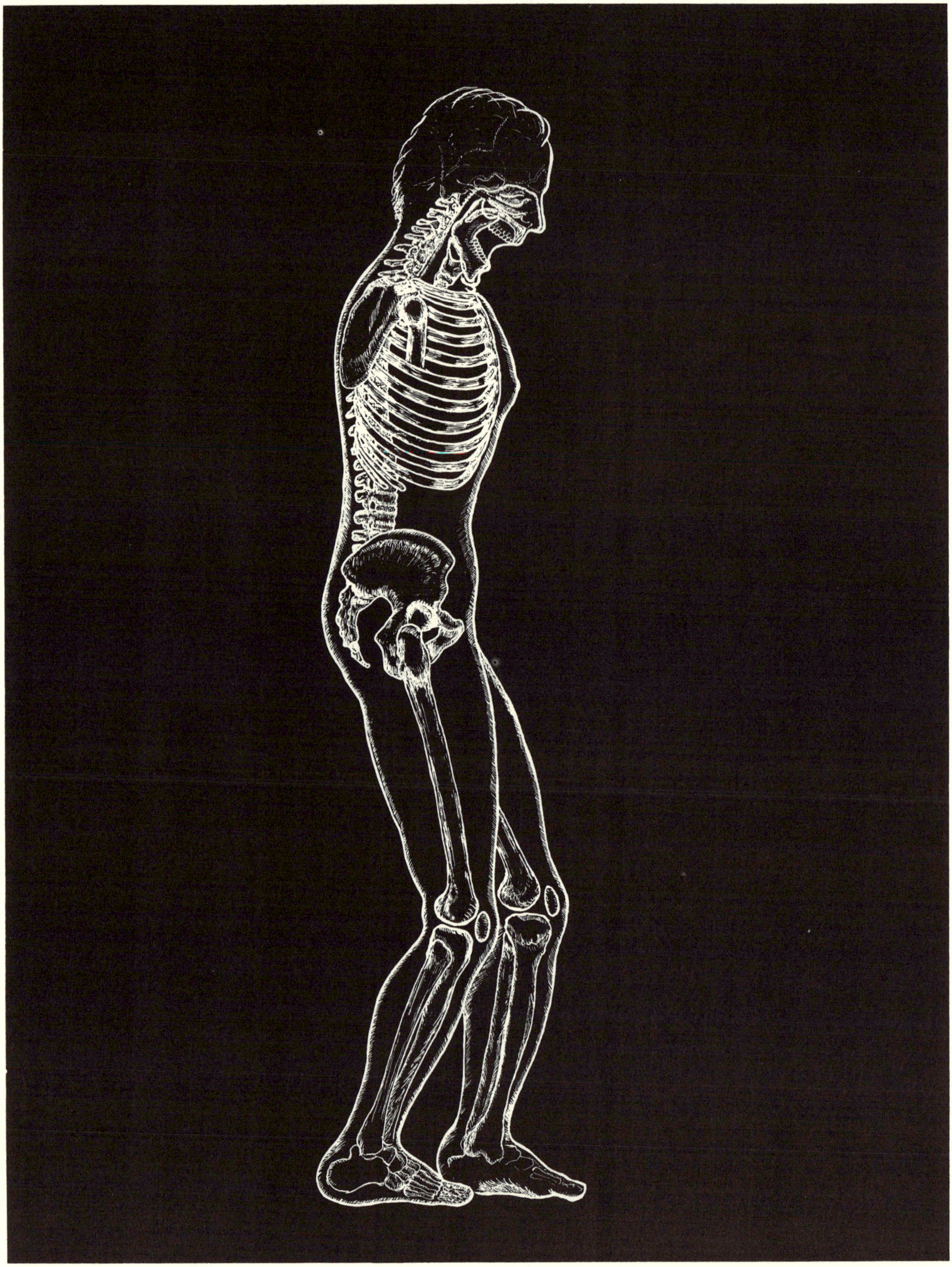

XVII. MAXIMUM ROTATION OF HEAD AND PELVIS IN ABSOLUTE JAW, LARYNX, BODY FUSION

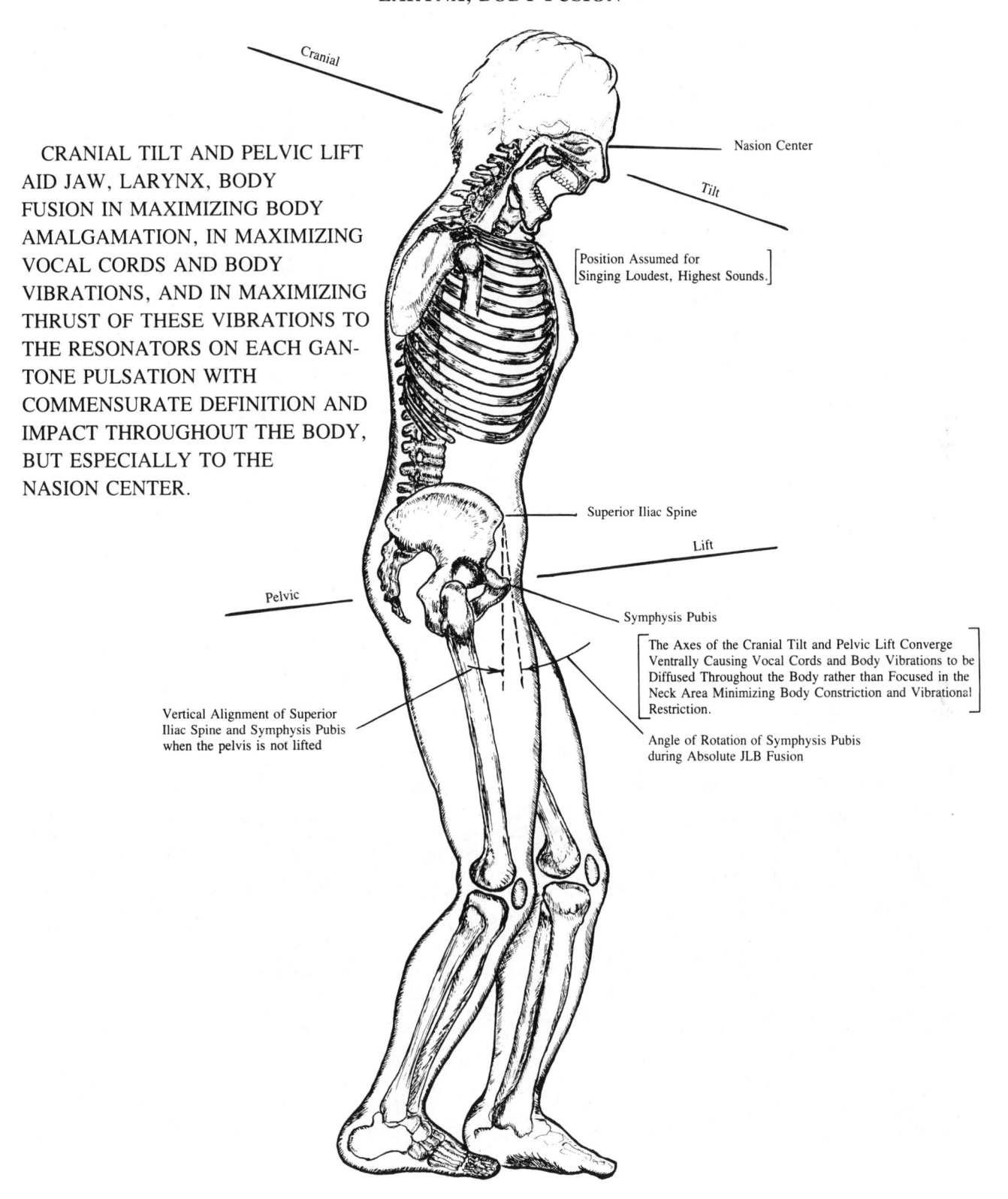

CRANIAL TILT AND PELVIC LIFT AID JAW, LARYNX, BODY FUSION IN MAXIMIZING BODY AMALGAMATION, IN MAXIMIZING VOCAL CORDS AND BODY VIBRATIONS, AND IN MAXIMIZING THRUST OF THESE VIBRATIONS TO THE RESONATORS ON EACH GAN-TONE PULSATION WITH COMMENSURATE DEFINITION AND IMPACT THROUGHOUT THE BODY, BUT ESPECIALLY TO THE NASION CENTER.

Cranial

Nasion Center

Tilt

[Position Assumed for Singing Loudest, Highest Sounds.]

Superior Iliac Spine

Lift

Pelvic

Symphysis Pubis

[The Axes of the Cranial Tilt and Pelvic Lift Converge Ventrally Causing Vocal Cords and Body Vibrations to be Diffused Throughout the Body rather than Focused in the Neck Area Minimizing Body Constriction and Vibrational Restriction.]

Vertical Alignment of Superior Iliac Spine and Symphysis Pubis when the pelvis is not lifted

Angle of Rotation of Symphysis Pubis during Absolute JLB Fusion

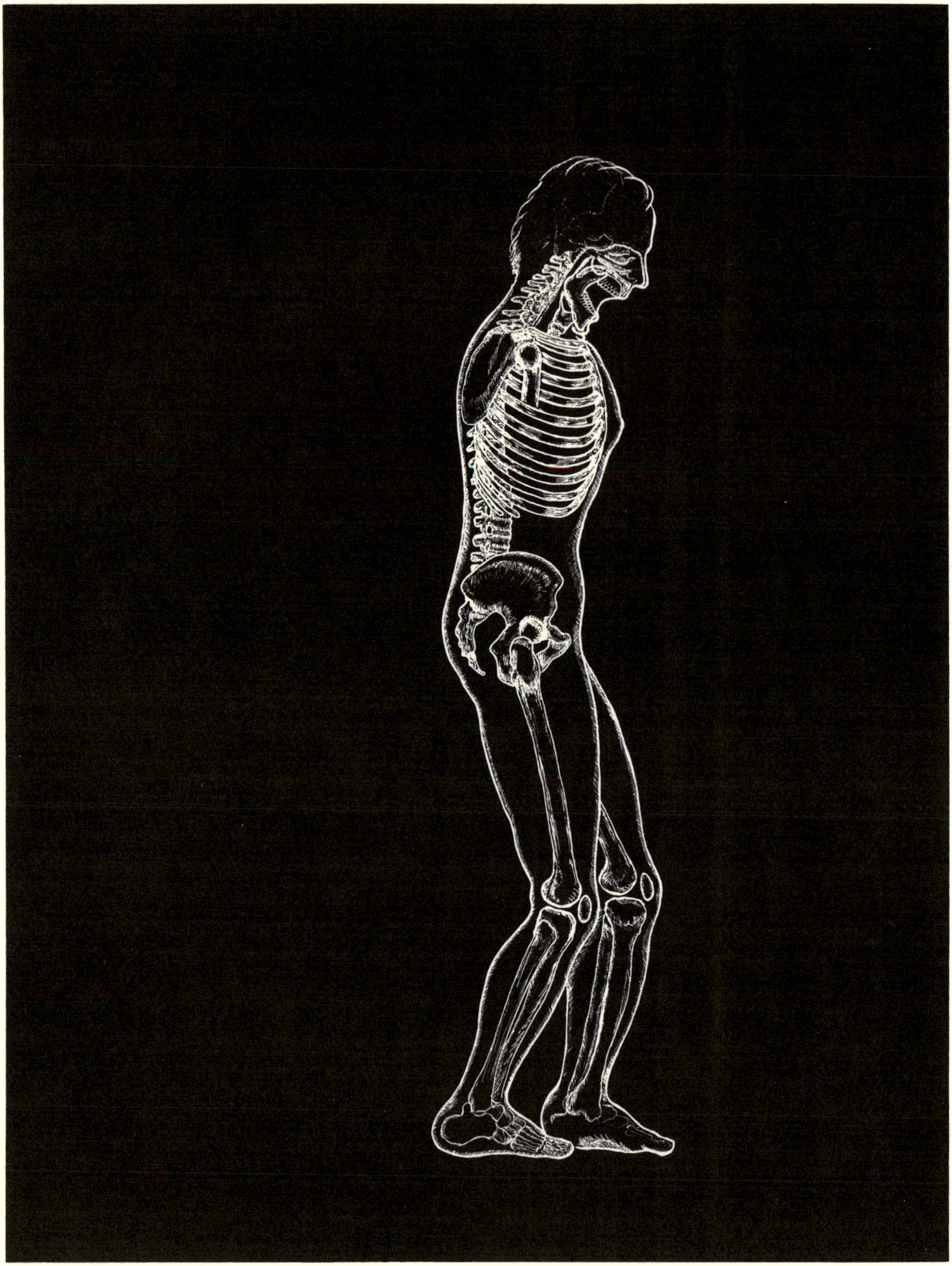

XVIII. BODY CURVE IN ABSOLUTE JAW, LARYNX, BODY FUSION

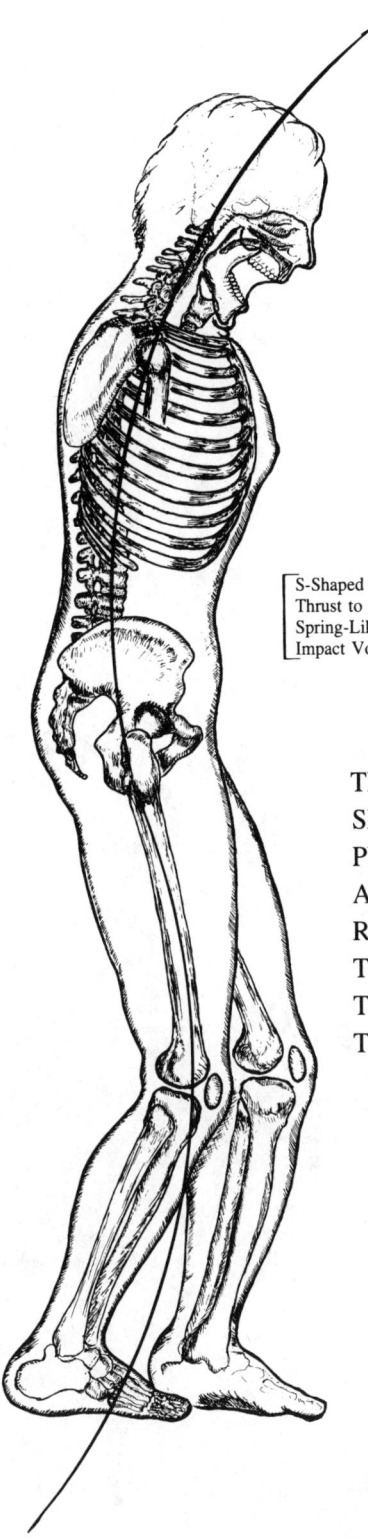

S-Shaped Body Curve Adds Resilient Thrust to Gan-Tone Pulsations as the Spring-Like Beats, about 6 per Second, Impact Vocal Energy to Head Resonators.

THE SPEED AND ACCURACY IN SUSPENDING THE MANDIBLE COMMENSURATELY WITH THE SPEED AND INTENSITY OF THE GAN-TONE PULSATIONS IMPOSED ON THE VOCAL CORDS AND BODY VIBRATIONS ALONG WITH THE RESILIENCE OF THE BODY CURVE DETERMINE THE FREEDOM OF VIBRATIONAL MOVEMENT THROUGHOUT THE BODY, BUT ESPECIALLY TO THE HEAD RESONATORS.

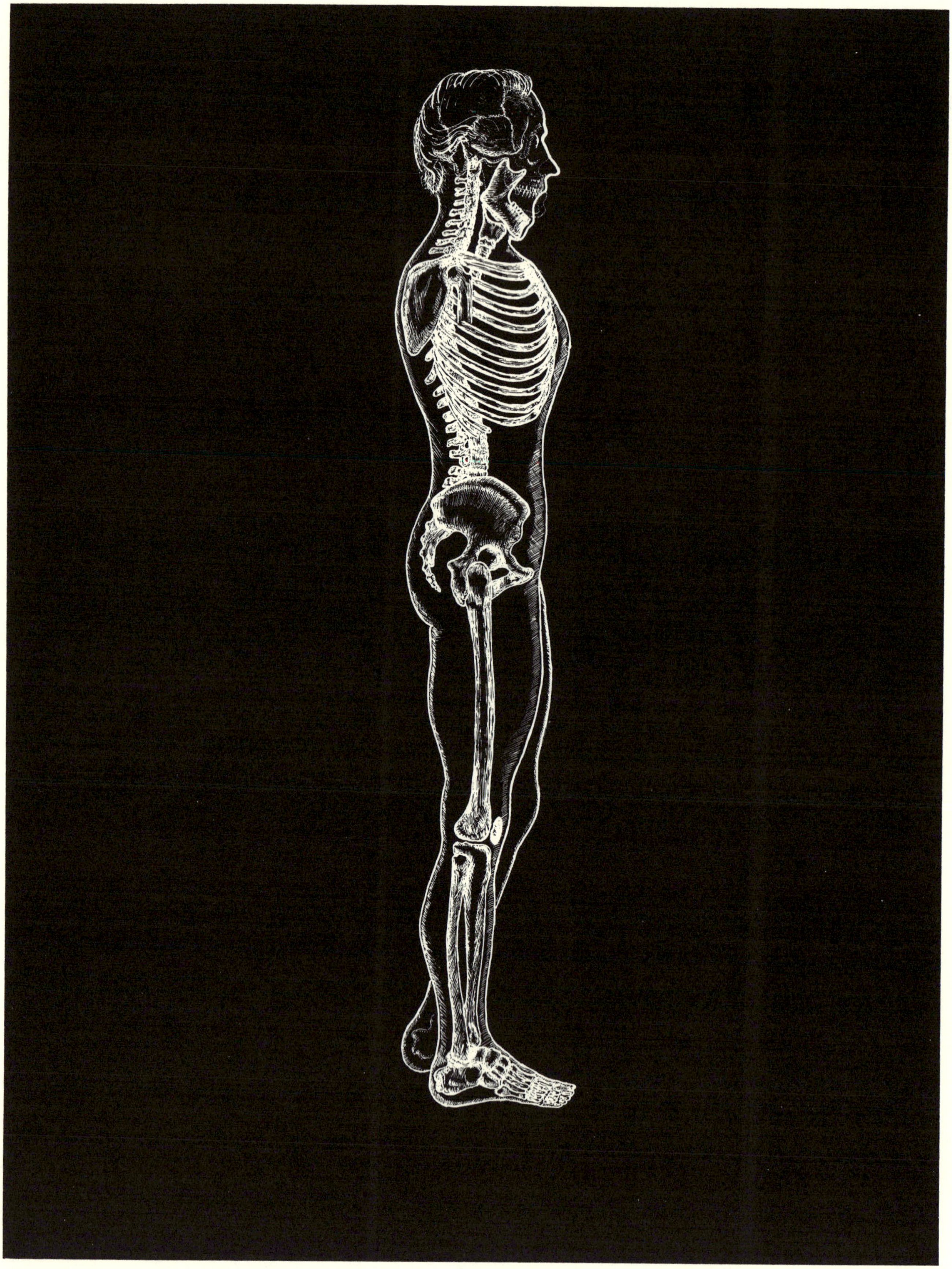

XIX. BODY POSTURE IN MODIFIED JAW, LARYNX, BODY FUSION

EFFECTIVENESS OF PISTON ACTION OF GAN-TONE PULSATION IS LESSENED, SINCE BODY IS MODERATELY FUSED PRODUCING LESS VOCAL CORDS VIBRATIONAL OUTPUT, THEREBY REDUCING THE ROLE OF THE BODY AS GENERATOR OF SINGING ENERGY.

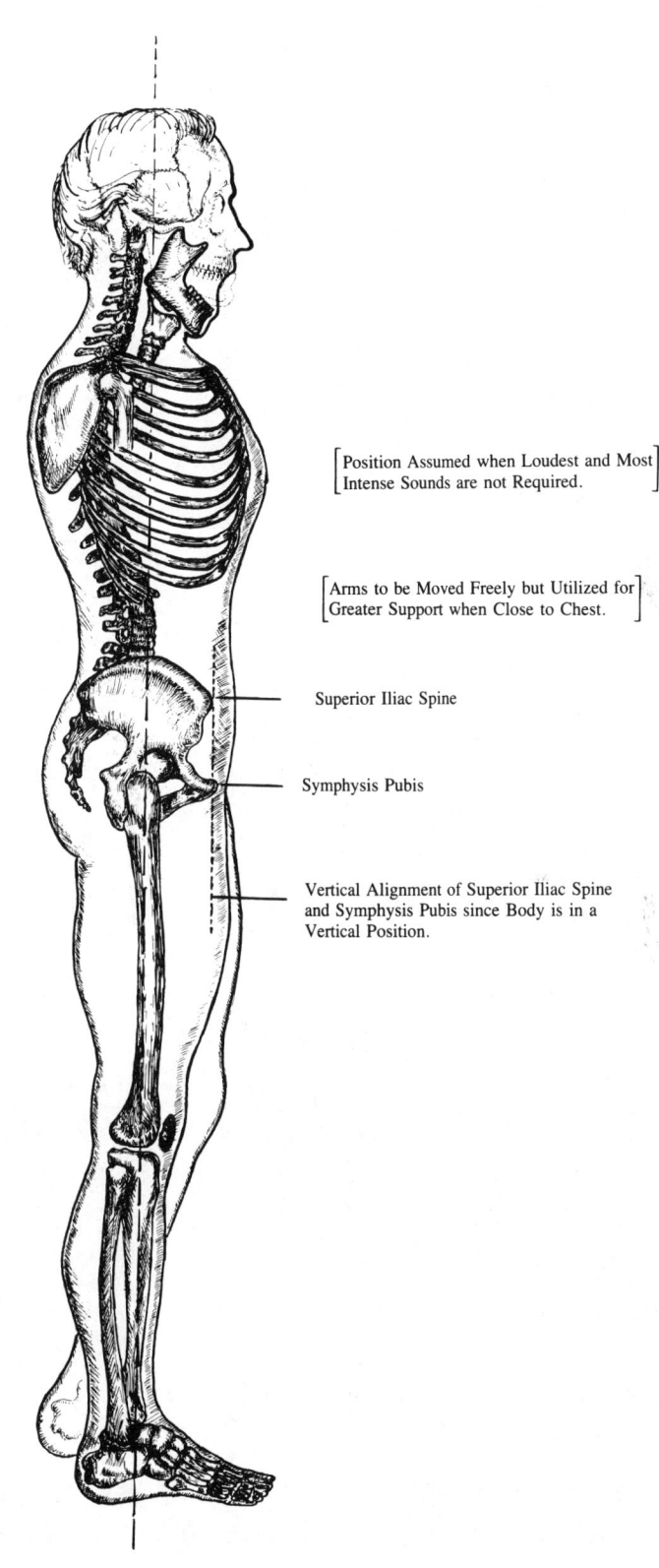

[Position Assumed when Loudest and Most Intense Sounds are not Required.]

[Arms to be Moved Freely but Utilized for Greater Support when Close to Chest.]

Superior Iliac Spine

Symphysis Pubis

Vertical Alignment of Superior Iliac Spine and Symphysis Pubis since Body is in a Vertical Position.

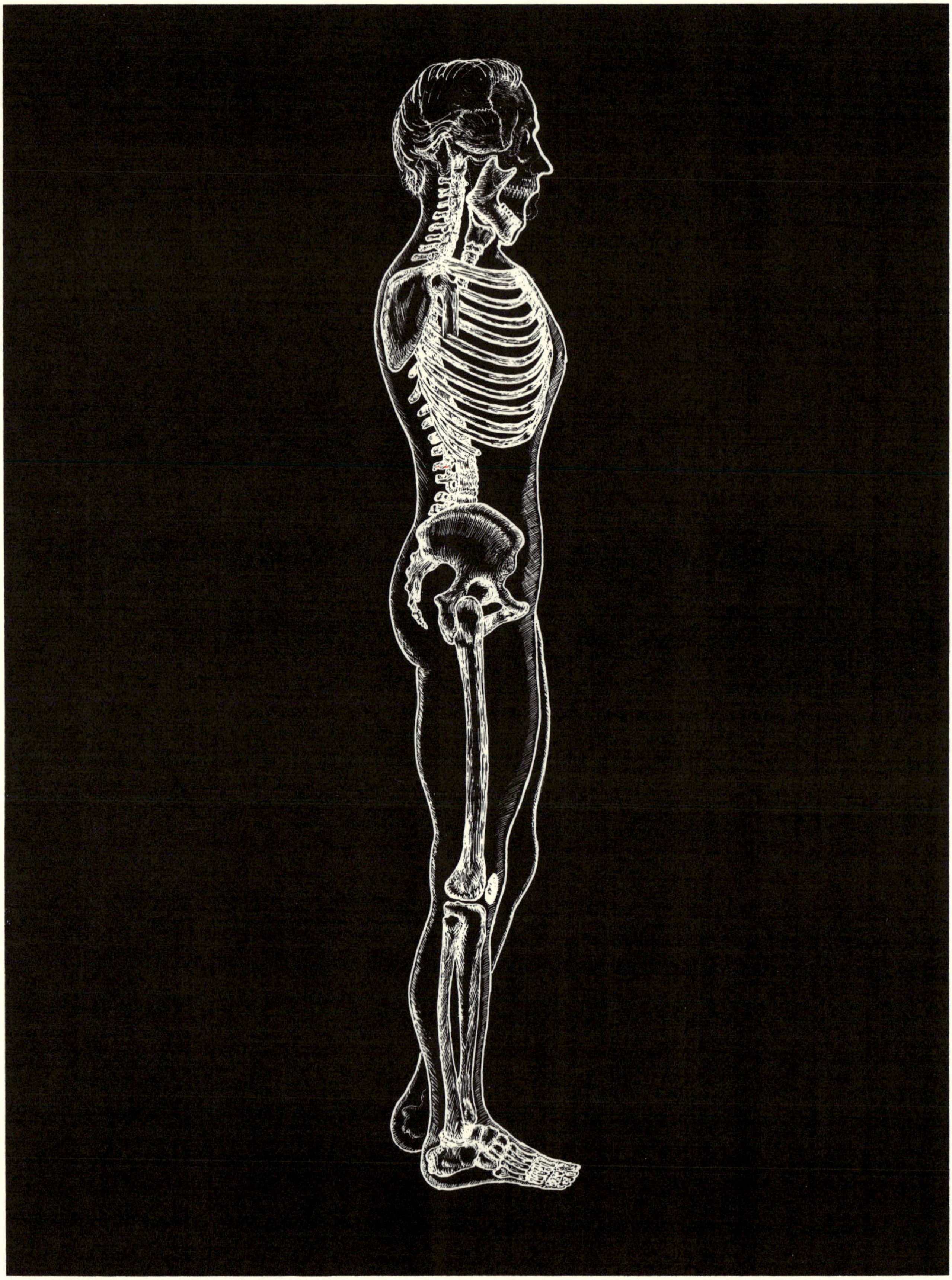

XX. POSITION OF HEAD, MANDIBLE AND PELVIS IN MODIFIED JAW, LARYNX, BODY FUSION

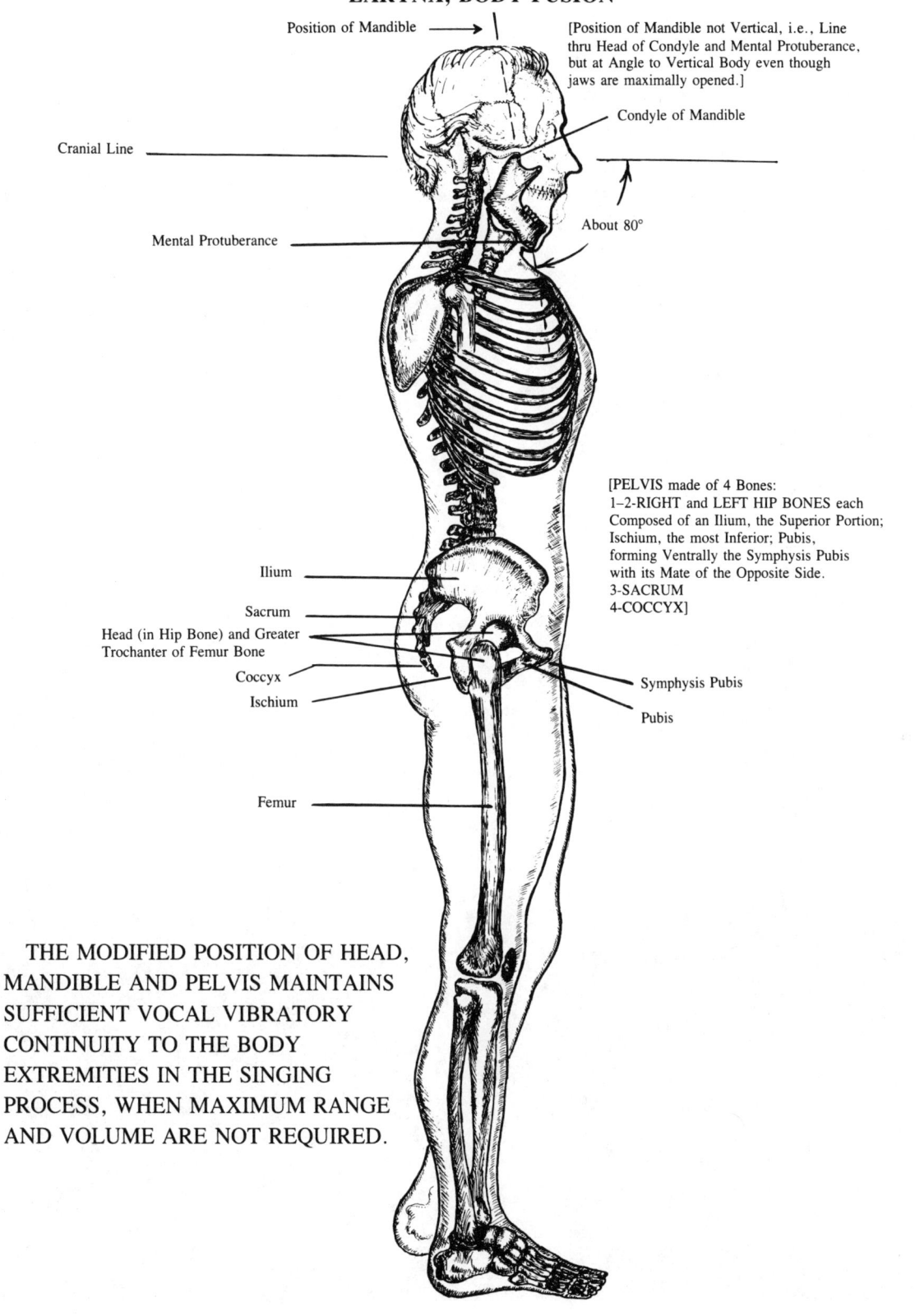

Position of Mandible

[Position of Mandible not Vertical, i.e., Line thru Head of Condyle and Mental Protuberance, but at Angle to Vertical Body even though jaws are maximally opened.]

Condyle of Mandible

Cranial Line

About 80°

Mental Protuberance

[PELVIS made of 4 Bones:
1-2-RIGHT and LEFT HIP BONES each Composed of an Ilium, the Superior Portion; Ischium, the most Inferior; Pubis, forming Ventrally the Symphysis Pubis with its Mate of the Opposite Side.
3-SACRUM
4-COCCYX]

Ilium

Sacrum

Head (in Hip Bone) and Greater Trochanter of Femur Bone

Coccyx

Ischium

Symphysis Pubis

Pubis

Femur

THE MODIFIED POSITION OF HEAD, MANDIBLE AND PELVIS MAINTAINS SUFFICIENT VOCAL VIBRATORY CONTINUITY TO THE BODY EXTREMITIES IN THE SINGING PROCESS, WHEN MAXIMUM RANGE AND VOLUME ARE NOT REQUIRED.

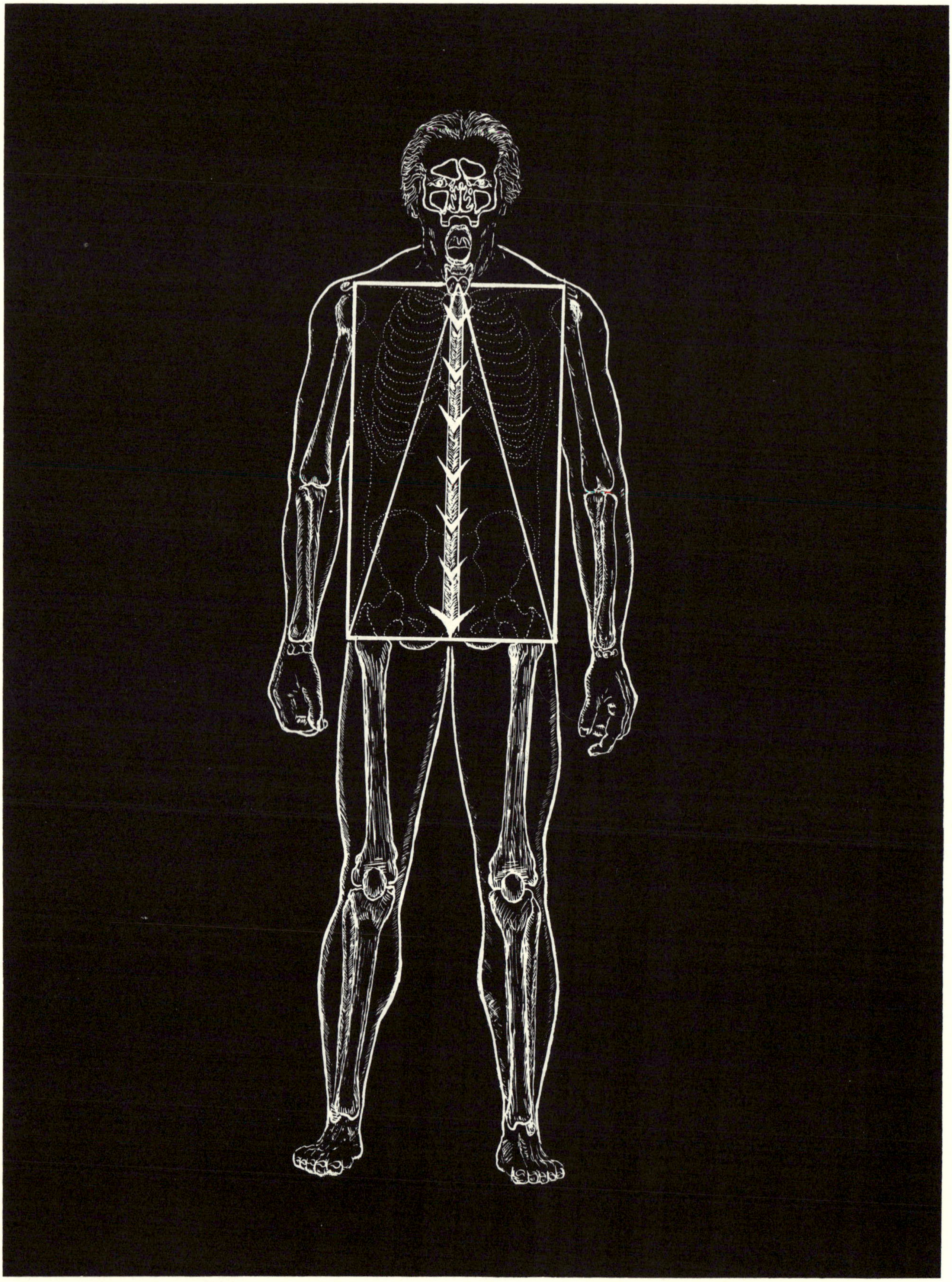

249

XXI. PRODUCTION AND AMPLITUDE OF GAN-TONE PULSATION

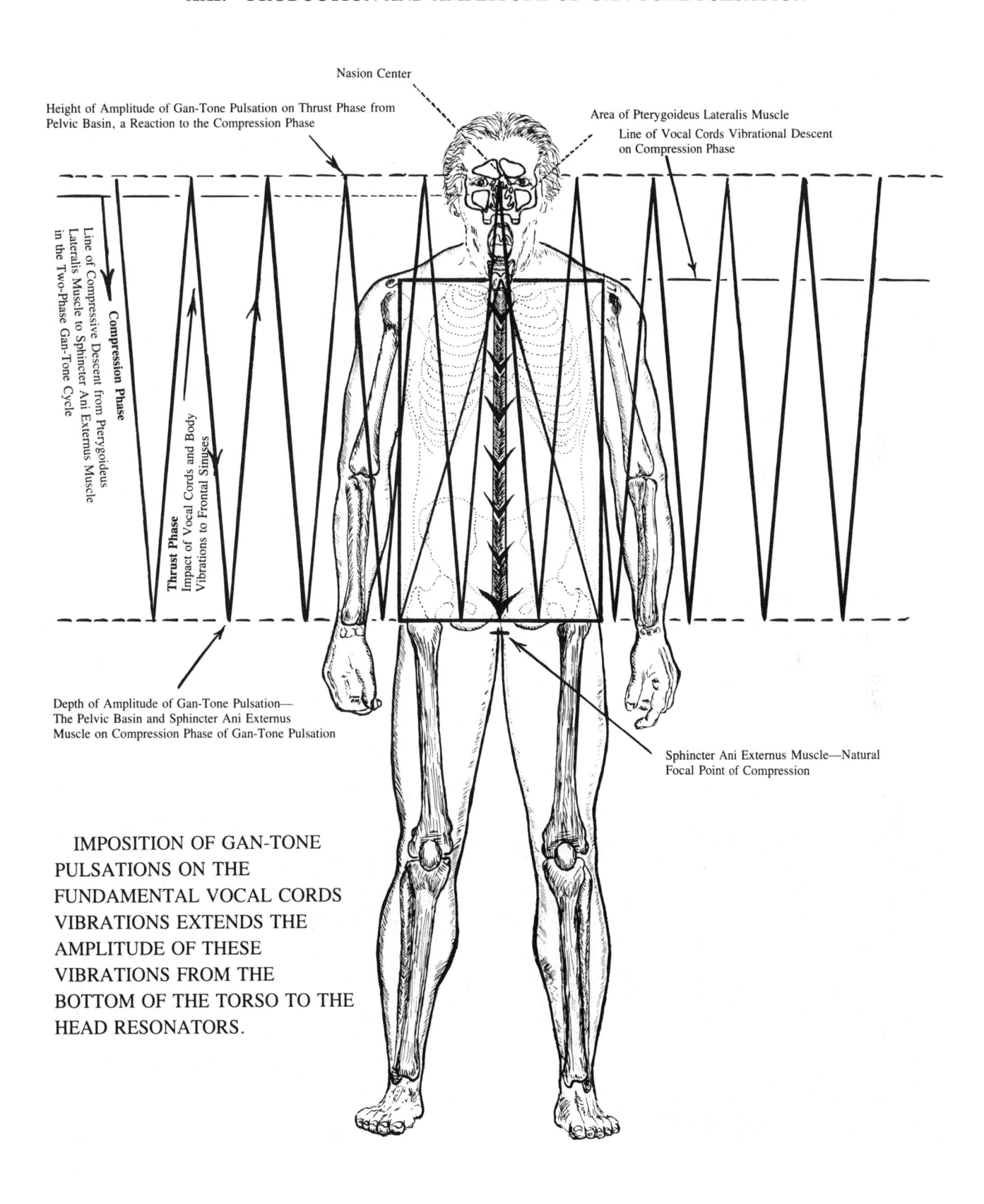

Nasion Center

Height of Amplitude of Gan-Tone Pulsation on Thrust Phase from Pelvic Basin, a Reaction to the Compression Phase

Area of Pterygoideus Lateralis Muscle
Line of Vocal Cords Vibrational Descent on Compression Phase

Line of Compressive Descent from Pterygoideus Lateralis Muscle to Sphincter Ani Externus Muscle in the Two-Phase Gan-Tone Cycle

Compression Phase

Thrust Phase
Impact of Vocal Cords and Body Vibrations to Frontal Sinuses

Depth of Amplitude of Gan-Tone Pulsation—
The Pelvic Basin and Sphincter Ani Externus Muscle on Compression Phase of Gan-Tone Pulsation

Sphincter Ani Externus Muscle—Natural Focal Point of Compression

IMPOSITION OF GAN-TONE PULSATIONS ON THE FUNDAMENTAL VOCAL CORDS VIBRATIONS EXTENDS THE AMPLITUDE OF THESE VIBRATIONS FROM THE BOTTOM OF THE TORSO TO THE HEAD RESONATORS.

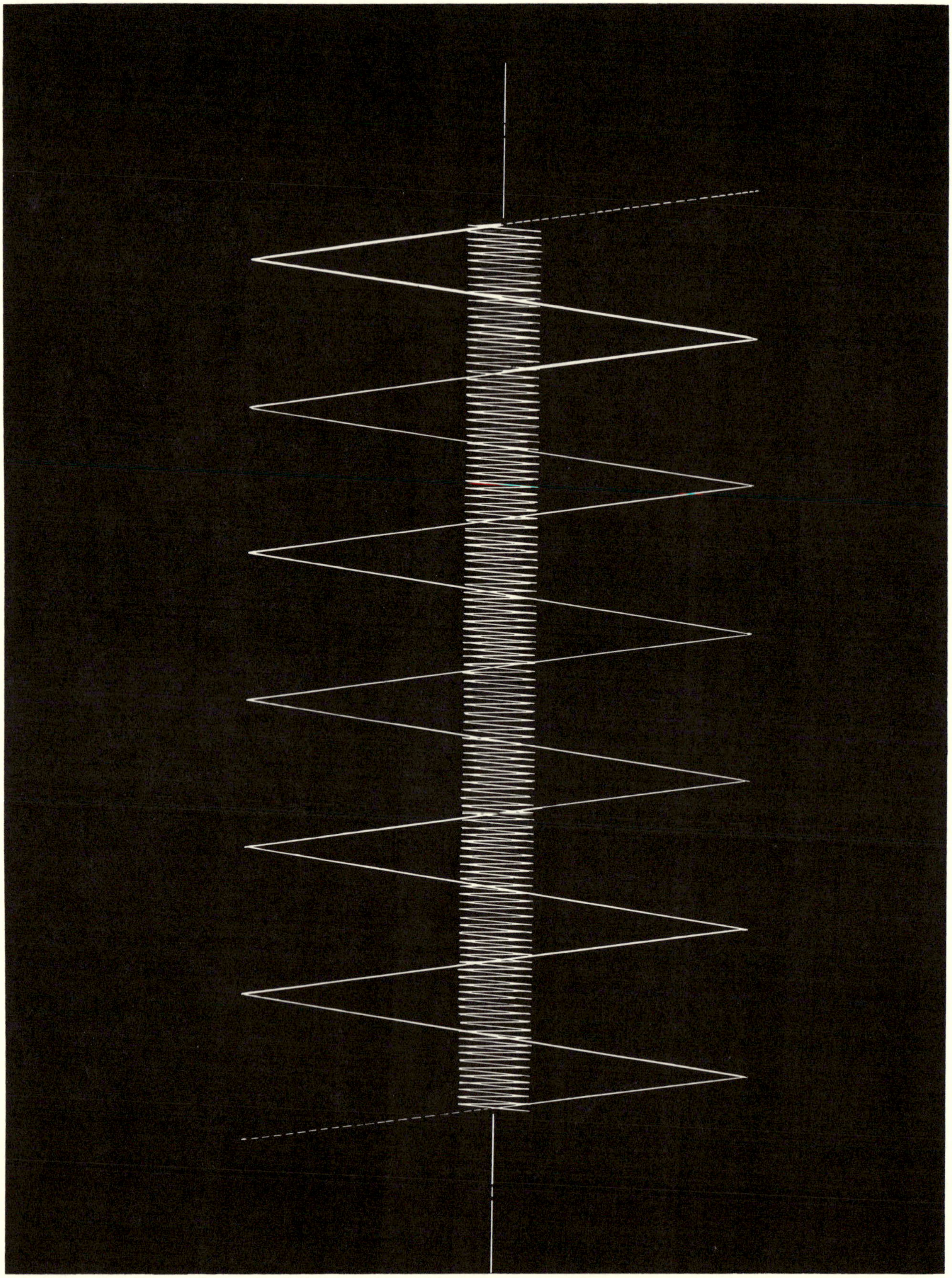

XXII. EXTENSION OF AMPLITUDE OF NOTE BEING SUNG WITH APPLICATION OF GAN-TONE PULSATION

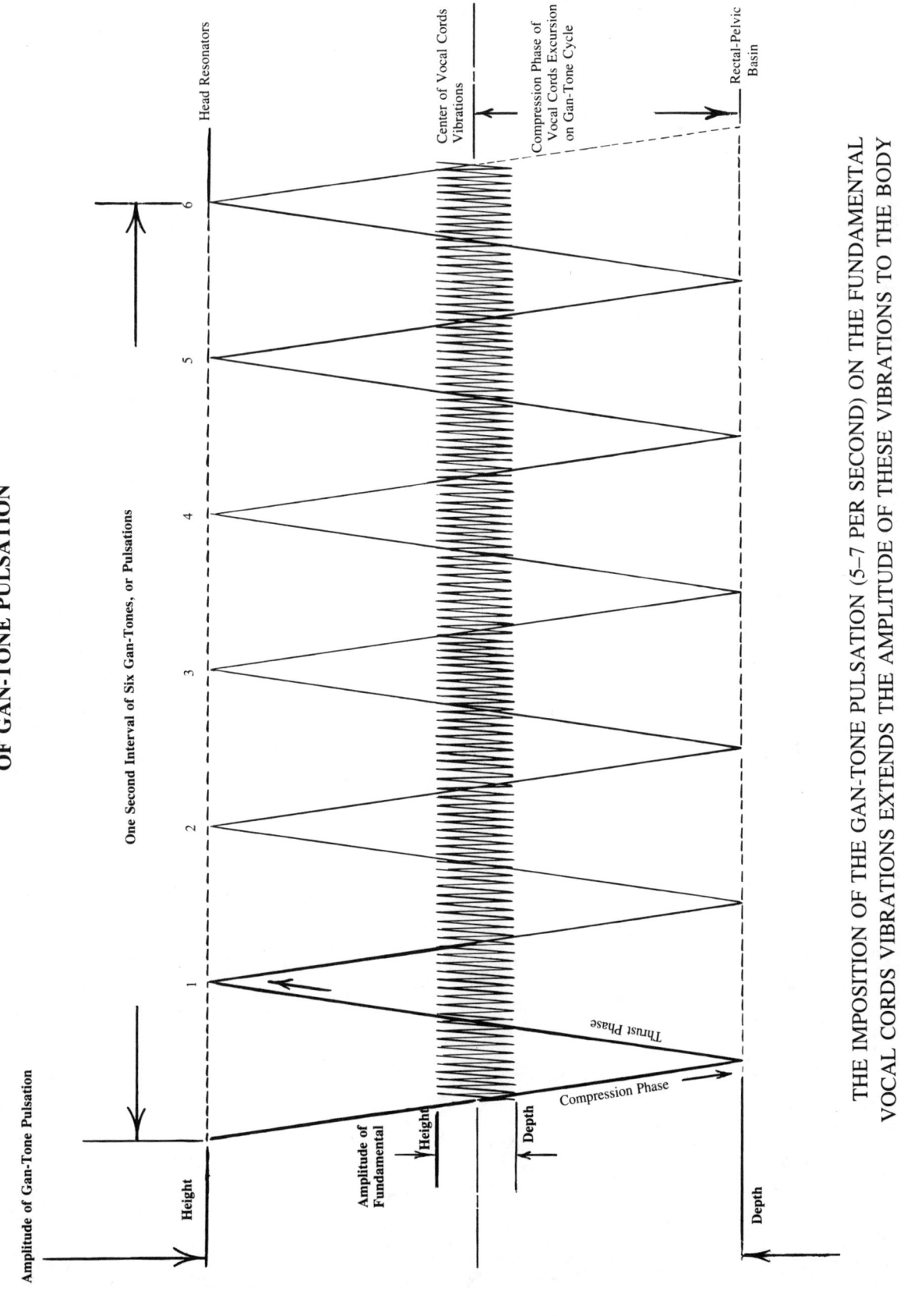

THE IMPOSITION OF THE GAN-TONE PULSATION (5–7 PER SECOND) ON THE FUNDAMENTAL VOCAL CORDS VIBRATIONS EXTENDS THE AMPLITUDE OF THESE VIBRATIONS TO THE BODY EXTREMITIES (RECTAL-PELVIC BASIN TO HEAD RESONATORS) WITHOUT ALTERING PITCH BEING SUNG.

251

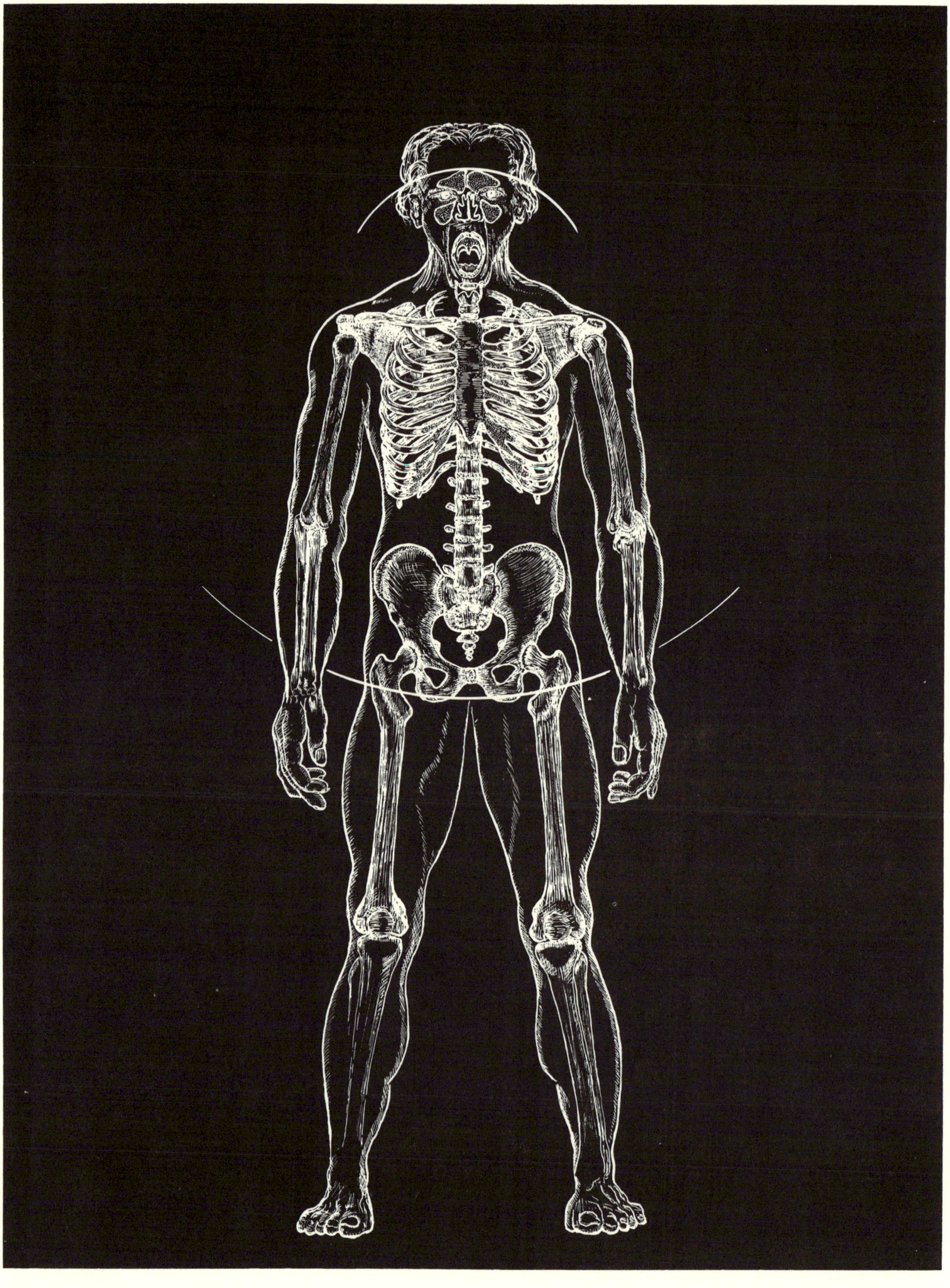

XXIII. STRUCTURAL BOUNDARIES FOR PRODUCTION OF VOCAL SOUND WITH APPLICATION OF JAW, LARYNX, BODY FUSION AND GAN-TONE PULSATION

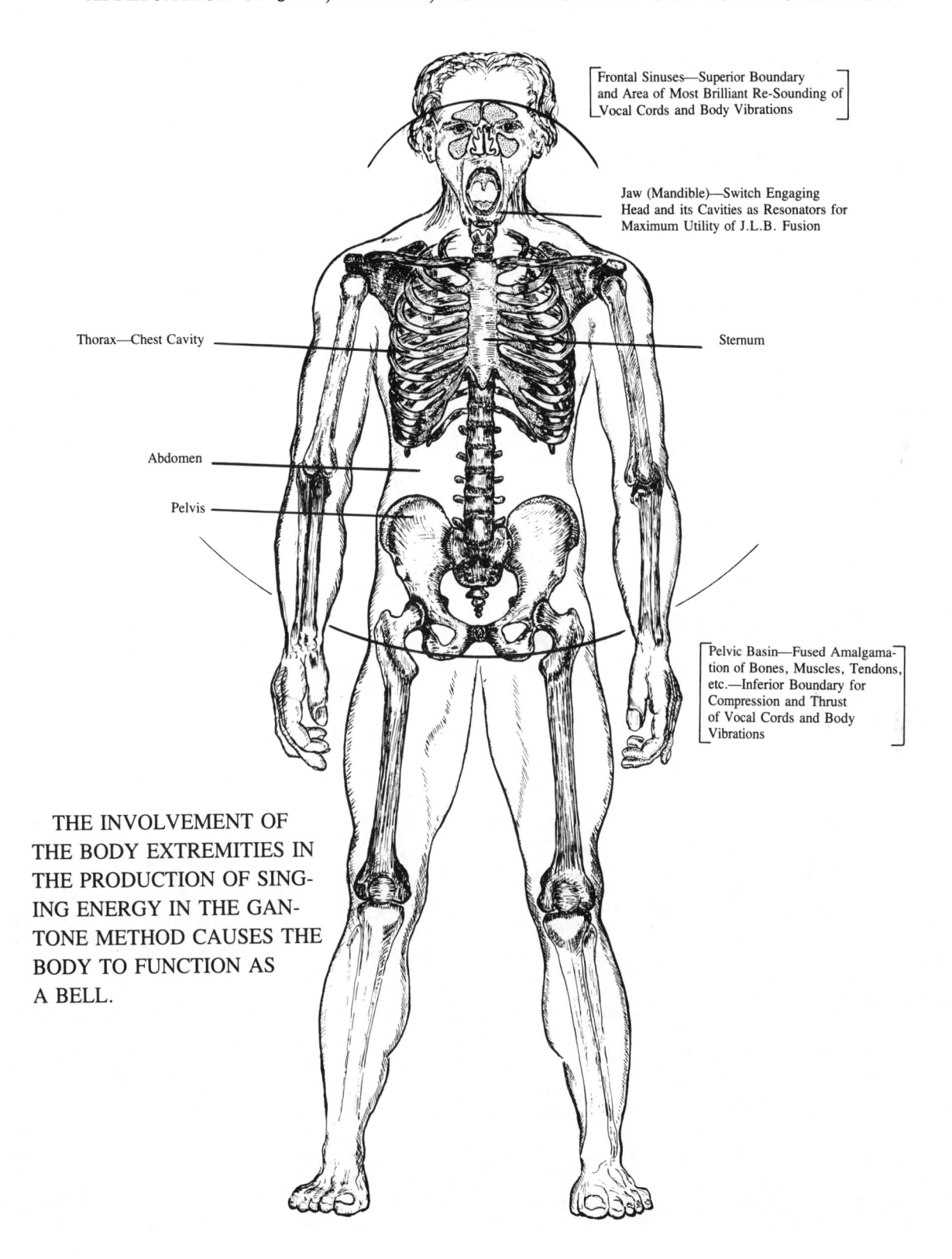

Frontal Sinuses—Superior Boundary and Area of Most Brilliant Re-Sounding of Vocal Cords and Body Vibrations

Jaw (Mandible)—Switch Engaging Head and its Cavities as Resonators for Maximum Utility of J.L.B. Fusion

Thorax—Chest Cavity

Sternum

Abdomen

Pelvis

Pelvic Basin—Fused Amalgamation of Bones, Muscles, Tendons, etc.—Inferior Boundary for Compression and Thrust of Vocal Cords and Body Vibrations

THE INVOLVEMENT OF THE BODY EXTREMITIES IN THE PRODUCTION OF SINGING ENERGY IN THE GAN-TONE METHOD CAUSES THE BODY TO FUNCTION AS A BELL.

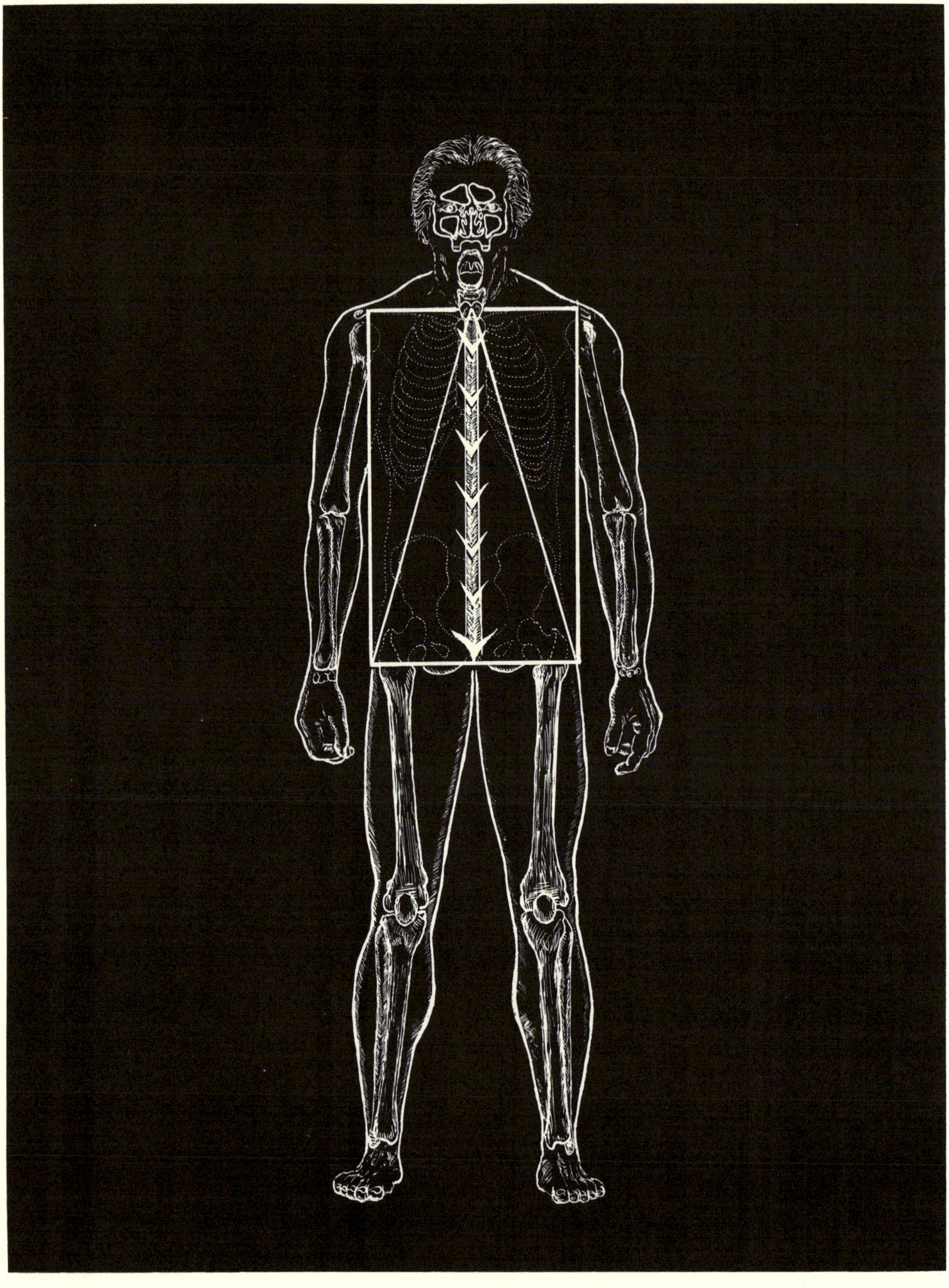

XXIV. BODY AS A PISTON AND CYLINDER

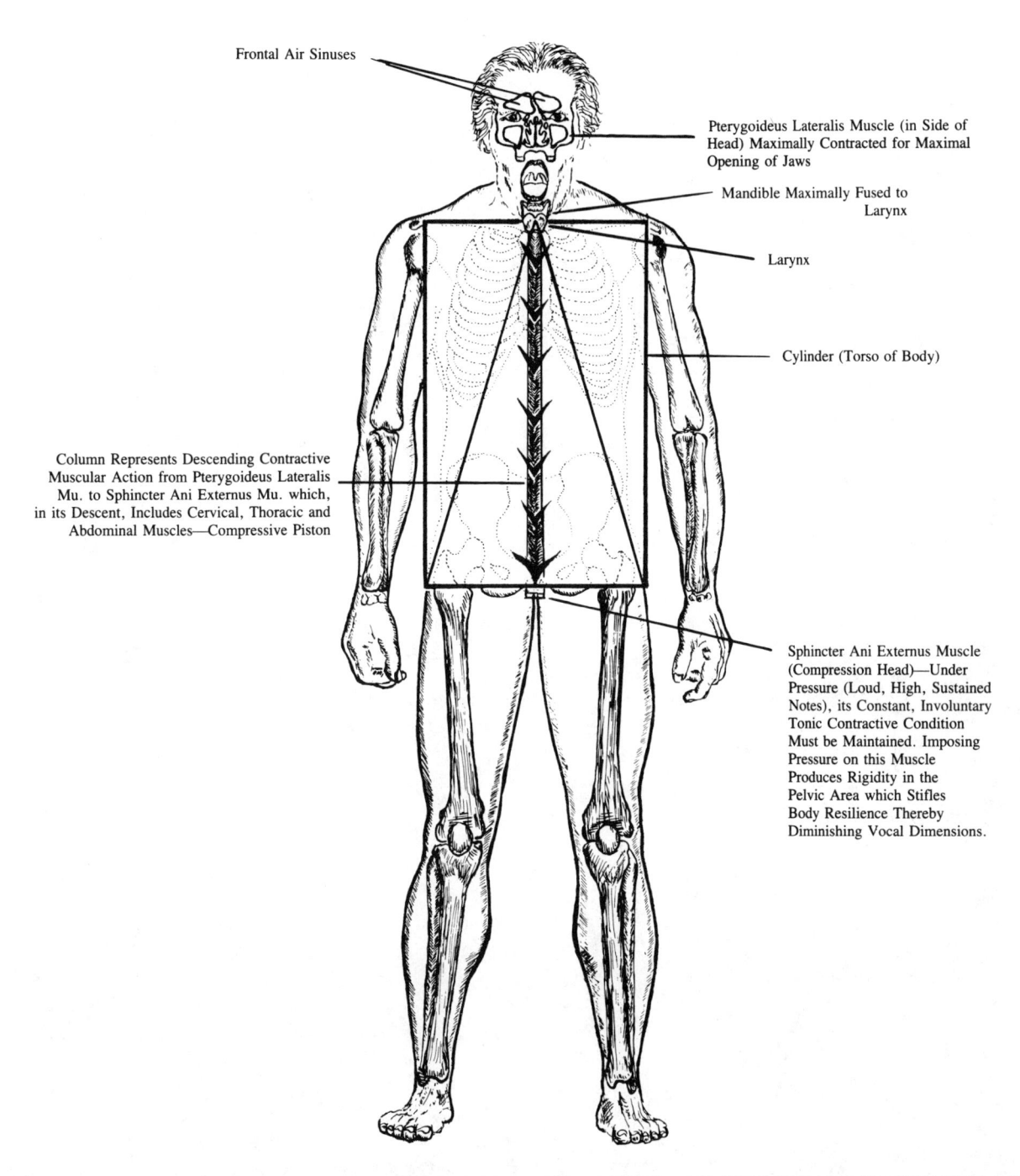

Frontal Air Sinuses

Pterygoideus Lateralis Muscle (in Side of Head) Maximally Contracted for Maximal Opening of Jaws

Mandible Maximally Fused to Larynx

Larynx

Cylinder (Torso of Body)

Column Represents Descending Contractive Muscular Action from Pterygoideus Lateralis Mu. to Sphincter Ani Externus Mu. which, in its Descent, Includes Cervical, Thoracic and Abdominal Muscles—Compressive Piston

Sphincter Ani Externus Muscle (Compression Head)—Under Pressure (Loud, High, Sustained Notes), its Constant, Involuntary Tonic Contractive Condition Must be Maintained. Imposing Pressure on this Muscle Produces Rigidity in the Pelvic Area which Stifles Body Resilience Thereby Diminishing Vocal Dimensions.

IN THE GAN-TONE METHOD, THE CYLINDER IS THE TORSO AND THE PISTON IS THE TWO-PHASE GAN-TONE CYCLE (COMPRESSION AND THRUST) WITHIN THE CYLINDER. THIS UNIT IS CAPABLE OF GENERATING VOCAL CORDS AND BODY VIBRATIONS OF GREAT MAGNITUDE WHICH ARE THRUST TO THE HIGHEST HEAD RESONATORS RESULTING IN SINGING ENERGY OF GREAT BRILLIANCE.

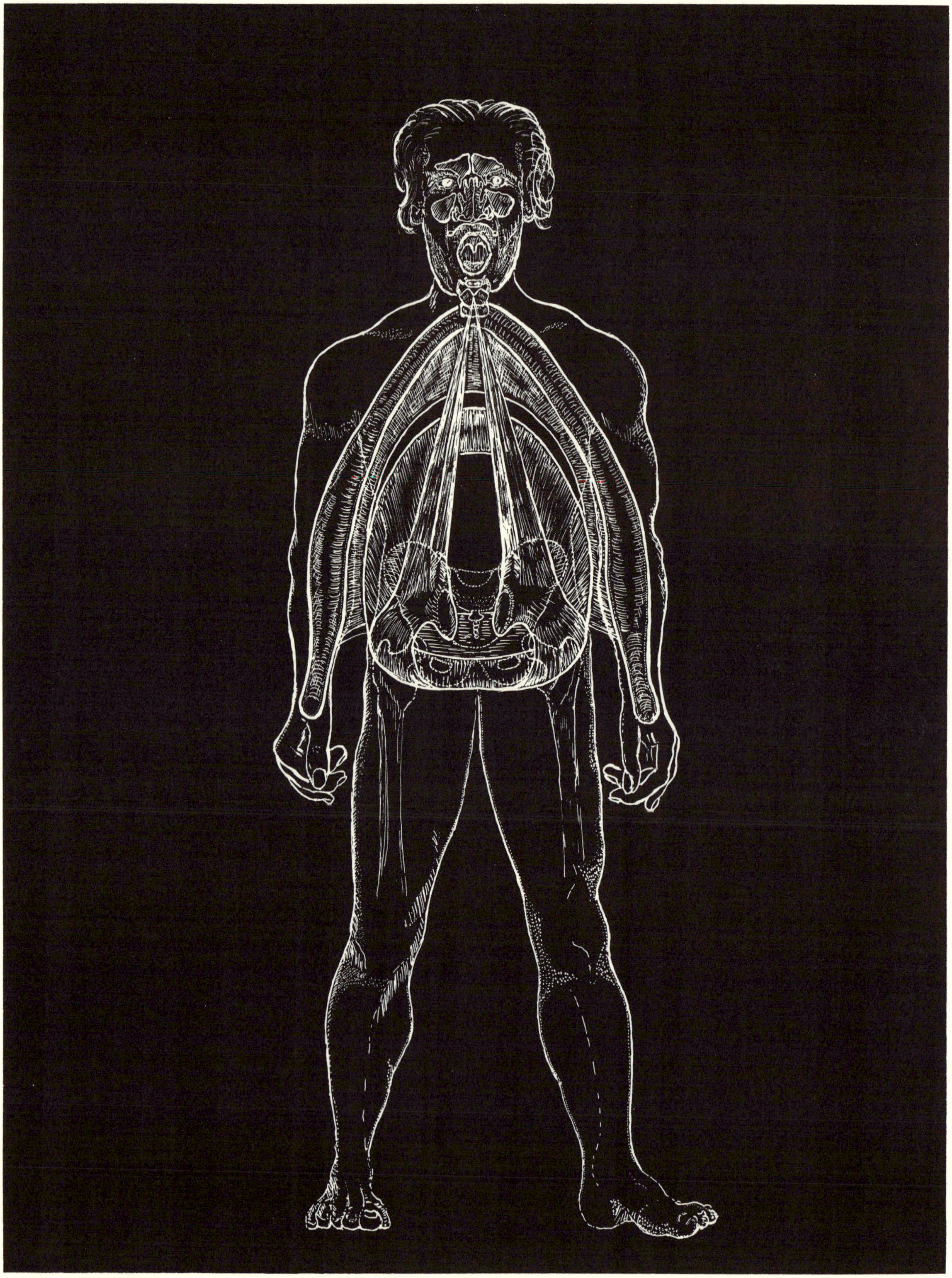

XXV. BODY AS EXTENSION OF VOCAL CORDS

THE JAW, LARYNX, BODY FUSION AND THE GAN-TONE PULSATION FUSE VOCAL CORDS VIBRATIONS TO THE BOTTOM OF THE TORSO FROM WHICH THEY ARE THRUST TO THE HIGHEST RESONATORS FOR BRILLIANT RE-SOUNDING CAUSING THE BODY TO FUNCTION AS AN EXTENSION OF THE VOCAL CORDS.

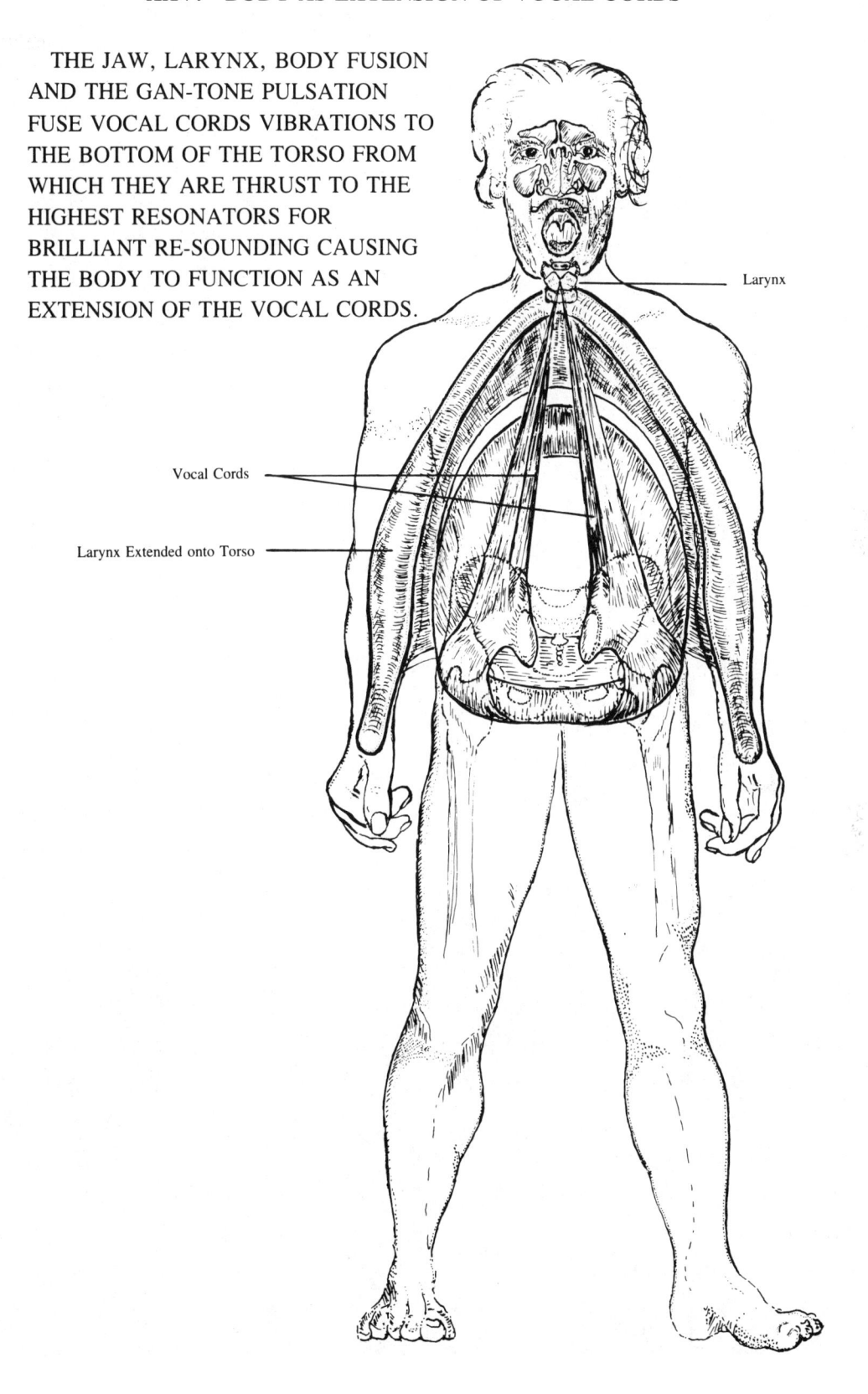

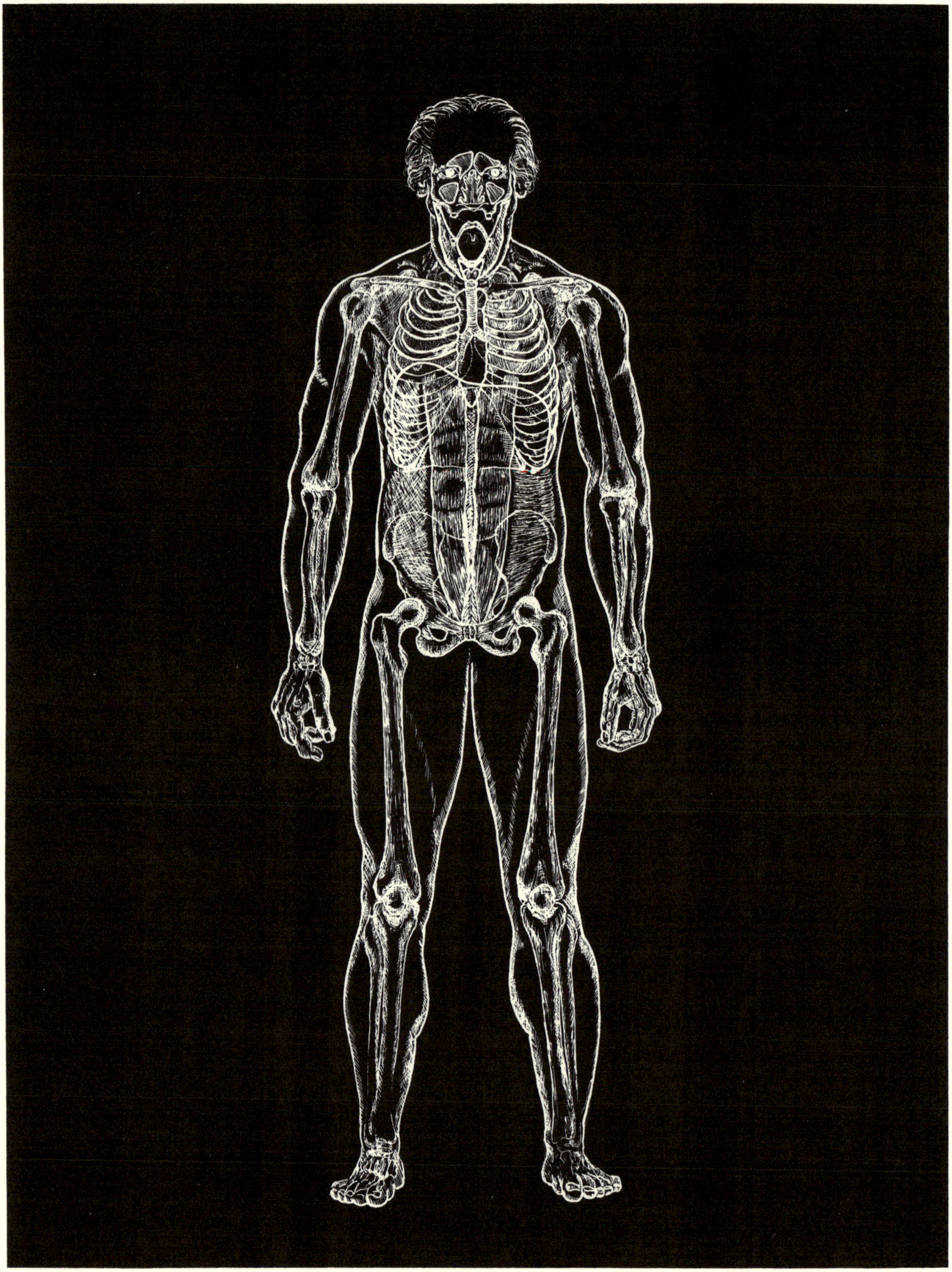

XXVI. KEY MUSCLES IN THE APPLICATION OF JAW, LARYNX, BODY FUSION AND GAN-TONE PULSATION

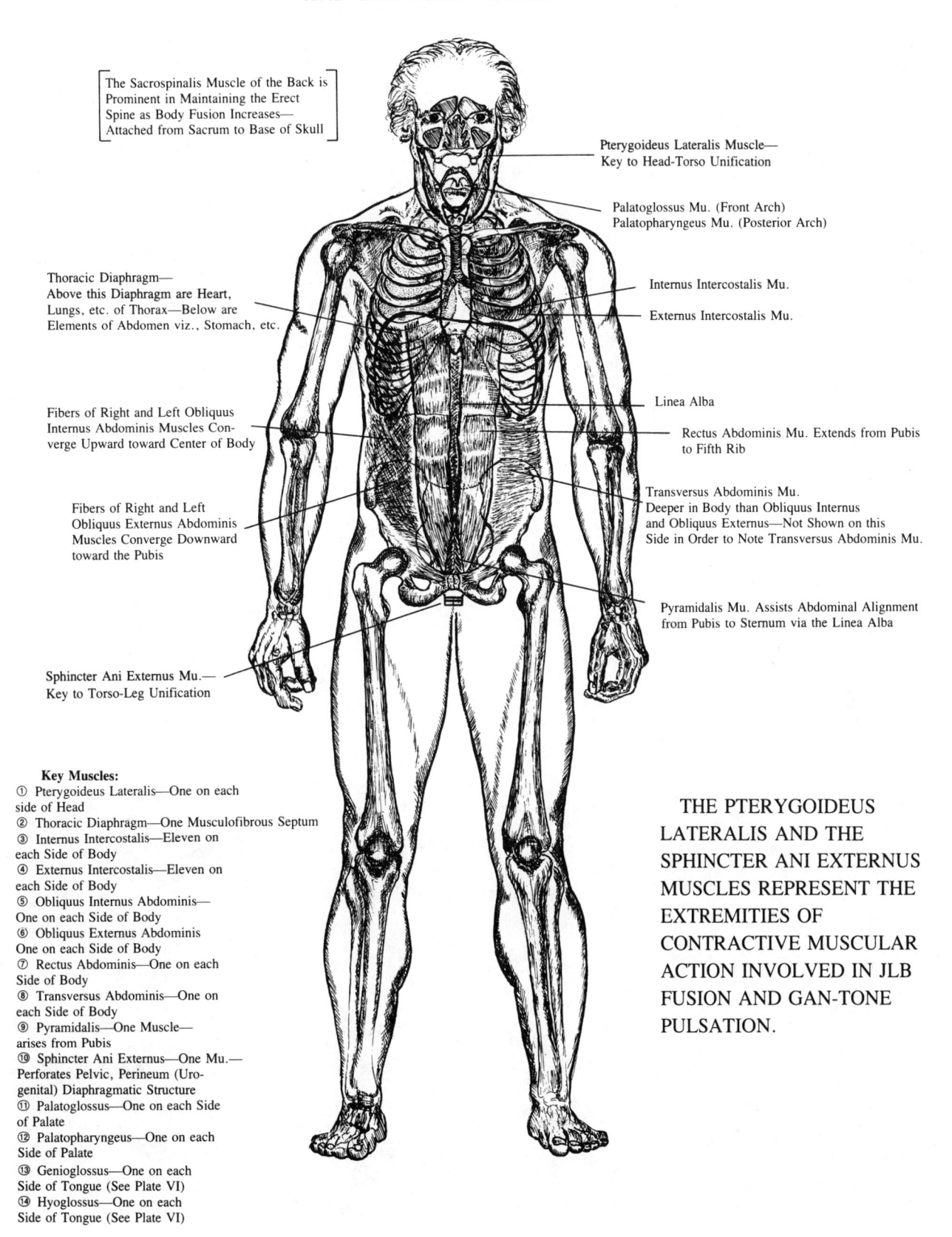

[The Sacrospinalis Muscle of the Back is Prominent in Maintaining the Erect Spine as Body Fusion Increases—Attached from Sacrum to Base of Skull]

Pterygoideus Lateralis Muscle—Key to Head-Torso Unification

Palatoglossus Mu. (Front Arch)
Palatopharyngeus Mu. (Posterior Arch)

Thoracic Diaphragm—Above this Diaphragm are Heart, Lungs, etc. of Thorax—Below are Elements of Abdomen viz., Stomach, etc.

Internus Intercostalis Mu.

Externus Intercostalis Mu.

Linea Alba

Fibers of Right and Left Obliquus Internus Abdominis Muscles Converge Upward toward Center of Body

Rectus Abdominis Mu. Extends from Pubis to Fifth Rib

Transversus Abdominis Mu. Deeper in Body than Obliquus Internus and Obliquus Externus—Not Shown on this Side in Order to Note Transversus Abdominis Mu.

Fibers of Right and Left Obliquus Externus Abdominis Muscles Converge Downward toward the Pubis

Pyramidalis Mu. Assists Abdominal Alignment from Pubis to Sternum via the Linea Alba

Sphincter Ani Externus Mu.—Key to Torso-Leg Unification

Key Muscles:
① Pterygoideus Lateralis—One on each side of Head
② Thoracic Diaphragm—One Musculofibrous Septum
③ Internus Intercostalis—Eleven on each Side of Body
④ Externus Intercostalis—Eleven on each Side of Body
⑤ Obliquus Internus Abdominis—One on each Side of Body
⑥ Obliquus Externus Abdominis One on each Side of Body
⑦ Rectus Abdominis—One on each Side of Body
⑧ Transversus Abdominis—One on each Side of Body
⑨ Pyramidalis—One Muscle—arises from Pubis
⑩ Sphincter Ani Externus—One Mu.—Perforates Pelvic, Perineum (Urogenital) Diaphragmatic Structure
⑪ Palatoglossus—One on each Side of Palate
⑫ Palatopharyngeus—One on each Side of Palate
⑬ Genioglossus—One on each Side of Tongue (See Plate VI)
⑭ Hyoglossus—One on each Side of Tongue (See Plate VI)

THE PTERYGOIDEUS LATERALIS AND THE SPHINCTER ANI EXTERNUS MUSCLES REPRESENT THE EXTREMITIES OF CONTRACTIVE MUSCULAR ACTION INVOLVED IN JLB FUSION AND GAN-TONE PULSATION.

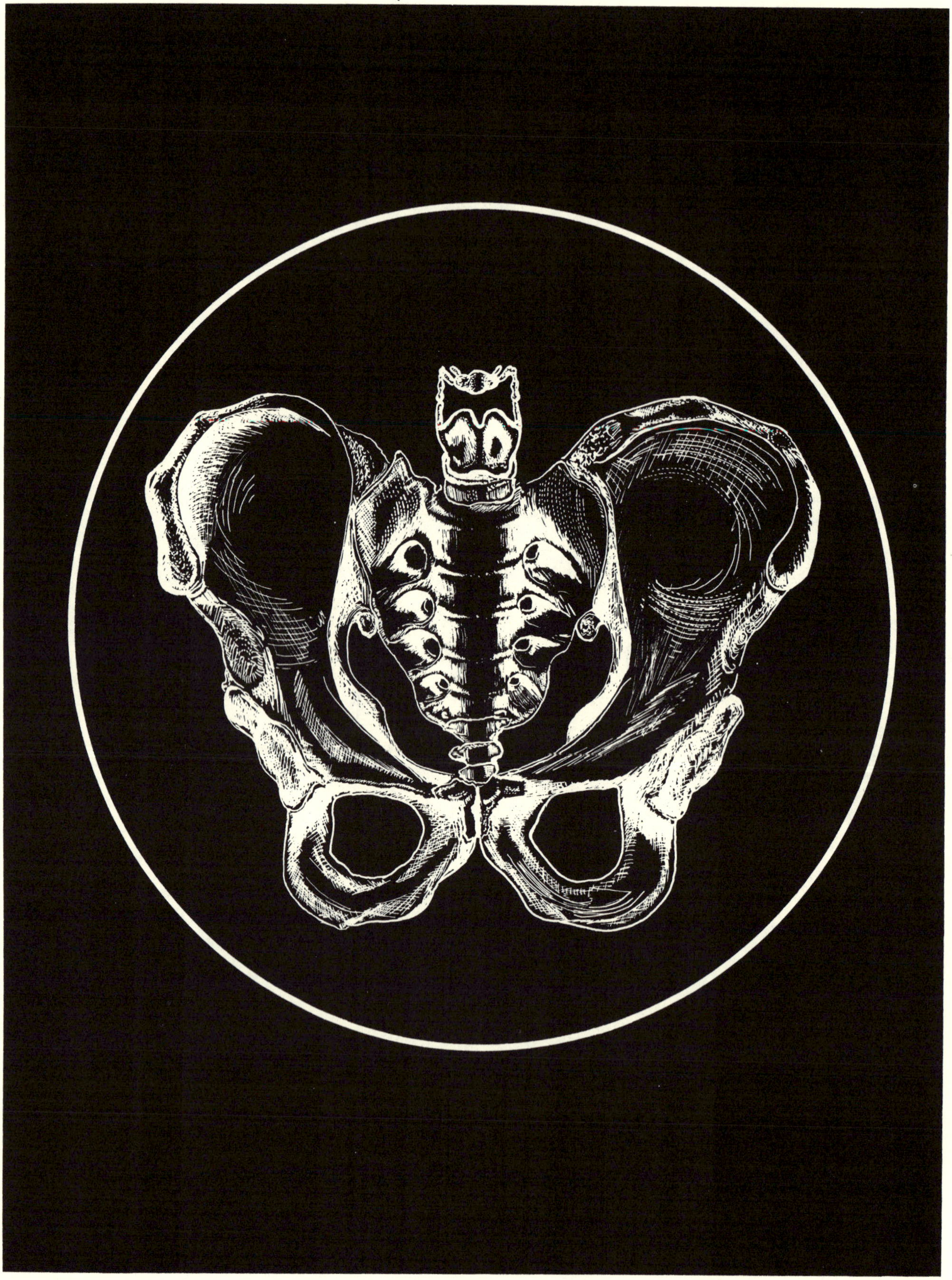

XXVII.   SYMBOL OF LARYNGEAL-PELVIC FUSION

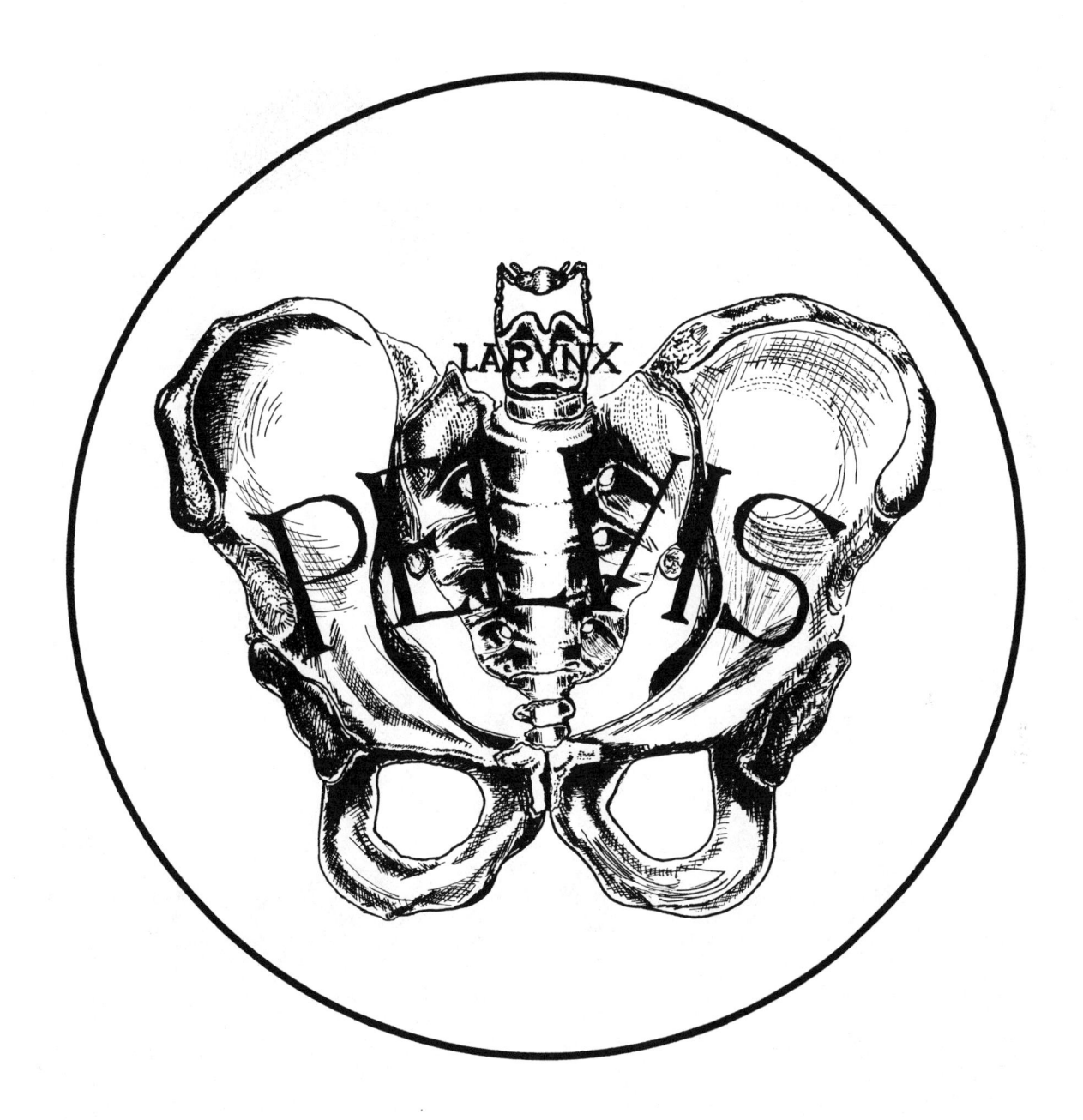

SYMBOL OF BODY UNIFICATION IN GENERATING VOCAL CORDS AND BODY VIBRATIONS FOR THE PRODUCTION OF VIBRANT SINGING ENERGY.

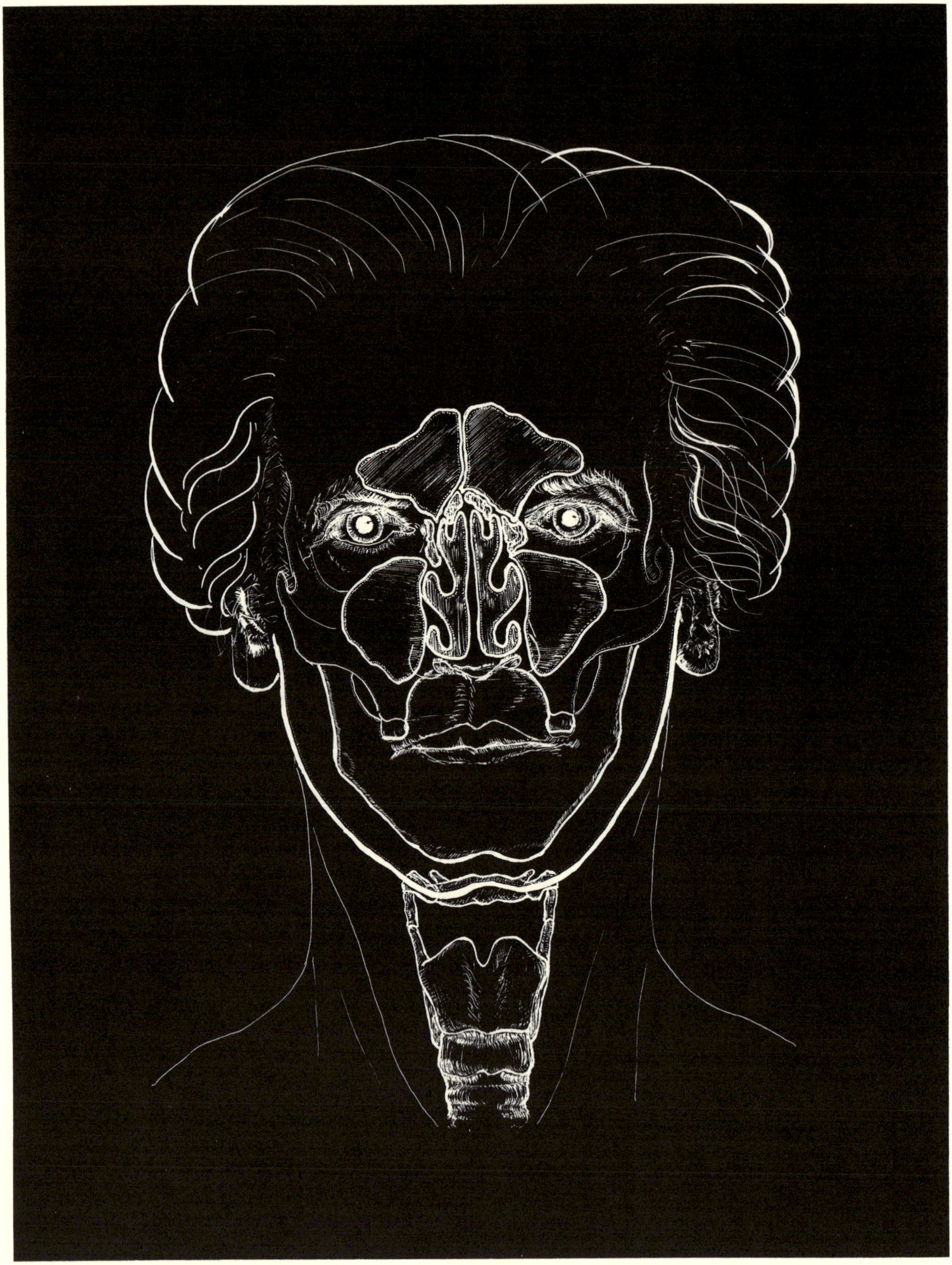

Nasion Center Line

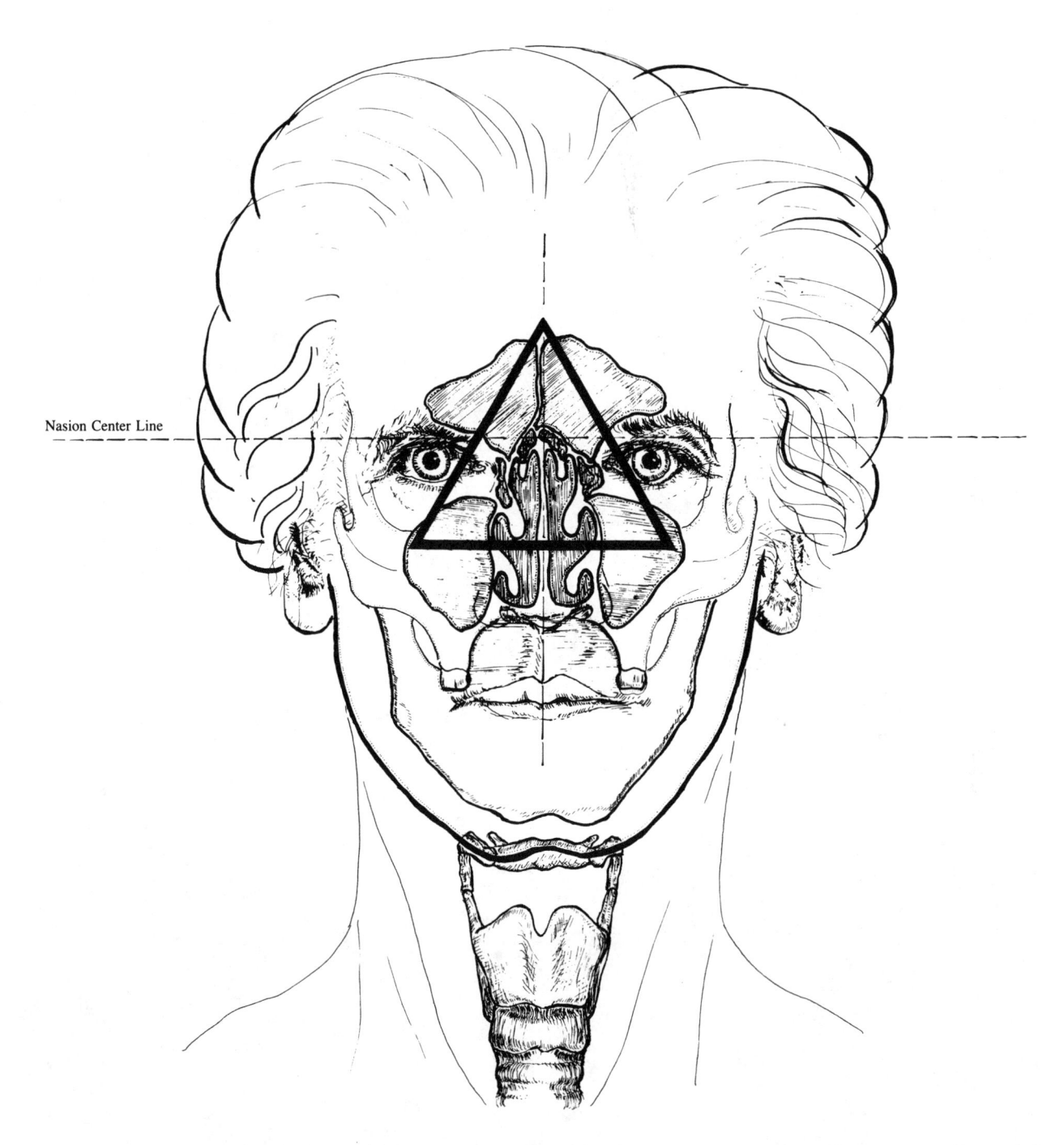

NASION CENTER—FOCAL POINT FOR RE-SOUNDING OF VOCAL ENERGY WHEN MIND, BODY AND AIR ARE SKILLFULLY COORDINATED IN THE GAN-TONE METHOD. JAW, LARYNX, BODY FUSION CONCOMITANTLY APPLIED WITH THE IMPOSITION OF THE GAN-TONE PULSATION ON THE VOCAL CORDS AND BODY VIBRATIONS CAUSE THESE VIBRATIONS TO BE RE-SOUNDED IN THE HEAD RESONATORS PRODUCING MAXIMAL ENERGY AND BRILLIANCE IN THE SINGING SOUND.

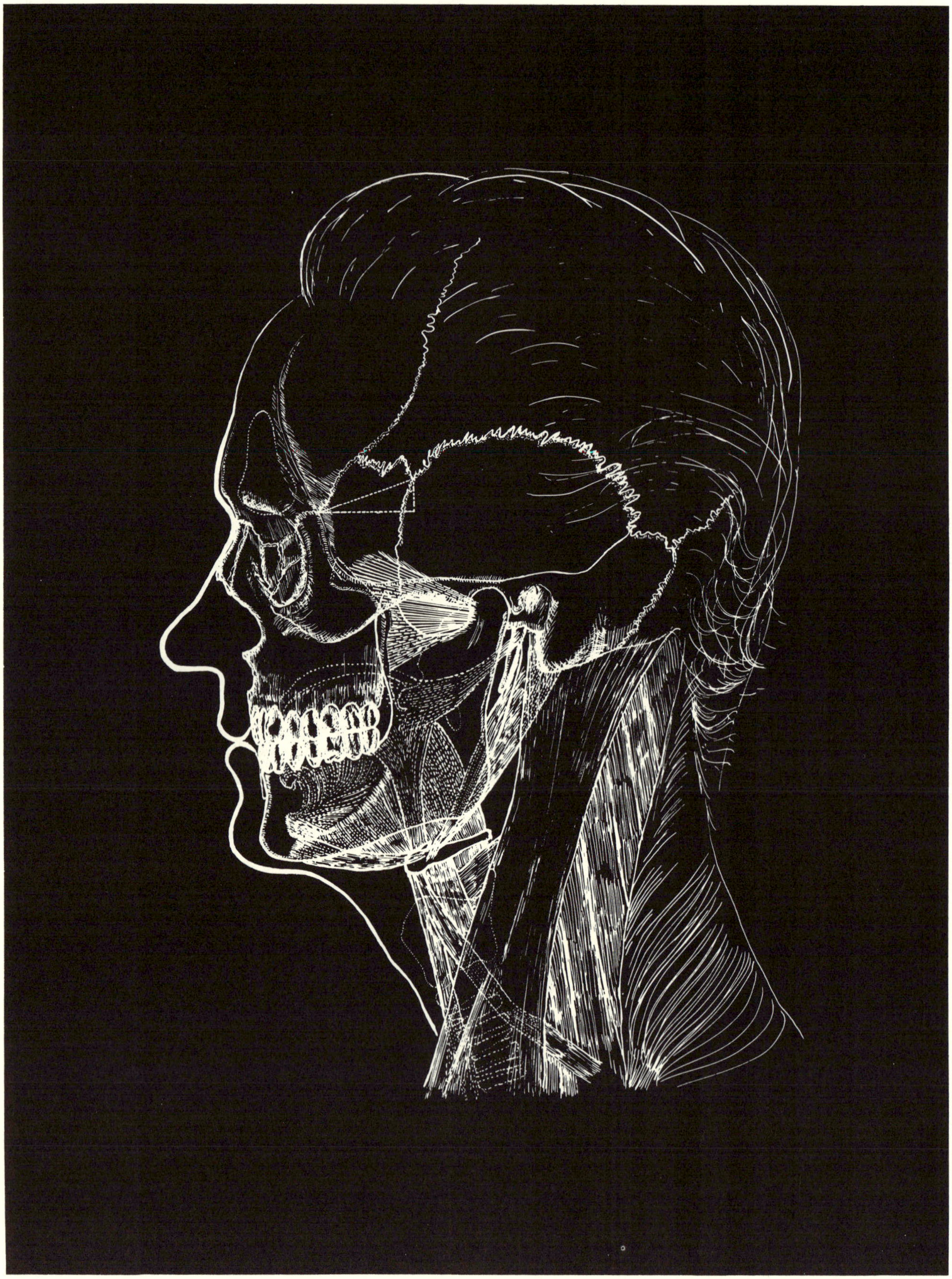

XXIX. NASION CENTER—LATERAL ASPECT

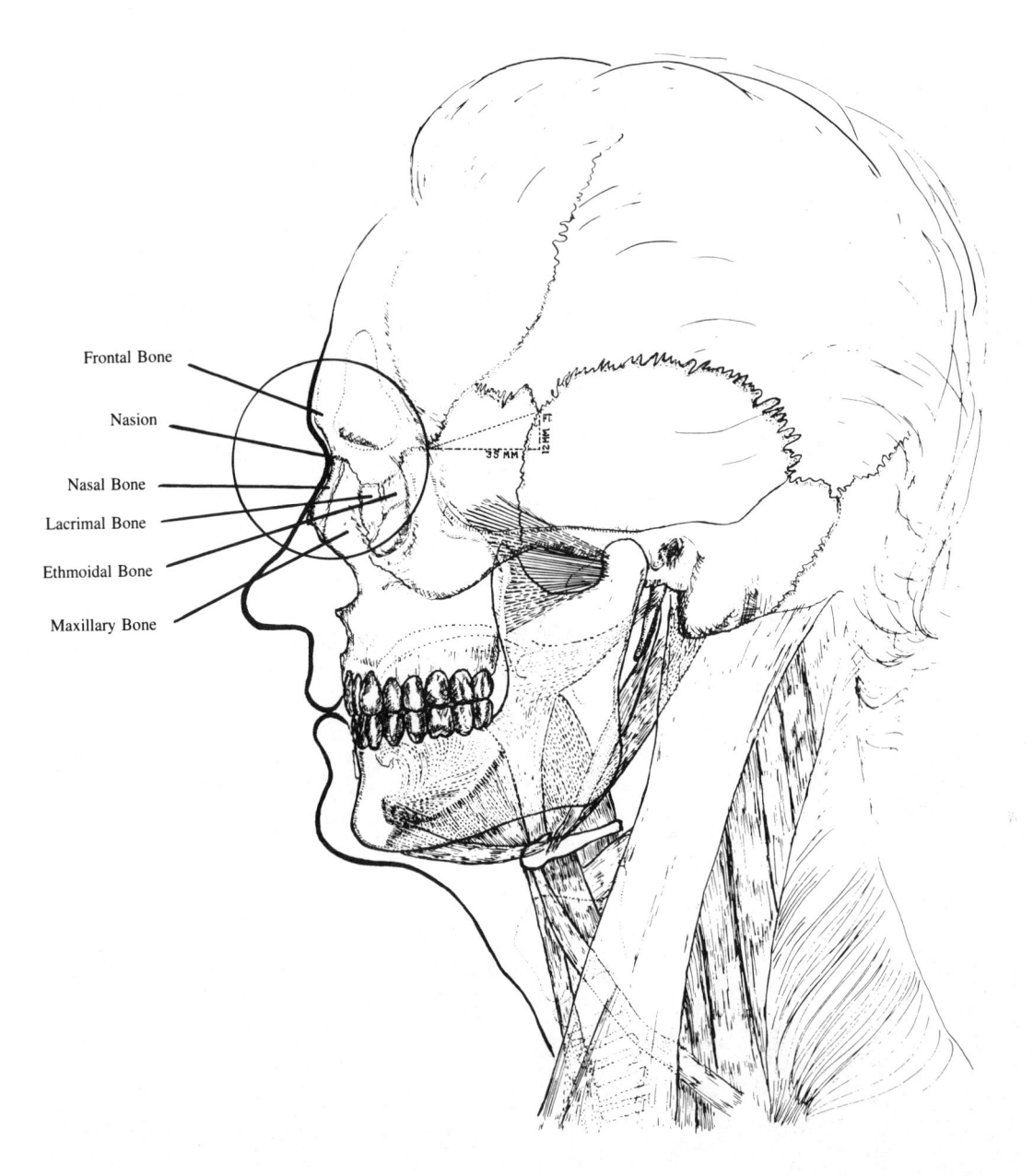

Frontal Bone
Nasion
Nasal Bone
Lacrimal Bone
Ethmoidal Bone
Maxillary Bone

THE CONVENTIONAL SEAT OF SUPPORT FOR THE PROJECTION OF THE HUMAN VOICE, THE THORACIC DIAPHRAGM, NEGATES THE FULL UTILIZATION OF THE MORE THAN TWENTY AIR SINUSES (CAVITIES) FOR THE BRILLIANT RE-SOUNDING OF VOCAL CORDS AND BODY VIBRATIONS THAT IS, HOWEVER, MADE POSSIBLE THROUGH THE GAN-TONE REFERENCE POINTS, THE SPHINCTER ANI EXTERNUS MUSCLE AND THE PELVIC-PERINEUM DIAPHRAGM, AS A RESULT OF THE JAW, LARYNX, BODY FUSION AND THE GAN-TONE PULSATION WHICH PROJECT VOCAL CORDS AND BODY VIBRATIONS FROM THE BOTTOM OF THE TORSO TO THESE HEAD RESONATORS THEREBY FULLY EMPLOYING THE BELL-LIKE CHARACTERISTICS OF THESE NUMEROUS AIR CAVITIES.

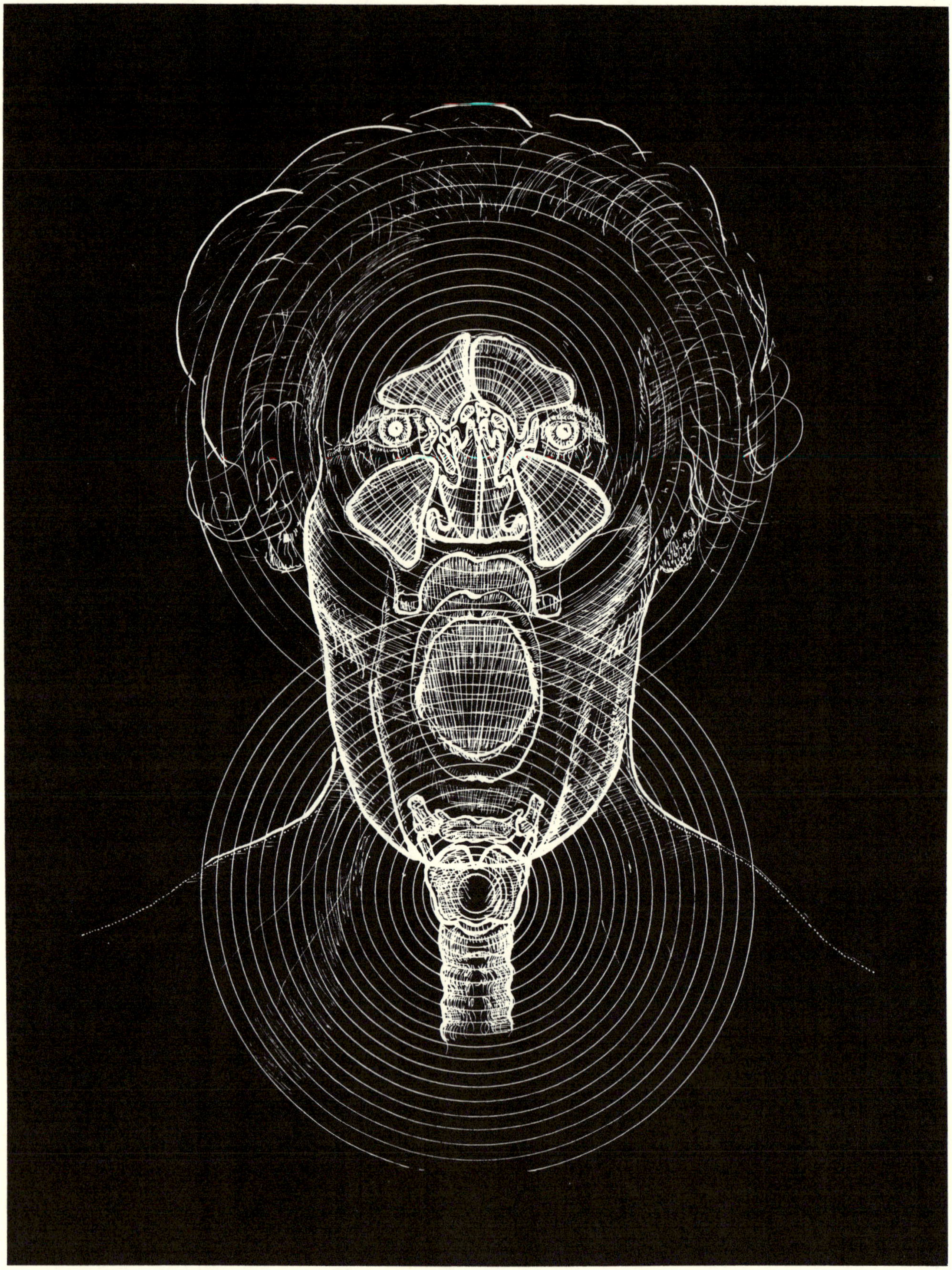

XXX. VIBRATORY AURA AS RESULT OF JAW, LARYNX, BODY FUSION AND GAN-TONE PULSATION

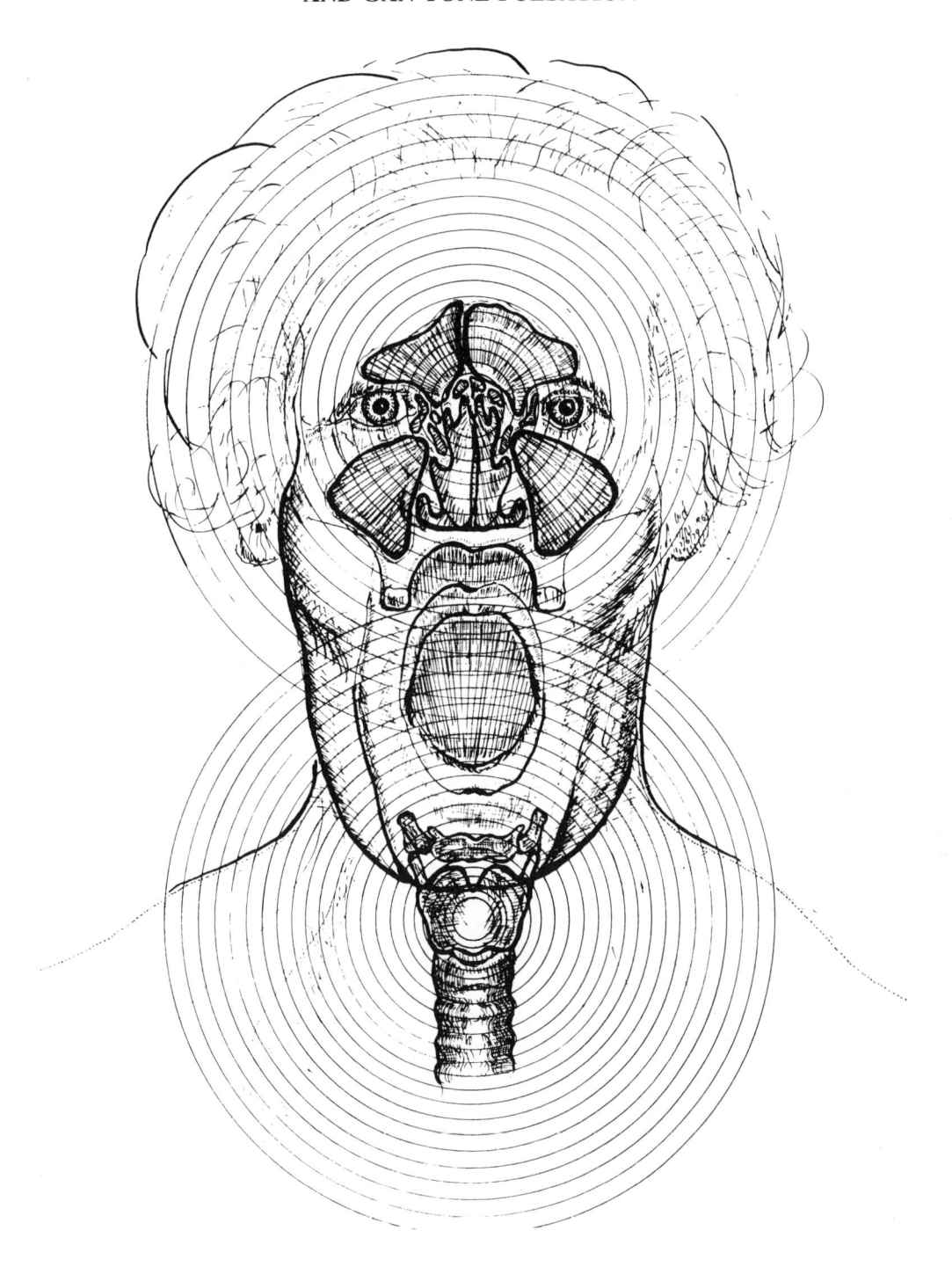

WHEN JAW, LARYNX, BODY FUSION AND GAN-TONE PULSATION ARE MAXIMALLY APPLIED, THE SINGING ENERGY PRODUCED MAKES THE BODY FUNCTION AS A BELL CAUSING IT TO BE SURROUNDED BY A VIBRATORY AURA.

GLOSSARY

SINGING ENERGY IN THE GAN-TONE METHOD OF VOICE PRODUCTION

CONTENTS—GLOSSARY

1- ABSOLUTE JAW, LARYNX, BODY FUSION
2- ACOUSTICS
3- ACTION REACTION
4- AIR TURBULENCE
5- ALTERNATING CURRENT
6- AMPLIFICATION
7- AMPLIFIER
8- AMPLITUDE
9- ANXIETY
10- ASPIRATE
11- ATTACK

12- BATTERY
13- BELL FACTOR
14- BELLOWS
15- BODY BEAT
16- BODY COLUMN
17- BODY DROP
18- BODY EXTREMITIES
19- BODY PERISTALSIS
20- BODY REGISTER
21- BODY RESILIENCE
22- BODY VIBRATIONS
23- BREAK IN THE VOICE
24- BREATH CONTROL
25- BRILLIANCE
26- BRILLIANT PEAKS

27- CENTER OF TONE
28- CLASSICAL SINGING
29- COLORATION OF SOUND
30- COLORATURA
31- COLUMNARIZATION
32- COMPACTING THE BODY
33- COMPLETE BODY INVOLVEMENT
34- COMPONENTS OF THE BODY
35- COMPRESS
36- COMPRESSION
37- COMPRESSION PHASE
38- CONDUCTOR
39- CONTACT
40- CONTROLLING CENTER
41- COVER OF TONE
42- CYCLE OF SOUND
43- CYLINDER AND PISTON

44- DIFFUSION OF PRESSURE
45- DILATED NOSTRILS
46- DIMENSIONAL POTENTIAL
47- DIRECT RESONANCE
48- DISEMBODIED SOUND
49- DOOR

50- EDUCATED LAUGH
51- EXALTATION OF SOUND
52- EXINVAC

53- FALSETTO VOICE
54- FEATHER-TOUCH CONTACT
55- FEATHER-TOUCH FOR THE PRODUCTION AND PROJECTION OF SOUND
56- FEEDBACK
57- FREQUENCY OF THE GAN-TONE PULSATION
58- FUNDAMENTAL FREQUENCY
59- FUNDAMENTAL VOCAL CORDS VIBRATIONS
60- FUSE
61- FUSION
62- FUSION LAPSE

63- GAN-TONE PULSATION
64- GAN-TONE REFERENCE POINTS
65- GENERATOR
66- GIGGLE
67- GLASS JAW
68- GRADUATED JAW
69- GROUNDING OF VIBRATIONS
70- GRUNTING DOWN

71- IDLING JAW
72- IMPASSE
73- IMPULSES
74- INAUDIBLE VIBRATIONS
75- INDIRECT RESONANCE
76- INNER LAUGH
77- INTENSITY OF THE GAN-TONE APPLICATION

78- JAW
79- JAW, LARYNX, BODY FUSION
80- JAW, MOUTH, NOSE COORDINATION
81- JAW SENSE

82- LAUNCHING PAD
83- LEGATO
84- LIFTED POSITION OF THE SINGING SOUND
85- LIPS

86- MANDIBLE
87- MASK
88- MAXIMAL VIBRATIONAL FLOW
89- MESSA DI VOCE
90- METHOD
91- MIND, BODY AND AIR
92- MODIFIED JAW, LARYNX, BODY FUSION
93- MULTIDIMENSIONAL SOUND

94- NASION CENTER
95- NATURAL LAUGH
96- NATURAL SINGING
97- NERVES
98- NODE

99- OMNIDIRECTIONAL TRANSMISSION

100- OPEN THROAT
101- OSCILLATION
102- OVERTONES
103- OVERTONES CYCLE

104- PAYLOAD
105- PELVIC BREATHING
106- PELVIC-PERINEUM DIAPHRAGM
107- PENETRATION
108- PISTON
109- PITCH
110- POPULAR SINGING
111- PRESSURE
112- PTERYGOIDEUS LATERALIS
113- PURE VOCAL CORDS SOUND
114- PYRAMIDAL STRUCTURE OF SOUND

115- RANGE
116- RECTAL-PELVIC BASIN
117- RECTAL-PELVIC BREATH CONTROL
118- REGISTERS
119- RESONANCE
120- RESONATORS
121- RE-SOUNDING
122- RESOUNDING BODY
123- ROCK AND ROLL SINGING

124- SEPTUM
125- SINGING
126- SINGING ENERGY
127- SINGING LINE
128- SINGING SOUND
129- SINKING THE BREATH
130- SINUS CAVITIES
131- SOUND CONFIGURATION
132- SPARK
133- SPEAKERS
134- SPHINCTER ANI EXTERNUS
135- SPINAL-PELVIC CURVE
136- SPIRIT
137- SPONTANEOUS APPLICATION
138- STACCATO
139- SUPERIMPOSED PULSATION
140- SUPPORT

141- SWITCH
142- TENSION
143- THRUST
144- THRUST PHASE
145- TIMBRE
146- TIME AND MOVEMENT RELATIONSHIP
147- TONGUE ENGLISH
148- TONGUE WHEEL
149- TOTAL VIBRATOR
150- TREMOLO

151- UNDERTONES
152- UNHINGED JAW
153- UVULAR TYMPANY

154- VARIABLE MOUTH AND JAW OPENINGS
155- VERTICAL-ELLIPTICAL MOUTH OPENING
156- VERTICAL FUSION
157- VIBRANCY
158- VIBRATING AIR
159- VIBRATIONAL ABSORPTION
160- VIBRATIONAL RESTRICTION
161- VIBRATIONS
162- VIBRATO

163- VIBRATORY AURA
164- VIBRATORY CHARACTERISTICS OF BODY MEDIUMS
165- VIBRATORY HARMONY
166- VOCAL CORDS
167- VOCAL CORDS EXTENSION
168- VOCAL CORDS VIBRATIONS
169- VOCAL FOCUS
170- VOCAL HOOK
171- VOCAL IMPACT
172- VOCAL STABILITY
173- VOCAL VIBRATORY CONTINUITY
174- VOICE PLACEMENT
175- VOICE PROJECTION
176- VOICE PROJECTION POTENTIAL
177- VOLUME
178- VOMITING PRINCIPLE

179- WEIGHT DIFFERENTIAL
180- WHISPERING
181- WHISTLE POSITION
182- WOBBLING JAW

183- YAWNING PROCESS
184- YODELING

GLOSSARY

The Gan-Tone Method establishes new reference points regarding the role of the body in the production of the singing voice. Current thought focuses on body parts in the production of the singing voice; whereas, the Gan-Tone Method unifies body parts extending the dimensions of singing energy to the body extremities thereby focusing on body unification. Appropriate terminology has, therefore, been created in order to explain this Gan-Tone approach, and existing terminology has been re-defined to include the scope of the Gan-Tone Principles.

ABSOLUTE JAW, LARYNX, BODY FUSION. The maximal involvement of body parts in fusion which results in the maximal application of the Gan-Tone Pulsation.

The head is tilted forward and downward. The pubis of the pelvis is tilted upward producing a cranial, pelvic, spinal curve. The knees are bent, one knee slightly in front of the other with the feet solidly planted on the gound. The mandible is diverged maximally from the upper jaw and resting, with a feather-touch contact, down and back on the larynx.

In this maximal position of the Jaw, Larynx, Body Fusion, there is maximal contact between the two Gan-Tone reference points (Pterygoideus lateralis muscle in the head and the Sphincter ani externus muscle at the bottom of the torso), as a result of maximal body fusion.

Since body fusion is applied concomitantly with the Compression Phase, or down-part of the Gan-Tone beat, the density of compression of vocal cords and body vibrations is maximal, as a result of maximal intensity in body fusion resulting in a maximal thrust of these vocal cords and body vibrations to the body resonators in the Thrust Phase, or up-part of the Gan-Tone beat.

This maximal fusion of the jaw, larynx and body is utilized by the Gan-Tone singer for the maximal dimension of sound in loud, high, sustained notes and for the dispersal of vocal pressure to the body extremities.

ACOUSTICS. Multidimensional sound scientifically produced through the application of the Jaw, Larynx, Body Fusion and the Gan-Tone Pulsation, enabling the singer to transmit vocal cords vibrations of the fundamental pitch through body components, activating them to vibrate, in order to achieve a desired vocal result, such as, depth in the sound, which is determined by the extent to which body components are penetrated.

Through fusion of body parts and compression of vocal cords vibrations to the bottom of the torso, the individual differences in the composition of body components are magnified producing an infinite variety of acoustical effects, since the size, shape and proximity of body parts vary in each individual making each voice uniquely different.

The degree of skill that the singer acquires in fusing body parts and compressing vocal cords vibrations to the bottom of the torso on the Compression Phase, or down-part of the Gan-Tone beat, will determine the degree of transmission of vocal cords vibrations through the body which will determine the degree to which body parts will vibrate. The singer focuses these vibrations to various parts of the resonators by the manipulation of the many apertures of the vocal hook, such as the throat, uvular tympany, mouth, nostrils and tongue, on the Thrust Phase, or up-part of the Gan-Tone beat, which determines the color, quantity and quality of the sound.

The singer's skill in coordinating the jaw with the body, while ascending or descending the scale, for maintaining maximum production, transmission and re-sounding of vocal cords vibrations throughout the range will determine the acoustical effect of the vocal sound.

The degree of intensity of the Gan-Tone beat determines the degree of intensity of body penetration to the pelvic basin which, in turn, determines the degree of vibration of body parts and the size and effective utilization of body cavities that, in turn, determine the acoustical effect of the emitted sound.

ACTION REACTION. Newton's Law which states that for every action there is an equal and opposite reaction. This law governs the function of the Gan-Tone Pulsation, i.e., the intensity of the Compression Phase, or down-part of the Gan-Tone beat, which fuses and compresses vocal cords vibrations to the rectal-pelvic basin, determines the intensity of the Thrust Phase, or up-part of the Gan-Tone beat, which transmits these vocal cords vibrations to the body resonators, but especially to the head resonators.

AIR TURBULENCE. The agitation of air in the throat during the singing process produced by the wobbling of irregular body parts, in the irregular vocal hook, causing these parts, as a result of instability under pressure, to interrupt the smooth movement of vibrating air through the vocal hook (curved tract from the vocal cords to the mouth and nostrils).

Coordinated fusion of body parts produced by the Jaw, Larynx, Body Fusion unifies and thus stabilizes these parts, preventing them from wobbling under pressure, enabling the vibrating air to move smoothly through the curved tract of the throat.

ALTERNATING CURRENT. The flow of vocal cords and body vibrations whose direction is periodically reversed by the imposition of the Gan-Tone beat. Each cycle of the Gan-Tone beat produces one pulsation in the flow which consists of two phases. The downward direction of the flow occurs in the Compression Phase, or down-part of the Gan-Tone beat, when vibrations are compressed and amplified at the rectal-pelvic basin, and the upward direction occurs in the Thrust Phase, or up-part of the Gan-Tone beat, which reverses the mainstream of vibrations by thrusting them to the resonators.

The frequency of this pulsation in the vibrational flow is dependent on the number of Gan-Tones applied per second. If, for ex., five Gan-Tones are applied in one second, the flow of vibrations would be reversed five times, producing five thrusts of vibrations to the resonators in one second, i.e., five times the vibrational flow is rapidly compressed to the rectal-pelvic basin and thrust from this area, in the opposite direction, to the resonators, giving great impact to these vibrations in the resonators which, in turn, produces great dimensions in the emitted sound.

AMPLIFICATION. The increase of vocal vibratory energy through body power by means of fusion of body parts and compression of vocal cords and body vibrations to the rectal-pelvic basin on the Gan-Tone beat.

Increased vocal vibratory energy, or amplification of vocal cords vibrations, is the function of the body, and the re-sounding of these vibrations, or vibrant air, is the function of the body cavities.

AMPLIFIER. The body, since it functions as a magnifier of vocal cords vibrations, when the Jaw, Larynx, Body Fusion and the Gan-Tone Pulsation are applied.

The fundamental vocal cords vibrations are fused and compressed to the rectal-pelvic basin on the Compression Phase, or down-part of the Gan-Tone beat, causing these vibrations to be amplified through the body mediums (bones, cartilages, muscles).

Amplification of vibrations occurs during the Compression Phase, or down-part of the Gan-Tone beat, which is the action downward through the body.

The re-sounding of these amplified vibrations occurs during the Thrust Phase, or up-part of the Gan-Tone beat, which is the re-action upward through the body.

The more intense the Compression Phase, or down-part of the Gan-Tone beat, the greater the amplification of vocal cords vibrations through the body producing a commensurate re-sounding of these vibrations in the body resonators during the Thrust Phase, or up-part of the Gan-Tone beat.

AMPLITUDE. The extent to which vocal cords vibrations penetrate the entire body, from the rectal-pelvic basin to the head resonators, on the Gan-Tone beat with the Jaw, Larynx, Body Fusion. The function of the Gan-Tone beat is to extend the amplitude, or distance, of the vocal cords vibrations (fundamental frequency) from the throat area, omnidirectionally, to the body extremities.

The degree to which the down-part of the Gan-Tone beat transmits vocal cords vibrations to the rectal-pelvic basin determines the degree to which the up-part of the Gan-Tone beat thrusts these vocal cords vibrations to the resonators that are now maximally opened. The degree of intensity of the Gan-Tone beat, therefore, determines the degree of omnidirectional penetration, or amplitude, of vibrations from the vocal cords throughout the body, but especially to the extremities.

ANXIETY. Uneasiness in the singer during the singing process, since he anticipates the spasm and collapse of the vocal line, as a result of the impedence and restriction of vibrations in the vocal cords and throat area during loud, high, sustained sounds, causing muscle tension. This excessive imbalance of vibrations in the throat area occurs as a result of the lack of dexterity in jaw movements and lack of dispersion of vocal cords pressure throughout the body, causing fatigue and collapse of the vocal structure.

ASPIRATE. To produce non-prescribed breath sounds while inspiring or expiring air during the singing process which denotes inefficient utilization of breath in the Gan-Tone Method.

These breath sounds are non-existent in the Gan-Tone Method, since breath is most efficiently utilized when the singer immediately coordinates mind, body and air in the singing process. Spontaneity in the coordination of the Jaw, Larynx, Body Fusion and the Gan-Tone Pulsation most efficiently utilizes breath eliminating any non-prescribed breath sounds.

Aspirated sounds often occur during the attacking, the slurring, the bellowing, the guffawing or the sobbing of a note. In the Gan-Tone Method, aspirated air is non-existent, since there is a complete sinking of the breath downward (as opposed to outward), extending the vocal cords and body vibrations to the bottom of the torso, as a result of the Jaw, Larynx, Body Fusion and the Gan-Tone Pulsation which add dimension to the attack and to whatever emotion is desired, while maximally utilizing the breath.

ATTACK. The onset used by the singer in the production of the singing sound which consists of directing a jet of air from the lungs through the tensed vocal cords with a feather touch, while maintaining the Jaw, Larynx, Body Fusion, thus diffusing the resulting vocal cords vibrations through the body mediums to the bottom of the torso on the Compression Phase, or down-part of the Gan-Tone beat.

The action phase of the attack, i.e., the Compression Phase, or down-part of the Gan-Tone beat, results in the reaction phase, i.e., the thrusting of these vocal cords and body vibrations to the resonators on the Thrust Phase, or up-part of the Gan-Tone beat.

The grounding of vocal cords and body vibrations at the rectal-pelvic basin provides the greatest foundation for launching the attack of the singing sound, since it makes possible a great quantity of vibrations, maximum thrust of these vibrations and accuracy in maintaining Vocal Focus in the resonators, regardless of the vowel being sung.

The effectiveness of the attack, or onset of the sound, is dependent on the spontaneity with which the singer articulates initial or final consonants, regulates the Uvular Tympany and applies the Jaw, Mouth, Nose Coordination, Tongue English, Jaw, Larynx, Body Fusion, Jaw Sense and the Gan-Tone Pulsation.

BATTERY. The combination of body parts that are consolidated, through fusion, to transmit, amplify and re-sound vocal cords vibrations in order to increase the dimensions of the emitted sound by increasing the vibrational current.

BELL FACTOR. The body is compared to the bell. The hollow, cup-shaped, metallic vessel that vibrates when struck is known as a bell. The degree to which body parts are fused and the Gan-Tone beat applied determines the degree to which the entire body vibrates and re-sounds vocal cords and body vibrations which, in turn, determines the degree to which the body resounds as a bell.

BELLOWS. The lungs and bronchial tubes that converge on the windpipe leading to the glottis (the opening between the vocal folds through which inhaled and exhaled air passes).

A jet of air from the lungs passes through the glottis during exhalation. When the vocal folds are tensed, this air activates the folds to produce audible vibrations.

In the Gan-Tone Method, the body becomes the bellows by the extension of the lungs to the rectal-pelvic basin through body fusion and compression. The body, rather than the lungs, furnishes the breath support which is controlled at the rectal-pelvic basin, the strongest area of the body.

Compression augments the lungs by increasing their size, power and resilience through body involvement thereby increasing their control and thrust of the air.

BODY BEAT. The pulsation through the body when the Gan-Tone beat is imposed on the fundamental frequency.

Fundamental vocal cords vibrations are fused to the bottom of the torso on the Compression Phase, or down-part of the Gan-Tone beat, and then thrust to the body extremities, such as the sinus cavities, on the Thrust Phase, or up-part of the Gan-Tone beat, making the entire body the vibrator and resonator of the singing sound, when a series of these beats are imposed on the singing line, producing a smooth, vibrant, energetic sound.

The mind causes Gan-Tone beats to pulsate the body by fusion and compression just as the mind imposes impulses through the nerves and muscles of the larynx that directly or indirectly control the ligamentous vocal cords.

BODY COLUMN. The upright pillar of vertical support created by the fusion of the jaw, larynx and body and the Gan-Tone Pulsation producing a dense, resilient amalgamation of body parts to the bottom of the torso which, in turn, creates a resilient conductor for the transmission, amplification and thrust of vocal cords and body vibrations throughout the body, but especially to the resonators, negating the need for horizontal spread (obesity) to produce support and volume in the singing sound.

BODY DROP. The spontaneous dropping of the torso by bending the knees (utilized in the martial arts, ballet and fencing to increase body thrust) in conjunction with the Jaw, Larynx, Body Fusion and the Gan-Tone Pulsation to launch the initial attack of a sustained sound with increased body weight in order to get more power and dimensions in the sound.

The body drop increases weight and body density in the singer, enabling him to spontaneously attain maximum dimensions of depth, height, resilience and volume in the sustained sound with a minimal need for physical obesity.

The body drop, the Gan-Tone Pulsation and the Jaw, Larynx, Body Fusion maximize body resilience as the projecting agent of the singing sound. However, the lack of body resilience, which occurs when the Jaw, Larynx, Body Fusion and the Gan-Tone beat are not applied, diminishes vibratory continuity, projection and dimensions of the emitted sound, even though the body drop is utilized, giving the sound a tight, reedy quality.

The weight differential which occurs when the knees are bent in the process of dropping the torso can be recorded on a scale.

BODY EXTREMITIES. The utmost parts of the body, such as the head and torso, to which vocal cords vibrations are transmitted and amplified on the Gan-Tone beat.

The rectal-pelvic basin controls the amount of amplification, support and thrust of vocal cords and body vibrations and determines the payload of vibrations that will be re-sounded in the highest resonators of the head, such as the sinus cavities. However, the efficiency of the rectal-pelvic basin as a controlling center is dependent on the intensity of the Gan-Tone beat. The more intense the application of the Gan-Tone beat, the more efficient the rectal-pelvic basin as a controlling center of vibrations causing the head resonators to be more effectively utilized.

BODY PERISTALSIS. The worm-like wave motion of the contractive muscular action produced by successive contractions of the muscle fibers of the body from the Pterygoideus lateralis muscle in the head to the Sphincter ani externus muscle at the rectal-pelvic basin during the application of the Jaw, Larynx, Body Fusion and the Gan-Tone Pulsation causing vocal cords and body vibrations to be transmitted downward to the pelvic-perineum diaphragm on the Compression Phase, or down-part of the Gan-Tone beat, and upward to the body resonators on the Thrust Phase, or up-part of the Gan-Tone beat. This peristaltic action of the body is synonymous with the application of the Gan-Tone beat and is two directional, i.e., downward (Compression Phase) and upward (Thrust Phase).

BODY REGISTER. The range of the singing voice, from low to high, produced by complete body involvement, without any change in quality, as a result of the Jaw, Larynx, Body Fusion. This coordination and fusion of body parts accommodate the increased pressure resulting from increased range, providing a smooth transmission of vocal cords vibrations, omnidirectionally, from the vocal cords throughout the body, for the entire range of the singing voice.

BODY RESILIENCE. The spring-like action of the body produced by fusion and compression of body parts to the rectal-pelvic basin on the spring-like action of the JLB Fusion and the Gan-Tone beat. This beat energizes and amplifies vocal cords and body vibrations and thrusts them to the resonators with great impact and buoyancy.

BODY VIBRATIONS. A composite of pulsations of different frequencies activated in the body mediums, such as bones, cartilages, fluids and flesh, each medium having its own pitch. The body is made up of many members, each one vibrating at a different frequency. These vibrations are activated as a result of vocal cords vibrations penetrating omnidirectionally from the vocal cords throughout the body on the Gan-Tone beat. The more intense the application of the Gan-Tone cycle, the more intense the vibrational energy, causing these body vibrations to be channeled to the resonators, thereby making them audible in the emitted sound, thus adding more facets to the dominant fundamental pitch.

BREAK IN THE VOICE. An abrupt change in the quantity of vibrational energy, in the process of ascending or descending the scale, producing an abrupt change in tonal quality, as a result of the collapse of Vocal Vibratory Continuity brought about by the divergence of body parts.

In ascending the scale, vibratory continuity is easily maintained in the lower notes. As the singer approaches the middle of the voice, pressure increases, as a result of increased vibrations characteristic of ascending pitch and increasing volume. Lack of coordination of body parts to accommodate this pressure causes a divergence and collapse of these body parts revealing a disembodied, or pure vocal cords, sound, sometimes referred to as a register break. This break can occur in different parts of the range.

BREATH CONTROL. The agile conversion of a quantity of air from the lungs into resonating sounds by means of the Jaw, Larynx, Body Fusion and the Gan-Tone beat in order to utilize a minimum of air in activating the vocal cords and transmitting these vocal cords vibrations to resonating areas of the body with speed and efficiency, enabling the singer to sustain long phrases, execute intricate passages and simultaneously shade and color the sounds without running out of breath.

During the fusion of body parts, air is compacted downward, along with the lungs and other body parts, to the rectal-pelvic basin, giving resilience and strength to the jet of air activating the vocal cords and simultaneously amplifying vibrations, thus producing great support and thrust for the re-sounded vibrations, enabling the singer to produce sound with a minimal quantity of breath and minimal use of the vocal cords.

BRILLIANCE. Radiant brightness in the aura of sound emanating from the body, as a result of the Gan-Tone Pulsations which give great depth, height, thrust and penetration to vocal cords and body vibrations enabling them to reach the body extremities, i.e., from the depth of the rectal-pelvic basin to the bony, perforated mask of the head, which is the most resilient area for the production of resonance in the body, when vibrations are thrust from the rectal-pelvic basin, which is the most productive area for the amplification of vocal cords vibrations.

The degree of brilliance evident in the emitted sound is dependent on the degree of amplification and thrust of vocal cords and body vibrations from the rectal-pelvic basin.

BRILLIANT PEAKS. The bright high points of the vibrant aura of sound radiantly emanating from the body. The height and brilliance of the sound is dependent upon the intensity and depth to which vibrational energy is compressed and amplified at the rectal-pelvic basin, creating an equal intensity of thrust to the resonators; maximized with the Gan-Tone Pulsation.

CENTER OF TONE. Sound produced with a perfect balance of depth and height which occurs when the body below and above the vocal cords is equally utilized in the omnidirectional penetration of vocal cords vibrations through the Jaw, Larynx, Body Fusion and the Gan-Tone beat, making resonance below and above the vocal cords equally present, eliminating the age-old belief of registers in the voice.

This state of equilibrium can only be attained with the coordination of the jaw to the body, since the jaw is the door that balances vibrations in the body extremities, below and above the vocal cords. Overtones and undertones are always present, regardless of how the tone is produced. The distortion, or eccentricity, of the vocal cords vibrations omnidirectionally throughout the body is the result of pressure produced by increased range and volume, and the inability to diffuse this pressure with the necessary jaw opening. The application of the Gan-Tone beat maximizes and balances tone by producing equal dimensions of depth and height in the sound.

If the jaw is not opened wide and resting on the larynx, while singing low notes, equilibrium of vibrational movement to the head resonators is diminished, producing less height in the emitted sound as a result of less depth. As vibrations increase, while ascending the scale, the restriction of these vibrations with increased muscular pressure results in a change in tonal quality, which is mistakenly referred to as a register demarcation, i.e., the termination of the chest register and the beginning of the head register. The change in tonal quality occurs when the singer can no longer involve the larynx and body, since the lack of jaw opening puts pressure on throat muscles and causes a divergence of the jaw from the larynx and body, divorcing their involvement in the production of sound. The so-called head register, therefore, is essentially pure vocal cords sound devoid of laryngeal and body amplification.

Lack of understanding regarding the relationship of the jaw opening to increased pressure explains why some singers can produce full sounds in the low range and are unable to negotiate the middle range without a register break, i.e., a change in tonal quality, and why some singers can negotiate the high range but yet are unable to descend the scale to the lower range of the voice without a change in tonal quality. In both cases, lack of jaw coordination and fusion restrict the movement of vibrations to areas below and above the vocal cords.

The vocal impasse met by the bass, tenor and soprano, in the process of ascending and descending the scale, which results in registers, can be attributed to ignorance regarding the position of the jaw in relation to vibrational movement.

Imbalance in the tone, i.e., lack of dimensional evenness (depth and height), causes eccentricity rather than concentricity in the emitted sound.

The application of the Gan-Tone beat on the fundamental frequency maximizes the omnidirectional penetration of vocal cords vibrations throughout the body, balancing the involvement of the body below and above the vocal cords, producing maximum concentricity in the vibrational energy of the emitted sound.

CLASSICAL SINGING. The most advanced vocal expression, since it involves the maximum understanding and demonstration of the Gan-Tone Principles in order to completely and effectively utilize the body in the amplification and re-sounding of vocal cords vibrations for producing maximum dimensions of depth, height and volume in the emitted sound, creating an energetic line of sound of such dimensions and radiance that it ultimately becomes the dominant component of communication as opposed to words.

COLORATION OF SOUND. The different tonal colors that can be achieved in the singing voice when vocal cords vibrations penetrate body mediums, such as bones, cartilages, muscles and fluids, activating these mediums to vibrate along with the orignal vocal cords vibrations. The degree to which these vibrations are amplified and re-sounded in the body cavities is dependent on the intensity of the Jaw, Larynx, Body Fusion and the Gan-Tone beat. The more intense the application of the Jaw, Larynx, Body Fusion and the Gan-Tone beat, the more evident the vibratory characteristics of these mediums in the emitted sound.

COLORATURA. A high soprano voice that sings florid vocal music, such as runs and trills, with Vocal Vibratory Continuity, producing a flute-like sound with body involvement, as a result of the Jaw, Larynx, Body Fusion and minimal focus of pressure on the vocal cords as a means of controlling the singing line, when performing runs and trills in a high range.

A true coloratura, in the Gan-Tone Method, can apply the Jaw, Larynx, Body Fusion and the Gan-Tone Pulsation to trills, staccati notes and the legato line in the highest range of the female voice to add dimensions of depth, height and brilliance, thus creating more vibrant energy in the singing line, as a result of the feather-touch contact of the jaw on the larynx which, in turn, produces complete body involvement.

The current vocal approach of the coloratura focuses on throat control for the amplification and thrust of vocal cords vibrations with a halted position of the jaw; whereas, the Gan-Tone approach focuses on the rectal-pelvic basin as a controlling center for the transmission, amplification and thrust of vocal cords vibrations with the fluid movements of the jaw, i.e., not setting or jutting the jaw to maintain pressure necessary for sustaining pitch and volume, but opening the jaw with a feather-touch to accommodate the increased energetic buildup of pressure and vibrations, when increasing volume or ascending the scale, thus shifting pressure from the neck area to the ultimate point of reference, which is the rectal-pelvic basin.

COLUMNARIZATION. The use of the body as a pillar, column, or cylinder, of vocal vibrational energy whose structural boundaries are the Pterygoideus lateralis muscle in the head and the Sphincter ani externus muscle at the bottom of the torso made possible through the Jaw, Larynx, Body Fusion and the Gan-Tone Pulsation which amalgamate body parts and compress vocal cords and body vibrations vertically to the bottom of the torso causing the body to function as a dense, resilient column for the amplifying, thrusting and re-sounding of vocal cords and body vibrations to the highest head resonators, thereby enabling the body to function as a shaft, or launching agent, for projecting, or cannonading, the vocal sound.

COMPACTING THE BODY. Fusing and compressing body parts, such as the jaw, larynx and torso, and elements of the body, such as bones, cartilages, muscles, ligaments, membranes, fluids and air, along with vocal cords vibrations to the rectal-pelvic basin in order to amplify vocal cords and body vibrations, increase space in the cavities, promote greater control of the breath by augmenting the strength of the lungs, and increase thrust and transmission of vibrations to the body extremities thereby producing greater dimensions in the emitted sound.

COMPLETE BODY INVOLVEMENT. Total body inclusion in the amplification and re-sounding of vocal cords and body vibrations below and above the vocal cords by means of the Jaw, Larynx, Body Fusion and the Gan-Tone Pulsation.

COMPONENTS OF THE BODY. The body parts, whether solid or liquid, such as bones, cartilages, muscles, fluids or cavities, in which vocal cords and body vibrations are amplified and re-sounded.

The degree of amplification and re-sounding of vocal cords and body vibrations in the body parts is dependent on the degree of fusion of these parts and the intensity of the Gan-Tone beat. The greater the body fusion and the more intense the application of the Gan-Tone beat, the greater the amplification and re-sounding of vocal cords and body vibrations in the body parts.

COMPRESS. To push down fused body parts and vocal cords and body vibrations to the rectal-pelvic basin by grunting deeply to the bottom of the torso with the Jaw, Larynx, Body Fusion in order to amplify these vibrations; to produce body density and resilience by contractive muscular action from the Pterygoideus lateralis muscle to the Sphincter ani externus muscle.

COMPRESSION. The act of compacting fused body parts and vocal cords and body vibrations to the rectal-pelvic basin on the Compression Phase, or down-part of the Gan-Tone beat.

COMPRESSION PHASE. The compacting and amplifying of vocal cords and body vibrations and fused body parts to the rectal-pelvic basin on the down-part of the Gan-Tone beat. This phase aids in maximizing space in the resonating cavities of the body and determines the intensity of the Thrust Phase, or up-part of the Gan-Tone beat, which thrusts these vibrations to the body resonators.

CONDUCTOR. The body under the influence of the Jaw, Larynx, Body Fusion and the Gan-Tone Pulsation, since the body becomes capable of readily transmitting, amplifying and re-sounding vocal cords vibrations.

The most effective utilization of the body as a conductor for transmitting vibrations occurs when the compression head is maximized at the rectal-pelvic basin on the Compression Phase, or down-part of the Gan-Tone beat.

CONTACT. The connection of the jaw, larynx and torso, with a minimal amount of muscular pressure, to produce the strongest path through the body for the transmission and amplification of vocal cords vibrations.

CONTROLLING CENTER. The rectal-pelvic basin, which is the area of the body that most effectively governs and registers the processes of fusion, compression and amplification of vocal cords and body vibrations. Since these processes converge in this area, developing a great pressure head, it becomes the only area in the body from which these vibrations can be thrust to the body extremities, particularly the resonators of the head, with the greatest strength and penetration.

COVER OF TONE. The aura, or dimensions of depth and height, surrounding the emitted sound, as a result of the deep penetration and re-sounding of vocal cords vibrations below and above the vocal cords produced by the Jaw, Larynx, Body Fusion. This fusion determines the amount of vocal cords vibrations that will be compressed and the degree of throat opening for the widest passage of these vibrations which, in turn, prevents throat constriction, vibrational restriction and diminished aura of sound. The Jaw, Larynx, Body Fusion also creates the framework for the imposition of the Gan-Tone Pulsation.

The dimension of height achieved in the tone is the result of the deep penetration of vocal cords vibrations downward to the rectal-pelvic basin on the Compression Phase, or down-part of the Gan-Tone beat. The greater the penetration of these vibrations to the rectal-pelvic basin, which is the action, the greater the reaction, i.e., the thrust of these vibrations throughout the body, but especially to the head resonators, on the Thrust Phase, or up-part of the Gan-Tone beat, producing greater height in the tone, as a result of the greater penetration of the body resonators.

Complete cover of tone occurs when the vocal cords are activated, with a Feather-Touch Contact, and the Jaw, Larynx, Body Fusion and the Gan-Tone Pulsation are maximally applied causing vocal cords vibrations to be maximally amplified and re-sounded in the body extremities, below and above the vocal cords.

CYCLE OF SOUND. The life of sound is conceived in the mind as thought vibrations that are channeled through the nerves as impulses registered as tension, or inaudible vibrations, on the vocal cords which are activated to audibility by a jet of air from the lungs. Through the Jaw, Larynx, Body Fusion and the Gan-Tone Pulsation, these vocal cords vibrations are fused, compressed, amplified and re-sounded throughout the body and then projected as multidimensional sound.

When the mind ceases to formulate and amplify these vibrations, sound ceases from the body.

CYLINDER AND PISTON. The cylinder, in the Gan-Tone Method, is the torso in which vocal cords and body vibrations are activated and generated, just as the cylinder in an engine is a container in which energy is generated.

The piston is the vertical column of pressure the singer imposes through the cylinder, or body, which consists of body fusion and compression of vocal cords vibrations to the bottom of the cylinder, or rectal-pelvic basin, produced by the down-part of the Gan-Tone beat, or Compression Phase.

The spark consists of the vocal cords vibrations that are fused and compressed through the body, which is comparable to the spark plug in the engine that ignites the gasoline and air producing compression and power of the piston through the cylinder.

Maximum compression and amplification of vocal cords and body vibrations are reached at the bottom of the cylinder, or rectal-pelvic basin, resulting in maximum thrust of these vibrations throughout the body, but particularly in the body cavities, producing resonance.

The intensity of the piston (fused and compressed vocal cords and body vibrations) is commensurate with the intensity of the Compression Phase, or down-part of the Gan-Tone beat, which results in an equal reaction of thrust of these vibrations to the vibrant and resonant areas of the body during the Thrust Phase, or up-part of the Gan-Tone beat.

DIFFUSION OF PRESSURE. The transfer of stress from the vocal cords and surrounding muscles to the body and its extremities during the singing process.

DILATED NOSTRILS. Distended nasal apertures for increasing the resonating space in the nasal passages.

Lenses for controlling the emission of nasal resonance (quantity and quality). The more constricted the nasal apertures, the more confined the vibrations within the nasal chambers, muffling and diminishing the emitted sound, giving it a quality of reediness. The more dilated the nostrils, the more resonance is emitted, giving the sound more brilliance.

DIMENSIONAL POTENTIAL. The degree of dimensions, i.e., depth, height, volume, coloration, buoyancy and brilliance, in the singing voice dependent on the degree of facility with which mind, body and air interact.

The greater the speed and intensity in the application of the Jaw, Larynx, Body Fusion and the Gan-Tone beat, the greater the Vocal Vibratory Continuity and resultant vibratory impact in the resonators, giving the singer a greater ability to manifest lyric as well as dramatic sounds in the singing voice.

DIRECT RESONANCE. Vibrational energy, in the singing process, emitted from the vocal cords directly and constantly to the body resonators for re-sounding without alternating the direction of this vibrational energy on the Gan-Tone beat.

DISEMBODIED SOUND. Falsetto voice; pure vocal cords sound produced with torso involvement but without vocal cords-laryngeal-torso fusion.

The falsetto voice is more pronounced in the male than in the female, since the larynx and the vocal cords are larger in the male, making the distance between the vocal cords and the laryngeal parts greater than in the female. This distance enables the male to produce pure vocal cords sound without laryngeal fusion, enabling him to produce much range in the falsetto, since the vocal cords can stretch more independently of the larynx, even though they are attached to it, creating quite a disparity between the falsetto voice and the vocal cords sound with laryngeal fusion.

The distance between the vocal cords and the laryngeal parts is much closer in the female, since the larynx is smaller, making it difficult for the vocal cords to stretch independently of the larynx thus limiting the range that the female voice can reach in the falsetto. The female falsetto voice is, therefore, less discernible than the male falsetto, since the larynx is more directly involved with the vocal cords, as a result of proximity.

However, the disembodied sound, extended to very high notes in the male voice, i.e., in the octave above the tenor's High C, and possibly beyond, indirectly involves the larynx and the torso, through muscular tension, producing very loud sounds as, for ex., the Indian war cry.

DOOR. The jaw, which functions as a valve for enabling vocal cords vibrations to move back and forth through the body, i.e., from the vocal cords through the narrow throat opening to the body extremities on the Gan-Tone beat.

The degree of jaw opening determines the quantity and quality of vocal cords vibrations that are transmitted through the solid parts as well as the open paths of the body. The more volume desired, the greater the jaw opening, or fusion of the jaw to the larynx and body, in order to produce more vibrations to be compressed to the rectal-pelvic basin during the Compression Phase, or down-part of the Gan-Tone beat. The widest jaw opening simultaneously maximizes the throat opening, permitting the unrestricted movement of vocal cords vibrations through the maximally opened passage.

Increased vibrations, produced by the increased opening of the jaw, enables more vibrations to be thrust to the body resonators, but especially to the head resonators, creating not only more volume, but also more aura (depth and height) in the emitted sound.

Any degree of jaw closing, while producing maximum volume or range, decreases the quantity of vocal cords vibrations that will be compressed and amplified and also restricts the passage of these diminished vocal cords vibrations, producing decreased re-sounding in the body resonators.

EDUCATED LAUGH. The disciplined, simulated laugh which extends vocal cords vibrations to the body extremities by the imposition of the Gan-Tone Pulsation on the natural vibrations of the singing voice.

The Compression Phase, or down-part of the Gan-Tone beat, takes the vocal cords vibrations and compresses and amplifies them to the rectal-pelvic basin from which they are thrust to the resonators on the Thrust Phase, or up-part of the Gan-Tone beat, extending the vocal cords from the bottom of the torso to the head resonators, since the entire body vibrates the frequency of the vocal cords.

Great speed is required of the singer in coordinating the feather-touch contact for activating the vocal cords to the desired frequency simultaneously with the vertical-elliptical mouth opening, the Jaw, Larynx, Body Fusion and the Gan-Tone Pulsation which, in turn, determines the speed with which the vocal cords vibrations penetrate the body to the rectal-pelvic basin and are thrust to the resonators. When this quick coordination is mastered by the singer, body suppleness is achieved, making the body resilient, enabling the singer to control the frequency of the simulated laugh, thus producing evenness and smoothness in the singing line. Great buoyancy and brilliance are also achieved, as a result of great depth and height in the simulated laugh.

EXALTATION OF SOUND. The maximum height achieved in the singing sound, regardless of pitch, when vocal cords vibrations maximally penetrate the depth of the body (rectal-pelvic basin), which is the action produced by the fusion and compression of vocal cords vibrations to the bottom of the torso on the Compression Phase, or down-part of the Gan-Tone beat, producing the reaction of maximal utilization of the body resonators on the Thrust Phase, or up-part of the Gan-Tone beat.

The frequency of the Gan-Tone imposition (5 to 7 Gan-Tones per second on the fundamental frequency) produces maximal height in the emitted sound, as a result of the maximal thrust of vocal cords vibrations to the body resonators on a series of Gan-Tone Pulsations, which results in a buoyant, resilient, scintillating, vibrant singing line.

The effectiveness of the Gan-Tone beat is dependent on the skill the singer achieves in fusing the jaw, larynx and body.

The degree to which the Gan-Tone beat amplifies, thrusts and re-sounds vocal cords vibrations in the body and its resonators is dependent on the body resilience developed by the Jaw, Larynx, Body Fusion which, in turn, determines the degree of exaltation, i.e., the height achieved in the singing sound, as a result of the degree of penetration of vocal cords vibrations to the depth of the body.

EXINVAC. The conscious application of a simulated yawn (inhalation) in the process of singing (exhalation) in order to draw air deeply into the body for the purpose of activating, compacting and thrusting vocal cords vibrations to the resonators, with speed and efficiency, on the Gan-Tone beat. EXhale is the emitted air and sound. INhale and VACuum are the characteristics of the natural yawn. Exinvac utilizes the two phases of the respiratory cycle (inhalation and exhalation) simultaneously in order to maximize body density.

The inhaled air is drawn downward through the body toward the rectal-pelvic basin along with the lungs, diaphragm and abdomen on the Compression Phase, or down-part of the Gan-Tone beat, creating vacuums in the cavities above the diaphragm. These vacuums cause a greater amount of air to rush into these expanded cavities, which intensifies compression, producing an equally intense thrust of vocal cords and body vibrations to the resonators on the Thrust Phase, or up-part of the Gan-Tone beat.

The speed and intensity produced in the vibrating air, as a result of the vacuums created by the Gan-Tone beats, enable vocal cords and body vibrations to be maximally re-sounded in the resonators of the body with a minimal expenditure of breath; enables the singer to attain one register in the voice.

FALSETTO VOICE. The natural male or female voice throughout the range of the vocal cords produced by not fusing the vocal cords to the larynx. Application of pressure while fusing the vocal cords to the larynx results in the so-called manly sound but limits the range of the vocal cords that can be utilized, as a result of increased pressure on the larynx, preventing the vocal cords from stretching upward for utilization of increased range.

The disparity between the falsetto and the laryngeal-body sound is greater in the male than in the female, since the laryngeal parts are larger and, therefore, further removed from the vocal cords than the female larynx, enabling the male to stretch the vocal cords to greater range than the female.

The falsetto is less discernible in the female than in the male, since the smaller laryngeal structure in the female causes a proximity of laryngeal parts, which include the vocal cords, making the vocal cords more directly involved with the larynx. Since the female sings an octave higher than the male, the vibrant frequency is doubled causing a more natural involvement of the larynx through fusion of laryngeal parts.

The male vocal cords are larger producing a lower frequency than the female vocal cords which are smaller. Since the male vocal cords are larger, they are capable of greater stretching, enabling the male to produce more range in the falsetto than the female.

Sound produced without descending vocal cords-laryngeal fusion.

FEATHER-TOUCH CONTACT. The minimum amount of pressure imposed on the vocal cords, the jaw, the throat muscles and the larynx to produce maximum compression of vocal cords and body vibrations to the rectal-pelvic basin which, in turn, produces maximum thrust of these vibrations to the resonators resulting in maximum resonance. Minimum pressure is maintained on these parts for the duration of the emitted sound with the maximum compression head maintained at the rectal-pelvic basin.

FEATHER-TOUCH FOR THE PRODUCTION AND PROJECTION OF SOUND. The spontaneity with which the mind activates vocal cords vibrations and deftly coordinates body parts for the amplification and thrust of these vibrations to the resonators.

FEEDBACK. The increase in the amplification of vocal cords and body vibrations by compression of fused body parts and vocal cords vibrations to the rectal-pelvic basin during the down-part of the Gan-Tone beat, or Compression Phase, and the omnidirectional thrust of these vibrations throughout the body on the up-part of the Gan-Tone beat, or Thrust Phase, causing a returning of these vibrations, by reverberation, to the area of fusion and compression for re-grounding at the rectal-pelvic basin and re-thrusting from this area. The degree of returning, by reverberation, is dependent on the intensity of the Compression Phase, or down-part of the Gan-Tone beat.

The vacuums created in the cavities by the Compression Phase, or down-part of the Gan-Tone beat, after compressing fused body parts and vocal cords vibrations to the rectal-pelvic basin, causes rarefaction in the resonating chambers. The vibrating air that is thrust to the resonators on the Thrust Phase, or up-part of the Gan-Tone beat, collides with the walls and the air in the resonators causing a thunderclap of sound. The volume and frequency of this thunderclap (reaction) is determined by the intensity and lightning speed of the Gan-Tone beat (action); produced by the simulated yawn (Exinvac Principle).

FREQUENCY OF THE GAN-TONE PULSATION. The number of times, per second, that the Gan-Tone Pulsation is imposed on the fundamental frequency, or pitch.

The Gan-Tone Pulsation can be imposed 5 to 7 times per second, regardless of the pitch, or frequency, being sung. The singing line is, therefore, composed of two frequencies: the fundamental frequency and the Gan-Tone frequency. The latter frequency does not alter the fundamental frequency but, instead, amplifies its dimensions.

FUNDAMENTAL FREQUENCY. The number of times per second that the vocal folds vibrate to produce the desired pitch being sung before the imposition of the Gan-Tone beat.

The vocal folds are extended through the body without altering the pitch, or fundamental frequency, when the Gan-Tone beat is imposed on the JLB Fusion. The body extremities reached by the vocal cords vibrations through this beat ultimately make up the structure of the singing sound.

FUNDAMENTAL VOCAL CORDS VIBRATIONS. The audible pulsations that emanate from the vocal cords, when a jet of air activates them to audibility.

The pitch of the sound, or fundamental, is determined by the number of pulsations per second that emanate from the vocal cords. These pulsations are registered by the mind as tension on the vocal cords. Frequency, or v.p.s. of the vocal cords, is equal to tension in the form of stretching or compressing through contraction of connecting muscles. The greater the tension, the greater the frequency, i.e., the higher the pitch.

FUSE. To closely unite body parts, from the vocal cords to the rectal-pelvic basin, on the JLB Fusion simultaneously with the compression of vocal cords and body vibrations to the rectal-pelvic basin on the Compression Phase, or down-part of the Gan-Tone beat.

FUSION. The blending of body parts, such as the jaw, tongue, hyoid bone, laryngeal cartilages, muscles and membranes, cricoid cartilage, rings of the trachea, chest bones and muscles, diaphragm muscle, abdomen and viscera, and the rectal-pelvic basin in order to create a column through the body for transmitting vocal cords vibrations to the rectal-pelvic basin and to create the structure necessary for the application of the Gan-Tone beat. This beat compresses, amplifies and thrusts vocal cords and body vibrations throughout the body, but especially to the resonators. The degree to which the singer can fuse body parts, maintain the vertical-elliptical mouth opening and apply the Gan-Tone beats to sustained sounds determines volume, or voice projection.

FUSION LAPSE. The period after the infant learns to speak, at which time he abandons the use of the Jaw, Larynx, Body Fusion in maximizing vocal cords vibrations to produce a loud, secure cry as a means of communication, until he becomes consciously aware of body fusion in the Gan-Tone Method.

The Jaw, Larynx, Body Fusion is a natural law with the non-speaking infant and is, therefore, a spontaneous, uninhibited action.

When the infant learns to communicate through speech, the need for loud sounds diminishes, since he is no longer helpless, but can walk and talk, making himself easily understood. Even though an infant's vocal apparatus is undeveloped, the volume he produces through fusion and compression of vocal cords vibrations is greater than the volume produced by many adults who are unaware of this Gan-Tone Principle. The involvement of the whole body as a vibrator, amplifier and resonator of vocal cords vibrations is a natural process with the infant.

GAN-TONE PULSATION. A superimposed vibration on the fundamental vocal cords vibrations which extends the amplitude of the fundamental vocal cords vibrations to the body extremities without altering the pitch. The increased amplitude of the vocal cords vibrations to the body extremities through the JLB Fusion and the Gan-Tone beat produces complete body involvement, causing the body to become the vibrator, amplifier and resonator of the vocal cords vibrations, thus extending the vocal folds through the body.

The Gan-Tone cycle consists of two phases: the Compression Phase and the Thrust Phase. The Compression Phase, or down-part of the Gan-Tone beat, consists of the feather-touch contact of air and muscle pressure on the vocal cords, Jaw, Larynx, Body Fusion, and compression of vocal cords vibrations to the rectal-pelvic basin for the amplification and grounding of these vibrations. The Thrust Phase, or up-part of the Gan-Tone beat, consists of the thrust of these vibrations from the rectal-pelvic basin to the body cavities for re-sounding. The degree of intensity of the Gan-Tone beat determines the degree of amplified vibratory energy to be re-sounded. Maximum intensity produces maximum re-sounding causing the body to resound as a bell.

The Gan-Tone beat maximizes vocal cords vibrations in the body while maximizing, and thus fully utilizing, the resonators. No instrument placed in the cavities of the mouth and chest for increasing the size of the cavities can be as effective as natural bodily functions, such as yawning and vomiting, which are simulated by the Gan-Tone beat.

The cycle of the Gan-Tone beat is governed by Newton's Law of Action and Reaction which states that for every action, there is an equal and opposite reaction. The intensity of the Compression Phase, or down-part of the Gan-Tone beat, determines the intensity of the Thrust Phase, or up-part of the Gan-Tone beat.

The degree of involvement of the Gan-Tone beat can consist of a superficial body penetration in conjunction with Jaw Sense for minimal vibratory aura to a maximal body penetration on the Jaw, Larynx, Body Fusion for maximal vibratory aura which encompasses the body extremities, thus making the amplitude of the Gan-Tone beat the controlling structure of the singing sound; coordinated contractive muscular action from the Pterygoideus lateralis muscle to the Sphincter ani externus muscle.

GAN-TONE REFERENCE POINTS. The Pterygoideus lateralis muscle in the head and the Sphincter ani externus muscle at the bottom of the torso. It is from these two reference points that the singing voice is controlled in the Gan-Tone Method making it possible to utilize the entire body as a bell in the production of the singing voice, when the Jaw, Larynx, Body Fusion and the Gan-Tone Pulsation are maximally applied, rather than focusing on parts, such as the vocal cords, throat muscles or diaphragm.

GENERATOR. The body, since it converts body energy, such as tension on the vocal cords, into audible vibrations, when this tension is acted upon by air from the lungs.

The body, since it generates, or creates, other vibrations as the Compression Phase, or down-part of the Gan-Tone beat, passes through body mediums, such as bones, etc.

The body, since it generates, or produces, an alternating current of these vibrations, i.e., vocal cords and body vibrations, with the Compression and Thrust Phases, or down-part and up-part of the Gan-Tone beat. The Compression Phase compresses vocal cords and body vibrations downward to the rectal-pelvic basin; the Thrust Phase thrusts these vibrations in the opposite direction to the body resonators.

GIGGLE. A laugh whose vibrations are confined to the vocal cords producing pure vocal cords sound, incorrectly referred to as the falsetto. The giggle is characterized by a high-pitched, feminine quality with a complete absence of resonant depth in the laugh.

GLASS JAW. The fragile quality of the jaw, when it is not coordinated to cope with the vocal tensions that develop in the singing process; jutting or wandering mandible.

When the jaw is not opened, down and back, and fused with the larynx and body in order to unify the solid parts, such as cartilages and bones, tension focuses on throat muscles and those muscles that control jaw movement, ultimately producing an oscillation of the jaw, making the jaw a weak link in the structure that sustains the singing sound, since this jaw oscillation, or series of uncontrollable spasms, causes the eventual collapse of the singing sound.

The Jaw, Larynx, Body Fusion and the Gan-Tone Pulsation make the jaw a strong link in the vocal structure, since the jaw becomes unified with the body. Any divergence, or moving outwardly, of the jaw, when sustaining loud, high sounds causes weakness to enter the body structure that produces the vocal sound.

GRADUATED JAW. The varied openings of the jaw in ascending and descending the scale, throughout the range, in order to maintain a minimum amount of vocal cords pressure, while maintaining maximum re-sounding of vibrational energy in the cavities of the head, throat and chest.

As pressure increases, while ascending the scale or singing extremely low notes, the jaw openings must increase in order to disperse this pressure.

Increased pressure, resulting from increased volume throughout the range, must be accommodated by increased jaw openings in order to transfer this pressure to the body, while maintaining minimum vocal cords pressure.

Diffusing increased pressure through the increased openings of the jaw involves the body in the production of the sound. However, lack of Jaw Sense, or alertness in opening the jaw to accommodate increased pressure, divorces the body in the production of the sound; governor of vocal vibrant energy.

GROUNDING OF VIBRATIONS. The fusion and compression of vocal cords and body vibrations to the rectal-pelvic basin, the foundation of the torso, in order to amplify and thrust these vibrations throughout the body and its cavities, where they are re-sounded, completing the circuit of one Gan-Tone Pulsation.

284 Singing Energy

GRUNTING DOWN. The act of compressing body parts to the rectal-pelvic basin, which is a constant action and a prerequisite for body support and the imposition of the Gan-Tone beat.

The act of fusing vocal cords and body vibrations through compressed body parts by descending, contractive, muscular action to the rectal-pelvic basin.

IDLING JAW. Lack of jaw (mandible) involvement in the fusion, compression and amplification of vocal cords and body vibrations, preventing the maximum amplification of these vibrations and the maximum utilization of the resonators, since the amount of fused and amplified vibrations are limited, producing minimal re-sounding in the resonators.

The jaw is uninvolved, uncontrolled, or idling, if it is not moved down and back and resting on the larynx as the need for more range, volume, depth and height increases. More volume necessitates more amplification and thrust of vibrations which can only be achieved when the jaw is fused to the larynx and body.

The idling, or uninvolved, jaw leads to the deterioration of the vocal structure by focusing pressure on muscles, rather than fused body parts, causing muscles to wobble and eventually collapse; wandering jawbone.

IMPASSE. The obstruction of vibrational movement throughout the body caused by vibratory absorption in the body mediums, such as, bones, cartilages and fluids, and the constriction of the re-sounding areas, or resonators, limiting the range and dimensions of the sound; produces nodes (swellings on the vocal folds) as a result of vocal vibratory complication.

This condition is remedied by fusion and compression of body parts, i.e., the Jaw, Larynx, Body Fusion, which maximize the transmission and amplification of vocal cords and body vibrations thereby maximizing the size of the re-sounding areas of the body, enabling the singer to encompass more range and dimensions of sound, since the pressures that result when ascending the scale are now diffused, from the vocal cords and surrounding muscles, to the body.

All singers who have limitations will develop more range and volume in the voice, when they master the coordination of the Jaw, Larynx, Body Fusion and the Gan-Tone Pulsation.

IMPULSES. The actions of mental energy through the nerves and muscle fibers which are registered as tension, or inaudible vibrations, in the vocal cords. This tension is brought to audibility as pitch, when a jet of air from the lungs passes through the vocal cords.

The actions of vibrant energy through the body produced by diffusing vocal cords vibrations to the body extremities on the Gan-Tone Pulsation.

INAUDIBLE VIBRATIONS. Mental impulses, registered in the vocal cords as tension, that are inaudible until made audible by a stream of air from the lungs passing through them.

INDIRECT RESONANCE. Vibrational energy in the vocal cords that is fused, compressed and amplified downward through the body by the Jaw, Larynx, Body Fusion and thrust upward to the resonators on the Gan-Tone beat. This energy is composed of vocal cords and body vibrations and is amplified in the body before it is re-sounded in the body cavities.

The direction of the vibrational energy is alternated, from the rectal-pelvic basin to the head resonators, on the Gan-Tone beat, at precise intervals per second that are determined by the singer, in order to penetrate the entire body for the purpose of amplification, thrust and re-sounding of this vibrational energy, making the entire body the vibrator, amplifier and resonator of this energy, giving the body a resounding quality, which results in an emitted sound of great depth and height.

The more intense the application of the Gan-Tone beat, the more intense the alternation of this vibrational energy, producing more effective vocal projection.

INNER LAUGH. The Gan-Tone Pulsations imposed on the fundamental frequency of the singing line, creating the effect of a simulated laugh through the body, from the rectal-pelvic basin to the head resonators, in order to amplify vocal cords and body vibrations and magnify the thrust of these vibrations, which are controlled from the rectal-pelvic center, thus maximizing the re-sounding of these vibrations in the body and its cavities. This maximum re-sounding produces brilliance, buoyancy, resiliency and vibrancy in the emitted sound.

The frequency of the Gan-Tone Pulsation, or inner laugh, is controlled by the singer (5 to 7 Gan-Tones per second) to produce a smooth line of sound; exalted vocal energy.

INTENSITY OF THE GAN-TONE APPLICATION. The degree of fusion applied to the jaw, larynx and body which determines the degree of effectiveness of the Gan-Tone beat.

The more fused the jaw, larynx and body, the more compressed and amplified the vocal cords vibrations on the Compression Phase, or down-part of the Gan-Tone beat, since the body becomes a strong conductor for the transmission and amplification of vocal cords vibrations to the rectal-pelvic basin, producing an equal amount of thrusting and re-sounding of these vibrations during the Thrust Phase, or up-part of the Gan-Tone beat.

The greater the degree of Jaw, Larynx, Body Fusion, the more effective the intensity of the Gan-Tone beat, producing greater depth and height in the emitted sound.

JAW. Mandible; the door of the body that controls the transmission, amplification and thrust of vocal cords and body vibrations throughout the body and its resonators, since the jaw is a circuit maker-breaker for the movement of vibrations throughout the body. When the jaw is opened and fused to the larynx and body, Vocal Vibratory Continuity is maximal. When the jaw moves toward closing and diverges from the larynx, Vocal Vibratory Continuity diminishes.

The jaw also determines the size of the resonators and mouth opening. The wider the door (jaw) opening, the larger the resonators and the greater the transmission and amplification of vocal cords and body vibrations which allows greater thrust of these vibrations to more spacious resonators; controls vocal vibrational output to the degree that it is fused to the larynx and torso.

JAW, LARYNX, BODY FUSION. The welding of the jaw and larynx to the torso in order to create a resilient body column through which the vocal cords vibrations can be grounded at the rectal-pelvic basin by means of the Feather-Touch Contact on the vocal cords and the Gan-Tone Pulsation.

The welding of body parts, from the jaw to the rectal-pelvic basin, includes the vocal cords, curve of the tongue, hyoid bone, nine laryngeal cartilages, spine, ligaments, muscles, cricoid cartilage, trachea, chest bones, lungs, diaphragm, and abdomen with viscera, in a voluntary tonic contractive muscular action.

The welding of body parts to the rectal-pelvic basin makes the body a dense, resilient agent for the transmission, amplification and thrust of vocal cords and body vibrations to the resonators on the Gan-Tone beat, while maximally opening the body cavities for maximal re-sounding of vibrations; descending contractive muscular action from the Pterygoideus lateralis muscle in the head to the Sphincter ani externus muscle at the bottom of the torso.

JAW, MOUTH, NOSE COORDINATION. The harmonious functioning of the jaw, mouth and nose as regulators for controlling the quantity and quality of the singing sound.

The unhinged position of the jaw with the Feather-Touch Contact on the larynx, the Jaw, Larynx, Body Fusion and the Gan-Tone Pulsation provide maximum Vocal Vibratory Continuity through body fusion and compression simultaneously opening the throat area for re-sounding a maximum of vocal cords and body vibrations to the body resonators. Any divergence of the jaw from the larynx constricts the throat opening, decreasing space in the resonators and the quantity of vibrations to be re-sounded. The restriction of vibrations in the throat causes a tight, reedy sound.

When the jaw is completely opened, the mouth opening determines the quantity and quality of re-sounded vibrations that will be emitted from the mouth. The wider the mouth opening, the greater the emission of resonant sound. The smaller the mouth opening, the more muffled and confined the resonant sounds within the mouth cavity.

When the jaw is unhinged, down and back, the mouth widely opened, the nostrils maximally opened and the Uvular Tympany maximally distended, nasal-oral-pharyngeal sound is emphasized without any reediness in the singing voice.

The smaller the opening of the jaw, mouth and nose, the greater the tightness and reediness of the emitted sound.

The wider the opening of the jaw, mouth and nose, the greater the depth and height in the emitted sound.

JAW SENSE. The sensitivity and speed the singer develops regarding the relationship of the jaw positions to the pressures encountered in the singing line that occur with increased range or volume.

Increased pitch, for ex., increases tension on the laryngeal muscles and vocal cords, as a result of increased vibrations. This tension is diffused as the jaw is moved down and back and resting on the larynx. This jaw movement welds the solid parts, such as bones and cartilages, protecting the muscles and membranes that are between the solid parts, through fusion. The solid parts become the stays for supporting the structure of sound under stress. This condition can occur only when the singer becomes sensitive to the absolute opening of the jaw as a valve for diffusing pressure from the vocal cords throughout the body; the swift perceptivity the singer develops to the jaw positions required for the diffusion of pressure from the larynx to the Sphincter ani externus muscle which simultaneously aids in generating and projecting vibrational energy from soft to loud sounds; the response the singer develops to the swift, maximal contraction of the Pterygoideus lateralis muscle for producing the maximal jaw opening necessary for the threading of vocal energy through vibrational complications (nodes) in the singing line.

LAUNCHING PAD. The floor of the rectal-pelvic basin from which vocal cords and body vibrations are thrust omnidirectionally throughout the body, but especially to the head resonators, on the Thrust Phase, or up-part of the Gan-Tone beat.

LEGATO. A singing line that sounds uninterrupted and is composed of, essentially, two vibrational frequencies: one called the fundamental, whose frequency determines pitch, and the other called the Gan-Tone Pulsation, which is imposed by the singer and does not alter the fundamental frequency but, instead, magnifies the dimensions of the fundamental pitch.

LIFTED POSITION OF THE SINGING SOUND. The expanded dimensions of the tone toward greater height, regardless of pitch or range, which is produced by the imposition of the Gan-Tone Pulsation on the fundamental frequency, causing vocal cords vibrations to penetrate omnidirectionally from the vocal cords throughout the body mediums.

The intensity of the Gan-Tone beat determines the degree of vibrational penetration through the body mediums (bones, air, cartilages and muscles) and its extremities. The greater the vibrational penetration to the body extremities, along with the Feather-Touch Contact on the vocal cords in the maintenance of pitch, the greater the vibrational aura omnidirectionally producing depth (penetration) and height (exaltation) in the emitted sound.

The degree of lift in the voice is, therefore, the reaction to the action, i.e., the intensity of the Compression Phase, or down-part of the Gan-Tone beat, downward through the body determines the intensity of the Thrust Phase, or up-part of the Gan-Tone beat, to the highest resonators of the body; exalted, vibrant sound.

LIPS. Two fleshy folds surrounding the orifice of the mouth which function as a lens for the focus and emission of vibrations.

The wider the opening of the lens, the less intense the focus of vibrations on the lips and the greater the emission of re-sounded vibrations, as a result of increased re-sounding space and increased mouth opening, giving the sound increased volume. The smaller the opening of the lens (lips), the more intense the focus of vibrations on the lips and the more confined the re-sounding vibrations, restricting and muffling the emitted sound. When the lips are completely closed, the nasal tract becomes the only vent for the emission of vocal cords vibrations.

The horizontal (smiling) position of the lips in the articulation of vowels decreases the size of the resonators, breaks vibratory continuity, constricts the throat opening, restricts vibrational movement and minimizes the thrust of vibrations, producing tightness, brittleness and reediness in the emitted sound.

The vertical-elliptical position of the lips, in the articulation of vowels, however, maximizes resonator size, vibratory continuity and thrust of vibrations, producing a maximally projected sound of great resilience, buoyancy, brilliance, depth and height, when the Gan-Tone Principles are deftly applied.

MANDIBLE. The lower jawbone which is attached to the skull essentially through muscles and ligaments; the switch, or link, that joins the head to the body during the singing process primarily through the contraction of the Pterygoideus lateralis muscle in the head making it possible to maximally augment the fundamental vocal cords vibrations to the two Gan-Tone reference points (Pterygoideus lateralis muscle in the head and the Sphincter ani externus muscle at the rectal-pelvic basin), when the Gan-Tone Pulsation is applied.

MASK. The face that conceals the cavities of the head for aiding in the re-sounding and projecting of the singing voice. The structure consists of the Frontal Bone, which is the forehead that extends across the supraorbital borders and contains an air sinus, or cavity, over each orbit, the Nasal Bones at the bridge of the nose, the Lacrimal Bones on either side of the Median Septum of the nose, the Nasal Fossae, the Sphenoid Bone and its two air sinuses, the Maxillary Bones (upper jaw), the Zygomatic Bones (cheek bones), the Palatine Bones (part of the roof of the mouth), Oral and Pharyngeal Cavities, the Ethmoid Bone (behind the Lacrimal Bones) with its numerous air sinuses, the Inferior Nasal Concha Bones, the Vomer Bone whose anterior point is the base of the nose, and the Mandible (lower jaw). The converging point of all these bones and cavities is the Nasion Center which is located near the bridge of the nose and can be considered the center of focus of the mask.

The anterior borders of the mask extend from the frontal sinuses (superior border) to the angle of the chin bone (inferior border). The lateral borders are the Zygomatic Bones, or cheek bones, which include the Zygomatic Arches, to where they meet the Condyle of the Mandible on each side of the head to the angle of the Ramus, which is the curve of the mandible (lower jaw), about 3 centimeters below the ear. The general configuration of the mask is conical. The profound, or posterior, apex is the median wall of the Sphenoid Sinuses within the cranium; and the base of the cone is the superficial area of the face.

In the Gan-Tone Method, the application of the Jaw, Larynx, Body Fusion and the Gan-Tone Pulsation causes vocal cords and body vibrations to be compressed to the bottom of the torso, at the Sphincter ani externus muscle, on the Compression Phase, or down-part of the Gan-Tone beat. These vibrations are thrust to this conical structure in the head on the Thrust Phase, or up-part of the Gan-Tone beat, for re-sounding in these cavities. The mask, therefore, is the loudspeaker whose cone shape aids in amplifying the dimensions of the projected sound; physical cover of tone; labyrinth of air cavities for compounding the cover of tone when the Gan-Tone Principles are applied.

MAXIMAL VIBRATIONAL FLOW. Minimal restriction, or maximum movement, of vocal cords vibrations, from the vocal cords throughout the body, below and above the vocal cords, when the Gan-Tone Principles are maximally applied with maximum speed in the coordination of body parts and the application of the Gan-Tone Pulsation, thus providing the framework for producing maximum freedom in the flow of vocal cords vibrations with minimal restriction and absorption of these vibrations, insuring maximal re-sounding of these vibrations which produces maximum dimensions of depth and height in the singing sound, giving this sound maximal buoyancy, projection, resilience and brilliance.

MESSA DI VOCE. The shading of a tone, from soft to loud and then diminishing to soft again, whose dimensions are determined by the Jaw, Larynx, Body Fusion, the Yawn (Exinvac Principle) and the Gan-Tone beat.

In shading a tone from soft to loud and then soft again (Messa di Voce), the depth and height of the softest as well as the loudest sound is maximized, when the Jaw, Larynx, Body Fusion, the Yawn and the Gan-Tone beat are maximally applied. Through compression, pressure and vocal cords vibrations are diverged from the vocal cords to the body. The Yawn causes the resonators to become enlarged. The penetration of vocal cords vibrations through the body mediums (bones, cartilages, muscles) to the rectal-pelvic basin on the Compression Phase, or down-part of the Gan-Tone beat, produces an aggregate of vocal cords and body vibrations, since the body mediums vibrate, producing body vibrations which are clustered together with vocal cords vibrations. Maximum compression of these vibrations to the rectal-pelvic basin on the Compression Phase, or down-part of the Gan-Tone beat, produces maximum depth which results in the reaction of maximum thrust of these vibrations to the enlarged resonators in the Thrust Phase, or up-part of the Gan-Tone beat.

The aggregate of vocal cords and body vibrations, the compression of these vibrations to the rectal-pelvic basin and the thrust of these vibrations throughout the body and its enlarged resonators add fullness, i.e., depth, breadth and height, to the softest as well as the loudest sound in the Messa di Voce.

METHOD. The application of principles, or laws, in an orderly procedure which results in similar reactions, if applied to similar subjects as, for ex., humans; otherwise, there are no rules and ultimately no method, since rules imply that, when applied, similar reactions will result.

Although the curved tract, or vocal hook, from the vocal cords to the mouth, the nostrils and jaw along with general body configuration vary with each individual, the basic structure is the same and characteristic of all humans implying that the procedure, or method, for mastering the aerodynamics in the vocal hook must be similar for all humans. However, the individual differences that result from the interaction of mind, body and air produce unique individual vocal characteristics in each human.

The Gan-Tone Principles are natural rules that are applied, in an orderly procedure, to all humans resulting in the generation, transmission, amplification, thrusting and re-sounding of vocal cords vibrations in the body and its cavities, producing maximum dimensions of vibrant energy in the singing sound.

Any infraction of these natural Gan-Tone laws focuses pressure in the vocal cords causing tension and rigidity through the body, producing anxiety in the singer, stifling the sound and decreasing the vibrant energy in the singing line, as a result of minimal Vocal Vibratory Continuity, as, for ex., when the jaw is allowed to ride up and away from the larynx, while sustaining loud, high sounds, it (jaw) acts as a circuit breaker separating the vocal cords vibrations from the body extremities, preventing these vibrations from flowing through the body. The responsibility for the expansion of the dimensions of vibrant energy in the singing line is, therefore, left to the throat muscles rather than the body.

The application of Gan-Tone laws which produce vocal harmony.

MIND, BODY AND AIR. The three forces whose interaction determines the pitch, compression, amplification and thrust of vocal cords and body vibrations throughout the body and its resonators, producing resonance that is emitted as vocal sound.

The mind formulates pitch as impulses, or vibrations, which are channeled through the nerves and muscles and focused in the vocal cords as tension, or inaudible vibrations, that is activated to audibility as air from the lungs passes through the tensed vocal cords. The coordination of body parts causes vocal cords vibrations to be compressed, amplified and thrust throughout the body and its cavities.

The degree of agile mental and physical coordination applied to the Gan-Tone Principles determines the quality and quantity of the emitted sound.

MODIFIED JAW, LARYNX, BODY FUSION. The moderate involvement of body parts in fusion, which results in a less intense application of the Gan-Tone Pulsation, as opposed to the maximal involvement in the Absolute Jaw, Larynx, Body Fusion which makes possible the most intense application of the Gan-Tone Pulsation.

The head is not tilted downward, but the jaw maintains contact with the larynx in order to insure fusion of the jaw, larynx and body. The pelvic pubis is not tilted upward from its vertical alignment. One knee is forward and slightly bent. One foot is solidly planted on the gound. The mandible is diverged maximally from the upper jaw and resting, with a Feather-Touch Contact, down and back, on the larynx.

In this modified position of the Jaw, Larynx, Body Fusion, contact is maintained between the two Gan-Tone reference points (Pterygoideus lateralis muscle in the head and the Sphincter ani externus muscle at the bottom of the torso), but the intensity of their involvement is modified, as opposed to their maximum involvement in the Absolute Jaw, Larynx, Body Fusion.

Since modified body fusion is applied concomitantly with the Compression Phase, or down-part of the Gan-Tone beat, the density of compressed vocal cords and body vibrations is lessened, as a result of less intensity in body fusion resulting in a less intense thrust of these vocal cords and body vibrations to the body resonators in the Thrust Phase, or up-part of the Gan-Tone beat. Nevertheless, these modified dimensions are ample for most types of singing, giving the sound unusual volume, depth, height and resilience. Vocal pressure is diverged to the body extremities rather than being focused in the neck area.

MULTIDIMENSIONAL SOUND. Tone of great depth, breadth, height, brilliance, buoyancy, resiliency and vibrancy produced by the spontaneous application of the Feather-Touch Contact on the vocal cords, the Jaw, Larynx, Body Fusion and the maximum application of the Gan-Tone beat, transforming the pure vocal cords vibrations into full-bodied sound, since these vibrations are fused, compressed and amplified throughout the body, and maximally resonant sound, since these amplified vibrations are re-sounded in maximally opened cavities and thrust, with great penetration, to the body extremities for great brilliance.

NASION CENTER. The focal point near the bridge of the nose where the bones and cavities, or sinuses, of the skull, i.e., the cranium and face, converge making this point the most concentrated area for the re-sounding of vocal cords and body vibrations, when the Jaw, Larynx, Body Fusion and the Gan-Tone Pulsation are applied.

The bones and cavities that converge at the Nasion Center are the Frontal Bone, which is the forehead, the Sphenoidal Bone, whose two sinuses are the most profound, and the Ethmoidal Bone and its numerous sinuses. These are Cranial Bones. The facial bones are the Nasal Bones, the Lacrimal Bones, the Maxillary Bones (upper jawbone), the Zygomatic Bones, the Inferior Nasal Concha Bones, the Vomer Bone, the Palatine Bones and the Mandible (lower jawbone). The remaining skull bones are two Parietal Bones, two Temporal Bones and one Occipital Bone which are not bones of the mask but they do complement the vibratory quality of the emitted sound.

The current of vocal cords and body vibrations thrust to this focal point (Nasion Center) on the Thrust Phase, or up-part of the Gan-Tone beat, from the Sphincter ani externus muscle at the rectal-pelvic basin, at a frequency of about 5 to 7 Gan-Tones per second, provides an intense impact of vibrations at this point defining the vibratory quality of every recess, bone and cavity of the entire head thereby giving the emitted sound the head tone peculiar to the characteristics of each skull. The more intense the application of the Gan-Tone Pulsation, the more defined the characteristics of coloration, or nuance, in the projected sound, since the vocal cords and body vibrations are being re-sounded in the Nasion Center with more intensity magnifying the vibrant and resonant qualities of the bones and cavities that are peculiar to each skull.

NATURAL LAUGH. A series of imposed vibrations on the natural frequency, or vibrations, of the laugh's pitch, i.e., a high-pitched or low-pitched laugh. The frequency and dimensions of the imposed vibrations are determined by the degree of emotional reaction to happiness, satisfaction, derision or thought sensations and are ultimately controlled and thrust from the rectal-pelvic area. The more spontaneous and intense the laugh, the greater the elation, producing more buoyancy, resiliency, depth and height in the laugh. The more sluggish the laugh, the greater the depression, producing a calculated, static laugh which lacks buoyancy and resilience.

288 Singing Energy

NATURAL SINGING. Singing without any signs of stress, as a result of the application of Gan-Tone Principles that consciously simulate natural processes, such as the Jaw, Larynx, Body Fusion which is characteristic of yawning, and the compression of body parts to the rectal-pelvic basin which is characteristic of vomiting, along with the simulated inner laugh which is characteristic of the Gan-Tone beat, for diffusing vocal cords pressure and muscle strain from the throat area to the body extremities, thus creating a systematic involvement of the entire body in the transmitting, amplifying, thrusting and re-sounding of vocal cords vibrations causing the body to resound as a bell.

NERVES. Channels for transmitting mental impulses which are registered as tension on the vocal cords through the contraction of attached muscles. This tension is vibrant energy, or inaudible vibrations that are brought to audibility as pitch by a jet of air from the lungs.

NODE. Knot, impasse, or break in ascending or descending the scale produced by the lack of awareness of Jaw Sense which constricts the vocal hook causing the restriction of vibrational energy; register in the voice; an irritation; a lesion such as a lump, or swelling, which occurs in the attempt to force a uniform dimension of vibrational energy through the constricted vocal hook.

OMNIDIRECTIONAL TRANSMISSION. The movement of vocal cords and body vibrations in all directions of the body, but especially to the resonators, through the application of the Gan-Tone beat and the Jaw, Larynx, Body Fusion.

Vocal cords vibrations are compressed to the rectal-pelvic basin, through fused body parts, becoming more amplified and also accumulating body vibrations, as a result of activating body mediums (bones, muscles, etc.) on the Compression Phase, or down-part of the Gan-Tone beat. These vocal cords and body vibrations are re-sounded in the body cavities after being thrust from the rectal-pelvic basin on the Thrust Phase, or up-part of the Gan-Tone beat.

OPEN THROAT. The perfect condition of the throat during the singing process, since it provides the widest passage for the maximum transmission of vocal cords vibrations throughout the body which, in turn, insures the maximum utilization of the resonators, enabling them to produce an emitted sound of maximum depth and height, regardless of volume and range, causing the body to function as a bell.

The open throat is achieved through mastery of Jaw Sense, Jaw, Mouth, Nose Coordination, Tongue English, Jaw, Larynx, Body Fusion, Uvular Tympany and Gan-Tone Pulsation, since these Gan-Tone procedures create the widest opening for the maximum flow of vibrations through the throat area which, in turn, determines the efficiency of the body cavities as resonators. The greater the Vocal Vibratory Continuity through the open throat, the more vibrations reach the resonators for re-sounding, causing the resonators to be maximally utilized in producing a multidimensional sound of great depth and height, regardless of volume and range.

If the jaw is partially closed, for ex., when singing loud, high, sustained sounds, the throat opening is diminished causing Vocal Vibratory Continuity and body fusion to be interrupted. The body's ability to amplify vocal cords vibrations is, therefore, diminished (regardless of the singer's bodily strength or weight) which, in turn, limits the body's ability to thrust these vibrations to the resonators, causing a minimal payload of vibrations to be re-sounded thus preventing the resonators from being maximally utilized.

The degree to which the throat is opened determines the degree to which the body functions as a bell. The wider the throat opening, the greater the Vocal Vibratory Continuity, allowing greater amplification, thrust and re-sounding of these vibrations, causing the body to become a complete vibrator and resonator.

The singer's vocal strength, in the Gan-Tone Method, is equated in terms of his ability to fuse and compress body parts, irrespective of muscular development and weight.

OSCILLATION. The dimensions of the Gan-Tone vibration in one cycle. This oscillation begins at the vocal cords, extends downward to the rectal-pelvic basin on the Compression Phase, or down-part of the Gan-Tone beat, and upward to the septum and sinus cavities above the bridge of the nose on the Thrust Phase, or up-part of the Gan-Tone beat, creating the structure, or amplitude, of the singing sound.

The frequency of the Gan-Tone beat (5 to 7 Gan-Tones per second on the fundamental frequency) projects a singing sound whose dimensions are determined by the intensity of the application of the Gan-Tone beat. The greater the intensity of the Compression Phase, or down-part of the Gan-Tone beat, the greater the amplitude of the penetrating wave of fused body parts and amplified vocal cords and body vibrations to the rectal-pelvic basin, producing a commensurate reaction of re-sounding of these vibrations in the body cavities on the Thrust Phase, or up-part of the Gan-Tone beat, provided the Jaw, Larynx, Body Fusion is applied, with great speed, in order to insure that the cavities are maximally opened and maximal Vocal Vibratory Continuity is maintained, in a strong columnar structure, to the bottom of the torso.

No conventional, traditional method of singing can produce a sound that so thoroughly utilizes the body cavities and the body extremities as the Gan-Tone Method. Sound produced by the Gan-Tone Method is characterized by great buoyancy, resiliency, depth, height and brilliance.

Oscillation of body parts, such as the jaw, throat muscles, larynx, diaphragm and abdomen, (since they are not aligned with body fusion) or oscillation produced by a vibrato, in order to give the emitted sound dimensions of depth and height, will result in muscle spasm and collapse of the vocal structure. The only oscillation for vocal control is a unified body oscillation produced by the JLB Fusion and the Gan-Tone Pulsation, which is controlled from the Pterygoideus lateralis muscle in the head to the Sphincter ani externus muscle at the bottom of the torso.

Any oscillation of body parts in isolation divorces the vocal structure from the body, preventing the complete utilization of the body as a bell and contributing to the instability and ultimate collapse of the vocal structure.

The Gan-Tone beat, however, produces a body oscillation that gives great cohesion, direction and resilience to body parts by fusing and compressing these parts, along with vocal cords vibrations, to the rectal-pelvic basin. This body oscillation, therefore, is a composite of vocal cords vibrations and vibrations produced by vibrating body mediums.

OVERTONES. Undertones that are produced by the fusion and compression of vocal cords and body vibrations to the rectal-pelvic basin on the Compression Phase, or down-part of the Gan-Tone beat, and thrust from this basin to the body cavities for re-sounding as overtones on the Thrust Phase, or up-part of the Gan-Tone beat; audible venting of undertones; the higher tones, or upper partials, which are a reaction to the action of undertones.

Current belief stresses the presence of overtones in isolation without realizing that overtones cannot exist without the presence of undertones, since overtones are the reaction of undertones.

The Jaw, Larynx, Body Fusion and the Gan-Tone Pulsation add dimensions of depth and height to the emitted sound unattainable by any other procedure, since the greater the intensity of the Compression Phase, or down-part of the Gan-Tone beat, the greater the production of undertones which, in turn, creates an equal amount of overtones in the Thrust Phase, or up-part of the Gan-Tone beat, giving the emitted sound greater height, which is the result of greater depth.

OVERTONES CYCLE. The many higher sounds which, with the fundamental pitch, make up the complex brilliant tones created by the imposition of one Gan-Tone Pulsation, or cycle, on the fundamental frequency. The imposition of this beat 5 to 7 times per second on the fundamental frequency, for the duration of a sustained sound, constitutes the singing line.

The more swift and intense the application of the Gan-Tone beat, the more audible the integral pitches that occur in the fundamental pitch, producing more audible facets for brilliance in the emitted sound, since the degree of intensity of the Gan-Tone Pulsation determines the degree of amplification of vocal cords and body vibrations which produces undertones of equal depth on the Compression Phase, or down-part of the Gan-Tone beat, resulting in overtones of equal height on the Thrust Phase, or up-part of the Gan-Tone beat, caused by more intense vibratory penetration in the body extremities.

PAYLOAD. The amount of vibrations generated by the vocal cords and body and re-sounded in the body cavities.

The amount of vibrations, or payload, re-sounded in the body cavities is dependent on the speed and intensity of the application of the Gan-Tone beat. The greater the intensity, the greater the amplification and transmission of vocal cords and body vibrations to the resonators.

PELVIC BREATHING. Maximal utilization of air in producing the singing sound by fusing and compressing air, body parts and vocal cords vibrations to the rectal-pelvic basin, the controlling center for the amplification and thrust of vocal cords and body vibrations to the resonators, thus making the body an extension of the vocal cords and lungs.

Pelvic breathing extends the dimensions of the singing sound from the area of the vocal cords and throat to the body extremities, causing the body to become the amplifier and thrusting agent of vocal cords vibrations, therefore, requiring less stress on the vocal cords and lungs and less breath to produce the singing sound, giving greater support and strength to the lungs and greater control over the air impinging on the vocal cords.

PELVIC-PERINEUM DIAPHRAGMATIC STRUCTURE. The partition that separates the torso from the legs and is composed of muscles and sinews. Its center is the Sphincter ani externus muscle. This partition, in the Gan-Tone Method, is considered the most profoundly resilient point of the body for determining body fusion, breath control, amplification of vocal cords and body vibrations, and thrust and re-sounding of these vibrations to the body resonators. It is, therefore, the controlling center for the projection of the singing voice; Pelvic-Urogenital diaphragm.

PENETRATION. The profound diffusion of vocal cords vibrations omnidirectionally throughout the body on the Gan-Tone beat, which maximizes vibrations and resonance, making the body resound as a bell.

The intense application of the Compression Phase, or down-part of the Gan-Tone beat, fuses and compresses vocal cords vibrations to the rectal-pelvic basin, making the entire body the vibrator and amplifier of vocal cords and body vibrations. This action produces the commensurate reaction of thrusting these vibrations to the body resonators (Thrust Phase, or up-part of the Gan-Tone beat), causing a profound permeation and re-sounding of these vibrations in the bones and cavities of the body.

PISTON. The vertical column of pressure imposed by the singer through the cylinder of the body, which consists of fused and compressed body parts and vocal cords vibrations to the rectal-pelvic basin, or bottom of the cylinder, on the Compression Phase, or down-part of the Gan-Tone beat.

PITCH. The balance of mind, body and air that is responsible for the characteristic quality of a musical tone by producing the appropriate frequency of vibrations per second of the vocal cords. This frequency of vibrations is channeled by the mind through muscles and is registered as tension, or inaudible vibrations, in the vocal cords. A jet of air from the lungs makes these vibrations audible.

The frequency of vibrating sound waves, which produces pitch, is extended to the body extremities, i.e., the bottom of the torso and the head cavities, on the Gan-Tone Pulsation through the Jaw, Larynx, Body Fusion establishing a balance of undertones and overtones, below and above the vocal cords. This balance of undertones and overtones enables the singer to achieve the center of the tone for any pitch, or frequency of vibrations being sung.

Pitch produced with the Gan-Tone beat has the highest degree of definition, since the Gan-Tone Pulsation has a controlled frequency of its own (5 to 7 Gan-Tones per second on the fundamental). The amplitude of each Gan-Tone Pulsation extends to, and is controlled from, the rectal-pelvic basin thus extending the amplitude, or dimensions, of the fundamental from the rectal-pelvic basin to the most remote, vibrant areas of the head, such as the frontal air sinus cavities. Control of vocal cords and body vibrations from this basin makes possible a maximum definition of thrust, impact and re-sounding of these vibrations in the body cavities which could not be achieved from any other area of the body.

POPULAR SINGING. Conversation-like singing that emphasizes lyrics as the dominant element of communication rather than the singing line. Vocal cords vibrations are confined primarily to the vocal cords rather than diffused and amplified throughout the body requiring, therefore, a minimal application of the Jaw, Larynx, Body Fusion and the Gan-Tone beat; singing requiring minimal control of vocal energy.

PRESSURE. Body Fusion utilized in the production of the singing voice through the JLB Fusion and the Gan-Tone Pulsation; the natural inclination to focus tension on neck muscles during the singing process, as a result of the divergence of body parts preventing the diffusion of pressure, or tension, from the vocal cords and neck to the bottom of the torso. Fusion of the jaw, larynx and body and the application of the Gan-Tone beat remove tension from the vocal cords and neck muscles that results from increased range and volume, and diffuse this tension throughout the body. This tension becomes the structure for amplifying, thrusting, re-sounding and projecting the voice from the body.

PTERYGOIDEUS LATERALIS. A short, thick muscle on either side of the head, just below eye level, which is inserted into the condyle of the mandible. This muscle opens the jaws, when it contracts, by pulling the condyle forward thereby rotating the chin down and back causing the mandible (lower jaw) to rest on the larynx, consequently, providing the structure for the application of the Jaw, Larynx, Body Fusion and the Gan-Tone Pulsation. The movement downward of vibrant energy from this muscle to the Sphincter ani externus muscle comprises the Compression Phase, or down-part of the Gan-Tone beat; the superior Gan-Tone reference point in the head that makes possible body fusion to the Sphincter ani externus muscle in the rectal-pelvic basin, which is the inferior and most profound Gan-Tone reference point, thereby providing the extreme boundaries for the vibratory structure of the fundamental frequency, when the Gan-Tone Pulsation is imposed on this frequency; the muscle in the head that is responsible for minimizing stress on throat muscles during the singing process.

PURE VOCAL CORDS SOUND. Audible vocal cords vibrations without the involvement of the fused larynx throughout the entire range of the voice referred to as the falsetto voice.

PYRAMIDAL STRUCTURE OF SOUND. The conical path through which vocal cords and body vibrations alternate on the Gan-Tone beat. The base of the pyramid, or cone, is the rectal-pelvic basin. The apex of the pyramid is the septum of the frontal sinus cavities.

During the Compression Phase, or down-part of the Gan-Tone beat, vocal cords and body vibrations are fused and compressed downward along with body parts, such as the tongue, hyoid bone, thyroid and cricoid cartilages, muscles and ligaments of the larynx, trachea, chest bones, and organs, such as the lungs, diaphragm, abdomen and viscera, to the rectal-pelvic basin. This grunting down process is a conscious, contractive, muscular action which is produced in many natural body functions, such as yawning and vomiting.

Vocal cords and body vibrations are, therefore, compressed to the rectal-pelvic basin, which can be considered the base of the pyramid and the controlling center for the amplification and thrust of vocal cords and body vibrations. During the Thrust Phase, or up-part of the Gan-Tone beat, which is the equal and opposite reaction to the action of the Compression Phase, or down-part of the Gan-Tone beat, vocal cords and body vibrations are thrust throughout the body and its cavities for re-sounding, reaching the apex of the pyramid, which is the septum of the frontal sinus cavities.

RANGE. The gamut of the male and female voice produced through the vocal cords without laryngeal fusion and through a limited portion of the vocal cords with laryngeal fusion.

RECTAL-PELVIC BASIN. The controlling center for the fusion of body parts; the controlling center for the compression, generation and magnification of vocal cords and body vibrations during the Compression Phase, or down-part of the Gan-Tone beat; the controlling center for the thrust and focus of vocal cords and body vibrations to the resonators for re-sounding on the Thrust Phase, or up-part of the Gan-Tone beat.

The contractive merging of muscles, such as the cervical, thoracic, diaphragmatic and abdominal, fuses and compresses body parts with vocal cords and body vibrations to the rectal-pelvic basin on the Gan-Tone Pulsation producing an amplification of these vibrations in this basin not possible in any other area of the body as, for ex., the throat or chest. The amalgamation of muscles and body parts with vocal cords and body vibrations in the rectal-pelvic basin, produced by the JLB Fusion and the Gan-Tone Pulsation, determines the dimensions of the singing sound. The degree of intensity of the Compression Phase, or down-part of the Gan-Tone beat, produces a compression, or grounding, of vocal cords and body vibrations in the rectal-pelvic basin which results in a commensurate thrust of these vibrations to the highest head resonators on the Thrust Phase, or up-part of the Gan-Tone beat, resulting in intense re-sounding of these vibrations and, therefore, giving the emitted sound great height.

The thrusting of vocal cords and body vibrations to the highest head resonators would be an impossibility, if the controlling center were not the rectal-pelvic basin.

RECTAL-PELVIC BREATH CONTROL. The utilization of the breath in the singing process whose efficiency is controlled from the rectal-pelvic basin. Control of the breath from this center maximizes the strength, quality, quantity and thrust of this air pressure enabling the singer to focus and re-sound vibrating air in the highest resonating cavities, which would be impossible if the air were controlled from the thoracic diaphragm or from any other area of the body; regulation of the breath in the singing process through contractive muscular action from the Pterygoideus lateralis muscle (head) to the Sphincter ani externus muscle (bottom of the torso).

REGISTERS. Non-existent in the Gan-Tone Method; the change in tonal quality when moving from low to high sounds and vice versa, which has led to the belief of registers, occurs when Vocal Vibratory Continuity is interrupted, i.e., when the movement of vibrations throughout the body, especially in the throat area and other cavities, is impeded causing aerodynamic changes which result in variations in tonal quality.

Orienting the beginner to the coordination involved in the Jaw, Larynx, Body Fusion, when ascending or descending the scale, makes the student completely free of so-called registers, since he develops an even scale from the beginning, as a result of becoming sensitive to vocal vibratory harmony. The student also becomes aware of the degree of Vocal Vibratory Continuity in other singers.

Registers, therefore, are the result of the singer's ignorance regarding the natural laws that govern the coordination of body parts for transmitting the varied quantities of vocal cords vibrations throughout the body that are produced in the singing scale, i.e., the higher the range, the greater the frequency of vibrations and the greater the need to coordinate body parts in order to prevent the impedence of these vibrations and thus prevent changes in tonal quality. Increased vibrations and increased amplitude, for ex., require that the jaw be completely down and back and fused to the larynx and body in order to increase the throat opening which, in turn, prevents the impedence of vocal cords vibrations.

RESONANCE. The dimension of vibrational energy produced in the singing sound which is dependent on the degree of body fusion and the intensity of the Gan-Tone beat.

The greater the intensity of the Jaw, Larynx, Body Fusion and the Gan-Tone beat, the greater the penetration, amplification and re-sounding of vibrations through body mediums, whose vibratory characteristics color the fundamental pitch, giving the emitted sound greater volume, depth, height, resilience, buoyancy, brilliance and the distinct timbre that is peculiar to each individual, as a result of individual differences in size, shape and position of body mediums (bones, cartilages, muscles, etc.).

RESONATORS. Cavities of the body, such as the sinuses, head and chest, in which vocal cords and body vibrations are re-sounded.

The degree to which these cavities are utilized for re-sounding these vibrations is dependent on the intensity of the application of the Jaw, Larynx, Body Fusion and the Gan-Tone Pulsation.

RE-SOUNDING. The reverberating of amplified vocal cords and body vibrations throughout the body, but specifically in the resonating cavities, or speakers, of the body during the Thrust Phase, or up-part of the Gan-Tone beat.

RESOUNDING BODY. The entire body involved as a vibrator and resonator of the original vocal cords vibrations, making the body appear to be filled with sound.

ROCK AND ROLL SINGING. A form of popular singing that is greatly influenced by a conversation-like production of sound. Melodic lines, involving a wide range and loud, high sounds, are produced by blatantly attacking the vocal cords. Extremely high range is produced by pure vocal cords sound with no laryngeal fusion.

SEPTUM. The partition that separates the frontal air sinus cavities, which is the point in the head for the most brilliant re-sounding of vocal cords and body vibrations. Any partition, whether bony, cartilaginous or muscular, is a vibrator and re-sounder of vibrations, such as the pelvic-perineum diaphragm in the rectal-pelvic basin, which separates the torso from the legs; the thoracic diaphragm, which separates the chest cavity from the abdomen; the palate, or roof of the mouth, which separates the oral from the nasal tract.

SINGING. Musical tones created by physical tension which is produced by mental tension in the form of impulses transmitted to the muscles that control the vocal cords through nerves causing these muscles to relax and contract thereby producing tension on the cords, or inaudible vibrations, that is brought to audibility by a jet of air from the lungs passing through them. These vocal cords vibrations are amplified and re-sounded in the body extremities (rectal-pelvic basin and head resonators) through the Jaw, Larynx, Body Fusion and the Gan-Tone Pulsation, producing musical tones of great depth and height.

SINGING ENERGY. The audible manifestation of vocal cords vibrations, from the pure vocal cords sound, produced without laryngeal fusion, to the full-bodied, open-throated, head-resonant sound, produced with laryngeal fusion, the Feather-Touch Contact on the vocal cords, the Jaw, Larynx, Body, Fusion and the Gan-Tone beat to the rectal-pelvic basin and the head resonators.

The more intensely body fusion and the Gan-Tone beat are applied, the more intense the singing energy, producing intense radiance, buoyancy, resilience, depth, height, brilliance and volume in the emitted sound, as a result of more intense compression of vocal cords vibrations to the rectal-pelvic basin resulting in more intense thrust of these vibrations to the body resonators and especially those resonators of the head.

SINGING LINE. A series of superimposed pulsations, or Gan-Tones, on the fundamental vibrations of musical tones which extends the amplitude of these fundamental vocal cords vibrations to the body extremities, i.e., to the rectal-pelvic basin downward and upward to the head resonators.

SINGING SOUND. Tone produced by two concomitant processes of oscillation; the first process is the fundamental frequency

292   Singing Energy

and its integral parts, such as harmonics, overtones and partials, and the second process is the imposition of the Gan-Tone Pulsation on the fundamental frequency which extends the dimensions of the fundamental vibrations and increases the number of integral parts of these vibrations.

The Compression Phase, or down-part of the Gan-Tone beat, causes the fundamental vocal cords vibrations to penetrate deeply through the body, vibrating the body mediums, thus adding more facets to the fundamental sound.

The Thrust Phase, or up-part of the Gan-Tone beat, causes the fundamental vocal cords vibrations and body vibrations to be transmitted to the body cavities for re-sounding, with special emphasis on the head resonators.

SINKING THE BREATH. The compacting of inspired air toward the rectal-pelvic basin on the Compression Phase of the Gan-Tone Pulsation.

The degree of intensity of the Gan-Tone beat determines the degree of compression of fused body parts and air pressure. The greater the compression, the greater the air pressure, since the lungs are now fused with the elements of the chest and the abdomen to the rectal-pelvic basin giving the lungs great power and control over the thrust of air, as a result of being reinforced by complete body involvement, extending the strength of the lungs to the rectal-pelvic basin.

The degree to which the breath is compacted to the rectal-pelvic basin is dependent upon the intensity of the Gan-Tone Pulsation. The more intense the Compression Phase, or down-part of the Gan-Tone beat, the greater the sinking of the breath to the rectal-pelvic basin.

The sinking of the breath to the bottom of the torso can only occur through the fusion and compression of body parts and vocal cords vibrations on the Gan-Tone Pulsation.

SINUS CAVITIES. The hollow caves below, above and beyond the bridge of the nose that re-sound vocal cords and body vibrations, as a result of the amplification and thrust of these vibrations from the rectal-pelvic basin on the Thrust Phase, or up-part of the Gan-Tone beat.

SOUND CONFIGURATION. The utilization of the greatest amount of vibrational energy in the process of singing vowels and consonants made possible through the imposition of the Gan-Tone beat on the fundamental vocal cords vibrations.

SPARK. The minimum jet of air required to activate the vocal cords to vibrate at any pitch with a minimum amount of pressure, or tension, on the vocal cords to maintain the pitch. The jet of air is the spark that brings inaudible vibrations to audibility.

SPEAKERS. The cavities of the body in which audible vocal cords vibrations are re-sounded, such as the sinus, nasal, oral, pharyngeal, laryngeal, tracheal, bronchial and thoracic cavities; the cavities of the body that function as vents for projecting the singing voice.

SPHINCTER ANI EXTERNUS. The rectal muscle at the bottom of the torso which is about one inch wide and about three and one half inches in anteroposterior length and is constantly in a state of involuntary tonic contraction. This muscle is the focal point of body fusion, compression of vocal cords and body vibrations and is the controlling center for thrusting, re-sounding and projecting vocal cords and body vibrations on the Thrust Phase, or up-part of the Gan-Tone beat;   the inferior reference point at the bottom of the torso to which vocal cords and body vibrations are compressed when the Pterygoideus lateralis muscle, the superior Gan-Tone reference point, contracts, causing the mandible to be fused to the larynx thereby uniting the head to the body, which provides the two extreme boundaries for the amplification of the fundamental frequency as long as the Jaw, Larynx, Body Fusion and the Gan-Tone Pulsation are applied;   the focal point of the pelvic-perineum diaphragm for the support of sound, in the Gan-Tone Method, rather than the thoraco-abdominal diaphragm, which is the conventional belief.

SPINAL-PELVIC CURVE. The position of the head, spine and pelvis assumed by the Gan-Tone singer during the Absolute Jaw, Larynx, Body Fusion.

The head is tilted forward and downward. The jaws are maximally diverged. The lower jaw, or mandible, is resting on the larynx. The pubis, or front part of the pelvis, is pulled upward by the Rectus Abdominis Muscle causing the spine to curve and making the anterior part of the body concave. Since the head is forward and downward and the pelvis is forward and pulled upward at the pubis, the head, spine and pelvis assume an arched configuration. In this position, the knees are bent to aid pelvic rotation.

This arched configuration of the head, spine and pelvis compacts the body reducing the distance between the Pterygoideus lateralis muscle in the head and the Sphincter ani externus muscle at the bottom of the torso, thus insuring maximal body density and maximal compression of vocal cords and body vibrations to the Sphincter ani externus muscle on the Compression Phase, or down-part of the Gan-Tone beat, which results in maximal resilience and thrust of these vibrations to the head resonators on the Thrust Phase, or up-part of the Gan-Tone beat. The definition of intensity of the Gan-Tone beat to the Sphincter ani externus muscle, made possible by the curve of the head, spine and pelvis along with the bent knees, determines the involvement of the legs in producing total body density and resilience for the production and projection of the human voice;   spring-like curve of the entire body upon which Gan-Tone Principles are structured and maximized.

SPIRIT. Energy;   the principle of life which is manifest in the human as vibrations.

The degree of energy, or spirit, in the singing sound, which is manifested as brilliance, is determined by the degree of speed and intensity with which the Gan-Tone Pulsation is imposed on the fundamental vibrations, or pitch, of the sound being sung.

The more quickly and efficiently the Jaw, Larynx, Body Fusion is applied and the greater the intensity of the Gan-Tone Pulsation, the greater the fusion and compression of vocal cords and body vibrations and body parts to the rectal-pelvic basin enabling the body to resist deformation, thus reducing the absorption of vibrations and increasing the speed and intensity of the vibrational flow throughout the body, but especially to the resonators and the body extremities, thereby maximizing the body as a conductor for the transmission, amplification and thrust of vocal cords and body vibrations.

The greater the speed and intensity in applying the Jaw, Larynx, Body Fusion and the Gan-Tone Pulsation, the greater the degree of energy, or spirit, in the singing sound which is characterized by great billiance that is produced by the vibrant energy emitted from vibrant body parts, such as the vocal cords, larynx, chest, head and rectal-pelvic basin.

SPONTANEOUS APPLICATION. The utilization of the Gan-Tone Principles with instantaneous action in order to maintain maximum dimensions and uniformity in the emitted sound.

Lack of spontaneity in the coordination of body parts diminishes the dimensions of the emitted sound, since sluggishness constricts body parts, particularly the resonators, restricting the movement, amplification and re-sounding of vibrations. If, for ex., maximum volume and height are desired, the mouth must be opened wide instantly. If the mouth is only partially opened during these moments, the sound is diminished in volume and height, since the resonating chambers are smaller and vibratory continuity and amplification are, therefore, decreased.

STACCATO. A singing line that is comprised of detached sounds of short duration and is characterized by an interrupted flow of vocal cords vibrations throughout the body, since body fusion and compression of vocal cords vibrations to the bottom of the torso are interrupted according to the frequency of the staccato.

SUPERIMPOSED PULSATION. The Gan-Tone beat that extends the amplitude of vocal cords vibrations to the body extremities, i.e., from the rectal-pelvic basin to the head resonators, by fusing and compressing vocal cords vibrations to the rectal-pelvic basin on the Compression Phase, or down-part of the Gan-Tone beat, and then thrusting and re-sounding these vibrations in the head resonators on the Thrust Phase, or up-part of the Gan-Tone beat, in order to attain the maximum dimensions of depth, height and volume along with maximum control of the emitted sound.

SUPPORT (APPOGGIO). The amount of fusion and compression of vocal cords and body vibrations to the bottom of the torso necessary to sustain a quantity of resonant sound. These vibrations are fused and compressed to the rectal-pelvic basin, the controlling center for the maximum support of sound, on the Compression Phase, or down-part of the Gan-Tone beat. The degree of sound sustained is commensurate with the degree of fusion and compression produced and the intensity with which vocal cords vibrations penetrate from the vocal cords throughout the body.

SWITCH. The jaw, which acts as a circuit maker or breaker for uniting or separating the head, larynx and body as a circuit for transmitting a current of vibrations.

When the jaw rests on the larynx in an unhinged positon, close to the collar bone, or jugular notch, and the back of the tongue is forward and downward, the head is fused to the larynx and torso, producing the strongest circuit for the current of vibrations. Any divergence of the jaw from this position breaks the circuit limiting Vocal Vibratory Continuity.

TENSION. The focus of mental energy in the vocal cords causing them to vibrate producing inaudible vibrations which are brought to audibility by a jet of air from the lungs; the tightening of throat muscles when vocal cords vibrations are restricted in the throat area, rather than diffused through the body on the Jaw, Larynx, Body Fusion and the Gan-Tone Pulsation, producing a tightening of other body parts, such as the face, shoulders, neck and abdomen, which increases anxiety in the singer and causes a shrinking, or converging, of the dimensions of depth and height of the sound to the throat area; isolated strain harnessed as body resilience with the Jaw, Larynx, Body Fusion and the Gan-Tone Pulsation.

THRUST. The projection and reverberation of vocal cords and body vibrations in the body and its resonators on the Thrust Phase, or up-part of the Gan-Tone beat. The intensity of this projection and reverberation is dependent on the intensity of the Compression Phase, or down-part of the Gan-Tone beat.

THRUST PHASE. The reaction to the Compression Phase, or down-part of the Gan-Tone beat, which projects vocal cords and body vibrations to the body extremities, but especially to the head resonators. The intensity of the Thrust Phase is equal to the intensity of the Compression Phase demonstrating Newton's Law of Action and Reaction which states that for every action there is an equal and opposite reaction.

TIMBRE. The quality of tone that distinguishes different voices, as a result of the variations in the vibratory frequency of body mediums, such as the vocal cords, larynx, bones and abdomen.

Vibratory frequency is affected by the individual differences in size, shape and position as, for ex., larger male chest bones produce a lower frequency than smaller male chest bones because of their larger size, giving the emitted sound greater depth.

These variations become more manifest in the emitted sound as the Gan-Tone Pulsation is applied more intensely, since vibrations become more magnified.

TIME AND MOVEMENT RELATIONSHIP. The spontaneity applied to the movement from consonants to vowels and the spontaneity in the application of the Gan-Tone Pulsation suspends time and the movement of sound.

Sluggishness in the articulation of consonants and vowels makes tone labored, which lays heavy on the listener.

Spontaneity of application makes sounds of long or short duration or prolonged singing move quickly for the listener, since the maximized dimensions of the sound demand total absorption of the listener, making him lose track of time. Therefore, however prolonged the sound, it seems to be terminated too quickly.

TONGUE ENGLISH. The movement of the tongue, from the tip to the root, by the mental imposition of pressure on this curved surface. These pressure points on the tongue provide maximum flow and amplification of vocal cords vibrations through the vocal hook, or curved tract, from the vocal cords to the mouth and nostrils, by maximally opening and stabilizing this curved tract, thus creating more vibrations and more space for the re-sounding of these vibrations which aid in producing body fusion and promoting the efficiency of the other body cavities, since they are being more fully utilized as resonators, as a result of increased vibrations.

TONGUE WHEEL. The curve of the tongue midway from the tip to the root can be considered the hub of a wheel. The tongue is stabilized by the contraction of the Genioglossi and Hyoglossi muscles. The Genioglossi moor the tip to the back of the lower teeth and gum. The Hyoglossi fuse the tongue downward. The spokes of the wheel are the points on the surface where pressure is imposed. The rim of the wheel is the aura of resonance created by the increased vibrations and resonating space resulting from the variety of pressure points, or spokes, on the hub, or curve, of the tongue. This aura is reflected in all the resonators and the resultant emitted sound.

The greater the imposition of pressure points, or spokes, on the hub, or curved surface, the greater the aura, or dimensions of resonance, in the throat, pharynx and other body cavities thereby minimizing vibrational absorption and maximizing vibrational energy.

TOTAL VIBRATOR. The complete involvement of the body as an oscillator of vocal cords and body vibrations in the singing process, as a result of the application of Gan-Tone Principles.

TREMOLO. An exaggerated vibrato that creates a wobbling in the singing line which vacillates between two pitches. The higher of the two pitches is the intended tone.

This exaggerated vibrato, which is undesirable, is produced through lack of fusion of body parts, such as bones, cartilages, ligaments and muscles, causing pressure to be focused on muscles which spasm, distorting the vibratory pattern by interfering with the air intensity focused on the vocal cords and the pressure within the laryngeal cavity and throat, resulting in two pitches.

This condition is comparable to the tongue movement in the process of whistling. While maintaining a constant pitch, or tension, on the vocal cords, moving the tongue back and forth changes the size of the oral cavity and the intensity of the air passing through the tensed lips causing a pulsation. If the movement of the tongue is rapid, a vibrato is produced. If the movement is sluggish and exaggerated, two pitches, or a tremolo, become evident.

The Jaw, Larynx, Body Fusion and the Gan-Tone Pulsation stabilize the structure on which the sound is built, causing tension on the vocal cords, or frequency, to be true to the pitch, as a result of eliminating distortions. By fusing body parts, pressure is focused on the hard parts, such as bones and cartilages, which can withstand pressure (rather than on muscles which cannot of themselves adequately cope with pressure) thereby minimizing muscle spasm. Since muscles are now fused with the hard parts, they maintain their stability under pressure enabling the jet of air from the lungs to bring inaudible vibrations from the vocal cords to audibility without any interference in the air flow from spasming muscles. The Gan-Tone Pulsation insures the most effective fusion of body parts, especially during moments of great pressure (loud, high, sustained notes), since the Compression Phase, or down-part of the Gan-Tone beat, insures total contractive muscular focus in the rectal-pelvic basin thus providing the strongest amalgamation of body elements, such as air, liquids, membranes, muscles, tendons, cartilages and bones, but especially the great pelvic bone. Muscles under pressure, therefore, become a part of the whole body and their strength is controlled at the rectal-pelvic basin rather than functioning as isolated parts which would cause them to spasm thereby interfering with the air flow to the vocal cords that causes the tremolo or any other undesirable involuntary action.

UNDERTONES. The lower tones, or lower partials, which, with the fundamental, create the overtones that produce musical tones of great depth and height.

Undertones are vocal cords and body vibrations that are not directly re-sounded, i.e., those vibrations that do not pass directly through the air to the resonators but, instead, are amplified and compressed to the rectal-pelvic basin on the Gan-Tone Pulsation and re-sounded concomitantly with the vocal cords vibrations that move directly to the resonators.

Undertones amplify the fundamental frequency and its integral parts, add facets to the sound that reflect the vibratory characteristics of body parts, such as bones, cartilages, etc., generate overtones commensurate to the undertones and thrust these overtones from the greatest depths of the body to the greatest heights of the body, the distance covered by the amplitude of the Gan-Tone Pulsation.

The structure of the emitted sound is, therefore, not based on the fundamental and overtones alone, but on the undertones, as well. The height of the overtones is dependent on the depth of the undertones, i.e., the intensity of the reaction of overtones is dependent on the intensity of the action of undertones.

The greater the intensity of the Gan-Tone Pulsation, the more undertones and integral parts are created in the Compression Phase, or down-part of the Gan-Tone beat, resulting in an equal amount of overtones during the Thrust Phase, or up-part of the Gan-Tone beat, which create more height and vibratory aura in the emitted sound.

UNHINGED JAW. The position of the jaw down and back and resting on the larynx which creates recesses in front of the tragi located in front and above the ear lobes. This maximum opening of the jaw, along with the vertical-elliptical mouth opening, makes possible the fusion of the jaw with the larynx and body, producing the structure for the maximum transmission, amplification and re-sounding of vocal cords and body vibrations.

UVULAR TYMPANY. The M-shaped, flexible membrane located at the back of the mouth which is an extension of the hard and soft palates. Since the uvula is a flexible membrane, it functions as a tympany, that is, it is capable of distention; a flexible partition for determining the size of the cavities, or resonators, the amount of vibrations that will pass through them and the amount of resonance that will be produced. When the uvula is completely distended and lifted high, it aids in maximizing resonator size, vibratory continuity and resonance.

VARIABLE MOUTH AND JAW OPENINGS. The gamut of mouth and jaw openings, from the widest opening, created by the unhinged jaw and the vertical-elliptical position of the mouth, to the smallest opening, where the size of the oral cavity is minimal and the upper and lower lip meet. The mouth opening can be completely independent of the jaw opening, i.e., the mouth can be closed even though the jaw is unhinged.

The maximum opening of the jaw is produced when the jaw is unhinged and resting on the larynx, and the widest opening of the mouth is created with the vertical-elliptical position. It is from this absolute opening of the jaw and mouth that the greatest amount of pressure can be allayed, and the greatest amount of vibratory continuity can be sustained, since it is in this position that the body cavities are maximally opened, and the greatest amount of vocal cords pressure is controlled by diffusion through the body.

Any divergence from this absolute opening converges pressure to the vocal cords and throat muscles, diminishes the ability to control pressure, decreases vibratory continuity and amplification of vibrations throughout the range, and also decreases the size of the body resonators which diminishes the re-sounding of these vibrations.

Since this absolute opening of the jaw and mouth cannot be sustained without interruption, as a result of the rapid articulation of words, in the process of singing, the singer must develop spontaneity in positioning the mouth and jaw to the widest openings possible, with minimal mouth and jaw movements, in order to maintain the greatest degree of body involvement, vibratory continuity, amplification of vibrations and size of body resonators, thus maximizing the dimensions of depth and height in the sound, even though the mouth and jaw openings vary, as a result of articulating words in the singing process.

A singing line that involves a rapid articulation of words causes instability in the structure necessary to maintain maximum dimensions in the emitted sound, since the jaw and mouth openings oscillate, compounding tension in the throat muscles and converging pressure and the dimensions of the sound to the throat area. Agile positioning of the mouth and jaw stabilizes the structure that produces the singing sound, even though a rapid articulation of words occurs in the singing line, since the fast movements enable the jaw to be fused to the larynx more often, insuring greater vibratory continuity and diffusion of pressure through the body.

Deft positioning of the mouth and jaw in the rapid articulation of words minimizes mouth and jaw movements, thus maximizing the Jaw, Larynx, Body Fusion which insures maximum dimensions in the emitted sound.

VERTICAL-ELLIPTICAL MOUTH OPENING. The opening of the mouth that maximizes the flow of vibrations to the body extremities, when the Gan-Tone Principles, such as the Jaw, Larynx, Body Fusion and the Gan-Tone Pulsation, are applied.

This mouth opening prevents constriction of body cavities and restriction of vibrational flow, enabling vibrations to maximally penetrate the body extremities during the Thrust Phase, or up-part of the Gan-Tone beat.

This opening of the mouth and lips stresses the converging of the corners of the mouth vertically (covering the upper and lower teeth) rather than spreading these corners horizontally. The widest opening of this mouth position follows the plumb line of the body.

The maximum opening of the mouth in the vertical-elliptical position provides the structure for the maximum amplification, unrestricted transmission and re-sounding of vocal cords vibrations to the resonators.

The horizontal spreading of the mouth negates the plumb line of the body, constricting the throat opening and, thereby, restricting the movement of vocal cords vibrations. The spreading of the corners of the mouth horizontally spreads, flattens and tightens neck muscles and the tone, diminishing the dimensions of depth and height in the sound by restricting these dimensions to the throat area rather than extending them to the body extremities.

VERTICAL FUSION. The blending of body parts downward to the rectal-pelvic basin enabling vocal cords vibrations to be compressed to the rectal-pelvic basin on the Compression Phase, or down-part of the Gan-Tone beat, thus maximizing the body as a conductor for transmitting, amplifying, thrusting and re-sounding vocal cords vibrations which eliminates the need for the horizontal spread of the girth (obesity) or the corners of the mouth for attaining volume in the emitted sound.

VIBRANCY. The brilliance, i.e., the depth and height, in the emitted sound, as a result of the superimposed pulsations (Gan-Tones) on the vibrations of the fundamental frequency (pitch).

The Compression Phase, or down-part of the Gan-Tone beat, fuses vocal cords vibrations, i.e., pitch, through the body to the rectal-pelvic basin, generating and amplifying vibrations through the body mediums. These vibrations are thrust to the resonators on the Thrust Phase, or up-part of the Gan-Tone beat.

The height, or brilliance, in the emitted sound is, therefore, the result of compound vibrations: the vibrations of the fundamental frequency (pitch), the vibrations of the body mediums and the vibrations of the Gan-Tone Pulsations. The intensity of the Gan-Tone beats on the fundamental frequency determines the degree to which the vibrations of the body mediums will be evident in the emitted sound.

The degree of penetration of vocal cords vibrations to the depths of the body on the Gan-Tone Pulsations and the unrestricted movement of these vibrations through the body (especially the throat area) and its resonators determine the brilliance, or depth and height (vibrancy), in the emitted sound.

VIBRATING AIR. Oscillating air; the reaction to the frequency of the fundamental vocal cords vibrations (pitch), whose amplitude (depth and height of oscillation) is dependent on the intensity and frequency of the Gan-Tone Pulsation on the fundamental frequency (pitch). This oscillating air is re-sounded in the resonators and results in the singing sound.

The composition of the oscillating air consists of vocal cords and body vibrations whose quantity and quality is determined by the intensity of the Gan-Tone Pulsation. The more intense the application of the Gan-Tone beat, the greater the magnification of vocal cords and body vibrations producing more intensity in the air which results in greater depth, height, brilliance and volume in the emitted sound. The greater the intensity of the vibrating air, the greater the degree of life, or energy, in the singing sound.

VIBRATIONAL ABSORPTION. The assimilation of vocal cords vibrations in the body mediums, such as bones and cartilages, preventing the transmission and amplification of these vibrations in the body resonators. The application of the Jaw, Larynx, Body Fusion and the Gan-Tone Pulsation minimizes vibrational absorption and promotes Vocal Vibratory Continuity.

VIBRATIONAL RESTRICTION. The confinement of vocal cords vibrations in the throat area during the singing process, when the Jaw, Larynx, Body Fusion and the Gan-tone Pulsation are not applied.

If the jaw is not opened to accommodate the increased vibrations produced by increased volume or range, the throat area constricts causing vocal cords vibrations to be restricted in this area, rather than being transmitted to the body resonators, producing tension in the vocal cords and surrounding muscles. This tension on muscles leads to the weakening of throat muscles which diminishes range, volume and dimensions of depth and height in the singing sound resulting, eventually, in total collapse of the sound.

Each beat of the Gan-Tone, when applied to the fundamental frequency, maximizes Vocal Vibratory Continuity throughout the body, increasing the amplification, transmission and re-sounding of vibrations as well as maximizing the size of the re-sounding areas.

The Compression Phase, or down-part of the Gan-Tone beat, transmits vocal cords vibrations through a highly resilient body column to the rectal-pelvic basin, as a result of the Jaw, Larynx, Body Fusion. This basin is the most solid area for the launching of vibrations throughout the body on the Thrust Phase, or up-part of the Gan-Tone beat.

The imposition of the Gan-Tone beat, which requires the Jaw, Larynx, Body Fusion, minimizes vibrational restriction in the throat area and maximizes the amplification and transmission of these vibrations to the body resonators.

VIBRATIONS. Pulsations; manifestation of the principle of life whether audible or inaudible; spirit; energy.

VIBRATO. Voluntary or involuntary pulsations on the fundamental vocal cords vibrations, or pitch, focused at the vocal cords, that promote warmth and beauty in musical tones.

Involuntary pulsations exist in some voices by nature, without conscious mental imposition.

Voluntary pulsations are mentally imposed by adding pressure to the vocal cords, while maintaining the fundamental pitch.

The vibrato is essentially an embellishment with a superficial involvement of the body; whereas, the Gan-Tone Pulsation creates the structure of the singing sound by imposing a calculated number of beats per second on the singing line. Each beat fuses and compresses vocal cords and body vibrations to the rectal-pelvic basin, which is the controlling center for the transmission, amplification, thrust and re-sounding of vocal cords and body vibrations throughout the body and its cavities.

VIBRATORY AURA. The resounding atmosphere that surrounds a singer, when the Jaw, Larynx, Body Fusion and the Gan-Tone beat are maximally applied, producing total re-sounding of vocal cords and body vibrations through total involvement of the body as vibrator and resonator, making the body resound as a bell.

VIBRATORY CHARACTERISTICS OF BODY MEDIUMS. The qualities in the tone produced by the variations in vibratory frequency of body mediums, such as the vocal cords, larynx, bones, abdomen and fluids.

The variations in the vibratory frequency of chest bones, for ex., produced by the variations in size and shape of the different bones cause a gamut of vibrational frequencies, from slow to rapid, creating a combination of depth and height in the tone. The mediums of slower frequencies create depth, and the mediums of higher frequencies create height in the emitted sound. The degree to which this depth and height is audible in the emitted sound is dependent on the intensity of the Gan-Tone beat.

VIBRATORY HARMONY. The smooth flow of vocal cords and body vibrations throughout the body, but especially to the extremities, i.e., the rectal-pelvic basin on the Compression Phase, or down-part of the Gan-Tone beat, and the head resonators on the Thrust Phase, or up-part of the Gan-Tone beat, producing aesthetically pleasing loud and soft, full-bodied sounds, as a result of the smooth adaptation and coordination of body parts made possible through the Jaw, Larynx, Body Fusion.

The more rapid and intense the coordination and fusion of body parts, the more ease in the vibrational flow, producing a minimum of tension in the vocal cords, a very desirable condition, since tension in the vocal cords and surrounding areas of the throat results in vocal and physical disharmony.

VOCAL CORDS. The two ligamentous folds attached within the larynx that converge horizontally in the angle of the thyroid cartilage (the narrowest area of the wind tube) and are brought together when mental impulses are focused (primarily through contractive, laryngeal, muscular action) as tension, or inaudible vibrations. These vibrations are brought to audibility when air from the lungs passes through them; make up part of the rim of the glottis (hole).

In the Gan-Tone Method, the vocal cords are the primary source of audible vibrations, or sound, but the extension of these cords, by fusion and compression, through the body makes the body, rather than the vocal cords, the total vibrator and resonator of the original vocal cords vibrations.

VOCAL CORDS EXTENSION. The increase in the size of the vocal cords to include the body through fusion of the vocal cords with other body parts on the Jaw, Larynx, Body Fusion and the Gan-Tone beat. The original vocal cords vibrations are extended and amplified to the rectal-pelvic basin on the Compression Phase, or down-part of the Gan-Tone beat, producing body vibrations. The rectal-pelvic basin is the controlling center for the amplifying and thrusting of these vocal cords and body vibrations throughout the body, but especially to the head resonators, on the Thrust Phase, or up-part of the Gan-Tone beat.

The vocal cords, therefore, are not isolated parts located in the throat area but are, instead, the instruments for venting vibrant energy that is produced through the interaction of mind, body and air. Gan-Tone Principles establish the vocal cords' oneness with the body.

VOCAL CORDS VIBRATIONS. Vibrant energy manifested as tension on the vocal cords, as a result of mental impulses transmitted through the nerves to the vocal cords. These inaudible vibrations, or tension, are brought to audibility when a jet of air from the lungs passes through the vocal cords.

The fundamental vocal cords vibrations are a product of the two vibrating cords. Since the two folds, or cords, are naturally dissimilar, as, for ex., the variations between the left and right hand, the left and right foot and the articulates of the arytenoid cartilages, the vibrations from these two cords will vary to the extent of their dissimilarity, thus affecting the quality of their vibrations, which is an integral factor in the individual timbre of each voice. Unnatural dissimilarities in the two folds, or cords, can be attributed to lesions as, for ex., a node on one cord can produce a disparity in the pitch of the two cords.

VOCAL FOCUS. The convergence of vibrational energy in the most vibrant and resonant areas of the body produced by the Jaw, Larynx, Body Fusion and the Gan-Tone Pulsation.

The more intense the application of the Compression Phase, or down-part of the Gan-Tone beat, on the fundamental frequency of the vocal cords vibrations, the more intense the compression of vocal cords and body vibrations to the rectal-pelvic basin producing an equally intense thrust of these vibrations throughout the body on the Thrust Phase, or up-part of the Gan-Tone beat, which, in turn, determines the degree of vibrational energy focused in the resonators, but specifically in the head resonators. The intensity of this focused vibrational energy in the resonators determines the depth, height, resilience, buoyancy and brilliance of the emitted sound.

The greater the intensity of the Gan-Tone beat on the fundamental frequency, with the Jaw, Larynx, Body Fusion, the more resilient the body to the extremities (rectal-pelvic basin and head resonators) and, therefore, the less the vibrational absorption in the body, allowing a greater quantity of vibrations to be focused, with greater impact, in the resonators.

VOCAL HOOK. The curved tract leading from the vocal cords, larynx, pharynx, nasal cavities and nostrils, mouth and lips, and includes the tip of the chin and the sinus cavities.

The opening of this tract is determined by the position of the jaw, the fusion of body parts and the yawn which, in turn, determine not only the utilization of this tract as a resonator, but the entire body, as well. The acoustical qualities of the vocal hook are fully utilized for producing innumerable effects through the JLB Fusion and the Gan-Tone Pulsation.

VOCAL IMPACT. The collision-communicating force, or the acoustical effect, of sound on the listener's ear created by magnified undertones and resultant overtones of the fundamental frequency as a result of the imposition of Gan-Tone Pulsations on this fundamental.

The Gan-Tone Pulsations extend the amplitude of the fundamental vocal cords vibrations to the body extremities (rectal-pelvic basin and head resonators), producing great depth (undertones) and great height (overtones) in the emitted sound.

These disciplined beats (Gan-Tone Pulsations) are graphic piston-like actions on the singing line which define vibrational amplitude through magnified undertones (great intensity of vibrational depth at the rectal-pelvic basin) and magnified overtones (commensurate intensity of vibrational height in the head resonators).

The degree of audibility of undertones and overtones is dependent on the intensity with which the Gan-Tone Pulsations transmit fundamental vocal cords vibrations to the rectal-pelvic basin.

VOCAL STABILITY. The steadiness of the singing line which is determined by the degree of skill attained in coping with the pressures encountered in the singing process.

Fluid, swift and resilient movement of Gan-Tone Pulsations on the fundamental vocal cords vibrations concomitantly with the Jaw, Larynx, Body Fusion insure the greatest stability, or steadiness, of the softest as well as the loudest sounds, therefore, producing a smooth line of singing that appears effortless, since the responsibility of coping with pressures and amplitude of sound waves is allocated to the body, whose controlling center is the rectal-pelvic basin, rather than isolated parts.

VOCAL VIBRATORY CONTINUITY. The movement of vocal cords vibrations, continuously and omnidirectionally, throughout the body without restriction during the singing process, as a result of the Jaw, Larynx, Body Fusion and the Gan-Tone Pulsation which fuse body parts and vocal cords and body vibrations to the rectal-pelvic basin on the Compression Phase, or down-part of the Gan-Tone beat, and thrust these vibrations to the body resonators on the Thrust Phase, or up-part of the Gan-Tone beat, thus creating an uninterrupted path through the body for these vibrations and thereby minimizing vibrational absorption.

VOICE PLACEMENT. The mobility of vibrational energy to the body resonators with specific direction and definition of these vibrations to the head resonators throughout the range, as a result of the Feather-Touch Contact on the vocal cords, Jaw, Larynx, Body Fusion and the Gan-Tone Pulsation producing great brilliance in the emitted sound.

Placement of the voice, i.e., the re-sounding of vocal cords and body vibrations in the head resonators, occurs automatically with the application of the Gan-Tone Principles, such as the Jaw, Larynx, Body Fusion and the Gan-Tone Pulsation, since the fusion of body parts and vocal cords and body vibrations to the bottom of the torso on the Compression Phase, or down-part of the Gan-

Tone beat, involves the rectal-pelvic basin which is the controlling center for the thrusting of these vibrations to the head resonators, with great impact and definition, on the Thrust Phase, or up-part of the Gan-Tone beat.

When the singer applies the Jaw, Larynx, Body Fusion and the Gan-Tone Pulsation, therefore, vocal cords and body vibrations are re-sounded in the highest resonators of the body, since these vibrations penetrate the depths of the body and are thrust to the body resonators from this body extremity.

The singer, consequently, who wishes to place the voice high in the mask applies the Gan-Tone Principles that will enable him to utilize the highest resonators of the body thereby producing an emitted sound of great depth, height and brilliance.

VOICE PROJECTION. The distance at which the singing voice is heard. This distance is dependent on the degree of inward penetration and amplification of vocal cords and body vibrations to the bottom of the torso on the Gan-Tone beat (Compression Phase, or down-part of the Gan-Tone beat) which determines the degree of thrust of these vibrations to the resonators (Thrust Phase, or up-part of the Gan-Tone beat) and, in turn, determines the carrying power of the emitted sound; a casting out of vocal sound from the body produced by vocal cords and body vibrations that have been amplified by the Jaw, Larynx, Body Fusion, compressed to the rectal-pelvic basin on the Compression Phase, or down-part of the Gan-Tone beat, and thrust throughout the body, particularly to the resonators, on the Thrust Phase, or up-part of the Gan-Tone beat.

The degree of intensity of the Gan-Tone beat determines the degree of vibratory energy that is amplified and thrust which, in turn, determines the degree of impact of this energy to the resonators. The resonance produced determines the carrying power, or distance at which the emitted sound can be heard.

VOICE PROJECTION POTENTIAL. The possible distance at which the emitted sound will be heard is dependent on the degree of efficiency with which mind, body and air interact.

The greater the speed and intensity in the application of the Jaw, Larynx, Body Fusion and the Gan-Tone beat, the greater the carrying power, or distance at which the emitted sound will be heard.

VOLUME. The degree of fullness and quantity of tone that is evident in the emitted sound which is dependent on the Feather-Touch Contact of air on the vocal cords and the intensity with which the vocal cords and body vibrations are fused, compressed, amplified and thrust from the rectal-pelvic basin to the body resonators on the Gan-Tone beat.

VOMITING PRINCIPLE. Maximum opening of the throat, nose and mouth, and fusion and compression of body parts to the rectal-pelvic basin characteristic of the vomiting process and simulated in the Gan-Tone Method in order to give vibrating air the greatest amount of thrust to the resonating cavities.

This vomiting principle is basic in the Jaw, Larynx, Body Fusion and the Gan-Tone Pulsation.

WEIGHT DIFFERENTIAL. The difference in body weight that can be created by the singer in the Gan-Tone Method for affecting the amplification, thrust and re-sounding of vocal cords vibrations which, in turn, will affect the volume, brilliance, depth and height, i.e., the vibrant energy of the singing sound.

The process of fusion and compression of body parts to the rectal-pelvic basin virtually increases the weight of the body, providing more vibrant area for the transmission and amplification of vocal cords vibrations.

The imposition of the Gan-Tone Pulsation does, in fact, increase body weight. The Compression Phase, or down-part of the Gan-Tone beat, acts as a piston going down through the cylinder of the body and developing its compression head at the rectal-pelvic basin. This increase in weight can be recorded while the singer stands on a scale as he applies the Gan-Tone beat. This action is analogous to placing an open cylinder vertically on a scale and striking downward to the bottom of the cylinder with a hammer. As the hammer falls and hits the bottom of the cylinder, the surplus weight differential is recorded on the scale. The hammer is analogous to the Gan-Tone beat, and the cylinder is analogous to the body.

The physical dropping of the torso by bending the knees, which is characteristic in the martial arts, ballet and fencing to increase body thrust, increases body weight and density in the singer. This weight differential can also be recorded on the scale.

The coordinated action of fusion and compression of body parts, the Gan-Tone Pulsation and the Body Drop maximizes the surplus weight differential, thoroughly utilizing body weight in the production of the singing voice, thus minimizing the need for obesity in obtaining the maximum dimensions of depth, height and volume in the singing sound. Contrary to traditional belief, excessive weight interferes with body fusion and resilience and hinders the body coordination required for the Gan-Tone Pulsation.

It should be noted that the Body Drop in coordination with the Jaw, Larynx, Body Fusion and the Gan-Tone Pulsation produce the greatest dimensions of the vocal attack where depth, height, volume and projection of the sound are concerned bringing the essence of abandon in the singing sound which, however, is perpetually governed by the Gan-Tone laws.

WHISPERING. Speech produced by air impinging on the periphery of the lips of the glottis primarily in the attitude of expiration, when the vocal cords are not tensed by the mind for the creation of frequency, or pitch. The degree of mouth and jaw opening and the degree of air pressure through the glottis coordinated with the tip of the tongue, the lips and the teeth in the articulation of sounds, or words, determine the pitch of the whisper, as opposed to tension on the vocal cords for pitch in the singing voice.

The volume, pitch and dimensions of the whisper can be increased by increased air and body thrust from the rectal-pelvic basin.

WHISTLE POSITION. The vertical-elliptical mouth opening which stresses the tautness of the lips (periphery of the mouth) for focusing vibrating air thus making the lips function as a lens for regulating the intensity of the emitted sound.

As the mouth opening contracts and the lips become more taut, the vibratory frequency of the lips increases. Vibrating air impinging on this position vibrates the lips augmenting the dominant fundamental pitch of the vocal cords with a lower pitch thus adding more vibrant energy to the singing sound.

The pitch of the vibrating lips is lower than the fundamental pitch of the vocal cords, since the opening of the lips is wider than the opening of the vocal cords producing a lower frequency of minimal volume, as a result of less air intensity through the lips than through the vocal cords.

WOBBLING JAW. An involuntary, irregular oscillation of the jaw while sustaining tones, as a result of pressure focusing on the throat muscles causing these muscles to spasm which, in turn, sets up a vacillating movement of the jaw (clonic spasm) producing a distortion in the pitch being sung and creating a singing line that alternates between two pitches; the higher of the two pitches is the intended pitch.

Some singers impose a vacillating movement of the jaw to affect a vibrato. However, this action causes a wobble and eventual collapse of the singing line, since the throat muscles producing this oscillation fatigue and collapse.

The remedy for the wobbling jaw is the Jaw, Larynx, Body Fusion and the Gan-Tone Pulsation which stabilize the jaw by removing pressure from the throat and other muscles and diffusing this pressure downward through the body.

The Gan-Tone Pulsation, whose amplitude, from the rectal-pelvic basin to the head resonators, is the structure of the singing line, naturally controls the vibrato. An embellishment, the vibrato is a superficial penetration of vibrations in the throat area and not the structure of sound. The Gan-Tone Pulsation makes the point of reference for the structure and stability of sound the rectal-pelvic basin, rather than the throat muscles, making the whole body the vibrator; whereas, the vibrato is localized in the throat area. The frequency of Gan-Tone Pulsations produces a true, one-tone pitch by stabilizing the wobbling jaw, as a result of fusing the jaw to the body.

YAWNING PROCESS. An involuntary action which stresses a maximal opening of the mouth in order to inspire a maximal amount of air omnidirectionally in the body cavities. The yawn is simulated in the Gan-Tone Method as an aid to the effective utilization of the Jaw, Larynx, Body Fusion and the Gan-Tone Pulsation; Exinvac Principle.

The yawning process maximizes space in the cavernous system of the body for re-sounding vibrations, relaxes the entire muscular system of the body and, at the height of inspiration, fuses body pressures to the rectal-pelvic basin. The more deeply the yawning process is simulated, the more definite the release of isolated body pressures to the rectal-pelvic basin. Maximum simulation of the yawn is attained when the Gan-Tone Pulsation is applied with maximum intensity, maximizing space in the body resonators for maximal re-sounding of vibrations.

The yawn position is simulated when the jaw is unhinged, down and back, and straddles the larynx. The recesses in front of the ear lobes are maximally opened. The tongue is pressed forward and downward and laying flat. The tip of the tongue is touching the back of the lower teeth. The Uvula is raised, thus producing a maximally opened mouth for the accommodation and transmission of vibrations. The pharyngeal-nasal tract is opened and the nostrils are dilated, producing maximum space in the head cavities (sinus, nasal, pharyngeal and oral cavities).

YODELING. Singing produced by alternating pure vocal cords sound (dispersion of body parts) and fused sound (fused body parts), i.e., sound produced with no laryngeal fusion (falsetto) and sound produced when the vocal cords and its vibrations are fused to the larynx and surrounding area.

This alternation consists of breaking the connection of laryngeal fusion after singing a low note and moving to a higher note with no laryngeal fusion, producing a disembodied, effeminate sound.

Q   Gansert, Robert
784.
932   SINGING ENERGY IN THE GAN-TONE
GAN   METHOD OF VOICE PRODUCTION
        273856

PATCHOGUE-MEDFORD
LIBRARY
PATCHOGUE, N.Y. 11772

DEC 29 1983